Terrorism in the Twenty-First Century

Seventh Edition

CINDY C. **COMBS**

University of North Carolina at Charlotte

Routledge
Taylor & Francis Group

LONDON AND NEW YORK

First published 2013, 2011, 2009, 2006 by Pearson Education, Inc.

Published 2016 by Routledge
2 Park Square, Milton Park, Abingdon, Oxon OX14 4RN
711 Third Avenue, New York, NY, 10017, USA

Routledge is an imprint of the Taylor & Francis Group, an informa business

ISBN: 9780205851652 (pbk)

Library of Congress Cataloging-in-Publication Data

Combs, Cindy C.
 Terrorism in the twenty-first century / Cindy C. Combs. — 7th ed.
    p. cm.
 Includes bibliographical references and index.
 ISBN-13: 978-0-205-85165-2
 ISBN-10: 0-205-85165-7
 1. Terrorism. 2. Terrorism—Forecasting. I. Title.
 HV6431.C6472 2012
 363.325—dc23
                                          2011042081

BRIEF CONTENTS

Contents   v
Preface   xiii

CONTENTS

v

PART II   Who are the Terrorists?

PART V   Current Trends and Future Prospects

CHAPTER 14   The New Terrorist Threat: Weapons of Mass Destruction   327

PREFACE

Confronted with the sudden death of a leader, terrorist
group become cornered animals. When wounded, they lash out.
Not only in hopes of surviving, but also to demonstrate
their continuing power and continued relevance.
Al-Qa'ida is no different.

Bruce Hoffman

Bruce Hoffman, terrorism expert and professor at Georgetown University's School of Foreign Service Security Studies, clarifies the continuing danger that terrorism poses today. The death of a prominent leader does not nullify the threat, but may actually intensify it. Individuals and organizations carrying out terrorist attacks today are not static; hey continue to learn and to translate their learning into new methods of attack in spite of governments' best efforts to counter them. Just as terrorism is not static but constantly evolving and surviving, understanding of terrorist groups, tactics, and training cannot be static if counterterrorism measures are to be effective. Terrorism is not a subject we can afford to comfortably ignore, nor can we safely build effective counterterrorism policy without an evolving understanding of this phenomenon. The death of Osama bin Laden, although a pivotal point in the strategy of the "war on terror," does not mark the end of terrorism. Instead, terrorism is likely to become a larger, not a smaller, player in international politics, as more individuals and groups seek political change by violent attacks on vulnerable civilian targets.

September 11, 2001, was, in some respects, a wake-up call not only for the United States but for the world that terrorism constitutes a clear and present danger, a weapon evolving faster and more effectively than the world community's responses to it. The targeted death of bin Laden, al-Qaeda's founder and leader, does not end the threat, but does change the playing field in ways that are important to understand. Evaluating present conditions and attempting to predict future trends can offer useful insights for policymakers and citizens throughout the world, as terrorism today is a transnational threat.

In the wake of the September 11, 2001, attacks in the United States, al-Qaeda spokesman Suliman Abu Geith suggested that the perpetrators of the attacks had "destroyed America with their airplanes," evoking an image of terrorists at war with a country. Geith's comment that these individuals had "moved the battle into the heart of America" was reflected in the response of the U.S. government, which issued a declaration of "war" on terrorism in the wake of these attacks. The subsequent war in Afghanistan and the war initiated by the United States in Iraq were premised on the threat of terrorism and the need of states, individually and collectively, to respond. The early years of the twenty-first century clearly demonstrate the changing nature of terrorism and its challenge to international peace and security. This challenge is one that the international communities, as well as individual nation-states, are in many respects ill-prepared to meet. *Terrorism in the Twenty-First Century* is intended to strengthen our ability to cope by improving our understanding of the problem of terrorism today.

NEW TO THIS EDITION

This new edition—of a text first published years before the September 11 attacks—focuses on the evolving ability of nations and institutions to generate effective counterterror measures using the force of law and investigative resources. The death or capture of leaders, combined with the emerging threat of leaderless movements and lone-wolf terrorists, present us with a constantly changing threat of terrorism today. Focus in this edition on the effort to "deal with" terrorism legally highlights the importance of an operational definition of terrorist acts in a world engaged in a "war" on this phenomenon.

Terrorism is not new, but it is changing in tactics, in scope of operations, and in the structure of the organizations responsible for terrorist acts. This new edition examines carefully the nature of these changes, retaining the historical basis of our understanding of terrorism, emphasizing the differences in modern terrorism as it presents new challenges on a global as well as a national scale. The specific revisions made to this edition include the following.

- Regional terrorism centers and institutes and counterterror legislation with an emphasis on intelligence-sharing and capacity building are explored in several chapters.
- The role of the Internet in the training, recruitment, planning, and funding of terrorist groups—and the successful use of the Internet in law enforcement to counter these efforts—is the focus of several new case studies.
- David Rapoport's theory of the "four waves" of modern terrorism is utilized to discuss the role of religion as a transnational force linking groups and individuals in all parts of the globe and as a recruiting tool for terrorist acts.
- The link between failed states and terrorism in the form of either piracy or terrorist training grounds is explored with case studies involving Somalia and Afghanistan.

- The escalation of suicide bombings and the use of IEDs (improvised explosive devices) in transnational attacks is examined in several chapters, using case studies and statistics to clarify this rapidly emerging threat.
- The effectiveness of counterterror measures is illustrated in new case studies on the attack by special forces on bin Laden's compound in Pakistan, the International Criminal Court's (ICC) indictments of national leaders, enemy combatants, new links between narcotics and terrorism, terrorism in Mumbai, allocation of resources based on threat and risk assessment, and cyber security and cyber terror.
- The Selective Chronology of Recent Terrorism has been updated to focus on political violence in this century.

The ongoing "war on terror" declared in 2003 is a transnational effort to combat the threat of terrorism, and the steps taken in this "war" have impacted terrorist groups and stimulated terrorist acts in many countries as well. Counterterrorism efforts, such as the emerging international conventions on terrorism and the building of regional efforts to gather and share intelligence, offer insights into the counterterror learning curve, as do the national legislations enacted in several nations both before and after the September 11 attacks, with varying degrees of success. New efforts, including "fusions centers" of a domestic as well as an international nature, offer potential for increased success in information sharing, but also raise concerns about privacy rights and civil liberties protections.

In order to keep this new edition user-friendly for students, it retains the original structure of chapters, but has substantially more case studies in each chapter. These case studies, beginning with one on redefining terrorism in Chapter 1, offer ways for students to apply the ideas discussed in the chapter with real events, organizations, or materials, which help them apply the more abstract concepts to reality. The idea of women involved in terrorism, for example, is made real by a small case study of the Black Widows group in Russia. The reality of genocide is easier to accept using the case study in Chapter 5 on the events in Darfur and the indictment by the ICC of Sudan's president on charges of genocide. An understanding of the transnational threat of terrorist training camps is clarified in the case studies of such camps in the United States, in the United Kingdom, and on the Internet.

Since terrorism as well as counterterrorism today utilizes the Internet, in this edition the Analysis Challenge at the end of each chapter is focused on the use of Internet resources. These challenges are designed to provide opportunities to further explore at least one concept from each chapter, using the Internet to increase understanding and to provoke further analytical efforts. If individuals who are engaged in effectively countering this threat, today and in the future, are to adapt their responses and countermeasures as successfully as those who are initiating terrorism, their skills in the use of the Internet as a tool must be continuously enhanced and analytical skills challenged. This small challenge is designed to further the evolution of successful counterterror efforts by increasing the learning curve.

The transnational nature of terrorism today is the focus of case studies on the regional counterterrorism institute in Singapore and on the emerging role of instruments of international law, particularly the ICC, in countering this threat. The growing list of failed and failing states generated by the U.S. Department of State each year is examined in terms of the growing threat of terrorism generated in these areas, particularly piracy, as the case study of Somalia illustrates. The potential for cyberterror, explored from alternative angles in different chapters, offers further insights into the transnational nature of this threat. The transformation of terrorism into a form of "netwar," the potential for cyberterror, and the ability of nations to deal with this asymmetric threat are illustrated in graphs, tables, and case studies as well.

FEATURES

To understand terrorism in the twenty-first century, it is important to examine terrorism in historical context. Political science is founded upon a need to explain and to predict actions in the political realm. For that purpose, this text examines the elements of contemporary terrorism, attempting to explain the primary characteristics of what, who, why, and how. Predictions about forthcoming patterns of terrorism can then be based on an understanding of previous and current patterns of behavior.

It has always been important that this text be easy for both students and professors to use, with material organized clearly and concisely, and presented without prejudice. In order to prevent, as far as possible, a pejorative use of the material, the examination of the concept of "terrorism" emphasizes a legal, operational definition applicable to terrorist acts, rather than to the individuals, groups, or states who carry out such acts. This makes the term much less likely to be applied with prejudice; if the term is applied in a legally correct context, it can be done objectively rather than subjectively. This also facilitates the use of the book by a wider audience, since each individual, group, and state can be evaluated in the context of the actions taken.

The purpose of this text is to facilitate an understanding of what terrorism is in this new century: both an old and a new phenomenon—constantly evolving, yet retaining basic characteristics, an asymmetric form of warfare with the ability to dramatically impact the peace and stability of the world. The first part of the book, therefore, explores the definitions offered for this phenomenon, looking at the recent efforts by agencies and governments to clarify what a terrorist act is. Since these definitions emerged from historical context, Chapter 2 explores the roots of modern terrorism, from assassinations to bombings, looking specifically at the cycles of violence engendered by terrorism perpetrated by both state and nonstate actors.

Building on this historical analysis, Chapter 3 examines the causes of modern terrorism, from frustrated nationalism to radical religious fundamentalism, building toward an understanding of why groups of people resort to terrorist acts. From an understanding of the causes of terrorist violence, Chapter 4 offers insights into the mind of a terrorist, helping to differentiate between types of terrorists and the socialization patterns that help to create these mind-sets.

Recognizing that states have demonstrated more capacity to commit acts of terror than any individual or group throughout history, Chapter 5 shifts the focus in the study of terror to include terror by states, exploring the spectrum of such terror from relatively mild intimidation to coerced conversion to the practice of genocide. Modern terrorism, as Chapter 6 makes clear, networks across state lines, acting in many ways as a multinational corporation, often engaged in profitable business enterprises to support the commission of the terrorist acts.

These networks serve to recruit and train a wide range of individuals to the commission of terrorism today. The scope of modern terrorist training and networking is explored in Chapter 7, with Chapter 8 adding a careful look at the role of the media today in this networking, recruitment, and implementation process, comparing the goals of terrorists with those of the media reporting the acts to an increasingly international audience. The next chapter, Chapter 9, serves as a larger case study, briefly examining terrorism in the United States in terms of its history, the types which have evolved, the networking evident in modern incidents, leading into an exploration of the responses explored in this country to combat modern terrorism.

Since, as Chapter 9 indicates, a large part of U.S. counterterror response is based in law (the PATRIOT Act), it is logical that the next chapter deal with law as a counterterrorism tool. Indeed, Part Four of this text focuses on the efficacy of several different counterterror tools: international law (Chapter 10), military special forces (Chapter 11), legislation and intelligence-gathering (Chapter 12), and security measures (Chapter 13). However, since none of these measures have been completely successful in eliminating terrorism, the need to prioritize the problems faced, and to analyze the success of the responses initiated, is critical. Chapters 14 and 15 of the text, thus, explore the expanding threat of the use of weapons of mass destruction in terrorist incidents, and the challenges of the future in a world in which global terrorism is a norm, rather than an aberration.

Understanding what terrorism is must be rooted in an understanding of the causes of terrorist actions. Individuals are not born terrorists, nor are most individuals engaged in revolution guilty of terrorist acts. Clearly, terrorism evokes a wide range of responses from governments and peoples today, so a study of those responses should clarify the options for counterterrorism, highlighting the strengths and weaknesses of each, making it unnecessary for each nation to reinvent the wheel in devising a response to the challenge of terrorism today. Moreover, there is no single terrorist type that fits all individuals carrying out acts of terrorism, so this text takes a quick look at the types of modern terrorists, based on available studies. Applying such criteria to individuals, groups, and states makes it possible to differentiate to some degree between such terms as *crusaders* and *criminals,* between *state-sponsored terrorism* and *terrorism-sponsored states,* and between *separatist* and *nationalist groups.* Familiarity with these operationalized terms makes it easier to apply such terms without prejudice and, more significantly, to evaluate the response options for each type.

The text is organized in a style intended to be quite comfortable for use in a lecture or a seminar-style course. Lists of key concepts at the beginning of each chapter, case studies throughout the chapters designed to illustrate key points, discussion sections after the conclusion of each chapter, significant endnotes to alert readers to important works in this field of study, and a list of suggested readings for those interested in pursuing ideas further allow people with a variety of learning styles and reading approaches to master the content of this text fairly easily. Internet site listings for further readings and research have been added to this edition. Faculty can readily accentuate, elaborate, or correlate examples that are similar, parallel, or contrary, to create a sound framework for student understanding. With this format, I hope to engage the interest of a wide range of readers of varied preparatory backgrounds and academic experience in the vitally interesting subject of terrorism.

SUPPLEMENTS

Please visit the companion website at www.routledge.com/9780205851652

ACKNOWLEDGMENTS

The opportunity to share research and to interact with the International Centre for Political Violence and Terrorism Research in Singapore, courtesy of Dr. Rohan Gunaratna, was particularly useful in this new edition, strongly impacting its focus on regional counterterror efforts.

I would also like to thank the reviewers for this edition for their thoughtful comments—James Creagan, University of the Incarnate Word; Michael Deaver, Sierra College; and Mary Payrow-Olia, University of San Francisco.

Focus in this new edition on the utility of legal responses to contemporary terrorism reflects the impact of my teaching associate, Matthew Smither, whose passion for peaceful resolution of conflict led me to research more intensely the legal counterterror instruments. My husband, Lee, is always my strongest critic and best researcher, downloading information about the use of special forces in Afghanistan, the raid on bin Laden's compound, and countless other aspects of the ongoing "war on terror."

CINDY C. COMBS

Selective Chronology of Recent Terror

2000	March 21	**India:** Armed militants kill 35 Sikhs in Chadisinghpoora Village. Members of two groups, the Lashkhar-e-Tayyba and the Hiab-ul-Mujahideen, militant Muslim groups in Kashmir, are arrested.
	October 12	**Yemen:** In Aden, a small dinghy carrying explosives rams the U.S. destroyer, *USS Cole,* killing 17 sailors and injuring 39 others. Supporters of Osama bin Laden are suspected in this attack.
2001	June 1	**Israel:** HAMAS claims responsibility for the bombing of a popular nightclub in Tel Aviv that causes over 140 casualties.
	September 11	**United States:** Two hijacked airliners crash into the twin towers of the World Trade Center in New York City. Soon thereafter, the Pentagon is struck by a third hijacked plane. A fourth hijacked plane, headed for a high-profile target in Washington, DC, crashes into a field in southern Pennsylvania. More than 3,000 people are killed in these attacks. U.S. intelligence information indicates that Osama bin Laden, based in Afghanistan, is responsible for coordinating the attacks. **United Nations:** A global "war on terrorism" is declared by the United Nations.
	October	**United States:** Letters containing anthrax are sent through the U.S. Postal Service in the Washington, DC, and New York areas. Several people are infected—a few fatally.
2002	June 18	**Israel:** A 22-year-old member of HAMAS detonates a suicide bomb in a bus in Jerusalem, killing 19 and wounding at least 55, many of whom are high school students.
	October 12	**Indonesia:** A bomb explodes in a pub in Kuta, a town on the Indonesian island of Bali. As patrons and others rush into the street, a more powerful second bomb hidden inside a van is detonated. 202 people are killed and 209 injured in these attacks. Jemaah Islamiya Organization claims responsibility.
2003	May 12	Three housing compounds for expatriate workers in Riyadh, Saudi Arabia, are bombed, killing dozens and wounding about 140. Al-Qaeda cells are implicated.
	October 23–26	Chechen rebels take more than 200 people hostage at a Moscow theater, demanding that Russian troops leave Chechnya. After nearly three days, special forces troops pump an anesthetic gas into the theater and attack. All of the rebels and 129 of the hostages are killed, with most of the hostages dying from the gas.
2004	March 11	10 bombs are detonated on several commuter trains in Madrid, Spain, killing 191 and wounding more than 1,500. Al-Qaeda cells are responsible for the attacks.
	September 1–3	Beslan, Russia. Chechen extremists take more than 1,100 people hostage, primarily children. After a three-day stand-off, Russian forces storm the building. At least 334 hostages are killed.

2005	July 7	Four bombs explode in London: three simultaneously aboard London Underground trains and one aboard a bus. The attacks, carried out by suicide bombers, kill more than 50 people and injure more than 700.
	July 23	Three suicide bombers detonate bombs at the Egyptian resort town of Sharm el-Sheikh in Sinai. More than 60 people are killed, including over 40 Egyptians and at least 15 foreign tourists, mainly Europeans.
	September 30	In Darfur, Sudan, a group of 300 armed assailants attack a camp for refugees, killing 29 civilians, wounding 10 others, and destroying 80 temporary shelters. No group claimed responsibility.
2006	July 11	Mumbai, India. 203 civilians, 8 children killed, and another 863 civilians, 27 children wounded in IED transit attacks.
	November 20	Darfur, Sudan. 80 civilians killed in armed attack by suspected Janjaweed Militia.
2007	August 14	Four coordinated suicide bomb attacks in Yazidi communities in northern Iraq kill 796 and wound 1,562 people near Mosul. Al-Qaeda-in-Iraq believed to be responsible.
	November 27	Prime Minister Benazir Bhutto of Pakistan assassinated in a suicide attack in Rawalpindi.
2008	February 1	In Baghdad, two mentally disabled women are strapped with explosives and sent into busy markets, where they are blown up by remote control. The bombs kill at least 98 people and wound more than 200.
	November 26–29	Mumbai, India. Coordinated attacks by Islamic extremists on hotels, cafes, a women and children's hospital, a Jewish community center, and other targets kill at least 164 people and wound 308. The surviving attacker indicates that the Lashkar-e-Taiba (a Pakistani-based group) is responsible and was assisted by the ISI, Pakistani's Secret Service.
2009	January 17	Several hundred children are killed in assault and incendiary attacks by suspected LRA forces in the Democratic Republic of Congo.
	September 17	In Mogadishu, Somalia, 16 peacekeepers are killed and another 21 wounded in suicide VIED attacks by Shahaab al-Islamiya.
2010	March 29	40 civilians killed, 91 others injured in a double suicide bombing attack in Moscow by the Caucasus Emirate.
	August 23	87 people, including 8 children, killed with another 231 injured in an armed attack by al-Shabaab al-Islamiya in Mogadishu, Somalia.
2011	January 24	A suicide bomber in the Domodedovo Airport in Moscow set off a blast killing 35 people in the waiting area, before the security checkpoints.

An Idea Whose Time Has Come?

The terrorist of yesterday is the hero of today, and the hero of yesterday becomes the terrorist of today. In a constantly changing world of images, we have to keep our heads straight to know what terrorism is and what it is not.

— *Eqbal Ahmad*

Will the death of Osama bin Laden, leader of al-Qaeda, signal an end to the threat of terrorism today? Probably not, most experts agree. Is there evidence that terrorism has been decreasing since the declaration of a "war on terror" in 2001? Given the terrorist attacks in Madrid, London, Baghdad, and Kabul, this is clearly not the case. But the violence of the past two decades was clearly less than that of the decades during which the world experienced the trauma of two global wars. There was certainly less loss of life than during the years in which the Indo–China conflict raged. In fact, fewer lives were claimed by political violence during recent years than by traffic accidents on U.S. highways annually.

So why is so much attention directed toward developing policies to cope with terrorist violence today? It is easy to simplify or to generalize too much about this critically important phenomenon, and it has attracted what could be considered an inordinate amount of attention, compared to other major problems of our times, such as global debt and world hunger. Terrorism has been the subject of countless speeches by political leaders and the impetus for numerous initiatives and conferences by foreign policy experts. The drama of terrorist-directed events such as those outlined in the Selective Chronology of Recent Terror (see pp. xxi–xxiv) attracts enormous attention in the press and on television worldwide. Terror-violence did, in many respects, become a method of warfare during the latter part of the twentieth century. In the twenty-first century, terrorism itself has become a target of "war" on the part of the international community, clearly increasing the level of violence and the number of victims.

In the wake of the events of September 2001, a global "war on terrorism" began to be waged, led by the United States and sanctioned by the United Nations. While the initial context of the "war" took place in Afghanistan, neither the toppling of the Taliban leadership nor the disruption of the al-Qaeda network in Afghanistan sufficed to "win" this new war. Terrorism is an ancient "enemy" with roots in many cultures and followers in many creeds. A "war" against such an enemy will not be quickly brought to a successful conclusion.

Certainly, terrorism has been waged by a wide variety of individuals and groups. It has been a favorite tactic of national and religious groups, individuals whose ideologies fall on both the left and the right of the political spectrum, and nationalist and internationalist movements. It has been used as an instrument of state policy. It has been directed against autocratic as well as democratic regimes although political democracies have been the most frequent targets. At times, it has been an instrument of last resort for movements of national liberation whose political attempts to change the system have failed; at other times, it has been deliberately chosen by such movements *before* other political options have been attempted.

States have sponsored terrorism outside their own frontiers and have used terrorism as a weapon against their own citizens. Terrorism remains, paradoxically, both an instrument designed to force radical social and political changes and an instrument of oppression in seeking to prevent such changes.

Even with the increased use of terrorist violence, or perhaps because of its proliferation, there remains a great deal of confusion as to what the term *terrorism* really encompasses. Many definitions of terrorism are encoded political statements. Too often the term is used in a pejorative sense, attached as a label to those groups whose political objectives one finds objectionable. To study this phenomenon, we must first establish a workable definition—workable in that it has sufficient precision to allow us to identify the phenomenon when it occurs. *Terrorism* is a politicized term; its definition must, therefore, be politically acceptable.

MODERN DEFINITIONS OF AN OLD CONCEPT

Terrorism is a phenomenon that is becoming a pervasive, often dominant, influence in our lives. It affects the manner in which governments conduct their foreign policies and the way corporations transact their businesses. It causes alterations in the role and even the structure of our security forces. It forces us to spend huge amounts of time and money to protect our public figures, vital installations, citizens, and even our systems of government. It influences the way we travel and the places we travel to see. It even affects the manner in which we live our daily lives. Our newspapers, radios, and televisions inundate every waking moment with vivid details of terrorist spectaculars from all corners of the globe.

But what *is* terrorism—this "it" to which we attribute so much influence today? Before we can assess just how great a threat "it" poses and exactly whom "it" threatens, we need to determine what "terrorism" is. And it is precisely this problem of definition that has caused political, legal, and military leaders to throw up their hands, metaphorically, in discouragement.

Because terrorism is a political as well as a legal and military issue, its definition has been slow to evolve. Not that there are not numerous definitions available—there are hundreds. But few of them reflect sufficient legal scholarship to be useful in international law, and most of the legally useful definitions lack the necessary ambiguity for political acceptance. As Eqbal Ahmad noted, "Officials don't define terrorism because definitions involve a commitment to analysis, comprehension, and adherence to norms of consistency."[1]

The problem of defining *terrorism* is not insuperable, but it must be handled with caution in order for subsequent use of the term to have meaning. To say that the number of terrorist incidents is rising annually has little meaning unless it is precisely clear what such an incident *is* and *is not*.

It helps to put the term into an historical perspective. Terrorism is not a modern phenomenon. The admixture of religion and politics fomenting terrorism in many areas today has a counterpart in the *hashashin* of the Middle Ages. Incidents such as the *Achille Lauro* hijacking in 1985 have precedents dating back many centuries. The statement that "one man's terrorist is another man's patriot" illustrates the historical continuum of conflict under which terrorism is operationally defined.

Ideology has always had an ambiguous relationship with terrorism—at one point justifying and at another condemning the same act. Theorists (and practitioners) of both the left and the right have advocated the use of what has been termed "terrorist" violence. Understanding the context of the ideological debate helps to illuminate the justifications offered in contemporary times for terrorist acts.

It also helps to assess the ideological commitment of the perpetrators of terrorism. Profiling modern terrorists is one way of assessing terrorism's current commitment. An understanding of the impact of group dynamics is also useful in critiquing the rationale behind such acts. Patterns in the type of recruiting done among groups committing terrorist acts lend substance to these profiles of modern terrorists.

While the official definition of *terrorism* adopted by many countries today limits application of the term to nonstate actors, terrorism is not strictly a phenomenon committed by individuals or groups. In fact, *terrorism* as a political term derived from *state* terror. So any analysis of the ways in which states use terrorism as an instrument of foreign and domestic policies offers vital insights, particularly when a war, such as the one initiated by the United States in Iraq in 2003, is premised to some degree on the commission of state terrorism by the leader deposed in the ensuing conflict.

Some states are involved in the network emerging among individuals and groups involved in the commission of terrorist acts. Opinions differ as to the extent, cohesiveness, and ideological commitment of this network, but evidence of its existence is beyond reasonable dispute. Nations such as Iraq, Syria, and Iran have repeatedly been accused of involvement in state-sponsored terrorism. The linkage between states and terrorism will be explored in depth later, focusing on questions such as: How is the terrorism financed? What are its targets? The emergence of what is termed *netwar* as a pattern for some modern terrorist groups and the creative use of money transfer systems like *hawala* offer opportunities to plumb the murky depths of the "terror network."

Understanding of *why* and *who* leads to questions of *how*. Profiles of terrorist events offer thumbnail sketches and disturbing insights into the *how* of terrorism. The depth of media involvement in the making of a "terrorist spectacular," for instance, can provide useful clues to why this is so sensitive an area of democratic policymaking. Analysis of potential targets and weapons raises crucial and frightening questions for democratic systems.

The response of the systems—legal, military, and political—to the threat and reality of terrorism is, of course, crucial to any understanding of the problem of terrorism today. The willingness as well as the capacity of the international community, and of an individual nation, to respond to this form of "warfare" is critical to any assessment of the role of terrorism in shaping our world. The difference between the responses to domestic, as opposed to international, terrorism may also be critical as democratic nations seek ways to respond to terrorism without sacrificing fundamental principles.

Democracies, throughout history, have been the effective targets of terrorist attacks, because democratic systems must "play by the rules" and thus cannot respond in comparable fashion to terrorist attacks. Autocracies and totalitarian systems are able to respond more easily to terrorist acts *with* terrorist acts, which sometimes serve as an effective deterrent, but democracies cannot make such responses. A comparative look at counterterrorism in the democratic systems of the United States and New Zealand in Chapter 12, with their enactment of laws and security systems, offers insights into the patterns of terrorism and response characteristic of democracies today.

Ultimately, the question may not be how nations can eliminate terrorism but rather how much the likelihood of terrorist acts can be prevented, and the amount of terrorism a state can tolerate. New laws and new technology are changing the face of terrorism, but since it is not vanishing, then new thresholds for "acceptable" violence may well be emerging. With the development of effective and accessible chemical and biological as well as nuclear weapons, these thresholds may determine the survival of humanity.

This discussion in no sense covers *all* that could be said about terrorism. This is a contemporary review of current acts of terrorism. Definitions of *terrorism*, like the act itself, continue to undergo changes. The definition suggested in the following section highlights certain important facets of the issue, answering some questions while raising a multitude of others. Such a study can provide a frame of reference from which it should be possible to analyze this phenomenon—the instrument and the nemesis of rulers, governments, and citizens.

CRUCIAL COMPONENTS OF TERRORISM

While it has not been possible, yet, to create a universally acceptable definition of *terrorism*, it is both possible and necessary to specify certain features common to the phenomenon. This in turn makes it feasible to create an operational definition of this term. Acts possessing *all* of these attributes could then be identified as terrorist acts with some consistency, making data analysis of this phenomenon more meaningful. Without falling into the political quagmire of attempting to label individuals or groups as "terrorist," certain types of *actions* could be identified as terrorism, regardless of who commits them, for however noble a cause.

Let us consider a loose definition of *contemporary terrorism*. It must of necessity be "loose," because its elements tend to form a variety of compounds, which today fall within the rubric of terrorism. For the purposes of this investigation, **terrorism** will be defined as *a synthesis of war and theater, a dramatization of the most proscribed kind of violence—that which is deliberately perpetrated on civilian noncombatant victims—played before an audience in the hope of creating a mood of fear, for political purposes.*

This description of terrorism has a number of crucial components. Terrorism, by this definition, involves an act of violence, an audience in which a mood of fear is created, targeted civilian noncombatant victims, and political motives or goals. Each of these elements is contained in the definitions currently in use by national and international agencies.

While there are significant differences in established American definitions of *terrorism*, they do share common elements suggested in the definition above. For example, the U.S. Department of State uses the following definition:

> premeditated, politically motivated violence perpetrated against noncombatant targets by subnational groups or clandestine agents, usually intended to influence an audience.[2]

The U.S. Department of Defense defines terrorism as:

> the unlawful use, or threatened use, of force or violence against individuals or property to coerce and intimidate governments or societies, often to achieve political, religious, or ideological objectives.[3]

The U.S. Federal Bureau of Investigation (FBI) also includes these key elements in its definition of terrorism:

> the unlawful use of force or violence against persons or property to intimidate or coerce a government, the civilian population, or any segment thereof, in furtherance of political or social objectives.[4]

There are a few significant points to note from this quick examination of definitions:

1. The definitions are of *acts* of terrorism, not of people or of groups. Thus, applying the term "terrorist" to an individual or a group is not supported by the definitions at this point.

2. The definitions do *not* include state terrorism; although, states have certainly committed far worse acts of terror than any group or individual has yet accomplished. State terrorism is often ignored in state-generated definitions of terrorism, for political reasons. Although the United Nations has generated a dozen treaties dealing with terrorism, it has not reached agreement on a universal definition of terrorism.

The basic criteria—acts of violence, designed to create a mood of fear in an audience, for political/social motives, targeting people not engaged in combat—are incorporated into many modern definitions of terrorism in use today. Each term deserves some clarification in order to formulate a clear set of parameters for this frequently misunderstood and misused concept.

Violence, Audience, and a Mood of Fear

First, note that terrorism is fundamentally a violent act. Sit-ins, picket lines, walkouts, and other similar forms of protest, no matter how disruptive, are *not* terrorist acts. Violence—the threat of violence where the capacity and the willingness to commit violence are displayed—is endemic to terrorism. The violence need not be fully perpetrated—that is, the bomb need not be detonated or all of the passengers aboard an airliner killed—in order for it to be considered a terrorist act. But the capacity and the willingness to commit a violent act *must* be present.

This violence need not be lethal to human targets to meet these definitional criteria. Violence is destructive, but the destruction need not necessarily take lives; it may instead disrupt lives without destroying them. For instance, the modern phenomenon known as cyber attacks could be called a form of terrorism, because it is certainly potentially disruptive, although not necessarily lethal to human targets. The violence is against a system, rather than a physical human body, but the disruption and the mood of fear induced are potentially devastating.

This means, then, that it is the *perception* of the audience of that violent potential that is crucial to classifying an act as terrorism. Terrorism is, as Brian Jenkins noted two decades ago, essentially theater, an act played before an audience, designed to call the attention of millions, to an often-unrelated situation through shock—producing situations of outrage and horror, doing the unthinkable without apology or remorse. Unlike similar acts of murder or warfare, acts of terrorism are neither ends in themselves, nor are they often more than tangentially related to the ends sought. They are simply crafted to create a mood of fear or terror in that audience.

This mood is not the result, moreover, of the numbers of casualties caused by the act of violence. Automobile accidents cause greater numbers of injuries and deaths each year in the United States, without necessarily invoking a mood of terror among other drivers. Nor is it the deliberate nature of the death inflicted that causes the audience response. Individuals are murdered in nonpolitical, nonterrorist acts throughout the world each year without provoking widespread fear.

Victims: The Right Place—But the Wrong Time

Instead, the creation of this mood of intense anxiety seems specifically linked to the nature of the victim of terrorist acts. As one scholar notes:

> To qualify as an appropriate victim of a terrorist today, we need not be tyrants or their sympathizers; we need not be connected in any way with the evils the terrorist perceives; we need not belong to a particular group. We need only be in the wrong place at the wrong time.[5]

Terrorism is, thus, distinguished from guerilla warfare by deliberate attacks upon civilians not engaged in combat and the separation of its victims from the ultimate goal—the "playing to an audience" aspect of a terrorist act. Terrorism can be distinguished from legal acts of warfare and ordinary crimes of murder. As David Fromkin points out:

> Unlike the soldier, the guerilla fighter, or the revolutionist, the terrorist . . . is always in the paradoxical position of undertaking actions the immediate physical consequences of which are not particularly desired by him. An ordinary murderer will kill someone because he wants the person to be dead, but a terrorist will shoot somebody even though it is a matter of complete indifference to him whether that person lives or dies.[6]

Put more simply, the difference between a terrorist act and a similar crime or war activity is that terrorist acts are perpetrated *deliberately* upon civilian noncombatant third parties in an effort to coerce the opposing party or persons into some desired political course of action. Victims are chosen not primarily because of their personal guilt but because their deaths or injuries, the disruption of their lives, will shock the opposition. Terrorist acts, in other words, are constructed to deliberately "make war" on persons not involved in combat situations.

This distinction will need some explanation. The laws of war permit waging war between national armies, within certain humanitarian limits. Even for the enemy in a violent protracted conflict, some types of behavior (such as genocide and torture) are expressly forbidden, and certain basic amenities are required to be preserved (regarding such issues as the treatment of prisoners of war).[7] "War" as waged by terrorist acts violates these rules in that those deliberately destroyed are not principally armed military opponents, but hapless civilians. Rules of international behavior, particularly those that pertain to political responsibility and military obligations, offer maximum protection to civilian noncombatants, regarded as "innocent persons" even in time of war. Terrorism makes a practice of persistent, deliberate harm to precisely that type of person.

The distinction between a terrorist act and a legitimate act of guerrilla warfare is not always clear. In Iraq today, the distinction between terrorist acts and acts of revolutionary violence (which are legal under the laws of war) is often difficult for soldiers and civilians alike to determine. An individual explosive device (IED) planted at a roadside or near a recruiting station is not clearly targeted at civilians, but frequently generates nonmilitary casualties. If the device is placed in a market, frequented by primarily civilians, then the line is clearer in marking the event as a terrorist act. But if it is placed on a highway most often used by military forces and is not triggered deliberately when a busload of ordinary people passes, this is less clearly terrorism and more likely to be judged an act of revolutionary or insurgency violence—destructive, but not terrorist in nature, as it did not deliberately target innocent people.

The point here is that a terrorist deliberately chooses to invoke injury on the civilian noncombatant in an effort to shock the political or military audience. Injury to those not engaged in combat, thus, is not an undesirable accident or by-product, but the carefully sought consequence of a terrorist act.

A terrorist act is committed, not against a military target necessarily nor against the person in direct opposition to the perpetrators, as the ultimate goal is not usually the death of one leader. Unlike the terrorism practiced by nineteenth-century anarchists, twentieth-century terrorist acts are deliberately aimed against civilian noncombatants, third parties whose loss of well-being can be expected to evoke a desired response from the opposition and/or the audience watching the event throughout the world.

It is important to note here that the terms *civilian* and *noncombatant* are used in this working definition of terrorism. There are two critical problems with this designation. The first is that the term *civilian* is not easily applied in low-level guerrilla warfare, where many who engage in such conflict are never formally enrolled in any army nor are they issued any materials that would identify them as soldiers (uniforms, identification tags, and the like). Therefore, their status as "civilians" will always be called into question, making application of the term *terrorism* to the acts against them potentially subjective.

The problems with using the term *noncombatant* are similarly rooted in a desire to prevent subjective use of the term *terrorism*. Many of the world's military are engaged today in what are termed *peacekeeping* activities, which in theory at least should be a noncombat status. The term *peacekeeping* itself does not appear in the UN Charter, so there is a lack of clarity as to what peacekeeping really is and what the rules for such activity should be. Thus, the soldiers engaged in this type of activity could be regarded as combatants or noncombatants, depending on the political view of the group or government reacting to their activities. This confusion as to definition, and hence to status, makes the application of the term *terrorism* to attacks on such military units potentially pejorative and legally vulnerable. When clarity of definition for *peacekeeping* makes it possible to determine whether or not military engaged in such activity are combatants or noncombatants, it is potentially confusing to use this term in a working definition.

The problem with confusion in the definition of "terrorism" is clearly demonstrated in the data tracking and analysis of contemporary acts of terrorism. As Case Study 1.1 illustrates, the "real" number of terrorist incidents altered dramatically in 1998 and again in 2006, not necessarily reflecting an actual increase in incidents but indicating a difference in the *definition* of the attacks being recorded.

Redefining "Terrorism"

Until 1998, the database used by the U.S. Central Intelligence Agency (CIA) considered terrorism incidents carried out within one country "domestic" rather than international, even if the group planning and carrying out the operation had international ties. Thus, most of the incidents occurring inside of Israel and the occupied territories carried out by Harakat al-Muqawamah al-Islamiyyah or Islamic Resistance Movement (HAMAS) or Hezbollah were not included in the data pool, as they were "domestic," by this definition. The change in definition clearly provided a much larger number of incidents for inclusion, but the definition was not retroactive in the data pool at that time.

In 2006, the number of terrorist incidents appears to dramatically increase again, with the increase partially explained by the confusion over the classification of attacks occurring in Iraq and Afghanistan. As noted earlier, such acts often had a combination of civilian noncombatant as well as military deaths and injuries, so determining whether these acts were genuinely "terrorist attacks" or were instead the

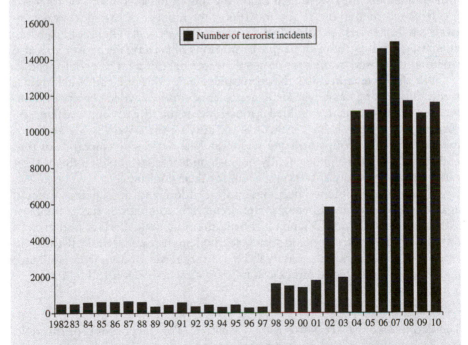

FIGURE 1.1
Number of Terrorist Incidents Each Year.

Source: U.S. Department of State "Report on Terrorism," issued annually, 1982–2010.

(continued)

legitimate actions of an insurgency targeting military with a perhaps excessive number of civilian casualties was extremely difficult. The acts could legitimately be classified as "crimes of war" for the number of civilian casualties, but were not as clearly identifiable as acts of terrorism. Indeed, the United States at this point separated the acts of "terrorism" in Iraq and Afghanistan from other acts of international terrorism recorded, highlighting this data collection and analysis problem. The impact of the "redefinition" of the acts of terrorism being recorded was clear, and not desirable, for a country and a world engaged in a "war on terrorism." ■

The need for a universally applicable definition of terrorism is clear, but the ability to generate such a definition and to apply it consistently has not yet developed, even within one country. Tracking "trends in terrorism" when the definition of such acts remains in flux makes such data analysis questionable. While engaged in a "war on terrorism," it is clearly vital that an operational definition be both developed and consistently applied today.

Although the definitional problem is not yet resolved, the focus on civilian noncombatant victims highlights another disturbing aspect of modern terrorism. Until recently, although most of the victims of terrorism were civilian noncombatants, they were also relatively few in number. In those terrorist incidents recorded in the 1950s and 1960s, the number of casualties was relatively small. Experts speculated that perhaps the terrorists felt a need to avoid alienating certain groups of people or portions of society. Perhaps it was also true that terrorists "want a lot of people watching, not a lot of people dead."[8]

But the attacks in 2001 that took place in New York and Washington, using fully loaded passenger airplanes to crash into crowded centers of commerce and government, heralded a loosening of the threads constraining terrorists in their search for victims. As the craving for a worldwide audience increases among groups utilizing terrorism, the increasing tolerance of that audience for violence may actually be pushing terrorists to widen their target range to create a more spectacular event for their audience.

Thus, as the violence becomes more randomized, it is being directed against a wider range of persons. Children are becoming targets, as the massacres at the Rome and Vienna airports, the tragedy at Beslan, and attacks on school buses in Ireland and Israel clearly demonstrated. Ironically, this increase in innocent targets may well be a direct result of a viewing audience no longer as interested in attacks on military attachés or political figures.

Political Quicksand

The definition of an act of "terrorism" matters. For the purposes of this text, *terrorism* will be defined as an act of violence perpetrated on innocent civilian noncombatants in order to evoke fear in an audience. One further component, however, is necessary for this definition to be operational. As it stands, such a definition could reasonably be applied to actions taken by professional football players on the playing field!

The addition of a "political purpose" to the concept of terrorism continues to create enormous legal problems. Although establishing parameters for this concept of political purpose is crucial, particularly in light of the fact that political crimes and criminals have enjoyed special status under international law for centuries, the concept remains largely undefined.

Much of the confusion today results from a misperception that the presence of political *motivation* is sufficient to establish the political character of an action. An extradition case in 1980 clearly stated that, "An offense is not of a political character simply because it was politically motivated."[9] The prevailing Anglo-American rule of law, derived from *in re Castroni,* contains two basic criteria for determining the "political" quality of an action. These requirements, simply stated, were that (1) the act at issue must have occurred during a political revolt or disturbance and (2) the act at issue must have been incidental to and have formed part of that same revolution or disturbance.[10]

A political motive thus may be termed *necessary* but it is not sufficient to earn for an action a "political offense" status under international law. Nicholas Kittrie suggested that a "pure political offense" would consist of acts "which challenge the State but affect no private rights of innocent parties."[11] By this definition, a political revolution or disturbance is an essential ingredient in which the political offense plays only a part. Moreover, the offense must bring harm *only* to the state, while protecting innocent parties from harm through reasonable precautions. This has the effect of narrowing the classes of acceptable victims.

Political assassination by organized revolutionaries careful to cause as little harm as possible to innocent persons remains protected to some extent within the political offense provisions of international law. Hence, the assassination of the Grand Duke Sergius might qualify for political offense status, while the mob violence of the Paris Commune would clearly not.

Obviously, the political element of an act of terrorism adds considerable confusion, both in the legal and in the political realms. Although it is a necessary component to a definition of *terrorism*, it is so ambiguous a concept that it is often a two-edged sword, offering insights into the causes of an act while providing gaping loopholes in the law through which perpetrators of heinous acts continue to slither.

What distinguishes terrorism, then, from purely political actions may be the illegality of the violence employed, primarily in terms of the victims of the offenses. What distinguishes the terrorist of today from the football player, the political assassin, and the revolutionary engaged in regular or irregular warfare may be the *lack* of legitimacy that his or her actions enjoy under international norms. By its very nature, terrorism involves the deliberate disruption of norms, the violation of generally accepted standards of decency, including the laws of war as they apply to the innocent and helpless.[12]

Because this is a confusing and contradictory area in the definition of terrorism, it is useful to review the issue once more. What is it, then, which distinguishes the terrorist act from other acts of war, as well as from other political or common crimes? Few would argue that wars, whether between or within states, could or should occur without violence, without the inflicting of injury and death. As individuals we may deplore the violence, but as nations we have recognized its inevitability and have accorded it a limited legitimacy.

But international rules have been created and accepted that govern the acceptable types of violence, even in war. The international community does not forbid the use of *all* violence; it does, however, suggest basic rules for the use of violence. Many of these rules are directed toward the protection of civilian populations. Even in the life-and-death struggles between nations, these laws focus on minimizing of danger of injury or death to noncombatants, civilians with neither military or political rank nor involvement in the conflict.[13]

Political motivation, then, is *not* a lever by which acts of terrorism can be justified under international law. On the contrary, international law makes it clear that, regardless of the motive, some acts of political violence are never acceptable.

TYPOLOGIES OF TERRORISM: USEFUL TOOLS

At this point, let us look at some typologies of terrorism. Feliks Gross, a leading authority on revolutionary terror, has suggested that at least five types of terror-violence exist:

1. **Mass terror** is *terror by a state, where the regime coerces the opposition in the population, whether organized or unorganized, sometimes in an institutionalized manner.*
2. **Dynastic assassination** is *an attack upon a head of state or a ruling elite,* precisely the kind of terrorism that the international community tried to criminalize in the mid-nineteenth century.
3. **Random terror** involves *the placing of explosives where people gather (such as post offices, railroads, and cafes) to destroy whoever happens to be there.* "Algerian revolutionaries left bombs in public places in Paris," one scholar notes, "apparently convinced that one Frenchman blown to bits was pretty much like any other."[14]
4. **Focused random terror** restricts *the placing of explosives, for example, to where significant agents of oppression are likely to gather* (as in the aforementioned case of the attack on Grand Duke Sergius).
5. Finally, **tactical terror** is *directed solely against the ruling government as a part of a "broad revolutionary strategic plan."*[15]

Table 1.1 summarizes some of the types of terrorism in use today. Although not all of the possible categories of terrorism are included, it is useful to compare the tactics, targets, and perpetrators of such types of terrorism.

Such a typology leaves some guerrilla activity enmeshed in the terrorist label. Although numerous other typologies of terrorism have been offered by various scholars, review of them in detail would not significantly contribute to the development of a workable definition of *contemporary terrorism.* However, a few important points of interest can be made about these typologies.

TABLE 1.1

Types of Terrorism

Type	Committed by	Target	Tactics
Mass terror endemic authorized enforcement repressive	Political leaders (e.g., Joseph Stalin's rule in the USSR)	General population	Coercion organized or unorganized
Dynastic assassination	Individuals or groups (e.g., assassination of Anwar Sadat)	Head of state or ruling elite	Very selective violence
Random terror	Individuals or groups (e.g., attacks on the World Trade Center in New York City)	Anyone in "the wrong place at the wrong time"	Bombs in cafes, markets, and similar places
Focused random terror	Individuals or groups (e.g., Provisional Irish Republican Army and Ulster Defense Force bombings in Northern Ireland)	Members of the "opposition"	Bombs in specific cafes and markets
Tactical terror (revolutionary)	Revolutionary movements (e.g., M-19 attacks on Colombian justices)	The government	Attacks on politically attractive targets

One is that most typologies developed today include some form of state terrorism as well as individual and group terrorism. What Feliks Gross terms "mass" terrorism is described by U.S. Department of State analyst Thomas Thornton as "enforcement" terror,[16] and by political scientist Paul Wilkinson as "repressive" terror.[17] Whatever the label applied to this particular type of terror, it is obvious that some consensus exists on the propriety of including some repressive state tactics in the classification of terrorist acts.

The typologies also suggest that a wide variety of acts have been encompassed under the rubric of terrorism, including many engaged in by revolutionary groups, and composed of both internal activities and activities that cross state lines, but all of which are politically motivated and directed toward some end other than the immediate act of violence. These observations serve both to fortify the conclusions already drawn concerning the distinctive nature of terrorist acts and to highlight certain points of dissension that may contribute to the clouding of our understanding of this term.

USING TACTICS AS LABELS

Before summarizing the conclusions concerning a working definition of *terrorism*, one further point needs to be emphasized. Both the typologies of terrorism and the working definition of terrorism being offered treat terrorism as a *tactic*, not as a *goal*. This is important if the term *terrorism* is not to be used or misused by governments unsympathetic to a group's cause. To describe a particular action as a terrorist action does not, and should not, in any sense define either the group or the cause for which it uses that tactic as terrorist.

It is true that if an individual, a group, or a government chooses to use this particular tactic repeatedly, those observing the actions will associate the tactic with those individuals. Continued or prolonged use of such a tactic by any group or government contributes to the perception of that group or government as terrorist by the audience for whom the crime is committed. This is not necessarily accurate, nor is it inaccurate: it is simply a natural phenomenon.

This is true to some extent of groups that repeatedly engage in terrorist acts. The frequency with which they engage in such actions, and to some degree the openness with which they do so, will certainly have an effect on whether their audience views them as terrorists. This does not mean that the ends toward which they strive are bad, somehow tainted with the opprobrium of terrorism. It simply means that the audience for whom the terrorist acts are generally staged has mentally associated the actors with the actions taken in pursuit of the cause.

This is, of course, a very narrow line of reasoning, one not clearly understood by the general public, which is often the audience for terrorist events. That same public frequently attaches a terrorist label to individuals and even to groups who engage on a fairly regular basis in terrorist acts. But in terms acceptable in the legal and political community, it is only the *act* that can accurately be labeled as "terrorist"—not the individual or the group and certainly not the cause for which the tactic is employed.

Members of a group cannot engage in questionable or even blatantly illegal actions on a regular basis and not be tainted with the negative labels associated with such actions. Members of Mafia families, although they may themselves be several steps removed from the actual commission of organized crimes, are nevertheless viewed by both the general public and by law enforcement agencies as being linked to, and part of, those deplorable actions.

So it is with terrorism. Those who commit it, and those whose groups or governments have chosen to use it as a tactic, cannot escape the label of "terrorist" given them by the very audience toward which such acts are directed. The justice of a cause rarely is sufficient, in that audience's view, to excuse the use of such a tactic. Certain acts can be described by definition as terrorist acts whether they are carried out by democratic governments in pursuit of reasonable policy goals or by armed revolutionaries fighting for freedom against tyranny.

CONCLUSIONS

Terrorism, then, is an act composed of at least four crucial elements: (1) It is an act of violence, (2) it has a political motive or goal, (3) it is perpetrated against civilian noncombatants, and (4) it is staged to be played before an audience whose reaction of fear and terror is the desired result. This definition eliminates football players, lunatics on a killing spree, and the assassin who tries to kill a bad ruler from the label of terrorist. All acts of violence are not terrorist acts, however heinous the acts may be.

Unfortunately, the line between acceptable types of violence and unacceptable types is not always clear. Violence by revolutionaries and by the state is sometimes difficult to categorize clearly as terrorist, even given the working definition evolved here. Further study of the history, ideology, and individuals involved in terrorist acts may increase our understanding of this important but confusing term.

DISCUSSION

Using the definition in a practical application is one method of increasing one's understanding of the usefulness and limitation of the definition. Listed next are two brief sketches of what were termed by some observers to be terrorist acts. Use the four criteria in the definition of terrorism suggested in this chapter to decide whether these incidents were, in fact, terrorist acts. Try also to decide which type of terrorism, if any, was involved, using any one of the typologies mentioned.

1. In November 2003, a U.S. transport plane carrying soldiers engaged in peacekeeping and nation building in postwar Iraq was shot down by a surface-to-air missile. Sixteen of these soldiers, who were being transported to planes to take them on the first stage of their journey home for a brief leave, were killed. Iraqi groups seeking to force the United States out of their country claimed responsibility for the attack.
2. In April 2011, a U.S. unmanned drone attack killed at least 25 people in Pakistan's North Waziristan region. The dead included 3 women and 4 children, as well as 18 suspected militants.
3. Just before dawn on October 23, 1983, a vehicle laden with about 2,500 tons of TNT blew up the U.S. Marine headquarters near the Beirut, Lebanon, airport. Around 230 people were reported killed, most of them as they slept. The Free Islamic Revolutionary Movement claimed responsibility for the action.
4. In April 1999, an attack by two students at Columbine High School in a suburb of Denver, Colorado, resulted in the deaths of 15, while more than 20 people were wounded, some of them critically. The attackers, identified as Eric Harris, 18, and Dylan Klebold, 17, both juniors at the school, reportedly laughed and hooted as they opened fire on classmates after they had booby-trapped the school with pipe bombs. Harris and Klebold were members of a group calling itself the Trenchcoat Mafia, outcasts who bragged about guns and bombs, and hated Blacks, Hispanics, and student athletes.

ANALYSIS CHALLENGE

Go to the following websites and try to find a clear, legally applicable definition of "terrorism."

http://www.state.gov/s/ct/rls/crt/2009/140901.htm
http://www.fbi.gov/albuquerque/priorities
http://legalift.wordpress.com/2010/11/24/u-n-remains-deadlocked-on-defining-terrorism/

Which do you think is the best? Why?

KEY TERMS

terrorism 5   random terror 12   tactical terror 12
mass terror 12   focused random
dynastic assassination 12   terror 12

SUGGESTED READINGS AND RESOURCES

Hoffman, Bruce. *Inside Terrorism.* New York: Columbia University Press, 2006.
Howard, Russell D., and Reid Sawyer, eds. *Terrorism and Counterterrorism: Understanding the New Security Environment.* Guilford, CT: Dushkin/McGraw-Hill, 2002.
Kegley, Charles W. *The New Global Terrorism: Characteristics, Causes, Controls.* Upper Saddle River, NJ: Prentice Hall, 2003.
Laqueur, Walter. *The New Terrorism: Fanaticism and the Arms of Mass Destruction.* Oxford: Oxford University Press, 1999.
———, ed. *Voices of Terror: Manifestos, Writings and Manuals of al-Qaeda, Hamas, and other Terrorists from Around the World and Throughout the Ages.* New York: Reed Press, 2004.
Martin, Gus. *Understanding Terrorism: Challenges, Perspectives, and Issues.* Thousand Oaks, CA: Sage Publications, 2006.
Sederberg, Peter. "Explaining Terrorism." In *Terrorism: Contending Themes in Contemporary Research,* ed. Peter Sederberg. Boston: Houghton Mifflin, 1993.
Wilkinson, Paul. *Terrorism and the Liberal State.* New York: New York University Press, 1979.

NOTES

1. Eqbal Ahmad, "Terrorism: Theirs and Ours," in *Terrorism and Counterterrorism: Understanding the New Security Environment,* ed. Russell D. Howard and Reid Sawyer (Guilford, CT: Dushkin/McGraw-Hill, 2002), 47.
2. U.S. Department of State, Title 22 of the United States Code, Section 2656f(d).
3. U.S. Departments of the Army and the Air Force, *Military Operations in Low Intensity Conflict.* Field Manual 100-20/Air Force Pamphlet 3-20. (Washington, DC: Headquarters, Departments of the Army and the Air Force, 1990), 3–1.
4. Terrorist Research and Analytical Center, National Security Division, Federal Bureau of Investigation, *Terrorism in the United States, 2003.* (Washington, DC: U.S. Department of Justice, 2004), p. ii.
5. Irving Howe, "The Ultimate Price of Random Terror," *Skeptic: The Forum for Contemporary History,* 11, no. 58 (January–February 1976): 14.

6. David Fromkin, "The Strategy of Terror," *Foreign Affairs* 53 (July 1975): 689.
7. See Treaty and International Agreements Series no. 3365.
8. Brian M. Jenkins, *International Terrorism: A New Kind of Warfare* (Rand: June 1974): P-5261, 4.
9. *Escobedo v. United States*, 633 F2d. 1098, 1104 (5th Cir. 1980).
10. *In re Castroni* 1 Q.B. 149, 156, 166 (1891).
11. Nicholas N. Kittrie, "Patriots and Terrorists: Reconciling Human Rights with World Order," *Case Western Reserve Journal of International Law,* 13, no. 2 (Spring 1981): 300.
12. Robert Friedlander, *Terrorism: Documents of National and International Control,* vol. 1 (Dobbs Ferry, NY: Oceana, 1979), 286.
13. *Principles of the Nuremberg Charter and Judgment*, formulated by the International Law Commission, 1950 (U.N. General Assembly Records, 5th Session, Supp. 12 A/1315).
14. Feliks Gross, *Political Violence and Terror in Nineteenth and Twentieth Century Russia and Eastern Europe* (New York: Cambridge University Press, 1990), 8.
15. Ibid.
16. Thomas Thornton, "Terror as a Weapon of Political Agitation," in *Internal War,* ed. H. Eckstein (London: International Institute for Strategic Studies, 1964), 77–78.
17. Paul Wilkinson, *Political Terrorism* (Cambridge, MA: Harvard University Press, 1974), 38–44.

Not a Modern Phenomenon

Ironically, perhaps, terrorism in its original context was also closely associated with the ideals of virtue and democracy. The revolutionary leader Maximillien Robespierre firmly believed that virtue was the mainspring of a popular government at peace, but that during the time of revolution must be allied with terror in order for democracy to triumph.

—Bruce Hoffman

HISTORIC ROOTS

Terrorism is an act with deep historic roots, and one that has evolved, like the individuals, groups, and systems that commit it, over time. The fundamental characteristics of a terrorist act have not, perhaps, changed, but the associated tactics, targets, weapons, support systems, and even motivations have substantially changed in recent years. Understanding that this phenomenon has been a part of human history for centuries is useful as long as it is balanced with an awareness that, while the basic elements identifying the act as "terrorism" remain the same over time, the act itself continues to evolve in sometimes startling and often challenging ways.

Even though the word *terrorism* originated during the French Revolution and the Jacobin Reign of Terror (1792–1794), individual acts of terror-violence can be traced back at least to the ancient Greek and Roman republics. By some definitions, the assassination of Julius Caesar in 44 B.C. was an act of terrorism, to the extent that a modern political assassination is defined as terrorism. Modern political science, at any rate, tends to treat **assassination,** *the murder of a political leader*, as a terrorist act.[1] During ancient times, conquerors created a mood of fear in their realms by exterminating whole populations or forcing them into exile. The Romans created terrifying symbols of the consequence of opposition by crucifying prisoners—nailing or tying them to a cross or wooden platform on which they would slowly die a very painful, very public death. Terrorism carried out by rulers was clearly not uncommon centuries ago.

Group terrorism became more common as early as the Middle Ages. In fact, the word *assassin* comes from an Arabic term, **hashashin**, which means "hashish-eater," or "one addicted to hashish."[2] It was used to describe *a sectarian group of Muslims who were employed by their spiritual and political leader, Hassan I Sabah, to spread terror in the form of murder and destruction among religious enemies, including women and children.*

Accounts of Marco Polo's travels include tales of murder committed by these assassins, acting, it was supposed, under the influence of hashish or other such drugs. Even the crusaders, who killed not only fighting men but also women and children in their effort to take Jerusalem from Muslim hands, made mention of this group of fanatics and the terror they inspired.[3] This religious sect, a splinter group of Ismaili Muslims in the late eleventh century, was believed to take the drug hashish prior to committing acts of terrorism on the spiritual and political opponents of their caliph, Hassan I Sabah.

The potent combination of religious and political fanaticism with intoxicating drugs made the legacy of the "Brotherhood of Assassins" formidable. **Narco-terrorism**, as the *linkage between drugs and terrorism* is often termed today, will be described in greater depth in Chapter 7. The impact of religion in stimulating terrorism must also be examined further, as it has become once again a potent force in the modern world, as the events of September 11, 2001, demonstrated.

Another Brotherhood of Assassins emerged from a combination of religion and politics in the 1890s. The Hur Brotherhood, whose roots were in the Sind region of British India, resembled the earlier Islamic Brotherhood of Assassins. Although this later brotherhood was suppressed, after considerable bloodshed, another Hur rebellion occurred in Pakistan in the mid-twentieth century. Much of modern Pakistan's terrorism from its Sikh minority derives from that group's religious and political dissatisfaction with Muslim Pakistan's leaders. Religion and politics continue to take innocent lives in this turbulent region of the world as India and Pakistan, both nuclear powers, stand poised on the brink of war over Kashmir.

There is an important point, which must be made here. Islam is not, in any sense, a violent religion. Neither is Christianity, Judaism, nor any of the other religions in whose name violence has been carried out. However, the mixture of religion and politics has throughout history resulted in violence, frequently against innocent victims, which makes it, according to the definition suggested in Chapter 1, terrorism. The Middle East, as the home of three major world religions, has been plagued by a variety of violent religious sects. Today, nations such as Iran have witnessed—and some have fostered—the creation of violent sects, whose blending of religion and politics resembles that of the Brotherhood of Assassins. Table 2.1 offers a brief insight into the diversity of a few of the larger of these radical religious groups and their locations.

TABLE 2.1

Radical Religious Groups

Group	Description	Activities
al-Qaeda	Islamic extremist group, maintaining a network of supporters with cells in many countries, based in Afghanistan	Attacks on the World Trade Center and Pentagon in the United States Bombing of U.S. embassies in Kenya and Tanzania Links to Madrid and London mass transit attacks
Jemaah Islamiyah (a.k.a.) JI	Islamic extremist group, operating in Southeast Asia	Bombing attacks, including 2002 attack on hotel in Bali, killing over 200
Sikh groups include, among others: *Dashmesh* (active in India, Germany, and Canada); *Dal Khalsa* (active in India, Pakistan, and Germany); *Babbar Khalsa* (active in India, Germany, and Canada)	Several domestic and international groups that seek to establish an independent Sikh state called Khalistan	Regular and bloody attacks against Hindus Blamed for bombing of Air India airline (329 people killed) Desecration of Hindu holy places, bombings, and assassinations
Aryan Nations (active in the United States)	Advocates race war against non-Christian, non-Aryans to protect Christian values	Linked to wide range of attacks on individuals in state and national governments
Ansar al-Islam	Islamic extremist group, operating in northern Iraq	Bombings, assassinations, and destructions of schools for girls and beauty salons
HAMAS (Harakat al-Muqawamah al-Islamiyyah or Islamic Resistance Movement)	Palestinian militant group, seeking to gain control of the Palestinian movement toward statehood, and the creation of an Islamic state	Bombings, including suicide bombings, of Israeli civilian and military targets in West Bank and Gaza
Christian Identity Movement	Racist Christian extremist movement	Eric Rudolph (member)—bombing of abortion clinic Timothy McVeigh (member)—Oklahoma City bombing

The **fedayeen**, *the Islamic "self-sacrificers,"* perceive themselves as engaged in a "holy war" against threats to their religion and culture. This type of war—being waged by more militant sects such as the Taliban in Afghanistan and Osama bin Laden's al-Qaeda network—is similar in many respects to the Brotherhood of Assassins of the Middle Ages. Like the Assassins, modern fedayeen find strength in the promise of a reward in paradise. Unlike the earlier sect, however, these modern zealots believe they will receive their reward in a spiritual paradise, not in the courtyard of the caliph, with drugs and sex. Religion serves as the narcotic that motivates their actions and deadens their consciences to the horror of the slaughter that they inflict on innocent persons.

Thus, the mixture of religion, politics, and narcotics in the commitment of terrorism today is not new, but continues to be quite deadly. History enables us to place current mixtures such as these in context, which makes understanding easier. It has not yet made it possible for governments or organizations to prevent the explosion of these potentially lethal elements.

STATE TERRORISM

The use of "irregular, illegal, and violent means" has never been limited to lone political assassins. The execution of Marie Antoinette on October 16, 1793, was one of the first incidents actually called terrorism. In this instance, the terrorists were not trying to *overthrow* the government—they *were* the government! The Committee of Public Safety, led by Robespierre, chief spokesman of the Jacobin party, governed France during the tumultuous period known as the Reign of Terror (September 1793–July 1794). It is from this period, during which an estimated 20,000 people were killed, that the word *terrorism* evolved. Throughout history, terrorism by a state has been much more lethal, claiming many more lives than that carried out by individuals or groups.

Modern terrorism thus derives its name from a gross example of **state terrorism,** *acts of terrorism that a state commits against defenseless victims,* rather than from terror-violence by a lone assassin or small, fanatic, nonstate group. Although most state-crafted definitions of *terrorism* do not include terrorism initiated by a state (focusing instead on substate groups), states continue to be involved in a wide variety of violent acts, many of which meet the criteria of terrorism, against their own citizens and those of other nations.

Consider the case of piracy. From the sixteenth century forward, pirates have been considered by lawmakers to be the "common enemies of humanity." William Blackstone's *Commentaries* referred to piracy as "an offense against the universal law of society."[4] Yet both England (for whom Blackstone wrote) and America (whose law frequently cites his precepts) licensed **privateers,** *private ships outfitted as warships and given letters of marque and reprisal, allowing them to make war on vessels flying foreign flags.*

Under the reign of Queen Elizabeth I of England, the Elizabethan Sea Dogs, privateer ships sailing under the protection of the English flag, carried out acts of piracy against the Spanish fleet. American privateers played a fairly significant role in both the American Revolution and the War of 1812. Both nations commissioned pirates to carry out acts of terror-violence for them on the high seas, acts that both nations publicly deplore as "offenses against humanity" in their courts today. Modern terrorism continues to occasionally take the form of piracy, but today the piracy is of aircraft as well as sea vessels.

TYRANNICIDE: "TO GO TOO FAST"

The leaders of state perceived by individuals or groups as "unjust" or "terrorist" have been historically the target of another type of act characterized as "terrorism." Assassination has been both an ideological statement and a powerful political weapon, using the vehicle of the doctrine of **tyrannicide**, *the assassination of a (tyrant) political leader.* Throughout Italy during the Renaissance, tyrannicide was widely practiced, while in Spain and France during the Age of Absolutism, it was at least widely advocated. One of the leading advocates of the doctrine of tyrannicide as an acceptable solution to political repression was a Spanish Jesuit scholar, Juan de Mariana, whose principal work, *De Regis Institutions,* was initially banned in France.[5]

In the words of Mariana we find much of the same political justification as that used by leaders of national liberation movements today. Mariana asserted that people necessarily possessed not only the right of rebellion but also the remedy of assassination, stating that "if in no other way it is possible to save the fatherland, the prince should be killed by the sword as a public enemy."[6]

Only ten years after Mariana's words were uttered, the king of France, Henry III, was assassinated by the monk, François Ravaillac. Many leaders since that time have been struck down by persons who claimed to have acted as instruments of justice against a tyrant. Even U.S. President Abraham Lincoln's assassin, John Wilkes Booth, saw his act in such a light, as evidenced by his triumphant shout, *"Sic semper tyrannis!"* (Thus always to tyrants!).[7]

During the latter part of the eighteenth century and early nineteenth century, the **divine right of kings** theory, *that kings rule by divine appointment,* began to lose its political grip on Europe. As the theory of the existence of a social contract between a people and their government began to gain acceptance, those who carried out political offenses such as tyrannicide gradually found a more benign atmosphere in which to act.

As someone acting to right the wrongs committed by government, the political assassin was no longer regarded with universal disfavor. Georges Vidal, a leading French legal scholar, noted:

> Whereas formerly the political offender was treated as a public enemy, he is today considered as a friend of the public good, as a man of progress, desirous of bettering the political institutions of his country, having laudable intentions, hastening the onward march of humanity, his only fault being that he wishes to go too fast, and that he employs, in attempting to realize the progress which he desires, means irregular, illegal, and violent.[8]

Not until the middle of the twentieth century was the murder of a head of state, or any member of his family, formally designated as terrorism. Even today, those who commit the political crime of murder of a head of state often enjoy a special protection in the form of **political asylum,** a type of *sanctuary or refuge for a person who has committed such a crime granted by one government against requests by another government for extradition of that person to be prosecuted for this political crime.*

Just as rulers in previous centuries claimed a "divine right" to rule, political assassins, like those committing murder in the name of religion, frequently claimed to be acting as "divine instruments" of justice. The robes of martyrdom have been donned as readily by political as by religious zealots. Like religious fanatics, political assassins have no hesitation in acting as judge, jury, and executioner, assuring themselves and others that their appointment to these offices were made, not by them, but by a "higher" will or authority.

The concept of **jihad,** or *holy war,* continues to permeate the mixture of religion and politics in the many parts of the world today. The words of al-Qaeda spokesman Suleiman Abu Gheith in a videotaped statement on Al Jazeera in October 2001 echoed this ancient concept when he stated that:

> Allah says fight, and for the sake of Allah, uphold the name of Allah . . . I thank Allah for allowing us to start this *jihad* and ask Allah to give us victory in the face of our enemy.[9]

GUERRILLA WARFARE: SELECTIVE VIOLENCE

Since the French Revolution, terrorism and guerrilla warfare have become increasingly difficult to separate clearly. **Guerrilla warfare** is, essentially, *an insurrectionary armed protest, implemented by means of selective violence.*

To the extent that the violence remains "selective" and the choice of targets military rather than civilian, it is possible to distinguish between guerrilla warfare and terrorism.

The term *guerrilla,* meaning "little war," evolved from Spanish resistance to the invasions of Napoleon in 1808. This war on the Iberian peninsula, in which Spanish guerrillas were aided in making increasingly successful attacks on French encampments by the British military, has become a prototype for the twentieth-century wars of national liberation. In such contemporary struggles, indigenous vigilante groups are often supported openly or covertly by the military of other nations.

Ideology and nationalism combined with terror-violence in the Internal Macedonian Revolutionary Organization (IMRO), a group that made its first appearance in 1893. For several years, the IMRO waged guerrilla warfare, sometimes employing terrorist tactics, against the Turkish rulers of their region. As in the Iberian conflict, other nations both assisted and interfered in the struggle. Bombings and kidnappings, as well as the murder of civilians and officials, were frequent in this "little war." Violence escalated into the Saint Elijah's Rebellion in August 1903, which was dealt with ruthlessly by Turkish authorities. This struggle left thousands dead on both sides, at least 70,000 homeless, and 200 Macedonian villages in ashes.

Turkey's suppression of nationalist struggles by its Armenian population in the early part of the twentieth century generated accusations of genocide and helped to create Armenian groups willing to engage in terrorist activities today. These activities, which include bombings and murders reminiscent of the IMRO, have been directed less by nationalism than by a desire to have revenge for the ruthless suppression of that earlier nationalism. Savagely suppressed nationalism spawned vengeful terrorism by individuals and groups whose demands are perhaps even harder to satisfy than were those of the nationalists of earlier decades.

Events of the 1990s in the former Yugoslavia give credence to the concept that repressed nationalism can, in a resurgent form, exact a bloody toll on innocent civilian populations. In the turbulent years before World War I, the Balkan states were engaged in a wide variety of revolutionary violence. Brigands, calling themselves *comitatus* (committee men), covertly sponsored by Greece, Serbia, and Bulgaria, roamed the countryside. In the worst, not the best, tradition of revolutionaries, these brigands terrorized their fellow citizens, burning, murdering, and robbing all who stood in their way.

World War I was, in fact, triggered by a transnational assassination that had its roots in revolutionary terrorism. A secret Serbian revolutionary organization, popularly known as the Black Hand, was both an organization employed by the Serbian government as an unofficial instrument of national foreign policy and a lethal weapon of political protest against the Austro-Hungarian Empire. On June 28, 1914, a 19-year-old Serbian, Gavrilo Princip, trained by the Black Hand, murdered the heir to the imperial throne of that empire, Archduke Franz Ferdinand, in Sarajevo. This assassination was the catalyst for a series of events that, within a month's time, grew into a global conflagration.

Revolutionary terror-violence triggered international devastation on a scale unprecedented at that time. Conflict in and around Sarajevo in the 1990s is partially explained by this early pattern of revolutionary terror-violence. At least twice within the twentieth century, revolutionary terror-violence was unleashed by groups, governments, and militias against the civilian population within the same region. Memory of violence against women and children within families are hard to relinquish, and repetition of such violence within less than a century makes the creation of a sense of common identity (nationalism) and reconciliation between populations within that region perhaps an impossible goal.

Revolutions are not by definition terrorist events. Indeed, many have been successfully carried out without resort to terrorist tactics. It is increasingly difficult, however, for an untrained and sparsely equipped indigenous army to wage a successful guerrilla war against a strong national standing army. With mounting frustration in the face of apparently insurmountable odds, it is easy to resort to terror-violence to achieve by psychological force what it is not possible to achieve by force of arms.

Perhaps nowhere else in this century has the role of liberationist combined more thoroughly, until recently, with that of terrorist than in the actions of the militant group usually known as the Irish Republican Army (IRA). Britain's suppression of Irish nationalism in the early twentieth century generated "martyrs" for the cause of the rebellion led by the fledgling IRA. This group's guerrilla campaign of murder and terror, growing out of the Sinn Fein movement in 1916, provoked the British to respond with a counterterror campaign. Although this revolutionary terrorism may be said to have stimulated the creation of an independent Irish Republic, the violence did not end with this "success." In the mid-1950s, the Provisional IRA (PIRA) began a second wave of anti-British terror, which continued until 1994. For the next decade, efforts to secure a just and lasting peace have been repeatedly damaged by the groups that splintered from the PIRA, unwilling to move toward peace without fully achieving independence for the whole of the island.

This struggle offers insights in several respects. In addition to being a blend of nationalism and terrorism, it is also a contemporary example of the potent mixture of religion and politics. Catholic Ireland has long resented Protestant Britain's domination of its politics. Northern Ireland, which remains under British rule, is predominantly Protestant, with a Catholic minority.

Thus, the lines of battle are drawn along both nationalistic and religious lines. Catholics in Northern Ireland have tended to support a unification of those Northern provinces with the Republic of Ireland, while Protestants in Northern Ireland have demanded continued British rule. The legacy of hatred and mistrust bred by generations of violence is so bitter that an end to the violence seemed, until the end of the twentieth century, unlikely.

CYCLICAL NATURE OF TERROR

Violence, particularly terrorist violence, has too often created a **cycle of violence,** *with those against whom the terror-violence is first carried out becoming so angered that they resort to terrorism in response, directed against the people or institutions regarded as responsible for the initial terrorist acts.* Each violent act frequently causes equally violent reactions. When the violence is unselective, when innocent people are victimized, the reactive violence is also likely to break all the rules in the selection of targets and thus be terrorist.

Most revolutionary groups assert that it is terrorism by the *state* that provokes, and by its presence justifies, acts of terror-violence by nonstate groups. The relationship between terror-violence by the state and that of nonstate groups and individuals is evident in the history of many modern nation-states. But the nature of that relationship is still the subject of much debate.

Since the French Revolution, terrorism and guerrilla movements have become inextricably intertwined. Perhaps the most prominent proponents of individual and collective violence as a means of destroying governments and social institutions were the Russian anarchists, revolutionaries within Russia who sought an end to the Czarist state of the latter nineteenth century. "Force only yields to force," and terror would provide the mechanism of change, according to Russian radical theorist Alexander Serno-Solovevich.[10]

In the writings of two of the most prominent spokesmen for revolutionary anarchism, Mikhail Bakunin and Sergei Nechaev, one finds philosophies often echoed by modern terrorists. Bakunin, for example, advocated in his *Revolutionary Catechism* (1866) the use of "selective, discriminate terror." Nechaev, in his work *Revolutionary Catechism* (1870), went further in advocating both the theory and practice of pervasive terror-violence. He asserted of the revolutionary:

> [D]ay and night he must have one single thought, one single purpose: merciless destruction. With this aim in view, tirelessly and in cold blood, he must always be prepared to kill with his own hands anyone who stands in the way of achieving his goals.[11]

This is a very large step in the evolution of a terrorist from the lone political assassin of earlier centuries. Even the religious fanatics of the Assassins' genre and the privateers of Elizabethan times were arguably less willing to kill anyone to achieve a political objective. But this difference may have existed more on paper than it did in practice. In spite of this written willingness to kill anyone who stood in the way, the Socialist Revolutionary Party resorted primarily to selective terror-violence and took special pains to avoid endangering innocent bystanders. For instance, the poet Ivan Kalyayev, who assassinated the Grand Duke Sergius on the night of February 17, 1905, had passed up an opportunity earlier that evening to throw the bomb because the Grand Duchess as well as some of her nieces and nephews was riding in the Grand Duke's carriage.[12]

With the creation of the *Narodnaya Volya* (The Will of the People) in 1879, political assassination of a wide range of targets began to become a more common form of political protest, becoming part of an intense cycle of terror and counterterror. This revolutionary group believed terrorism should be used to give constant proof that it is possible to fight the government and to thereby strengthen the revolutionary spirit of the people and its faith in the success of the cause.[13]

It is quite easy to note the blending of revolutionary and state terror-violence during this time. The assassinations of Czar Alexander II in 1881 and of First Minister Peter Stolypin in 1911 were incidents that produced periods of counterterrorism (in the form of state repression). Thus, the terrorist acts of assassination, inspired by brutal repression in the Czarist state, provoked further state terrorism, which in turn inspired revolutionary movement to further acts of violence.

The formation of the Union of Russian Men to combat the growing revolutionary movement "by all means" was not only sanctioned by the Czar but also granted special protection by him. This reactionary group engaged in a variety of terrorist activities, including, but not limited to, political murders, torture, and bombing. The Okhrana (the Czarist secret police) also wreaked fierce counterterror against the militant revolutionaries in an unabated attack until World War I.

TABLE 2.2

Assassinated Leaders, 1881–1912

Individual	Nation	Year of Death
President James Garfield	United States	1881
Czar Alexander II	Russia	1881
Lord Frederick Cavendish—chief secretary	Ireland	1882
President Sadi Carnot	France	1894
Premier Antonio Canovas del Castillo	Spain	1897
Empress Elizabeth	Austria-Hungary	1898
King Umberto I	Italy	1900
President William McKinley	United States	1901
First Minister Peter Stolypin	Russia	1911
Premier Jose Canalejas y Mendez	Spain	1912

George Kennan, commenting on the rising tide of terrorism in Russia during the last half of the nineteenth century, explained the relationship of state and revolutionary terrorism in this way:

Wrong a man . . . deny him all redress, exile him if he complains, gag him if he cries out, strike him in the face if he struggles, and at the last he will stab and throw bombs.[14]

While some of the seeds of a more widespread and random terror-violence were sown in the revolutionary and anarchistic movements of the late nineteenth century, by the beginning of the twentieth century, terror-violence was still principally directed toward political assassination. Between 1881 and 1912, at least ten national leaders had lost their lives to assassins, as Table 2.2 indicates.

CASE STUDY 2.1

Cycle of Violence: From Germany to Israel to Palestine

The cyclical nature of terror is also evident in the events surrounding the creation of the state of Israel. The terrorism spawned in Nazi Germany helped to create a cycle of violence that still grips the Middle East today. After the military collapse of the Central Powers and the Armistice Agreement of November 1918, a large number of largely right-wing paramilitary organizations grew within Germany. In ideology, terrorist method, and political role, these groups were in many respects

(continued)

the historical heirs of the Brotherhood of Assassins. They were also the nuclei for the German *Reichswehr*.

Under the leadership of these organizations Germany perpetrated upon innocent persons the greatest atrocities the world has ever recorded. Organized state terrorism reached its zenith in Nazi Germany, and its victims numbered in the millions. Of those victims, the majority were Jewish. Many who sought to flee the terror tried to emigrate to Palestine, which at that time was under British mandate. Britain had, in 1917, issued the so-called Balfour Declaration, offering a "homeland" for Jews in this mandate in return for help in defeating Germany in World War I. But the British-mandate government, by 1940, was engaged in another world war and was engaged in closing the gates to Jewish immigration into this land, which was, in fact, already occupied by Arabs, most of whose families had lived there for centuries. As the population balance began to swing away from the indigenous Arab population toward the immigration of Jews from Europe fleeing German persecution, the British government sought to stem the tide of refugees, actually turning away shiploads of Jews fleeing the concentration camps of Hitler.

The *Haganah*, a Zionist underground army, and the *Irgun Zvai Leumi*, a Zionist militant force, waged terrorist warfare on the British forces in Palestine. Bombing, murder, and assassination became the order of the day as British counterviolence met with escalating Irgun and Haganah intransigence. With the Irgun bombing of the King David Hotel in 1946, in which many innocent people died or were seriously injured, British determination to quell the rebellion diminished. In 1947, Britain turned Palestine over to the fledgling United Nations.

But during the struggle to gain a homeland free of Nazi terror, the Irgun had practiced terror against the indigenous population. When Israel declared itself to be an independent state in 1948, some of the dispossessed people within its borders and those who fled to surrounding states began a war of revolution and of terror against the new state of Israel.

Israel's initial revolutionary terror-violence against the Palestinian people and the resulting Palestinian terror-violence against the people and the state of Israel spawned a conflict that continues today. Born in bloodshed, violence, and desperation, Israel struggles against the terrorist violence that its very creation evoked. The violence of the Palestine Liberation Organization (PLO), HAMAS, and many other Palestinian groups engaged in terrorism against Israel traces its roots to this cycle. ■

CONCLUSIONS

Is contemporary terrorism different? In what ways? One reason for briefly reviewing the historical patterns and roots of terrorism is to be able to discover what patterns remain accurate in the contemporary world. If terrorism today is just like terrorism of previous centuries, then we can use historical patterns to predict behavior and to construct responses based on successful attempts to combat this phenomenon in the past.

If terrorism today is different, however, then historical patterns will still be useful in designing responses and in understanding the dynamics of the phenomenon. We need to know whether twenty-first-century terrorism is significantly different from its historical counterparts.

David Rapoport, in a critical analysis of historical trends in terrorism, identified what he described as **four waves of modern terror.**[15] According to Rapoport, *the initial "Anarchist" wave began in the 1880s, which lasted for about forty years, and was followed by the "Anti-Colonial" wave, stretching from the 1920s and ending within about forty years in the 1960s. The third wave, which he called the "New Left" wave, began in the late 1960s and dissipated in the 1990s, to be followed by the "Religious" wave, which we are now experiencing.*

Although each of these waves was different, none ended with a complete stoppage of that type of terrorism. So most or all of the historical patterns of terrorism remain today. But there are important differences in modern terrorism. Examination of these differences may help us to understand our contemporary terrorism.

Political Assassinations

Terrorist acts are still directed at heads of state, as the assassination of Benazir Bhutto demonstrated, but state heads are no longer the primary target of most attacks. Security precautions to guard such persons against attack have made it very difficult for a lone assassin to successfully murder such a person. The assassination of Yitzhak Rabin, prime minister of Israel in 1995, demonstrated that it is not impossible for such an attack to occur with success. However, in the latter part of the twentieth century, attacks have been made with greater frequency on individuals of less significance but easier access. This broadens the range of acceptable victims well beyond those justified under the early doctrine of tyrannicide.

Drugs, Religion, and Political Murders

This lethal combination still exists in the contemporary world, but the relationship among these elements has changed considerably. During the Middle Ages, the caliph rewarded his assassins with drugs for successfully completed murders of religious opponents. Today, drugs are used to finance religious zealots whose targets are not only those of another religion within their community but also whole nations or groups of nations whose citizens are regarded by the zealots as legitimate targets for murder. This is a drastic broadening of the category of acceptable potential victims and the use of the "tool" of drugs. Osama bin Laden's call for Muslims to attack any American in the waging of a holy war dramatically illustrated this broadening of targets, particularly in the September 11 attacks. The use of drug trafficking to finance terrorism is emerging in many regions, including, but not limited to, Central and South America, the Middle East, and Southeast Asia.

Piracy

Although piracy of the sea waned somewhat in the early part of the twentieth century (the incident involving the *Achille Lauro* reminded us that such piracy still occurs), air piracy has become fairly commonplace. Where sea pirates sought primarily material gains (with political gain a pleasant by-product for certain governments), modern air pirates tend to seek political gain first. So although the treatment of victims of piracy has remained essentially the same (pirates throughout the ages have tended to treat their victims as completely expendable), the

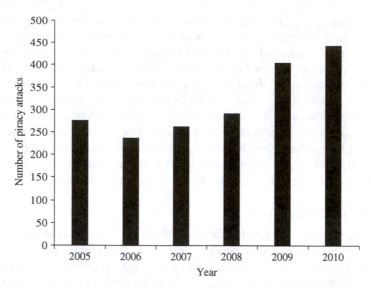

FIGURE 2.1

2005–2010 Worldwide Maritime Piracy Incidents

Source: International Maritime Organization, Reports on Acts of Piracy and Armed Robbery against Ships, Annual Report (annual issues), MSC.4/Circ.133, available at http://www.imo.org/home.asp

purpose or goal of the act has changed. Piracy of the sea, which is occurring with increasing frequency today, still meets the criteria of having a political or social motive in terms of the political unrest or collapse of the states in whose waters it occurs and is still almost exclusively for material profit. Modern piracy of the air, while it meets the political criteria for terrorism quite clearly, is not increasing at the rate of the more historic maritime form, as Figure 2.1 indicates.

Terror-Supported States

While terrorism was, for many states in the twentieth century, an institutionalized form of foreign policy, in recent years states have instead begun to be supported by terrorist organizations. State sponsorship and state support for terrorism differs significantly from the old forms of state terrorism in which the state had obvious and usually controlling interest in the terrorist acts being committed against its citizens. The trend in recent years, however, for failed or failing states to be financially supported and to some extent controlled by organizations carrying out terrorism is a new—and disturbing—pattern. Nonstate actors controlling states with funding make the actions of both the states and the nonstate actors far less predictable and much harder to punish or control with any accuracy.

Technological Changes

Technology has widened the field of possible targets and tactics for terrorism. Modern methods of travel, for example, make it possible to carry out an assassination in the morning in Country Q and be halfway around the world from that nation within a matter of hours. Modern communication has made this a smaller world in that events, for instance, in Yemen are of immediate notice and interest in New York. Such communications also have served to expand the theater to which the terrorist plays. Thus, to catch the attention of the United States, the terrorist need not travel to New York City with a bomb—he needs only to plant a bomb in a boat in Yemen's harbor. The role of the Internet, in particular, needs examination, as it offers linkage, training options, weapons purchase, and critically important information—an incredible and virtually uncontrolled access to people, weapons, and information—making modern terrorism transnational in ways that terrorism in previous centuries could not manage. In this important sense, terrorism today is becoming truly a "new" phenomenon.

Terrorism today seems to be evolving into a violent form of **netwar** as well. The term *netwar* refers to

> an emerging mode of conflict and crime at societal levels, involving measures short of traditional war, in which the protagonists use network forms of organization and related doctrines, strategies, and technologies attuned to the information age.[16]

Groups such as al-Qaeda and HAMAS appear to consist of loosely organized, semi-independent cells that often lack any central command hierarchy. These decentralized, flexible structures make counterterrorism efforts, such as the war on terrorism, very difficult to wage successfully, since it is difficult to determine who the "enemy" is and when the enemy is truly defeated or captured.

Weapons

Modern technology has also rapidly expanded the arsenal available to groups and individuals committing terrorism. No longer does the would-be assassin need to rely on a small handgun to eliminate his or her victim. A letter bomb will do the job without endangering the perpetrator, as the Unabomber in the United States and the sender of the letters contaminated with anthrax demonstrated. Revolutionaries are no longer confined to simple rifles: surface-to-air missiles are quite accessible, as are a wide range of plastic explosives.

The events in Japan in 1995 and the United States in 2001 gave ample evidence of the potential for destruction through chemical and biological weapons when used in the vulnerable mass transit or the mail system of modern nation-states. Perhaps, until recently, the consequences of using such weapons were too dramatic for most groups to contemplate. But modern technology has certainly put at the terrorist's disposal a vast array of lethal and largely indiscriminate weapons, of which the sarin toxin used in Japan and the anthrax sent through the mail in the United States represent only simple examples. With this arsenal, the selection of victims has become devastatingly indiscriminate. One can be a victim simply by riding a subway train or bus to work, or by opening the mail—basic and essential acts for millions of innocent people.

As historical precedents for terrorism grow, it becomes very hard to distinguish between legitimate and illegitimate violence. As nations born in violence such as Northern Ireland and Israel become states, it is often difficult to condemn as illegitimate the methods employed in the struggles for independence and survival of persons within those states.

DISCUSSION

Modern Piracy and Government Responses

On April 8, 2009, pirates hijacked a U.S.-flagged, Danish-owned container ship with 20 American crewmembers. The 17,000-tonne *Maersk Alabama* was seized by the pirates off the coast of Mogadishu, Somalia, a "failed state" on the northeastern coast of Africa. All of the crew were unharmed in the attack and were able to retake the ship, but the captain of the *Alabama*, Richard Phillips, agreed to be a hostage for the pirates in order to secure his crew's safety.

The USS *Bainbridge*, an American warship (named for a U.S. naval hero who was himself once a prisoner of Barbary pirates), was at the scene of the piracy within hours, but was not able to facilitate a quick rescue of the captain, who was held hostage on the small boat in which the pirates had fled. By the next day, the U.S. Navy called in the Federal Bureau of Investigation hostage negotiators from Quantico, Virginia, to negotiate with the pirates for the captain's release.

During the third day of the event, April 10, Captain Phillips attempted to escape from his captors, but within a few moments of his entering the waters, the pirates fired their weapons at him in warning, and he was forced to return to the lifeboat in which he and his pirate captors were drifting. The *Bainbridge* was unable to help the captain in his escape attempt, but two days later, on April 12, the captain was rescued by U.S. Navy SEALS, who shot and killed three of his captors.

This modern incident of terrorism and counterforce raises some important questions for discussion:

1. Were the hijackers pirates, "common enemies of mankind," or just sailors using the means at their disposal to secure a living in a failing economic system?
2. Was Somalia at fault for not stopping the hijackers from operating off its coast?
3. Would the United States have been justified in taking the law into its own hands by going into the Somali port, which at that time operated as a "safe harbor" for many of the Somali pirates, and using force to stop the pirates' use of this port?

Cyberterror

In 2007, the movie *Live Free or Die Hard* depicted a "cyberterror" attack on the U.S. government. In this attack, computer hackers were used to gain access to government data banks and equipment. The resulting traffic accidents and fatalities, panic, and loss of electrical power over a large part of the eastern United States cost the government and its people millions of dollars and much effort to ensure survival and recovery. This scenario raises interesting questions regarding modern terrorism:

1. Is an attack on computer systems really "terrorism"? Does it meet the criteria for a "violent" act, even if no person is deliberately physically injured?
2. If the attack is not on a government computer system, but on a banking system or that of a medical facility, is it still terrorism, or could it just be a sophisticated form

of theft, which is still a crime and does cause harm but is not generally listed as "terrorism" because the motive is usually not political?

3. Do we need to redefine the term *violence* to incorporate this new potential method of attack?

ANALYSIS CHALLENGE

The Convention on Genocide is very short, so read it quickly at http://www.hrweb.org/legal/genocide.html. Then read about alleged genocides in one of the following countries: Rwanda, Bosnia, Cambodia, or Sudan. Use a search engine to find an article on one of these alleged atrocities. How well does what is described in the Genocide Convention fit the description of events? You can even find links to satellite images of a region's destruction as well as a brief history of the "ethnic cleansing" that has happened. Genocide by a state is occurring today, as these websites indicate. What should be the international community's response?

KEY TERMS

assassination 18	privateers 21	guerrilla warfare 23
hashashin 19	tyrannicide 22	cycle of violence 25
narco-terrorism 19	divine right of kings 22	four waves of modern
fedayeen 21	political asylum 23	terror 28
state terrorism 21	jihad 23	netwar 31

SUGGESTED READINGS AND RESOURCES

Laqueur, Walter. "Postmodern Terrorism: New Rules for an Old Game." *Foreign Affairs* (September/October 1996).

Miller, Judith, Stephen Engelberg, and William Broad. *Germs: Biological Weapons and America's Secret War.* New York: Simon & Schuster, 2001.

Nyatepe-Coo, Akorlie A., and Dorothy Zeisler-Vralsted, eds. *Understanding Terrorism: Threats in an Uncertain World.* Upper Saddle River, NJ: Prentice Hall, 2004.

Rapoport, David C. "The Four Waves of Rebel Terror and September 11." *Anthropoetics,* vol. 8, no. 1. (Spring/Summer 2001).

Simonsen, Clifford E., and Jeremy R. Spindlove. *Terrorism Today: The Past, the Players, the Future.* Upper Saddle River, NJ: Prentice Hall, 2004.

Slann, Martin. "The State as Terrorist." In *Multidimensional Terrorism,* eds. Martin Slann and Bernard Schechterman. New York: Rienner, 1987.

NOTES

1. George Fetherling, *The Book of Assassins: A Biographical Dictionary from Ancient Times to the Present* (Edison, NJ: Castle Books, 2001), 7.
2. Funk and Wagnall's *Standard Dictionary: Comprehensive International Edition,* vol. 1, 86, col. 3.
3. Fetherling, *The Book of Assassins,* 5.
4. William Blackstone, *Commentaries on the Laws of England* (Oxford: Clarendon Press, 1749), vol. 4, 71.

5. Walter Laqueur, ed., *Voices of Terror: Manifestos, Writings and Manuals of al-Qaeda, Hamas, and other Terrorists from Around the World and Throughout the Ages* (New York: Reed Press, 2004), 34–38.
6. *Ibid.*, 36.
7. Carl Sandburg, *Abraham Lincoln: The War Years* (Cambridge, MA: MIT Press, 1939), vol. 4, 482.
8. Georges Vidal, *Cours de Droit Criminal et de Science Pententiare*, 5th ed. (Paris: Rousseau, 1916), 110–112.
9. "Allah Says Fight." Transcript of Statement by al-Qaeda Spokesman. *ABCNews. com*, October 9, 2001. http://abcnews.go.com/International/story?id=80500&page=1
10. Quoted by F. Venturi, *Roots of Revolution: A History of the Populist and Socialist Movements in Nineteenth Century Russia,* trans. F. Haskell (New York: Norton, 1966), 281.
11. Venturi, *Roots of Revolution,* 366.
12. Irving Howe, "The Ultimate Price of Random Terror," *Skeptic: The Forum for Contemporary History* 11 (January–February 1976): 10–19.
13. Sandra Stencel, "Terrorism: An Idea Whose Time Has Come," *Skeptic: The Forum for Contemporary History* 11 (January–February 1976): 4–5.
14. Quoted by Robert Friedlander, *Terrorism: Documents of International and Local Control* (Dobbs Ferry, NY: Oceana, 1979), 26.
15. David C. Rapoport, "The Four Waves of Rebel Terror and September 11," *Anthropoetics*, Vol 8, no. 1 (Spring/Summer 2001). Retrieved from http://www. anthropoetics.ucla.edu/ap/0901/terror.htm.
16. John Arquilla, David Ronfeldt, and Michele Zanini, "Networks, Netwar, and Information-Age Terrorism," in *Terrorism and Counterterrorism: Understanding the New Security Environment,* ed. Russell D. Howard and Reid L. Sawyer (Guilford, CT: McGraw-Hill, 1999), 101.

Ideology and Terrorism: Rights from Wrongs?

"I have always dreamed," he mouthed, fiercely, "of a band of men absolute in their resolve to discard all scruples in the choice of means, strong enough to give themselves frankly the name of destroyers, and free from the taint of resigned pessimism which rots the world. No pity for anything on earth, including themselves, and death enlisted for good and all in the service of humanity. . . ."

—Joseph Conrad

J ust as terrorism as an action is not "new" today, but has certainly changed in significant ways, the motivation for carrying out acts of terror, while fundamentally similar in many ways to that which existed in the past, has also changed. Men and women still claim that their "right" to commit acts of extreme violence derives from the "wrongs" done to them by an unjust system. What has changed about the "causes" for which acts of terrorism are committed are the perceived initial injustices, the "justified response."

Some have continued to spark terrorism for centuries, while others are clearly phenomena of the last two centuries. In this chapter we examine not only the fundamental "causes" for which terrorism has been, and continues to be, committed, but also the more recent provocations to terrorist violence.

Can one injustice truly justify the commission of another injustice? There are, of course, no easy answers to such loaded questions. Understanding the "cause" for which an act of terrorism is committed does not in any sense "justify" the commission of that act, but it can enable us to both understand and thereby more accurately predict such acts as they continue to occur.

Most individuals or groups who claim that an act is justified mean that it is "the right thing to do." So we must study the reasons or justifications given for the terrorist acts in order to understand the driving force behind them. Because we have already reviewed the transformation of terrorism over the centuries, we confine our study of the reasons for terrorism to the terrorism that has existed in the twentieth century.

This will not limit the usefulness of our observations, since the basic reasons for terrorism have not, in many ways, changed as rapidly as have the tactics of terror. The forces of oppression that have caused men to rebel have not changed over the centuries; what has changed is the willingness of the oppressed to use previously unthinkable means to achieve their objectives.

THE RATIONALIZATION OF VIOLENCE

The terrorist revolution is the only just form of revolution.

Nikolai Morozov (1880)

The reasons for the willingness to use extraordinary means are important; they are, in many ways, the "justification" for modern terrorism. It has always been possible to murder innocent persons. Why is it no longer an unthinkable option for revolutionary groups?

This is the crucial question. States throughout history have used terrorism on their citizens, on the citizens of other nations, and as an instrument of war. Biblical and historical accounts abound of conquering armies who slaughtered innocent men, women, and children; armies who took slaves and captives, perpetrating all manner of atrocities.

But those rebelling against such tyrannous brutality have, for the most part, eschewed a comparable brutality. Indeed, the lodestar of revolutionary theory has been its vehement condemnation of the brutality of the existing regime.

Why, then, during the twentieth century did revolutionary groups become more willing to perpetrate equally brutal acts against similarly innocent persons? Oppression is not new, nor is the presence of a few desperate people willing to risk all to oppose a system they abhor. What is new is the willingness of these "desperate people" to use tactics that, until very recently, were the sole provenance of the "oppressive" state.

This is the phenomenon of modern terrorism: that revolutionaries rebelling against state oppression are now willing to use weapons of terror against an innocent citizenry. In the past, revolutionaries and the theorists who espoused their causes defended their actions in terms of ridding the world of oppressive states whose leaders committed unthinkable acts upon the citizenry. By committing similar acts upon the citizenry, revolutionaries have fundamentally altered their philosophy. It is important to understand the substance of this changed philosophy, and the reasons for the change, in order to understand modern terrorism.

Just as in earlier empires the "divine right to rule" had been the criterion for justifying the abuse of citizens by tyrants, with the French Revolution the "will of the people" became a justification for terrorism by the people seeking to overthrow regimes. Yet when the efforts at revolution failed or produced results that did not satisfy the desire for "justice" by those seeking to change the system, the revolutionaries became intensely frustrated, and more willing to use terrorism to achieve change. As one scholar put it:

> Modern non-state-sponsored terrorism, or terrorism from below, emerged during the last third of the nineteenth century because liberal, revolutionary changes failed to materialize. Frustration mounted as the revolutions of 1830 and 1848 failed to bring sweeping changes—Russia remained an autocracy controlled by the Czar, the French Republic was perverted into an empire, and Germany remained unchanged.[1]

Revolutionaries such as Nikolai Morozov came to view terrorism as the only chance for successful revolution in czarist Russia. **Anarchism,** *which advocated that "individual freedom should be absolute, and that all government and law is evil,"* became increasingly involved in nonselective violence, as the possibility of forcing change within the structure of the existing state became less feasible.

Indeed, anarchism, as a theory, is less strict in its adherence to the injury of only "guilty" persons than were most revolutionaries of the nineteenth-century. Louis Auguste-Blanqui asserted that the transformation of society could only come about from a small, well-organized group of "terrorists" acting as the vanguard of the revolutionary process.[2] With the imperial abdication in France in 1870, and the establishment of the Paris Commune in March 1871 (composed as it was of a Blanquist majority), "a red terror once again came into being, accentuated by class division and violence."[3]

The anarcho-syndicalist credo expressed by American revolutionary propagandist Emma Goldman offers another insight into the transition of revolutionary theory. Goldman advocated "direct action against the authority of the law, direct action against the invasive meddlesome authority of our moral code."[4] This rejection of a moral code as "invasive" and "meddlesome" and belonging to those in authority is certainly a shift in philosophy. Revolutionaries of previous centuries had claimed that such a code "justified" their actions against a clearly immoral state.

Franz Fanon, the theoretical architect of the Algerian independence movement, offered some changes to traditional revolutionary theory. He argued for the use of "the technique of terrorism" that, he asserted, consisted of individual and collective attempts by means of bombs or by the derailing of trains to disrupt the existing system.

Both of these theorists express a philosophy radically different from that espoused by the early Russian revolutionaries or advocates of tyrannicide. The legitimate victim of violence need no longer be exclusively either the soldier or the government official. Rather, with increasing frequency, he or she is an innocent civilian third party, whose injury or death is intended to hurt or frighten the entire body politic.

In the United States, anarchist philosophy began to engender radical demands for indiscriminate violence. Anarchist publications in the 1880s were candid in their enthusiasm for the widespread use of explosives. One letter that appeared in one extremist paper, *Alarm,* enthused:

> Dynamite! Of all the good stuff, this is the stuff. . . . Place this in the immediate vicinity of a lot of rich loafers who live by the sweat of other people's brows, and light the fuse. A most cheerful and gratifying result will follow.[5]

Anarchist violence did indeed claim innocent lives, often through the use of dynamite, during the following decades. Although strains of both nonviolent socialism and violent anarchism mixed in the labor movement, tainting much of labor's legitimate attempts to organize, acts of random violence were unabashedly carried out by anarchist extremists within the movement.

On October 1, 1910, the *Los Angeles Times* building was destroyed by dynamite. Two young ironworkers eventually confessed to this crime, in which 20 innocent people died and another 17 were injured. On September 16, 1920, an explosion on New York City's Wall Street claimed an even larger number of innocent lives. Forty people were killed in this blast, and another 300 were injured. A hitherto unknown group, calling itself the American Anarchist Fighters, claimed credit for this devastating attack on victims who were ordinary working people.

▶ **CASE STUDY 3.1**

Tupamaros (Uruguay Faction)

Violence among groups seeking to correct societal injustices has not been limited to anarchistic rationalization. In Uruguay, terrorism was justified by the Tupamaros on nationalistic and socialistic grounds. Uruguay, until the late 1950s a model of democracy and prosperity in a largely authoritarian sea of South American nations, began to falter economically in 1958. Young middle-class professionals and intellectuals, hit especially hard by the economic difficulties and moved by the wretched living and working conditions of many groups in the country, began to seek radical solutions to the nation's woes.

The Tupamaros, named for Tupac Amaru, a Peruvian rebel Indian leader who was burned at the stake in the eighteenth century, began a nationalist movement in 1962. It was led in the beginning by Raúl Sendic, born in 1925 in the Flores Province of Uruguay into an upper middle-class family. Sendic became frustrated with his law studies and dropped out of school, heading to the northern part of Uruguay to work among poor sugar beet laborers. In 1962, Sendic went to Cuba for a few months, returning to organize the sugar plantation laborers in their first march on the capital, Montevideo. As support grew for Sendic and the sugar beet laborers, the Tupamaros movement was launched.

Over the next few years, their activities ranged from the hijacking of trucks carrying food (which they subsequently distributed to needy people) to bank robbery and kidnapping for ransom. Seeing themselves as the "Robin Hood" of their country, they robbed banks and corporations and distributed the money to the poor. Kidnapping was another profitable method of financing their activities, and their victims included a Brazilian consul, a U.S. advisor to the Uruguayan police (whom they later killed), and the British ambassador to Uruguay. They also assassinated leading figures, including the chief of the civil defense forces.

Convinced that the Tupamaros constituted a threat to democracy in Uruguay, President Gestido banned the Socialist Party in 1967, and the government declared an internal war against the Tupamaros. By 1972, more than 4,000 Tupamaros sympathizers had been arrested, and the government passed the Law of State Security, suspending the normal time period allowed for the holding of suspects. It also permitted military trials of suspected Tupamaros supporters. Free press and free speech were suspended by the government in order to curb the media coverage of the Tupamaros.

The desire to drive out foreign influence and to forcibly redistribute wealth served, in the case of the Tupamaros, as the justification for its acts of terror-violence. In response, the government declared a state of war, making it difficult to justify the killing of innocent persons by the group, since the consequences for much of the population were retaliatory acts of state terrorism. The cycle of violence generated by terrorist acts by this group spiraled out of control, making the justification for the terrorism by the revolutionaries much less credible, since it failed to bring about the desired results, but instead brought down more government action against the population of the state. ■

Source: http://latinamericanhistory.about.com/od/20thcenturylatinamerica/a/tupamaro.htm

REBELLION AND THE RIGHT OF SELF-DETERMINATION

The evolution of revolutionary violence into terrorism is significant. It has long been a stumbling block in the creation of effective international law concerning terrorism. Revolutions have occurred throughout history without recourse to terror-violence; an effort must be made to understand why such revolutions do not continue to occur without the use of terrorist tactics.

Although rebellion cannot be separated from violence, certain types of violence have not been acceptable. Violence directed deliberately against innocent parties is destructive not only of law and of legal systems but also of civilized society, according to one expert on international law.[6]

As the United Nations (UN) Secretariat, in its study of the nature and causes of terrorism, concluded: "The legitimacy of a cause does not in itself legitimize the use of certain forms of violence, especially against the innocent." Paragraph 10 of the Secretariat's study notes that this limit on the legitimate use of violence "has long been recognized, even in the customary laws of war."[7] Both the General Assembly and the Security Council of the United Nations have passed resolutions stating that "criminal acts intended or calculated to provoke a state of terror in the general public, a group of persons or particular persons for political purposes are in any circumstances unjustifiable, whatever the considerations of a political, philosophical, ideological, racial, ethnic, religious, or other nature that may be invoked to justify them."[8]

Two points here are worth noting. One is that the community of nations regards the limits on the legitimate use of violence as long standing—not the product of twentieth-century governments seeking to prevent rebellions.

The second point is that the community of nations, not just in the Secretariat's report but in many documents and discussions, has agreed that there are in fact limits to the legitimate use of violence, regardless of the justice of the cause. Moreover, these limits are acknowledged to exist even in times of war. Indeed, it is *from* the laws of war that we obtain our clearest understanding of precisely what these limits on the use of violence are.

Therefore, a condemnation of terrorism is not a denunciation of revolutionaries or guerrillas. It does not in any sense preclude the right to revolution, which is a recognized and protected right under international law.

> As one scholar pointed out, those who attack "political and military leaders . . . will not be called terrorists at all" in international law.[9] Another knowledgeable expert remarked that "today's revolutionaries want to be guerrillas, not terrorists," as there is no stigma attached to the status of rebels.[10] Most resolutions passed by the UN General Assembly on terrorism contain a reaffirmation of "the inalienable right of self-determination and independence of all peoples."[11] Kofi Annan, former secretary-general of the United Nations, expressed the international community's feelings concisely when he stated that: "Terrorism strikes at the very heart of everything the United Nations stands for. It presents a global threat to democracy, the rule of law, human rights and stability."[12]

No pejorative status is attached to rebels and revolutionaries, but even armies engaged in warfare must by law recognize certain limits on the use of violence. The right to revolution and self-determination cannot be predicated upon the wrongful deaths of innocent persons, nor is it prevented in any meaningful way from other nonprohibited activity by the condemnation of terrorist tactics.

To cite a venerable legal maxim, *jus ex injuria non oritur,* meaning *"rights do not arise from wrongs."* Revolutions have occurred throughout history without depending on the use of terrorism for success. There seems no legitimate reason why they cannot continue to occur successfully in spite of a ban on terrorist tactics. The position of governments committed to this concept was stated by former U.S. Secretary of State William Rogers when he spoke at the 1972 opening of the UN General Assembly:

> [T]errorist acts are totally unacceptable attacks against the very fabric of international order. They must be universally condemned, whether we consider the cause a terrorist invoked noble or ignoble, legitimate or illegitimate.[13]

Not all nations, governments, or individuals agree with this assessment. Even the nations that subscribe to this assessment are not unfailingly willing to adhere to it. For instance, during World War II, Nazism was regarded as "an ultimate threat to everything decent . . . an ideology and a practice of domination so murderous, so degrading even to those who might survive it, that the consequences of its final victory were literally beyond calculation, immeasurably awful."[14]

But nonstrategic, random terror bombing by those same nations that authored and defended the current laws against terrorism resulted in the deaths of thousands of German civilians. These persons were apparently sacrificed for "psychological" purposes (i.e., to create fear and chaos in an audience). Such "sacrifices" and indiscriminate destruction of civilians today would be roundly condemned by those same nations if they were performed by a revolutionary or guerrilla force or by a rogue state carrying out terror-violence against its own citizens.

So the distinction between acceptable and unacceptable use of force is not always clear and is influenced by the nations responsible for making the rules. But the *mores* prohibiting certain forms of violence are not of recent vintage: They have been evolving over many centuries.

One of the ingredients in the formulation of the rules that govern civilized society today that *is* new is the **right of self-determination**. The UN Charter, written in 1945, states that *people have a right to determine for themselves the form of state under which they choose to live.*[15] Since that time, nations and legal scholars have been trying to work out just which people have this right and how extensive a justification this right confers on individuals engaged in wars of self-determination.

The answers to these and related questions are not readily attainable. As one scholar noted:

> [A]ccording to United Nations practice, a "people" is any group with a shared identity, identified by that international organization most often in the context of an organization wishing to liberate the "people" from a regime not sharing that identity. Thus, the Puerto Ricans are a people but the Kurds are not; the Namibians are a people and possess their own state but the population of East Timor (or what remains of it) is without identity and without hope.[16]

East Timor is now a state (making the observation by Robert Friedlander in the 1980s no longer completely accurate), but the lack of clarity as to who are a "people" by law remains. Nor is it clear just how fundamental this right to self-determination is. Is it more fundamental than the right to life? If not, then the pursuit of self-determination cannot intentionally jeopardize any person's right to life. Does the right to self-determination supersede the right of a state to protect itself and to provide for its citizens a safe and stable system of government?

No people seeking to exercise their right to self-determination do so today in a vacuum. Their actions in the course of their struggle necessarily have an effect, often a negative one, on other persons within their community. As in any armed struggle, there must remain limits within which their right to pursue self-determination must operate, to limit the adverse effects of such a course of action on the rights of others.

The problem that this newly articulated right to self-determination has created in terms of the limitation of armed warfare is important. This right is readily conferred upon, or claimed by, many groups who do not enjoy, and probably can never gain, majority support among the indigenous population of their state. This means that many groups of disaffected persons who have no hope of ever waging a successful guerrilla war against an established state may claim this right. The argument has been made that these groups cannot reasonably be held to conventional rules of warfare, for to hold them to those rules is to condemn them to inevitable failure.

Faced with the overwhelming odds in favor of the well-established and well-armed state, many of the peoples seeking to exercise their right to self-determination are increasingly willing to use less conventional methods of waging war. Lacking large popular support from the indigenous population and facing a state whose trained army and weaponry make conventional resistance a mockery, such groups are willing to use the illegal tactic of terrorism to achieve their right.

The difficulties facing such groups seeking self-determination are very real, but the problems that they create are also formidable. What happens, for example, if two "peoples" claim that their right to self-determination gives them the right to occupy and control the same piece of land? Who decides which group's right should prevail?

This is not a hypothetical situation. The rival claims of the Palestinians and the Israelis to the same land have provoked decades of bloodshed and bitter fighting. People in this struggle claim a historical right to the land.

▶ **CASE STUDY 3.2**

The Palestinians

In Chapter 2, we examined the situation of Israel and Palestine in the context of a "cycle of violence." Now, let us look at it in terms of a "right of self-determination."

Declaring its right to be a state in 1948, Israel exercised its right to determine its own form of government and to maintain control over its own people. But it has had to do so through force and to maintain, through the end of the twentieth century, its existence through occupation of additional land. Peace is seldom achieved, in the long term, through occupation, and Israel struggled with the difficult issue of the need to pull out of those occupied lands. But as Israeli settlements in the occupied territories continue to expand, there are Jewish settlers who have now lived in those lands for years, whose identity and security as a people are threatened by the withdrawal and whose right to self-determination may be lost in the peace process.

The assassination in late 1995 of Yitzhak Rabin, prime minister of Israel, by a Jewish student seeking to derail the withdrawal of Israel from the occupied territories, makes this threat very clear. The satisfaction of the Palestinians' right to self-determination will be difficult to achieve in any way that is acceptable to all of the people of Israel. One Israeli military officer noted that even children born and raised in Palestinian refugee camps will state that they are from Jaffa and other coastal cities (of what used to be Palestine). Since this land is now an integral part of Israel, there seems little likelihood that the aspirations of Palestinian adults who have fostered this sense of belonging to old homelands can ever be satisfied.

Violent actions taken during the peace process that began in 1993 made it clear that some factions of Palestinians do not want independence in the West Bank or the Gaza Strip. They want to claim their "homeland" of Palestine, including the land that is today Israel. It would appear impossible to satisfy their right to self-determination without infringing upon Israel's right to exist. Just as the Jewish people rejected other offers of homelands around the turn of the century, insisting on their right to return to the homeland of their theological ancestors, Palestinians have found it difficult to accept alternatives that fall short of a return of *their* homeland.

On whose side does "right" rest in this conflict? The right of self-determination that the Palestinians seek is the same one for which the Haganah fought against the British occupying forces in the 1930s to 1940s. Just as the Jewish Irgun and its radical offshoot, the Stern Gang, used terror tactics to force out an occupying power, the Palestinians have resorted to terrorist acts to rid themselves of what they perceive to be an occupying power. This right to self-determination is, by its very lack of clarity, a dangerous justification for unlawful violence. Because neither the peoples nor the extent of the right itself appears to have any specific legal limitations, the exercise of such rights can lead to vicious spirals of violence.

In 2011, the Palestinian leadership submitted a request to the secretary-general of the UN for admitting Palestine as a state, moving the conflict from the realm of terror to the halls of international diplomacy. While the Security Council had not, by October of that year, taken action on this request for recognition of statehood, this effort to shift the battle for a right of self-determination to a diplomatic "battleground" may offer hope that the spiral of violence may be resolved without destruction of either of the peoples who claim the same land. ■

Source: http://topics.nytimes.com/topics/reference/timestopics/organizations/p/palestinian_authority/index.html

TERRORISM IN THE NAME OF GOD

Just as terrorism for political goals has deep historic roots, so does terrorism carried out for religious reasons. Cases such as that of the Palestinians and the Israelis offer examples of the complex web of religious and political goals of those carrying out terrorist acts. Under the leadership of Hassan I Sabah, Muslim extremists seeking to purify their communities carried out terrorism in medieval times, justifying their actions by their desire to hasten the arrival of the Imam, "the heir to the Prophet, the Chosen of God, and the sole rightful leader of mankind, who would establish a new and just society."[17]

An extreme Jewish Zealot sect, the Sicarii, carried out similar assassinations, targeting mainly Jewish "moderates" who accommodated the Romans in the first century C.E. Their immediate goal was to end Roman influence, but they ultimately sought to initiate the coming of the Messiah by forcing an apocalyptic conflict between Rome and Jerusalem, in a belief that by initiating such a confrontation, they could force God's direct intervention for the people of Israel.[18]

The role of religion as a guiding force in the commission of acts of terrorism will be explored further in succeeding chapters. It is important here to note four points:

Terrorism in the name of religion is *not* a modern phenomenon. For centuries, religious zealots have been willing to take the lives of innocent people to bring about radical religious goals. While the extent of the damage to people and property that occurred with the events of September 11, 2001, may have set new records in deaths and destruction carried out and/or called for by a religious zealot, it is not unique.

Contrary to their claims, the zealots who carry out the acts of terror "in the name" of their religious beliefs do *not* reflect the beliefs of the vast majority of those who share the basic faith. Zealotry denotes extremism, and religious zealots are extremists. Thus, the religions of Judaism, Islam, and Christianity (which generated crusades and extremes of violence as well) are not fundamentally violent, but can be cited by extremists to justify violent acts. It is essential to understand the basic faith in order to interpret and identify the exaggerations of those misusing it to justify their extreme actions.

Religious zealots act for two audiences: the state, which they seek to change, and their divine leader (God, Allah, Jehovah, or by whatever name their leader is known). The sought political change is real, but it is often tangled inextricably with religious goals. For the zealot, if actions do not achieve the desired reaction from the divine audience, more action is clearly necessary, making political resolution of conflicts difficult.

The entangling of religious and political goals often makes resolution of conflicts difficult, if not impossible, to achieve. While groups carrying out acts of terror may share some of the same goals, they may not agree on the primacy of the goals, making it unclear to those seeking to diffuse the conflict what they could offer that would satisfy the demands for change. For instance, while the Palestinian Liberation Organization sought political solutions in its conflict with Israel (the creation of a Palestinian state), HAMAS (Harakat al-Muqawamah al-Islamiyyah, another Palestinian faction) seeks the establishment of an Islamic state to rule the area. Differing goals continue to make a solution to this problem almost impossible to achieve.

Religion certainly complicates the process of conflict resolution, making the goals sought hard to determine, and failure impossible to accept (as the Sicarii demonstrated at Masada).[19] The actions of religious zealots are intended to improve human existence both politically and religiously, with the religious changes sought paramount.

The attacks by al-Qaeda on September 11, 2001, were described by leaders of the group, including Osama bin Laden, as acts of *jihad* against globalization and the spread of Western influence. The radicalized Islam advocated by bin Laden, while not acceptable to most Muslims, does indicate an element that needs to be explored here: the impact of globalization as interpreted by religious extremists.

Globalization is an umbrella term that refers to *increasing global connectivity, integration, and interdependence in the economic, social, technological, cultural, political, and ecological fields.* As cultures, societies, and economic and political systems become increasingly connected with modern technology that makes transportation, communication, and trade so much easier than ever before, religious fundamentalism finds itself challenged with a need to accept changes that may not be compatible with traditional belief systems. As long as societies allow fundamental religious sects to maintain separate lifestyles as dictated by their religious beliefs, there are few problems. But as globalization makes the possibility of "separateness" and seclusion more difficult to maintain, the more fundamentalist elements of the faith community may become more radicalized as they seek to maintain the "purity" of their faith community.

Another element of globalization has also begun to trigger terrorist attacks. As people become more aware of the vast differences in lifestyles, resources, and wealth that exist in our global society, it becomes increasingly easy to resent, and even to hate, those who have wealth but do not share it. This is not a sudden transformation for most individuals, but a gradual radicalization as globalization allows the realization of the levels of "unfairness" that currently exist. It is usually a slow process, but as the speed of globalization increases, so may this process.

To understand the transition now evolving in the perspectives of many today, let us examine the process briefly. It can be broken down into four phases or steps of understanding: a view of the world in context, in comparison, in attribution, and in reaction.

Most people experience a feeling of frustration at wanting something they do not have, or in needing something they cannot get. For example, if you are hungry, and you need food, a natural reaction would be that *it is not right* that you do not have food, for you have done nothing wrong to deserve a punishment of hunger. Your anger is relatively undirected because you have nothing with which to compare yourself, and there is no one to fault for your lack of food. This is the first and least destructive stage in the process of radicalization by globalization.

The second stage can begin when you have something or someone with which to compare your state of hunger. When you start to realize that others like you are not hungry, but have sufficient food, you begin to think that *it is not fair.* You should not have to be hungry while others have all the food they need. There is no justice in such a situation. As the world becomes more globalized, the differences in poverty and plenty and hunger and gluttony become increasingly apparent. Your anger is becoming more focused, but it is more likely against your leaders, who have failed to achieve justice for you as have the leaders of other cultures.

The third stage in this process arises from this need to attribute fault for your lack of food. Savvy leaders will direct your attention to the fact that those with abundance are not sharing and have in fact established trade barriers that make it impossible for them to get a fair share of the resources to you. Your anger can then be focused on those who have abundant resources while you do without basic essentials. If you watch those you die for lack of food, it is understandably easy to be angry with those whom the media (to which you have increasing access) describe as suffering from obesity. As global networks make these comparisons possible, it is simple to transfer your anger about your situation to those pictured in the media as having too much.

But even this level of anger will seldom result in an act of terrorism. It may result in murder or armed attacks aimed at obtaining the things needed. The targets of your anger, though, are very specific, and still, in your view, people. You are, perhaps, bitterly angry and want those with too much to have to share with you and to be aware of your needs. But your faith teaches you to still regard them as human beings: misguided; perhaps unaware and even uncaring; but still people who can be reached and made aware and who might, when made aware, help you.

The fourth stage involves a transition from a general anger with those in the world who could be helping to protect and support those in need, to a reaction of impersonal commitment to destroy an evil. In this stage, you see those who are not preventing the starvation; who are causing their technology to invade your life; and who are impinging on your culture, as not just uncaring but as wicked and monstrous. Killing such an enemy is therefore not a problem, but an obligation. Table 3.1 offers a simple view of this four-step process.

This last stage has historically required the emergence of a leader or leadership cadre to focus the anger and define the enemy as not human but monstrous. Religious zealots have found this transition simple, and as the forces of globalization combine today with increasing radicalization of religious groups, it is unsurprising that acts of terrorism also have risen in number and scope, to become global problems.

TABLE 3.1		
It's not right	—	anger in context
It's not fair	—	anger in comparison
It's your fault	—	anger directed by attribution of fault
You are evil	—	anger in reaction

CAUSES OF THE LEFT, RIGHT, AND CENTER

In addition to having belief systems that help the individual to justify terrorist actions, there are a wide variety of causes for which men and women have committed terrorism. Let us briefly consider a few of the motives for modern terrorism.

Religious Fanaticism

The al-Qaeda network has given the world a dramatic example of the destructive power of *individuals committed to waging holy war on religious principles,* disciples of **religious fanaticism.** The holy war called for by bin Laden supported by Islamic fundamentalists caused the death of thousands of innocent people in the attacks on the World Trade Center and the Pentagon in 2001 and continues to feed the flames of conflict within Afghanistan, Iraq, and the rest of the world.

In their religious fervor, religious fanatics of all faiths have been unrepentantly responsible for the loss of thousands of lives. Planes are sabotaged, temples stormed, and unrelenting guerrilla warfare waged, all in the name of "religion." Such a war pits Shi'a Muslims against Sunni Muslims, Catholics against Protestants, and Hindus against Muslims across all forms of political and physical boundaries.

Modern "crusaders," often taking the form of suicide bombers in the Middle East today, offer some of the most chilling evidence of the impact of religion on terrorism. Martyrdom is a compelling lure, and self-sacrifice is valued above many other virtues. In the name of a supreme being, rivers of blood have flowed and will no doubt continue to flow, for fanatics of any sort are seldom satisfied by any gain.

Anarchism

Few groups that still operate today hold strictly to this cause. The last three decades of the twentieth century witnessed the growth and demise of the Weather Underground and the Symbionese Liberation Army in the United States. The Japanese Red Army has espoused anarchistic beliefs, as did the Red Army Faction in Germany. Such groups tended to be small and short-lived, perhaps because their goals are somewhat nebulous, and thus they find it difficult to draw others into their ranks. Anarchism's more extreme form, nihilism, in which the destruction of *all* structure and form of society is sought, still exists as an ideology among certain terrorist groups.

Neo-Nazism/Neofascism

In recent years, a number of groups have sprung up throughout Western Europe and the United States embracing **neo-Nazism/neofascism.** In the United States, for example, the Aryan Nations and several related groups including the Christian Identity Movement (CIM) and the Christian Patriots have been involved in armed conflict with the authorities and have been responsible for several bombings in which innocent people were killed. Indeed, many of these groups have been involved in the arming and training of paramilitary troops in almost every state in the United States. The devastating bomb blast in Oklahoma City in 1995, after which a shocked nation watched the bodies of small children being carried lifeless or dying from the rubble, was carried out by a person who had been a member of a paramilitary group in Michigan and whose mother had involved him at an early age in the CIM.

Separatism

Perhaps the best-known group embracing **separatism** *is the Euskadi Ta Askatasuna (ETA), the Basque separatists who seek independence or at least autonomy from Spain,* and have used bombs and machine guns to try to force the Spanish government to accede to their demands for independence. The violent group of French-Canadian separatists, the Quebec Liberation Front, was essentially inactive by the 1990s, but was responsible for several acts of terrorism during the 1960s and 1970s. The Abu Sayyaf Group in the Philippines carried out numerous kidnappings for ransom in an effort to gain separation for the Muslim portion of the country from the government in Manila.

Nationalism

It is difficult to separate **nationalism** from separatism as a motivator of terrorism. *Groups whose motivation is nationalism are those who seek for their portion of society, which is sometimes but not always a minority, to gain control of the system of government and the allocation of resources within that nation-state.* Such groups do not seek independence or separation from the nation. With this in mind, the Irish Republican Army, whose terrorist acts in Northern Ireland are the source of infamous legend, could conceivably have been classed in this category prior to the peace process of the 1990s. The Tupamaros in Uruguay and the Shining Path (Sendero Luminoso) in Peru could also be placed within this category.

Issue-Oriented Terror

During the latter part of the twentieth century, various forms of **issue orientation** emerged, where issues *aroused such violent sentiments that adherents to one side or another resorted to terrorist violence to enforce their beliefs.* Abortion is one such issue; its opponents have actually bombed abortion clinics. Oddly enough, during the last decade of the twentieth century environmental and animal protection activists became increasingly militant in their insistence that protection of the environment, animals, or both is critically important and worth fighting for. Placing spikes in trees and in paths through the woods and burning down animal-testing centers have become common actions by such groups. Just as doctors have been killed by individuals violently opposed to abortion to "save the fetuses that those doctors may have been willing to abort," the Earth Liberation Front, a militant environmental group in the United States, rationalized that if it was necessary to kill people to save the trees, then they would be justified in killing people! This group, now listed by the Federal Bureau of Investigation (FBI) as a terrorist group, has been responsible for much property damage in its efforts to stop building projects that its members deem destructive to the environment.

The issue of nuclear power and nuclear weapons has also provoked violence. Several modern novelists and screenwriters have created all-too-realistic scenarios concerning the possibility of antinuclear activists detonating a nuclear weapon to illustrate their contention that such weapons must be banned. Thus far, such an incident exists only in fiction, but the growing intensity of the debate on this issue makes such an incident uncomfortably close to reality.

As Table 3.2 indicates, the causes for which terrorism is committed today encompass a wide spectrum. Many of these reasons for terrorism do not fit comfortably into the lineup but may be associated with a cause, depending upon the type of group or state perpetrating it. Visualizing this line of causes is useful, but it helps to remember that the causes of the extreme left and the extreme right too often meet on the fringe of a circle rather than being separated to the ends of a straight line because groups at both ends of this spectrum may desire the same thing: an absolute end to the authority structure that currently exists.

Ideological Mercenaries

The legendary Ilich Ramirez Sanchez, known to the world as Carlos the Jackal, and more recently Sabri al-Banna (Abu Nidal) have given rise to a fear of the proliferation of *"terrorists-for-hire,"* or **ideological mercenaries**. Although it is beyond debate that such persons do exist and cause considerable

---

TABLE 3.2

Spectrum of Causes, from Left to Right, with Groups

New Revolutionary Alternative	Continuity Irish Republican Army	ETA (Basque)	Aryan Nations	al-Qaeda
Anarchist	Nationalist	Separatist	Neo-Nazi/ neofascist	Religious zealot
		Single-issue extremists		
		Ideological mercenaries		
		Counterterrorism		

violence, little evidence suggests the development of a mercenary army of terrorists. Indeed, the arrest of Carlos from his abode in Sudan and his removal for trial in France indicates that the twenty-first century may have less tolerance politically for such individuals. Instead, the rise of individuals like Osama bin Laden suggests that terrorists who can themselves hire or fund terrorist activities constitute a greater threat.

Pathological Terrorists

Some persons kill and terrorize for the sheer joy of terrorizing, not for any "cause" or belief. Charles Manson was perhaps an example; those who commit so-called serial murders are of the same cast. **Pathological terrorists** *have no cause; they are sick and twisted individuals,* whom Frederick Hacker, in his book *Crusaders, Criminals, Crazies: Terror and Terrorism in Our Time,* has called "crazies." Perhaps the youths responsible for the massacres in schools during the 1990s were enjoying terrorizing and were thus pathological but not necessarily terrorists, because they lacked a definable political motive.

Counterterror Terrorists

Perhaps the most frightening development toward the end of the twentieth century is the proliferation of so-called **counterterror terrorists,** the *death squads that mete out summary justice to those judged by their leaders to be terrorists.* Several authoritarian states, threatened by political change, have resorted to these semiofficial troops, inspiring a spiral of terror-violence. Several countries in Central and South America have fallen prey to the lure of counterterror tactics to control terrorism. Even Israel, itself prey to countless terrorist suicide bombings, has resorted to the use of helicopter gunship attacks on civilian communities in its attempts to kill suspected leaders of militant groups.

CONCLUSIONS

Terrorism *is* different today, with many different forms and causes. The argument continues to be made that the justice of the cause, the nobility of the motive, in some way makes the terrorist act less heinous. To understand the cause for which one fights and the belief system in which one operates, it is said, makes it less likely that one will wholeheartedly condemn the actions taken.

But does the woman whose legs are blown off in an explosion in the supermarket understand that the bomb was placed by persons who bore her no personal grudge but were merely seeking independence or separatism for a disenfranchised minority? Will the family of a child killed in an airline explosion accept the explanation that the group responsible for the explosion had not enough weapons to fight a legitimate battle with an authoritarian government? Can those who lost loved ones in the World Trade Center attacks accept their losses more easily by understanding the desperation of those who saw their faith threatened by the presence of the United States in the Middle East?

No cause, however just or noble, can make such actions acceptable. Understanding cannot diminish the horror of the atrocity committed against the innocent. If the right of self-determination must be secured by the wrongs of the murder and maiming of innocents, it is not worth the price in the eyes of the rest of the world.

DISCUSSION

If a group is exercising its right to self-determination, does this give it the right to commit a wrong against other persons? To what extent is one justified in committing a wrong in order to secure a right? Is there ever a time in which, as some have argued, the needs of the many—for example, to secure the right of self-determination or freedom—can be said to outweigh the needs of the few—the victims of the violence?

Consider and discuss the following incidents, keeping in mind several questions: Were these acts of terrorism? For what cause were they committed? Were they in any sense justified?

1. *Assassination of Franz Ferdinand.* Shot to death by a man who felt that the rights of the minority of which he was a part were being cruelly ignored in the carving up of Europe. Ferdinand's death precipitated the events leading up to World War I. His death was in some ways the catalyst to that calamity.

2. *Assassination of Anwar Sadat.* Shot by men who felt that he had betrayed the Arabs by his willingness to establish a peaceful relationship with Israel, Sadat's death slowed down considerably the peace process in the Middle East. His successor, Hosni Mubarak, was understandably reluctant to take similar unpopular steps.

3. *Bombing of the U.S. Marine barracks in Lebanon.* Carried out by militants who regarded the U.S. military presence in Lebanon as an invasive influence in their civil war, this attack resulted in over 200 deaths and the diminishing of the U.S. presence in that war-torn country. Syrian and Israeli influence and presence remain strong in Lebanon's territory, however.

4. *Bombing of Hiroshima.* Carried out by U.S. bombers carrying atomic weapons, this attack was designed to bring a quick halt to the devastating war in the Pacific. It did indeed achieve this, at the cost of countless thousands of Japanese civilians dead or maimed and many more who bore disease and deformity for generations.

ANALYSIS CHALLENGE

Go to the United Nations website, http://www.un.org/apps/news/infocusRel.asp?infocusID=129&Body=North+Africa&Body1=change, and read the article "Winds of Change: North Africa and the Middle East." Is the violence occurring there terrorism, by individuals, groups, or states? Peaceful protests met with oppressive government violence can generate cycles of violence, as history indicates. Which of the states undergoing these "winds of change" have, in your opinion, a chance to achieve this change without resorting to terrorism? Why?

KEY TERMS

anarchism 37
jus ex injuria non
  oritur 40
right of
  self-determination 41
globalization 45

religious fanaticism 47
neo-Nazism/
  neofascism 47
separatism 48
nationalism 48
issue orientation 48

ideological
  mercenaries 49
pathological
  terrorists 50
counterterror
  terrorists 50

SUGGESTED READINGS AND RESOURCES

Bergen, Peter L. *Holy War, Inc.: Inside the Secret World of Osama bin Laden*. New York: The Free Press, 2001.

Crenshaw, Martha. "Ideological and Psychological Factors in International Terrorism," paper presented to the Defense Intelligence College Symposium on International Terrorism. Washington, DC: December 2–3, 1985.

Gunaratna, Rohan. *Inside Al-Qaeda: Global Network of Terror*. New York: Columbia University Press, 2002.

Jenkins, Brian. *The Terrorist Mindset and Terrorist Decisionmaking: Two Areas of Ignorance*. Santa Monica, CA: Rand Corporation, 1979.

Ranstorp, Magnus. "Terrorism in the Name of Religion." In *Terrorism and Counterterrorism: Understanding the New Security Environment*, eds. Russell D. Howard and Reid Sawyer. Guilford, CT: McGraw-Hill, 1999.

"Turner Diaries: Blueprint for Right-Wing Revolution." *Law Enforcement News*. June 30, 1987.

NOTES

1. John Weinzierl, "Terrorism: Its Origin and History," *Understanding Terrorism Threats in an Uncertain World*, eds. Akorlie A., Nyatepe-Coo, and Dorothy Zeisler-Vralsted. (Upper Saddle River, NJ: Pearson Prentice Hall, 2004).
2. R. Blackey and C. Payton, *Revolution and the Revolutionary Ideal* (New York: Pergamon Press, 1976), 91–93. See also B. Croce, *History of Europe in the Nineteenth Century*, trans. H. Furst (New York: Rienner, 1953).
3. Sandra Stencel, "Terrorism: An Idea Whose Time Has Come," *Skeptic: The Forum for Contemporary History* 11 (January–February, 1976): 51.
4. Emma Goldman, *Anarchism and Other Essays* (New York: Dover, 1969), 66. This is a republication of the original 1917 edition. Of particular note to the student of terrorism are Goldman's essays on the meaning of anarchism and the "psychology of political violence."
5. Quoted by Jonathan Harris, *The New Terrorism: Politics of Violence* (New York: Messner, 1983), 141.
6. Robert Friedlander, "On the Prevention of Violence," *The Catholic Lawyer* 25, no. 2 (Spring 1980): 95–105.
7. UN Secretariat Study, "Measures to Prevent International Terrorism" (November 2, 1973), U.N. Doc. A/C.6/418. Prepared as requested by the Sixth Legal Committee of the General Assembly.
8. United Nations General Assembly Resolution 51/210, "Measures to Eliminate International Terrorism" (January 16, 1997).

9. C. Leiser, "Terrorism, Guerrilla Warfare, and International Morality." *Stanford Journal of International Studies* 12 (1974): 39–43.

10. J. Bowyer Bell, "Trends of Terror: Analysis of Political Violence." *World Politics* 29 (1977): 476–477.

11. UN General Assembly Resolution 44/29, "Measures to Prevent International Terrorism Which Endangers or Takes Innocent Human Lives or Jeopardizes Fundamental Freedoms and Study of the Underlying Causes of Those Forms of Terrorism and Acts of Violence Which Lie in Misery, Frustration, Grievance, and Despair and Which Cause Some People to Sacrifice Human Lives, Including Their Own, in an Attempt to Effect Radical Changes" (December 4, 1989).

12. Kofi G. Annan, "Preface," *International Instruments Related to the Prevention and Suppression of Terrorism* (UN Publications, 2001).

13. For the full text of his remarks, see State Department Bulletin no. 67 (1972), 425–429.

14. Quoted by Robert Friedlander, "On the Prevention of Violence," 67.

15. The UN Charter entered into force on October 24, 1945.

16. Robert Friedlander, "The PLO and the Rule of Law: A Reply to Dr. Annis Kassim," *Denver Journal of International Law and Policy* 10, no. 2 (Winter 1981): 231.

17. Bernard Lewis, *The Assassins: A Radical Sect in Islam* (New York: Oxford University Press, 1967), 27.

18. Weinzierl, *Understanding Terrorism Threats in an Uncertain World*, 31.

19. Ibid., 32.

Criminals or Crusaders?

Nothing is easier than to denounce the evil doer; nothing is
more difficult than to understand him.

—*Fedor Dostoevsky*

What kind of person becomes a terrorist? Perhaps an understanding
of the dynamics of becoming a terrorist will increase our understanding of this phenomenon. As noted in Chapter 3, terrorist acts
are committed for a wide variety of causes. It is also true that there are a wide
variety of individuals and groups who commit terrorist acts.

The political world changed a great deal in the last decade of the twentieth and the beginning years of the twenty-first century. These political changes
influenced the type of persons more likely to be recruited into terrorist groups.
A study of the type of individuals known to be drawn to terrorism in the twentieth century will, perhaps, help us to predict the most probable type of twenty-
first-century terrorist. This could be an extremely useful tool for governments
and institutions confronted with the need to plan to cope with terrorism.

PROFILE OF A TERRORIST

Is there any way to tell who is likely to become a terrorist? This question provides a clue as to why political scientists and government officials are particularly interested in the psychological factors relating to terrorism. If one could
identify the traits most closely related to a willingness to use terrorist tactics,
then one would be in a better position to predict, and prevent, the emergence
of terrorist groups.

Unfortunately, identifying such traits is not easy. Just as not all violence
is terrorism and not all revolutionaries are terrorists, not all persons who
commit acts of terrorism are alike. Frederick Hacker suggests three categories of

persons who commit terrorism: *crazies*, *criminals*, and *crusaders*. He notes that an individual carrying out a terrorist act is seldom "purely" one type or the other, but suggests that each type offers some insights into why an individual will resort to terrorism.[1]

Understanding the individual who commits terrorism is vital, not only for humanitarian reasons but also to decide how best to deal with those individuals *while they are engaged in planning or carrying out terrorist acts*. From a law enforcement perspective, for example, it is important to appreciate the difference between a criminal and a crusading terrorist involved in a hostage-taking situation. Successful resolution of such a situation often hinges on understanding the mind of the individuals perpetrating the crime.

Consider the three categories of terrorists suggested by Hacker: crazies, criminals, and crusaders. For the purposes of this study, we need to establish loose descriptions of these three types. Hacker offers some ideas on what is subsumed under each label. **Crazies**, he suggests, are *emotionally disturbed individuals who are driven to commit terrorism "by reasons of their own that often do not make sense to anybody else."*

Criminals, on the other hand, *perform terrorist acts for more easily understood reasons: personal gain*. Such individuals transgress the laws of society knowingly and, one assumes, in full possession of their faculties. Both their motives and their goals are usually clear, if deplorable, to most of mankind.

This is not the case with the **crusaders**. These individuals commit terrorism for reasons that are often unclear both to themselves and to those witnessing the acts. Their ultimate goals are frequently even less understandable. While such individuals are usually idealistically inspired, their idealism tends to be a mixed bag of half-understood philosophies. Crusaders, according to Hacker, *seek not personal gain, but prestige and power for a collective cause*. They commit terrorist acts in the belief "that they are serving a higher cause," in Hacker's assessment.

What difference does it make what kind of terrorist is behind the machine gun or bomb? To the law enforcement personnel charged with resolving the hostage situation, it can be crucial to know what type of person is controlling the situation. Criminals can be offered sufficient personal gains or security provisions to induce them to release the hostages. Crusaders are far less likely to be talked out of carrying out their threats by inducements of personal gains, since to do so they would have to betray, in some sense, that higher cause for which they are committing the action.

For the same reason, it is useful for security agents to know what type of individual is likely to commit a terrorist act within their province. A criminal would be more likely to try to smuggle a gun aboard an airline than a bomb, since the criminal usually anticipates living to enjoy the reward of his or her illegal activities. Crusaders are more willing to blow themselves up along with their victims, since their service to that higher cause often carries with it a promise of a reward in the life to come.

The distinction between criminals and crusaders with respect to terrorism needs some clarification. Clearly, when anyone breaks the law, as in the commission of a terrorist act, he or she becomes a criminal, regardless of the reason for the transgression. The distinction between criminal and crusader, though, is useful in understanding the differences in the motives and goals moving the person to commit the act.

The majority of the individuals and groups carrying out terrorist acts in the last decade of the twentieth and the beginning years of the twenty-first century have been crusaders. This does not mean there are not occasional instances in which individuals decide to take a machine gun to the target of their anger. Nor does it mean there are not individual criminals and criminal organizations that engage in terrorist activities.

Nonetheless, it is true that the majority of individuals who commit modern terrorism are, or perceive themselves to be, crusaders. According to Hacker, the typical crusading terrorist appears to be normal, no matter how crazy the cause or how criminal the means used for this cause may seem. He or she is neither an idiot nor a fool. Instead, the crusading terrorist is frequently a professional, well trained, well prepared, and well disciplined in the habit of blind obedience to a cause.

Table 4.1 indicates a few dramatic differences between the types of terrorist Hacker profiles. One is that crusaders are the least likely to negotiate a resolution to a crisis, both because such action can be viewed as a betrayal of a sublime cause and because there is little that the negotiator can offer, since neither personal gain nor safe passage out of the situation is particularly desired by true crusaders. Belief in the cause makes death not a penalty, but a path to reward; therefore, the threat of death and destruction can have little punitive value. What can a police or military negotiator offer to a crusader to induce the release of hostages or the defusing of a bomb?

TABLE 4.1

Hacker's Typology of Terrorists

Type of Terrorist	Motive/Goal	Willing to Negotiate?	Expectation of Survival
Criminal	Personal gain/ profit	Usually, in return for profit and/or safe passage	Strong
Crusader	"Higher cause" (usually a blend of religious and political)	Seldom, since to do so could be seen as a betrayal of the cause	Minimal, since death offers reward in "afterlife"
Crazy	Clear only to perpetrator	Possible, but only if negotiator can understand	Strong, but not based on reality

Similar problems exist with crazies, depending upon how much in touch with reality such an individual is at the time of the incident. Negotiation is difficult but not impossible if the negotiator can ascertain the goal or motive of the perpetrator and offer some hope (even if it is not real) of success in achieving that goal. One of the critical elements is that crazies, according to Hacker's evaluation, have a limited grip on the reality that they themselves may die in the course of this action, making the threat of death by a superior force carry diminished weight. Just as very young children find the reality of death a difficult concept to grasp, Hacker suggests that crazies offer serious difficulties for negotiators because they often cannot grasp this reality.

Criminals, then, are the preferred perpetrators, since they will negotiate; their demands are generally logical (although often outrageous) and are based in terms that can be met or satisfied with rational alternatives. Criminals know they can be killed and have a strong desire to live to enjoy the rewards of the actions they are taking. Thus, negotiators have specific demands to be bartered, and their "clients" can be expected to recognize superior force and to respond accordingly in altering demands and resolving the incident.

These differences are critically important in at least two contexts: (1) resolving situations in which hostages are held by terrorists and (2) establishing security measures and training for vulnerable targets. Negotiators in hostage situations need to know whether they are dealing with a crusader or a criminal to know whether there is any potential for negotiation. If crusaders are holding hostages, an immediate hostage rescue attempt may be more appropriate than initiating negotiations.

In terms of security devices and training, the profiles become even more vital. The events of September 11, 2001, illustrate dramatically the consequences of training and equipping for the wrong type of perpetrators. Airline pilots in the United States had been trained to respond to attempts to take over flights as hostage situations. Thus, the pilots of the doomed September 11 flights were engaged in trying to keep the situation calm and to "talk down" the plane, to initiate a hostage release without violence. But the individuals taking over the planes were not criminals or crazies but crusaders who did not plan to live through the incidents. Only the passengers on the flight that crashed in Pennsylvania were able to offer substantial resistance— perhaps in part because they had not been trained to assume that a peaceful solution could be negotiated.

This does not suggest that the pilots and crew were not vigilant and did not make every effort to save the lives of the passengers. But because the profile they had been trained to respond to did not match the profile they confronted, they were unable to respond successfully to the demands of the situation. Thus, inaccurate profiling in pilot training was a serious contributing factor to the sequence of events on September 11.

To political scientists, as well as to military, police, and other security and intelligence units assigned the task of coping with terrorism, an understanding of the type of person likely to commit acts of terrorism is invaluable. As our understanding of a phenomenon increases, our ability to predict the behavior of its adherents with some accuracy also increases. Thus, as we try to understand who terrorists are and what they are like, we should increase our ability to anticipate their behavior patterns, thereby increasing our ability to respond effectively and to prevent more often the launching of successful terrorist attacks.

TERRORIST BELIEFS AND IMAGES

Terrorism has been justified by relatively sophisticated theories, such as anarchism, by less well-defined concepts, such as the right of self-determination, and by religious zealotry. But how do modern terrorists justify themselves, on a personal level, for their actions?

The content of terrorist belief systems has not been the subject for much systematic study. The reasons for this neglect are in some respects understandable. For one thing, the study of terrorism is an emerging field, with increasing emphasis placed today on understanding the view of the world held by those committing acts of terrorism.[2]

Another serious problem in analyzing terrorist belief systems lies in the difficulties in acquiring and interpreting data. Since the initiation of a "war on terror" by the international community, a flood of documents has been recovered about training camps and online meetings of people engaged in terrorist activities although a limited number of "decision makers" from functioning groups engaged in terrorism are available to facilitate a reconstruction of events. Much of the existing data are classified by governments in ways that make it virtually inaccessible to academic researchers.

This does not mean that there are no studies of terrorist belief systems. In 1984, Gerald A. Hopple and Miriam Steiner employed content analysis to evaluate 12 factors as potential sources of action and applied the techniques to 46 documents from the German Red Army Faction (RAF), the Italian Red Brigades, and the Basque Euzkadi Ta Azkutasuna (ETA). Their findings indicated that emphasis within belief systems changes over time and that different groups stress different motivations.[3] *Voices of Terror: Manifestos, Writings and Manuals of al-Qaeda, Hamas, and Other Terrorists from Around the World and Throughout the Ages*, edited by Walter Laqueur, offers one of the best collections of the words of those willing to engage in terrorism.

Some significant components of terrorist belief systems emerged from these and other studies. A brief review of these, although not sufficient to explain why *all* terrorists do what they do or believe what they do, will offer insights into the framework of logic by which a terrorist justifies his or her actions.

One of the significant components of a belief system is the **image of the enemy**. Dehumanization of the enemy is a dominant theme. *The enemy is viewed in depersonalized and monolithic terms.* It is not human beings whom the terrorist fights; rather, it is this dehumanized monolith.

As one group of researchers noted, for many terrorists, "the enemy is nonhuman; not good enough. He is the enemy because he is not the hero and is not friendly to the hero."[4] This rationalization is particularly prominent among right-wing terrorists, whether neofascist or religious extremist. Such groups tend toward prejudicial stereotyping based on class, ethnic, or religious attributes.

Making war—even illegal, "unthinkable" war—on an inhuman enemy is easy. As long as that enemy does not have a face, a wife or child, a home, grieving parents, or friends, the destruction of that enemy is a simple matter, requiring little or no justification beyond the enemy status.

Viewing the enemy in these terms also makes depicting the struggle in which the terrorists see themselves as engaged relatively simple. It is a struggle in which good and evil are very obvious. The enemy is often seen as much more powerful in its monolithic strength, with many alternative courses of action from which to choose. The terrorists, on the other hand, have no choice except to resort to terrorism in confronting this "monster," which becomes, in their view, a response to oppression—not a free choice on their part, but a duty. Osama bin Laden, in his call for a jihad against America, stated, "The ruling to kill the Americans and their allies—civilians and military—is an individual duty for every Muslim who can do it in any country which it is possible to do it."[5]

Also of interest in this belief system is the terrorists' **images of themselves.** Terrorists of both the left and right tend to think of themselves as belonging to an *elite*. Most left-wing revolutionary terrorists view themselves as the *victims* rather than the aggressors in the struggle in which they are engaged—an obligation, a duty, not a voluntary choice—because they are the enlightened in a mass of unenlightened.[6] For the religious zealot, the image tends to be of being *chosen* by a supreme being to lead the struggle and to be a martyr in confronting the monster that threatens the world of the *faithful*.

Like terrorists of the right, revolutionary terrorists seem to view themselves as above the prevailing morality, as morally superior. They do not deem themselves in any sense bound by conventional laws or conventional morality, which they often regard as the corrupt and self-serving tool of the enemy. It would clearly be useless to condemn as immoral an action by a terrorist, because it is quite likely that those embracing terrorist tactics have already reached the belief that the morality condemning their action is inferior to their own morality.

This view of morality is integral to the terrorists' view of the **nature of the conflict** in which they are engaged. *Not only is this a moral struggle, in which good and evil are simplistically defined, but terrorists tend to define the struggle also in terms of elaborately idealistic terms.* Terrorists seldom perceive what they do as the murder of innocent persons. Instead, they are to describe such actions as executions committed after trials.

Menachem Begin offered insights into this legalistic rationalization. He noted that, in terrorist struggles, "what matters most is the inner consciousness that makes what is 'legal' illegal and the 'illegal' legal and justified."[7]

Also of importance in understanding the belief system of terrorists is the **image of the victims** of the violence. *If the victims are fairly easily identifiable with the enemy, then as representatives of the hostile forces, they are despised and their destruction is easily justified, even if such victims have committed no clear offense against the terrorist or his group.* As Michael Collins, founder of the Irish

Republican Army (IRA), noted with reference to the killing of 14 men *suspected* of being British intelligence agents, such persons were "undesirables . . . by whose destruction the very air is made sweeter." This remained true, according to Collins, even though not all of the 14 were guilty of the "sins" of which they were accused.[8]

Innocent victims, persons whose only "crime" was in being in the wrong place at the wrong time, are generally dismissed as unimportant by-products of the struggle. Thus, the persons in the airplanes flown into the World Trade Center towers and the Pentagon were only victims because they were on the wrong flight; those killed in the towers and at the Pentagon were part of the American "monster" against which bin Laden had called for a jihad.

This brings up one last important point about terrorist belief systems: the predominant **theme of millenarianism.** *Personal redemption through violent means* is a millenarian theme found in many terrorist belief systems. Violence is often viewed as being essential to the coming of the millennium, whose coming may be hastened by the actions of believers willing to violate the rules of the old order in an effort to bring in the new order.

Such beliefs have led to a deliberate abandonment of restraints. Coupled with the tendency to divide the world into clear camps of good and evil, this abandonment of restraints usually entails a strong conviction that no mercy can be shown to the evil that the enemy embodies. Terrorists are wrapped in an impenetrable cloak of belief in the absolute righteousness of their cause and the ultimate success that will inevitably come. If all violence brings the millennium closer, then violence, regardless of its consequences, cannot be regarded as a failure. The terrorist always "wins" in this struggle.

Other elements are common to some terrorist belief systems. Some, for instance, place a premium on martyrdom, suggesting this as a desirable goal.

A statement from the "Ladenese Epistle" illustrates the strength of this commitment to martyrdom:

> Those youths know that their rewards in fighting you, the USA, is double than their rewards in fighting someone else not from the people of the book. They have no intention except to enter paradise by killing you.[9]

Understanding at least these few fundamental elements of terrorist beliefs may facilitate an ability to deal with terrorism in its many forms and to anticipate its future growth patterns. Certainly the modern terrorist appears to hold belief systems very different from those of either soldiers or criminals.

CAN WE GENERALIZE ABOUT A "TYPICAL" TERRORIST?

What do we know about the type of individual who becomes a terrorist? Until recently, with the in-depth coverage given to Osama bin Laden, we had very limited personal data about successful perpetrators of terrorist attacks, because successful terrorists depend upon secrecy for protection. Through the capture of those less efficient in the art of terrorist operations, we have learned some useful information, and our security and intelligence organizations continue to add substantially to that data pool.

Nevertheless, it is difficult to generalize about the "typical" terrorist with any degree of accuracy. The search for a "terrorist personality" is a legitimate exercise, but it is unlikely to produce any common denominator capable of uniting a wide variety of countries, periods of time, cultures, and political alliances. In other words, the community of nation-states is unable, at this point, to agree on such a profile.

As Louise Richardson notes, "the emergence of terrorism requires a lethal cocktail with three ingredients: a disaffected individual, an enabling group, and a legitimizing authority."[10] She points out at least two reasons why it is difficult to generate convincing explanations for terrorism: there are both so many terrorists (since terrorism is a tactic carried out by many different groups in many different locations for many different reasons), and so few terrorists (as religions and social movements have millions of followers, but relatively few are terrorists). She notes that terrorists come from democracies, autocracies, and (more often) transitional or failed states; some come from wealth, others from poverty. Social class and/or political system are not enough to identify "likely" terrorists.

Some scholars suggest that the application of Social Identity Theory (SIT) in terrorism research yields an understanding of the individuals who commit acts of terror that is more comprehensive than the focused study of individuals, since SIT places individuals in a social context. Arena and Arrigo, two scholars who use SIT to study terrorism, suggest that the identity of individuals who engage in terrorism derives from three different sources: personal, social, and group/collective.[11] Their studies of four extremist organizations, including the Provisional Irish Republican Army (PIRA), HAMAS (Harakat al-Muqawamah al-Islamiyyah), the Peruvian Shining Path (Sendero Luminoso), and the Liberation Tigers of Tamil Eelam, lend strength to this theoretical approach, as it helps to explain the roles of individuals within the organizations, as well as the role of the organizations within the culture.

Some scholars have attempted to create a profile of a typical terrorist. Their successes are mixed, at best, but offer some ideas that help us not only to understand what a typical terrorist may be like but also to evaluate how terrorists and terrorism have changed in recent years.

Edgar O'Ballance offers a critique of what he calls a "successful" terrorist (by which he appears to mean one who is neither captured nor dead). In his book, *The Language of Violence,* O'Ballance suggests several essential **characteristics of a "successful" terrorist:**

> *Dedication.* To be successful, a terrorist cannot be a casual or part-time mercenary, willing to operate only when it suits his convenience or his pocket. He must become a **fedayeen**, a *"man of sacrifice."* Dedication also implies absolute obedience to the leader of the political movement.

Personal Bravery. As a terrorist must face the possibility of death, injury, imprisonment, or torture if captured, O'Ballance regards personal bravery as important, in varying degrees, depending upon one's position within a terrorist group's hierarchy.

Without the Emotions of Pity or Remorse. Since most victims will include innocent men, women, and children, who must be killed in cold blood, a terrorist must have the killer instinct, able to kill without hesitation on receipt of a code or signal. As this expert notes, many can kill in the heat of anger or in battle, but few can do so in cold blood.

Fairly High Intelligence. As a would-be terrorist has to collect, collate, and assess information; devise and put into effect complex plans; and evade police, security forces, and other hostile forces, intelligence appears to be a requisite.

Fairly High Degree of Sophistication. This is essential, according to O'Ballance, for a terrorist to blend into the first-class section on airliners, stay at first-class hotels, and mix inconspicuously with the international executive set.

Be Reasonably Well Educated and Possess a Fair Share of General Knowledge. By this, O'Ballance means that a terrorist should be able to speak English as well as one other major language. He asserts that a university degree is almost mandatory.

O'Ballance notes that "all terrorists do not measure up to these high standards, but the leaders, planners, couriers, liaison officers, and activists must."[12] This assertion is difficult to challenge effectively, because if the terrorist is successful, then the implication is that he or she has succeeded in evading law enforcement, security, and intelligence officers, and hence the information about the individual is necessarily either scant or unconfirmed.

We could conclude, with some justice, that most of O'Ballance's assertions are at least half true, half false, and largely untestable. But these generalizations, with their grains of truth, are still useful in analyzing terrorism and terrorist behavior. Let us instead examine each of his suggested attributes of a terrorist to discover whether they can be substantiated by insights into contemporary behavior.

Dedication certainly appears, on the surface, to be characteristic of modern terrorists. Palestinians involved in various groups have indicated a willingness to wait for as long as it takes them to realize their dream of a nation of Palestine. They have been willing to wait as long as the Irgun waited, or longer, and many are reluctant to accept the current peace settlements, because that represents at this point less than full national independence for a nation of Palestine.

The progress toward a comprehensive peace settlement in the Middle East in the first decade of the twenty-first century indicated that this tenacity is still massive. wall that slices through the West Bank and decimates parts of Palestinian territory, Palestinian leadership from the West Bank has taken to the

United Nations a request/demand for recognition of Palestine as a state, with membership in the United Nations. Although this matter remains unresolved, the determination of Palestinian leaders to the restoration of the state of Palestine is strong.

Anger by the Palestinian group now in elected leadership in Gaza, **HAMAS,** *a radical Islamic movement supported by Iran throughout the Middle East,* indicates that a significant portion of the Palestinians remains committed to full restoration of Palestine to the Palestinian people. The suicide bombings in this area beginning in 1994, which claimed the lives of innocent men, women, and children and which provoked a harsh response by Israel in the form of attacks that have claimed far more Palestinian lives, have given credence to this absolute resolve.

However, unlike the continuing violence in the Middle East, progress is being made toward a political settlement of the problem in Northern Ireland. Like the situation of Palestine, though, the solution will probably not satisfy all of the truly dedicated terrorists. The willingness of the **Provisional Irish Republican Army (PIRA),** *the organization of radical Irish Catholics committed to the removal of British forces from Northern Ireland and to the unification of Ireland which succeeded the original IRA,* to negotiate peace has angered radical elements in the Catholic community. The movement of the British to negotiate with the PIRA openly raised equal anger in militant Protestant groups. As resolution of the dispute between the British and the PIRA was reached and a merging of Northern Ireland with the Republic of Ireland planned, similarly dedicated groups of terrorists determined to force the United Kingdom into retaining sovereignty (thus keeping Protestant control) emerged in the form of the Continuity IRA and the Real IRA.

Such dedication is not always directed at so specific a nationalist cause. The Japanese Red Army (JRA), founded in 1969, describes itself as **soldiers of the revolution,** *pledged to participate in all revolutions anywhere in the world through exemplary acts.* This group was responsible for the massacre of 26 tourists at Lod Airport in Tel Aviv, Israel. These dedicated revolutionaries undertook numerous terrorist attacks, many of which, like the Lod Airport massacre, were essentially suicide missions, because escape was scarcely possible.

The dedication of Osama bin Laden and his **al-Qaeda** network—*created by bin Laden in the late 1980s to bring together Arabs in Afghanistan against the Soviet Union and now engaged in attempting to establish an Islamic caliphate throughout the world*—has also become apparent, as evidence has emerged that most of the attacks generated by this network involved years of preparation. Some of the individuals who carried out the September 11 attacks came to the United States years in advance, slowly and carefully planning each stage of the operation. The dedication involved for those willing to leave home and live for years in the country to be attacked—learning about its airport security systems, taking lessons in order to pilot its airliners, even traveling on the airline's planes to time and plan each step with accuracy—is clear from the evidence of their activities.

Personal bravery is also a characteristic often attributed to modern terrorists. There are, however, two views of the bravery that terrorists may possess. One might argue that it can scarcely be termed "brave" to use weapons against unarmed and defenseless civilians. The men, women, and children at Lod Airport were wholly unable to defend themselves against the attack of the JRA. Was it "brave" of the JRA to slaughter these innocent and unarmed people?

The opposing view is that to be willing to carry out missions in which one's own death or imprisonment is inevitable argues no small degree of personal courage. A willingness to give one's life for a cause has commanded, throughout history, at least a reluctant admiration, even from one's enemies.

Bravery is a very subjective term. One may feel oneself to be cowardly but be perceived by others to be quite fearless. The audience for one's deeds is often able to judge one's bravery only by the commission of the deed and is unaware of the inner doubts or demons that may have driven one to the act.

The question as to whether terrorists who murder innocent persons with the knowledge that their own survival is problematic are brave may never be answered to anyone's satisfaction. Much depends on the way in which one describes the situation.

According to O'Ballance, a successful terrorist should be without the emotions of pity or remorse. Given the necessity of being able to kill, in cold blood, unarmed and innocent persons, this would appear a reasonable assumption regarding the terrorist personality. Unlike criminals who may kill to prevent being captured or to secure some coveted prize, terrorists must, by the very nature of the act, kill persons against whom they have no specific grudge, whose life or death is not really material to their well-being or security.

Hacker states:

> Often, the terrorists do not know whom they will hurt, and they could not care less. Nothing seems important to them except they themselves and their cause. In planning and executing their deeds, the terrorists are totally oblivious to the fate of their victims. Only utter dehumanization permits the ruthless use of human beings as bargaining chips, bargaining instruments, or objects for indiscriminate aggression.[13]

Consider the following case: On July 22, 1946, an Irgun team, dressed as waiters, rolled seven milk churns full of dynamite and TNT into the empty Regency Grill of the King David Hotel in Jerusalem. At 12:37 p.m., the TNT in the milk cans exploded, creating pressure so great that it burst the hearts, lungs, and livers of the clerks working on the floors above.

Thurston Clarke gives a gruesome description of the fate of the people in the King David Hotel at that time:

> In that split second after 12:37, thirteen of those who had been alive at 12:36 disappeared without a trace. The clothes, bracelets, cufflinks, and wallets which might have identified them exploded into dust and smoke. Others were turned to charcoal, melted into chairs and desks or exploded into countless fragments. The face of a Jewish typist was ripped from her

skull, blown out of a window, and smeared onto the pavement below. Miraculously it was recognizable, a two-foot-long distorted death mask topped with tufts of hair.

Blocks of stones, tables and desks crushed heads and snapped necks. Coat racks became deadly arrows that flew across rooms, piercing chests. Filing cabinets pinned people to walls, suffocating them. Chandeliers and ceiling fans crashed to the floor, impaling and decapitating those underneath.[14]

Ninety-one people died in that bomb blast. Of these, 28 were British, 41 were Arabs, and 17 were Jews. Another 46 were injured.

Listen to the words of the person who commanded this attack:

There is no longer any armistice between the Jewish people and the British administration of Eretz Israel which hands our brothers over to Hitler. Our people are at war with this regime—war to the end.[15]

Was this bombing the deed of a fanatic, a person who could murder many innocent people in cold blood in this "war to the end"? Certainly it would seem the case.

Yet the perpetrator of this atrocity, the man responsible for the terrible destruction of 91 lives, was Menachem Begin, who in the 1970s served as prime minister of Israel. The Irgun terrorist who plotted to destroy the hotel was the same man who, working with President Jimmy Carter of the United States and President Anwar Sadat of Egypt, made significant efforts to move Israel on the road to peace with its Arab neighbors, signing the famous Camp David Accords, bringing a measure of peace between Israel and Egypt.

Just as there is no safe generalization with regard to the personal bravery of terrorists, so there seem pitfalls in making too broad a characterization of a terrorist as incapable of pity or remorse. Perhaps of all that O'Ballance had to say about this particular aspect of a terrorist's characteristics, it is accurate only to say that terrorists appear to have an image of the enemy that allows them to be willing to use lethal force.

The characteristics that O'Ballance suggests of sophistication and education are less true of post-1970s terrorists than they were of terrorists prior to that time. Many nineteenth-century revolutionary terrorists were indeed intelligent, sophisticated, university educated, and even multilingual. Those responsible for the murder of Czar Alexander II of Russia in March 1881 were men and women who possessed a much higher level of education and sophistication than most other young people of their nation.

Similarly, the Tupamaros of Uruguay were primarily composed of the young, well-educated liberal intellectuals who sought, but never fully gained, the support of the masses. The Baader-Meinhof gang in West Germany, which terrorized that nation throughout the 1970s, was also composed of middle- and upper-class intellectuals. This gang's master strategist was Horst Mahler, a radical young lawyer, and it drew its membership and support system heavily from the student body of German universities.

The founder of one of Italy's first left-wing terrorist bands, the Proletarian Action Group (GAP), was Giangiacomo Feltrinelli, the heir to an immense

Milanese fortune and head of one of Europe's most distinguished publishing houses. Like the Red Brigades, which would succeed this group as Italy's leading left-wing terrorist group, the GAP drew much of its initial membership from young, often wealthy, intellectuals.

Terrorists, in fact, tended to be recruited from college campuses until the 1980s. Many came from well-to-do families, so that sophistication and an ability to mix with the international set were well within their grasp. Intelligence, sophistication, education, and university training: not only the leaders but also many of the practitioners of both nineteenth-century anarchism and contemporary terrorism possessed these attributes.

But standards and modes of behavior among terrorists as we move forward in the twenty-first century are changing. The French anarchists did not abduct children and threaten to kill them unless ransom was paid. The Narodnaya Volya did not send parts of their victims' bodies with little notes to their relatives as the right-wing Guatemalan National Revolutionary Unity did. Neither French nor Russian anarchists tormented, mutilated, raped, and castrated their victims, as too many terrorist groups have done in the latter part of the twentieth century. The Baader-Meinhof would not have flown passenger airlines into the World Trade Center, killing thousands.

As Walter Laqueur pointed out:

> Not all terrorist movements have made a fetish of brutality; some have behaved more humanely than others. But what was once a rare exception has become a frequent occurrence in our time.[16]

According to Laqueur, the character of terrorism has undergone a profound change. Intellectuals, he contends, have made "the cult of violence respectable."

Nevertheless, Laqueur is correct in his assertion that the terror of recent decades is different. Modern terrorists are significantly different; the type of person becoming a terrorist today has a great deal to do with the difference in terrorism. No "profiling" of a terrorist can be complete without factoring in an individual analysis of modern terrorist leaders and followers, even if such analysis must be general, with specific examples, rather than comprehensive examples.

INDIVIDUAL-LEVEL ANALYSIS: WHY DOES SOMEONE BECOME A TERRORIST TODAY?

Based on psychological literature and countless interviews with terror suspects and those imprisoned for the crimes, Richardson suggests that there are three essential points that stand out in the analysis of why individuals become terrorists today: simplicity, identification, and revenge.[17] Let us explore each of these motivations to better understand the important *why* of individual terrorist action. In terms of counterterrorism, it is essential to understand *why* a particular action is chosen by an individual, if one is intending to accurately predict such actions, thereby making prevention and/or response to such actions possible. Understanding does not connote sympathy or justification, but it can make prevention and response much more feasible for the general public as well as for those charged with securing public safety. Linking the "causes" discussed in Chapter 3 with the "who" of the profiles in this chapter makes the picture of modern terrorism more easily understood.

Simplicity

Individuals carrying out acts of terrorism tend to see themselves as engaged in a struggle of good against evil, right against wrong. This oversimplified view of the world allows them to blame their adversaries for all of their problems, as the "you are evil" discussion from Chapter 3 suggests. This view helps them to see themselves as defenders, not aggressors; as altruistic, not terrorists. Mark Juergensmeyer notes in his interview with Dr. Abdul Aziz Rantisi, one of the founders of HAMAS, that this leader stated: "You think that we are the aggressors. That is the number one misunderstanding. We are not; we are the victims."[18] **Osama bin Laden** frequently described the world and the struggle in which he was engaged in simplistic terms, asserting that, "The truth is the whole Muslim world is the victim of international terrorism, engineered by America and the United Nations."[19] Simplicity of worldview, then, is one vital aspect of individual motivation toward terrorism.

Identification

Identification with others is frequently cited by both leaders and followers in conversations about the commission of terrorist acts. A report prepared by the New York Police Department's (NYPD) Intelligence Division suggested that the process of **radicalization,** or *socialization toward politically violent extremism and terrorism,* has four stages: preradicalization, self-identification, indoctrination, and jihadization.[20] While this report focuses on the attacks in the West (those carried out in London and Madrid as well as those prevented in Canada and the United States) by Islamic radicals, similar studies of such radicals living in the Middle East suggest similar phases of development.

The "identification" stage of this process is important, because it transitions the individual, who may have initially been simply feeling a bit marginalized and unhappy with his or her current social system. As the FBI (Federal Bureau of Investigation) director noted in his remarks in June 2006,

> Radicalization often starts with individuals who are frustrated with their lives or with the politics of their home governments . . . Some may be lonely or dissatisfied with their role in society. Others may have friends or mentors who encourage membership for social reasons . . . Once a person has joined an extremist group, he or she may start to identify with an ideology—one that encourages violence against a government and its citizens. They may become increasingly isolated from their old lives, drift away from family and friends, and spend more time with other members of the extremist group.[21]

Group identity, then, is regarded as a critical phase of the radicalization process, by which individuals become willing to carry out terrorist acts. Not everyone who joins a group carries out a terrorist act, but identification lends strength to the individual's motivation, as interviews and memoirs of those who have carried out such acts suggest.

As Richardson notes, "terrorist group leaders have told similar stories of being radicalized by identifying with the suffering of others."[22] For example, Omar Sheikh, a British citizen who became a radicalized member of the Pakistani group Jaish-e-Mohammed , was convicted of the murder of Daniel Pearl, a reporter for the *Wall Street Journal* in Pakistan in 2002. Sheikh wrote that, while he was a student at the London School of Economics in 1992, he observed the film, *The Death of a Nation*, depicting the murder of Bosnian Muslims by Serbs, which he claimed began his "political awakening" and eventual radicalization.[23] His story of radicalization by identification with the suffering of others is similar to that of Abimael Guzman, academic leader of Peru's militant group, the Shining Path (Sendero Luminoso), who "saw the fighting spirit of the people during the uprising in Arequipa in 1950."[24]

Not only intellectual leaders of groups are radicalized toward terrorism by the force of identity with a group. Accounts of Protestant paramilitaries in Northern Ireland who became radicalized by the sight of neighbors injured in bombs detonated by the Catholic-based IRA in Northern Ireland parallel similar stories of IRA members being radicalized by being driven from their homes by Protestant mobs. Identity with a group of one's faith that is experiencing violent attacks obviously can foster a willingness to carry out acts of violence in support of the group under attack.

Identity, then, is not dependent upon actually being victimized by attackers. The "self-identification" referred to in the NYPD analysis suggests that this is an intentional act of identification, rather than the outgrowth of natural socialization processes; a choice, rather than an accident of fate. According to sociologists, the need for "identity" is critical for mankind. Individuals who are impacted by forces of globalization that threaten or challenge their identity (such as migration to another culture, without assimilation into that culture; loss of traditional norms, jobs, or opportunities; the breaking down of communities as cultures mesh and clash) are vulnerable to this need for identity and today can easily "identify" with groups they may never meet whose needs are depicted daily on the news and the Internet. As the NYPD report makes clear, the identification with a group often occurs today on the Web, rather than in the more tangible personal interaction of group meetings.

Revenge

The identification with the suffering of others is often linked with the desire to avenge the "wrongs" done to those in the identity group. Renato Curcio, the intellectual leader of the Italian group the Red Brigades, asserted that he was "converted" to violence and terrorism in response to an incident in which the Italian police fired on farmworkers, killing some adults and injuring several children. Certainly many of bin Laden's speeches were laden with calls for, and claims to, vengeance against the United States. Shortly after the events of September 11, 2001, he stated on Al Jazeera television:

> America has been filled with horror from north to south and east to west, and thanks be to God that what America is tasting now is only a copy of what we have tasted. Our Islamic nation has been tasting the same for more than eighty years, humiliation and disgrace, its sons killed and their blood spilled, its sanctities destroyed.[25]

Richardson suggests that combined desire for revenge, renown, and reaction are important elements of the profile of modern terrorism. These are, she suggests, short-term goals of the followers of terrorist movements, while the leadership of such movements generally seeks long-term goals that include philosophical or political aspirations.[26] This point is important if we are trying to profile modern terrorists. The rank and file will seek **revenge**, in the form *of inflicting suffering on those responsible for causing or allowing suffering to occur on their identifying group of people*, and perhaps **renown**, often gauged in terms of *making headline news around the world*. They will seldom, however, link the success of their "mission" or attack in terms of reaction, or *the forcing of political or philosophical change to occur*. That measure, if it is used at all, is applied by leaders seeking long-term goals by the commission of multiple short-term, focused actions.

Individuals today have become more radicalized and therefore are more likely to carry out terrorist acts as they assimilate a very simple view of their world as being full of good and evil, as they identify with a group they consider "good" in the conflict of good with evil in this world, and as they seek to "right" the "wrongs" that are inflicted on their people of identity. The processes of globalization, desocialization, dislocation within systems, and forced relocation into refugee communities have intensified the radicalization of individuals today.

TERRORISM IS DIFFERENT TODAY

Terrorism today is different from terrorism that occurred in previous centuries. While there are many types and levels of changes that have evolved in terrorism, we will explore some of the most significant changes in terms of understanding contemporary terrorism: aims or goals, group dynamics, religious fanaticism, demographic changes, and socialization patterns. Each offers useful insights into modern terrorist activity.

Aims or Goals

Part of the difference between terrorism as it occurred in previous generations and modern terrorism lies in the **motivation** that drives individuals to embrace terrorism. Walter Laqueur summed up the situation very well in the 1980s:

> Whatever their motives may be, the "ardent love of other" which Emma Goldman observed is not among them. The driving force is hate not love,

ethical considerations are a matter of indifference to them and their dreams of freedom, of national and social liberation are suspect. Nineteenth-century nationalist terrorists were fighting for freedom from foreign domination. More recently, appetites have grown, the Basques have designs on Galicia, the Palestinians not only want the West Bank but also intend to destroy the Jewish state, and the IRA would like to bomb the Protestants into a united Ireland. The aims of terrorism, in brief, have changed, and so have the terrorists.[26]

In the twenty-first century, a less-than-clear political purpose seems involved in much of the terrorism perpetrated. Although idealism, a social conscience, or hatred of foreign oppression can serve to drive one to commit acts of terrorism, so can boredom, mental confusion, and what psychologists term "free-floating aggression."

What difference does it make whether terrorism is committed by social idealists or persons suffering from free-floating aggression? We could speculate that a social conscience would be more likely to inhibit a perpetrator from using indiscriminate violence against the unprotected masses. Perhaps mental confusion contributes to an inability to recognize limits on the use of terror-violence.

Terrorists of the twenty-first century appear more willing to use weapons of mass destruction than terrorists of preceding decades, perhaps because more states have used such weapons in internal wars in recent years. Iraq's use of cyanide gas on the Kurds in Halabja in March 1988 dramatically illustrated the willingness of states to use such weapons. Thus, the news that al-Qaeda tested an air dispersal mechanism for cyanide, although a chilling thought, should hardly be surprising. If states, which set the norms that limit the use of such weapons, are using these weapons openly against their own citizens, then individuals engaged in terrorist acts can scarcely be expected to continue to refrain from the use of such weapons.

Group Dynamics

Before considering demographic information that might help to substantiate and explain the differences, let us first consider the impact of the terrorist *group* upon the terrorist. **Group dynamics,** *forces of group behavior that help to shape terrorist thought and action*, must certainly be understood in order to comprehend the contemporary terrorist.

Modern terrorists are for the most part fanatics whose sense of reality is distorted. They operate under the assumption that they, and they alone, know the truth and are therefore the sole arbiters of what is right and what is wrong. They believe themselves to be moralists to whom ordinary law does not apply because the law in existence is created by immoral people for immoral purposes.

They are not, however, consistent in their logic. For example, terrorists demand, when captured, that governments treat them as prisoners of war, as they are involved in a war against either a specific government or society in general. But terrorists vehemently deny the state's right to treat them as war criminals for their indiscriminate killing of civilians. In other words, they invoke the laws of war only in so far as they serve their purposes but reject any aspect of such laws that limit their ability to kill at will.

Two other points should be made with respect to understanding the impact of group dynamics on the contemporary terrorist. The first point is relatively simple and involves what seems like a truism. *The less clear the political purpose that motivates terrorism, the greater its appeal is likely to be to unbalanced persons.* A rational individual will be more likely to require a clear purpose for the commission of an extraordinary act. Thus an irrational mind is more likely to accept the appeal of an act with an unclear political purpose.

Contemporary terrorism has significantly less clear political purpose than terrorism of earlier centuries. Thus, it seems fair to say that a larger proportion of contemporary terrorists may well be less rational persons, making the ultimate goals they are seeking more difficult to articulate. This certainly makes counterterrorism more difficult, as it will be increasingly unclear what political motives and goals are behind the acts of individuals plotting to carry out terrorist attacks.

The second point relates to what psychologists term *group dynamics. If it is true that a terrorist's sense of reality is distorted* as discussed earlier in the context of terrorist images, *then the greater the association the terrorist enjoys with his or her group of fellow terrorists, the greater that distortion will be.* In other words, the more an individual perceives his or her identity in terms of a group of fellow terrorists, the less he or she will be able to see the world as it really is. For the terrorist who is a member of a close-knit organization, reality is defined by the group.

Thus, conventional moral and legal constraints have little meaning to an individual deeply involved in a terrorist group. The group determines for itself what is moral and what is legal. An individual who has just joined the group may be able to perceive the difference between what the group and society declare to be morally or legally justified. The longer the individual remains with the group or the more strongly he or she identifies with the norms of the group, the less the individual is able to see the difference between reality and "reality" as it is defined by the group.

The strength of the individual's acceptance of the group's definition of reality is particularly evident in situations in which terrorism has been a significant part of the culture for several generations. In Northern Ireland, for instance, young people have been "brought up to think of democracy as part of everyday humdrum existence, but of recourse to violence as something existing on a superior plane, not merely glorious but even sacred."[28]

Religious Fanaticism

Certainly **religious fanaticism,** *religious advocacy that involves a pattern of violently and potentially deadly opposition to anyone perceived as not in agreement with the faith,* is today as strong a motivator for the commission of terrorism as it has been in previous centuries. The holy war waged by some Muslims on Christians and fellow Muslims is no less violent than that waged during the Middle Ages. The mixture of political and religious fanaticism has always been a volatile and often violent combination.

Consider the case of the individual who commits terrorism as a member of a fanatic religious group. Religions, as a rule, offer their own versions of reality, as well as a promise of reward for conformity to the norms of that reality. The reward is usually promised for a future time, when the present reality has passed away.

Thus, religious zealots committing an act of terrorism are assured by their religious leaders that their acts are acceptable to a higher morality. They are reinforced in their belief that what they are doing is right by the approval of their fellow zealots. Further, religious fanatics are assured of immortality and a suitable reward if they should die in the commission of the act of terrorism.

It would be difficult if not impossible to persuade such persons out of their beliefs. Little could be offered to such persons as an inducement to discontinue the acts of terrorism. What reward can compete with the promise of immortality, approval by one's peers, and religious sanctification?

Obviously, the dynamics of some groups are much more powerful than those of others whose reward system and expensive spiritual support system is less organized or persuasive. Certain types of terrorists are, thus, much more difficult to deal with on a rational basis due to this ability of a group to distort reality.

Like some of the earliest forms of terrorism, terrorists in the twenty-first century are increasingly motivated by religious zealotry, seeking not only to change a political system but also to purify a religious community. Seeing themselves as called upon to engage in a holy war against infidels who threaten their faith, these modern zealots have begun to have an impact not enjoyed by their predecessors of earlier times. The **Sicariis**, *dagger-wielding Jewish zealots of ancient Rome who sought to provoke an apocalyptic confrontation between Rome and the Jewish nation,* and the Assassins (noted in Chapter 2) who tried to purify the Muslim community by assassination in order to hasten the arrival of the Imam—the heir of the Prophet, who would establish a new and just society—had either a negative or at best a relatively insignificant impact on the growth of their faith community.

Modern religious zealots emerging today have been able to seriously impact both political systems and the strength of faith communities in their movement toward holy wars. Extremists carrying out terrorism—by the state, by groups, or by individual suicide bombers—are making the emergence of a political state of Palestine and the survival of the state of Israel problematic. Religious leaders in several countries in the Middle East advocate instructing the very young to commit themselves to religious fanaticism, which makes peace in that region unlikely. Religiously inspired terrorists carried out the attacks of September 11 and impeded the rebuilding of both Afghanistan and Iraq with calls for a holy war to purify and protect a faith community. Clearly, religious motivation for terrorism today has not only increased but is also becoming more successful.

Demographic Trends in Group Membership

Some **demographic trends** in recruitment and membership in modern terrorist affiliations offer clues as to who is currently becoming a terrorist. While this falls short of providing a precise profile of a modern terrorist, it does yield insights into not only who modern terrorists are but also the impact of such a demographic configuration on contemporary terrorism.

Age Terrorism is not only a pursuit of the young. In the late 1970s and 1980s, it became a pursuit of the *very* young. Although terrorists during the time of the Russian anarchists tended to be at least in their mid-twenties, during the two decades in the late twentieth century, the average age steadily decreased. During the turbulent 1960s, many terrorists were recruited from college campuses throughout the Western world. This brought the average age down to around 20; the leaders were several years older, often in their early thirties.

As early as the spring of 1976, however, evidence of a change in the age level of terrorists began to emerge. Arrests of Spanish ETA members revealed a number of youths in their teens. In Northern Ireland, some of the terrorists apprehended were as young as 12 to 14.[29]

Today, although the majority of active terrorists are in their twenties, there has been a tendency, particularly among groups in the Middle East, Southeast Asia, and Africa, to recruit children of 14 or 15 years of age. These children are used for dangerous, frequently suicidal missions, partly because their youth makes them less likely to question orders and partly because their extreme youth makes them less likely to attract the attention of the authorities.

One explanation of this phenomenon is that the anarchistic-revolutionary philosophy that had begun to infiltrate the province of university students has begun to infiltrate the secondary school level, but this is a less persuasive explanation. Instead, researchers note the increasing level of media violence, access to weapons, development of satanic cults, and other sociological phenomenon are more likely to be found in young people today than in earlier decades.

Although these social patterns may explain part of this demographic trend, another explanation may lie in the number of children growing up in cultures in which violence is a way of life. In the Middle East and in Northern Ireland, for instance, children growing up in violent community struggles easily become a part of terrorist activities spanning successive generations within the same family. Children were thus recruited, not by philosophy learned at university or secondary school, but by the dogma and lifestyles of their parents.

However, by the 1990s, this trend became less clear, as peace within at least one of these regions came closer to reality. Religious fanaticism is still a highly motivating factor compelling young teenagers into roles as suicide bombers; yet, studies of groups such as HAMAS and Ansar al-Islam indicate most members are closer in age to the early 1970s' terrorist profile. The individuals responsible for the bombing of the Pan Am flight over Lockerbie and those involved in either the 1993 bombing or the dramatically more successful 2001 attacks on the World Trade Center in New York City were certainly not 12 or 13 years of age!

One pattern remains relatively consistent among groups engaging in terrorism from all regions of the world: leaders tend to be older than followers. While the leaders of European groups continue to be younger than their counterparts in Latin America, they are still older than their followers. This age difference is important in the context discussed earlier concerning goals, as the long-term leader goals of significant political or social change may not always mesh with those of the short-term revenge goals of the followers.

Education   Until the mid-1970s, most of the individuals involved in terrorism were well educated. Almost two-thirds of the people identified as terrorists were persons with some university training, university graduates, or postgraduate students. Among the Tupamaros, for example, about 75 percent of their members were very well educated, and among the Baader-Meinhof organization in West Germany, the figure reached almost 80 percent.

In the Palestinian groups, most members were university students or graduates, frequently those who, by virtue of their middle-class wealth, had been able to study at foreign universities. This group of students became an important recruiting pool for the Popular Front for the Liberation of Palestine (PFLP). Indeed, George Habash, the chief of the PFLP for decades, was a medical doctor who obtained his degree abroad.

Marc Sageman, who researched the biographies of 172 members of al-Qaeda, found that 60 percent had gone to college; several had doctorates.[30] Peter Bergen's study of the background of 75 Islamic terrorists responsible for the most damaging attacks in recent history indicated that more than half had attended college, and 2 had doctorates from Western universities, while 2 others were working on their PhDs.[31]

But the level of education of the terrorist "followers" in many other groups is declining today, partly because of the trend in recruitment age of the last two decades of the twentieth century already noted. If young people are being recruited out of secondary school rather than out of college, then the number of individuals in terrorist groups with college educations will necessarily decline as well.

This trend brings with it another important decline: a diminishing of the understanding by the rank and file among terrorists of the political, religious, and social philosophies that motivated the groups to adopt terrorist activities. As a rule, elementary school children are unable to grasp the impetus of Marxist philosophy toward social revolution. Unlike the college students of the 1960s who studied and at least half-understood radical political philosophies, today's new terrorist recruits are fed watered-down versions of Marx and Lenin, radicalized religious dogma, and other distortions that they are not able to challenge effectively.

Economic Status   During the 1960s, many young people joined terrorist organizations as a way of rejecting the comfortable, middle-class values of their parents. Often children of parents who could afford to send them to private colleges, they were rejecting the comparative wealth of their surroundings to fight for justice for those less fortunate.

Today's terrorist followers tend to be drawn more from the less fortunate than from comfortable middle-class homes. Although some come from families who have had wealth, most are from absolute destitution, individuals for whom terrorism represents the only way to lash out at society's injustices. In the terrorist group, these individuals find a collective wealth and ability to improve one's financial situation that is enormously appealing to the impoverished.

Abu Nidal provides insight into the change in the economic circumstances of the type of person who becomes a terrorist today in many parts of the world. Nidal, born Sabri al-Banna, was the son of wealthy Palestinian parents who lost everything. From the lap of luxury, his family moved into the extreme poverty of refugee camps. The bitterness and frustration of a life of endless poverty and statelessness may well have been the catalyst for the terrorist he was to become.

Leaders of groups today, however, are increasingly emerging from middle- to upper-class families. Mohammed Atta, the leader of the al-Qaeda team that carried out the September 11 attacks, was the son of an Egyptian lawyer and had himself earned a doctorate in urban planning. Sageman's study of al-Qaeda members indicated that about two-thirds of them were from middle- or upper-class families, findings supported by Gilles Keppel's studies of 300 Islamic militants, who were from higher socioeconomic backgrounds.[32]

Osama bin Laden clearly illustrates this trend in economic status. The son of a multimillionaire who inherited substantial wealth, bin Laden was similar to the terrorists of the 1970s, rejecting a life of wealth and perceiving himself as fighting on behalf of those victimized by the very economic system from which his family benefited. This emergence from a background of privilege to identify intensely with and eventually lead a group perceived (by its leaders) to be "victimized" is similar to that of Raúl Sendic, one of the founders of the Tupamaros in Uruguay.

Gender   During the earlier part of the twentieth century, the leaders of terrorist cadres included some women among their numbers, but the rank and file was usually predominantly male. In many such groups, women were assigned the less life-threatening roles of intelligence collection, courier, nurse or medical personnel, and maintenance of "safe houses" for terrorists on the run.

Terrorism of the late twentieth century, however, was an equal opportunity employer. The commander of the JRA for years, Fusako Shigenobu, was a woman, and of the 14 most wanted West German terrorists in 1981, 10 were women. Studies show that female members of terrorist groups have proved to be tougher, more fanatical, and more loyal, and they have a greater capacity for suffering. In some terrorist groups, women on average tended to remain members longer than men.

One example of the difference in the roles played by women in terrorism today is a pregnant woman who was given the task of carrying a suitcase loaded with explosives aboard an airplane in the 1980s. Only a few decades ago, she would have been, at best, allowed to provide a safe haven for the man entrusted with that task. This is *not* to suggest that this is in any way "progress," but it does indicate a difference in the role women now play in terrorism. Indeed, women as suicide bombers are becoming an increasingly common role today in troubled areas, as Case Study 4.1 indicates.

Disturbing Patterns of Socialization

Although the trends in recruitment of individuals into terrorist acts offer insights into the demographics of groups engaged in terrorism today, there are also several more disturbing patterns emerging. Many individuals who engage in terrorist acts share either a lack or a rejection of the desire for a peaceful society. Among many groups, too, is an emerging and violent antipathy toward Western cultures. When these two factors combine with religious fanaticism, the potential for escalating terrorism against Western targets by individuals and groups who share a common enemy and even a common religious motivation easily becomes a holy war of immense proportions.

Socialization toward Violence: Suicide Bombing   Intellectuals have, during the past few decades, helped to make the cult of violence respectable. But for

---

CASE STUDY 4.1

The Black Widows

This group of women, known as *Chyornyye Vdovy* in Russia, originated in 2000 in Chechnya and operates primarily in this region. Its first terrorist attack was carried out by Khava Batayeva, a young woman who was a suicide bomber attacking a Russian military base in June of 2000, killing three soldiers and injuring five others. The actual size and membership of this group is unclear, as the Russian media dubs any woman who carries out a suicide bombing in Russia a "Black Widow." Most of the women known to belong to this group lost their husbands in the Chechen wars against the Russian Federation. Reports suggest that many of the women were encouraged by other Chechen separatists to carry out suicide bombings as a last resort, a final act of defiance in the wars that had cost them their marriage partners.

Reports from the Russian government indicate that this group has caused extensive damage, resulting in the deaths of several hundred Russians, with about 150 killed in the summer of 2003 alone. The Global Terrorism Database 2 suggests that the Black Widows will undoubtedly continue to gain recruits as the reservoir of widowed Chechen women grows commensurate with the death of rebel Chechen fighters. ∎

today's terrorists, there has been **socialization toward violence** in ways never before experienced in civilized society. Intellectual terrorists of the 1960s were, for the most part, first-generation terrorists. Today we see an increasing number of third- and even fourth-generation terrorists. Young people recruited in such circumstances have been *socialized to accept violence as a normal pattern of life*. Peace, as much of the rest of the world knows it, has no meaning for them, and the related values of a civilized society have little relevance in their lives.

Patterns of successive generations of terrorism produced terrorists in Northern Ireland and parts of the Middle East who had no understanding of the limits on the use of violence regarded by much of the world as fundamental until the peace efforts of the 1990s. The role of violence is made vividly clear in remarks made by the Reverend Benjamin Weir, a former U.S. hostage held by terrorists in Lebanon in the 1980s. He suggested that for many Lebanese youths the only employment open to them that offered both an income and some form of security for their families was with one of the warring militia factions. Life as a terrorist was, in some respects, the *only* alternative for many young people in that war-torn country.

In states experiencing economic and political system failure today, young people are vulnerable to this socialization, to the extent that violently killing themselves and others is becoming almost a norm. The spiraling rate of people willing to be suicide bombers, destroying their lives and as many other people as possible, offers grim evidence of this trend.

Alienation toward Western Systems

Globalization has left at least 20 percent of the world's population completely stranded, alienated, and desperate, without hope of catching a ride on the accelerating economic train led by the West. Terrorism and violent religious fundamentalism, however complex their causes, grow well in the soil of poverty and hunger. For people who struggle to feed their families and feel left behind by economic globalization, the call to radicalism is powerful. More than 800 million people globally are chronically undernourished, a condition with devastating consequences for their health and for the welfare of their communities. The poverty and hunger in the developing nations threaten social and political stability, while providing fertile ground for those who want to blame the Western governments for these conditions.

Clearly, many who responded to bin Laden's call for holy war against the United States were among those stranded and alienated by the Western-led pattern of globalization. Not only did the poverty and hunger breed resentment of those who appear to enjoy so much of the world's wealth, but the presence of the West, particularly the United States, in the Middle Eastern region provided a focus for the anger. When the U.S. presence could be described as desecrating the holy sites of Islam, then the fires of religious zeal could be added to the desperation of poverty and hunger, creating a lethal combination.

CASE STUDY 4.2

Osama bin Laden

Mastermind of the attacks on the World Trade Center and the Pentagon, as well as the alleged architect of the bombings of the U.S. embassies in Kenya and Tanzania and the attack on the USS *Cole* in Yemen, Osama bin Laden is perhaps the world's best-known terrorist. A brief review of his life offers interesting insights into the profile of this modern crusader terrorist.

Osama, which means "young lion" in Arabic, was born on March 10, 1957, in Riyadh, Saudi Arabia. His family moved to Medina when he was six months old, later dividing their time between Jeddah and the holy cities of Mecca and Medina.

At seventeen, bin Laden married a Syrian relative (the first of his four wives) and soon began his studies at King Abdul-Aziz University in Jeddah, receiving his degrees in economics and public administration in 1981. At the university, bin Laden became acquainted with both the Muslim Brotherhood and the leading teachers in Islamic studies, Abdullah Azzam and Muhammad Qutb. Both of these men would influence bin Laden's life significantly. Azzam would eventually create the first contemporary international jihadist network, and Qutb was the brother of Sayyid Qutb, author of *Signposts*, the key text of the jihadist movement.

Bin Laden absorbed Sayyid's writings with intensity; indeed, they shaped the way he saw the world and his role in it. Sayyid Qutb suggested that the way to establish the Islamic order desired by true Muslims is through an offensive jihad against the enemies of Islam, whether they be non-Islamic societies or Muslim societies that are not following the precepts of the Koran. As one scholar notes, "This is the ideological underpinning of bin Laden's followers, who target not only the West but also such rich Muslim regimes as Saudi Arabia, which they regard as apostates."[33]

In the middle of his studies of these writings, the Muslim world was undergoing a period of substantial change. In 1979, the shah of Iran was overthrown and Iran became a Muslim state under the leadership of Ayatollah Khomeini. Egypt and Israel signed a peace agreement in March of that year; in November, hundreds of armed Islamic militants seized the Grand Mosque in Mecca; and the Soviets invaded Afghanistan in late December.

Muslims from around the world were drawn to fight the Soviets in Afghanistan during the 1980s. Rob Schultheis, one of the few journalists who covered this largely ignored war, called it "the holiest of wars," as the Afghans rose up under the banner of Islam to drive the infidels out and to stop the carnage, which ultimately cost more than a million Afghan lives and displaced at least another five million.[34]

Bin Laden, then 22, headed to Pakistan to meet with the Afghan leaders who were calling for support from the Muslim world. He then returned home to Saudi Arabia to lobby his family and friends for support of the mujahideen. During the next few years, he made several trips to Afghanistan, taking hundreds of tons of construction machinery from his family construction business, which he made available to the mujahideen to build roads, dig tunnels into the mountains for shelter, and build simple hospitals for the wounded.

Having lost his deeply religious father at a very early age, bin Laden was influenced throughout his life by older religious men, often radicals, but always men of strong faith. He told a Pakistani journalist that his father "was very keen that one of his sons should fight against the enemies of Islam," and he clearly saw himself as fulfilling his father's wishes.[35]

Bin Laden's contribution to the Afghan war was primarily in terms of fund-raising and the intensity with which he advocated support for the mujahideen. Like most Afghans who fought in the war, the significance of their interaction lay in the lessons they learned from it, the network that emerged from contact with militants from dozens of countries, and the indoctrination in the most extreme ideas of jihad. All received at least some military training and a little battlefield experience, and went home to continue this jihad on another front.

The war in Afghanistan profoundly affected bin Laden in what he viewed as a spiritual rather than a political or military context. In an interview with CNN, he stated:

I have benefited so greatly from the jihad in Afghanistan that it would be impossible for me to gain such a benefit from any other chance. . . . What we benefited from most was [that] the glory and myth of the superpower was destroyed not only in my mind, but also in [the minds] of all Muslims.[36]

Bin Laden's subsequent willingness to call for a jihad against the remaining superpower, the United States, clearly grew from his experiences in the Afghan war. This, from his perspective, was his destiny. The events of September 11, 2001, although not necessarily planned by him, were certainly a fulfillment of his desire for such an attack on what he viewed as enemies of Islam. ■

Source: http://www.biography.com/people/osama-bin-laden-37172

CONCLUSIONS

The trends discussed in this chapter present an alarming portrait of modern terrorists. Some are younger, much younger than in previous centuries. As any parent (or older sibling) knows, younger children are harder to reach by logical argument. Their values are less clearly formed or understood. They are, as a whole, less rational and more emotional than their elders. They are also less likely to question the orders of their leaders, more likely to follow blindly where their trust is given.

However, the exception to this pattern appears to be found in Islamist groups, where the followers, while still younger, are on average in their mid-twenties. This creates the potential for forming autonomous cells of groups carrying out terrorist acts, rather than having such cells clearly under the leadership of a central command.

Younger or older, the followers in most groups are less educated than their leaders, are less likely to be following the dictates of a strong social conscience or clearly formed political philosophy, and are thus more likely to be simply following orders. It is very difficult to reason with someone who is "just following orders." Some of the world's worst atrocities have been committed by those who were just following orders—who did not even have the excuse of being children.

The majority of individuals committing terrorist acts today are less likely to have a comfortable home to cushion their failure. As the largest percentage in most groups are followers rather than leaders, their families are increasingly likely to be extremely poor. For these new recruits, membership—and success—in a terrorist group is the only way out of abject poverty for themselves, or for their families. For them, there can be no turning back.

They are used to violence; for them it is a daily occurrence. They neither understand nor recognize the need for limits on that violence. They have seen homes destroyed and families killed in endless wars of attrition. The idea that civilization wishes to impose limits on the types or victims of violence is beyond their understanding because they have seen almost every type of violence used against almost every conceivable victim.

Too often, their faith and the teachings of their religious leaders not only justify their actions but call upon them to do more. The agents of socialization—family, community, religion—are now offering increasing support for young people to carry out extreme acts of violence against enemies of their faith community. Western concern about the role of **madrassas**, *the Arabic word for any type of school, secular or religious*, in Saudi Arabia reflects awareness of the pivotal role of these socialization agents.

These are the new terrorists, and they are a formidable force. Whether it is possible for modern civilization to successfully counter this radicalization of the very young toward the violence of terrorism is questionable. What is beyond question is that unless we *can* reverse these trends, civilization will have to cope with an increasing spiral of terror-violence.

DISCUSSION

The modern terrorist *is* different. Profiling to "detect" terrorists is a challenge, and the indicators suggested by O'Ballance are not particularly useful in all parts of our world. Too often, "profiling" has entailed only physical or cultural identification, rather than the generic socio-political-demographic attributes suggested by O'Ballance.

Using the U.S. Counterterrorism Center's website and a website giving background information about the perpetrators of the 9/11 attacks, compare the "profiles" of three or four terrorists on these lists.

http://www.nctc.gov/site/profiles/index.html
http://www.biography.com/profiles-of-9-11/terrorists.jsp

1. What attributes on these profiles would be generally useful in profiling modern terrorism? (Look for general similarities.)
2. Is there additional information about these suspected terrorists that would be useful to include, making it possible to create a generally applicable profile?
3. How is such profiling counterproductive, in terms of domestic terrorism?

ANALYSIS CHALLENGE

Two attacks in public schools in the United States generated serious concerns about safety, training, and planning for school officials, parents, and community workers. Read about one or both of these events, and look for the elements discussed in this chapter (alienation, desocialization, etc.), which you think may help explain these events. How can we be more proactive in identifying individuals, as well as groups, who are becoming alienated?

Columbine High School: http://www.acolumbinesitea.com/columbine.html
Virginia Tech: http://www.techtragedy.com

KEY TERMS

crazies 55
criminals 55
crusaders 55
image of the enemy 58
image of themselves 59
nature of the conflict 59
image of the victims 59
theme of millenarianism 60
characteristics of "successful" terrorist 61

fedayeen 61
HAMAS 63
Provisional Irish Republican Army 63
soldiers of the revolution 63
al-Qaeda 63
Osama bin Laden 67
radicalization 67
revenge 69

renown 69
motivation 69
group dynamics 70
religious fanaticism 71
Sicariis 72
demographic trends 73
Black Widows 76
socialization toward violence 77
madrassas 80

SUGGESTED READINGS AND RESOURCES

Arena, Michael P., and Bruce A. Arrigo. *The Terrorist Identity: Explaining the Terrorist Threat.* New York and London: New York University Press, 2006.

Bergen, Peter L. *Holy War, Inc.: Inside the Secret World of Osama bin Laden.* New York: The Free Press, 2001.

Clarke, Thurston. *By Blood and Fire: The Attack on the King David Hotel.* New York: Putnam, 1981.

Hacker, Frederick J. *Crusaders, Criminals, Crazies: Terror and Terrorism in Our Time.* New York: Norton, 1976.

Hoffman, Bruce. "Defining Terrorism." In *Inside Terrorism.* New York: Columbia University Press, 1998.

Juergensmeyer, Mark. *Terror in the Mind of God: The Global Rise of Religious Violence.* Berkeley: University of California Press, 2000.

Laqueur, Walter, ed. *Voices of Terror: Manifestos, Writings, and Manuals of al-Qaeda, HAMAS, and Other Terrorists from Around the World and Throughout the Ages.* New York: Reed Press, 2004.

O'Ballance, Edgar O. *The Language of Violence: The Blood Politics of Terrorism.* San Rafael, CA: Presidio Press, 1979.

Pillar, Paul R., ed. "Dimensions of Terrorism and Counterterrorism." In *Terrorism and U.S. Foreign Policy.* Washington, DC: Brookings Institute Press, 2001.

Richardson, Louise. *What Terrorists Want: Understanding the Enemy, Containing the Threat.* New York: Random House, 2006.

NOTES

1. Frederick J. Hacker, *Crusaders, Criminals, Crazies: Terror and Terrorism in Our Time* (New York: Norton, 1976), 8–9.
2. Brian M. Jenkins, *The Terrorist Mindset and Terrorist Decisionmaking: Two Areas of Ignorance* (Santa Monica, CA: Rand, 1979), P-6340.
3. Gerald W. Hopple and Miriam Steiner, *The Causal Beliefs of Terrorists: Empirical Results* (McLean, VA: Defense Systems, 1984).
4. Franco Ferracuti and Francesco Bruno, "Italy: A Systems Perspective," in *Aggression in Global Perspective,* ed. A. Goldstein and M. H. Segall (New York: Pergamon, 1983), 274.
5. Osama bin Laden, "World Islamic Front Statement: Jihad against Jews and Crusaders," *Washington Post,* February 23, 1998.
6. Martha Crenshaw, "Ideological and Psychological Factors in International Terrorism," paper prepared for the Defense Intelligence College Symposium on International Terrorism, Washington, DC: December 2–3, 1985.
7. Quoted by Martha Crenshaw, "Ideological and Psychological Factors in International Terrorism," 8.
8. Rex Taylor, *Michael Collins* (London: Hutchinson, 1958), 17.
9. Osama bin Laden. "Ladanese Epistle: Declaration of War (Part III): A Martyr Will Not Feel the Pain of Death," *Washington Post,* September 21, 2001.
10. Louise Richardson, *What Terrorists Want: Understanding the Enemy, Containing the Threat* (New York: Random House, 2006), 40.
11. Michael R. Arena and Bruce A. Arrigo, *The Terrorist Identity: Explaining the Terrorist Threat* (New York and London: New York University Press, 2006), 27.
12. Edgar O'Ballance, *The Language of Violence: The Blood Politics of Terrorism* (San Rafael, CA: Presidio Press, 1979), 300–301.
13. Hacker, *Crusaders, Criminals, Crazies,* 105.
14. Thurston Clarke, *By Blood and Fire: The Attack on the King David Hotel* (New York: Putnam, 1981), 45.
15. Quoted by Milton Meltzer, *The Terrorists* (New York: Harper & Row, 1983), 111.
16. Walter Laqueur, *The Age of Terrorism* (Boston: Little, Brown, 1987), 92.
17. Richardson, *What Terrorists Want,* 41.
18. Mark Juergensmeyer, *Terror in the Mind of God* (Berkeley: University of California Press, 2000), 74.
19. John Miller, "Interview with Osama bin Laden," *ABC News,* May 1998. www.pbs.org/wgbh/pages/forntline/shows/binladen/who/interview.html (accessed May 30, 2007).
20. "Radicalization in the West: The Homegrown Threat," report produced by Mitchell D. Silber and Arvin Bhatt of the Intelligence Division of the New York Police Department, 2007. www.nyc.gov/html/nypd/pdf/dcpi/NYPD_Report-Radicalization_in_the_West.pdf (accessed August 31, 2007).
21. Remarks prepared for delivery by Director Robert S. Mueller, III, Federal Bureau of Investigation, speaking to the City Club of Cleveland, Cleveland, Ohio, June 23, 2006, from the website http://www.fbi.gov/pressrel/speeches/mueller062306.htm (accessed August 31, 2007).
22. Richardson, *What Terrorists Want,* 42.
23. "Omar Sheikh's Diaries, Part II," *Indian Express,* October 11, 2006.

24. Richardson, *What Terrorists Want,* 42, from the Shining Path website, www.blythe.org/peru-pcp/docs_en/interv.htm
25. Osama bin Laden, statement, October 7, 2001.
26. Richardson, *What Terrorists Want,* 81.
27. Laqueur, *The Age of Terrorism,* 93.
28. Connon Cruise O'Brien, "Reflecting on Terrorism," *New York Review of Books* (September 16, 1976): 44–48.
29. Charles Russell and Bowman Miller, "Profile of a Terrorist," *Terrorism: An International Journal* 1, no. 1 (1977): 20.
30. Marc Sageman, *Understanding Terror Networks* (Philadelphia: University of Pennsylvania Press, 2004), 23.
31. Peter Bergen and Swati Pandey, "The Madrassa Myth," *New York Times,* June 14, 2003.
32. Gilles Keppel, *Muslim Extremism in Egypt: The Prophet and the Pharaoh* (Berkeley: University of California Press, 1995), 58.
33. Peter L. Bergen, *Holy War, Inc.: Inside the Secret World of Osama bin Laden* (New York: The Free Press, 2001), 48.
34. Rob Schultheis, *Night Letters: Inside Wartime Afghanistan* (New York: Crown, 1992), 155.
35. Bergen, *Holy War,* 52.
36. Osama bin Laden. Interview by Peter Bergen and Peter Arnett, CNN, May 1997.

Terrorism by the State

Terror is an outstanding mode of conflict in localized primitive wars; and unilateral violence has been used to subdue satellite countries, occupied countries or dissident groups within a dictatorship.

— *Thomas Schelling*

Individuals and groups are not the only perpetrators of terrorism. Political leaders have used terrorism as an instrument of both domestic and foreign policy for centuries. From the time when centralized governments were first organized, rulers resorted to the use of terror tactics to subdue their subjects and to spread confusion and chaos among their enemies.

Terrorism remains a formidable weapon in the hands of a ruthless state. It is still used primarily for two purposes: to subdue a nation's own people or to spread confusion and chaos among its enemies. **State terrorism,** as defined by *Britannica,* is terrorism "*employed by governments—or more often by factions within governments—against that government's citizens, against factions within the government, or against foreign governments or groups.*"[1] For the purposes of this text, state terror activity will be divided into two categories: internal terrorism and external terrorism.

Internal terrorism, *practiced by a state against its own people,* has produced some of the most flagrant violations of human rights that the world has ever known. **External terrorism,** *practiced by one state against citizens of another,* is less often cited as a form of state terrorism. Its perpetrators tend, as a rule, to try to conceal their roles as the instigators or supporters of the terrorist acts.

INTERNAL TERRORISM: THE BEAST THAT LURKS WITHIN

No matter how chilling the atrocities committed by individuals or groups, these crimes pale in comparison with the terror inflicted by a state on its own people. Because governments have a much greater array of power, they are capable of inflicting a much greater degree of terror on their citizenry.

A look at casualty figures gives some perspective on the magnitude of the harm states can inflict on their people, compared to the damage caused by nonstate terrorists. In the decade between 1968 and 1978, about 10,000 people were killed worldwide by terrorist groups. In just *one* of those years, 1976–1977, the military dictatorship in Argentina was responsible for almost that same number of deaths.

Throughout history, states have used terrorist acts of violence to subdue groups or individuals. States have used such violence to create a climate of fear in which citizens will do whatever the government wants.

The history of state terrorism stretches back at least to the legacy of ancient Rome. The Roman emperor Nero ruled by fear, ordering the deaths of anyone who either opposed him or, in his mind, constituted a threat to his rule, including members of his own family. He was responsible for the slaughter of many of the nobility and for the burning of Rome in A.D. 64. To him, everyone was an enemy, and with his power he made them all victims of his terrorism.[2]

What a state does to its own people was, until very recently, strictly its own business. Neither the rulers nor concerned citizens in other countries usually interfered with what a sovereign government chose to do with its citizens. Even today such interference is largely limited to diplomatic or economic pressures and to the problematic effects of an informed world opinion.

At least three levels of internal state terrorism have been identified as useful gradations in understanding the scope of terrorism practiced by the state. The first is **intimidation**, *in which the government tries to anticipate and discourage opposition and dissent*, frequently through control of the media and prolific use of police force. This form of state terrorism has existed in almost every nation-state at some point in its history, most often during times of war. North Korea, Myanmar (Burma), and Syria offered, in recent years, compelling examples of this type of internal state terrorism. **Coerced conversion,** *involving government efforts to create a complete change in a national lifestyle*, is not unusual in the aftermath of a revolution, as Iran experienced in the 1980s.

Nations in the twentieth century also practiced the third level of internal state terrorism, **genocide,** *the deliberate effort to exterminate an entire class, ethnic group, or religious group of people*, for ideological reasons, while the rest of the civilized world watched in horror, disbelief, or studied indifference.[3] Nor was this destruction of innocent persons confined to Nazi Germany or Stalin's Soviet Union. Certain tribes in African nations were all but obliterated by rival tribal leaders who grasped the reins of government. Rwanda, in the

> **▲ TABLE 5.1**
>
> **Spectrum of State Terrorism**
>
> | Intimidation | Coerced Conversion | | Genocide |
> |---|---|---|---|
> | State-tolerated | Covert state supported | Overt state supported | Genocide |
> | Ku Klux Klan | "hit squads" | "dirty war" | Holocaust |

mid-1990s, experienced at least one wave of this form of terror. In the early 1990s, Bosnia was the scene of mass slaughter of people of one ethnic group by leaders of another. Sudan, in the first decade of the twenty-first century, has been internationally accused of this crime.

State internal terrorism can be placed on a spectrum to facilitate understanding, because state internal terror takes a variety of forms with varying degrees of state participation. Using the gradations of terrorism—intimidation, coerced conversion, and genocide—it becomes clear that state terror can range from forms of intimidation in which the state simply allows terrorist acts to occur, to the commission of terrorist acts for which the state is fully responsible. Placing state-tolerated terrorism at one end of the spectrum, moving on to covert state terror, then to overt state terror, culminating in genocide organized by the state offers a useful tool in visualizing the range of internal state terrorism. (See Table 5.1.)

Let us look at some of these examples of state terrorism to better gauge a comparison between their destructiveness and the destructiveness of terrorist groups. State terrorism during the twentieth century was not confined to one nation or to one continent. Although history is sprinkled with examples of gross state terrorism, many modern nations must share the "honors" as states committing terrorism today.

Examples of Genocide

Dictatorial regimes have found it easier to commit terrorism without world censure than have individuals, because state terrorism is committed, generally, in secret. The shadowy world of state terrorism is, thus, less susceptible to the pressures of world opinion than the activities of terrorist groups, who actively seek this spotlight of global attention.

A quick review of several genocidal events in recent years serves to illustrate this point. Like the Holocaust perpetrated by Nazi Germany during World War II, governments have killed millions of their own people, often without generating even overt world condemnation, much less any form of global intervention to prevent these acts.

During its rule of less than four years, the systematic state terrorism under the Khmer Rouge was responsible for over 1 million deaths in **Cambodia**, a land of only 7 million people. In the early 1990s, conflict between Hutu and Tutsi in **Rwanda** led, as noted earlier, into an explosion of genocide, killing hundreds of thousands and displacing millions. Attacks with guns, grenades, and machetes continued to cost the lives of aid workers, UN personnel, and ministers even after the explosion of violence gradually ended in the mid-1990s. Hundreds of thousands of people displaced by the violence fled to neighboring Zaire, where refugee camps, filled to overflowing, became the focus of a revolution that eventually led to the overthrow of Mobutu Sese Seko. The ethnic conflict sparked in Rwanda, by overflowing into Zaire, continued to spark violent conflict throughout central Africa for years. During the first five years of the twenty-first century, an armed force that included former soldiers and supporters of the previous government that orchestrated the genocide in 1994, the Democratic Forces for the Liberation of Rwanda (known as the Army for the Liberation of Rwanda (ALIR) until 2001), continued to operate in Rwanda and the Democratic Republic of the Congo. An ALIR unit was responsible for the kidnapping and murder of nine people in Bwindi Park in 1999. Under the auspices of the International Criminal Tribunal for Rwanda (ICTR), established by UN Security Council in 1994 to prosecute crimes occurring in the 1994 genocide, 28 members of this force have been convicted. In accordance with Security Council Resolution 1503, all first-instance cases were to have completed trial by the end of 2008, and all work by the tribunal completed by 2010. However, these goals were not realistic, and have changed. As of May 12, 2011, the tribunal has completed the work at the trial level with respect to 62 of the 92 accused. Appellate proceedings by the ICTR have been concluded for 35 persons, but 10 fugitives who were indicted by the tribunal remain at large.

As the state of Yugoslavia erupted into civil war, Muslims in **Bosnia and Herzegovina** *experienced, during the tumultuous disintegration of the former state of Yugoslavia, acts of genocide carried out by the Serbs with the aid and direction of Serbian leadership* in Yugoslavia's capital, Sarajevo. Mass murders at Srebrenica and several other towns were attributed to Serb leaders who were indicted, many in *absentia*, at the special court established in The Hague to respond to these massacres.

The term *genocide* is currently in dispute in reference to the treatment of the Armenians by the Turks in the violence of that region in the early twentieth century. What the Turkish government today calls "civil war" casualties is decried by other governments as genocide, which cost the lives of more than a million Armenians.

Coerced Conversion and Genocide in Stalin's USSR

Not all of the examples of state terrorism fit into the extreme category of genocide. Some states employed a mixture of coerced conversion as leadership sought to radically alter a country's culture, with genocide aimed at removing or reducing the number of those opposing these changes.

Hitler's destruction of millions of people is only *almost* unparalleled: The Soviet Union under Stalin was responsible for millions of deaths as well. Only estimates have been given for the number of people who fell victim to

Stalin's totalitarian society. By the time of Stalin's death in 1953, between 40 and 50 million people were sent to Soviet jails or slave labor camps, where between 15 and 25 million died—by execution, hunger, and disease.

In some ways it is difficult for the world to grasp the magnitude of the terror inflicted by such regimes because the numbers are so large and the masses of individuals relatively faceless. We are able to identify with Alexander Solzhenitsyn in his description of the terrors of the psychiatric-ward prison in his book *The Gulag Archipelago,* but we find it difficult to identify with the 25 million who died, unheralded, in the labor camps.

Countries in many regions of the world have experienced, and continue to cope with, less openly destructive forms of state terrorism. The continent of Africa, for example, has had its share of state terrorism. Colonial powers used terrorism, often in the form of summary imprisonment and execution, to suppress national liberation movements. But this was not the only form of terrorism in Africa. Uganda, under Idi Amin, was clearly a terrorist state. Between 1971 and 1979, over 100,000 Ugandans lost their lives.

CASE STUDY 5.1

Genocide in Darfur

In the twenty-first century, the nation of Sudan is visibly struggling with accusations of state-tolerated terrorism, carried out in the region of **Darfur,** *a portion of southern Sudan populated by Black African communities from which more than a million people have fled, victims to what the UN officials investigating have described as "ethnic cleansing," carried out by a group of Arab militiamen called Janjaweed.* Thousands in this region have been killed, and human rights groups assert that there has been a systematic campaign of rape, intended to create a mood of fear, to humiliate and to punish the non-Arab population.

The Janjaweed have killed, raped, maimed, looted, and burned down tens of thousands of village houses, displacing hundreds of thousands of people. The Janjaweed has ruthlessly attacked Black Africans from the Fur, Massaleet, and Zagawa ethnic groups, driving most away, and murdering those daring to remain. The number of the Janjaweed is reported to be very small, perhaps a few thousand, but they are apparently well armed with automatic weapons and ride well-fed horses and camels. The Government of Sudan has been unable—or unwilling—to stop the attacks.

The ongoing violence in Darfur and the unwillingness of the Sudanese government to accept responsibility for the violence or to effectively restrain and punish the Janjaweed provoked the United States to condemn this state in the Security Council of the United Nations for acts of genocide. The United Nations has sponsored several efforts to determine the extent of the tragedy, which was made "visible" to the world through the Internet by a link provided by the Web search engine Google. The International Criminal Court (ICC) issued an arrest warrant for Sudanese President Omar Hassan al-Bashir for a five-year campaign of violence in Darfur. He was charged with seven counts of crimes against humanity and war crimes. The warrant did not mention genocide, but the court reserved the right to include that charge later.

Thousands of Sudanese from this region have fled to refugee camps across the borders in neighboring countries, and the death toll is at least in the thousands, perhaps hundreds of thousands. For most of these refugees, survival is a daily struggle. ■

Source: http://www.unitedhumanrights.org/genocide/genocide-in-sudan.htm

South America continues to have regimes that practice terror on their people. At least five nations on this continent—Argentina, Bolivia, Chile, Paraguay, and Uruguay—have suffered under cruel and repressive regimes. In Uruguay, the terrorism instigated by the leftist Tupac Amaru was repaid hundredfold by the repressive military regime that came to power in the wake of the collapse of what was, at the time, South America's only democracy.

State terrorism has also been rife in Asia. States such as North Korea and Myanmar suffer under oppressive regimes, which, while not committing genocide, have carried out overt internal terrorism.

CASE STUDY 5.2

Myanmar's Overt Internal Terrorism

Myanmar offers a chilling example of the potential for state terrorism in all three gradations to be carried out, unchecked, for almost fifty years. It clearly meets the criteria for internal terrorism by a state and indicates the desire of a state to "clean up" its own problems and to punish, if necessary within, rather than submit to international adjudication.

This country, also known as Burma, achieved independence as a modern state in 1948, emerging from British colonial rule engaged in one of the longest running civil wars. A military junta seized power in 1962, led by General Ne Win, who ruled for almost twenty-six years. From this point until 1974, Ne Win led a military council, which nationalized or brought under government control almost all aspects of society (businesses, the media, and manufacturing). Under his rule, Burma became a modern **stratocracy,** *a term used by the ancient Greeks to describe a form of military government in which the state and the military are traditionally the same thing and government positions are always occupied by military leaders.* Under this regime, Burma became one of the world's most impoverished states.

Almost from its inception, the military regime faced protests, initially led by students. On July 7, 1962, demonstrations at Rangoon University led to a government crackdown that killed 15 students. Similar protests from 1974 to 1977 were violently suppressed with overwhelming force. Ne Win's regime also relentlessly persecuted resident aliens (immigrant groups not recognized as citizens

(continued)

of Burma), leading to the exodus or expulsion of more than 300,000. Shortly after the new constitution of the Socialist Republic of the Union of Burma was adopted in 1974, hundreds of thousands more fled from Burma, primarily Rohingya Muslims, into neighboring Bangladesh.

In 1988, widespread demonstrations provoked by unrest over economic problems and political oppression, erupted into what was called the 8888 Uprising. In response, government security forces killed thousands of the demonstrators, culminating in a coup d'etat led by General Saw Maung, who formed the State Law and Order Restoration Council (SLORC), which then declared martial law. This council renamed the state the Union of Myanmar the following year.

Although in May 1990 free elections were held for the first time in almost thirty years, the election results were nullified by the SLORC, since the National League for Democracy won 382 of the 489 seats in the legislature. Aung San Suu Kyi, leader of this party, was placed under periods of house arrest until November 2010. Under the continued control of the military, Myanmar's government continued its oppressive policies, driving large ethnic communities to flee the country in large numbers, albeit engaging sporadically in cease-fire agreements with various minorities engaged in insurrection.

In 2006, the International Labour Organization (ILO) announced that it would seek through the ICC to prosecute members of the ruling military junta in Myanmar for "crimes against humanity." The specific crime involved the forced labor of its citizens by the military. According to the ILO, approximately 800,000 people have been forced by the government into labor by the military, in a continuing form of criminal oppression. While the ability of the ICC to prosecute in this case would be curtailed by the fact that the military government was not a party to the ICC statutes, the simple fact that an international organization recognized and documented the persecution of the Myanmar government makes a strong case for the charge of internal state terror still leveled today against that regime. ∎

Source: http://www.amnesty.org/en/library/info/ASA16/011/2008

THE CONTINUING REALITY OF STATE TERROR

In 1972, a young woman named Ayse Semra Eker was abducted off the street by Turkish military police. For the next ten days she was tortured. She was tied spread-eagle to pegs on the floor and beaten repeatedly, on her naked thighs, on her palms, and on the soles of her feet. She was beaten so hard and so often that her feet turned black, and she was unable to walk. Electric wires were attached to her fingertips and toes, and she was shocked again and again. Then the wires were moved to her ear lobes, and the current was turned up until her teeth broke and her mouth spewed blood. Electric probes were inserted in her anus and vagina, and she passed out from the pain. She awakened to find her fingernails had been burned with hot cigarettes.[4]

Dozens of nations today use terrorism as (unofficial) government policy to secure and ensure control over their citizens. The use of torture, defined by the UN Convention Against Torture as being *any act by which severe pain or suffering, whether physical or mental, is intentionally inflicted on a person for such purposes as obtaining from him . . . information or a confession, punishing him for an act he . . . has committed or is suspected of having committed, or intimidating or coercing him,*[5] continues to be a tool used covertly by many governments today. Amnesty International reports that foreign "experts" in torture have been sent from country to country. Schools of torture teach methods to government officials, particularly electroshock techniques, because that is the easiest and most commonly used form of scientific torture.

Modern torture equipment is exported regularly. Some of the shock machines used by governments to torture their citizens are made in the United States.[6]

The United Nations crafted a Convention Against Torture and Other Cruel, Inhuman or Degrading Treatment or Punishment, which was adopted in 1984 for signature and ratification, and came into force three years later. More than two decades later, a substantial majority of states, approximately 144, have ratified the convention. Yet a review of the reports of torture collected by the UN's Special Rapporteur indicates that torture continues to be a weapon that states use, covertly, today.[7]

Torture falls within the form of state terrorism called "covert state terror," because few states openly admit to practicing this lethal abuse of citizens. In using the power of the state to stifle dissent and compel the people through fear into compliance, the ability of a state to intimidate or to force a change in its people is almost unchecked. The use of murder, slavery, and terror to subjugate and intimidate people taints the history of almost every modern nation.

Even the United States has experienced such abuses of power by persons in authority. The events in Ludlow, Colorado, offer a poignant vignette of state terrorism. On Easter night in 1914, members of the Colorado National Guard, aided by the company police of Colorado Fuel and Iron Company (owned by John D. Rockefeller, Sr.), poured oil on the tent city of miners and set it ablaze. The miners, who had been on strike and evicted from their homes in the company town, had dug a cave under the largest tent and placed their children there for safety. Even so, eleven children and one pregnant mother burned to death, while five men and one boy were shot to death as they tried to run to safety.

Similar blots on U.S. history also exist in the treatment of Blacks. Slavery was enforced by government law and police power for decades. Even through the Thirteenth Amendment to the Constitution, unofficial persecution of Blacks continued unchecked. The Ku Klux Klan and similar groups murdered, lynched, beat, and raped in a concerted effort to terrorize the freedmen after the Civil War and Reconstruction. Although such groups were not arms of the state, they were allowed until the 1960s to carry out their terror campaigns relatively unhampered by an unsympathetic or uncaring government.

The recently initiated "war on terror" and the U.S.-led war in Iraq have provided vivid and disturbing evidence that the United States may still engage in torture, justifying its actions on the irregularity of its enemy in the war on terror, and the critical need for intelligence that this war generates. Since many acts of torture are committed to gain information considered vital, the war on terror, with its irregular patterns of conflict and lack of clearly defined participants, offers many opportunities for states to justify the use of such tactics, as Case Study 5.3 suggests.

◤ **CASE STUDY 5.3**

U.S. Prisoners in the "War on Terror"

The United States, in the wake of the terrorist attacks of September 11, 2001, led the United Nations to declare a "war on terrorism." In the effort to find and punish those responsible for the attacks, the United States not only led a multinational force to attack Afghanistan, where the individuals who had carried out the attack had received training under the leadership of Osama bin Laden, but also in 2003, led an invasion of Iraq, which the U.S. executive leadership blamed for assisting in the attacks on the United States.

In terms of state terrorism, these wars generated serious accusations against the United States for its treatment of prisoners, both in a now-infamous prison named Abu Ghraib in Iraq and in the U.S. military base in Guantánamo Bay, Cuba. In the immediate aftermath of September 11, the United States arrested or captured many prisoners, both at home and abroad, believed to be involved in terrorism against the United States. Hundreds of these prisoners were sent to Guantánamo to be held, as the Geneva Conventions on the Treatment of Prisoners during Time of War permits, until the end of hostilities. Similarly, when the U.S.-led incursion in Iraq began in 2003, many individuals were captured and imprisoned in facilities like that of Abu Ghraib.

The legal problems and confusion that resulted in the capture and treatment of these prisoners will be discussed more fully in Chapter 10 on the use of law as a tool to prevent or restrain terrorism. But the charges that the U.S. military engaged in acts of torture against those prisoners deserve serious consideration.

On August 1, 2002, the U.S. Department of Justice issued what became known as the "torture memo." This memo carefully and narrowly defined what constituted torture, stating that physical pain must be "equivalent in intensity to the pain accompanying serious physical injury, such as organ failure, impairment of bodily function, or even death."[8] The memo went on to state that, to be considered torture, the infliction of such pain must have been the "specific intent" of the one inflicting the pain. Furthermore, the memo asserted that the U.S. ratification of the 1994 torture statute could be considered unconstitutional, as it would interfere with the president's power as commander in chief.

While this memo was rescinded by the Justice Department in December 2004, it sheds some light on the actions of military and civilian personnel at Abu Ghraib and at Guantánamo, some of whom were brought to trial over allegations of torture and prisoner abuse. Abu Ghraib was, until the summer of 2006, used by both the U.S.-led coalition occupying Iraq and the Iraqi government. When the story broke in the spring of 2004, the American public, and that of its allies, were shocked.

The stories painted a grim picture of the treatment of prisoners at this U.S.-held facility. The acts depicted in the article in the *New Yorker* magazine by Seymour M. Hersh, and the *60 Minutes II* news report, which were published and aired in April 2004, were committed by personnel in the U.S. 372nd Military Police Company and the Central Intelligence Agency (CIA). One of the most infamous pictures is that of a hooded prisoner, dressed in a costume similar to that of a member of the Ku Klux Klan, standing on a box with electrical wires connected to various parts of his body. Another prisoner interviewed told of being punched, stomped on, stripped, and forced to simulate homosexual acts—all under the direction of U.S. soldiers. As this prisoner noted, "Saddam [Hussein] didn't do this to us."[9] Another prisoner testified at the court martial of one of the military personnel accused of this abuse that he (the military guard) smashed a stick against his injured legs, forced inmates to eat from a toilet, and threatened them with snarling police dogs. The picture of a female guard, an army private first class, holding a naked male prisoner on a chain as he lay on the floor shocked the public and stimulated a cry for an investigation.

Ultimately, the military and political leaders conducted a total of 12 inquiries into prisoner abuse at U.S.-held Iraqi facilities, as well as at Guantánamo. Several of those responsible were convicted, primarily those of the lowest rank. The use of highly coercive interrogation techniques having been displayed in vivid detail in 2004 forced a reassessment of U.S. policy for the treatment of the prisoners in the "war on terror." While the U.S. government held that the war in Iraq was a conventional conflict in most respects in which the Geneva Conventions would apply, it continued to insist that the war on terror was not a conventional war. Without a clearly delineated "enemy" and thus without a signatory on the opposing side to be held to those rules of warfare, the United States held that the prisoners obtained in this "war" would not necessarily be treated according to all of the provisions of the Geneva Conventions.

Perhaps one of the most unfortunate effects of this policy regarding torture is reflected in the statement of one of the prisoners from Abu Ghraib, who noted that "These American guards shaped our view of what America [is] like."[10]

States use many weapons to conduct terrorism, including arrest (usually in the dead of night to maximize the psychological impact), summary deportation of dissidents or subversives, incarceration without trial for indefinite lengths of time, and of course, torture. It is torture that is the ultimate weapon of state terrorism.

Amnesty International's Report on Terrorism provides horrifying details of state torture and terror, including the following description of torture in Chile:

> Many people were tortured to death by means of endless whipping as well as beating with fists, feet and rifle butts. Prisoners were beaten on all parts of the body, including the head and sexual organs. . . . There were many cases of burning (with acid or cigarettes), of electricity, of psychological threats including simulated executions and threats the families of the prisoners would be tortured. At times the brutalities reached animalistic levels.[11]

The report goes on to tell of rape, sexual depravities, abortions forced by rifle butts, force-feeding of excrement, immersion in ice-cold water or tanks of petrol,

(*continued*)

and countless other atrocities too horrible to recount. They sicken the reader—but they are true, and they are happening now.

If, as Hannah Arendt suggests, "lawlessness is the essence of tyranny, then terror is the essence of totalitarian domination." In her essay "On Violence," this same expert notes that "terror is not the same as violence; it is, rather, the form of government that comes into being when violence, having destroyed all power, does not abdicate but, on the contrary, remains in full control." State terrorism, thus described, is the quintessential form of terrorism.[12] ■

Source: http://projects.washingtonpost.com/guantanamo/timeline/

It is useful to remember that the word *terror* derives from the actions of a government—the Jacobin government of revolutionary France. In fact, terrorist regimes have been far more deadly than group or individual actors in this century, even after the end of World War II.[13] The word *totalitarian* has become part of the political lexicon of the twenty-first century as a result of state terrorism in Nazi Germany and Stalinist Russia. Both systems relied upon organized, systematized discriminate terror to create bondage of the mind as well as of the body.[14]

State terrorism is frequently a nasty combination of personality and ideology. "Nazism and Stalinism were personifications of the evil genius of their leaders, but they could not have succeeded without a disoriented, terrorized citizenry," according to one expert.[15]

Totalitarianism and state terrorism aim not only at the transmutation of society but also at the fundamental change in human nature. The basic goal of terrorist states is mass disorientation and inescapable anxiety. Modern governments whose actions have earned for themselves the soubriquet "terrorist," have employed terror-violence as an integral part of the governing process.[16]

Governments continue to be as likely to commit terrorist acts as individuals and groups. Moreover, it is probably true that "as violence breeds violence, so terrorism begets counter-terrorism, in an ever-increasing spiral."[17] So state domestic terrorism not only transgresses international law, but it often creates the political, economic, and social milieu that precipitates acts of individual and group terrorism. It is thus a causal factor in the perpetration of further terrorism.

EXTERNAL TERRORISM: WAGING WAR BY PROXY

Coercive measures within the state are only one form of state terrorism. Terrorism has been used by national leaders as an instrument of foreign policy, particularly in the waging of irregular warfare. This has usually taken the form of covert terrorism, because the acts are generally expected to be committed without the state being openly involved.

This state form of terrorist behavior usually falls into one of two categories: state-directed terrorism and state-supported terrorism. In **state-directed terrorism,** *there is more involvement by the state, sometimes as direct as decision making and control of the group's activities.* In **state-supported terrorism,** *the state usually aids or abets existing terrorist groups that have varying degrees of independence.*[18] In both types of state terror, the state uses groups engaged in terrorist acts to advance state goals in other countries. Unlike the internal coercive diplomacy, clandestine operations are, by their very nature, conducted in secrecy. Consequently, they are often difficult to document. Thus, there are often little verifiable data that can be used to study this phenomenon. This makes the use of terrorism an attractive, but potentially dangerous, weapon for states seeking to carry out hostile acts without initiating a war.

Because it is almost impossible to distinguish whether a state is engaging in state-directed or state-supported terrorism in the absence of clear lines of connection, the use of external terrorism by states continues to be an attractive foreign policy option. State-directed and state-supported terrorism are primarily used to produce fear and chaos within potentially unfriendly or hostile states. They are used, for example, to weaken the resistance or diminish the intransigence of states. Such activities are also designed to demonstrate the weaknesses and vulnerabilities of opponents in an effort to make such adversaries more willing to bargain.

These activities have been described as attempts to "destabilize" unfriendly regimes. CIA efforts in Chile in the early 1970s took this form. This organization was not only involved in clandestine efforts—including the assassination of René Schneider, the commander in chief of the Chilean Army who refused to approve plans to remove President Salvador Allende from office—but it was also involved in numerous other efforts to remove Allende. Records indicate that at least $7 million were authorized by the United States for CIA use in destabilizing Chilean society, including the financing of opposition groups and right-wing terrorist paramilitary groups.

Similar clandestine efforts in Nicaragua provoked a great deal of undesirable attention. Efforts to destabilize the Sandinista regime supposedly came to an official halt in 1982, when the U.S. House of Representatives voted to halt covert activities abroad by the CIA for the purpose of overthrowing the government of Nicaragua.[19] But, as the *Iran-Contra* affair indicated, efforts to conduct clandestine terrorist operations did not cease with the passage of that law. Instead, such activities became one step *more* covert.

Claire Sterling conducted serious research into the networks of support and sponsorship that terrorist organizations enjoy. According to Sterling, nations such as the former Soviet Union were heavily involved in sponsoring terrorism:

> Direct control of the terrorist groups was never the Soviet intention. All were indigenous to their countries. All began as offshoots of relatively non-violent movements that expressed particular political, economic, religious or ethnic grievances.[20]

States have chosen to support terrorism abroad more often, indirectly. Let us consider at least one compelling reason for indirectly supporting terrorism: Such support offers a low-risk avenue for redressing an international grievance. Some Arab states chose to sponsor Palestinian groups engaged in terrorist acts as a less risky method of redressing the Palestinian problem—less risky than provoking another open and costly war with Israel.

Certainly Iran, under the direction of religious leaders, engaged in this practice throughout the Middle East. Some nations within the former Communist bloc also offered support to terrorist groups in the form of equipment and training camps, purportedly as a way of exporting the Communist revolution or perhaps as a means for weakening an adversary state (a reason often cited to explain support for terrorist activities against Israel). Libya used terrorism to help the state track down and eradicate exiled dissidents (or intimidate them into silence), offering sanctuary and assistance to the Abu Nidal Organization and a variety of other Palestinian resistance groups.

Again we can turn to Sterling's assessment of the former Soviet Union's reasons for becoming involved in state-supported terrorism. She suggests that "[t]he heart of the Russian strategy was to provide the network with the goods and services necessary to undermine the industrialized democracies of the West."[21]

Even in the light of information unearthed by Sterling and other journalists who sought to uncover the support network by which terrorist organizations operate, a significant lack of verifiable data exist to link states thought to have logical policy reasons for supporting such groups with actual instances of substantive support. Although few would dispute the evidence of relatively low-level sponsorship (providing safe houses, travel documents, and similar assistance), there is a lack of hard evidence of "control" exercised by the states or participation by states in any hostile events.

Most researchers recognized that the Soviets had an interest in actions that would spread fear and chaos in the Western world. What is often referred to as "fishing in troubled waters"—that is, offering assistance to those already engaged in opposition to states that are one's enemies—is not an unusual policy nor is it necessarily illicit. Does such "fishing" make the state giving the assistance culpable for the offenses committed by those receiving the assistance? Efforts in the early twenty-first century to link Iran with various terrorist groups are often premised on this assumption.

Sterling suggests that "the Soviet Union had simply laid a loaded gun on the table, leaving others to get on with it."[22] By inference, the issue of whether a state directs or merely benefits from terrorist actions carried out with that "loaded gun" is less significant, while the linkage to the state and its state policy is fairly clear. Activities carried out by groups provided with those "loaded guns" are nonetheless incidents of state-supported terrorism. Governments may engage in terrorism for a variety of reasons, which become blurred even in their own minds and are often indistinguishable in the eyes of horrified observers. One cause may be the principal motivator for a particular act, but it may have numerous desirable side effects that become prime motivators in time, too. A state may decide, for example, to assist an organization carrying out terrorist acts or field an organization of its own to try to redress a particular international grievance. In the course of events, the state may discover that the terrorism has helped to weaken an adversary state against which it would not ordinarily have had the strength to wage a regular war. After a time, it becomes difficult for the state to decide what the most important reason is for its decision to engage in terrorism by proxy.

There are at least two tangible and potentially traceable venues of state support for terrorism that continues to be strong, even with the end of the cold war and the global unity against terrorism engendered for a time by the events of September 11. These are the provision of weapons to groups and individuals engaged in terrorism either without cost or at low cost and the offer of **safe haven** given by states to such individuals and groups, *permitting the groups to organize, plan, raise funds, communicate, recruit, and even train within the territory of the state.* The former venue—the provision of arms—is usually an economic as much as it is a political decision, stimulated by economic needs or opportunities important to the state offering this form of assistance. The latter—the provision of safe haven for terrorists—occurs more often in rogue or troubled states. For the purpose of this text, a **rogue state** refers to a *recalcitrant or outlaw state that not only chooses to remain outside the community of nation-states but also assaults the community's basic values.* **Troubled states,** on the other hand, are *fragile and dysfunctional states that lack either the capacity or the intent to fulfill the basic needs of a substantial element of their populations, often casting doubt on the legitimacy of the regime in power.*[23]

THE ARMS BAZAAR: SUPPLYING THE WEAPONS

Let us examine the booming sales of arms to individuals, groups, and nations engaging in terrorist acts that made no secret (until after the September 11 attacks) of their propagation of terrorism. Even among the Western allies, who on paper oppose these regimes and groups, there remained strong support channels until the close of 2001. Through these channels, with the knowledge and support of the state, many companies circumvent national law, selling arms to hostile or warring nations or groups.

France sold dozens of Exocet antiship missiles to Libya, which were subsequently used by Muammar al Qadhafi to attack the U.S. Sixth Fleet. Germans traveled to Iran to work out a contract for the sale of four diesel submarines, which would be added to the armada with which Iran threatened the shipping lanes in the Persian Gulf. Austria officially condemned Iraq's use of gas in the Iran–Iraq war and offered the use of its hospitals for the treatment of Iraqi victims of gas attacks. Yet Austria exported the chemicals used to make the poisonous gas—to Iraq! From the former West Germany, via Greek shipping offices, Iran obtained optics and range-finding equipment, as well as the G-3 assault rifle, its standard infantry weapon.

Nor is it only Iran and Iraq who benefited from industrial nations' desires to cash in on the arms market. Libya, which made little secret during the last three decades of the twentieth century concerning its support for and commitment to groups and individuals engaging in terrorism against the West, was the recipient of considerable European assistance, only part of which took the form of arms sales. Italy, too, has had a strong trade relationship with Libya, averaging approximately $5 billion per year during the 1980s, when Libya owned 15 percent of Fiat Corporation. In May 1986, the former chief of the Italian intelligence service admitted that his service had helped Qadhafi get arms and assisted him on intelligence matters. Italy also sold a wide variety of arms to Libya, including Augusta antitank helicopters, Assad-class missile corvettes, self-propelled howitzers, Otomat missiles, and acoustic mines and torpedoes. Many of these weapons have subsequently found their way into the hands of terrorists.

Athens, Greece, known as the *cradle of democracy*, has for years been the middleman through which transactions from the West are channeled to various protagonists in the Middle East and North Africa. Members of the Islamic Jihad, the Abu Nidal Organization, and Abbu Abbas operated freely through Greek borders.

Cooperation between governments in the sales of arms has resulted in some strange bedfellows. None is perhaps stranger than the relationship between Israel and Iran in the 1980s, when Israel was one of Iran's biggest suppliers of armaments. In 1984, Israel sold 20 F-4 jet engines to Iran, routing the transaction through Greece to Tehran. In January 1985, Israel offered to sell (via telexes to brokers, including those in Iran) 150 U.S. Sidewinder air-to-air missiles.

Defenders of such sales argue that the nations or groups would purchase such arms anyway, so why should Western nations not make the profit in these "inevitable" transactions? Such an argument is merely a rationalization of an economic reality that contravenes political policy.

The economic ties forged by such transactions make it difficult for nations to take firm stands against terrorism or terrorist groups sponsored by the recipient nations. The stronger the economic linkage, the weaker is a government's response to restrict terrorism. The uneasy relationship between these buyers and sellers of arms clouds the issue of each nation's policy on terrorism. The seller nations—the purveyors of arms—find themselves in the dubious position of appearing to sponsor terrorism indirectly, which is an allegation they cannot completely dismiss.

WEAPONS OF MASS DESTRUCTION ON THE ARMS BAZAAR

As the **arms bazaar** *expands today to include weapons of mass destruction (WMDs)*, the stakes for the peace and security of the international community escalates dramatically. A quick look at several suppliers of WMDs makes clear the potential dangers:

> *Russia.* Because Russia's defense, biotechnology, chemical, aerospace, and nuclear industries are eager to raise much-needed funds, there is a large potential for the export and transfer of weapons, as well as training in the use of these weapons. During the first half of 2002, Russian entities were a key source of dual-use biotechnology, chemicals, production technology, and equipment for other states seeking to develop WMD capabilities, such as Iran.

North Korea. North Korea continues exporting significant ballistic
   missile-related equipment and technical expertise. Selling WMDs is
   a critical source of hard currency for this cash-strapped system.
China. China has, since the mid-1990s, provided material support for
   Iran's chemical weapons program. Since Iran continues to arm many
   groups engaged in terrorism and is not a party to the Chemical-
   Biological Warfare agreement, the probability of Chinese chemical
   weapons supplies reaching the hands of terrorists is high.[24]

SILENT PARTNERS: OFFERING ARMS AND HAVENS

States have played both roles in the support of terrorism: arms suppliers
as well as providers of havens. A quick look at one or two such states offers
useful insights.

Syria

Syrian president Hafez al-Assad sought to become the dominant power broker
in the Middle East, and until the fall of 1986, he came close to achieving that
objective, masking his support for terrorists beneath a cloak of state secrecy.
By distancing himself from the terrorists, he managed to preserve deniability;
and when it seemed strategically expedient, he renewed his credit with the
West by intervening on behalf of Western hostages.

Assad's secure power base at home and close ties with Moscow made diplomats hesitant to openly criticize him. In the absence of evidence to the contrary, some observers even assumed that he was a "helpful partner" in Middle
East negotiations concerning Lebanon.

Evidence of his duplicity came to light after the demise of the Soviet
Union. As *U.S. News & World Report* noted, "even in the diplomatic world
of studied indirection and strategic dissembling, the evidence has become impossible to ignore, and it points straight at Syrian strong man Hafez Assad."[25]

Former Secretary of State George Schultz noted that the case of Nezar
Hindawi's unsuccessful attempt to blow up an El Al jetliner in London provided "clear evidence" of Syrian involvement in terrorism. Ariel Merari, director of Tel Aviv University Project on Terrorism, suggested that "there is
no doubt that the general policy of sponsoring terrorist activity in Western
Europe is done with Assad's approval and probably his initiative."[26]

The same report contained one expert's comments that

> For years, Libya's Muammar Qadhafi has been the international outlaw,
> condemned for his wide-ranging support of terrorism. But now it is clear that
> Qadhafi is an erratic bumbler compared with Assad, a hard-eyed strategist
> who uses terror as an essential tool of statecraft.[27]

Assad's preferred tool of persuasion was terror, according to some Middle
East experts. During the early 1980s, he began exporting his deadly product,
by increasingly indirect means. The CIA made public evidence that the Syrian

intelligence services gave logistical support to the individuals who bombed the U.S. Marine barracks in Lebanon. After the attack, the National Security Agency intercepted messages showing payments were sent through Damascus to the Iranian-sponsored group responsible for the bombing.

There were five base camps near Damascus and at least twenty other Syrian-controlled camps where instruction in the techniques of terrorism was provided. Yarmouk, in Damascus, was the camp most often used for advanced terrorist training. Skills acquired at these camps were tested in Lebanon's Bekaa Valley, which Syria controlled.

Unlike Libya's Qadhafi, Assad seemed to prefer secrecy to the spotlight of international attention in the drama of terrorist involvement. Assad relied on sporadic, preferably untraceable attacks, which allowed him to avoid retribution. Qadhafi, in the 1980s, treated terrorism like a banner to be waved before the troops; for Assad, it was instead as quick and silent as an assassin's bullet.

One expert at the Foreign Policy Research Institute summed up sponsors of terrorism during the 1970s and early 1980s in this manner:

> Of the four major sponsors of terrorism—the Palestinian Liberation Organization (PLO), Libya, Iran, and Syria—the first two get all the attention. But it's the other two we should be watching, and particularly Syria. It is quiet and deadly in its effectiveness, and until this slipup with Hindawi, it has always managed to stay in the shadows.[28]

Assad's death near the end of the 1990s did not substantively change Syria's role as a quiet supporter of terrorism. Under his son Bashir's leadership, Syria continued to provide safe haven and support for several groups that engage in terrorist attacks. Osama bin Laden's al-Qaeda, Ahmad Jibril's Popular Front for the Liberation of Palestine–General Command (PFLP–GC) and the Palestinian Islamic Jihad (PIJ), and George Habash's PFLP have maintained their headquarters in Damascus. The Syrian government allowed HAMAS (Harakat al-Muqawamah al-Islamiyyah) to open a new main office in Damascus in March 2000. In spite of abundant evidence to the contrary, Syrian officials still describe the Damascus headquarters of these terrorist groups as "media offices," although the offices also facilitate recruitment, training, co-ordinating, funding, and even directing group operations in Israel and the Palestinian-controlled territories.

With Syria's blessing, Hezbollah deployed some 10,000 rockets in southern Lebanon, most of which were supplied by Syria or transferred from Iran via Syria. These rockets became the focus of the conflict between Israel and Lebanon in July 2006. The conflict, which officially lasted thirty-four days, involved engagement between Hezbollah paramilitary forces and the Israeli military and began when Hezbollah fired rockets at Israeli border towns. Syria, pressured during the conflict to "rein in" Hezbollah, asserted that it does not control the group, although Hezbollah had bases within Syria's borders and was firing rockets supplied by Syria.[29]

Although Syria is today a signatory to 9 of the 13 international conventions and protocols relating to terrorism, and Syrian officials publicly condemn terrorism, large numbers of foreign fighters from groups engaged in terrorism continue to transit through Syria, gathering assistance and sanctuary. Syria's affiliation with al-Qaeda in Iraq (AQI) continues to be strong.

Iran

According to the U.S. State Department, Iran was clearly the most active state sponsor of terrorism through the year 2010. Following their success in the 2004 elections, conservative clerics and the more radical anti-Western fundamentalists continue to be actively involved in the planning and execution of terrorist acts and to support a variety of groups that use terrorism to support their goals. Iran has been a strong sponsor of extremist Islamic and Palestinian groups, providing safe haven, funds, weapons, and training. The Lebanese Hezbollah, one of Iran's most important "clients," was responsible for some of the most lethal acts of the 1980s and early 1990s, including the 1983 suicide truck bombing of the U.S. embassy and U.S. Marine barracks in Beirut, the hijacking of TWA Flight 847 in 1985, the 1992 car bombing of the Israeli embassy in Argentina, and rocket attacks on civilians in northern Israel.

Iran openly supported many other radical organizations that resorted to terrorism, including the PIJ, the PFLP–GC, and HAMAS. The last group was particularly active during the 1994–1996 portion of the peace process, with numerous car and suicide bombings carried out in Israel, the West Bank, and the Gaza Strip. The *intifada*, which emerged when the peace process faltered during the late 1990s, was marked by suicide bombers encouraged by HAMAS and the Islamic Jihad and supported by Iran.

Iran's support of terrorism has been somewhat open, unlike Syria's more covert assistance. This made it easier to link the state to the terrorist acts, but difficult to prevent such support, because the government appeared unconcerned with international disapproval or condemnation until the international community came together to condemn terrorism after the attack on September 11, 2001. Iran, in some respects, has been a crusader in state terrorism, willing to accept death for a cause in the confident expectation of eternal reward. Moreover, Iran's strong position as an oil-producing nation made nations unwilling to support direct action against Iran in retaliation for such support.

Tehran conducted 13 assassinations in 1997, according to the U.S. *Global Report on Terrorism*, the majority of which were carried out in northern Iraq. The targets of Iran's attacks were members of the state's main opposition groups, such as the Kurdish Democratic Party of Iran (KDPI) and the Mujahedin-e Khalq, an Iranian group that opposes the current Iranian regime and is based in Iraq.[30]

Perhaps the most compelling evidence of Iran's involvement in terrorism was reviewed in the trial in Germany of an Iranian and four Lebanese for the 1992 killing of Iranian Kurdish dissidents in Berlin's Mykonos restaurant. Finding the four guilty of murder, the court stated that the government of Iran had followed a deliberate policy of assassination of enemies of the regime living outside of Iran. The judge noted that the Mykonos murders were approved at the most senior levels of the Iranian government by an extralegal committee that included the president, the foreign minister, the supreme leader, and the minister of intelligence and security.

Iran continues to provide support (training, money, weapons, or all three) to several groups engaged in terrorism. The government has encouraged the violent rejection of the Middle East peace process. In the fall of 1997, Tehran hosted a conference of "Liberation Movements" in which there was open discussion of the jihad and of establishing greater coordination between certain groups.

Israel continues to be the biggest target of Iranian-based terrorism, with Tehran supporting, as Syria does, several Palestinian groups from Lebanon. Support for these groups, in the forms of funding and safe haven, gives Iran prestige in the Muslim world, as they undermine the peace process. The terrorist groups also offer Tehran an avenue to strike at the United States without actually initiating the strikes.

After September 11, international attention turned to discovering and eliminating al-Qaeda's support network. The fact that several senior al-Qaeda figures, including Osama bin Laden's son Saad, were in Iran intensified interest in Iran's link to terrorist groups. While Iran claimed to have Sunni extremists under careful watch, it refused to turn the extremists over to international authorities for questioning, suggesting that Iran's interests might entail the use of these individuals as foreign policy leverage, perhaps in the struggle over the issue of Iranian nuclear power development.

Essentially, the overt and covert support Iran continues to offer for terrorism gives Iran something that it considers vital: options in its foreign policy decisions. A middle-weight contender in terms of economic power (due to its oil reserves), with a military that is in many respects in a state of disrepair, Iran appears to view support for terrorist groups as giving it a role in the struggle with Israel, a voice in Iraq's future, and a method of interfering with U.S. interests in the region.[31]

Libya

Libya, while also an oil state, has been less obvious in its support for terrorism since 1985, when linkage to a terrorist act in West Germany evoked a bombing attack on Tripoli by the United States. Indeed, Libya's support for acts of terrorism continued to cause economic and political penalties during the 1990s, following the bombing of Pan Am Flight 103 in 1988 over Lockerbie, Scotland. The UN Security Council passed Resolution 731, which demanded that Libya take steps to end its state-sponsored terrorism, including extraditing two Libyan intelligence agents indicted by the United States and the United Kingdom for their role in that bombing. The resolution also required that Libya should accept responsibility for the bombing, disclose all evidence related to it, pay appropriate compensation, satisfy French demands regarding Libya's alleged role in bombing UTA Flight 772 in 1989, and cease all forms of terrorism.

In 1992, the UN Security Council adopted Resolution 748, imposing an arms and civil aviation embargo on Libya. This resolution demanded that Libyan Arab Airlines offices be closed and required that all states reduce Libya's diplomatic presence abroad. When these measures failed to elicit full compliance from Libya, the Security Council adopted Resolution 883 in 1993, imposing a limited assets freeze and oil technology embargo on Libya and strengthening existing sanctions against that nation.

In 1999, Libya surrendered the two suspects accused of the 1988 bombing of Pan Am Flight 103 to a court in The Hague, presided by international jurists. On January 31, 2001, the court found Abdel Basset al-Megrahi guilty of murder, concluding that he caused an explosive device to detonate on board the airplane, resulting in the murder of the flight's 259 passengers and crew as well as 11 residents of Lockerbie, Scotland. The judges found that he acted "in furtherance of the purposes of . . . Libyan Intelligence Services." The other defendant, Al-Amin Kalifa Fahima, was acquitted based on a lack of sufficient evidence of "proof beyond a reasonable doubt."[32]

In the wake of UN intervention in the Lockerbie case, Libya largely avoided open association with acts of terrorism and terrorist groups. Although Qadhafi offered public support for radical Palestinian groups opposed to the PLO's Gaza-Jericho accord with Israel in 1993, and openly threatened to support extremist Islamic groups in neighboring Algeria and Tunisia, the level of open support by Libya for terrorism decreased substantially.

Instead, Libya played a high-profile role in negotiating the release of a group of foreign hostages seized in the Philippines by the Abu Sayyaf Group, reportedly in exchange for a ransom payment. Libya also expelled the Abu Nidal Organization and distanced itself from Palestinian groups engaged in terrorism against Israel, although it maintained contact with groups such as the PIJ and the PFLP–GC.

In the wake of the September 11, 2001, attacks on the United States, Libya was vehement about its noninvolvement and in its condemnation of the actions. Clearly, Libya is seeking to redefine itself with regard to the soubriquet of "state supporter of terrorism." In 2004, Libya joined the international community in condemning terrorism, and sanctions were lifted against its economy as it began to rebuild relations damaged by its long-term role as state supporter of terrorism.

Instead of being engaged in state-supported external terrorism, Libya's leader, Qadhafi, was indicted by the ICC in June 2010 for crimes committed against his own people. From state support of terrorism, Libya appears to have moved into the status of a state perpetrator of internal terrorism, in part no doubt due to the ongoing internal war against Qadhafi's regime, a war supported by many Western states. In the democracy movements that swept the Middle East in 2011, Libya's opposition groups toppled the Qadhafi regime, offering the hope that this nation will not, in the immediate future, be a state sponsor of terrorism in other systems, and that internal terrorism, such as that of which Qadhafi is accused, will cease as well.

TERRORIST-SUPPORTED STATES

Globalization, corruption, poverty, and a variety of factors are generating "failed states," whose governments are too weak and often too impoverished to provide for themselves or for their citizens. Some of these failed states have become the anomaly of **terrorist-supported states,** *states that receive support from affluent terrorist groups.* The groups then use these states as training grounds, recruitment centers, and procurers of useful technologies, making the state a partner in the terrorism being planned or perpetrated.

Few, if any, states today can afford, politically or economically, to openly support terrorism. Instead, the phenomena of the twenty-first century may well be the emergence of states supported by terrorist groups. There are groups today with sufficient resources, economic and personnel, that can receive safe haven and access to land for training facilities from political systems too weak to survive as effectively without their support. A brief look at two case studies—Afghanistan under the Taliban and the emerging state of Palestine under the Palestinian Liberation Authority (PLA) and Yasser Arafat—may help to make this new development clearer.

> **CASE STUDY 5.4**
>
> ## Afghanistan under the Taliban Leadership
>
> Afghanistan under the leadership of the Taliban was a primary hub for terrorists and a home or transit point for the loosely organized network of **Afghan alumni,** *a web of informally linked individuals and groups that were trained for and fought in the* Afghan war. These alumni have been involved in several major terrorist plots and attacks against enemies, including but not limited to the United States and other Western nations. The leaders of some of the most dangerous groups engaged in terrorism emerging during the last two decades of the twentieth century have had headquarters or major offices in Afghanistan.
>
> From this network have come attacks throughout the world, from the Philippines to the Balkans, Central Asia to the Persian Gulf, Western China to Somalia, and South Asia to Western Europe. But the most visible group in recent years has been al-Qaeda, bin Laden's group, blamed for the attacks on September 11, 2001. International concern for this state sponsorship of terrorism was articulated in 2000 by UN Security Council Resolution 1333, which levied sanctions on the Taliban for harboring Osama bin Laden and failing to close down terrorist training camps established and funded by bin Laden in Afghanistan.
>
> The problem was that bin Laden's organization provided financial and material support for the Taliban, and espoused the more fundamentalist view of Islam popular with both bin Laden and the Taliban leadership. Thus, it was not a situation in which a state government offered support and protection to a group practicing terrorism; rather, it was a group that offered support and assistance to a shaky leadership that controlled only a part of a state and lacked international diplomatic recognition as a state government.

Lacking this recognition, it was clearly impossible to bring diplomatic pressure on the Taliban to evict bin Laden and the al-Qaeda network from Afghanistan. Moreover, it is unclear whether the Taliban, even if they had wished to do so, could have mustered the force necessary to capture or evict bin Laden and his followers. ■

Source: Council on Foreign Relations report at http://www.cfr.org/afghanistan/taliban-afghanistan/p10551

CASE STUDY 5.5

Palestinian Liberation Authority

In the case of Palestine, the leadership responsible for supporting terrorism is not a recognized state entity in the international community. The Palestinian Liberation Authority (PLA) has a limited role in the governing of the territories relinquished by Israel according to the 1994 Oslo accords. Yet in this limited territory, more acts of individual and group terrorist violence have occurred than in virtually any other context during the 1990s. With the encouragement and support of groups such as HAMAS, suicide bombers have killed people in shopping centers, on buses, in a wide range of public venues during the *intifada,* which in this case refers to *the violent civil disobedience of Palestinians in the occupied territories to Israeli rule*, which arose after the Oslo accords began to fall behind schedule.

Israel blamed Yasser Arafat, elected as the first president of the PLA, for failure to control the violence, accusing him of sponsoring terrorism within the territories by failing to arrest and punish those responsible for attacks. Arafat argued that he did not support the attacks, but was unable to control the violence within the extremely limited context that Israel allowed for his police to exercise power.

Again, the ability of a not-quite state to exercise effective control over groups and individuals engaged in terrorism within its territories is debatable. Given the high political and economic costs engendered by the attacks by HAMAS on the future of Palestine, it was unlikely that Arafat actually supported the attacks. But his government's ability to control such individuals and groups was problematic, and he had to depend on some of these people for support in maintaining his leadership role in ongoing negotiations for the future of the state of Palestine.

However, with the elections of January 2006 in Palestinian territories, HAMAS emerged as the leading party in the Palestinian Authority government, precipitating a crisis of international concern. Since HAMAS played a leading role in the suicide bombings that rocked the peace process and continued to support efforts in Gaza to launch missile attacks on Israel, the ability of the emerging state of Palestine to separate itself from terrorism became increasingly questionable. In the case of Palestine, it may be less a state "sponsoring" terrorism than a group of individuals using terrorism to "sponsor" the emergence of the state.

The letter sent by the Palestinian authority to the secretary-general of the United Nations in 2011 requesting admission of Palestine as a state, with

(continued)

recognition as a state by formal vote, indicated a willingness of Palestinians of both the West Bank and Gaza to press for statehood, precipitating a crisis for its ally, the United States, in Security Council, where such a vote would first be taken. Recognition, long sought, in exchange for an end to violence and a final demarcation of the boundary lines of this state—the two-state solution long discussed by all parties—offers hope for an end to the conflict in this troubled area. ■

Source: http://www.worldstatesmen.org/Palestinian_National_Authority.htm

CONCLUSIONS

State terrorism, whether it is internal or external, offers a real threat to international peace and security. Internal terrorism breeds resistance movements, which often resort to terrorist tactics. This cycle of terror-violence can result in a whirlwind that will destroy all within its reach—innocent and guilty.

External terror, as practiced by some states, has resulted in the proliferation of terror worldwide. States whose policy specifically rejects the use of terror have been guilty of giving aid, often clandestinely, to states or groups that promote terrorism. With the exception of a few states such as Iran, most states have sought to keep their dealings with terrorists a secret.

Overt state support for terrorism decreased during the last decade of the twentieth century. This became increasingly evident in the fall of 2001, as the international community became a part of the "war" declared by the United States on terrorism in the wake of the September 11 attacks. Open support for terrorism, or for groups actively engaged in terrorist activities, became too politically costly and, because of the increasingly globalized economy, too economically costly as well. As the case studies of Afghanistan and Palestine graphically illustrate, although groups carrying out terrorist acts continue to find safe haven of a more discreet sort in some countries today, most are tolerated rather than openly supported by states whose ability to govern is frequently questionable and thus whose ability to control the use of its territory by such groups is marginal.

The effects of the winds of democratic reform sweeping the Middle East and North Africa in 2011 during the so-called Arab Spring offer hope for a decrease in state terror in that region, as Egypt's president of more than three decades steps down and faces potential trial for his alleged crimes as leader of that state. But the fighting in both Libya and Syria, noted earlier for their support of groups engaged in terrorism, has evoked claims of state terror against governments of both states, as the civilian casualty toll mounts. Although both states have argued that there is a distinction between terrorist attacks and attacks taken by groups engaged in national liberation struggles, it is clear that when such struggles are occurring within their own borders, these states are willing to carry out acts of extreme violence against their own civilian population to repress them. The winds of change appear to be stirring states previously engaged in primarily externally supported terrorism to acts of internal terrorism today.

DISCUSSION

As more states emerge that cannot govern their territories effectively enough to control the access of their territory to terrorist groups, can the international community cope with this emerging challenge? This may be a critical question, as an increasing number of "failed" or "troubled" states become a haven for pirates, militia groups, and warlords willing to carry out terrorism. Consider each of the following situations, using the Web links to get information to support your answer:

1. The situation in Darfur, and for those who are refugees in neighboring countries, is becoming critical. Not only does the violence continue, but the lack of fresh water is critical, and may cost the lives of many. Yet the ICC's effort to indict and bring to trial Sudan's president has resulted in the closing of many of the UN and other international aid groups who had been working to save lives in that region, as Sudan's leadership declared these groups "unwelcome." What can be done to resolve this crisis without more loss of life and without damaging national sovereignty issues?

2. Somalia is now a "safe haven" for pirates in that region, as the continued conflict between warlords makes the ability of any governing body there minimal. Hunger and desperation as the state system continues to collapse make the turn to piracy more popular by the day, and relief aid is again not able to be delivered with any regularity in this "failing state." Again, tough decisions about intervention into sovereign territory to rescue prisoners of pirates, to destroy pirate safe havens, or to simply rescue people who are starving must be made.

ANALYSIS CHALLENGE

State terrorism in the form of genocide and piracy continues to occur today, not just in your history books. Explore one of the following websites to learn more about the examples just discussed. Are these examples of genocide and piracy, and if so, what is the responsibility of the international community?

Darfur, Sudan: http://www.ushmm.org/maps/projects/darfur/
Somalia: http://www.heritage.org/Research/HomelandSecurity/wm2397.cfm

KEY TERMS

state terrorism   84
internal terrorism   84
external terrorism
   84
intimidation   85
coerced conversion   85
genocide   85
Cambodia   86
Rwanda   86

Bosnia and
   Herzegovina   87
Darfur   88
stratocracy   89
state-directed
   terrorism   94
state-supported
   terrorism   94
safe haven   97

rogue state   97
troubled states   97
arms bazaar   98
terrorist-supported
   states   104
Afghan alumni
   104
intifada   105

SUGGESTED READINGS AND RESOURCES

Andersen, Martin Edwin. *Dossier Secreto: Argentina's Desaparecidos and the Myth of the "Dirty War."* Boulder, CO: Westview Press, 1993.

Guest, Ian. *Behind the Disappearances: Argentina's Dirty War Against Human Rights and the United Nations.* Philadelphia: University of Pennsylvania Press, 1990.

Martin, Gus. *Understanding Terrorism: Challenges, Perspectives, and Issues.* Thousand Oaks, CA: Sage Publications, 2006.

Simonsen, Clifford E., and Jeremy R. Spindlove. *Terrorism Today: The Past, the Players, the Future*, 2nd ed. Upper Saddle River, NJ: Pearson Prentice Hall, 2004.

U.S. Department of State. 2003 *Global Terrorism Report.* Washington, DC: Government Printing Office, 2004.

Wolosky, Lee S. Statement before the first public hearing of the National Commission on Terrorist Attacks upon the United States. April 1, 2003.

NOTES

1. http://www.wip.britannica.com/eb/article-217762/terrorism (accessed September 2, 2007).
2. Milton Metzer, *The Terrorists* (New York: Harper & Row, 1983), 193.
3. Martin Slann, "The State as Terrorist," in *Annual Editions: Violence and Terrorism 91/92*, ed. Martin Slann and Bernard Schecterman (Guilford, CT: Dushkin, 1991), 69.
4. Robert A. Liston, *Terrorism* (New York: Elsevier/Nelson Books, 1977), 67.
5. United Nations Convention on Torture, Article 1.
6. Amnesty International, *Report on Terrorism* (New York: Farrar, Straus, and Giroux, 1975), 27.
7. Amnesty International. http://webamnesty.org/library/Index/ENGIOR510042007 (accessed September 2, 2007).
8. Public Broadcasting Service. "Redefining Torture?" http://www.pbs.org/wgbh/pages/frontline/torture/themes/redefining.html (accessed September 2, 2007).
9. T.R Reid, "Case against Soldier Is Presented," January 12, 2005. *Washington Post*, January 12, 2005. http://www.washingtonpost.com/wp-dyn/articles/A1164-2005Jan11.html (accessed September 2, 2007).
10. Ibid.
11. http://www.amnesty.org/en/library/info/ASA16/011/2008.
12. Hannah Arendt, *The Origins of Totalitarianism* (New York: Harcourt, Brace, & World, 1973), 464.
13. See, for further documentation of this trend, the Annual Reports by Amnesty International, as well as that organization's *Report on Torture* (2005).
14. Carl J. Friedrich, "Opposition and Government Violence," *Government and Opposition* 7 (1972): 3–19.
15. See Erich Fromm, *The Anatomy of Human Destructiveness* (New York: Holt, Rinehart, and Winston, 1973), 285–288.
16. Ted Gurr, *Why Men Rebel* (Princeton, NJ: Princeton University Press, 1970), 213.
17. United Nations Secretariat Study, "Measures to Prevent International Terrorism," U.N. Doc. A/C.6/418 (November 2, 1973). Prepared as requested by the Sixth Legal Committee of the General Assembly.
18. Bernard Schechterman and Martin Slann, eds. *Violence and Terrorism 98/99* (New York: Dushkin/McGraw-Hill, 1998), 42.

19. Robert Slater and Michael Stohl, eds. *Current Perspectives on International Terrorism* (New York: Macmillan/St. Martin's Press, 1988), 169.
20. Claire Sterling, "Terrorism: Tracing the International Network," *New York Times Magazine* (March 1, 1981): 19.
21. Ibid., 54.
22. Claire Sterling, *The Terror Network* (New York: Holt, Rinehart, and Winston, 1981), 293.
23. *Strategic Assessment 1999: Priorities for a Turbulent World* (Washington, DC: National Defense University Press, 2000), 120.
24. http://www.fas.org/irp/threat/bian_apr_2003.htm
25. "The Unmasking of Assad," *U.S. News & World Report* 101, no. 19 (November 10, 1986): 27.
26. Ibid., 26.
27. Ibid., 28.
28. Ibid., 29.
29. "Timeline: Decades of Conflict in Lebanon, Israel," *CNN*, July 14, 2006. http://www.cnn.com/2006/WORLD/meast/07/14/israel.lebanon.timeline/ (accessed September 3, 2007).
30. U.S. Department of State, "State-Sponsored Terrorism," in *1997 Global Terrorism Report* (Washington, DC: Government Printing Office, 1998), 6.
31. Daniel L. Byman, *"Proxy Power: Understanding Iran's Use of Terrorism."* Accessed from the Brookings Institute website on September 3, 2007. http://www.brookings.edu/views/op-ed/byman/20060726.htm
32. U.S. Department of State, "Overview of State-Sponsored Terrorism," in *Patterns of Global Terrorism* (Washington, DC: Government Printing Office, April 2000), 3.

Terrorism, Inc.

> Terrorism can be viewed as a warped
> mirror image of the new economy.
>
> —*Don van Natta, Jr.*

Terrorism today is a transnational problem, no longer contained within the borders—or the jurisdiction—of a single state. As states become increasingly unable to openly support or to control terrorism, and more troubled states become safe havens for terrorist groups, modern terrorism has become an "international business," networked across state borders as terrorists carry out, and finance, the business of terror. Let us consider modern terrorism as a network with business activities and funding that cross the globe, and with an increasingly loose affiliation among groups with shared interests or goals.

NETWORKING

The three Japanese who disembarked from Air France Flight 132 at Lod International Airport in Tel Aviv, Israel, in May 1972 appeared no different from the other tourists bound for the Holy Land. Chatting pleasantly with the other passengers, they made their way swiftly to the luggage conveyor belt, where they retrieved their bags.

Opening one suitcase, they extracted a lightweight, Czech-made submachine gun and a few hand grenades. They then opened fire on the crowd of disembarking passengers and visitors, using their weapons to strafe the airport lounge from side to side. From time to time they lobbed the grenades into the groups of terrified people.

Twenty-six people died in this attack. At least six of them were decapitated. One child of about seven was cut in half twice by the barrage of bullets.

More than half of the dead were Puerto Ricans on a tour of the Holy Land. An additional 78 people were wounded, many of them dismembered. The entire episode was over in seconds.

As an example of the **networking** of international terrorists, *in the creation of an interconnected system linking groups with common goals,* this incident excels. Forty years ago, Japanese members of the Japanese Red Army killed Puerto Ricans on behalf of Palestinian Arabs who sought to punish Israelis.

Cooperation between terrorist groups with, if not a common cause, at least a shared hatred, has occurred with alarming frequency for four decades. Anti-NATO sentiment, for example, drew several European groups into co-operative action. A communiqué on January 15, 1986, declared that the Red Army Faction (RAF) of West Germany and Action Direct (AD) of France would together attack the multinational structures of NATO. Shortly thereafter, assassins killed the general in charge of French arms sales and a West German defense industrialist. On August 8, 1985, two Americans were killed in a bomb blast at a U.S. air base in Frankfurt, West Germany. The RAF and AD claimed joint responsibility for this attack.

Linkage between terrorist groups exists. It appears in the form of shared members, training camps, weaponry, and tactics. It is obvious in the propaganda being disseminated by the groups. Perhaps the most obvious linkage—funding—became evident after the September 11, 2001, attacks.

Study of contemporary terrorist groups suggests that terrorists share intelligence information, weapons, supplies, training facilities and instructors, sponsors, and even membership. Such frequent *ad hoc* sharing does not necessarily constitute an organized "network of terror," as some have suggested. But the dimensions of cooperation between groups with unrelated or even opposing ideological bases offer useful insights to police, military, intelligence, and academic personnel who understand the web that does from time to time link terrorists.

That web is tenuous for the most part, constructed in a pragmatic fashion to meet common needs for relatively scarce resources. This does not, of course, diminish the potential for serious damage posed by such linkages. It simply makes the danger more difficult to assess, as the linkages are not only usually covert but also appear to be in an almost constant state of flux.

Let us examine, then, some of those linkages as they have been shown to exist (usually after the fact in a terrorist event or confrontation). It is not necessary to study *all* of the available data on such linkages to establish that such connections exist. A brief survey of some of the evidences of cooperation or collusion will suffice to illustrate both the reality and the hazards of this insidious merging of terrorist interests and assets.

SHARED STRATEGIC PLANNING

Attempts at coordinating activities are made by many terrorist groups, and proof of shared strategies demonstrating a "terrorist conspiracy" perhaps driven by a common bond of faith or a common target is growing. One expert, James Adams, suggests that terrorist groups act more like a "multi-national corporation with different divisions dotted around the world, all of which act in an essentially independent manner."[1]

In his book, *The Financing of Terrorism,* Adams illustrates his analogy by suggesting that these "independent divisions" offer to the head of another operation, when he or she comes to town, the use of the company apartment, advances against expenses, and perhaps access to local equipment. In a similar manner, terrorist groups carrying out an operation in a foreign country may be granted such assistance by the "host" country's terrorist groups.

This analogy between different divisions in a multinational corporation and terrorist groups is more credible than that of a conspiracy, which is supported by only fragmentary and often subjective evidence. The cooperation in terms of **strategic planning** that has been authenticated to date between terrorist groups has been (1) ad hoc, *focused on the planning of just one particular operation between groups whose other contacts remain fragmentary;* and/or (2) bombastic, *consisting primarily in the issuing of declarations by "congresses" or transient alliances between groups briefly united against a perceived common target.*

In 1975, French police learned that the international terrorist known as "Carlos the Jackal" was running a clearinghouse for terrorist movements. His clients included the Tupamaros, the Quebec Liberation Front, the Irish Republican Army (IRA), the Baader-Meinhof gang from West Germany, Yugoslavia's Croatian separatists, the Turkish People's Liberation Army, and the Palestinians.[2]

An **international terrorism congress,** *a meeting of terrorists from all over the world to work out agendas and to organize cooperative efforts,* took place in Frankfurt, Germany, in 1986, reportedly attended by no less than 500 people. Meeting under the slogan "The armed struggle as a strategic and tactical necessity in the fight for revolution," it proclaimed the U.S. armed forces in Europe to be the main enemy.

At this congress, it was decided that the correct strategy was to kill individual soldiers in order to demoralize their colleagues and lower their collective capacity to kill. Among those represented at this congress, or present as guests, were German, French, Belgian, Spanish, and Portuguese terrorists, as well as members of the Palestine Liberation Organization (PLO), the Popular Front for the Liberation of Palestine (PFLP), the African National Congress, the IRA, the Tupamaros, the Italian Red Brigades, and the ETA (Basque separatists). Most of the manifestos issued by this congress were basically Marxist-Leninist in style. The congress was financed largely by Libya.[3]

This "congress" of terrorist actors was not an anomaly. Actually, Western intelligence believes that between 1970 and 1984, 28 meetings involving different terrorist groups were held around the world. Although these meetings were generally called to discuss cooperation rather than coordination or revolutionary activities, it is difficult to establish precisely what plans and agreements have emerged from these contacts.

In 2004, for example, two such "congresses" were held in two different countries. Northern Lebanon, in early February of that year, was the meeting site for a range of Muslim groups, including but not limited to HAMAS, Hezbollah, al-Qaeda, Islamic Jihad, and Ansar al-Islam. At this conference, the focus was reportedly on renewed offensive attacks on Israelis and Israeli interests abroad, according to an interview with an Arab diplomat in Amman, Jordan.

That same year, Iran reportedly sponsored a 10-day conference of major terrorist organizations, purportedly to discuss anti-U.S. strategy. The conference date was chosen to mark the 25th anniversary of the return to Iran of the late Ayatollah Ruhollah Khomeini, leader of the revolution against the shah of Iran in 1979. Titled "The Days of Dawn," the conference was ordered by Iran's supreme leader, Ali Khamenei, and demonstrated Iran's involvement in sponsoring insurgency groups in the Middle East, Asia, and South America.[4]

Contact between various terrorist groups does exist and has been documented. Adam Cohen, writing for *Time* in the aftermath of September 11, suggested that Osama bin Laden led a "global terrorist network," where bin Laden "creates the service and brand, but the cells largely fund their activities."[5]

TERRORISM IS BIG BUSINESS

If the PLO were an American corporation, it would have been on the list of Fortune 500 companies. What was the PLO worth in the mid-1980s? James Adams calculated the organization's financial empire at $5 billion. Return on investments was the group's largest source of income at that time, bringing in about $1 billion per year.

Let us take a look at the financial headquarters of this group, as Adams describes it:

> Just off Shah Bander Square in downtown Damascus is a five-story building of light brown cement. It looks more like the office of a low-level government department, unpainted since the colonials departed, than the headquarters of one of the wealthiest multinational corporations in the world.[6]

On the top floor of this building were banks of Honeywell computers, which were tended by young Palestinians. Most of these computer experts were trained in the United States, some at MIT and some at Harvard. From this world of high technology and superefficiency, the Palestinian National Fund managed investments that generated a total annual income greater than the total budget of some Third World countries, an income that made the PLO the richest and most powerful terrorist group in the world during the 1980s.

Almost all of the PLO's assets were held indirectly through private individuals and in numbered bank accounts in Switzerland, West Germany, Mexico, and the Cayman Islands. Its primary banking institution was the Palestinian-owned Arab Bank, Ltd., headquartered in Amman, Jordan. The chairman of the Palestine National Fund at that time, Jawaeed al-Ghussein, administered the PLO finances.

PLO financiers invested money in the European market, as well as in a few blue-chip stocks on Wall Street. The PLO also held large amounts of lucrative money certificates in the United States. These and other investments were said to provide as much as 20 percent of all the group's revenues.

The PLO, like many multinational corporations, was also involved in a wide variety of business ventures, not all of which generated a monetary profit. Some were primarily political, made to win friends for the PLO. PLO money flowed covertly, through dummy corporations established in such places as Liechtenstein and Luxembourg, into investments in Third World countries. Much of this investment money passed through the Arab Bank for Economic Development in Africa and the Arab African Bank.

The PLO owned dairy and poultry farms and cattle ranches in the Sudan, Somalia, Uganda, and Guinea. It reportedly purchased a duty-free shop in Tanzania's Dar es Salaam International Airport and then negotiated for similar shops in Mozambique and Zimbabwe.

The point is that the PLO not only had cash assets of staggering proportions, but that it also succeeded in investing them for capital, political, and strategic gains. Its stock and bond investments were exemplary and brought in considerable revenue; its investment in Third World ventures brought it considerable support and goodwill from many nations; and its ventures into such operations as duty-free airport concessions provided it with security-proof access through which to transfer materials from country to country. The PLO not only had money—it learned how to use much of it wisely.[7]

Not all groups carrying out terrorist acts are so well endowed. Most have to depend on the largess of patrons or on their own success in carrying out robberies, marketing drugs, and kidnapping for ransom. The ETA, which had close ties with the IRA and the PLO, adopted one of the PLO's less-publicized methods of raising money. Funds for this group, which received training and support from Libya and the PLO, were generated through **revolutionary taxes,** which were *levied on Basque businessmen.* The PLO levied such a *tax against the wages of Palestinians working abroad throughout the Arab world.*

Of the financial patrons of contemporary terrorist groups, two nations and one individual created networks that deserve special attention. These networks alone have been responsible for the training and arming of countless terrorist teams during the latter part of the twentieth century. Under their aegis, international terrorism took on a truly international flavor.

▶ **CASE STUDY 6.1**

Somalia: Robbery on the High Seas

Torn by civil war among warlords for more than two decades, Somalia has many of its citizens today engaged in the business of piracy. Piracy has become an expensive problem for international maritime commerce and a lucrative "business" for many of the people of Somalia. Studies suggest piracy off the coast of Somalia and in the Indian Ocean has cost the global community around $10 billion. The average ransoms for ships caught by pirates has grown from about $150,000 in 2005 to about $5.4 million in 2011, with the number of attacks also steadily increasing. In the first three months of 2011, 98 such attacks were reported.

The business of piracy has become an attractive career option for many Somalis. Although the high risk—of capture, death, imprisonment, and more—associated with piracy is very real to these people, the lucrative nature of this "business" continues to draw new recruits. Some carrying out piracy regard the ransom demanded of the foreign vessels captured by pirates to be a form of "tax" on the foreign ships utilizing their waters. Others see this career as an escape from the grinding poverty crushing so much of Somalia.

The local economy, particularly the fishermen, benefit from the business of piracy as well. As the pirates forced the fishing fleets of Spain, India, and Italy to go to other waters, there was substantial benefit to the local fishing industry. Indeed, piracy was, according to some historians, initiated in recent years to combat two problems exacerbated by the lack of a strong central government with organized coast guard capacities: the dumping of toxic wastes off Somali shores by foreign vessels and the overfishing of Somali waters by fishing fleets of other nations.

In fact, one of the pirate networks operating in these waters calls itself the National Volunteer Coast Guard (NVCG). At least three other networks of pirates have been identified to date in this region: The Marka group, comprised of several scattered and marginally organized groups, operates near the town of that name, while the Puntland group is a large consortium of local fishermen operating off the Puntland coast of Somaliland, the portion of Somalia that declared itself to be independent during the civil war. The most powerful and sophisticated of the pirate groups is the one calling itself the *Somali Marines*, which has a military structure, including a fleet admiral and a head of financial operations.

Piracy has had mixed impact on the local communities. Some have complained that the presence of large gangs of armed men has increased their feeling of personal insecurity, particularly in a land still torn by domestic strife. Others, however, have noted the "boomtown" effect that the on-shore spending by the pirates has had on the local economies. This rejuvenating effect of this spending has provided jobs and opportunities in areas of destitute populations. Entire communities have been transformed by this influx of pirate wealth, with local shop owners and residents using their profits to purchase "luxury" items such as electric generators. In a country whose per capita GDP is, according to the UN, about $600 per year, with most of its citizens therefore living on less than $2 per day, this "wealth" is valued, and the draw to a career in piracy is very strong.

While much of the pirates' weaponry comes from Yemen, a considerable amount also comes from Mogadishu, Somalia's capital. The funding of pirate operations, including the purchase of armaments, is today structured in a stock exchange, with investors buying and selling shares in upcoming attacks. Piracy ransom money is generally paid in large-denomination U.S. dollar bills. The pirates use currency-counting machines to authenticate the currency, just as foreign exchange businesses do throughout the world. Much of the money is then invested in weapons and shares in the next venture.

The benefits of these piracy ventures extend beyond these markets, however. In neighboring Kenya, local fishermen have begun to enjoy a replenished fish stock, as Somali pirates force away foreign fishing fleets which had been depleting this important resource. Piracy, in the eyes of some in this region, does indeed pay. ■

Source: John Norton and Bronwyn Bruton, "The Price of Failure," *Foreign Policy* (October 5, 2011) at http://www.foreignpolicy.com/articles/2011/10/05/the_price_of_failure

Iran's Support Network

Libya was certainly not the only Middle Eastern nation to support terrorism—openly during the 1970s and 1980s, more discretely in the 1990s. As James Adams noted, when one prime supporter falls away, another tends to rise to take its place. Iran was able, to a large degree, to take Libya's place as the leading patron of terrorism in the Middle East, Europe, and the Americas.

In order to understand Iran's commitment to terrorism, one can look back 900 years to the time of al-Hassan ibn-Sabbah. Sabbah, a leader of the dissident Muslim Ismaili group (which in turn is one of the two divisions of the Shi'a sect), was the founder of the previously mentioned "Assassins," the hashish-smoking terrorists of the Persian Gulf region in the twelfth century. Sabbah called his followers **fedayeen**—meaning either adventurers or men of sacrifice, a label adopted by many terrorists today. Palestinian suicide bombers in Israel and those engaged in the holy war initiated by bin Laden against the West have both been called fedayeen.

Iran is the home of the Shi'a branch of Islam, which has been in conflict with the majority Sunni branch for centuries. When Ayatollah Khomeini came to power after the fall of the shah, he began to rally Shi'a globally to this ancient conflict. In March 1982, clergy and leaders of Shiite revolutionary movements from all over the world came to Tehran. At this meeting, in addition to agreeing to establish a number of training camps for terrorists in Iran, it was agreed that $100 million would be immediately allocated as a **fighting fund**, established by Iran to support worldwide terrorism. Moreover, an additional $50 million was designated to be spent each year for an indefinite period of time to bankroll specific acts of terrorism.[8]

From this capital outlay have come a variety of terrorist activities. Several powerful groups operating in Lebanon were financed by Iran during the last two decades of the twentieth century. Bomb attacks on moderate Arab states, including Kuwait, Saudi Arabia, and Egypt, caused serious human casualties and monetary expense. Islamic fundamentalism, supported by substantial cash infusions, rose rapidly in southern Asia. Hit squads were dispatched throughout Europe to eliminate "enemies" of Shi'a Islam. A global network of clergy-dominated religious groups was also formed, whose purpose was to mastermind further terrorism and recruit new assassins to serve in Iran's holy war. (The concept of a holy war against the West did not originate—nor will it end—with bin Laden.)

Faced with the threat of continuing Iranian-sponsored terrorist bombings and hijackings, some wealthy Kuwaiti citizens began taking extended vacations during the late 1980s in other Arab states and Western Europe. The Kuwaiti government naturally was concerned that too large an exodus of such persons could set off panic among foreign guest workers, who made up 70 percent of the Kuwaiti workforce. Accordingly, Kuwait moderated its antagonism toward Iran, fearing that Iran's terrorist retaliation might cripple beyond repair the Kuwaiti economy.

Saudi Arabia, which was also a victim of Iranian-directed terrorism, was also very cautious in taking public stands in the Iran–Iraq conflict. Although many Saudi officials urged a tough stance toward Tehran, King Fahd maintained an extremely cautious approach. Remembering the violence of the Iranian-provoked riot in Mecca in July 1987, which left more than 400 dead, the Saudis were careful not to deliberately antagonize the state of Iran. The bombing in late 1995 of the building used as U.S. military training headquarters for years in the city of Riyadh indicated that such caution might not have been sufficient.

Despite Saudi political wariness, however, terrorism continued to pour from Iran in an unpredictable flow, encompassing friend and foe alike in the Arab world. Originating from Bangkok, Kuwait Airways Flight 422 was hijacked on April 5, 1988, in a plot hatched four months earlier in Tehran by Shi'a radicals from Bahrain, Lebanon, and Iran. The world, with the possible exception of Iran, watched in horror as the bodies of innocent persons on Flight 422 were thrown from the plane by the terrorists, whose demands for the release of other terrorists held in Kuwaiti prisons were steadfastly refused by the Kuwaiti government. Those imprisoned terrorists were responsible for Iranian-directed bombings of the U.S. and French embassies in Kuwait.

Iran provides substantial financial assistance to Hezbollah—millions of dollars each year, by some estimates. This support is not always covert. The general secretary of Hezbollah publicly noted in an interview in March 1996 that this group receives financial assistance to continue what he termed "the legitimate struggle against Israel."[9]

As a State Department official, in his testimony before a congressional subcommittee, noted in 2006, "Iran is the 'central banker' of terrorism."[10] Since funding is the essential "oxygen" of terrorist groups, Iran's role in the support of the "business" of international terrorism cannot be overstated. ■

Source: U.S. Department of State Country Reports on Terrorism at http://www.state.gov/s/ct/rls/crt/2010/170260.htm

---

CASE STUDY **6.3**

Al-Qaeda's Funding

Osama bin Laden, son of a billionaire Saudi construction magnate with an estimated worth of hundreds of millions of dollars, ran a portfolio of businesses across North Africa and the Middle East. Companies in sectors ranging from shipping to agriculture to investment banking throw off profits while also providing al-Qaeda's movement of soldiers and procurement of weapons and chemicals. Saudis, Pakistanis, Yemenis, Egyptians, Algerians, Lebanese, Mauritanians, Palestinians, and more have carried out terror operations linked to al-Qaeda. Many of these men were originally affiliated with a specific national organization like Egypt's Islamic Jihad or Algeria's Armed Islamic Group, but their allegiance shifted to bin Laden, and they fight for his causes.

Some of bin Laden's money is in mainstream institutions, as investigations after the September 11 attacks indicated when the United States requested banks worldwide to cooperate in freezing al-Qaeda's assets. But al-Qaeda also clearly makes

(*continued*)

use of **hawala**, an informal Islamic banking network that links brokers around the world who advance funds to depositors on a handshake and, sometimes, a password. *Hawala*, Hindi for "in trust," has operated for generations in Asia and the Middle East. In remote areas, a broker may have little more than a rug and a phone, and the transfers leave little or no trail for investigators to follow, because they involve no wire transfers, balance sheets, or financial statements.

Hawala is used to transfer small amounts of money—usually less than $1,000—around the world. The transaction is almost immediate, based entirely on trust, and requires no certification that might leave a paper trail. This system is an excellent example of the Islamic world's unique approach to finance. Services and training are provided interest-free for rich and poor, personal relationships and trust replace collateral, and accounting is a luxury often not included. Donating money for the advancement of Islam—building a mosque or funding an Islamic exhibit—is a religious obligation.

Financial services such as hawala are a quick and inexpensive way for Muslims in the West to send funds to poorer relatives back home. For example, Al-Barakaat, a Somali-based organization, has outlets in cities across Europe and North America through which Somalis abroad send vital cash to families at home.

Extremists have begun exploiting the religious rather than the financial motives of hawala, and its lack of detailed bookkeeping makes it difficult to track the source of money used by groups engaged in terrorist acts. Islamic charities also take in billions each year, most of which is used for good causes, but not all. Some of these millions make it into the hands of Islamic fighters and terrorists. Al-Qaeda's financial structure was built, as a recent report noted,

> from the foundation of charities, nongovernmental organizations, mosques, web sites, fundraisers, intermediaries, facilitators, banks and other financial institutions that helped finance the mujahideen throughout the 1980s. This network extended to all corners of the Muslim world.[11]

Bin Laden established himself in Sudan in 1991 and launched several companies. One of these, the Al Shamal Islamic Bank, had a complete website with a list of correspondent banking relationships, including institutions in New York, Geneva, Paris, and London. Bin Laden also set up agricultural and construction companies.

One former al-Qaeda member, a Sudanese man named Jamal Ahmed al-Fadl, suggested in testimony at the trials of those accused of bombing the U.S. embassies in Kenya and Tanzania that bin Laden's organization has been beset by the usual office politics, ruthless cost cutting, and even corruption by some of its members. Al-Fadl complained bitterly about his $500 monthly salary, which was lower than other members' salaries, particularly certain Egyptians who seemed to enjoy preferential treatment. Bin Laden's response, according to al-Fadl, was that the Egyptians were paid more because they had more skills than the Sudanese, such as the ability to obtain forged documents.

In this sense, terrorism in the al-Qaeda network resembles a warped mirror image of an international corporation in its financial structure with corporate chieftains who manage lean, trimmed-down firms and bring in consultants and freelancers to perform specific jobs. As one author notes, "The specialists work as a team to complete an assignment, then move on to other jobs, often for other companies."[12] In this image too, bin Laden was much like a terror "mogul," a man with the power to approve projects suggested to him, who had final veto over the content or timing but often little to do with the project's actual creation. His most important contribution was the money.

The formal merging of al-Qaeda with the Egyptian Islamic Jihad in 1998 greatly enhanced bin Laden's global reach and organizational ability. In early 1998, when the two groups announced they had formed the World Islamic Front for Jihad Against Jews and Crusaders, the focus of Islamic Jihad shifted from overthrowing the current Egyptian government to attacking U.S. interests—bin Laden's focus.

The leaders of this expanded network used the Muslim pilgrimages to Islamic holy sites in Saudi Arabia as a cover for recruiting new members or passing cash from one member to another. They shifted money around the world to bail members out of jail in Algeria or Canada and to finance applications for political asylum to enable the planting of terrorist cells in Western Europe.

Evidence of al-Qaeda cells emerged in more than 40 countries after the September 11 attacks, as the United States urged other states to "follow the money" to determine the extent of the network of terrorism and its financial support structure. Bin Laden's degree in economics and his experience as part of a multibillion dollar, multinational construction company made this task quite challenging.

Al-Qaeda resources have been invested in industries as diverse as trade in honey and in diamonds. American officials noted evidence that bin Laden used a network of shops that sell honey—a staple of Middle Eastern life since biblical times—to generate income as well as to secretly move weapons, drugs, and agents throughout his terrorist network. Honey is deeply rooted in Middle Eastern culture, religion, and trade. The honey business is less significant for the income it generates, however, than for the operational assistance it provides. The shops allow al-Qaeda to ship such contraband as money, weapons, and drugs. The *New York Times* reported that "the smell and consistency of honey makes it easy to hide weapons and drugs in shipments. Inspectors don't want to inspect that product. It's too messy."[13]

Al-Qaeda, like other groups, have exploited the corruption and chaos endemic to the Democratic Republic of the Congo (DRC) to tap into the diamond trade and funnel millions of dollars into their organizations. U.S. officials investigating the financing of al-Qaeda indicated that they had greatly underestimated the amount of money this group and other organizations controlled, not only in the diamond trade but also in the trade of gold, uranium, and tanzanite in this troubled region. The diamonds and other precious and semiprecious materials are bought at a small fraction of their market value, then smuggled out of the country and sold, frequently in Europe, for sizable profits.

Viewed in this context, al-Qaeda is clearly a financial structure willing to break moral laws to further its cause. Preying on failed or collapsed states, such as the DRC, Liberia, and Sierra Leone, this organization profits from the chaos, violence, and intimidation of this region to secure funds for its operatives to carry out terror in other states. There is one further important point to remember in the analysis of al-Qaeda as a terrorist "organization." Expert opinion remains divided about the strength of the structure of al-Qaeda, as it has operated increasingly more like a loose network of affiliates joined by a common general vision and less like a

(continued)

structured organization with clear leadership roles and functional plans. It appears to be increasingly more of a network of terrorist groups than a tightly structured organization. However, "terrorism is cheap," as an analyst studying al-Qaeda's financing observed in 2010, and a "group" like al-Qaeda, with major affiliates whose leadership remains relatively intact despite the death of bin Laden, could easily fund a bombing attack such as the one that occurred in London in 2005 and cost only about $15,000.[14] ∎

Source: Council on Foreign Relations at http://www.cfr.org/terrorist-organizations/al-qaedas-financial-pressures/p21347

THE INTERNATIONALIZATION OF TERRORISM

Like many businesses in today's global market, terrorism is increasingly trans-national. What had once been the "problem" in only one national or regional "market" is now more likely to be planned, supported, and carried out across many national borders, "internationalizing" the crime. Although terrorism "internationalized" in the Middle East long ago, frequently around a religious war against a commonly hated heretic state, Europe has also had to cope with the networking of terrorist groups into a web whose strength is difficult to measure. Study of one of Europe's earliest "networked" groups, the RAF, offers insight into this phenomenon.

The RAF was the oldest and the most ruthlessly violent left-wing terrorist movement in Germany in the late twentieth century. Emerging from a small residue of left-wing extremists from the Baader-Meinhof group and others involved in the student protests of the late 1960s, it was responsible for half a dozen bombing attacks in 1972. Although it suffered large defeats in 1977 and again in 1982 (due to the arrest of many of the original leaders), it continued to successfully regroup and reemerge as a violent political force until Germany was reunited in the early 1990s.

Early generations of the RAF were to some degree international in the struggle that they waged against imperialism. In 1977, the RAF carried out a PFLP plan to hijack a Lufthansa aircraft to Mogadishu. The PFLP plan was designed to capitalize on the Schleyer kidnapping. Two members of the RAF, Hans-Joachim Klein and Gabriele Krocher-Tiedemann, were recruited by Carlos the Jackal to assist in the raid on the Vienna OPEC conference in 1975. Another two members of the RAF, Wilfried Böse and Brigitte Kuhlmann, participated in the 1976 hijack to Entebbe Airport in Uganda.

But in July 1984, West German police found documents indicating that the RAF planned to further internationalize its struggle by uniting with other terrorist groups in attacks on the representatives of repression, specifically NATO allies. This anti-imperialism brotherhood of bombers and assassins began to wage war throughout Europe in the 1980s.

German, French, and Belgian radicals assassinated prominent members of Europe's defense establishment and set off explosives at such targets as a U.S. air base, military pipelines, and a variety of other NATO installations. The targets did not remain specifically military. A Berlin nightclub filled with off-duty soldiers and German civilians was bombed in 1984, allegedly by this terrorist alliance.

One source close to the German underground noted,

> From the Red Army Faction point of view, the only opportunity to fight NATO suppression around the world is to organize a kind of illegal guerrilla war and get in contact with more and more people.[15]

This transformation apparently took concrete form first in 1981. Italian counterterrorist forces revealed that in that year, exiles from the RAF, the Italian Red Brigades, and other groups met in Paris. From this meeting, the order went out to kidnap James L. Dozier, a U.S. Army brigadier general stationed in Rome. From being indigenous terrorist groups, operating primarily on their own soil for essentially nationalistic purposes, these groups began to focus their attention and activities against an international enemy: NATO.

Working together, these European terrorists created an informal network helping them to strike at a variety of NATO targets throughout that region. With relatively open borders between nations in the European Union, these terrorists managed to operate in a manner that made it difficult for

---

CASE STUDY 6.4

Al-Qaeda's Network

In the year of intense effort on the part of the United States and its allies in the international community to "search out and destroy" al-Qaeda, it became obvious that the organization had developed new bases and a looser structure; it was still quite capable of attacking Western targets. An examination of some of the individuals, the cells scattered worldwide, and the pattern of activities still taking place offers insights into the new "netwar" being waged by this particular brand of "terrorism, inc.," today.

The "Lieutenants"

Osama bin Laden could not have carried out the attacks of September 11, 2001, without widespread help from a network of talented and committed "lieutenants." These men were sought intensely by the United States following the attacks in 2001, because their participation was believed to be crucial to the attack's success:

> *Ayman al-Zawahiri:* Widely believed to have been bin Laden's deputy, al-Zawahiri was the leader of the Egyptian Islamic Jihad, the group blamed for the assassination of President Anwar el-Sadat in 1981, and a member of the **Shura**—a body of al-Qaeda that contains members of other terrorist groups. Al-Zawahiri, a surgeon, was sought by the U.S. military in Iraq in 2004, where it was believed that he continued to coordinate attacks against U.S. military in that country. "Al-Zawahiri's experience is much broader than even bin Laden's," according to Dia'a Rashwan, one of Egypt's top

(continued)

experts on militants. "His name has come up in nearly every case involving Muslim extremists since the 1970s."[16] In the wake of bin Laden's death, he is widely expected to take leadership of this networked organization.

Muhammad Atef: Thought responsible for carrying out the detailed mechanics of the plan to hijack four aircraft simultaneously on September 11, 2001, Atef is also believed to be responsible for planning the 1998 bombings of U.S. embassies in Kenya and Tanzania. Responsibility for these attacks was claimed by the Islamic Army for the Liberation of Holy Sites, led by Sobhi al-Sitta, also a bin Laden lieutenant. Atef operated his own military training camps in Afghanistan, where he apparently trained members of the Islamic Army group. He was killed in Kabul, Afghanistan, by a U.S. Predator.

Mustafa Ahmed al-Hawsawi: Ahmed, as Osama's "money man," financed the hijackers while they were in the United States. In fact, he was in the United Arab Emirates before the September 11 attacks, waiting for the hijackers to return their unused U.S. dollars to him there.

Abu Zoubaydah: This Palestinian was responsible for overseeing al-Qaeda's training camps. He is thought to have masterminded the "millennium bombings," including a plot to blow up the Los Angeles airport on New Year's Eve in 1999. Zoubaydah was arrested by Pakistani agents in Faisalabad.

Saif al-Adel: Described by the FBI as one of the most dangerous al-Qaeda leaders, al-Adel responsible for training elite terrorist recruits in handling explosives. Several of the September 11 hijackers were reportedly schooled by al-Adel in Afghanistan. He is believed to be in Iran. ∎

Source: Council on Foreign Relations backgrounder on "Al-Qaeda" updated August 2011 at http://www.cfr.org/terrorist-organizations/al-qaeda-k- al-qaida-al-qaida/p9126

law enforcement officials to predict and prevent their attacks or to capture them after the events. Evidence suggests that they shared personnel, resources (explosives and weapons), and safe houses, as well as the low-level support system involved in such activities as the production of travel documents.

This networking of groups with common ideas, common enemies, and overlapping memberships has become even more common today, particularly among groups united behind religious zealots. As the world discovered in the wake of the attacks of September 11 in the United States, this networking encompasses individuals of vastly different cultures, socioeconomic groups, even languages. The uniting force for the network appears to be the radicalized faith and, in part, the charisma of the leadership. Take a quick look at the actors involved to understand the extent of the network of al-Qaeda.

THE NETWORK AND NETWAR

Terrorism is clearly taking on a new dimension, described as **netwar**, an *asymmetric mode of conflict and crime at societal levels, involving measures short of conventional war carried out by protagonists using network forms of organization and related strategies and information-age technologies to carry*

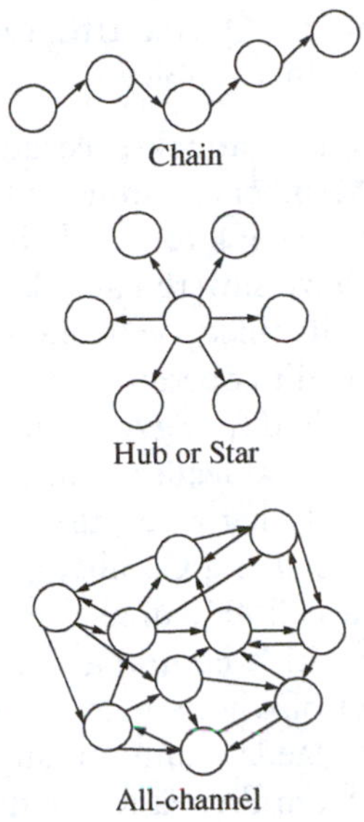

FIGURE 6.1

Terror Networks

Source: Networks of terror for text chapter 6.

out attacks. The individuals involved in a netwar usually connect in small groups, which communicate and coordinate their activities, but which generally lack an organized central command authority. When fighters returned to their home countries after passing through training camps in countries like Afghanistan, the groups to which they returned became, in a sense, the "international franchises" of al-Qaeda, local outposts in the Muslim world, capable of networking and interacting but also of acting independently.

Networks of terror groups, similar to the structures emerging in the world of business, generally organize in one of three types: chains, hubs, or all-channel. As Figure 6.1 shows, **Chain networks** are organized much like an organization of smugglers, where *goods, information, and even people are passed along a line of separate contacts, from one end of the chain to the other.* In contrast, **hub or star networks** are similar to the structure of a drug cartel, *with actors and cells tied to a central cell or actor that controls communication and coordinates action.* In the **all-channel network**, however, *each small group or cell is connected to every other group in a collaborative effort, but without a central command cell.*[17]

After the destruction of the Afghan training camps in 2001, many al-Qaeda operatives returned to their homelands or to third countries, where they made common cause with other Islamic groups to wage a jihad against the United States and its allies. These separate cells or factions, inspired by the events of September 11, do not appear to have needed contact with one another or a central authority to carry out successful terrorist attacks on al-Qaeda's behalf. As one news agency reported, "Al-Qaeda supporters in 60 countries range from small cells to allied terrorist groups to guerrilla gangs."[18]

First, a quick look at the "al-Qaeda affiliates" in this netwar helps to make the dimensions of the conflict visible:

In Europe, small cells plot new attacks, recruiting second-generation European Muslims. Members of some cells report directly to al-Qaeda, while others belong to allied North African groups. London and Madrid have suffered attacks on their transit systems by al-Qaeda "affiliate" cells since the September 11 attacks.

In North Africa, al-Qaeda allies operate from Morocco to Egypt. The Islamic Group and al-Jihad (in Egypt) remain active. Al-Zawahiri was the operational and political leader of al-Jihad before he "merged" it with al-Qaeda in 1998. Other allies, the Armed Islamic Group and the Salafist Group for Call and Combat (in Algeria), continue to carry out attacks. In Tunisia in 2002, an al-Qaeda cell attacked North Africa's oldest synagogue with a natural gas truck rigged with explosives, killing 19 people, most of whom were tourists.

In Sub-Saharan Africa, al-Qaeda maintains support for a variety of Muslim rebel groups from Eritrea to South Africa, including the Eritrean Islamic Jihad Movement and al-Ittihad al-Islamiya. This cell of al-Qaeda is known as al-Qaeda of the Maghreb (AQM).

In Pakistan, al-Qaeda members network with local groups, such as Jaish-e-Muhammad, Lashkar-e-Tayyiba, and Harakat ul-Mujahedin, to launch attacks on foreigners, and are suspected of involvement in the assassination of Benazir Bhutto in 2007. *Wall Street Journal* reporter Daniel Pearl was kidnapped and murdered in 2002 in Karachi by members of a Pakistani organization with ties to al-Qaeda. In 2002, a group linked with al-Qaeda bombed a church in Islamabad frequented by Westerners, killing five people.

In Southeast Asia, an al-Qaeda affiliate, the Jemaah Islamiyah (operating in Indonesia), was allegedly responsible for the attack on a Bali nightclub in October 2002 that killed 180 people. In 2007, an explosion in a karaoke bar in Zamboanga, on Mindanao Island in the Philippines, killed three people, and two bombs exploded in a department store in the same city, killing seven. The local Abu Sayyaf group, an al-Qaeda affiliate, claimed responsibility.

In Yemen, bin Laden's ancestral home, al-Qaeda maintains a very active cell (Al-Qaeda in the Arabian Peninsula, or AQAP), because the government here remains able to exert very little control over much of the country. In the fall of 2002, the French oil tanker *Limburg* was rammed by an explosives-laden boat off the coast of Al-Mukalla, Yemen.

In Central Asia, trouble continues to foment from the Islamic Movement of Uzbekistan and the Eastern Turkestan Islamic Party, whose members trained in Afghanistan under al-Qaeda. As one expert working with the Washington Institute noted, while the United States had assumed initially that al-Qaeda could be destroyed effectively by eliminating bin Laden and his headquarters in Afghanistan.

The Bali bombing and the attack on the French Tanker *Limburg* in Yemen that fall demonstrated . . . that al-Qaeda's power and reach stemmed from a network of small and local groups that work as "subcontractors" for terrorist attacks all over the world, even as bin Laden and his top lieutenants hid in distant caves. In other words, the al-Qaeda network was able to be resilient because it relied not only upon its top leaders and clandestine cells, but also "affiliate groups," which are larger, homegrown, organic Islamist terror groups that became volunteer fighters for the al-Qaeda matrix.[19]

Clearly, al-Qaeda *is* decentralized, but its capacity to commit acts of terror has in some respects actually increased as its territory and targets have expanded. Terrorism, in this netwar form, offers a challenge to international security unlike that faced by most modern law enforcement or military.

NARCO-TERRORISM

Transnational terrorism is less dependent on the sponsorship of patron states or individuals to create a network to support their violent activities. A new source of revenue has come into the hands of terrorist groups in the last decades of the twentieth century, prompting some experts to decry the existence of what they call **narco-terrorism**, *a networking of the trade in drugs and terrorism.* U.S. News & World Report called this "the unholiest of alliances, a malevolent marriage between two of the most feared and destructive forces plaguing modern society—terror and drugs."[20]

The use of drugs to underwrite the costs of terrorism adds a new dimension to law enforcement efforts to combat both drugs and terrorism. The drug trade offers vast profits, too, for nations that, while wanting to continue to sponsor terrorist groups, find their coffers seriously depleted in recent years. Syria, for example, and more recently Afghanistan, engaged in international drug smuggling to help finance their support for terrorist groups.

The netherworld of narco-terrorism has three main players: the terrorist groups such as al-Qaeda, the Revolutionary Armed Forces of Colombia, or Sendero Luminoso; the government officials and intelligence services of nations, such as Iran and Cuba, whose foreign policy includes the exporting of revolution; and the narcotic-dealing gangsters, such as Juan Matta Ballesteros, who also deal in political violence and terror. Through a complex network of contacts, these narco-terrorists deal in weapons, launder money, share intelligence information, trade false passports, share safe havens, and offer other forms of assistance.

It is a loose global alliance of two elements of the criminal world. In spite of the apparent callousness in such groups as the PLO toward the taking of human life, these groups are very sensitive to charges that they deal in drugs. Indeed, PLO treasurer Jaweed al-Ghussein vehemently repudiated such charges. "We are fighting for our homeland. We are not drug smugglers. That is against our values."[21]

Regardless of such denials, it is true that in war-torn Lebanon, the annual 1,500-ton hashish trade (recently supplemented by opium and heroin) has supported terrorists of many ideologies for years. "Lebanese hashish helps to pay for everything from hijacking and bombing spectaculars in Europe and the Middle East to a simmering revolt by Moslem insurgents in the Philippines."[22]

It is certain that Syria would be unable to conduct its assistance to insurgent groups without the infusion of millions of dollars in drug profits. Without such profits, the Syrian economy would be even more threadbare than it became in the years since the collapse of the Soviet Union. Intelligence agencies suggest that Syrian government involvement in the drugs-for-terrorism trade involves persons at high levels of the Syrian government.

Nor is the Middle East alone in experiencing the impact of narco-terrorism. In the so-called Triple Frontier, where the borders of Brazil, Argentina, and Paraguay meet, Hezbollah has recruited many Muslims who left Lebanon after the 1948 Arab-Israeli war and after the 1985 Lebanese civil war. Linking with those dealing in the drug traffic in this area has proved profitable for Hezbollah, as there is much relatively ungoverned and unpatrolled area available for training camps as well as young Lebanese refugees politically vulnerable for recruitment. One of the most wanted men on the terrorist lists in Europe and the United States, Imad Mugniyah, has been identified as masterminding several terrorist attacks killing more than 100 people in Argentina from a base in this region.

Moreover, according to the U.S. Drug Enforcement Agency, links between the drug trade in Mexico and Hezbollah have been strengthening in recent years. Hezbollah relies on the same criminal weapons smugglers, document traffickers, and transportation experts as the drug cartels, smuggling both people and, allegedly, weapons into the United States.

What are the implications of this new source of financial independence for terrorist groups and states? Is this alliance of drugs and terror a result of temporary coincidence of needs, or does it have long-term, broader, more strategic aims? It has been said that drugs could destroy the Western world; is the **unholy triangle** *of drug traffickers, terrorists, and state officials committed to the destruction of that world* just a mischance, or is it of deliberate design? How will this affect the way nations deal with drug traffic? Will there be any attempts to effect cooperation between agencies charged with combating drugs and those pledged to combating terrorism, similar to that attempted between Mexico and the United States in the mid-1990s?

CONCLUSIONS

Terrorism today is big business. No one state is wholly responsible for terrorism's scope, nor is any single individual so essential to the existence of terrorism that his or her loss would seriously diminish terrorism's spread. The continuation of terrorist attacks, in Europe, the Middle East, and now in the United States, after the collapse of the Soviet Union, has made it clear that no one state's support is essential to the survival of international terrorism. States such as the former Soviet Union made it *easier* for terrorists to network, but such support, while no longer available, is clearly not critical to the survival or the networking of many groups.

Similarly, even in the wake of U.S. attacks on Afghanistan that destroyed the physical terrain of bin Laden's camps and headquarters, terrorism by his supporters has not ended. In spite of the successful U.S. effort to eliminate bin Laden, his death did not end al-Qaeda's capability as a terrorist network. Cells within that network have continued to carry out successful attacks in many countries.

Three final points need to be made with regard to this concept of a terror network. The first has to do with the transition of terrorist organizations into "corporations." As such groups become institutionalized, in terms of formalized government contacts and offices, entrenched in the local economies of many nations, and independent of a need for sponsor financing, *terror financial networks become increasingly difficult to destroy*. Affiliates to terror finance networks begin to include government bureaucrats whose offices regularly deal with them, businesses that share joint economic interests, and communities whose livelihood depend upon their employment.

The second point is that, with the increasing contact and sharing of support between terrorists, *there is a potential for greater sophistication in the carrying out of terrorist acts*. Terrorists operating in a foreign country, if they are able to avail themselves of the local expertise of indigenous groups, can carry out more efficient operations.

The final point is that, after the September 11 attacks on the United States, *a concerted effort has begun worldwide to infiltrate the network of terrorism,* particularly but not exclusively that of al-Qaeda. The United States began to use a Foreign Terrorist Asset Tracking Center (FTAT), designed to dismantle terrorists' financial bases. The FTAT examines terrorist organizations worldwide, not just pinpointing financial data relating to a single crime. The information gathered will be used to identify and disrupt terrorists' funding, according to U.S. officials.

In this effort to cut off sources for terrorist funding, some Islamic charities have been impacted. Nada Management, founded in 1987 under the name Al Taqwa, is one of the world's largest financial institutions dedicated to Muslim clients and Islamic business activities. Organizations such as Nada Management have offices in scores of countries, some of which may see no justification for the legal crackdown on these funds.

But Italy has deployed a new 600-strong multidisciplinary force to investigate the finances of al-Qaeda and other terrorist groups. In September 2001, the United States released a list of 88 groups and individuals it suspects of aiding al-Qaeda. In at least nine countries, law enforcement officials made concerted efforts to freeze millions of dollars in assets and shut off affiliates of two groups that the United States accused of bankrolling al-Qaeda's terrorist activities.

Police in Italy raided the homes of Youssef M. Nada and Ali Ghaleb Himmat, top executives of Nada Management, whose offices in nearby Lugano, Switzerland, were searched. Both men were detained for questioning and released; both are members of the Muslim Brotherhood, a fundamentalist group whose long struggle to establish an Islamic state in Egypt could make it a natural ally for the Egyptian Islamic Jihad, with which al-Qaeda has networked.

Since the September 11 attacks, governments across the globe have frozen some $140 million in terrorists' assets, but terrorist groups have thus far adapted fairly well to remain financially intact. In an effort to broaden attempts to financially disrupt the "industry" of terrorism, governments have engaged in an increasingly wider range of options, including overt as well as covert actions. These efforts to disrupt terror financing have revealed an important counterterror point: Tracking terrorists' financial footprints can thwart attacks, as well as disrupt the logistical and financial support networks, and identify operatives not known to authorities.

While these efforts to break up terrorist support networks are certainly an encouraging development, the ability to do so effectively remains unproven. On the other hand, terrorists have clearly demonstrated in recent years that they can survive the loss of support states and can even internationalize and establish diverse funding structures quite effectively. In spite of the Convention for the Suppression of the Financing of Terrorism, drafted before September 11 but now fully operational, terrorism remains, essentially, a thriving international business.

DISCUSSION

Consider two examples of both the networking of terrorism and its impact on the states supporting its practice:

1. On December 22, 2001, Robert Reid, a British citizen, was restrained by passengers on a Paris-to-Miami American Airlines flight after flight attendants noticed a burning smell and found him using matches in an attempt to ignite his sneakers. Preliminary FBI tests on the shoes detected the presence of two compounds—pentaerythritol tetranitrate, one of the most powerful bases of plastic explosives, and triacetone triperoxide, another explosive compound. According to reports, Reid was the son of Jamaican and British parents, and had converted to Islam recently. He was networking with individuals in Europe to aid in his efforts to follow the dictates of holy war as a suicide bomber.
2. Two states, Libya and Syria, who were sponsors of terrorism in other states, supporting terrorist training camps and providing havens for leaders and financiers of such groups, were accused in 2011 of carrying out acts of internal state terrorism against their own people. As the Arab Spring spawned demands for democratic change across the region, these two states were the only two openly willing to engage in ruthless suppression of their own people. Libya's leader, Qadhafi, was indicted by the ICC for these crimes.

The networking of terrorism, including the funding, the training, and the willingness of people from very diverse backgrounds to cooperate to carry out terrorist attacks, raises many concerns for the nations seeking to secure themselves from terrorist attacks. As the events of September 11 graphically demonstrated, terrorist activities are global in reach—in nationality of perpetrators and in sophistication. The ability to cope depends on the degree to which one is able to understand and predict. As the scope of individuals and nations involved in carrying out attacks broadens, can states adequately predict and thereby protect themselves against future attacks by terrorists trained, armed, and carrying how-to manuals?

For states, a willingness to condone, or even support, acts of terror may generate in the state a willingness to actually carry out acts of terror against their own people. Terrorism was rejected by the international community, after much intense deliberation, even in times of warfare, as being illegal and unjustifiable. Any state which condones or supports the use by another individual or group of such methods of attack weakens its own ability to maintain a rule of law when confronted with threats to the regime. Syria and Libya offer sobering examples of this potential threat.

ANALYSIS CHALLENGE

Terrorism is truly international today, with groups existing all over the world and cells of many groups found in different countries. Go to the *Washington Post* website (http://www.washingtonpost.com/wp-dyn/world/issues/terrordata/) and choose a group, or a nation, and "map" the group's activities. You might also consider using the Community Walk website (http://www.communitywalk.com/africa/terrorist_groups/map/181855) to consider making a map of a particular region, indicating the groups that operate within it.

KEY TERMS

networking   111
strategic planning   112
international terrorism
   congress   112
revolutionary taxes
   114

fedayeen   116
fighting fund   116
hawala   117
Shura   121
netwar   122
chain networks   123

hub or star
   networks   123
all-channel network
   123
narco-terrorism   125
unholy triangle   126

SUGGESTED READINGS AND RESOURCES

Adams, James. *The Financing of Terrorism.* New York: Simon & Schuster, 1986.

American Foreign Policy Council. *Confronting Terrorism Financing.* Lanham, MD: University Press of America, 2005.

Arquilla, John, David Ronfeldt, and Michele Zanini. "Networks, Netwar, and Information-Age Terrorism." In *Terrorism and Counterterrorism: Understanding the New Security Environment,* eds. Russell D. Howard and Reid L. Sawyer. Guilford, CT: McGraw-Hill, 2003.

Ehrenfeld, Rachel. *Funding Evil: How Terrorism Is Financed—and How to Stop It.* Santa Monica, CA: Bonus Books, April 2005.

Gunaratna, Rohan. *Inside Al-Qaeda: Global Network of Terror.* New York: Columbia University Press, 2002.

Katzman, Kenneth. *CRS Report for Congress: Al Qaeda: Profile and Threat Assessment.* August 17, 2005.

Laqueur, Walter. *The New Terrorism: Fanaticism and the Arms of Mass Destruction.* Oxford: Oxford University Press, 1999.

McCormick, Gordon H. *The Shining Path and the Future of Peru.* Santa Monica, CA: The Rand Corporation, 1990.

Napoleoni, Loretta. *Terror Incorporated: Tracing the Dollars Behind the Terror Networks.* New York: Seven Stories Press, 2005.

Trinkunas, Harold, and Jeanne Giraldo, eds. *Terrorism Financing and State Response: A Comparative Perspective.* Palo Alto, CA: Stanford University Press, 2007.

NOTES

1. James Adams, *Financing of Terrorism* (New York: Simon & Schuster, 1986), 16.
2. When French police moved in to capture Carlos at his headquarters, he escaped in a spectacular shoot-out, during which he killed two French police officers. For further information and commentary, see Thomas P. Raynor, *Terrorism* (New York: Franklin Watts, 1982).
3. Walter Laqueur, *The Age of Terrorism* (Boston: Little, Brown, 1987), 290. Laqueur describes both the participants and the agenda of this congress in some detail.
4. "Iran Hosting Global Terrorist Conference," *WorldNetDaily.com*, February 20, 2004. http://www.worldnetdaily.com/news/article.asp?ARTICLE_ID=37000 (accessed September 8, 2007).
5. Adam Cohen, "How Bin Laden Funds His Network," *Time*, October 1, 2001, 63.
6. Adams, *Financing of Terrorism*, 107.
7. Marvin Scott, "What Is the PLO Worth?" *Parade Magazine*, September 21, 1986, 17.
8. Adams, *Financing of Terrorism*, 73.
9. Interview given to al-Wast, March 11, 1996. http://www.mehr.org/iran_terrorism. htm (accessed September 8, 2007).
10. Frank C. Urbancic, Principal Deputy Coordinator for Counterterrorism. Testimony Before the House Committee on International Relations, Subcommittee on International Terrorism and Nonproliferation and Subcommittee on Middle East and Central Asia. Washington, DC. September 28, 2006. http://www.state.gov/s/ct/rls/rm/2006/73352.htm (accessed September 8, 2007).
11. Statement of Lee S. Wolosky to the National Commission on Terrorist Attacks Upon the United States, April 1, 2003.
12. Don van Natta, Jr., "Running Terrorism as a Business," *New York Times*, November 11, 2001, A1.
13. Judith Miller and Jeff Gerth, "Trade in Honey Is Said to Provide Money and Cover for bin Laden," *New York Times*, October 11, 2001, A3.
14. Greg Bruno, "Al-Qaeda's Financial Pressures." Council on Foreign Relations. February 1, 2010, at http://www.cfr.org/terrorist-organizations/al-qaedas-financial-pressures/p21347.
15. Charles J. Hanley, "Reborn Terrorist 'Armies' Target NATO," *Winston-Salem Journal* (April 9, 1986): 1.
16. Douglas Jehl, "Egyptian Doctor Believed to Be Bin Laden's No. 2," *New York Times*, September 24, 2001, 1.
17. John Arquilla, David Ronfeldt, and Michele Zanini, "Networks, Netwar, and Information-Age Terrorism," in *Terrorism and Counterterrorism: Understanding the New Security Environment*, ed. Russell D. Howard and Reid L. Sawyer (Guilford, CT: McGraw-Hill, 2003), 101.
18. "Terror's New Wave," *Time*, October 28, 2002, 28.
19. Jonathan Schanzer, *Al-Qaeda's Armies: Middle East Affiliate Groups & the Next Generation of Terror*. Interview by Jamie Glazov, FrontPageMagazine.com, March 3, 2005. Accessed on September 8, 2007.
20. *U.S. News & World Report*, May 4, 1987, 17.
21. Scott, "What Is the PLO Worth?" 8.
22. "Narcotics: Terror's New Ally," *U.S. News & World Report*, May 4, 1987, 37.

Terrorist Training

So in the Libyan fable it is told
That once an eagle, stricken with a dart,
Said, when he saw the fashioning of the shaft, "With our own
feathers, not by others' hands, Are we now smitten."

—*Aeschylus*

The networking of terrorism, including the funding, the training, and the willingness of people from very diverse backgrounds to cooperate to carry out terrorist attacks, raises many concerns for the nations seeking to secure themselves from terrorist attacks. As the events of September 11, 2001, graphically demonstrated, terrorist activities are global in reach, in nationality of perpetrators, and in sophistication. The ability to cope depends on the degree to which one is able to understand and predict. As the scope of individuals and nations involved in carrying out attacks broadens, can states adequately predict and thereby protect themselves against future attacks by terrorists who are increasingly transnational in arms and training?

THE "HOW" QUESTIONS

Thus far we have noted who is likely to become a terrorist, who supports a person's decision to become a terrorist, and for what purposes a person might resort to terrorism. We have, in part, attempted to answer the *who* questions (who becomes a terrorist and who supports him or her) and some of the *why* questions. Elements of the *where* questions—relating to where terrorists operate and where they are trained—have also been discussed.

There remains a need to discuss the important question of *how* terrorists operate. How are they trained—at what sites and on what topics? How are they equipped, in terms of weapons available to them? How do they tend to operate—that is, what tactics do they choose and why do they choose to use or not use certain weapons? How do they select their targets?

Some of these *how* questions can be answered simply by listing the important points. Others, such as those relating to the type of weaponry available to contemporary terrorists, require considerable explanation. None of these questions needs to be answered in depth here, for two reasons. One is that this is, at best, a cursory look at terrorism, a brief sketch of only a few of the points relating to this complicated subject. The other is that just as terrorism is itself in considerable flux today, so the lists of training sites and topics of today's terrorists may well be inadequate for understanding and predicting the actions of tomorrow's terrorist. The topics and tactics are unlikely to become obsolete, but the list may well expand as the twenty-first century unfolds.

TRAINING SITES

Until the final decade in the twentieth century, more than a dozen nations were offering training camps for terrorists. The list of such countries included Algeria, Bulgaria, Cuba, Czechoslovakia, East Germany, Hungary, Iran, Iraq, Lebanon, Libya, North Korea, the People's Republic of China, South Yemen, Syria, and the USSR. Since many of these countries operated the training facilities within the structure of their own military services, it was difficult to designate such facilities as "terrorist training camps" with any accuracy.

Some nations were more discrete than others in the training opportunities they provided. Moreover, information concerning such camps necessarily came from some national intelligence services, meaning that the information was certainly biased according to how that nation defined terrorism. It is unlikely, for instance, that such an intelligence assessment would list "friendly" nations as hosts for terrorist camps, instead citing such camps as training sources for legitimate insurgent or revolutionary groups.

In addition, the dramatic changes that occurred in the world in the early 1990s seriously impacted the ability of states to offer training, arms, or specific support to terrorist groups. Of the states on the current list of those with training sites, only a few offered significant levels of training and support in the 1990s, and fewer still in the first decade of the twenty-first century. Iran remains a major supporter, providing weapons, funds, and training primarily to Hezbollah and HAMAS. Iraq, however, after the US-led invasion in 2003, is not a current sponsor of terrorism, although parts of it remain a safe haven to groups such as Ansar al-Islam, Al-Mahdi Army, and al-Qaeda in Iraq.

Nations such as Syria and North Korea became similarly unable or unwilling to openly offer terrorist training and support after 1987. Although Syria continued to offer **safe haven**, or *sanctuary in which a group and its members can safely organize, plan, raise funds, communicate, recruit, and even train within the territory of the state,* to the PFLP–GC, HAMAS, the PIJ, and other groups, the training assistance and access to weapons was no longer made freely available. The political costs, lacking the shelter of a superpower, were simply too high.

Perhaps one of the most dramatic highlights of the diminishing role of states involved in providing sanctuary to terrorists came in August 1994, when the Sudanese government handed over notorious terrorist Illich Ramirez Sanchez (a.k.a. "Carlos"). Carlos was given sanctuary in the Sudan in 1993, but was peacefully handed over to French authorities one year later. Open sanctuary to internationally known terrorists is obviously a less attractive policy option today.

Afghanistan became a base for several radical Islamic organizations under the rule of the Taliban in the 1990s. While al-Qaeda was the largest of these organizations, recruiting individuals from Pakistan, Afghanistan, Saudi Arabia, and throughout the world, other groups, including Al-Jihad, Lashkar-e-Jhangvi, Islamic Group, Armed Islamic Group, Harkak-ul-Mujahideen, and the Islamic Movement of Uzbekistan, also enjoyed the ability to operate openly in this country.

Pakistan also remains a staging ground and planning center for Islamic extremist groups operating in South Asia. In the wake of Operation Enduring Freedom (the UN-mandated effort to end the use of Afghanistan as a base for terrorism), a large number of those fleeing Afghanistan are found refuge in neighboring Pakistan. Indeed, Pakistan's secret service (ISS) has been accused of training and funding several Islamic terrorist groups operating in India's Kashmir province. Groups using Pakistan as a training base include al-Qaeda, Lashkar-e-Taiba, Jaish-e-Muhammad, Lashkar-e-Jhangvi, Al Badr, Harkat ul-Ansar, Hizb-ul-Mujahideen, and the Muslim United Army.

As Table 7.1 indicates, training camps for terrorists today are less likely to be openly state funded, but are often located in states where no government controls all of the territory effectively or in states where the governments will permit the establishment of such camps but do not staff or support them. Instead, as noted in Chapter 6, individuals and groups with funding and leadership are establishing camps in these countries, with often no more than the tacit consent of the state.

TABLE 7.1		
Some Terrorist Training Camps Identified After the Cold War		
Country	Camp Location	Additional Information
Iran	Many locations	Had at least 20 military camps run by the Islamic Revolutionary Guards to train in terrorist tactics
Iraq	Ramadi Salman Pak	Suspected biological/chemical weapons facility
Afghanistan	Impossible to identify all, but significant ones at:	
	Khalden	Open from Soviet invasion until 2000; closed by Taliban

(*continued*)

Country	Camp Location	Additional Information
	Al-Farouq	Most Guantánamo detainees allegedly trained here, training on all types of weapons; each session about 1 month long
	Derunta	Bomb-making; possible training in WMDs
	Tarnak Farms	One of bin Laden's homes, turned into training facility
Algeria		Offered arms training, funding, safe haven, diplomatic, and passport assistance
Syria/Lebanon	Bekaa Valley, various locations	
Bosnia-Herzegovina	Fojnica (suburb of Sarajevo)	
Greece	Euboea (island northeast of Athens)	
India	Near Mumbai	
Pakistan	Numerous, along border with Afghanistan	
Somalia	17 identified camps, including Center of Operations in Mogadishu	

After the September 11 attacks, information surfaced about terrorist training camps in Afghanistan established by al-Qaeda under bin Laden's leadership and funding. Islamic militants from more than 40 countries have received training in these camps, which the Taliban permitted to operate for years. U.S. bombing attacks in the fall of 2001 devastated many of these facilities. Although such attacks were aggressive acts of war in the territory of another state, the United States declared, and the international community in UN debates agreed, that the willingness of a state to allow the training of terrorists in its territory made that government's leadership responsible for the actions of the camps' trainees. Since the Taliban refused to help close the camps and turn over the al-Qaeda leadership, including bin Laden, to U.S.-led forces,[1] the destruction of the camps was argued to be a legal means to end a form of state support for terrorism.

Unfortunately, terrorist camps of the sort built in the mountains of Afghanistan were not buildings, but were caves that had existed for centuries and were merely reinforced and used to harbor the training facilities. Thus, the bombs certainly made the use of those particular caves as terrorist camps impossible but did not necessarily cost the terrorist leadership much in terms of lost facilities. Indications initially were that most personnel had fled in relative safety to neighboring states, possibly to regroup and rebuild in another passive host state.

The discussion thus far, and the lists of states with supported training camps, imply that such camps exist today only in certain regions or in a small number of states. But camps for terrorist training are being discovered all over the world, even in the heartland of democracies such as the United States and the United Kingdom. Since these democracies also have diverse populations and great freedom of association, this should not be a surprise—but it has shocked many.

CASE STUDY 7.1

Terrorist Camps in the United Kingdom and the United States

In the course of a four-year investigation, which culminated in trials in 2008, security officials in England discovered that national parks in the Lake District of northern England; the New Forest in the south; and peaceful corners of the southern counties of Berkshire, Kent, and East Sussex were used for training camps for radical Islamic extremists. The officials, during the course of the trials of the seven members of the group, indicated that hundreds of men—including a gang that made a failed attempt to bomb London's transit network—participated in the camps, which were set up across the quiet countryside. As the international news media reported, "Clad in mud-smeared combat fatigues, the young Muslims trained on picturesque British farmland, hurling imaginary grenades, wielding sticks as mock rifles and chopping watermelons in simulated beheadings."[2]

A video stolen from the camp by an undercover police officer showed recruits marching with backpacks (similar to those used by London's transit network attackers to carry their suicide bombs in 2005) and conducting weapons drills used by insurgents in Iraq and Afghanistan. In fact, the group of North African men who made an unsuccessful attempt to bomb London's transit network on July 21, 2005 (two weeks after the July 7 subway and bus attacks that killed 52 commuters), met and were trained at one of these camps.

The leaders of the camps were two London-based "preachers"—Atilla Ahmet, a longtime aid of radical cleric Abu Hamza al-Masri, and Mohammad Hamid. Hamid, originally from Tanzania, selected recruits from mainstream mosques, inviting them to his home for meetings and then choosing a few to attend the camps. Ahmet's friend al-Masri is an Egyptian whom the United States was, at the time of the

(continued)

trials for these camp leaders, trying to have extradited for his alleged plan to set up terrorist training camps in Oregon.

In May 2009, Oussama Abdullah Kassir was found guilty of charges related to his participation in an attempt to establish a jihad training camp in Bly, Oregon. The Bly jihad training camp was created as a place where Muslims could receive various types of training, according to trial records, including military-style training and the stockpiling of weapons and ammunition.

Kassir was apparently sent from London by Abu Hamza in late 1999 to help with this camp. He had, however, been trained at an al-Qaeda camp in Pakistan and demonstrated his jihad training at a mosque in Seattle, Washington, including lessons on how to assemble and disassemble an AK-47 and how to alter such a gun to launch a grenade. Trial records indicate that Kassir also possessed a compact disc with instructions on how to make bombs and poisons. Kassir is a Lebanese national and a citizen of Sweden, a truly transnational terrorist training camp leader. ■

Source: The Heritage Foundation, retrieved October 17, 2011, from http://www.heritage.org/research/reports/2009/10/islamist-terrorist-plots-in-great-britain-uncovering-the-global-network

TRAVELING TRAINING CAMPS

With the loss of training camps in Afghanistan from U.S.-led attacks in late 2001, al-Qaeda began to establish a **traveling terrorist training camp** system, *a system in which individual instructors offer skills classes at different locations, essentially generating mobile classrooms for terrorists to finalize their weapons skills.* Although this organization had developed a proficient use of the Internet to share training manuals, it still needed hands-on training, particularly for the use of explosives and for the art of bomb-making. Within a year, some of these training courses were reestablished in remote areas along the border between Afghanistan and Pakistan.

Al-Qaeda leaders became proficient at offering quick and covert courses for Afghans, Pakistanis, and others from the region, teaching classes in bomb-making and other operations. While the U.S. Central Intelligence Agency (CIA) and the Pakistani police inflicted some casualties when they caught courses as they met, the mobile class approach appears to be still operational. This concept has, in fact, spread through Southeast Asia, and possibly Europe and the United States, although these latter areas are not yet clearly established, as the need for truly remote areas for the testing of student bomb-making skills is more difficult to meet.

The capture of some of the traveling instructors of terrorist tactics has perhaps diminished the supply, but the classes continue to be offered. While the training system's use of mobile camps does not seem to have trained the thousands who were processed by the camps in Afghanistan prior to the events of September 11, it is reasonable to expect that many future terrorist attacks will be traced back to skills acquired in these mobile classrooms for terrorists who have emerged since 2001.

Terrorist groups are utilizing the accessibility, audience, and anonymity of the Internet to offer "training camps" to their global network. Al-Qaeda's

Al-Battar (The Sword) is an online training camp available to its cell members throughout the world. Posted on an al-Qaeda website, there is a continuing selection of editions, each of which focuses on some aspect of terrorist training. Edition nine, for example, is devoted to kidnappings and includes methods, potential targets, negotiating tactics, and directions on how to videotape the beheading of the victims and how to post these videos on the Web. This edition became available before the round of kidnappings and beheadings in Iraq in 2004.

The Revolutionary Armed Forces of Colombia has posted on its website children's games—games teaching children to play the role of terrorists, to be suicide bombers, and to assassinate political leaders. HAMAS, in Palestine, also has a children's section on its website, which features cartoon-type stories meant to recruit young people to join in the intifada, and to become a suicide bomber.[3]

TRAINING TOPICS: WHAT DO THEY LEARN AT CAMP?

In 2001, four people were convicted by a New York court for their roles in the August 1998 bombing of the American embassies in Kenya and Tanzania, a double atrocity that cost 224 lives and apparently took five years to plan. From this case, and a separate hearing in New York on the conspiracy by a group of Algerians to set off a suitcase bomb at Los Angeles airport at the turn of the millennium, evidence emerged about what is taught at training camps today.

One witness, who gave evidence for the prosecution, disclosed that he had received six months of training at a camp in Afghanistan in 1998. He, along with volunteers from many other places, including Algeria, Jordan, Yemen, Saudi Arabia, France, and Chechnya, was trained in how to blow up the infrastructure of a country, including "airports, railroads, and large corporations."[4] They were also taught how to wage urban warfare by blocking roads, storming buildings, and assassinating individuals.

Terrorists do not go to training camps just to acquire arms, intelligence information, or funding. At most such camps they undergo a rigorous program of activities to gain proficiency in a variety of skills. A brief, though not exhaustive, review of some of the topics taught at these training camps provides useful insights into the type of tactics that terrorists employ in their ventures.

Such a review also yields a better understanding of the depth and breadth of the training available to terrorists today. In fact, many terrorists are more highly trained in a wider array of tactics than the police forces of the nations whose task, often times, is to combat terrorism.

Arson and Bombs

Since about 50 percent of all terrorist incidents involve bombings, this ranks as one of the most prevalent and most popular training topics. Terrorists are, as a rule, taught how to make and use two types of bombs: explosive and incendiary. **Explosive bombs** are *generally of either fragmentation or blast type*. The most commonly utilized fragmentation bomb at these camps is the pipe bomb, usually employing gunpowder as the explosive agent. Terrorists are taught how to use commercial- or military-type dynamite with a blasting cap for detonation in the creation and use of blast-type bombs.

Information about camps in Afghanistan yielded useful insights into the training in bombs. The "Encyclopedia of Jihad," for example, gave directions in Arabic paired with diagrams for a host of explosive devices, including instructions on how to turn a wide range of common objects, such as hairbrushes, radios, and whistles, into lethal devices. According to experts who reviewed portions of the information on explosives, the writers had obviously gotten their hands on, among other things, U.S. special forces manuals, training guides the CIA produced in the late 1950s and early 1960s, and other explosives literature available from Paladin Press, the militia's favorite guide to weaponry and guerrilla tactics.[5]

Terrorists are also taught how to create and use incendiary bombs, as such bombs are quickly and easily constructed. **Incendiary bombs** are simply *fire bombs, generating extensive fire damage.* These are also inexpensive yet capable of inflicting extensive damage. Terrorists are often taught, for instance, how to make a simple fire bomb, consisting of a glass bottle filled with an inflammable mixture, to which a fuse is attached. Fire bombs can vary in sophistication from time-delay fused and barometric bombs to fertilizer mixed with fuel oil. The bomb blast in Oklahoma City in 1995 was clearly the latter type of incendiary bomb, simple in construction but incredibly destructive.

Not every training camp offers instruction on all such bombs, nor is every trainee instructed in the construction and use of all bomb types. **Plastic explosives,** *made of plastique,* are the newest additions to the weapons for which terrorists may receive training in camps. Access to such material is supposedly restricted, but Libya's stockpile of the plastique Semtex made it possible for terrorists to use this more sophisticated explosive, which is virtually undetectable by most modern airport security devices.

Assassination and Ambush Techniques

Terrorists are usually taught how to penetrate personal security systems in order to kill at close range. They are instructed in the proficient use of handguns and silencers. Methods of clandestine approach, disguise, and escape are generally incorporated into this part of every terrorist's training. Increasingly, modern terrorists are instructed in the commission of flamboyant, execution-style assassinations, instead of the unobtrusive-gunman-in-a-crowd techniques favored previously. The assassination in 2007 of former prime minister Benazir Bhutto at an election rally in Rawalpindi, Pakistan, offers clear evidence of this trend.

Extortion and Kidnapping for Ransom

Contemporary training courses for terrorists often include information on how to raise money for indigent terrorist groups. Among the instructions offered in this part of the curriculum is information on how to extort money from wealthy sources, usually the families or employers of kidnap victims.

In the 1970s, this was a source of considerable wealth, particularly for groups operating in Central or South America. U.S. firms in these areas were at first willing to pay large sums for the safe return of their kidnapped executives. However, during the 1980s, businesses began making it a formal part of their policy *not* to submit to ransom demands. As a result, kidnapping for ransom money became, for a time, a less profitable enterprise.

In the 1980s, terrorists were trained in the use of kidnap victims for the extortion of *political* rewards or concessions as well as money. Although many governments have a stated policy of not conceding to terrorist extortion demands, most have from time to time found it expedient to yield rather than allow a kidnap situation to drag on indefinitely or to end disastrously.

Events in the Philippines, however, particularly the actions of the Abu Sayyaf Group during the late 1990s, give credence to the credible and profitable use by terrorist groups of this tactic, at least to the kidnapping of tourists for ransom. Libya's payment of a ransom in 2000 for an international group of tourists held by this organization made this clearly a low-risk, high-profit operation.

Disguise Techniques, Clandestine Travel, Recruitment, and Communications

Terrorists today are trained in many of the same techniques the counterintelligence services utilize. They are taught methods of **disguise techniques** and **clandestine travel**, including *how to travel inconspicuously* (contrary to popular media images, an Arab engaged in a terrorist attack does *not* routinely wear a burnoose, nor does he or she travel by camel). Instruction is also given in *the procuring of false passport and identification papers,* and in *the skill of altering one's appearance to permit one to slip through surveillance nets.*

The trainees are taught how to blend in with the country in which they will operate. As one official speaking of a cell uncovered by the French put it, "They all carefully applied the technique taught in Afghan camps: act, look, talk and dress like the impious and corrupt people around, in order to better plan the blow against them."[6]

With training like this, the people who carry out terrorist attacks are most often those you would never suspect, the handful of "sleepers," *agents recruited, trained, sent to blend in unnoticed, but not put into operation for a period of time.* Hiding among millions of potential suspects and victims, such sleepers, if well trained in blending in, may evade security systems for years, as some of those who carried out the September 11 attacks clearly did.

Most terrorists are also trained in the techniques of **recruitment**, as all terrorist groups must seek to *draw in new members* but must constantly beware of the dangers of counterintelligence penetration. The screening and selection of potential recruits is thus a vital talent for every successful terrorist group.

Terrorists are also trained in sophisticated methods of **communication**. Recognizing the importance of *reliable and secure means of communicating during a terrorist incident,* leaders of terrorist organizations are having larger numbers of their recruits trained in the advanced technology of communication. Simple two-way radios still favored by many police forces are considered too primitive for modern terrorists.

Intelligence Collection and Counterintelligence Methods

Not surprisingly, many modern terrorists are more skilled at the collection of intelligence information than are many members of the intelligence organizations of some nations. Terrorists can now receive comprehensive training not only in the techniques of intelligence gathering but also in the equally important methods of counterintelligence operations.

Intelligence collection instruction involves teaching terrorists *how to infiltrate target areas, gather relevant data, and return that information to headquarters.* The use of codes and the translation of intelligence data bits into comprehensible information are basic to the education of today's terrorist.

Terrorists are also being taught methods of **counterintelligence,** including *how to disseminate misinformation designed to confuse their enemies.* Such instruction generally also includes information on how to *protect the organization from infiltration by police, military, and governmental intelligence operatives.*

This does not mean, of course, that all terrorists are trained in all of these methods. Most organizations can usually afford to train only a carefully selected number in the more sophisticated techniques; however, the ability of most terrorist organizations to have at least a few such skilled recruits is becoming a matter of survival. Lack of information or misinformation can seriously cripple an organization's ability to carry out a successful operation.

Weapons

This last item is by no means the least important in the repertoire acquired by terrorists in training facilities. The number and variety of **weapons** *available to terrorists through the different training camps over time certainly has varied considerably, making generalizations difficult.* Without detailing all of the weapons available to modern terrorists (which is covered in the following section), it is well to note the types of weapons for which terrorists are being trained.

In addition to being trained in the use of small firearms, including handguns, rifles, sporting and combat shotguns, and a wide range of explosives, terrorists are currently trained in the use of automatic and semiautomatic weapons. Training is regularly given in the use of machine guns and machine pistols, particularly those manufactured in the former Soviet Union, Eastern Europe, Israel, the United Kingdom, and the United States.

Training is also available in light-tank antirocket launchers, or **rocket-propelled** grenades, *a term used for any hand-held, shoulder launched anti-tank weapons capable of firing an unguided rocket equipped with an explosive warhead.* The training is focused principally on the RPG-7, RPG-26, and RPG-29; M72-LAW; and the FIM92 Stinger. Such weapons offer an easy way to deliver an explosive payload over a distance with moderate accuracy; they are also portable and relatively easy to conceal. Surface-to-air missiles (SAMs), known to be in the hands of terrorists, are part of some training programs, including those led by the United States.

There is now evidence of training being given to terrorists in the use of more exotic weapons, such as chemical or biological agents. While use of such weapons remains relatively infrequent today, the use of sarin gas by the Aum

Shinrikyo group in a Japanese subway in the mid-1990s raised the specter of vast destruction by such weapons.

The anthrax attacks in the United States following September 11 should not, therefore, have been a complete surprise to government experts, but they were. Agencies in the United States charged with responding to such a crisis were unprepared to deal with it expeditiously, giving those responsible for the attack a fairly low-cost victory in terms of the disruption of the system. Part of the problems seems to have been that these agencies were preparing to respond to a massive attack by an enemy at war who would seek destruction by the use of such a weapon. Terrorists, however, would seek only disruption, inflicting pain but not destruction—goals which the U.S. response allowed them to achieve.

The training process for terrorists appears quite comprehensive in its potential for turning out proficient terrorists. The camps created by bin Laden in Afghanistan became a kind of "university of terrorism, offering courses in murder and mayhem to which radical Islamic movements all over the world were invited."[7] The September 11 attacks on the United States demonstrated dramatically how well such training can work. No longer the gun- or knife-wielding assassins of earlier times, these men were trained to commit acts of mass destruction in sophisticated urban centers of arguably the most powerful country in the world—and they succeeded.

CASE STUDY 7.2

September 11, 2001, Attacks on the United States

In the bloodiest day on American soil since the Civil War, the United States experienced a terrorist attack in two cities, New York City and Washington, DC, which resulted in thousands of casualties and billions of dollars in damage. The events chronicled offer insight into the most devastating terrorist attack to date.

Sequence of Events

The cycle of events on September 11, 2001, began with the departure of two planes from Boston's Logan Airport. One was a Boeing 767, American Airlines Flight 11, bound for Los Angeles with 81 passengers, which took off at 7:59 A.M. and headed west over the Adirondacks before taking a sudden turn south and diving toward the heart of New York City. The second flight involved in the incident was United Airlines Flight 175, which left Boston at 7:58 A.M. Meanwhile, American Flight 77 had left Dulles Airport in Washington, DC, bound for Los Angeles, and United Flight 93 left Newark at 8:01 A.M., bound for San Francisco. Because all of these flights were transcontinental, they were heavily loaded with fuel.

At 8:45 A.M., American Airlines Flight 11 hit the World Trade Center's (WTC) north tower, ripping through the building's skin and setting its upper floors ablaze. Bits

(continued)

of plane, a tire, office furniture, glass, a hand, a leg, and whole bodies began falling all around, stunning the people in the streets who had at first assumed it was perhaps a sonic boom, or a construction accident, or at worst a dreadful airline accident. Inside the building, people began to run down the flights of stairs from the offices below the crash point. The lights stayed on, but the lower stairs were filled with water from broken pipes and sprinklers. The smell of jet fuel filled the building as hallways collapsed and flames erupted. Others leaped to their deaths from the 110-story tower as the fires trapped them in the upper floors. Pedestrians watched in horror as a man tried to shimmy down the outside of the tower, making it about three floors before flipping backward to the ground. Many escaping the tower were burned over much of their bodies.

At 7:58 A.M., United Airlines Flight 175, also a Boeing 767 filled with fuel for the transcontinental flight from Boston to Los Angeles with 65 passengers aboard, left the airport about twenty minutes behind schedule. After passing the Massachusetts–Connecticut border, it made a 30-degree turn, then an even sharper turn, and flew down through Manhattan, between the buildings, slamming into the south tower of the WTC at 9:06 A.M. The short delay at the Boston airport caused this flight to hit the WTC more than twenty minutes after the first crash, a delay that allowed time for escape from the blazing north tower.

After the initial impact in the north tower, employees ran to the windows and saw debris falling, and sheets of white building material, and bodies. As one employee, Gilbert Richard Ramirez, employed by BlueCross/BlueShield on the twentieth floor, noted, "Someone pulled an emergency alarm switch, but nothing happened. Someone else broke into the emergency phone, but it was dead. People began to say their prayers."

Stumbling out of office doors and down smoky stairs, those fleeing saw suffering on every side—people who had been badly burned, their skin appearing to be dripping or peeling from their bodies. Apparently some were thrust out of windows by the force of the blast and their bodies rained down on those below along with others who jumped to escape the inferno engulfing the building.

Each of the towers, more than 200 feet wide on each side, contained a central steel core surrounded by open office space. Eighteen-inch steel tubes ran vertically along the outside, providing much of the support for the buildings. One of the planes damaged the central core, redistributing the weight to the outer steel tubes, which were slowly deformed by the added weight and the heat of the fires. Steel starts to bend at 1,000 degrees Fahrenheit. The floors above where the second plane hit in 1 WTC—each floor weighing millions of pounds—were resting on steel that was softening from the heat of the burning jet fuel, softening until the girders could no longer bear the load. Because each floor dropped down onto the one below, the building did not topple—it came straight down, flattening all of the floors below, with all of the people trapped on those floors.

At 10:00 A.M., the sudden collapse of the south tower trapped hundreds of rescue workers and thousands of workers in the building. The debris from this collapse gutted the 4 WTC building below it. Twenty-nine minutes later, weakened by its imploded twin, the north tower collapsed, pouring more debris and crushing buildings and rescuers below. The third building to collapse was 7 WTC, which fell at 5:25 P.M.

The first crash was shocking, but the second changed everything. The event became not a dreadful accident or an isolated incident. Facing the catastrophe and the clearly demonstrated threat, the New York City systems responded with emergency plans. Traffic stopped—the bridges and tunnels in the city were shut down at 9:35 A.M. as warnings were issued. The Empire State Building, the Metropolitan Museum of Art, and the UN buildings were evacuated. The airports in New York, then Washington, and then nationwide were closed for the first time in U.S. history.

As the second plane was crashing into the south tower, President Bush was in an elementary school in Sarasota, Florida, meeting second graders. Informed of the first crash just after he arrived, news of the second plane striking the south tower came as he was watching the students' reading drills. The president continued to listen to the students, but at a news conference after his time with the students, he ordered a massive manhunt to find the people responsible for the attacks. Bomb dogs checked Air Force One—the president's plane—again, and an extra fighter escort was added.

The attacks continued in a different city: Washington, DC. At 9:40 A.M., American Airlines Flight 77 hit the Pentagon. As the jet came in, its wings wobbled and it appeared to be aimed straight for the Pentagon. The plane was about 50 feet off the ground when it came in, sounding to spectators on the ground as though the pilot had the throttle wide open. The plane rolled left and back to the right, then the edge of the wing touched down at the helicopter pad to the side of the Pentagon and the plane cartwheeled into the building.

Within minutes, a "credible threat" prompted the evacuation of the White House and eventually all of the federal office buildings, including both the State and Justice departments. Although Washington had contingency plans for emergencies, such as this, the chaos on the streets by 10:45 A.M. gave evidence that the plans needed improvement. Traffic in and around the Capitol and the government buildings was gridlocked by 11 A.M. with people trying to leave. Although most plans to evacuate government leaders, including the vice president and the Senate's president pro tempore (fourth in line to the presidency), worked fairly efficiently, most government workers were unable to escape the city. Security units had closed both the 14th Street Bridge and the Arlington Memorial Bridge, which leads past the Pentagon and into Virginia, as well as the airports and Union Station.

The aircraft carrying Federal Reserve Chairman Alan Greenspan en route from Switzerland was ordered to turn back. Greenspan, however, reached his vice chairman Roger Ferguson by phone, and Ferguson coordinated contacts with Reserve banks and governors around the country to ensure that U.S. banks would continue to function. Vice President Dick Cheney told the president, who was returning from Florida, that law enforcement and security agencies believed the White House and possibly Air Force One were targets, suggesting that Bush head to a safe military base. Air Force One made a brief touchdown at Barksdale Air Force Base outside of Shreveport, Louisiana, at 11:45 A.M., with fighter jets hovering beside each wing during the descent.

By this time a third attack had occurred as well. United Flight 93, which had taken off from Newark, New Jersey, headed for San Francisco, took a sudden, violent left turn as it passed south of Cleveland, Ohio, and headed back into Pennsylvania. Although air-traffic controllers tried frantically to raise the crew via radio as the plane and its 38 passengers passed Pittsburgh, there was no response from the plane. At 9:58 A.M., the Westmoreland County emergency-operations

(continued)

center, 35 miles southeast of Pittsburgh, received a frantic cell phone call from a man who said he was locked in the restroom aboard United Flight 93 and who repeated frantically, "We are being hijacked!"

Many citizens later reported having cell phone messages from loved ones on the plane, who described the planned efforts of the passengers to thwart the hijackers' intent, if possible. The plane flew over woodland, pastures, and cornfields, crashing into a reclaimed section of an old coal strip mine at 10:06 A.M., barely two miles short of the Shanksville-Stonycreek School with its 501 students.

Insights into Those Responsible

At Dulles International Airport in Virginia, two polite young men of Arab origin handed over their prepaid $2,400 each first-class tickets to the American Airlines agent. Both men appeared to be around 20 years of age, had valid identification, and gave the right answers to standard security questions. The two brothers, Nawaq Alhamzi and Salem Alhamzi, boarded American Airlines Flight 77 for Los Angeles. They were two of the nineteen men who hijacked the four planes on September 11.

The real names of those 19 involved were not immediately known, since intelligence officials found that many used false identities. On American Airlines Flight 11, which crashed into the north tower of the WTC, Mohamed Atta al-Sayed, Satam Al Suqami, Waleed M. Alshehri, Wail Alshehri, and Abdulaziz Alomari were the names of those who carried out the hijacking. Hani Hanjour, Khalid Al-Midhar, Majed Moqed, Nawaq Alhamzi, and Salem Alhamzi carried out the hijacking on American Airlines Flight 77, which crashed into the Pentagon. Aboard United Airlines Flight 175, Marwan Al-Shehhi, Hamza Alghamdi, Ahmed Alghamdi, Fayez Ahmed, and Mohald Alshehri hijacked the plane and crashed it into the south tower of the WTC. Only four have been identified as being aboard the flight that crashed in Pennsylvania, United Airlines Flight 93: Ziad Jarrahi, Ahmed Alnami, Ahmed Alhaznawi, and Saeed Alghamdi.

As investigators and intelligence services worldwide rushed to trace the movements of these 19 men, it became increasingly clear that they were part of a much larger network and that years of planning had been a part of this operation. Hani Hanjour, for example, may have lived in Arizona since 1990. He took flight lessons nearby in 1996 and 1997. Nawaq Alhamzi joined him later at this location. Nawaq and Khalid Al-Midhar lived together in San Diego, California, from 1999 to 2000 and took a few flying lessons from a school close to their home. From July 2000 until September 2001, Mohamed Atta and Marwan Al-Shehhi traveled around South Florida, taking flying lessons and meeting accomplices. All five Flight 175 hijackers and some of those on Flight 93 appear to have lived in Delray Beach, Florida, and in nearby Deerfield Beach during the summer of 2001.

U.S. authorities believe Mohamed Atta was the ringleader of the 19 hijackers, but that he was working under the direction of someone from the network of Osama bin Laden and his al-Qaeda organization. The 19 blended in well with their American neighbors, living in inexpensive apartments, eating pizzas, wearing khakis and polos, and working out at local gyms. Experts think that it cost at least several thousand dollars to carry out the attack and that the money for both the attack and the support network for the agents in place came from bin Laden's resources.

This whole operation demonstrated to the world that terrorists were indeed capable of performing carefully planned, brilliantly executed, relatively low-cost attacks. Reconnaissance, timing, and planning were clearly techniques with which terrorists were becoming increasingly familiar. In time, an increasingly sophisticated arsenal of weapons would make such an attack many times more lethal. ∎

Source: Report of the 9/11 Commission, available at http://www.9-11commission.gov/report/index.htm

POTENTIAL FOR DESTRUCTION: A TERRORIST'S ARSENAL

Before examining the tactics chosen by trained terrorists, it is appropriate to look briefly at the arsenal of weapons and tactics available to the terrorist today. In training camps, individuals and groups are not only given exposure to a wide range of weapons but are also taught different tactics for the use of these weapons. Explosives, guns, and computers are tools with great diversity in potential use by camp members, with expert training.

Explosives

As noted earlier, terrorists worldwide continue to use explosives, frequently in the form of homemade devices. These are most often blast rather than fragmentation bombs. Explosives "offer many advantages to a terrorist: they are available everywhere and crude bombs can be fabricated locally; they are concealable and can be readily disguised so that X-ray and magnometer inspections are ineffective defenses."[8] Also note that the planes flown in the September 11 attacks were themselves fully fueled "bombs" flown into their targets with devastating results—and the terrorists did not have to smuggle bombs aboard the planes.

The destructive quality of bombs does not depend necessarily on the sophistication of their construction. Trucks packed with forms of TNT have created substantial damage and caused innumerable deaths. One truck laden with fertilizer and gasoline in Oklahoma City in 1995 destroyed a federal building and left hundreds of casualties, dead or injured.

The ability of a small amount of explosive to create a large amount of damage has been enhanced by terrorists using the **shaped-charge principle,** *focusing the force of the explosion in a desired direction.* Terrorists have shown themselves to be proficient in the use of both conical or "beehive" bombs (which increase the charge's penetration), and linear bombs, which have a "cutting" effect.

A new version of an old type of explosive has recently emerged, one dubbed as an **improvised explosive device,** or IED. An IED *is a homemade bomb, designed to maim or kill an enemy, typically thrown or left concealed on the side of a road.* These devices can be made using various household chemicals of the right combustible combinations, and can be put in paper bags, cardboard boxes, or more resilient containers, such as steel pipes, and can be set off by a timer or something as common as a cell phone. U.S.

security forces as well as local law enforcement and civilians in Iraq have been victims of these modern versions of the Molotov cocktail.[9]

Improvised Explosive Devices

The conflicts in Iraq and Afghanistan have highlighted the use of rapidly increasing use of IEDs by insurgents and terrorists—insurgents in attacks on military opposition forces and terrorists in attacks on civilian markets and checkpoints. An IED is, as its name suggests, a homemade device designed to cause death or injury by using explosives alone or in combination with other materials. These devices can be made in varying sizes, functioning methods, containers, and delivery methods, using commercial or military explosives, homemade explosives, or military ordinance components. There is much potential diversity since the IED builder will have used whatever materials are at hand to make the bomb, and generally using one of three types of structures: package-type IEDs; vehicle-borne IEDs; and person-borne, or suicide bomb, IEDs.

Package-type IEDs have been used extensively in terrorist attacks in Iraq, and with increasing frequency in Afghanistan. Such devices have been thrown from overpasses or in front of approaching vehicles or placed in potholes and covered with dirt. Artillery shells have been rigged to detonate as IEDs, sometimes hidden in bags along roads or in plaster shaped to look like a concrete block. Some are command detonated, either by wire or by a remote device; others are designed to be time-delay detonations, set off using cordless phones from vehicles or vantage points. These simple but lethal devices can kill and injure people in vehicles or walking by the road, standing in markets or traveling in armored cars.

A **vehicle-borne IED (VBIED)** uses a vehicle as the package or container of the explosive device. These IEDs vary by type, from small cars to large cargo trucks, even donkey-drawn carts and ambulances. VBIEDs generally carry from 100 lbs to 1,000 lbs of explosives. One technique using this type of IED, seen with increasing frequency in Iraq in 2007–2008, involves the use of other vehicles in the attack. A lead vehicle is used as either a decoy or a barrier breaker, which, when it is stopped or destroyed, draws opposition forces in to inspect the damage. The VBIED follows the lead vehicle, driving into the crowd of forces before detonating, causing more casualties among those gathered around the decoy.

A suicide or **person-borne IED (PBIED)** constitutes a singularly difficult threat to civilians and soldiers, since such a bomb generally uses a high-explosive wrapped with potential fragmentary objects and is detonated by a switch or button held by the person wearing the device. These devices are often contained in a vest, belt, or other article of clothing modified to carry the explosives and to conceal them. This makes detection and defense extremely difficult but absolutely mandatory, as failure to detect will give time for the carrier to detonate, but presumed detection and use of lethal force without certainty may result in the murder of an unarmed civilian. ■

Review of a few examples of the use of different types of bombs by terrorist groups indicates that the use of such weapons is becoming common throughout the world and that such attacks are extremely lethal.

December 1988, Lockerbie, Scotland. Pan Am Flight 103 exploded by a bomb, killing over 200 people. Responsibility for planning and support for the bombing was traced to Libya, Iran, and Syria.

August 1995, Oklahoma City. A truck bomb at a federal building injured or killed hundreds, including children in a day care center. A member of a militia group was charged with the crime.

September 11, 2001, United States. Two airplanes were flown into the WTC in New York City; another was flown into the Pentagon in Washington, DC. More than 4,000 people were killed in these attacks.

April 2004, Madrid, Spain. Bombs exploded in train stations, killing hundreds of commuters and wounding many more. Muslim extremists linked with al-Qaeda were arrested and brought to trial.

July 7, 2005, London, England. Three bombs exploded in subways, with a fourth detonating an hour later in a double-decker bus. Fifty-two people were killed, and more than 700 injured. Four Muslim men, British citizens, each detonated one of the bombs.

July 11, 2006, Mumbai, India. A series of bombs exploded in commuter trains, killing 209 and wounding 714 civilians. Muslim extremists were responsible.

July 22, 2011, Oslo, Norway. A bombing attack in Oslo killed 7 people, but an attack by the same individual that day killed another at least 87, in an ambush on a youth camp on island close to the capital. A religious white-supremacist zealot was responsible.

This does not, of course, detail all of the bombings that occurred in the recent years. It is intended only to demonstrate the wide range of bombs used, the variety of targets chosen, and the global nature of the utilization of this tactic.

Assassinations and Ambushes

Targets for assassinations and ambushes have been selected both for their publicity and their symbolic value. This tactic, since it requires an element of surprise, usually involves careful planning and execution. Assassins and their victims come in all shapes and sizes. Although government officials make attractive targets, a variety of others have come under assassin gunfire. Note in the following brief list the diversity of targets.

1981: Anwar el-Sadat, president of Egypt, is assassinated. Egyptian Islamic Jihad claims responsibility and begins to link with al-Qaeda. The Middle East peace process, initiated at Camp David, is derailed substantially.

1984: A coalition of Palestinian and JRA terrorists attacks tourists at airports at Rome and Vienna with grenades and machine guns, killing 18 and wounding 116. Abu Nidal's Revolutionary Fatah group is responsible. The Egyptian tourist industry declines dramatically for years.

1991: Former Prime Minister Rajiv Gandhi is assassinated by a suspected Liberation Tigers of Tamil Eelam (LTTE) suicide bomber while campaigning in southern India.

1995: Yitzhak Rabin, prime minister of Israel, is assassinated by a Jewish student claiming that Rabin had given away too much of Israel in the peace process. The Oslo peace agreements are derailed by the election in Israel forced by this assassination.

1996: A bomb explodes at the home of the French archbishop of Oran, killing him and his chauffeur. The Algerian Armed Islamic Group is believed to be responsible.

2007: Benazir Bhutto, the first woman prime minister in Pakistan, a pre-dominantly Islamic state, is killed when her car was hit by a bomb as she left an election rally in Rawalpindi. At least 20 other people died in the attack, for which Islamic militants are blamed.

Small Arms

In recent years, terrorists have continued to use pistols, rifles, and such crude weapons as the sawed-off shotgun. The supply of such weapons is vast, the cost relatively small, and the training for their use fairly simple to accomplish, making these popular weapons for small or underfinanced terrorist groups.

Handguns continue to be the weapon of the political assassin, but more important in terms of modern terrorism; they are often the preferred weapons of hostage-takers. Moreover, unlike automatic weapons, laws limiting the sale and possession of handguns are lax or nonexistent in many countries.

Automatic Weapons

The automatic weapon is essentially an antipersonnel weapon, but it has also been used by terrorists to assault cars and even airplanes. It is a favorite weapon of terrorist groups for several reasons: its availability, ease of conceal-ment, high rate of fire, and, perhaps most important, its psychological impact on unarmed civilians or lightly armed security forces.

There are two basic types of automatic weapons: the assault rifle and the submachine gun.[10] Both are easily obtained through arms dealers or the military of various nations, particularly since the demise of the Soviet Union. The Soviet AK-7 was one of the most popular weapons of terrorists, due to its accessibility as well as to its performance record.

In recent years, the machine pistol has become popular among terrorist groups and police forces. This is particularly true for terrorists in Europe, where such weapons can easily be procured.

Portable Rockets

Training of terrorists in the use of **precision-guided munitions (PGMs)**—*devices that can launch missiles whose trajectories can be corrected in flight*—has also increased dramatically. Most PGMs are portable, meaning they are fairly light-weight and can be both carried and operated by one or perhaps two persons.

Such weapons are designed to destroy aircraft and tanks. There are documented incidents, in which terrorists have attempted to use weapons such as the Soviet-made SA-7 (code-named *Strela*) against aircraft. Air Rhodesia Flight 827 was shot down in February 1979 by ZIPRA guerillas armed with a Strela 2 missile, killing all 59 passengers and crew. In 1993, Tranair Georgian Airline had two separate aircraft shot down a day apart in Sukhumi, Abkhazia, Georgia, killing 108 people. Of the surface-to-air rocket systems currently available, the most popular appear to be those of the United States, Russia, and the United Kingdom. The U.S. Stinger, the aforementioned Russian-made SA-7, and the British Blowpipe are popular among contemporary terrorists. Most such rockets employ infrared devices, heat-seeking sensors that, as a rule, serve to guide the missile to a heat source, presumably the aircraft engine. They generally weigh between 30 and 40 pounds, with an effective range of at least several kilometers.

Worst of all, from a security standpoint, such weapons are becoming all-too-readily available to terrorist organizations. Rand Corporation's terrorist expert, Brian Jenkins, noted in the 1970s that, since 30 to 40 developing countries had access to these PGMs, hundreds of these weapons would be "loose" on the world by the early 1980s.[11]

Jenkins was correct: Such weapons *were* loose in at least the hundreds if not the thousands in the 1980s. Not only did Third World nations allow and even assist in their dissemination, but Western nations were also guilty of allowing these missile systems to come into the hands of terrorists. Moreover, the catastrophic effect of missiles taking down one plane with only a small number of crew and passengers cannot be overstated. On April 6, 1994, two SAMs struck one of the wings of the Dassault Falcon carrying Rwanda's and Burundi's presidents as it prepared to land in Kigali, Rwanda, causing the plane to erupt into flames in mid-air and crash into the presidential palace gardens, exploding on impact. This incident, with the deaths of these men, ignited the genocide that would devastate Rwanda and was the catalyst for the destruction of the government of neighboring Zaire, which bore the brunt of the tidal waves of refugees. Two SAMs triggered the loss of millions of lives.

Aerial Hijacking

If the plane is not simply blown from the sky by a SAM, then it can be hijacked. Skyjacking, as such events have been called, has been used by terrorists to maximize shock value and to grab world attention.

These spectacles have provided extensive media coverage at fairly minimal cost to the hijackers. Although the psychological costs for the victim are high, the loss of lives has also tended to be less than in other types of terrorist events—except when things go wrong.

1994: Air France Flight 8969 was hijacked from Algiers by four Armed Islamic Group (GIA) members planning to crash the plane into the

Eiffel Tower in central Paris. French special forces GIGN commandos stormed the plane in Marseilles, killing the hijackers and freeing the remaining passengers after three passengers were murdered by the GIA. This aerial hijacking was the first-known effort of its kind where the intention was to destroy the aircraft and passengers, using the fuelled aircraft as a missile to destroy ground targets.

1996: Ethiopian Airlines Flight 961 crashed into the Indian Ocean near the Comoros Islands after hijackers refused to allow the pilot to land and refuel the plane. Of the passengers, 125 were killed and 50 survived with minor injuries.

2001: Nineteen terrorists hijacked American Airlines Flights 11 and 77, and United Air Flights 93 and 175. The four heavily fueled planes were used as missiles to attack targets of economic, military, and political significance in the United States. Two of the planes struck the WTC twin towers in New York City, destroying the complex and killing almost 3,000 people. One plane crashed into the Pentagon in Washington, DC, causing over one hundred deaths, and the fourth plane crashed into a field in Pennsylvania, killing all aboard.

Sabotage

Highly industrialized Western nations are particularly vulnerable to this type of terrorist tactic. It is possible, for example, to disrupt utility services or shut down industrial complexes. Japan in 1987 suffered a disruption of its commuter rail services by terrorists armed with nothing more than a few sharp blades. Such an incident can clearly have tremendous symbolic value and serves the terrorist goals of disrupting and perhaps destabilizing governments. However, they are not necessarily terrorist acts because no innocent victims are injured or killed in the action. This will be discussed further in several other contexts, including the potential for sabotage of nuclear facilities and the prospect of cyberterror designed to sabotage critical infrastructure.

Weapons of Mass Destruction

Robert Kupperman, in a report prepared for the U.S. Department of Justice in October 1977, made a useful analysis of the devastation that could be wrought by chemical, biological, and radiological weapons and nuclear explosives:

> In terms of fatalities, conventional weapons such as machine guns and small bombs constitute the least threat. They can produce tens or hundreds of casualties in a single incident. Chemical weapons such as nerve agents constitute a substantially greater threat, being capable of producing hundreds to thousands of fatalities. A small nuclear bomb could produce a hundred thousand casualties, but biological agents—both toxins and living organisms—can rival thermonuclear weapons, providing the possibility of producing hundreds of thousands to several millions of casualties in a single incident.[12]

Let us consider the possibilities of a terrorist group using chemical, biological, radiological, or nuclear weapons of mass destruction. That most groups have not yet done so is less a factor of the difficulties and dangers involved in producing such weapons than in the problems in effectively disseminating the toxic material.

Chemical or Biological Attacks

Agents for this type of tactic are commercially available or can be developed without undue difficulty by some groups. The possibility of a successful poisoning of a city's water supply has concerned some governments in recent years. Individuals in the United States have already demonstrated that it is possible to poison medicines on drugstore shelves and food supplies. Use of toxic agents against the Kurds by the government of Iraq during its conflict with Iran had already made it clear that states were increasingly willing to use this weapon against women and children.

There are tens of thousands of highly toxic chemicals, some of which are available to the general public in the form of, for instance, rodenticides. **Organophosphates,** *the so-called nerve agents,* could be synthesized by a moderately competent chemist with limited laboratory facilities. Indeed, for terrorist groups lacking even such a chemist and laboratory, some forms of these agents, such as tetraethyl pyrophosphate, are commercially available as insecticides.

The use of an organophosphate by a group in Japan in 1995 demonstrated both the effectiveness of the agent and the vulnerability of major urban centers to such attacks. The injury to thousands, generated by a relatively small amount of substance, makes clear that Kupperman's assessment was distressingly accurate. The relatively small number of casualties from the incident is attributable to the inability of the Aum Shinrikyo to place the agent in the appropriate place for maximum dissemination, according to experts.

The dissemination of such agents of destruction is not simple. Aerosol dispersal would be difficult and risky in some areas, although subways, trains, planes, and buses make inviting targets. Contamination of a large water supply is normally inhibited by factors such as hydrolysis, chlorination, and the required minimum quantity of toxic material per gallon of water for effectiveness.

Similar problems inhibit the dissemination, if not the production, of even more lethal **botulinal toxins,** *highly toxic nerve agents created by anaerobic bacterium,* often found in spoiled or ill-prepared food. Although compared to the most toxic nerve agent, botulinal toxin is at least a thousand times more dangerous, there are problems in the dissemination of botulinal toxins. Dissemination through the food supply is an obvious route and one that concerns the food industries.

Unfortunately, botulinal toxins are easily produced. There is a vast array of literature on their growth; serological typing for virulence; and the techniques for continuous culturing, separation, and purification of the toxin. The toxin that causes botulism is produced by the organism *Clostridium botulinium,* which is found almost everywhere.

Many chemical and biological agents are fairly readily produced or obtained, often through legitimate sources. They are also incredibly deadly, capable of killing thousands, even hundreds of thousands, of people. Thus far, the difficult step of dissemination may be one of the only remaining reasons why contemporary terrorists have not yet used these agents of mass destruction. The success of the use of such an agent in Japan in 1995 and the use by states of such weapons in times of conflict may well encourage other groups to begin to use these unconventional weapons.

In the Iran–Iraq War, as noted earlier, Iraq spread poison gas against its enemies. For a time such measures were reserved for desperate military situations, when confronted with overwhelming Iranian forces. But there was gruesome evidence of an increase in the use of this lethal weapon against villages and cities. The city of Halabja, near the Iran–Iraq border, was covered with a poison cloud, which one survivor described as "a dense choking pancake that settled over many square blocks."[13] Very few of those left in the center of town survived. Medical evidence suggests that Iraq dropped mustard gas, a relatively common poison; hydrogen cyanide, a chemical combination used for executions in U.S. prisons; and possibly sarin, a nerve gas that is one of the deadliest chemical weapons ever developed by mankind.

When nation-states themselves use such weapons, even on civilian populations, how can the civilized world prevent or even proscribe the use of such weapons by terrorists? Certainly the use of such weapons by nations engaged in conflict both lessens the strength of the laws designed to control or prohibit their use and makes more difficult the means by which the production of such weapons are controlled. If production of such chemical weapons cannot be effectively limited, then the dissemination of such weapons becomes even more difficult to control.

CASE STUDY 7.4

Al-Qaeda's Quest for a Biological Toxin

Material and testimony recovered from the training camps in Afghanistan have indicated that al-Qaeda at one time was interested in acquiring chemical weapons, biological weapons, or both. It is becoming clear, however, that this organization is still involved in attempts to manufacture and utilize such weapons. The efforts of recently discovered cells of this group appear to have focused on the production of ricin, a biological toxin found in castor beans.

In France in 2001, one al-Qaeda trainee, Menad Benchellali, set up a laboratory in his family's spare bedroom in Lyon and began to manufacture ricin. Blending the ingredients in a coffee decanter and scooping the dough-like mixture onto newspapers to dry, he was able to produce a powdered substance, which he stored in small jars. Benchellali and others like him have discovered that it is inexpensive and reasonably easy to produce a WMD for their group to use.

Unfortunately, this is hardly a surprising choice of weapon, since ricin is very accessible, relatively easy to make, safe to handle, and extraordinarily lethal. In fact, a single particle of ricin, the size of a pinhead, could kill an adult if injected into the bloodstream. Although a biological weapon, ricin also has the advantage of being noncontagious and is therefore not likely to set off epidemics that could kill the very persons for whom the politically motivated action is being taken. It cannot be absorbed through the skin, like the very lethal nerve agent VX, meaning that inhalation or injection must occur for dissemination to be successful—neither of which is easy to deploy.

To date, no ricin attacks by al-Qaeda have been carried out, perhaps because the problem of creating a weaponized form capable of effective dissemination is not yet solved. But it is clear that al-Qaeda and many other groups (domestic as well as international) are trying to create this new weapon. As one expert notes, "Biological and chemical weapons are more important than ever to al-Qaeda."[14] While ricin is not, in many respects, a feasible WMD (given its limitations in contagion and dissemination), it appears that groups such as al-Qaeda will continue to seek to acquire such substances and to learn how best to use them. The reported deaths in 2009 in Algeria of at least 40 members of al-Qaeda in the Land of Islamic Mahgred (AQLIM) from an apparent accident in the weaponizing of pneumonic plague highlights this continuing interest. ∎

Source: http://cns.miis.edu/npr/pdfs/123salama.pdf

Today, according to the 2011 Organization on the Prohibition of Chemical Weapons, which implements the Convention on Chemical Weapons, destruction/elimination of the category 1 (high risk) chemicals and precursors is significantly behind schedule. According to the convention, all were to have been destroyed by 2007, but stockpiles and production facilities remain. Iraq, for example, has an indefinite delay in its requirement to comply, due to the difficult in ascertaining the location of both production and storage facilities at this time. The United States and Russia have also announced delays in completion of this process, projecting completion by 2015 (Russia) and 90% completion by 2012 (United States).

Brian Jenkins, in 1975, suggested that

Terrorists want a lot of people watching, not a lot of people dead—which may explain why, apart from the technical difficulties involved, they have not already used chemical or bacteriological weapons, or conventional explosives in ways that would produce mass casualties.[15]

However, as we have seen in this chapter, it is no longer true that all modern terrorists eschew mass violence. It seems, then, that Jenkins' earlier premise regarding terrorists' reluctance to use WMDs proved less accurate in the twenty-first century. The reason few groups have not yet used such weapons may well rest upon the difficulty in disseminating the toxic substance in sufficient quantities. That is, surely, a frail defense for those nations who may find themselves the target of such attacks.

Radiological and Nuclear Attacks

For years, modern nations have tried both to secure the materials necessary for the development and production of radiological and nuclear weapons and to remain secure in their belief that, even if some small portions of such materials should fall into terrorist hands, the terrorists would lack the technical skill to manufacture such weapons. The former is a manifestly false premise, particularly since the breakup of the former Soviet Union, and the latter is, unfortunately, not true today.

While not truly constituting a WMD, a "dirty bomb" in which *explosives are attached to nuclear waste products to disperse radioactive materials* is increasingly possible. Radiological materials are relatively available today, and the dispersal of such materials, with the intent to cause harm, is comparatively easy. Nuclear reactors and power plants, nuclear waste and dump sites, medical facilities and medical waste, industrial facilities using radiological materials, and even university research facilities using such materials make access very difficult to control on a global scale. The good news is that devices designed as weapons to disperse such materials would generally cause only low to moderate serious injury and very few deaths. But the economic, psychological, and political disruption caused by the use of such a weapon could be catastrophic. Evacuation, decontamination, and the essential rebuilding of public confidence in safety could potentially cost millions in dollars and loss of economic momentum from this simplest of nonconventional weapon.

Experts have estimated that, in order to produce a crude nuclear weapon, terrorists would perhaps need to have a half dozen technologically trained individuals (trained in subjects such as nuclear chemistry, physics, metallurgy, electronics, and the handling of high explosives) and considerable time, space, and money. Let us consider each of these requisites to determine whether such a weapon does in fact lie within the realm of possibility for some terrorists today.

An organization such as al-Qaeda could perhaps generate the necessary funds to procure the materials, trained technicians, and facilities necessary to build such a weapon.

For small, poorly financed groups, a lack of time as well as money could inhibit the production of a nuclear weapon. Well-financed groups can afford, however, to wait while personnel are put into place in an adequately constructed facility. With their contacts among friendly governments, they might even be able to secure a safe testing ground for the weapon prior to its use, although such a step would not be essential. Military experts are concerned with such matters as high reliability and predictability yield. All terrorists need be concerned with is that the bomb produces a sufficiently audible "bang" and visible mushroom cloud.

The requirement of space is one that well-established and funded groups can manage. Because considerable hazards are attendant upon working with radioactive materials, a laboratory of fairly substantial size, equipped with specialized equipment, would be necessary. Like the fissionable materials, it has become increasingly probable that the acquisition of such facilities is within the grasp of some terrorist groups. If such groups can gain access to military training facilities as described earlier, then the possibility exists that they can also gain access to suitable research and development facilities.

After the demise of the Soviet Union, many trained personnel became available to terrorist groups and states that can afford market prices for such personnel. Thus, even though it might not be feasible to train a recruit with only a grade school or even a high school education in the technology necessary for the construction of nuclear weapons, terrorists have a large pool of university graduates from which to select, as well as a large number of trained scientists seeking employment following the crash of the Soviet system. Or such groups could obtain, on the global arms market, **backpack nukes** (*small, portable nuclear devices developed by the military of both sides of the cold war*).

However, the terrorists who may possess or be able to obtain the necessary resources to construct a crude nuclear weapon are those who are least likely to benefit from the commission of such a barbarous act. Well-established terrorist organizations have tended to try to distance themselves from acts of barbarity, as did the group leadership in Japan following the use of toxic gas on the subways. The reason for such distancing is obvious: These organizations have attachable assets, locations, and personnel upon which retribution could be meted out.

Yasser Arafat, for instance, when he led the Palestine Liberation Organization (PLO), would have been extremely reluctant to use the resources of his organization for the construction and subsequent detonation of a nuclear device. To do so, even before the peace process began in the 1990s, would have irreparably damaged his credibility with the United Nations and would have played into the hands of his enemies.

Two forms of nuclear terrorism remain feasible, however. One is the **threat/hoax** *by which leaders are frightened or blackmailed into acceding to terrorist demands, based on the threat of detonating a hidden nuclear device in a crowded area, such as a city.* This is another low-cost tactic, with varying potential for disruption, without making innocent victims of anyone. It forces governments to assess the vulnerability of the targets and the history of the group claiming responsibility. The cost of reacting to such a hoax may well be crippling to the authority involved, whereas the consequences of not responding could be equally dreadful.

To date that is all they have been: threats and hoaxes. But the time may well be at hand when leaders may no longer be so confident that terrorists do not truly possess a nuclear device that they are prepared to detonate. The increasing willingness of some terrorists to commit carnage on a large scale must surely give pause to those who would claim that the devastation wrought by a nuclear device would be on too large a scale for contemporary terrorists. As terrorism continues to become more violent, nuclear terrorism becomes a greater possibility.

The greatest potential for a nuclear disaster, and one that has concerned governments more, is the possibility of an attack or sabotage of an existing nuclear facility. With the growing number both of nuclear power plants inside countries that have for some years produced nuclear power and weapons and of nuclear facilities in previously non-nuclear states, the possibility of these types of situations has dramatically increased.

As noted earlier, nuclear technology and materials are available to terrorists today. While the devices may be difficult to manufacture, it is not impossible to do so, and they could be stolen, purchased, or supplied by a supporting state. Sabotage or bombing of a nuclear facility is also feasible and far less expensive.

The "science fiction" terrorism of earlier years is rapidly becoming part of the potential pattern of terrorism today and tomorrow. Chemical, biological, radiological, and nuclear terrorism is technically within the grasp of some terrorists today. That they have, for the most part, not chosen to pursue such tactics—yet—is a subject for conjecture. It would be unwise to rely, however, on the terrorists' need for popular approval or goodwill as an indefinite defense against an attack with weapons of this kind.

The recent record in the use of nontraditional weapons will be explored in more depth in Chapter 9 "Domestic Terrorism in the United States," and Chapter 14, "The New Terrorist Threat: Weapons of Mass Destruction." At this point, it is simply important to be aware of the very real and rapidly increasing possibilities for the use of chemical, biological, and nuclear agents.

Suicide Bombing: A "New" Weapon

Warriors throughout the ages have been told by their leaders that "there are no dangerous weapons, only dangerous men, implying that the warriors themselves were the true 'weapons' and their hardware (guns, swords, knives, bombs) were the tools they used in their fight."[16] Today, however, terrorism has added a new twist to this "truism," in the form of **suicide bombing**, *in which an individual carries explosives on his or her person or transport with the intention of detonating himself or herself in an effort to generate casualties among the enemy.* In such an attack, both the warrior and his or her tool (explosives) are weapons; the separation between warrior and weapon/tool is lost, intentionally. Those who carry out suicide bombings today have not invented a new method of warfare. Suicide attacks have been a method of combat for centuries. The hashashin, described in Chapter 2, committed suicidal attacks, as did the Sicarii and, more recently, Japanese kamikaze pilots during World War II. Today's suicide bombers, however, are a challenge that most Western democratic systems find hard to handle effectively.

Ideology, Not Psychology, of Suicide Bombing The difficulty, in part, lies in the fundamental lack of understanding in Western cultures of those who attempt suicide. The willingness to commit suicide is viewed, in these cultures, as an illness, not an outgrowth of religious ideology. Treating this willingness to commit suicide as an illness, in the context of those motivated by religious zealotry, has led to a fundamental misunderstanding of the root causes of such action and equally fundamental mistakes in trying to offer "treatments" or to "find cures" for this "ailment." The primary motivation for most suicide bombers today is the attack itself; in committing a terrorist act, the goal is to create a mood of fear, to gain attention to a cause, to cause chaos, and perhaps to destabilize a system—it is not to simply kill oneself.

Indeed, the suicide bomber today does not, according to most experts, consider himself or herself as a murderer, or as suicidal. Instead, today's suicide bombers in Pakistan, Afghanistan, Iraq, and a host of other countries see themselves as martyrs in a holy cause, fighting and dying in the name of Allah.[17] This is important in several respects. First, the purpose of the action is *not* to commit suicide, but to carry out a destructive action for a "higher purpose." Thus, there is neither a threat (of punishment, since an outcome of death is already accepted) nor a promise (since spiritual reward in an afterlife would doubtless be more attractive than any tangible physical reward on this earth to the "martyr") that can be effectively employed to stop the action. Moreover, the person is not suffering from a form of mental illness, which could perhaps be treated, as he or she is not seeking to commit suicide, but to fulfill a spiritually directed action; in that case, psychological counseling is unlikely to be a useful tool in diverting the action.

Suicide Bombings in Iraq In Iraq, and increasingly in Afghanistan, police and military authorities are confronted with the challenge of deterring suicide bombing of civilian and military targets. Since a state of war does not technically exist in either country, and the military are engaged in "peace-keeping" operations, neither the police nor the military has the authority to "shoot on suspicion" to prevent a possible suicide bombing attack, unless a "reasonable threat" is believed to exist. This puts the security forces in a difficult position: If they shoot and are correct in their judgment, thereby preventing a suicide bombing, then they will be commended; but if they are wrong and shoot an innocent person who "looked" as though he or she presented a threat, then the security officers may well be charged with a crime.

A suicide bomber does not wear a "uniform" to designate his or her role, although certain types of clothing offer loose concealment for belts of explosives. If the clothing in the region tends toward loose-flowing robes, the ability to conceal explosive packs is easier, and the "reasonable threat" is harder to determine. When the suicide bombers use vehicles, the ability to detect the threat is even more difficult. Judgment calls are often flawed, and the consequences disastrous. In 2003, U.S. soldiers, in part to offer security from suicide bombing attacks, fired on a van carrying thirteen passengers (women and children), killing seven of them, when the driver failed to stop at a military checkpoint.

Yoram Schweitzer and Shaul Shay, in their book *An Expected Surprise: The September 11th Attacks in the USA and Their Ramifications*, analyze general characteristics of suicide attacks worldwide. Perhaps the most important point that they make is that there is no single profile of a suicide bomber. They note that the motivations for such attacks include acting in the name of God/Allah, for a nationality, a particular leader or organization, peer pressure, and revenge. While modern suicide attacks appear to have surfaced with the actions of the Tamil Tigers in Sri Lanka, suicide terror activities have occurred over a wide geographic area, from the Middle East to Europe, and from South Asia to South America. According to researchers, women as well as men take part in these acts.[18]

Consider the following case study, an account by a news agency reporter who visited an Afghan village and talked with young people who had come to train to be suicide bombers.

> **CASE STUDY 7.5**
>
> # Suicide Bomber Training Camp
>
> In 2007, a *Newsweek* reporter visited a village in a Taliban-held territory in Afghanistan, southwest of Kabul and more than an hour's walk from the main road. As he came to a mud-brick house, a boy of about 10 years of age came out dragging a heavy sack. The guide who led the reporter picked up the sack, and carrying it over his shoulder as he walked to another house, told the reporter it contained a pair of suicide vests stuffed with explosives, enough to kill anyone within a football field, if detonated.
>
> One of the Taliban commanders, Mullah Dadullah Akhund, has boasted of having 1,800 trained suicide bombers waiting to carry bombs. Whether this is a realistic figure is not the point: The Taliban committed 139 suicide bombings in 2006, which was more than five times the number of similar attacks in 2005. The guerrillas call themselves "Mullah Omar's missiles," and the Taliban commander reminds them that they are the new "cruise missiles." The bombers see themselves as part of the jihad.
>
> The *Newsweek* reporter noted that his guide took the bag with the vest to another house, where eight heavily armed men were waiting, and they were joined by three intense-looking young men, who were introduced as fedayeen—in this case, meaning people who are literally ready to sacrifice their lives. The reporter met and talked with one of the young men, who declared, "I want my body and bones to hit the U.S. Army. I have come here for jihad, to drive the occupying U.S. and infidel forces from our Muslim country."
>
> This young man and about three dozen classmates went through two weeks of specialized training: learning how to pack cars, motorcycles, and vests with explosives; how to turn the packed explosives into bombs using batteries and detonators; and how to drive the motorcycles and cars to the targets selected. Their handlers help to smuggle them across borders and checkpoints, posting them in quiet villages until the time for their bombing attacks is at hand. They are not always competent and highly trained, not soldiers in most senses of the word. But they are prepared to wait, and to die, to achieve the jihad they believe is being fought.[19]
>
> Suicide bombing is, in many respects, a very challenging form of terrorist attack, as it requires security forces to make instant decisions on the use of force against what appear to be civilians. But perhaps the most frightening thing about this form of terrorist attack is the potential for an even more deadly form of suicide attack: that of a suicide patient. If young men and women are willing to volunteer and train, by the hundreds, to carry bombs on their bodies to destroy and defeat what they

perceive to be their enemies, what would happen if they were equally willing and able to carry a deadly disease to their enemies, infecting them silently but effectively. There would be no explosion, making it arguably a less attractive weapon, as there would be no immediate mood of fear created—but the results could be far worse than any bomb attack. As biological weapons stores were destroyed or removed at the end of the cold war, hundreds, perhaps millions of cubic feet of biotoxins disappeared. The potential for the use of such WMDs by any state remains small, but with suicide attackers multiplying in numbers—and perhaps in desperation and determination—the possibility of suicide patient attacks must be considered. ■

Source: Combating Terrorism Center at West Point

PHASES OF A TERRORIST INCIDENT: PUTTING THE LESSONS LEARNED AT CAMP INTO PRACTICE

Having assessed the training topics and chosen tactics of terrorists, it is also useful to note the patterns that have emerged in modern terrorist incidents. Much of what was taught in the training camps is clearly used in the structuring of the incident itself, at least by well-trained operatives.

Since it is clear that some organizations, like al-Qaeda, have very intelligent and organized lieutenants orchestrating the training of operatives, it should not be surprising to find that modern, well-planned terrorist attacks often have five discernible **phases of terrorist incidents,** which for the purpose of this study will be called *preincident, initiation, negotiation, termination, and postincident.* Each of these stages offers both insights into the sophistication of the group carrying out the operation and indicators that might be useful to law enforcement personnel seeking to prevent or resolve such incidents. Figure 7.1 illustrates the projected flow of a terrorist event, broken down into these five phases.

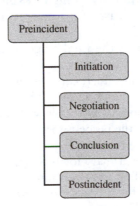

FIGURE 7.1
Phases of a Terrorist Incident: Putting the Lessons Learned at Camp into Practice

In the preincident phase, the individuals or groups planning the incident generally carry out two important functions: intelligence gathering and rehearsal of the event. Members of the group gather information about the target, make plans for the attack, and often rehearse the event. At this stage, training in clandestine travel and intelligence gathering becomes useful, as does training in evaluation of security systems and access routes.

This phase differs from the others in one critical respect: No law has yet been openly violated and therefore surveillance and intervention by law enforcement is difficult to justify. This issue will be pursued in more depth in the discussions in Chapters 9 and 10, as we consider the U.S. efforts to expand law enforcement capabilities in this area, particularly with the PATRIOT Act.

Phase two, the initiation phase, entails exactly what it suggests: the beginning of the implementation of the incident. This entails moving the individuals involved to the location(s) necessary for the event, as well as any equipment needed. During this phase a diversion is also planned, by the more well-organized groups, to draw the attention of law enforcement and the media away from the intended target. Thus, those seeking to protect the public from the planned attack may have to be able to discern which is the real target and which is the diversion during this initiation stage.

The third phase, negotiation, does not occur in every terrorist incident. If there is only the placing of a bomb or the driving of a truck filled with explosives to a desired target, there may well be no negotiation phase, because there is nothing to discuss about the act. This phase occurs when an individual or group has a demand (or a list of demands) to communicate and is willing to talk to someone in authority about meeting those demands. Generally, this involves the taking and negotiated release of hostages, the threatened detonation of a bomb or other weapon capable of mass destruction, or both. During this phase, the training that members of the group have received in the making of explosives and in the framing of demands for ransom or release of prisoners can significantly impact the flow of events.

What often appears to be the final stage, called here the termination phase, is not actually the end of the event in most cases today. This phase simply involves the escape, surrender, capture, or death of the individuals involved in the incident. Here, planning for a "back door" escape, a diversion to draw some of the attention away to allow this escape, or a demand that includes safe passage out for the perpetrators, often depends on the quality of training and experience of the terrorists.

For law enforcement, the primary focus is usually on the safety of the hostages, not the capture or killing of the criminals. If the event is handled by a military authority, however, the focus is most often on the capture or death of the individuals responsible. Thus, the success of this phase may depend on the nature of the enforcement officials seeking to end the incident.

The final phase is in many respects the most important, and unfortunately the least understood. In the postincident, or lessons learned, phase, the remaining members of the group who planned the attack regroup to *learn* from the mistakes as well as the successes of the incident. By studying what went right and what went wrong in the event, groups learn how law enforcement met the challenges and can then plan how to exploit the weaknesses of those protecting the public. The group members, in fact, do what military forces do in their debriefing after an incident.

The important point here is that *terrorists planning these events are not stupid*. They learn from mistakes and from successes, and they use those lessons in the next plans. Although there may be copycat perpetrators who will repeat the group's initial mistakes, the perpetrators, if they are well organized and trained, will not repeat their errors. Thus, if security forces only copy the attacks made by groups in planning security, they will miss a critical point, because no future attack by that group will be exactly like the one that occurred. Instead, the next incident will reflect the learning curve of the group from its postincident evaluation.

CONCLUSIONS

Terrorists today have a variety of tactics from which to choose and sufficient training and support systems to make the most of the tactics within their grasp, should they choose to use them. While most terrorist groups continue to rely on the tactics proven successful in earlier years, such as bombing and hostage-taking, recent developments make it possible that different choices may be made in the near future.

The attacks in Afghanistan in 2001 after the events of September 11 certainly precipitated the toppling of the regime of the Taliban, under which the al-Qaeda group had flourished. The training camps established in this area were seriously disrupted, destroyed, or forced to relocate. However, there appears to have been successful adaptation by some of the teachers in these camps in forming mobile training camps. The Internet continues to offer training manuals to interested persons, and these mobile camps appear to offer the final skills tests sessions needed for weapons training. Although the community of nations has come closer to tacit or explicit agreement that the use of WMDs is "unthinkable" for modern states, as the costs for the user are potentially too high, the same does not appear to be true for terrorist groups. Most of the information from terrorist training manuals and from individuals captured after participating in training camps indicates that the study of the procurement, development, and use of such weapons is a fundamental part of terrorist training today. The use of these weapons by states and groups will be explored in Chapter 14, but it is important to remember here that groups are actively training in the methods of acquiring, producing, and utilizing such weapons on a world that is ill-prepared to defend itself against such attacks.

DISCUSSION

Potentially conflicting forces seem to be influencing the terrorists' choice of tactics. Consider these factors carefully and decide what you think will be the trends in future terrorist attacks.

1. The training facilities that some states have given to favored regimes or insurgent groups have come under increasing criticism today as the world takes a harder look at the training received by those who later carry out terrorist acts. One such state-supported school is the Western Hemisphere Institute for Security Cooperation, known until 2005 as the School of the Americas (SOA), which is based in Fort Benning, Georgia, in the United States. This school has been in operation for more than fifty years, training over 60,000 Latin American soldiers and policemen. Among its graduates, as its critics point out, are some of the continent's most notorious torturers, mass murders, and state terrorists, including Colonel Byron Lima Estrada, whose infamous "D-2" military intelligence agency (40 percent of whose membership studied at SOA) obliterated 448 Mayan Indian villages, murdering thousands. Panama's Manuel Noriega and Omar Torrijos were also scholars at this school. It is described, by those who oppose it, as America's Terrorist Training Camp.[20] Is this an accurate description, or do states have a right/responsibility to help train the law enforcement and military of "friendly" regimes? Are they responsible for the actions taken by their "students" after they leave the school, just as those who train in camps in Afghanistan are held responsible for the actions of their "students?"

2. The use of traditional weapons, like suitcase bombs, in nontraditional fashion continues to present challenges today. The detonation of suitcase bombs in the nonsecured pre-ticketing area of airports, for example, occurred in a Moscow airport in 2011. Most nations have no system in place by which to scan persons prior to ticketing/boarding areas, making the use of such bombs, particularly when carried by suicide terrorists, almost impossible to prevent. How can nations cope successfully not only with new weapon technologies but also with the creative use of older weapons in different—and often unsecured—venues?

3. An ex-CIA officer discovered that bin Laden's al-Qaeda network had produced a bomb-making guide, written as part of an encyclopedia of the Afghan jihad. Volume one of this encyclopedia is titled "Explosives," and is, in this officer's words, a "portable university for the militant common man, nothing less than a terrorist's how-to guide." It starts with relatively simple stuff: how to rig letter bombs, exploding books, chairs, sofas, beds, and a variety of household items. It gradually moves to bigger items: bombs for trucks, cars, houses, buildings, laying out details on fuses, timing switches, even brewing instructions for the terrorist who can't get his hands on Libyan-stockpiled plastique Semtex explosives. Copies of this encyclopedia are held by individuals from many countries who have been trained in the jihad spreading from Afghanistan.

4. Dr. David Hubbard, a psychiatrist who has interviewed scores of imprisoned hijackers, contends that TV news broadcasts of ongoing terrorist events are "social pornography" because it "caters to the sick, unmet needs of the public" (*Skyjacker: His Flights of Fancy*).[21] He is convinced that world terrorism would decrease if television brought its coverage under control. How accurate do you think this assessment is? What kinds of controls can a democratic society afford to impose on its media? What are the dangers of such controls? How effective do

you think either voluntary or involuntary controls on media coverage of terrorism would be in reducing either the number or the violence of terrorist events?

ANALYSIS CHALLENGE

The concept of terrorist training camps in countries like the United Kingdom and the United States is often hard for its citizens to accept. Go to the Web links for the two accounts of terrorist training, and decide what you think about the reality—and the problems—such camps could present to democracies. As you make your analysis, you should check other sources for information about these events, to keep a balanced perspective.

United Kingdom: http://news.bbc.co.uk/2/hi/uk_news/7039608.stm
United States: http://www.canadafreepress.com/2007/cover061107h.htm

KEY TERMS

safe haven   132
traveling terrorist training
   camps   136
Al-Battar   137
explosive bombs   137
incendiary bombs   138
plastic explosives   138
disguise techniques   139
clandestine travel   139
sleepers   139
recruitment   139
communication   139
intelligence
   collection   140

counterintelligence
   140
weapons   140
rocket-propelled
   grenade   140
shaped-charge
   principle   145
improvised explosive
   device (IED)   145
package-type IED   146
vehicle-borne IED
   (VBIED)   146
person-borne IED (PBIED)
   146

precision-guided
   munitions (PGMs)
   148
organophosphates
   151
botulinal toxins   151
backpack nukes   155
dirty bombs   154
threat/hoax   155
suicide bombing
   156
deterrence   000
phases of terrorist
   incidents   159

SUGGESTED READINGS AND RESOURCES

Bergen, Peter L. *Holy War: Inside the Secret World of Osama bin Laden*. New York: Simon & Schuster, 2001.

Conboy, Ken. *The Second Front: Inside Asia's Most Dangerous Terrorist Network*. Jakarta, Indonesia: Equinox Publishing, 2006.

Gunaratna, Rohan. *Inside Al-Qaeda: Global Network of Terror*. New York: Columbia University Press, 2002.

Hoffman, Bruce. *Inside Terrorism*. New York: Columbia University Press, 1998.

International Institute for Counter-Terrorism. http://www.ict.org.il/

Laqueur, Walter. *The New Terrorism: Fanaticism and the Arms of Mass Destruction*. Oxford: Oxford University Press, 1999.

Mizzel, Louis R., Jr. *Target U.S.A.: The Inside Story of the New Terrorist War*. New York: John Wiley & Sons, 1998.

Raymond, Gregory. "The Evolving Strategies of Political Terrorism." In *The New Global Terrorism: Characteristics, Causes, Controls,* ed., Charles W. Kegley, Jr. Upper Saddle River, NJ: Prentice Hall, 2003.

Stern, Jessica. *The Ultimate Terrorists*. Cambridge, MA: Harvard University Press, 1999.

NOTES

1. "Background Note: Afghanistan," U.S. Department of State. http://www.state.gov/r/pa/ei/bgn/5380.htm (accessed April 18, 2008).
2. "Terrorist Training Camps in Rural England," MSNBC. http://www.msnbc.msn.com/id/23350557/print/1/displaymode/1098 (accessed June 4, 2009).
3. Retrieved from http://pcworld.about.com/news/Jul072004id116822.htm?p=1.
4. "The Spider in the Web," *Economist,* September 22, 2001, 5.
5. Reuel Marc Gerecht, "Blueprint for Terror," *Talk,* October 2000, 91.
6. Bruce Crumley, "Breaking a Web," *Time,* October 6, 2001, 2.
7. "How Bin Laden Set Up Shop in Southeast Asia," *Time,* October 10, 2001, 2.
8. Robert H. Kupperman and Darrell M. Trent, *Terrorism: Threat, Reality and Response* (Stanford, CA: Hoover Institution Press, 1979), 80.
9. "Improvised Explosive Devices," Military Factory website. http://www.militaryfactory.com/smallarms/detail.asp?smallarms_id=11 (accessed September 10, 2007).
10. Kupperman and Trent, *Terrorism,* 54.
11. Brian Jenkins, *Terrorism: Trends and Potentialities* (Santa Monica, CA: Rand, 1977), 80.
12. Kupperman and Trent, *Terrorism,* 83.
13. "New Horrors in a Long-Running Horror Show," *U.S. News & World Report,* April 4, 1988, 11.
14. "A Plague of 'Hellish Poison," *U.S. News & World Report,* October 26, 1987, 32.
15. Joby Warrick, "Al-Qaeda's Quest for a Toxin," *Washington Post National Weekly Edition,* May 17–23, 2004, 15.
16. Brian Jenkins, "Will Terrorists Go Nuclear?" P-5541 (Santa Monica, CA: Rand, November 1975).
17. Michael Hopmeier, Boaz Ganor, Tress Goodwin, and Debra S. Greinke, "'There Are No Dangerous Weapons . . .' Suicide Attacks and Potential Responses," *Homeland Security Journal* (July 2003).
18. Tovah Lazaroff, "Wexperts: Suicide Bombers Not Crazy," *Jerusalem Post,* May 27, 2002.
19. Yoram Schweitzer and Shaul Shay, *An Expected Surprise—The September 11th Attacks in the USA and Their Ramifications* (Herzilya, Israel: Mifalot, IDC & IST Publications, 2002).
20. Sami Yousafzai and Ron Moreau, "Suicide Offensive," *Newsweek,* April 16, 2007, 34–36.
21. Douglas J. Haggman, "Muslim Training Camps in North America." http://homelandsecurityus.com/special-investigative-reports/muslim-terrorist-training-camps-in-north-america (accessed October 16, 2011).
22. David Hubbard, Skyjacker: His Flights of Fancy (New York: Wilson, 1997), 133.

The Media: A Weapon for Both Sides?

> If terrorism is seen as political theater performed for audiences . . . clearly the mass media plays a crucial role. Without massive news coverage the terrorist act would resemble the proverbial tree falling in the forest.
>
> —*Brigette L. Nacos*

MASS-MEDIATED TERRORISM

Brigette Nacos, in her work exploring the central role of the media in terrorism, suggests that the relationship can be best described as **mass-mediated terrorism**. She asserts that such an understanding of terrorism focuses on *the centrality of communication via the mass media in the calculations by most terrorists of the consequences of their deeds, the likelihood of gaining media attention, and the likelihood of gaining entrance—through the media—into the triangle of political communication (between public interest groups, government officials and decision makers, and the mass media).*

Certainly the media have blurred the line between domestic and international terrorism, bringing the terrorist attacks occurring on remote Pacific islands into the homes of millions of listeners and viewers around the world. Since terrorists' "successes" and "failures" depend in some measure on the publicity that their actions receive, the actions of the mass media make the "audience" of the terrorist attack much larger than it would otherwise be, improving the calculus of "success" by the perpetrators. Even if, as Nacos notes, the terrorists fail to claim responsibility for acts of

terror, the mass media—simply by reporting extensively on the incidents—
"transmit the perpetrators' messages by warning citizens that even the most
powerful governments cannot protect them from this sort of violence."[1]

Nacos suggests that the media and terrorism do not simply have compatible goals but that communication and propaganda have an inevitable
and primary role in both the terrorist's planning and the contemporary
mass media's appetite for "feeding" the public. The "oxygen of publicity"
on which former British prime minister Margaret Thatcher suggested that
terrorism depended is now perhaps more plentiful than ever, because the
mass media thrive on feeding the public twenty-four-hour news of terrorist
events.

As terrorism becomes increasingly transnational, one of the "two-edged
weapons" used both by it and against it is the media. Terrorists seek to use the
media for specific purposes; the governments against which groups and individuals commit terrorist acts want to use the media for different but equally
important reasons; and the media itself have goals in the context of reporting
terrorist events. Understanding the relationship between the media, terrorist
groups, and the government responding to the actions is perhaps best achieved
by first examining these goals.

TERRORIST GOALS REGARDING THE MEDIA

In the view of many experts previously cited, terrorists have goals that the
media can help them achieve. Let us briefly examine a few of these goals to
determine more clearly the stakes in this very dangerous game.

Publicity

Because terrorism is an act of theater and requires an audience, most terrorist groups welcome the opportunity to acquire "free" **publicity.** *Getting information out to a large, even global audience* about the cause for
which an act is being committed is a vital part of the act itself. Press coverage that makes the world aware of the problem that the individual or
group is seeking to resolve is clearly advantageous. This publicity can offer both **tactical** (*short-term*) and **strategic** (*long-term*) **gains** for the operation itself and in some cases for the cause for which the terrorist act is
being committed.

Tactical gains in publicity are usually measured in terms of getting information concerning demands that must be met within a time frame to more
than just the law enforcement officers at the scene. If the general public can
be made aware of the demands and the consequences threatened for lack of
fulfillment, then pressure may be put on the legal officers to comply with
the concerned public. Strategic goals can be met by increasing that large
audience's awareness of the "justice" of the cause for which the act is being
committed and the seriousness of the "problem" that the terrorists are trying
to rectify.

Favorable Understanding of Their Cause

This is a vitally important goal of most terrorists today. Everyone wants to be understood, and individuals or groups that are clearly breaking important laws and norms of behavior have *an intense desire for* **favorable understanding,** *for their audience to understand why they are carrying out these acts.* Sympathy for their suffering, and more important, for their cause, can be generated by a press willing to convey their message to a wide audience. If, as discussed in Chapter 4, terrorists live with images of their world that are unlike those of most of their audience, then it is critically important to them that they convey to their audience the justice for which they struggle and the reasons that have driven them to carry out acts of terrorism.

As one expert has noted, "good relationships with the press are important here, and they are often cultivated and nurtured over a period of years."[2] Although not all terrorists have sufficient access or longevity to build such "friendly relations" with the press, most individuals and groups carrying out terrorist acts do want the press to share with the public a positive understanding of why the incident is occurring. This leaves the media in an invidious position of determining what is news and what is rhetoric from the terrorist's pulpit. As Rushworth Kidder suggests, "the decision whether or not to broadcast or publish interviews with admitted terrorists brings journalists to the fine line between news and a forum for propaganda."[3]

Legitimacy and Identity

To recruit effectively, groups must convey **legitimacy and identity,** *a clear sense of purpose and identity to those who might be seeking similar political goals.* Proving to be both committed and effective in kidnapping, bombing, assassination, and other dramatic terrorist events can be a very useful tool in the recruitment of new members to a group's cause. Moreover, if the group needs funding for its operations as most do, good publicity for a successful operation can be the key to drawing such support from nations and individuals who share a concern for the cause that motivates the group.

When numerous groups focus on a similar general problem, then a group may carry out bombings or assassinations simply to establish a separate and credible identity. Certainly in areas such as Northern Ireland and Israel this has been the case, as splinter groups commit acts of terrorism for which the tactical goal seems to be establishing a separate identity.

Destabilizing the Enemy

A goal often cited by terrorist groups has been to cause damage to the enemy by **destabilizing the enemy**—that is, *by generating a sense of unrest, enhancing a fear that the government is unable to offer security and stability to its people.* Because terrorism is an act designed to create a mood of fear, the press can be seen by terrorists as a valuable tool in the achievement of this goal. If the media can be used to amplify fear, then the terrorists will have achieved an important goal.

GOVERNMENT GOALS REGARDING MEDIA

In democratic systems journalists are usually given substantial freedom to report news, including that of terrorist events. But unlimited freedom of the press has led, as noted earlier, to an escalation of events and a loss of life—results that neither the press nor the government desires. In many ways, the goals of the government in terrorist incidents are quite similar to those of the group carrying out the act. (See also Table 8.1.)

Publicity

Most governments know that the event will be publicized and therefore will want the press to offer publicity designed to help the government achieve its goal of ending the situation without loss of innocent lives. This means that publicity, from the government's perspective, should be carefully disseminated in a manner that will not endanger lives and that will help the public to understand the positive actions undertaken by the government to resolve the situation. This clearly is not compatible with the terrorists' goals, because from the terrorists' perspective publicity should be used to spread fear, not reassurance, about the government's handling of the action. The media are thus left with difficult choices about what news to release and how it should be worded.

Criminality of Act

Certainly, law enforcement would prefer that the media paint the terrorists as the "bad guys," and the simplest method for achieving that goal is often to stress **criminality of act**, *the illegal nature of the act that is occurring.* The terrorists will seek to have the press convey the justice of the cause for which they fight, whereas law enforcement will want to focus on the serious breach of law being perpetrated. Because terrorism is by definition carried out against innocent victims, legal authorities will seek to have the criminal nature of the offense

---

TABLE 8.1

Comparison of Goals

Terrorists	Government	Media
1. Publicity	1. Publicity	1. Getting a scoop
2. Favorable understanding of their cause	2. Criminality of act	2. Dramatic presentation of news
3. Legitimacy and identity	3. Deny the terrorist a platform	3. Protection of rights
4. Destabilizing the enemy	4. Information and cooperation	4. Personal security

highlighted by noting the innocence of the victims. If the public views the terrorists as common criminals of a particularly nasty sort, then the government will be viewed as the "good guys" rescuing the victims and ending the violence. To achieve this goal, the government clearly needs the media's cooperation.

Deny the Terrorist a Platform

It is certainly in the government's best interest to enforce **denial of a platform—** that is, *not to allow terrorists to use the free press as a "bully pulpit" for their propaganda.* This platform can be used not only to generate understanding and perhaps sympathy for the terrorist's cause but also to generate tangible support. The 1986 hijacking of TWA Flight 847 in Beirut gave explicit indication of the dangers of this platform. The skyjackers reportedly offered the press tours of the plane for $1,000 and a session with the hostages for $12,500! Although not many situations ever become quite so chaotic, most government agendas include separating the terrorist from the media as far as possible so that neither propaganda nor funds can be generated from the event.

Information and Cooperation

For most law enforcement agencies the optimum solution would be exclusion of the media and other observers from the area where a terrorist event occurs, but this is seldom an option in democratic systems. Instead, governments may want **information and cooperation,** such as having *the media share information they may have about the individuals involved while being careful not to share information with the hostage-takers about data that might be of use to them.* Thus, the media will be asked by governments to be discrete, careful not to reveal how successful operations were performed, and cautious about revealing information about an event that might provoke or enable a **copycat operation,** *one in which a terrorist act is copied by an observer in a subsequent act.* In some cases cooperation may even be interpreted by the government as a willingness on the media's part to share **disinformation,** that is, *inaccurate information designed to confuse* when such cooperation will help in resolving the threat in the terrorist action.

MEDIA GOALS IN TERRORIST EVENTS

Few of these goals held by police and terrorists for working with the media are compatible. Indeed, most are absolutely incompatible because both sides seek "good" publicity, legitimacy, and cooperation. Before considering methods for resolving this problem in conflicting goals, let us briefly consider the goals of the media in reporting such events. (See also Table 8.1.)

Getting a Scoop

In a world with fast-breaking news reported twenty-four hours a day, **getting a scoop,** *being the first to report a story,* is a crucial goal. High-tech communications make it possible and increase the pressure to transmit news stories in real time—that is, as the event actually happens. This leaves little time for editing or carefully evaluating the impact of such a news release on the situation. In such cases, this pressure to be first may mean that discussing the impact of reporting with public safety officers, noted as part of several goals of the law enforcement community, may be costly to journalists, who stand to lose that scoop to a less scrupulous reporter.

Dramatic Presentation of News

The media, in this fierce competition for public attention, clearly *need to create a* **dramatic presentation** *of the event as well as a timely one.* During the hijacking of TWA Flight 847 in June 1985, ABC broadcasted extensive interviews with the hijackers and the hostages. Indeed, in one dramatic reel, a pistol was aimed at the pilot's head in a staged photo op for the interviewers.[4] The media argue that the intense scrutiny they give to each aspect of the event actually protects the hostages. This assumes that the primary goal of the act is to communicate a cause, drawing support from this explication. If drama is needed to demonstrate the seriousness of the cause, however, then the lives of hostages could be jeopardized by a media demand for drama. If killing a hostage or a planeload of hostages becomes the price of drama, then the media may be held responsible for raising the stakes in the hostage "game."

Protection of Rights

The media have a strong commitment to **protection of rights**, *specifically the public's "right to know" about events as they occur.* Usually, this does not mean that the media see their role in opposition to that of law enforcement. Most members of the media seek to be professional and accurate, careful not to give out disinformation, and to play as constructive a role as possible in the event. Freedom of speech is not an absolute and inviolable value; most democracies have experienced times when civil liberties, including free speech, have had to be curtailed in the interests of national security. As one scholar notes, the conflict discussed here between the media and law enforcement "is between our commitment to unhindered public discourse and the need for public security."[5] Censorship of the press in most democracies is unacceptable; voluntary restraints by the press on itself is advocated but difficult to evoke in a form flexible yet effective enough to satisfy all concerned. If democracies give up free speech to stop terrorism, then regardless of the "success" of this effort the terrorists win, because the government and its citizens lose a fundamental part of their system. But an absolutely free press can cost lives. In the hijacking of TWA Flight 847 mentioned earlier, radio broadcasts alerted the hijackers aboard the Lufthansa jet that the captain of the plane was transmitting information to authorities on the ground. The hijackers then killed the captain. The press was free and the cost was the life of the pilot.

Personal Security

The Committee to Protect Journalists, based in New York City, notes that more than 300 journalists have been murdered since 1986 as a result of their work. In 1995 alone, according to this group's records, 45 journalists were assassinated.[6] Thus, one of the goals of the media is increasingly **personal security,** *to be able to protect themselves, both during and after terrorist operations.* Journalists who interview terrorists are at risk, and those who fail to satisfy terrorists' goals of favorable understanding and publicity may be vulnerable to attack by the terrorists and their sympathizers. On January 23, 2002, *Wall Street Journal* reporter Daniel Pearl was kidnapped in Karachi, Pakistan, by members of a Pakistani organization with links to al-Qaeda. Its members beheaded him.

PROPAGANDA BY THE DEED

Terrorism has been called "propaganda by the deed." This particularly violent form of propaganda has captured the attention of millions of people. To what extent have the media become a weapon of the terrorists about whom they report? Who is exploiting whom in this vicious scramble for worldwide audience?

Many of today's terrorists have learned an important lesson about this technological age: TV news organizations can be forced into becoming the link between terrorists and their audience. What is needed to forge this link is a crime sufficiently newsworthy—which has come to mean outrageous, dramatic, or even barbaric enough. According to Brian Jenkins, an expert on terrorism, "terrorists want a lot of people watching and a lot of people listening, not a lot of people dead. . . . I see terrorism as violence for effect. Terrorists choreograph dramatic incidents to achieve maximum publicity, and in that sense, terrorism is theater."[7]

Terrorists benefit from what has been called an **amplification effect,** *when their activities are broadcast through the media to a much larger audience than would be available at the place where the action occurs.* For instance, insurgents carried on rural guerrilla warfare in several countries, including Angola and Mozambique, for more than a decade without receiving much attention from the rest of the world. But when a similar number of Palestinians carried their warfare into the urban centers of Europe and the Middle East, their actions and their causes became dinner table conversation for TV audiences around the world, because in the urban centers of Europe and the Middle East, the terrorists were within reach of TV news reporters and their cameras.

This confluence of interests between the media—which thrive on sensational news—and terrorists—who are only too happy to provide the sensational events—has raised questions about the possible complicity of the media in today's terrorism. Students of terrorism have suggested that the media today are in fact a contributing factor—a weapon—in the hands of modern terrorists. A quick survey of the opinions of a few of these experts is illuminating:

> *Frederick Hacker,* a California psychiatrist who has served as negotiator in terrorist incidents, notes that "if the mass media did not exist, terrorists would have to invent them. In turn, the mass media hanker after terrorist acts because they fit into their programming needs: namely, sudden acts of great excitement that are susceptible, presumably, of quick solution. So there's a mutual dependency."
>
> *Walter Laqueur,* chairman of the International Research Council of the Center for the Strategic and International Studies, stated, "The media are a terrorist's best friend. . . . [T]errorists are the super-entertainers of our time."
>
> *Raymond Tanter,* a political scientist at the University of Michigan, makes the relationship dilemma a bit clearer in his statement: "Since the terror is aimed at the media and not at the victim, success is defined in terms of media coverage. And there is no way in the West that you could *not* have media coverage because you're dealing in a free society."[8]

In Tanter's comments lies a key to the dilemma of the role of the media in terrorism. Censorship in any form is anathema to most free societies. Instead, it has been assumed that the media could be expected to exercise voluntary self-restraints where necessary in reporting such events. But the media are not wholly convinced that restraint is either necessary or desirable. There is still considerable conflict over the extent of the public's "right to know" in the coverage of terrorist events. Executives of most of the major news companies have stated that TV's "right to report" is absolute; that in any situation, it is better to report than not report. ABC's William Sheehan has said, "I don't think it's our job to decide what people should not know. The news media are not the reason for terrorism even though they may sometimes become part of the story."[9]

Which is the more accurate picture of the role of the media with respect to terrorism today? Is it the responsible means by which the public is kept informed on events and individuals who are interacting in the international arena? Or is it, as one hijacker said, a "whore" whose "favors" are available to anyone with a pistol?[10] If it is indeed true that the media are responsible for amplifying the effects of guerrilla warfare, to what extent are they responsible for the effects of that amplification? If terrorists have to move to increasingly spectacular crimes in order to satisfy TV audiences sated with violence, to what extent are the media responsible for whetting that appetite?

Some experts have suggested that the media are acting increasingly like a "loose gun," a weapon that terrorists are learning to use with rapidly increasing sophistication. It is, moreover, a gun that democratic governments have provided and continue to provide, essentially without controls, for use against themselves. It would indeed be ironic if one of the fundamental freedoms of the free world—a free press—were to be instrumental in its destruction.

MEDIA AS A "SHOWCASE" FOR TERRORISM

The media have, to varying extents in different cultures, become a tool of modern terrorists, offering a "showcase" through which those carrying out terrorist acts can impress and threaten an audience, recruit and train new members, and support and coordinate an emerging network of followers. The role of the media as a showcase—which by definition offers structure and support with a clear display of items arranged to attract the attention of an audience—offers useful insights into one method of "teaching terror" in the twenty-first century.

In order to understand the use of the media as a "teaching tool" for terrorism today, it is important to examine at least two important facets of showcasing: the audience for which the showcase is designed and the response sought from that audience. Clearly, all of those viewing the media do not share the same cultural, economic, political, religious, or demographic traits. Therefore, if the showcase is to be effective, it must be designed to have divergent appeals to differing audiences. The "effectiveness" of the showcase could be evaluated in terms of the responses sought and obtained from those audiences. So it becomes necessary to clarify both the types of audiences targeted and the types of responses sought to assess the role of the media as a showcase through which terrorism is taught.

There is one other perspective of the relationship between media and terrorism that must be a part of this analysis. Many terrorism scholars have identified a **symbiotic relationship** between terrorists, who seek attention from an audience, and news organizations, which seek dramatic stories to increase their readership and ratings. A symbiotic relationship is, according to *Webster's Dictionary of the English Language*, *"the intimate association of two dissimilar organisms from which each organism benefits."*[11]

Clearly, terrorists seeking attention and the media searching for dramatic events can benefit from an association. The intimacy of the association and the degree to which each benefits will depend on a variety of factors, including the goals sought by each "organism" and the limitations of the systems in which both operate. Thus, a look at the role of the governments involved in shaping the way in which media can interact in the event, as well as an examination of the goals of the media and those of the terrorists, may help to clarify the relationship that exists between these dissimilar organisms.

A *showcase* is a "glass-fronted cupboard, fitted with shelves, in which goods are set out on view for sale or objects for exhibition."[12] If terrorists are intentionally using the media as a showcase, then, like any good vendor, they will be *careful to display their causes, their actions, and their leaders in the best possible light, with the display designed to offer information in formats designed to evoke the desired response from their viewing audience.*

Terrorism is a crime of theater. In order for terrorism to be effective, terrorists need to be able to communicate their actions and threats to their audience as quickly and dramatically as possible. Statistically, terrorist incidents worldwide are insignificant—both in terms of the number of dead and injured and in terms of the number of incidents reported annually—compared to the number injured or killed in wars, famines, natural disasters, or even auto accidents. But massive media coverage of individual terrorist attacks reaches a vast audience, creating an impact far beyond that, which the incident in the absence of this media, could be expected to effect. It could be argued that without intensive media coverage, few would know of terrorist actions, motivations, and actors. Hence, the showcase in which terrorism is displayed amplifies the effect of the single act of terrorism dramatically.

There are at least three different audiences for which most terrorist media showcases are designed: *current and potential supporters,* the *general public,* and *enemy publics.* Each of these target audiences is offered a different view designed to convey a different message and thus to evoke a different response. Let us briefly examine each of these potential audiences in terms of the showcase structure most often used.

Current and potential supporters are most often drawn to the media window of the Internet. Most active terrorist groups today have established their presence on the Internet, with hundreds of websites existing worldwide utilized by terrorists and their supporters. These websites use slogans to catch attention and often offer items for sale (e.g., T-shirts, badges, flags, MP3 videos, DVDs, and similar items). Frequently the websites are designed to draw *local supporters, providing information in a local language and giving information about the activities of a local cell as well as that of the larger organization.* The website is, thus, a recruiting tool as well as a basic educational link for local sympathizers and supporters.

The **general public,** including the international public—though they are *not directly involved in a specific conflict—often have some interest in the issues involved* and are actively sought as an audience in most terrorist events today. Terrorists, seeking to draw sympathetic understanding and even support from this audience, will use the media to offer information about the cause for which an action is being taken, as well as historical background material about the organization and individuals involved in the cause. It is also this audience, however, which must be made to fear the consequences of not changing the policy or system which is the target of the attack. If terrorism is defined by the creation of a mood of fear, this is the audience that must be made to feel that fear.

The third type of audience, the **enemy public,** *includes not only the state but frequently the citizens of the state against which the terrorist act is committed.* While the enemy (that is the target) is not always clearly defined, at least one governing regime, or the policy of one regime, is usually a clear target, since terrorism by definition seeks to cause some type of political/social change. The enemy public, then, is the audience that the terrorist showcase is intended to demoralize and humiliate as well as threaten, thereby weakening public support for the targeted regime by facilitating a change in public opinion.[13]

Thus, terrorist events may be showcased in the media to impact at least three definable audiences. The critical difference is the type of reaction that the display is designed to evoke. These responses can be described as the *goals* of terrorists in their intentional interaction with the media. The extent to which these goals are achieved depends in part on the goals of the media in these interactions. Remember that the relationship *can be* symbiotic and that the media can be a showcase for terrorist activity, but that neither of these may be the case. If the goals of the media and of terrorists converge and are compatible, the relationship may be symbiotic and an effective showcase may be created. If not, the display may carry a message that differs from the intent of the terrorists, and the impact on the audience may not produce the desired effect.

LEGAL ISSUE OF THE RIGHT OF ACCESS

The issue of the relationship between terrorism, the media, and the law has received attention from scholars for more than a decade. Legal experts from law enforcement agencies and media services have benefited from the scrutiny of this complex web of relationships. A brief review of a few significant issues raised by experts on this subject may be of value at this point.

Experts on both the law and the media have frequently differed in their opinions of the nature of the relationships that should exist among law enforcement, the media, and terrorists. Members of the media often claim to have an unlimited right to have access and the right to report all news, including that relating to terrorist events. Those responsible for hostage rescue contend that such rights should not be regarded as unlimited and should never be exercised in ways that might endanger lives. The legal issues inherent in these contrasting viewpoints were explored extensively during the late 1970s and early 1980s. As one researcher succinctly noted, "The media must not be the dupes of the radical scriptwriters, nor should they be the mouthpiece of government. There is a mean. Law enforcement and the media cannot be locked in combat."[14]

The U.S. Supreme Court during Warren Burger's tenure as chief justice did not regard the media's right to access as superior to that of the general public. Abraham Miller created a significant review of case law decisions involving the issue of the press's **right of access** to terrorist events—that is, *the right of the press to get close to the events as they occur*. He noted that in the *Pell* decision, the Court stated that when the public is excluded from the scene of a crime or disaster, then the media may also be excluded without violating the First Amendment to the U.S. Constitution.

Miller's study suggests that the Court under Burger viewed access by the media to a site where news is being made (as in a terrorist incident) not as a First Amendment right but as a privilege to be granted or revoked at the discretion of the law enforcement agency entrusted with ending the breach of the law. Even access to the perimeter between the tactical squad and the public (frequently established by law enforcement units in hostage-taking and siege situations for the purpose of permitting access for the media) is not a right guaranteed to the media by the Constitution but is instead a privilege accorded at the discretion of the government law enforcement agency in charge of the situation. Miller concludes with this observation:

> Access to the site where news is being made cannot be claimed by the press if the general public is also being excluded. Press access, largely a privilege under the most sanguine of circumstances, can be revoked, and where the situation is fraught with imminent danger of people being injured or killed, the media's claim to special access rings especially hollow.[15]

An earlier study by Miller and Juanita Jones reached similar conclusions about the legality of excluding the press from certain areas during hostage situations, particularly those in which law enforcement procedures require secrecy in order to save lives. However, this study also noted that the Supreme Court did not allow blanket denial of access through a set of preconditions. Case law, according to this study, did not support a total or standard ban on news access to terrorist events; only, the circumstances surrounding each event could legally justify limitation of access.

Prior restraint, *establishing specific legal limits on the press before the action occurs,* has been a tool used successfully only during times of great national stress when the security of the state could reasonably be said to be at risk. During the Civil War and World Wars I and II, the United States imposed restraints on the press regarding the right of access to events. Fear that an unfettered press might irresponsibly jeopardize the lives of American soldiers or civilians by injudiciously printing too much information about an event led to restrictions on access of the press during time of war.

Even in such extreme circumstances, however, the right of the government to impose such restraints was vociferously challenged, not only by the press itself but by constitutional scholars who feared the precedent that such rules might set. In the first Gulf War (1990–1991), the media in the United States were permitted to have briefings near the front lines, shown flight recordings and raw data from the advancing armies often before the data had been fully analyzed by the military intelligence staff, and allowed to film much of the fighting. Still, the press chafed at the restrictions imposed and demanded unlimited access to all military information available in order to broadcast live to a worldwide audience.

If the world can watch a war being fought from start to finish by twenty-four-hour coverage via CNN, and if the press is allowed to broadcast live footage of special forces troops conducting a "stealthy" night landing in Somalia, it is difficult to imagine the circumstances surrounding a terrorism event that would engender the need to limit the access of the media.

It could be more effectively argued that self-restraint instead of prior restraint would be in both the media's and the nation's best interest. Few legal scholars have challenged court findings that restrictions on the media comparable to those imposed on the general public do not necessarily contravene the First Amendment's protection of a free press. Differences have arisen over the type of restrictions and the body empowered to impose them. Most recent research has focused on three alternatives: government-directed censorship, self-censorship by the media itself, and restraints imposed by a special commission. All three options have difficulties.

CENSORSHIP: THE UGLY WORD

No one wants to use the term **censorship,** referring to *efforts by a government to limit and edit what is said by the media about an incident,* in conjunction with the media in their coverage of terrorist events. Yet many democratic states are hard-pressed not to desire to filter what reporters say to a general public about the motives, the lives, the intentions, as well as the actions and individuals involved in perpetrating terrorist events. The power of the media to create heroes is sometimes frightening, and democratic governments are not blind to this danger. Few, however, are willing to sacrifice cherished liberal values in order to limit media coverage. Media in a democratic society would be to give to the perpetrators of the terrorist events a significant and unearned victory. When a democratic society, in panic and anger, abandons one of the cherished principles of law that makes it democratic, the society inflicts on itself a greater wound than the terrorists could achieve.

Miller, who conducted the study of the U.S. Supreme Court case law on this issue, expanded his study of this topic in 1990 with research on the struggles of the British government to balance the media's desire to be unfettered against special security needs generated by the struggle in Northern Ireland. As in the study of the U.S. Supreme Court decisions, Miller concluded that media access to information was not guaranteed by British law.[16] However, Miller found no evidence to support claims by the government of a need for censorship that extended beyond limiting access.

One of the most comprehensive research studies on terrorism and the media was conducted during the 1980s by Alex P. Schmid and Janny F. A. de Graaf, who examined the relationship between terrorist violence, the Western news media, and political actors.[17] This study is an excellent empirical exercise that includes scrutiny of terrorist violence beginning with nineteenth-century anarchists. The study evaluates interactions between terrorists, the media, and political actors in many regions of the world and concludes that much of the blame for the increase in terrorism can be attributed to the media.

Schmid and de Graaf summarize the arguments for and against censorship of terrorist news reporting. At the bottom of their list of 11 arguments against censorship is the only one relevant to the legality of censorship. This argument is simply that "the assertion of insurgent terrorists that democratic states are not really free would gain credibility if the freedom of the press were suspended."[18] This does not suggest that censorship in such events would be unconstitutional but that it might be counterproductive in constitutional democracies.

Government-directed censorship has been most often studied in the context of Great Britain's efforts to restrain the media on the subject of the conflict in Northern Ireland. Of particular interest in this situation is the legislation banning TV and radio broadcasts of interviews or direct statements by members of the outlawed Irish Republican Army, along with nine other organizations. Two of the organizations are legitimate (or at least not proscribed) groups: the Catholic group Sinn Féin and the Protestant Ulster Defense Association.

This broadcasting ban was intended, in the words of the prime minister at that time, Margaret Thatcher, to deprive terrorists of "the oxygen of publicity" on which they thrive.[19] Although the British legal system does not have a formal written constitution, it does possess a strong legal tradition of protection of civil liberties. There is considerable difference of opinion as to whether such measures are attacks on that legal tradition or simply reasonable precautions taken by a government faced with an extraordinarily difficult situation. As one British commentator noted, "Nobody calls it censorship when Mafia spokesmen are not allowed to explain, over the airwaves, why it is advisable to pay protection money."[20]

The controversy in Northern Ireland highlights one dilemma faced by law enforcement officials assigned the task of coping with terrorism. Terrorism is by definition a political crime in that it involves political motives. Yet most of the laws created by democracies to deal with terrorism have been crafted with a desire to prevent its classification as a political crime in order to prevent the use of the "political crime exception" included in most extradition agreements, as discussed in Chapter 1. Democracies in general allow a wide range of political dissent with political parties and interest groups representing extremes on both the right and the left of the ideological spectrum operating legally within the system. Thus, it is generally not the political motive that is illegal but the action taken by the individual or group.

It is easier to censure such actions than to censor them. If the motive is not illegal, then it is not reasonable to expect the press not to investigate, evaluate, and report on the motive as it relates to a specific act of terrorist violence. In a democratic system in which the media are allowed to interview perpetrators of violent crime (e.g., murder, rape, torture) and to interview their family, friends, coworkers, and any other "relevant" individuals, it seems unlikely that a clear standard could be established for the need to censor stories about individuals and groups involved in terrorist acts.

If terrorist acts are not political crimes, then the media cannot reasonably be censored from reporting information on the individuals and their motivations in such cases as long as they are permitted to publish similar insights relating to other violent crimes. Such reporting may be in poor taste or reflect bad judgment, but it is scarcely worthy of the serious punishment of censorship.

Broadcasters in the United Kingdom, confronted with the censorship system created by the government to control media coverage of the situation in Northern Ireland, were quick to note the ambiguity of this policy. Certainly it was inconsistent to prohibit Sinn Féin from having access to the broadcast media and to censor news stories about this political group when it was by law allowed to function openly as a political party. If it is legal to report on the activities and the causes espoused by other legal political parties, it is not rational for it to be illegal to report on those same items with regard to Sinn Féin.

Neither the United States nor the United Kingdom has been willing, moreover, to recognize violent acts carried out by radical political groups as acts of war. If they had done so, to justify censoring media reporting that might give "aid or comfort to the enemy during time of war" would have been a fairly simple matter. But if the governments were to declare that a state of war exists, then they would also be bound by international law to treat the individuals captured during the commission of those violent acts of terrorism as **prisoners of war**, *combatants who actively involved in a war have been* *captured by the opposing side.* This would make such prisoners subject to the appropriate Geneva Convention provisions and eligible for exchange. Governments are certainly aware that such a step would encourage the endless taking of hostages by groups committing acts of terror in order to exchange them for the prisoners of war held by the government. This could create an intolerable situation, one certainly not worth the comparatively small advantage that the legitimization of censorship would give.

Although the Northern Ireland situation has received the majority of research attention, other Western democracies also offer interesting viewpoints on the utility and effect of governmental restriction on the media's dissemination of information regarding terrorism. A study by Christopher Kehler, Greg Harvey, and Richard Hall offers interesting perspectives on the delicate balance that democracies are expected to maintain between the need for some form of media regulation and the need for a free press.

Kehler and his associates argue that some form of media regulation is essential simply because media coverage of terrorist events can endanger lives. They cite cases in which the press negotiated with terrorists—where press corps members entered lines of fire and secured zones—and cases in which hostage rescue efforts were endangered by live broadcasts of the rescue forces moving in for assault. Although such cases led these researchers to agree that it would be legally permissible for governments to regulate the media in its access to the scenes of these violent acts, it is interesting to note that these authors concluded that responsible standards created and enforced by the broadcast industry itself would be a preferable solution.

The conclusions of Kehler and his associates are consistent with those of most other researchers on this subject. Although almost all deplore the reckless endangering of lives that sometimes takes place when an unrestricted media abuses its privileges of access, few scholars advocate government censorship as a solution. Most appear to agree with Paul Wilkinson's assessment:

> [A]ny suggestion that any external body is bringing pressure to bear and altering editorial judgment as a result of political considerations undermines not only the credibility of the media, but the credibility of democratic government.[21]

Governments must decide the legal status of terrorist crimes before the option of censorship can ever be explored. If terrorism is a political crime, or even a crime of war, then certain restrictions by the government might be applicable. If, however, terrorism is treated by the government as simply a particularly vicious but essentially common crime, then the media should not be prevented from exploring its every facet in the same fashion as it is permitted to explore other violent criminal activity.

COMPLICITY: A VERY SERIOUS CHARGE

The relationship between terrorism and the media does not flow in a single direction; rather, terrorism reacts to and uses the media in a fashion similar to that in which the media react to and use (to sell newspapers or attract viewers) the terrorist events. This interactive relationship has prompted serious charges of **complicity,** *a legal charge indicating active participation of a primary or secondary nature,* in terrorist events to be leveled at the media by law enforcement and government counterterrorism officials.

The interaction of the media with terrorists in the Hanafi Muslim siege in Washington, DC, in March 1977 provides evidence of media interference in law enforcement efforts and of the proactive role of some media in terrorist events. Live broadcasts from the scene continued throughout the siege, and overzealous journalists tied up telephone lines interviewing the terrorists. This constitutes nuisance, perhaps, but not necessarily interference.

However, at least two incidents occurred that highlight the interactive nature of the media and the terrorists in this event. One of the reporters, observing law enforcement officers bringing something (food) to the terrorists, broadcast that the police were preparing for an assault. Eventually, the police were able to convince the Hanafi that the reporter was incorrect, but valuable negotiating time and trust-building efforts were lost. Another reporter called the leader of the hostage-takers, Hamas Abdul Khaalis, and suggested that the police were trying to trick him. Khaalis selected 10 of the older hostages for execution, and police again had to defuse the situation by removing some of their sharpshooters from the area.[22]

This certainly constituted interference in the hostage negotiation process and generated much legitimate criticism of the media. A reporter who was one of the hostages in this siege observed:

> As hostages, many of us felt that the Hanafi takeover was a happening, a guerrilla theater, a high impact propaganda exercise programmed for the TV screen, and . . . for the front pages of newspapers around the world. . . . Beneath the resentment and the anger of my fellow hostages toward the press is a conviction gained . . . that the news media and terrorism feed on each other, that the news media and particularly TV, create a thirst for fame and recognition. Reporters do not simply report the news. They help create it. They are not objective observers, but subjective participants.[23]

This charge suggests that the media play an active role in terrorist events, sometimes even impacting the course of the event. Such a claim goes well beyond that commonly made by many who research this issue: that terrorists use the media for their own purposes. Few would argue that terrorists do indeed use the media to reach a large audience and to carry a specific message to that audience as quickly as possible. The hijacking of TWA Flight 847 in 1985 was, as Grant Wardlaw notes, "cleverly choreographed to ensure maximum media coverage and maximum exposure of [their] propaganda."[24] It remains a disturbing example of the manipulation of the free world's news media by groups involved in terrorist acts.

To propose an interactive relationship suggests that it is possible that the media's impact on terrorism goes beyond that of a reluctant tool, tending instead toward that of a generator of action. This does not mean that anyone truly believes that the media plan, or deliberately suggest, terrorist attacks to groups or individuals. But the action of the media has been scrutinized intensely in recent years to determine whether media coverage of terrorist events caused, for instance, terrorists to choose one particular choice of action over another (e.g., bombings over hijackings).

Schmid offers three hypotheses that attempt to explain the media's effect on terrorism. The first, called the **arousal hypothesis,** *suggests that unusual or unique media content can increase a person's desire to act aggressively; that in fact any news story detailing some form of aggressive behavior can increase the potential for more aggressive behavior from members of the media's audience.*

The second is termed the **disinhibition hypothesis,** which *suggests that violence portrayed in the media weakens the inhibition of the viewer to engage in similar behavior, which in turn increases the person's readiness to engage in aggressive behavior.*

These are hardly as radical a set of concepts today as they were in 1982 when Schmid suggested them. Indeed, a great deal of time and attention has been devoted to determining whether the media encourage violent behavior in viewers, particularly young people. Results of research into these hypotheses have been mixed but have generated sufficient concern for the attorney general of the United States to issue a not-too-veiled warning to the TV networks, strongly suggesting they initiate self-regulation systems for limiting TV violence.

The third hypothesis suggested by Schmid involves the **social learning theory,** *which is premised on the belief that all behavior is learned by observation.* Thus, if television depicts successful terrorist acts, then viewers will learn all about them; this will, in turn, increase the likelihood of terrorism. The media would then be engaged in training individuals in terrorist behavior each time they report such acts.

Surely this is an extreme assessment of the situation. Live media coverage has perhaps given greater importance to events in remote parts of the world, but it seems unlikely that an individual would decide on the basis of a news report of a terrorist incident to engage in terrorist activities. Although TV newscasts are more visually exciting than printed news articles, it has been possible to test this hypothesis by tracking the articles generated by terrorist events over a decade to determine whether or not increased coverage of terrorist events actually resulted in an increase in the number of such events.

All that could be determined by such an analysis was that an **interactive relationship** appears to exist; that is, *one of the variables acts upon or influences the other.* It was not possible with these type of data to determine much more than a rough estimate of the strength of the relationship and its apparent direction. Because other variables could also affect the ones being studied, without controlling all other potential influences on terrorist behavior it would be difficult to generalize about the results of this research. It did become possible, however, to comment more on the utility of the third hypothesis posited by Schmid using this limited study.

According to the list generated by the U.S. State Department of terrorist incidents that took place from 1981 to 1989 (this was a time of fairly intense terrorist activity), a total of 119 incidents were recorded involving an American citizen in some respect. Because all of these incidents involved at least one U.S. citizen, it seems logical to assume they would be reported in national newspapers, such as the *Washington Post* and the *New York Times*. Using these two papers, most of whose stories on these incidents were supplied by the Associated Press (thus eliminating the majority of anomalies in the reporting of the data) and categorizing the incidents by type (to discover whether any type of event served better as a "learning tool"), it was possible to note several interesting phenomena.

First, cumulative regression analysis of the data resulted in a multiple r of 0.843 and a square multiple of r of 0.710. This generally indicates a strong relationship, in this case between the type of event and the amount of coverage.

Second, from 1981 to 1989 inclusive, the number of terrorist incidents increased overall while the number of articles generated in response to these incidents actually decreased. There were exceptions to these trends. The number of bombings resulting in deaths remained relatively constant, actually decreasing toward the end of the period. This occurred in spite of the enormous increase in the number of articles generated by these attacks.

The incidence of assassination (defined, in State Department terms, as any time an American is shot and killed) peaked in 1984, with four incidents that generated a record 14 articles. In spite of the rash of press coverage, however, the number of incidents fell the following year to the 1981 level (one incident), producing only four articles. The following year there were three incidents, showing that terrorist activity was clearly not impacted by the previous year's limited press coverage of these types of events. In other words, many articles in one year did not generate many attacks the following year; nor did a year when the number of articles dropped to only four result in a decrease in the subsequent number of incidents.

Hijackings (involving the willful seizure of a means of transportation for a political purpose) occurred in only three years during the decade studied. After three incidents generated a phenomenal 16 articles, there was only one further incident for the remainder of the decade.

Kidnappings of Americans actually generated fewer articles than other types of incidents, meaning that some incidents were not even reported in the national news. Nor was there a direct relationship between the number of articles and the number of incidents. Four incidents in 1985 generated only one article, whereas fewer incidents (three) in 1986 evoked seven articles.

These data suggest that, although a relationship appears to exist between the number of terrorist incidents in a given year and the number of articles they generate, this relationship varies with the type of incident. This implies, as suggested earlier, that other factors are at work in this process that are not accounted for in so simplistic an assumption as the "learned behavior" hypothesis. If all that was necessary for a terrorist to repeat his or her action, or for another terrorist to attempt a similar action, was news coverage of the event, then all of the types of events should have produced parallel growth lines between incident and article numbers. This was clearly not the case.

Instead, it is obvious that other factors influence the decision of an individual or group to engage in terrorist activities. Although the media may have some impact, it is erroneous to assume that the action of the media causes terrorist events to happen because of the coverage of previous events. Hijacking incidents did not become less frequent because of limited media coverage; instead, media coverage was extensive. However, the enactment of several aerial hijacking conventions and the subsequent closing of most safe havens for hijackers by the "extradite or prosecute" provisions in international agreements (discussed in Chapter 10) may as easily be given credit for reducing the number of hijacking incidents.

This limited study of news media in a role of "motivation" for potential terrorists suggests that although terrorism and the media show a strong relationship, this does not mean that media coverage results in terrorist acts. Certainly the mass media do serve to extend experience, present models, stimulate aspirations, and indicate goals for terrorists. But the media are clearly not responsible for terrorist acts occurring.

It is possible to infer from a variety of studies on this issue that the media can impact terrorists by what Schmid terms a **built-in escalation imperative,** *requiring that terrorists must commit more and more bizarre and cruel acts to gain media attention.* Because kidnapping failed to generate continued media attention, even though most articles suggested that many times the ransom demands were met, terrorists turned increasingly to the use of assassination. When the shooting of a single American stopped generating many articles (as it did between 1985 and 1989), bombings resulting in multiple deaths became the weapon of choice.

A relationship certainly exists between terrorists and the media. The strength and direction of that relationship is dependent on many variables and is thus probably not a suitable target for intervention by the government. Intervention could skew the relationship in an undesirable direction. As Schmid notes, "the assertion of insurgent terrorists that democratic states are not really democratic would gain credibility if the freedom of the press were suspended."[25]

Transformations in modern media, and in modern terrorism, have accelerated this mass-mediated growth of terrorism. During the past two decades, media venues have expanded to include the Internet, as more people connect through the World Wide Web today than ever before. Mergers and acquisition among media companies have accelerated as well, creating global media moguls. With technology linking the globe as never before, and with terrorist groups linking via the Web, mass transit, and mass communications, the role of the media today in reporting—and impacting—terrorist events must be carefully studied as we seek to come to grips with twenty-first-century terrorism.

Bin Laden's Tapes

A brief look at the skillful use of the media by one of the world's best-known terrorists, Osama bin Laden, makes many of the preceding points about the relationship of media and terrorism clearer. It also raises interesting questions about the impact of the media on events during a terrorist crisis.

As Judith Miller so aptly put it, "With his turban and camouflage jacket, his ornate Arabic and harsh vows of continued terror against America, Osama bin Laden revealed in his speech the instinctive cunning that has made him such a formidable foe."[26] Referring to one of bin Laden's taped speeches in which he articulated once again his call for jihad, she noted that the speech gave this al-Qaeda leader his most visible platform, because it was broadcast over a popular Arabic satellite channel and rebroadcast many times by CNN and many other networks.

Using this platform, bin Laden expressed righteous indignation over the suffering of Iraq and Palestine. With his pledge to end the eighty years of "humiliation and disgrace" that Muslims have endured since the demise of the Ottoman Empire and to recreate the caliphate, the Muslim empire based for about 500 years in Iraq, bin Laden made his appeal for understanding among the common Arab men of the region.

His timing of the appearance of this platform was excellent. Al Jazeera, the Arabic network, had followed bin Laden's instructions to delay release of the tape until after the start of the American bombing in Afghanistan. Using the West's media weapon very effectively, bin Laden issued his global statement just as President Bush was trying to declare war on terrorism. In his taped address, bin Laden suggested that the world was divided, not by those who stood with the United States in rejecting terrorism and those who stood against her, but in terms of people who were faithful to Islam and the infidels who opposed him.

Although this was not the first call by bin Laden to jihad against America—it was in fact the fourth such call—the video shown around the world in early October 2001 was perhaps the most effective. Bin Laden used the media to secure a platform with a worldwide audience to emotionally explain the cause for his anger and his anguish and to paint the enemies of his jihad in ways that shook the alliance that President Bush was trying to form. Ahmed Abdullah, a bin Laden lieutenant and the head of al-Qaeda's media committee, is believed to have arranged the filming and transmission of many of bin Laden's propaganda videos.

During the years following the September 11, 2001, attacks, videos of bin Laden continued to be released. The video released in September 2007 raised several new issues. Bin Laden's appearance, for example, had changed fairly dramatically. In previous videos, his hair and beard were clearly gray; in the 2007 fall video, both his hair and his beard had clearly been tinted to appear dark, raising interesting questions: Had the hair and beard been darkened to make bin Laden appear sufficiently young and vigorous to reassure his followers of his continued leadership? Or were they darkened in accordance with similar actions allegedly taken by

Mohammed in his time of leadership, to put fear in the hearts of his enemies? To which audience, in other words, was this change in appearance directed? ■

Source: The *Washington Post,* retrieved October 17, 2011 at http://www.washingtonpost.com/national/bin-laden-videos-other-data-released-by-obama-administration/2011/05/07/AFb2qLJG_story.html

CONCLUSIONS

Technological progress in communications systems has made the media a potentially significant weapon in the terrorist arsenal. Whether the media are "the terrorist's best friend," as Laqueur has suggested, or an unwitting ally, as described by Schmid and de Graaf's study, it seems clear that the media play a significant role in the "propaganda by the deed" which is modern terrorism.[27] The line between reporter of terrorist events and participant in these events is often quite thin and easily, if unintentionally, crossed.

Studies suggest that violent behavior can be learned and that copycat behavior among individuals and groups is common. Therefore, it is not unreasonable to assume that portrayal of terrorist events in the news may actually motivate terrorist behavior. This does not suggest that journalists are intentionally involved in the increase in terrorist incidents. Although journalists have, as noted earlier, sometimes interfered in situations to a degree that may have altered the course of the event, this is the exception rather than the rule.

A strong case can be made for the need for media to collaborate with the government to devise workable guidelines in matters of media coverage of terrorism. This should include guidelines for working with law enforcement in setting reasonable limits on access to events where appropriate, as well as self-regulating rules on the use, nonuse, or delayed use of information, technology, and opportunity in ways that will best protect the lives endangered by the situation and the needs of citizens for a full account of events.

The goals of terrorists, law enforcement, and the media are clearly related and fundamentally incompatible in many respects. There is no greater challenge for democracies in the struggle with terrorism today than that posed by the need to find a policy compatible with the tradition of a free and vigorous media. Democratic governments are confronted with the demand that they be able to reconcile the goals of the media with those of law enforcement in ways that do not satisfy the goals of terrorists. Prior restraints placed on access and censorship of media coverage of terrorist events create too high a price to pay for the dubious value of decreasing media reports of terrorist acts. Terrorists win significant victories against democracies when they force such measures.

Reconciling the goals of media with those of law enforcement with respect to terrorism is a formidable but not necessarily an impossible task. The *Report of the Task Force on Disorders and Terrorism* (1976) made constructive suggestions regarding the synthesizing of the protection of First Amendment rights with the need for public security:

1. Limiting interviews during hostage situations
2. Delaying the release of inflammatory or sensitive information
3. Minimizing the intrusiveness of the media in the course of the terrorist events
4. Striving for balanced and noninflammatory coverage of such incidents

The standards suggested by the media during the last decade of the twentieth century often coincide with these recommendations. Most call for balanced coverage, which avoids the use of provocative catchphrases. There is agreement as well on the need not to offer to terrorists a platform for propaganda. But the media have strongly resisted the concept of government regulation, regarding this as censorship. Although most constitutions have sanctioned powers of emergency that may be invoked, with a consequent limiting of freedom of speech, most democracies are unwilling to concede to terrorists their goal of destabilization by having to invoke such emergency provisions. Deciding which goals must be met and what the acceptable cost will be for meeting them is a challenge that governments in the twenty-first century *must* meet.

Ralph Perl, one scholar of this thorny issue, has stated the essence of this dilemma challenging democracies succinctly:

> The potential power of these [terrorist] groups seems to lie not in their threat to overthrow society by force of arms *per se,* but in their ability to symbolize the fragility and vulnerability of the social order and to force that order to subvert itself by eroding the liberal and democratic values upon which its own legitimacy is based.[28]

DISCUSSION

1. Ralph Perl suggests several voluntary press coverage guidelines that offer insights into the pattern of self-restriction that may emerge soon. Many are similar to those offered three decades ago in the study just discussed. Consider each guideline briefly and decide which goals are placed at risk by each.
   a. Limiting information about hostages that could harm them (e.g., number, nationality, official positions, personal wealth)
   b. Limiting information about military movements during rescue operations
   c. Limiting or agreeing not to air live interviews with terrorists
   d. Toning down information that may cause widespread panic
   e. Checking sources of information carefully
2. Ted Koppel, the former anchor of ABC television's *Nightline*, suggested that the U.S. media operate at the outer boundaries of what its European allies would view as acceptable. He notes that "[American television is] particularly vulnerable to misuse. We are vulnerable to misuse by our own leaders. . . . The fact that terrorism by definition tends to be dramatic [and] the fact that by definition it tends to involve acts which are pictorial, makes us even more vulnerable."[29] How can this "vulnerability" be diminished without allowing terrorists to use media as a weapon—eliminating the former two vulnerabilities by making it subject to a third?

3. David Hubbard, a psychiatrist who has interviewed scores of imprisoned hijackers, contends that TV news broadcasts of ongoing terrorist events are "social pornography" because it "caters to the sick, unmet needs of the public."[30] He is convinced that world terrorism would decrease if television brought its coverage under control. How accurate do you think this assessment is? What kinds of controls can a democratic society afford to impose on its media? What are the dangers of such controls? How effective do you think either voluntary or involuntary controls on media coverage of terrorism would be in reducing either the number or the violence of terrorist events?

4. Mary Strep and Rhonda Knox, assessing the impact of media portrayals and the events of September 11, 2001, raised troubling questions.[31] Noting that the media played a central role in the dissemination of information on September 11, these researchers ask the following: To what extent, then, did the media set the agenda on September 11, 2001? How were the most important stories selected? What images of September 11 do you remember most vividly? How important are those images in shaping your perceptions of what happened that day, what the causes were, and what should have been done about the attacks?

ANALYSIS CHALLENGE

The media are being used to recruit—and to get messages out—to potential audiences, and it is in many respects being used more effectively by terrorists than by counterterror forces. Visit this Marshall Center website to view a paper about jihadi use of the media: http://www.marshallcenter.org/mcpublicweb/MCDocs/files/College/F_Publications/occPapers/occ-paper_20-en.pdf. Visit the U.S. Military Academy's Countering Terrorism Center website, and look at the *Islamic Imagery Project,* where there are many symbols used by Islamic radicals in the electronic media: http://www.ctc.usma.edu/.

How can the media be used more effectively as a "weapon" to counter terrorism?

KEY TERMS

mass-mediated
  terrorism 165
publicity 166
tactical (short-term) and
  strategic (long-term)
  gains 166
favorable
  understanding 167
legitimacy and
  identity 167
destabilizing the
  enemy 167
criminality of act 168
denial of a platform 169
information and
  cooperation 169

copycat operation 169
disinformation 169
getting a scoop 169
dramatic
  presentation 170
protection of rights 170
personal security 171
amplification effect
  171
symbiotic
  relationship 173
showcase 173
current and potential
  supporters 174
general public 174
enemy public 174

right of access 175
prior restraint 176
censorship 176
prisoners of war
  178
complicity 180
arousal hypothesis
  181
disinhibition
  hypothesis 181
social learning
  theory 181
interactive
  relationship 181
built-in escalation
  imperative 183

SUGGESTED READINGS AND RESOURCES

Alali, A. Odasno, and Kenoye K. Eke. "Terrorism, the News Media, and Democratic Political Order." *Current World Leaders* 39, no. 4 (August 1996): 64–72.

Finn, John E. "Media Coverage of Political Terrorism and the First Amendment: Reconciling the Public's Right to Know with Public Order." In *Violence and Terrorism: 98/99*, ed. Martin Slann and Bernard Schechterman. New York: Dushkin/McGraw-Hill, 1998.

Forrest, James, ed., *Teaching Terror: Strategic and Tactical Learning in the Terrorist World*. Lanham, MD: Rowman & Littlefield Publishers, 2006.

Kidder, Rushworth M. "Manipulation of the Media." In *Violence and Terrorism 98/99*, ed. Martin Slann and Bernard Schechterman. New York: Dushkin/McGraw-Hill, 1998.

Nacos, Brigitte L. *Mass-Mediated Terrorism: The Central Role of Media in Terrorism and Counterterrorism*. Lanham, MD: Rowman & Littlefield Publishers, 2007.

Perl, Ralph F. *Terrorism, the Media, and the 21st Century*. Congressional Research Service, 1998.

Schmid, Alex P., and J. de Graaf. *Violence as Communication: Insurgent Terrorism and the Western News Media*. Beverly Hills, CA: Sage, 1982.

Strep, Mary, and Rhonda Knox. "Terrorism and the Media." *Council on Foreign Relations* (August 5, 2004).

NOTES

1. Brigette Nacos, *Mass-Mediated Terrorism* (Lanham, MD: Rowman & Littlefield Publishers, 2007), 17.
2. Rushworth Kidder, "Manipulation of the Media," *Annual Editions: Violence and Terrorism 98/99* (New York: Dushkin/McGraw-Hill), 151.
3. Ibid., 152.
4. On June 13, 1985, two Hezbollah gunmen hijacked this flight en route from Athens to Rome and murdered U.S. Navy diver Robert Stethem after the plane landed in Beirut for a second time. The U.S. State Department was highly critical of the impact of the media on this event.
5. John E. Finn, "Media Coverage of Political Terrorism and the First Amendment: Reconciling the Public's Right to Know with Public Order," in *Terrorism and the Media: Dilemma for Government, Journalism and the Public,* ed. Yonah Alexander and Robert Latter (Washington, DC: Brassey's, 1990).
6. See the website for the Committee to Protect Journalists: http://www.cpj.org/.
7. "Terrorism Found Rising, Now Almost Accepted," *Washington Post,* December 3, 1985, A4.
8. These quotes were gathered by Neil Hickey in "Gaining the Media's Attention," *The Struggle Against Terrorism* (New York: Wilson, 1977), 113–114.
9. Ibid., 117.
10. Ibid., 112.
11. *Webster's Dictionary of the English Language* (New York: Lexicon Publications, 1991), 923.
12. Ibid., 921.
13. Cindy Combs, "The Media as a Showcase for Terrorism," in *Teaching Terror: Strategic and Tactical Learning in the Terrorist World*, ed. James Forrest (Lanham, MD: Rowman & Littlefield Publishers, 2006), 140.

14. T. K. Fitzpatrick, "The Semantics of Terror," *Security Register* 1, no. 14 (November 4, 1974): 23.

15. Abraham H. Miller, "Terrorism, the Media, and the Law: A Discussion of the Issues," in *Terrorism, the Media, and the Law*, ed. A. H. Miller (Dobbs Ferry, NY: Transnational Publishers, 1980), 43.

16. Abraham H. Miller, "Terrorism and the Media: Lessons from the British Experience," in *The Heritage Foundation Lectures* (Washington, DC, 1990), 1–9.

17. Alex P. Schmid and Janny F. A. de Graaf, *Violence as Communication* (Newbury Park, CA: Sage, 1982), 160.

18. Ibid., 162.

19. Rushworth M. Kidder, "Manipulation of the Media," in *Violence and Terrorism 91/92*, ed. Martin Slann and Bernard Schechterman (New York: Dushkin, 1991), 118.

20. Ibid., 35.

21. Ibid., 44.

22. Schmid and de Graaf, *Violence as Communication*, 77.

23. Ibid., 72.

24. Grant Wardlaw, "State Response to International Terrorism: Some Cautionary Comments," paper presented to the Symposium on International Terrorism, Defense Intelligence Agency, Washington, DC, 1985, 8.

25. Schmid and de Graaf, *Violence as Communication*, 72.

26. Judith Miller, "Bin Laden's Media Savvy: Expert Timing of Threats," *New York Times*, October 9, 2001, A1.

27. Schmid and de Graaf, *Violence as Communication*, 172.

28. Ralph Perl, *Terrorism, the Media, and the 21st Century* (Washington, DC: Congressional Research Service, 1998), 2.

29. Ibid.

30. David Hubbard, *Skyjacker: His Flights of Fancy* (New York: Wilson, 1997), 134.

31. Mary Strep and Rhonda Knox, "Terrorism and the Media," *Council on Foreign Relations*, August 5, 2004.

Domestic Terrorism in the United States

> Terrorism is neither unique nor new to the United States.
> Nationalist terrorism began during frontier wars in the
> seventeenth century and has continued to the present day.
>
> —*Jonathan A. White*

To apply some of the concepts and definitions discussed thus far, study of terrorism as it has developed in one country may be helpful. Although the United States has been slower than some other Western democracies in developing definitions and coping strategies for domestic terrorism, the patterns observed may help to clarify the strengths and weaknesses of the profiles of terrorists, their patterns of training, and the philosophies that motivate them.

HISTORICAL ROOTS IN THE UNITED STATES

This nation was, as one historian noted, "conceived and born in violence,"[1] from early settlers and their wars with the Native American populations, to the Sons of Liberty and the patriots of the port cities during the 1760s and 1770s to the vigilante groups who enforced justice as the settlers moved West. Much of the violence of the nineteenth and twentieth centuries was rooted in these early patterns of terrorism, making a quick look at them useful in understanding and predicting terrorism in the twenty-first century.

Terrorism certainly occurred during the early years of colonial settlement in North America. The efforts of the British, and then the young American leaders, to eliminate the threat of the indigenous populations certainly became **genocide**, because, by definition, it evolved into *efforts to reduce in size (to facilitate control of) or to destroy ethnic groups.* This included massacres of men, women, and children, decimating entire villages or forcing the inhabitants of those villages on what became "death marches" to distant locations, as records of the treatment of the Cherokee of western North Carolina indicate.

Not all deaths of Native Americans at the hands of British or Americans were done by open violence; instead, evidence exists that some died from weapons of bioterror. Although diseases have historically killed large numbers of indigenous peoples as colonial intrusions brought diseases against which native populations had no resistance, the diseases were also used as weapons. There are accounts, for example, suggesting that certain local British commanders in 1769 planned to give to the Native Americans, as a peace offering, blankets from military hospitals that had been infected with smallpox. Although a smallpox epidemic did break out among the Native Americans in Pennsylvania, it is uncertain from historical records whether the blankets played any role in this outbreak.

Violence during the Revolution has often been justified by the Machiavellian philosophy of the ends justifying the means, an operational philosophy frequently claimed by modern revolutionary groups. Thus, the tarring and feathering of Tories in the seaport cities during the 1770s, a brutal act involving pouring tar over a victim and then dumping feathers over him or her (or rolling the person in a pile of feathers), was treated as a patriotic act of violence that helped to win the Revolutionary War.

The guerrilla warfare that encompassed the colonies from New York to Georgia was also marred by terrorism. Rival parties of Whigs and Tories bushwhacked houses and travelers, burning homes and often killing innocent family members. Neither Whigs nor Tories showed any mercy, and prisoners were frequently tortured and then hanged. Terrorism perpetrated against members of a family on one side often made the surviving members of that family willing to carry out equally atrocious acts of terror in revenge.

Although most of the Revolutionary War was no doubt fought according to the rules, at least in the sense that targets were primarily military rather than civilian and terrorism was the exception rather than the rule, it is evident from historical accounts that terrorism did take place. This pattern makes it clear, though, why nation-states such as the United States today are hesitant to condemn revolutionary violence in emerging states, even when such violence involves occasional acts of terrorism. Most nation-states, in their own history, have seen similar acts of terrorism, sometimes carried out by historically venerated "patriots," for reasons that touch cords of sympathy in modern times.

Like many modern nation-states, the United States also experienced a violent civil war. Although the practice of slavery in the twentieth century was declared an international crime, it was widely practiced in the United States until the mid-1860s and was a major contributing factor in generating the conflict. **Slavery,** which involves *the holding of a person as the property of, and completely subject to, another person,* was a violent act carried out legally at that time by thousands of families and businesses throughout the world. The practice of slavery and the violent conflict that tore the United States apart during efforts to end this practice left legacies of violence that endured through the twentieth century and are still inherent in many right-wing groups active today.

In the U.S. slave trade, individuals and families were captured and carried against their will in appalling conditions from one continent (usually Africa) to another continent (North America), and sold to U.S. citizens and businesses. This violent uprooting, brutal treatment, and degradation of an ethnic community would unquestionably today be classified as terrorism if it were carried out for political motives rather than economic ends. Regardless of its motives, its legacy has been both bitter and violent in the United States, contributing significantly to the right-wing terrorism currently emerging.

White supremacist groups that operate in the United States today trace their roots to the group that emerged after the Civil War during the period of Southern reconstruction, a group known as the **Ku Klux Klan** (KKK). This name has been applied to either of two distinct secret terrorist organizations in the United States. *One of these is the organization that was founded just after the Civil War and lasted until the 1870s. The other KKK began in 1915 and continued through the end of the century.* The first Klan was originally founded as a social club for Confederate veterans in Pulaski, Tennessee, in 1866. They apparently derived the name from the Greek word *kyklos,* from which comes the English term *circle;* the Klan part of the name came from an effort at alliteration. Rapidly becoming a vehicle for Southern White underground resistance, it drew members who sought to restore White supremacy to the South through intimidation and violence aimed at the newly enfranchised Black freedmen.

This Klan reached its peak between 1868 and 1870, its members dressing in white robes and sheets to intimidate the freedmen and to avoid being recognized. Klansmen beat and killed freedmen and their White supporters in nighttime attacks. The violence of this group caused its founders to order it to disband and the U.S. Congress to pass the KKK Act in 1871, which imposed heavy penalties on this terrorist organization. This Klan essentially disappeared in the following years, mostly because its goal of restoring White supremacy had been achieved and the need for such an organization was no longer evident.

The new Klan, which emerged in 1915, added a hatred of Roman Catholics, Jews, foreigners, and organized labor to its hostility toward Blacks. A burning cross became the symbol of this new organization. It peaked in membership in the 1920s, dropped drastically in activity in the Great Depression of the 1930s, and experienced a resurgence in membership and activities with the civil rights movement of the 1960s. Bombings, whippings, shootings, and lynchings were again committed by members of this group against innocent people.

By the end of the twentieth century, Klan membership was again fragmentary and dispersed. Many members left the Klan to become members instead of White supremacist groups active throughout the country. According to Bill Stanton, the Klan broke with the past in 1979 and emerged in North Carolina and Georgia as a paramilitary organization.[2] This emergence of a new form of right-wing extremism will be examined in more depth later in this chapter. It is sufficient to note here that the practice of slavery and the subsequent growth of racist groups carrying out violence against the newly freed slaves created a legacy of violence still generating terrorist acts today.

While the colonial period produced acts of genocide and slavery that were the genesis of much of modern right-wing terrorism, one form of this, **vigilante terrorism**, in which *individuals or groups seek to defend the status quo or return to that of an earlier period by using terrorist tactics on a population without legitimate authority to do so,* grew as the frontier of the new nation expanded. Settlers developed their own form of justice, with vigilante groups often composed of leading citizens holding moot, illegal "courts" to try and often execute those disrupting civil society.

This trend toward vigilante violence helps to explain the growth in the western United States of modern vigilante groups such as the Order, the Christian Identity Movement, and many of the militia organizations that exist nationwide. These groups tend to be based on the assumption that the current system of justice is inadequate and that vigilante action, often of a terrorist nature, is required to restore order to the system.

Several of these groups will be examined in more depth in the discussion of contemporary terrorism. At this point it is sufficient to conclude that most modern terrorist acts taking place in the United States have roots in its history.

CONCEPTUALIZING DOMESTIC TERRORISM IN THE UNITED STATES

Political violence in America has a long history; therefore, establishing categories for the types of domestic terrorism will make any analysis more coherent. Most of those who have researched violence in the United States have suggested three categories of terrorist types, although they differ somewhat in the naming of those types. Ted Gurr suggested that the categories be called vigilante terrorism, insurgent terrorism, and transnational terrorism.[3] This is very similar to that suggested in 1994 by Brent Smith, who grouped terrorism by motivation as well, but called the categories right-wing extremism; left-wing extremism, nationalist terrorism, and single-issue violence; and international terrorism.[4]

We will utilize an updated blend of Smith's and Gurr's categories but will define them to fit more clearly the forms of modern terrorism found within the United States. The three "types" of domestic terrorism examined here will be right-wing extremism, left-wing extremism, and transnational terrorism; these can be differentiated in terms of their differing views of the "status quo." The first category (using Smith's descriptive category), **right-wing extremism**, encompasses Gurr's vigilante terrorism and includes individuals or groups that *seek to retain or to reestablish an earlier status quo by the use of terrorist acts.* This would include radical religious groups seeking a return or expansion of "fundamental" faith strictures. It would also include some of the single-issue groups, such as the Army of God, that violently oppose current laws permitting abortion.

The second category of domestic terrorism, **left-wing terrorism**, derives from groups motivated by a desire to *seek to rebel against or radically change the political system through the use of terrorist tactics*. This is a fairly broad category, since it may include left-wing, nationalists, and some single-issue extremists (such as the Earth Liberation Front) and could fit comfortably in the category Gurr suggests of insurgent terrorism.

Finally, **transnational terrorism** is the same as international terrorism as both terms indicate *terrorism that involves two or more countries*. Some of the groups and individuals that have ideologies, which put them in the first two categories, also fall within this category; the difference is that for a group to be involved in transnational terrorism, it must have a desire to effect a change or restoration of the status quo that would go beyond the boundaries of one country.

LEFT-WING TERRORISM

Because this is, as the works of Gurr and Smith make clear, a very broad category, it will be useful to examine its different manifestations separately. Movements from the extreme left, the more moderate left, and issue-specific insurgency will be explored separately, with conclusions offered linking these "insurgent" movements in the context of U.S. terrorism.

Left-Wing Extremism

One of the early forms of insurgent terrorism to reach the United States was anarchism, which was imported from Europe during the late nineteenth and early twentieth centuries. Where Russia and parts of Europe experienced anarchists like Mikhail Bakunin and Sergey Nechaev, discussed in Chapter 2, America had **Johan Most,** *an anarchist who immigrated from Germany to the United States in 1882,* after serving a jail sentence in London for praising the assassination of the Russian Czar.[5]

Most was the first U.S. citizen to provide a philosophical rationale for terrorism, advocating the linkage of anarchism to the labor movement and arguing that violence was the only method available for overcoming the tyranny of the wealth and power of the state. In his revolutionary newspaper, *Freiheit* (which means "freedom" in German), Most discussed the value of organized violence in labor struggles, seeking to incite members of the labor movement to violence. In this newspaper, Most advocated a bombing campaign against the U.S. government and industry. He also developed plans for a letter bomb, which became a "unique American contribution to the terrorist arsenal."[6]

Most, like his occasional companion Emma Goldman, who emigrated from Russia to the United States in 1885, spent most of his time trying to incite others to violence. Both were closely linked to the labor movement, and strongly advocated social change and the use of violence to achieve those changes. Like many of their European counterparts, Most and Goldman were violent in words but not in deeds for the most part, limiting the extent to which they could accurately be accused of terrorism.

Like Europe, the United States experienced a surge of left-wing terrorism in the mid-to-late twentieth century, much of it initially on its college campuses rather than among its working poor in labor movements. Within the category of insurgent terrorism that flourished in the latter part of the twentieth century would fall the Puerto Rican nationalists who carried out terrorist acts, student-based revolutionary groups, and single-issue groups, according to Smith's analysis. These disparate left-wing groups tended to espouse Marxist philosophy, to be violently opposed to the economic "status quo," to seek to create bases for their movements in urban rather than rural areas, and like most other groups engaging in terrorism, to choose symbolic rather than strategically important targets for their attacks.

Unlike in much of Europe, however, the U.S. left-wing revolutionary movements did not generate widespread public support, nor were most groups long-lived or successful in efforts toward carrying out acts of violence. In 1967, several protest groups began to coalesce around the Students for a Democratic Society. The Weather Underground and the Symbionese Liberation Army (infamous for its kidnapping of heiress Patty Hearst) were active in the 1960s and 1970s. Many in these groups linked with Puerto Rican nationalist groups, such as the Macheteros. Fortunately for the United States, most of the student-based groups were active in ideological rhetoric but not skilled in violence. Many of the bombing attempts killed more of the student activists than they did the intended targets.

Nationalist Groups

Puerto Rican nationalists have been active for more than four decades, because the U.S. government has had difficulty deciding the ultimate status of this territory. In addition to the very violent Macheteros, the Armed Forces of National Liberation, the Volunteers for the Puerto Rican Revolution, the Armed Forces of Liberation, the Guerrilla Forces of Liberation, and Omega 7 operated in the United States. Many routinely joined other left-wing organizations. In addition to conducting one of the largest armored car robberies in U.S. history, Puerto Rican groups carried out several bombings, assassinations, and one rocket attack (on FBI headquarters in San Juan).

Although most of the left-wing revolutionary violence of the 1960s and 1970s has diminished substantially but not entirely vanished from the United States, the problem of violence erupting from Puerto Rico's status is likely to remain. Among Puerto Ricans, there is considerable division of opinion as to what is best for the islands: Some want statehood within the United States; others would like to have an independent country; and some are satisfied with its current commonwealth status. This ambivalence is compounded by the strategic importance placed on Puerto Rico by the U.S. military, which continues to use portions of the territory for target practice and military maneuvers. Regardless of which solution for Puerto Rico's future status is adopted, at least one or two groups will be angry and may well carry on the violent attacks on U.S. targets.

Single-Issue Groups

Within the category of insurgent terrorism are included, by Smith's categorization, groups and individuals motivated by a single issue such as protection of the environment or animal rights. These groups, according to Smith, are like the left-wing revolutionaries in their ideologies, their views of human nature, their economic views, and their fanatic devotion to their cause. Case studies 9.1 and 9.2 will illustrate these points.

CASE STUDY 9.1

Earth Liberation Front

The **Earth Liberation Front** (ELF), a violent environmental activist group, is believed to have splintered off from the Earth First! movement at a meeting in Brighton, England, in 1994. The notable difference between the Earth First! movement and the ELF is that the ELF advocates the destruction of property against corporations that it believes are hurting the environment.

The Federal Bureau of Investigation (FBI) upgraded the ELF to a terrorist organization in January 2001. This upgraded status was due to an incendiary attack on a ski resort under construction, as well as other destructive attacks. During the attack on the Vail Mountain ski resort in Colorado, the ELF burned three buildings and partially destroyed four ski lifts. The estimated cost of the damage exceeded $12 million. The ELF immediately claimed responsibility for the attack via an e-mail sent from Denver, Colorado. The reason for the attack, according to the e-mail, was that the Vail resort was planning an expansion of the ski resort that would encroach on the best lynx habitat in the state.

The FBI was unable to make immediate arrests or to uncover the identity of the group's members. One of the main reasons contributing to this sluggish legal response is the lack of a central hierarchy in the organization. The FBI believes members of the ELF work in small groups composed of members who know each other and do not keep membership lists or publicly release their identities. Because the ELF formed from a grassroots movement, its members are likely to remain in small groups and continue to lack a central government or leader.[7]

In March 2001, the FBI classified the ELF as the top domestic terror threat in the United States. While the events of September 11 drove the ELF from headlines, its activists clearly did not stop their actions.

In 2002, three students at Douglas S. Freeman High School in Henrico County, Virginia, in the name of the ELF, engaged in a spree of destruction using kerosene-soaked wicks to set fire to the fuel tanks of vehicles being used to construct a mall in Henrico. The three young men also vandalized 25 sport utility vehicles (SUVs) at an auto dealership, as well as several other SUVs parked at private homes. The three students, Adam Blackwell, Aaron Linas, and John Wade, pled guilty in January 2004, agreed to provide in excess of $200,000 in restitution for the damage, and were sentenced to short terms in jail.

Extremists from the ELF caused about $30,000 in damage to a Charlottesville, Virginia, building site in February 2004, setting fire to a bulldozer and damaging other construction equipment at the site. The site was being developed into a mix of retail, commercial, and residential units, a project to which the ELF obviously had objections. The ELF members responsible for this attack left behind a banner reading "YOUR CONSTRUCTION = LONG-TERM DESTRUCTION — ELF."

Activities by the ELF were not limited in the early years of the twenty-first century to the east coast of the United States. Fires set by ELF extremists early on the morning of April 20, 2004, in Snohomish County, Washington, caused an estimated $1 million in damage. The arsonists destroyed two new houses. According to a local newspaper, at a separate home-construction site near the firebombing, workers arrived the next morning to find soft drink and Gatorade bottles filled with flammable liquid and a threatening note written on a piece of cardboard.

In February 2006, a self-proclaimed member of the ELF was charged in California with demonstrating the use of a destructive device. Rodney Adam Coronado was arrested in Tucson, Arizona, by agents of the FBI and the Bureau of Alcohol, Tobacco, Firearms and Explosives (ATF). According to the indictment on August 1, 2003, at a gathering in San Diego, Coronado taught and demonstrated the construction and use of a destructive device, with the intent that the device be used to commit arson. The FBI has identified Coronado as a "national leader" of the ELF, although Coronado describes himself as an "unofficial spokesman."

According to FBI reports, the ELF has committed more than 1,200 acts of vandalism and arson in the United States, causing more than $200 million in damage but without causing loss of life.[8] With this record, the ELF's categorization as a group committing terrorism is regularly challenged, since it commits no violence against people, only to property. The ELF, however, has committed dramatic acts of violence to property that were certainly designed to create a mood of fear within a particular audience, in an effort to effect a change in policy. In that context, the ELF fits the definition of terrorism utilized by the FBI. ∎

Source: Federal Bureau of Investigation

Single-issue organizations do not exist only in the United States; indeed, many were formed first in Europe and have created cells in America, in a pattern similar to that of most other types of terrorism. This kind of terrorism appears to be increasingly prevalent and spans a wide range of issues, from abortion clinic bombings to the destruction of laboratories where cosmetics are tested on animals.

Conclusion: Left-Wing Terrorism in the United States Today

Although revolutionary and nationalist violence were fairly strong in the 1960s through the mid-1980s, the predominant type of insurgent terrorism in the United States in this new century appears issue-oriented, lacking in clear organizational structure and membership rolls and often carried out by individuals acting on their own rather than as a part of a planned group effort. Most groups are like the **Animal Liberation Front,** People for the Ethical Treatment of Animals, and the ELF: *movements, rather than groups, with no clear membership and few overt leaders.* This type of terrorist organization fits the category of an all-channel network, with each cell or individual operating separately, focused against a common enemy or toward a common goal. This is the most difficult structure of network to combat. Because it lacks a hub or chain, it is difficult to link the pieces and predict movement, membership, and resources with any accuracy.

RIGHT-WING EXTREMISM: FROM MILITIA GROUPS TO RELIGIOUS FANATICS

Abortion clinic bombings are at least ideologically linked to groups engaged in right-wing extremism in the United States, although they are also clearly a form of single-issue terrorism. Unlike the objective of vigilante groups prevalent during the early years of nationhood, the White supremacist groups and the militias that have been a part of the American landscape for much of the country's history share with those carrying out the bombing of abortion clinics a desire to return to the status quo of an earlier period. Individuals in right-wing terrorism have tended to be, in the United States as in Europe, those who want either to protect the system as it currently exists or to help the system return to an earlier status from which, in their view, it has mistakenly wandered.

Right-wing terrorism, unlike that of the left, has been strong in the United States, in both historical and contemporary times. In the last two decades of the twentieth century, in fact, there was an upsurge of right-wing groups, in membership and in activity. Just as the left-wing movements began to diminish in the mid-1980s, organizations like the Order, the Aryan Nations, the Christian Identity Movement, and hundreds of militia groups began to gain strength.

Militia Movements

Numerous local or state militias are in the forefront of the antigovernment movement in the United States. Some militias are very well armed and have assumed that they need to be for the ultimate conflict with federal authority they believe will inevitably occur. They have adopted April 19, the anniversary date of the Battle of Lexington in 1775 that launched the American Revolution, as a special date, since militia personnel consider themselves as instrumental in restoring values that the Revolution fought to protect.

At a gathering now known as the Rocky Mountain Rendezvous, held on October 23–25, 1992, at a YMCA in Estes Park, Colorado, plans were developed for a citizens' militia movement that exceeded anything the United States had yet experienced. The group of 160 White men who gathered there were White supremacists and pro-gun extremists meeting at an invitation-only gathering two months after FBI attempts to arrest Randy Weaver resulted in the deaths of Weaver's wife and son on April 19 at Ruby Ridge in Idaho. This meeting led, only three years to the day later, to the bombing of the federal building in Oklahoma City.

The bombing of the Alfred P. Murrah Federal Building in Oklahoma City on April 19, 1995, is the most violent expression of antigovernment sentiment by a member of a militia group. This was the most lethal terrorist attack ever perpetrated on American soil until the September 11, 2001, attacks on New York City and Washington, DC. One hundred sixty-eight people were killed and 850 others were injured. Two years earlier on April 19, 1993, after a fifty-one-day siege by the FBI and the ATF, a fire broke out at Mount Carmel in Waco, Texas, where David Koresh and his followers had stockpiled a large supply of illegal weapons. All these events have provided the militia movement with inspiration and martyrs.

Most of the militias firmly believe that the federal government is an aggressive force intent on undermining liberty in the United States and that they are only preparing to defend themselves against unconstitutional authority. However, not all militia members are advocates of violence or desirous of committing violent acts. The Constitution protects free speech, even if it is offensive or extremist. Only those militia members accumulating arsenals composed of illegal weapons have been targeted by government agencies.

The armed right-wing groups offer a significantly different challenge to government efforts to provide security than that offered by the left-wing college radicals of the 1960s and 1970s. Unlike the isolated, crudely unsophisticated pipe-bomb manufacturers who dominated most of the U.S.-based terrorist groups for at least two decades, members of right-wing groups are often well trained in the use of arms and explosives. They generally have skilled armorers and bomb makers and many members who are adept at guerrilla-warfare techniques and outdoor survival skills. As these skills are usually coupled with racial and religious intolerance and even an apocalyptic vision of imminent war, these groups have more potential to engage in lethal and increasingly sophisticated terrorist operations.

This form of right-wing activity has wide-ranging geographical dimensions, a diversity of causes its adherents espouse, and overlapping agendas among its member groups. There are militia groups from California to North Carolina and from Texas to Canada. Almost every state has at least one such group, and most have several. These groups share motivations spanning a broad spectrum: antifederalist, seditious, racial hatred, and religious hatred. Most have masked these unpleasant-sounding motives under a rather transparent veneer of religious precepts.

Writing generated by these groups indicates they are bound together by a number of factors, including a shared hostility to any form of government above the county level and even an advocacy of the overthrow of the U.S. government. Vilification of Jews and non-Whites as children of Satan is coupled with an obsession for achieving the religious and racial purification of the United States and a belief in a conspiracy theory of powerful Jewish interests controlling the government, banks, and the media.

These facets of right-wing ideology give interesting insights into the images that terrorists have of their world, their victims, and themselves. To view the enemy as "children of Satan" is to dehumanize them, as terrorists must in order to kill. To view the struggle of the group as an effort to purify the nation is to view it as a battle between good and evil, as terrorists must. The view of a coming racial war fits the millennial view that many terrorists maintain. A warrior fighting in a cause to purify a state from the children of Satan will have little problem in justifying the use of lethal force.

Although the United States has produced many different types of right-wing extremist groups, particularly in the last two decades of the twentieth century, the striking similarities in ideology and overlapping membership help to explain several important factors: the broad popular base enjoyed by militia groups; the assumption on the part of the general public and much of the law enforcement community, until the Oklahoma City bombing, that such groups are nonthreatening as a whole; and the inciting of support for hatred that such groups provide to individuals seeking someone or something to blame for the loss of jobs, income, family farms, and so on. A quick look at one umbrella group, one religious movement, and one militia organization offers examples of these factors.

CASE STUDY 9.2

Aryan Nations

The **Aryan Nations**, a White supremacist group, traces its origins back to the 1950s and early 1960s. Its current structure was organized in 1970 under the leadership of Richard Butler, with headquarters in Hayden Lake, Idaho. Its ideology is a mixture of theology and racism. The literature of this group indicates that its beliefs are couched in a religious doctrine of "identity," which holds that Jesus Christ was not a Jew but an Aryan, that the Lost Tribes of Israel were in fact Anglo-Saxon and not Semitic, and that Jews are the children of Satan.

The operational profile for this group derives from a book written by an American neo-Nazi, William Pierce. This book, *Turner's Diaries,* offers a blueprint for revolution in the United States based on a race war. It is a disturbing book, freely available on the market and used by many groups that have splintered from the Aryan Nations for tactical reasons. Pierce calls his book the "Handbook for White Victory," and says that it has been "effective in educating and inspiring a substantial portion of the people who have read it."[9] These groups include but are certainly not limited to the Order; the Silent Brotherhood; the White American Bastion; the Covenant, the Sword, and the Arm of the Lord; Posse Comitatus; the Arizona Patriots; and the White Patriot Party.

These groups have been linked to armored car and bank robberies, counterfeiting, assassinations, and assaults on federal, state, and local law enforcement personnel and facilities. One leader in the Aryan Nations, who was also the head of the Texas KKK, proposed a point system to achieve "Aryan Warrior" status. One could achieve this status (which required earning a whole point) by killing: members of congress = 1/5 point; judges and FBI directors = 1/6 point; FBI agents and U.S. marshalls = 1/10 point; journalists and local politicians = 1/12 point; president of the United States = 1 point (warrior status).

The Aryan Nations is regarded as an umbrella group for many factions involved in violent, often terrorist, activity. Its Hayden Lake property, which Richard Butler dubbed the "international headquarters of the White race," was the site of regular White supremacy festivals, where attendees were trained in urban terrorism and guerrilla warfare. This property was lost in 2000 in a lawsuit stemming from attacks by guards on African Americans whose vehicle was stranded near the property gates. The group has since splintered into three factions.[10] ∎

Source: Federal Bureau of Investigation

CASE STUDY 9.3

Christian Identity Movement

The **Christian Identity Movement** (CIM) in the United States links individuals by opposition to gun control, the federal government, taxes, environmental regulations, homosexuality, racial integration, abortion, and by support for home-schooling, states' rights, and a shared belief in an international one-world conspiracy that is about to take over the United States and the world. The CIM teaches that Aryans are God's chosen people, that Jews are the offspring of Satan, and that minorities are not human. Many CIM adherents are driving forces in the militia movement and believe the system no longer works because it has been taken over by the New World Order, a secret group that actually runs the world. The membership of this secret group is less clearly defined; for some it is the Jews, for others, the United Nations.

Many CIM members, particularly those in militias, define the enemy as the U.S. government, which is recast into the role of King George III, with members of the movement defining themselves as true patriots. They reject the normal democratic processes of change, including election, petition, assembly, and constitutional amendment, believing instead that they alone are the defenders of freedom in their country.

The CIM theology permeates many of the right-wing groups, militias, and their proponents. William Porter Gale, a former aide to General Douglas MacArthur and Robert DePugh, millionaire founder of the ultrarightist Minutemen, was a fervent Identity believer, as were Glenn and Stephen Miller, organizers of the White Patriot Party; Jim Ellison, founder of the Covenant, the Sword, and the Arm of the Lord; and James Wickstrom, former Posse Comitatus leader.

It is important to distinguish between the CIM and the Christian Patriots, even though there is considerable overlap in membership and philosophy. The CIM came from a nineteenth-century belief called British Israelism. A person can be a CIM member in Australia, Canada, and other former British colonial territories.

(*continued*)

Christian Patriots, in contrast, are found only in the United States. One could be a Christian Patriot without subscribing to CIM religious ideology.

It would be a large step for those moving from the Christian Coalition—which from its position on the religious right of the political spectrum wants to impose its ways on American society within the rules, not by breaking them—to a militia movement, which rejects the rules and flouts them with enthusiasm to "save" America. It is a much smaller step to go to the militias from the CIM, since the CIM also despises much of what comprises the system today and can rationalize, by religious doctrine, the death and destruction of children of Satan and other non-Aryan types. It is as unlikely that a militia leader will be elected to the U.S. Congress as it is that a Christian Coalition leader will consider poisoning a town's water supply. The CIM members could do either.

The Religious Right and the CIM were, for a long time, separated by many theological gaps. The cross-fertilization of these movements began occurring in the 1990s, sparked in part by the collapse of the Soviet Union. Although the CIM, with its focus on hatred of certain peoples and its distortion of biblical texts, has been an anathema to legitimate Christian groups, this began to change as the uncertainty of the 1990s engendered a fear that American society was "under attack," not from without but from within. Instead of an "evil empire" upon which both the Religious Right and the CIM could project their worst fears and personify as Satan, the enemy became internal: the U.S. government. It became easier to bridge the theological gaps when a common enemy was perceived at home. ∎

Source: Anti-Defamation League, at http://www.adl.org/learn/ext_us/Christian_Identity.asp?xpicked=4&item=Christian_ID

CASE STUDY 9.4

Sovereign Citizen Movement

The **Sovereign Citizen Movement** is the name taken by a wide range of individuals and groups located throughout the United States who refuse to recognize the authority of the federal government and assert their right as "sovereign citizens" to be free of any authority above that of the United States. This theory of common law and sovereign citizenship drew its roots from the Posse Comitatus, active in the 1970s and 1980s, and is today a loosely organized collection of people who espouse a desire to "restore" a minimalist governmental system, almost an anarchy, which they believe existed initially in the United States. To this end, members resort to what they term *paper terrorism*, taking the form of fraudulent liens, lawsuits, "common law courts," and a wide range of similar measures against judges and other federal or state government officials. In recent years, members of this movement have engaged in violence as well, taking the lives of police officers, firemen, and others who represent, to them, illicit authority.

In April 1992, an angry resident of Montana wrote that he was no longer a citizen of that state or of the United States, and was answerable only to the "common laws." A member of the Montana Freemen militia group, this "sovereign citizen" received considerable national attention after the Oklahoma City bombing attack, when he was convicted of conspiring with Timothy McVeigh in this attack. The angry rejection articulated by Terry Nichols in 1992 clearly found expression in this bombing attack on a federal building.

Most of the activities of the amalgam of groups and individuals who share the ideology of "sovereign citizens" have been disruptive, but not violent, although threats of violence are becoming more common. Members are encouraged, even expected, to act independently, taking action against state and federal laws, which "infringe" on their rights or impose responsibilities. Consequently, most of the actions by this movement in recent years have generated little national press, as most are nonviolent. As one expert noted,

> Sovereign citizens widely use fictitious financial instruments such as phony money, sight drafts, and controllers warrants . . . because it potentially allows the sovereign citizen to get something for nothing whenever a government agency, bank, business or private citizen mistakenly accepts one of the bogus instruments.[11]

Violent confrontations continue to erupt between members of this movement and state or federal authorities. On May 20, 2010, two West Memphis Arkansas police officers were killed and two county sheriff's officers wounded in shoot-outs involving Sovereign Citizen activists. Jerry Kane, while travelling around the country with his teenage son, Joseph, and holding seminars on his antigovernment theories, was pulled over by West Memphis police in the process of a drug interdiction exercise. The Kanes got out of their vehicle; the younger man pulled a gun and killed both officers, then they drove off. When the ensuing pursuit cornered the two Kanes at a Wal-Mart parking lot, another shoot-out ensued, resulting in the wounding of two officers and the death of both Kanes.

Sovereign Citizens as a movement has links with a wide range of right-wing groups, including the Christian Patriots, the CIM, and the Christian Coalition, but there are significant differences between each.

Networking of such groups occurs often in the United States. CP exists only in the United States, because its ideology focuses only on the U.S. government, its history, and related documents. CIM adherents and militia groups, however, have appeared in other countries and network with members of the Christian Patriots in the United States. Networking also occurs inside the country based on common positions on issues such as gun control and abortion.

The networks for most of the religious right are hub or spoke networks focused on and led by strong central figures and linked by common doctrines and belief systems. Sovereign Citizen groups, however, fit more easily into the all-channel pattern, with no specific group leader or hub; instead, each cell is capable of acting independently, with varying degrees of skill and success, against a common target, frequently a government, individual, or facility. When an individual such as Terry Nichols has membership in a leaderless movement (Sovereign Citizens), a religious group, (in the form of the CIM) and a militia group, his ability to act independently is enhanced, but it is more likely that he would see himself as a "holy warrior" in a good cause supported by his religious beliefs. This combination of independence, military expertise, and religious zeal can clearly be lethal. Take a quick look at the Field Manual of the Free Militia to understand the similarities between this terror network and that generated by al-Qaeda. ∎

Source: MSNBC, accessed October 17, 2011 at http://www.msnbc.msn.com/id/38668124/ns/ us_news-life/t/sovereign-citizens-st-century-counter-culture/#

CASE STUDY 9.5

Field Manual of the Free Militia

In order to understand the contemporary Christian militia movement in the United States, an excellent source is the Field Manual of the Free Militia, which is available on the Internet and cited or quoted in most militia group literature. This manual offers insights not only into the theology of this particular type of militia but also into the training of individuals and cells within this "leaderless movement." Marketed by the U.S. Taxpayers Party—a group organized by Howard Phillips, who attended the 1992 meeting in Estes Park—this manual contains a section on "Principles Justifying the Arming and Organizing of a Militia." Since its publication in 1994, the Field Manual of the Free Militia has become a staple within the militia movement, setting out in specific detail not only the principles/theology "justifying" the militia but also the command structure of militia and detailed instructions for countermeasures against the "enemy" who would be trying to subvert its actions.

Militias, using tools such as this manual, often operate within the context of a "leaderless resistance," in which groups and individuals conduct activities separately, without reporting to or receiving orders from a center of operations. The manual offers theological, constitutional, practical, and psychological training tools. Let us examine here two of these tools.

Theological Training

According the Field Manual of the Free Militia, the first and arguably the most important step toward training new members of the militia in the United States entails persuading novice associates to wholly accept the theological foundations prescribed in this manual, because this acceptance serves as a vital connecting link between militia members and cells. This theology connects cells of the militia in Montana to cells in California, Texas, or North Carolina, with or without personal contact among members of the different cells.

Theological foundations of the Christian militia movement can be found in detail in section I, subsection 1.1 of the manual, titled "The Morality of Arming and Organizing," which lays out step-by-step a biblical justification for the ideals and goals of the Christian militia movement. The biblical foundations for the militia movement are broken down into four primary theological pieces: biblical inspiration and authority, continuity of the Old and New Testaments, the premise that Jesus Christ was not a pacifist, and the principles of just war.

According to the Field Manual of the Free Militia, the New Testament scripture found in 2 Timothy 3:16 establishes both the divine inspiration and the divine authority of the Bible, stating that all scripture is "God-breathed." Using other scriptures to substantiate the "errorless truth" of the Bible, the manual is written in a manner designed to lead followers to accept that the Bible in its entirety must be believed and obeyed. The "leader" of the leaderless resistance may then be said to be the word of God and not of man. For new and old members alike, the "God factor" lends legitimacy and justification to their cause and actions, enabling people to participate in illegal activities they might otherwise avoid.

The authors of the manual negotiate the age-old conflict of Old Testament law versus New Testament law, arguing that the New Testament does not replace the Old Testament laws but instead builds upon, enhances, clarifies, or fulfills the Old Testament. Instructing the appropriate theological perspective for militia members on the issue of the testaments is vital to arguments concerning the use of force to which militia members may expect to be called. The Old Testament contains detailed laws by which people were to abide, laws that would be rendered invalid if movement members believed the New Testament law abolished the Old Testament law. Furthermore, the Old Testament abounds with examples of violence and war that are condoned rather than condemned by God, wars in which people fought against invaders and tyrannical rulers. This justification of the use of force is critically important to the training of new members in the militia.

The third theological basis addresses the nature of Jesus Christ, who emphasizes love throughout the New Testament, thus leading some contemporaries to argue that Jesus was himself a pacifist. The Field Manual of the Free Militia claims that Jesus was not a pacifist for the following reasons: Jesus did not condemn soldiering, only the abuse of power; Jesus allowed, even directed, his people to carry swords; Jesus used force when he cleared out the temple, as well as on other occasions; Jesus will, it is prophesied, one day use excessive force to separate the wicked from the righteous; and Jesus taught his disciples to use force, albeit as a last resort. Most of the points are certainly backed by carefully selected scriptures, except the idea that Jesus taught followers to use force as a last resort, which is instead inferred from various other scriptures. Again, the focus of this scripture "lesson" in the manual is clearly to justify, morally, the use of force.

Finally, the manual describes the biblical principles of "just war" to help members understand that it is not only acceptable to use force but that the use of such force may even be "commanded" by God, in order to prevent or redress a "wrong." Just war principles include the use of self-defense to protect one's life, the application of capital punishment for serious crimes, and the use of force for resistance to tyranny. Resisting tyranny applies to government institutions or leaders who commit murder, curb liberties, impose a tyrannical regime, or do all three. In these instances, people—according to the manual—must resist, including the use of force. In order to participate in a "just war," the warriors must ensure that the war is in the name of justice rather than revenge and that it is a collective action, not a personal one.

Understanding these four basic theological principles of the Field Manual of the Free Militia makes clear the manner in which theology becomes a training tool and in which the militia movement in the United States today is becoming the Christian militia movement. Members first become versed in the ideals and justifications of the group, using Section I of the manual; only after accepting the theology in this section are members fully integrated into the movement, which in some groups entails paramilitary training.

Equipment for a "Prepared" Militia Member

Following the development of a cause and a reason to fight in the manual is an introduction to what the militia should be prepared to fight with in forthcoming

(*continued*)

battles: their suggested armaments. The manual outlines extensively the weapons and other equipment considered necessary to be a genuinely "ready and armed militiaman." This begins with the choice of weapons, which the manual states, should ideally be a medium- to high-power semi-automatic rifle with a magazine that is detachable. After listing several different types of weapons and the reasons for and against each for use in the militia, the text then describes the other types of equipment needed to set up a fully armed and prepared cell of militiamen.

Much of what is suggested is basic military equipment, from inconspicuous clothing (e.g., camouflage), protective gear needed in direct combat (e.g., helmets and flak jackets), and basic radio equipment necessary to keep a small force of men in contact during a battle. This section of the manual is very detailed about what is needed and what it will probably cost to fully prepare for battle with the enemy, as well as offering instruction in how to conceal oneself from outside authorities. The manual points out the importance of not making public the information about what types of weapons and equipment that one owns, since one would then be an obvious target of the enemy when the time for battle comes. Suggestions such as buying weapons from private dealers and paying for equipment in cash (so that there are no records of the materials purchased) fill the manual. Indeed, the manual notes that, in an age of computers, practically anyone can get access to weapons online, with little to no checks on background and culpability.

This field manual describes how the cells should be organized and networked. The emphasis in the Christian militia groups is that the individual cells be small and able to operate independently of any larger organization. The cells are designed to include only eight men, and each cell is to be capable of acting without the direction or resources of any larger group of people, much like the al-Qaeda groups in bin Laden's network. The militias use the small groups or cells of eight men to encourage camaraderie and to ensure the group's ability to operate independently, since they would need more than just a few men to carry out any real military operations. While the manual does not encourage reliance between the cells for operation, it does encourage diversifying the cells to include different primary functions for each cell. The four different cell structures that are listed in the manual are the command cell, the combat cell, the support cell, and the communiqué cell. While each cell would have a specialized function to perform, the emphasis of the militia manual is that they all should still be able to perform without each other. Thus if one group is cut off, the others can and will still fight.

Much of the structure within the larger groups, or multiple cells, is very similar to the way a traditional army is organized. There is a commander (a general) and ranks that follow all the way down to a private. One of the unique aspects of the structure and network of the cells in the militia as a whole is that it includes no women. The last section of the manual even specifies that wives and children are to be left out of any planning or knowledge of the free militia completely. They are to know as little as possible beyond the basic principles of the Second Amendment. They are not to know the names of the other members of a cell, and they are not to know of any of the plans of that cell.[12] ■

Source: Elizabeth Combs and Lydia Marsh, "Militia Training." The Making of a Terrorist. Greenberg Press, 2005.

TRANSNATIONAL TERRORISM

Although right-wing terrorism flourished in the United States during much of its history, and left-wing extremists made some impact on the system during the 1960s and 1970s, the United States was aware of very little transnational terrorism—other than the connections of the Puerto Rican nationalists and some of the left-wing extremists to groups from Cuba and other socialist states—until the 1990s. Most of the efforts of the government agencies charged with domestic security from terrorist threats were focused on campus radicals, antiwar protesters, and groups with socialist or communist philosophies. The assumption was that most of the danger to the nation lay from these elements within the system, possibly supported by outside agents seeking to foment revolution rather than from external groups with cells operating within the U.S. system.

The networking of terrorists across national boundaries, in fact, was not researched with as much intensity in this country as it was in Europe and the Middle East. Since the United States is bordered on the east and west by oceans and on the north and south by friendly governments, the likelihood of a transnational attack seemed remote. The technology that made such linkage easier and transportation across oceans simple and convenient was not factored as thoroughly into the assessment of homeland security as it would be during the last decade of the twentieth century.

The first bombing of the World Trade Center (WTC) in 1993 made the nation aware, for the first time, of its vulnerability to attacks from transnational terrorist agents. According to the research of Steven Emerson, a network news correspondent who created a Public Broadcasting System program entitled *Jihad in America* after this incident, the United States had long been a target of hatred from groups in the Middle East that linked the United States with Israel and with European colonial policies. Until the 1990s, most such groups had lacked the infrastructure to provide support for an attack on Americans *in* the United States.

That infrastructure clearly existed by 1993, however, as this attack on the WTC was carried out by a network of internal and external individuals who shared this common hatred of the United States. A brief account of this event from news reports highlights several key points: the extent of the network of internal infrastructure uncovered, the obvious capability of transnational groups to carry out devastating terrorist acts, and the growing U.S. intelligence capacity for information gathering and analysis of such incidents.

On February 26, 1993, at approximately 12:18 p.m., an improvised explosive device detonated on the second level of the WTC parking basement. The resulting blast produced a crater approximately 150 feet in diameter and five floors deep in the parking basement.

The main explosive charge consisted primarily of approximately 1,200 to 1,500 pounds of a homemade fertilizer-based explosive, urea nitrate. Also incorporated in the device and placed under the main explosive charge were three large metal cylinders (tare weight 126 pounds) of compressed hydrogen gas. The resulting explosion killed 6 people and injured more than 1,000. More than 50,000 people were evacuated from the WTC complex during the hours immediately following the blast.

By Tuesday, March 2, 1993, four assistant U.S. attorneys were assigned to the prosecution. It was fortunate that the attorneys were assigned at that time because late on Monday night the vehicle fragment was identified by the FBI laboratory as having been a portion of the vehicle that contained the device and as having been reported stolen on February 25, 1993. FBI agents traveled to the Ryder Rental Agency in Jersey City, New Jersey, which had rented out the vehicle, and began an interview with the station manager.

While the interview was underway, an individual by the name of Mohammad Salameh telephoned Ryder and wanted his security deposit returned. A meeting was arranged so that Salameh would return to the Ryder Agency on March 4. When he returned for the $400 deposit, FBI agents were on hand to place him under surveillance. As Salameh was leaving, numerous media personnel were observed outside setting up their photography equipment. It was then decided that Salameh would be arrested on the spot.

Salameh's arrest and the subsequent search of his personal property led to Nidel Ayyad, a chemist working for the Allied Signal Corporation in New Jersey.

On March 3, a typewritten communication was received at the *New York Times*. The communiqué claimed responsibility for the bombing of the WTC in the name of Allah. The letter was composed on a personal computer and printed on a laser printer. Very little could be identified as to the origin of the printer, but a search of the hidden files in Ayyad's computer revealed wording identical to that of the text of the communiqué. Saliva samples from Salameh, Ayyad, and a third man, Mahmud Abouhalima, were obtained and compared with the saliva on the envelope flap. A DNA Q Alpha examination concluded that Ayyad had licked the envelope on the communiqué received by the *Times*. Abouhalima, who was an integral part of the conspiracy, had fled the United States the day after the bombing and had later been arrested in Egypt and extradited to the United States.

In September 1992, a man named Ahmad M. Ajaj had entered the United States from Pakistan at New York's JFK airport. He was arrested on a passport violation. In his checked luggage, Ajaj had numerous manuals and videocassette tapes. These tapes and manuals described methods of manufacturing explosives.

Interviews and latent fingerprint examinations identified two other individuals who were an integral part of the bombing conspiracy. The first, Ramzi Yousef, had entered the United States on the same flight as Ajaj but had been deported immediately. Yousef was identified through fingerprints and photos as having been associating with Salameh immediately prior to the bombing. His fingerprints were also found on the explosive manuals located in Ajaj's checked luggage. The second individual, known only as "Yassin," was identified in much the same manner and was probably involved in the packaging and delivery of the bomb on the morning of February 26.

During the six-month trial, more than 200 witnesses introduced over 1,000 exhibits. On March 4, 1994, exactly one year after Salameh's arrest, the jury found Salameh, Ajaj, Abouhalima, and Ayyad guilty on all 38 counts.[13]

The impact of this event on U.S. response to terrorism cannot be overstated. U.S. citizens began to assume that *any* large-scale terrorist attack would be carried out by foreigners, probably from the Middle East. Ironically, when the Oklahoma City bombing occurred a few years later, the immediate assumption on the part of the press and the public was that the perpetrator was Middle Eastern. The actual perpetrator, Timothy McVeigh, did not fit this profile at all.

Information gathered in the hunt for the individuals responsible led the United States to a better understanding of the existing networking of terrorism. When Ramzi Yousef's safe house in the Philippines was raided, information was discovered linking him to al-Qaeda (which would later be responsible for the 2001 bombing attacks on the WTC) and to Abu Sayyaf, the indigenous groups carrying out attacks in the Philippines. Intelligence agencies began to seriously investigate al-Qaeda and its leader Osama bin Laden, linking him to the bombing attacks on the U.S. embassies in Kenya and Tanzania in 1998, the attack on the USS *Cole* in Yemen's harbor, and the events of September 11, 2001.

An Egyptian-born Muslim and peace activist, Seifeldin Ashmawy, editor of the magazine *Voice of Peace,* testified before the U.S. Senate in 1997 about the spread of transnational terrorism into America. He warned that

> the heart, if not the soul, of the extremists is in fact largely in the United States, where these radicals have set up many of their fund-raising and political headquarters. These people have literally hijacked the mainstream Islamic organizations in the United States.[14]

The investigations by law enforcement and intelligence agencies since the events of September 11, 2001, revealed the existence of many organized cells of groups such as al-Qaeda, HAMAS, and Islamic Jihad throughout America. From Santa Clara, California, to Tucson, Arizona and from Detroit, Michigan, to Springfield, Virginia, these groups have organized membership cells, using the Internet to connect across state lines and to facilitate the transfer of funds. Although most of the activities of these cells have been nonviolent, the radical theology shared is in many respects similar to the radical form of Christianity shared by CIM members and militia groups. Such theology is not illegal, but it is troubling as the world slides closer to engagement in a holy war in which terrorism is justified by faith.

The "Lone-Wolf" Terrorists

Several types of domestic terrorism have generated so-called **lone-wolf terrorists,** *individuals who share an ideological or philosophical identification with an extremist group but do not necessarily communicate with the group about the terrorist act(s) he or she takes.* While the motivation of the lone wolf's actions may be to advance a group's goals, the methods and tactics to achieve the goals are generally conceived and implemented solely by the individual, without any command or control by the group.

This type of terrorism is thus even more unstructured than that discussed in Chapter 7, as there is not even a loose cell-structure connection to the actions being planned or executed. According to the FBI's Washington Field

Office, this type of terrorism is of serious concern, as it is difficult to track and hence almost impossible to prevent. As John Perren, head of that office, states:

> It could be anyone. It could be the guy next door, living in the basement of his mother's place, on the Internet just building himself up with hate, building himself up to a boiling point and finally using what he's learned.[15]

A terrorist acting alone rarely tells others what he or she is planning or give details as to where or when or how the attack will occur. This makes it incredibly difficult for authorities to determine who is actually prepared to commit a terrorist act to advance a cause, since the group advocating that cause may have little or no actual contact or information about the planned act.

While a lone wolf, acting outside of group direction or control, may kill only a single person or a small group of targets, he or she may also be responsible for a major terrorist incident. For example, the Washington area sniper, John Allen Muhammad, cost the region's governments and federal authorities serious man-hours and created a mood of fear in a wide audience through the apparently random shootings of individuals. Certainly more dramatic were the actions of Timothy McVeigh and his bombing of the federal building in Oklahoma City. While McVeigh was loosely linked with several militias or right-wing religious groups, he attended the meetings, read the materials of, and met with members of both regularly. William Pierce's *Turner Diaries*, used by both the CIM and radical racist groups, was an item over which McVeigh obsessed, taking it with him in his travels to gun shows throughout the United States.[16] Consider the attack by this "lone wolf," and understand why counterterror authorities in this country believe this type of terrorist is potentially our most dangerous and the most difficult to identify.

CASE STUDY 9.6

Oklahoma City Bombing

On April 15, 1995, the United States experienced the worst act of internal terrorism (prior to the attacks in 2001). At 9:02 A.M., a truck bomb exploded in front of the Alfred P. Murrah Federal Building in Oklahoma City, Oklahoma. The blast ripped away one-third of the building, killing 168 people and injuring 503 more. Many of those killed or injured were, in legal terms, innocent victims, women and children from a day care center, clerks, and typists who were simply "in the wrong place at the wrong time." Moreover, the resulting shock wave damaged over 300 surrounding structures. The 4,800-pound ammonium nitrate and nitromethane charge, stored in 55-gallon drums, was arranged in a conical form inside the truck to generate the maximum amount of blast force. Immediately following the explosion federal, state, and local emergency officials descended on the scene.

Early in the investigation, local law enforcement discovered the rear axle of the truck that was used to carry the explosives to the Murrah Federal Building. This rear axle proved to be the essential piece of information for the FBI. By using the vehicle identification number (VIN) on the axle, investigators found that the truck was owned by the Ryder Truck Corporation in Miami, Florida. It had been last rented in Junction City, Kansas. Agents quickly arrived in Junction City, and the first FBI sketches of the two men that rented the truck gave the suspects a face.

Around 10:30 A.M. the same day, an Oklahoma Highway Patrol officer pulled over a yellow 1977 Mercury Marquis near Perry, Oklahoma, for driving without a license plate. Officer Charles Hangar noticed that in addition to driving without a license plate, the driver had a concealed .45 caliber Glock pistol. The driver, Timothy J. McVeigh, was arrested and charged with driving without a license plate, without insurance, and carrying a concealed weapon.

After seeing the sketches of the two suspects, Officer Hangar realized that the man he had arrested a week earlier fit the drawing of the suspects. The FBI had narrowly avoided having their prime suspect escape. McVeigh was taken by the FBI just before being released on bond and was officially charged with the attack on the Murrah building on April 25, 1995. Fellow suspect Terry L. Nichols voluntarily turned himself in to authorities in Herrington, Kansas.

McVeigh and Nichols had met during Army Basic Training in Fort Benning, Georgia. Together they were stationed at Fort Riley, Kansas, along with Michael Fortier, who became the government's main informant, turning state evidence against his former friends. Timothy McVeigh had an excellent record in the Army and served in the Gulf War, in which he was awarded a Bronze Star. After being discharged, McVeigh became in some respects a drifter, traveling across the United States.

McVeigh and Nichols attended meetings of the Montana Militia but did not join, becoming frustrated with the willingness to talk but not take action of most members. Their shared view of government injustices apparently helped to solidify their friendship, and they continued to meet with members of other groups, including the CIM, without joining these groups. McVeigh, according to most records, joined only one "hate group"—the KKK—after his return from military service, but his meetings with member of the Aryan Republican Army and the CIM fed his belief that action against the government was both necessary and supported.

The attack on the Murrah Federal Building happened exactly two years after the fiery ending of the Waco, Texas, standoff. Both McVeigh and Nichols were supporters of groups that thought that the U.S. government had abused its power in ways that led to the death of 78 Branch Davidians. McVeigh traveled to Waco during the standoff to voice his discontent. This, combined with other incidents, such as another standoff at Ruby Ridge, was in McVeigh's mind proof of government infringement on the rights of U.S. citizens.

Timothy McVeigh stood trial and was sentenced to death by lethal injection for the Oklahoma bombing. His accomplice Terry Nichols was sentenced to life for his part in the act. McVeigh was given a lethal injection in June 2001. ∎

Source: Oklahoma City Memorial website http://www.oklahomacitynationalmemorial.org/

Lone-wolf terrorist attacks appear to be increasing in the United States, generated by a wide range of issue-orientations. A brief list of such recent attacks makes this diversity of ideology and impact clear:

- Between 1996 and 1998, Eric Rudolph, a CIM adherent (but not an official member), engaged in a series of attacks against abortion clinics, gay nightclubs, and events at the Olympics in Atlanta, killing 3 and injuring at least 150 people.
- On August 10, 1999, Buford O. Furrow, Jr., a member of the Aryan Nations, attacked a Jewish day care center in Los Angeles, injuring five and later shooting a Filipino-American mail carrier.
- On July 28, 2006, Naveed Afzal Haq penetrated the offices of the Seattle Jewish Federation in Seattle, claiming to be a "Muslim American, angry at Israel," shooting and killing one woman and injuring five others.
- On May 31, 2009, Scott Roeder was arrested for the killing of Dr. George Tiller, who provided abortions.

CONCLUSIONS

Clearly, terrorism escalated in the United States in the last decade of the twentieth century and during the first decade of the twenty-first century. Although many other developed countries, particularly in Europe, had dealt with a much higher level of terrorism for decades than that which afflicted the United States, the basic types of terrorism were approximately the same. The mistake by the United States, perhaps, was in its assumption that its physical isolation would make it less vulnerable to terrorism, since its democratic system tolerated a wide range of divergent views, multiple options for open disagreement without recourse to violence, and a general tolerance for many cultural and ethnic differences.

Blindness to the impact of globalization on the peoples and the economies of many in the developing world, ignorance of the anger felt against the United States for its policies in the Middle East, and a lambent isolationism that has colored U.S. domestic life since its birth have all contributed to its tardy awareness of the threat of domestic terrorism. The events of September 11, 2001, were a wake-up call, offering an opportunity to carefully assess the strengths and weaknesses of U.S. counterterrorism policy.

As analysis continues to be generated in the wake of the September 11, 2001, events, interesting insights can be seen in the differences between terrorists in the United States and those in other countries.

Age. Terrorists born in the United States tend to be older than terrorists indigenous to other countries. Foreign operatives carrying out operations in the United States appear to follow this trend. In recent years, most domestic terrorists tended to be over 30, which might be considered old compared to the profile of terrorists noted in Chapter 4. But this may be changing, as the arrests of terrorists in small al-Qaeda-linked cells in New Jersey and Florida in 2007 indicate, since some of those charged were in their twenties.

Infrequent Occurrence. As noted earlier, the United States has had a relatively low incidence of terrorism compared to other developed countries. This has made tracking of terrorist patterns and data analysis of terrorist incidents difficult, because the base of data is relatively small. This may also be changing, as small cells of those potentially plotting terrorism in the United States are arrested, without having perpetrated attacks, but with plans to do so.

Ordinary Criminal Act. Most terrorist activities, until the September 11, 2001, attacks, were treated under domestic law as violations of criminal laws. Criminal law enforcement agencies have normally been charged with responding to terrorism, unlike the apparatus and laws applied in Western Europe to this crime. Efforts to address this problem in the PATRIOT Act have met with mixed success and much criticism.

These three differences are significant. Older individuals tend to plan with more patience, waiting years if necessary to complete plans to carry out attacks; are better trained, if only because they have had more years to complete their training; and are overall more formidable enemies. Infrequency of events, while not a bad situation, does make it difficult to generate either funds or support for counterterrorism training, laws, or equipment. Until the events of the fall of 2001, the United States did not place a high priority on combating domestic terrorism, not even on tracking transnational terrorism that might emerge domestically. The lack of incidence led to a complacency in the security of the country.

Finally, because domestic terrorism until the fall of 2001 had been primarily handled as an ordinary criminal offense, there was little coordinated interagency preparation for dealing with terrorist events, insufficient training in detection of the differences between terrorists and ordinary criminals for the law enforcement units responsible, and a meager legal framework for the prosecution of terrorism as a unique form of criminal activity.

In the wake of the bombing attacks that occurred on September 11, 2001, the links between the attacks on the World Trade Center in 1993, the bombings at the U.S. embassies in Kenya and Tanzania, and the September 11 attacks became clear, focusing the attention of authorities on the specific threat of the al-Qaeda network and on transnational terrorism. The magnitude of the September 11 attacks fully captured the attention of the U.S. government and its citizens.

As intelligence agencies scrambled to secure information about those involved in the attacks, hundreds of people were taken into custody and questioned. Gradually, the links to bin Laden became sufficiently convincing for the administration to designate him as the prime suspect as leader of the al-Qaeda network. On September 27, 2001, President George W. Bush addressed a joint chamber of the House and Senate to pledge a war on terrorism, which he said would be a "lengthy campaign," committed to "find, stop, and defeat every terrorist group of global reach." In this speech, Bush demanded that the Taliban, leaders of the (unrecognized) government of Afghanistan where bin Laden had made his headquarters, hand over all terrorist leaders to U.S. authorities.

The United States sought support and assistance from allies and from states bordering Afghanistan in this war on terrorism. Support from NATO, in terms of invoking a crucial article of the organization's charter regarding collective self-defense in general and British military planes, ships, and missiles in particular, was offered. Through the efforts of Secretary of State Colin Powell, some degree of consent, but less tangible support, was built among nations near Afghanistan, including Pakistan, Iran, Saudi Arabia, and Uzbekistan. The ensuing bombing campaign initiated with British and U.S. missiles and followed by waves of U.S. bombers, stressed this uneasy alliance against terrorism.

Efforts to track the money that supported the terrorist attacks were less dramatic but seemed productive, as were efforts to engage nations within the international community to support the UN treaty on the financing of terrorism, which was by that time operative. Securing cooperation from international banking communities to track terrorist support funds through private accounts was somewhat difficult, because banking secrecy laws in many countries are designed to provide maximum anonymity for customers. However, this front of the war on terrorism generated peaceful results and useful evidence of links between terrorist cells in various countries.

The effort by the U.S. administration to lead a global effort to rid the world of terrorism has economic, financial, political, and religious elements. It has stretched to include many countries, and its initiators assume that it will take years to successfully conclude. In the early nineteenth century, it took the British Royal Navy almost fifty years to close down the Atlantic slave trade; the effort to eradicate terrorism is a task that may require at least that much time and much more military as well as political effort on the part of many nations.

The ability of U.S. agencies to deal effectively with domestic terrorism is vitally important. Problems in successfully and legally handling potential terrorist situations can themselves stimulate other terrorist attacks. Timothy McVeigh, the Oklahoma City bomber, clearly derived some of the motivation for his attack from the mistakes that the government made in the incident at Waco, Texas, two years earlier. Take a moment to review this incident, looking for reasons to see it as a potential stimulus for future terrorist actions by antigovernment individuals or groups.

DISCUSSION

Domestic terrorism in the United States highlights the weaknesses of many democracies in dealing with the problem of terrorism. Inadequate structure for coordinating response efforts, a lack of clear guidelines for law enforcement personnel for the successful resolution of terrorist situations, and complacency in security have marred much of counterterrorism efforts in the United States. Some of the more dramatic missteps by government agencies have actually fueled further terrorist events, as the evidence from the Oklahoma City bombing clearly indicated. Chris Temple, writing in *The Jubilee,* a major CIM newspaper, noted the following about the events in Ruby Ridge, when an FBI standoff resulted in the shooting of Randy Weaver's wife while she was holding their child:

> All of us in our groups . . . could not have done in the next twenty years what the federals did for our cause in eleven days in Naples, Idaho.

Read carefully the online account of a violent incident in the United States at http://www.u-s-history.com/pages/h2045.html. This is an account of the events at Waco, Texas, in 1993. Evaluate U.S. preparedness and response to such attacks. Examine the incident for the *type* of group perpetrating the incident (right-wing, left-wing, or transnational), and for the extent to which the perpetrators fit the profile of terrorists in the United States suggested earlier.

Consider carefully the following questions:

1. What kind of group was David Koresh leading at Waco? Would an understanding of the group have facilitated negotiations initially by the ATF? Was the ATF equipped to analyze and negotiate with such a group?

2. David Koresh actually left the compound several times to go to neighboring towns during the standoff's initial period. Would taking Koresh under arrest at one of his off-campus forays have resolved the issue? Why, or why not?

3. The FBI's decision to confer with the military's counterterror specialists in making plans to end the standoff was sharply criticized later. Why were the military assistance and resources perhaps not a good choice for the FBI in this situation? Was the FBI trained in the use of combat engineering vehicles and tear gas? Would this have impacted their ability to handle the situation without casualties?

4. The Oklahoma City bombing occurred on the date of the Waco violence, as did the shootings at Ruby Ridge. Can you see a pattern emerging in right-wing violence in the United States today?

5. Has the creation of the Department of Homeland Security improved the capacity of the United States to handle events like Waco? What part of the new agency would be most capable of dealing with such a situation?

ANALYSIS CHALLENGE

On December 25, 2009, Umar Farouk Abdulmutallab, a young Nigerian, set himself alight in a packed Airbus flight as it approached the Detroit airport. The young man had been in Yemen for several months, apparently connecting with al-Qaeda in the Arabian Peninsula. He bought a one-way ticket from Ghana on December 16, and was able to board Northwest Airlines flight 235 in spite of being on an American watch list and banned from entering Britain. He attempted to blow the plane up by setting alight an explosive device attached to his body. While his attempt failed, injuring him fairly severely, his statement that "more such attacks were being planned" renews concern about the potential for "lone wolf" terrorist attacks such as this.

Visit these websites and consider the differences in individuals constituting this type of threat:

http://www.newsweek.com/2010/01/01/a-thousand-points-of-hate.html
http://www.time.com/time/magazine/article/0,9171,1938698,00.html

Read this paper, searching for counterterror strategies for dealing with these increasing lethal phenomena.

http://www.transnationalterrorism.eu/tekst/publications/Lone-Wolf%20
    Terrorism.pdf

KEY TERMS

SUGGESTED READINGS AND RESOURCES

Animal Liberation Front. http:/animalliberationfront/com.

Dees, Morris, and James Corcoran. *Gathering Storm: America's Militia Threat.* New York: HarperCollins Publishers, 1997.

Free Militia. *Field Manual of the Free Militia.* Howard Phillips, ed., 1994. Available online at http://www.rickross.com/reference/militia/ilitia11mhtml.

Graham, Hugh Davis, and Tee Robert Gurr, eds. *Violence in America: Historical and Comparative Perspectives.* London, UK: Sage Publications, 1979.

Hildreth, Steven A. *Cyberwarfare.* CRS Report for Congress. Updated June 19, 2001.

Homeland Security, Department of. Available online at http://www.dhs.gov.

Kushner, Harvey, and Bart Davis. *Holy War on the Home Front: The Secret Islamic Terror Network in the United States.* New York: Sentinel Press, 2004.

Liddy, G. Gordon. *Fight Back: Tackling Terrorism, Liddy Style.* New York: St. Martin's Griffen, 2006.

Mizzler, Louis R., Jr. *Target U.S.A.: The Inside Story of the New Terrorist War.* New York: John Wiley & Sons, 1998.

North American Earth Liberation Front Press Office. http://www.elfpress.org.

Sargent, Lyman Towed, ed. *Extremism in America.* New York: New York University Press, 1995.

Smith, Brent L. *Terrorism in America: Pipe Bombs and Pipe Dreams.* Albany: State University of New York Press, 1994.

Stern, Kenneth S. *A Force on the Plain: The American Militia Movement and the Politics of Hate.* New York: Simon & Schuster, 1996.

———. "Militias and the Religious Right." *Freedom Writer* (October 1996).

The 9/11 Commission Report: Final Report of the National Commission on Terrorist Attacks Upon the United States. New York: W.W. Norton & Company, 2003.

NOTES

1. Richard Maxwell Brown, "Historical Patterns of American Violence," in *Violence in America: Historical and Comparative Perspective,* ed. Hugh Davis Graham and Ted Robert Gurr (London: Sage, 1979) 19–48.
2. Bill Stanton, *Klanwatch: Bringing the Ku Klux Klan to Justice* (New York: Grove Weidenfeld, 1991).
3. Ted Robert Gurr, "Political Terrorism in the United States: Historical Antecedents and Contemporary Trends," in *The Politics of Terrorism,* ed. Michael Stohl (New York: Dekker, 1988).

4. Brent L. Smith, *Terrorism in America: Pipe Bombs and Pipe Dreams* (Albany: State University of New York Press, 1994).

5. Bernard K. Johnpoll, "Perspectives on Political Terrorism in the United States," in *International Terrorism,* ed. Yonah Alexander (New York: Praeger, 1976), 32–33.

6. Jonathan R. White, *Terrorism: An Introduction* (Belmont, CA: West/Wadsworth, 1998), 161.

7. Ivan Blackwell, "Earth Liberation Front," in *Encyclopedia of Terrorism,* ed. Cindy Combs and Martin Slann (New York: Facts On File, 2002), 59.

8. Blackwell, "Earth Liberation Front," in *Encyclopedia of Terrorism: Revised Edition,* ed. Cindy Combs and Martin Slann (New York: Facts On File, 2006), 84.

9. Morris Dees, *Gathering Storm: America's Militia Threat* (New York: Harper-Collins, 1997), 205.

10. G. Gordon Liddy, *Fight Back: Tackling Terrorism, Liddy Style* (New York: St. Martin's Press, 2006), 75.

11. Anti-Defamation League, "Sovereign Citizen Movement—Extremism in America." http://www.adl.org/learn/ext_us/SCM.asp?LEARN_Cat=Extremism&LEARN_SubCat=Extremism_in_America&xpicked=4&item=sov (accessed July 7, 2011).

12. Elizabeth A. Combs and Lydia Marsh, "Militia Training," in James J. F. Forest, ed., *The Making of a Terrorist* (Greenfield Press, 2005), 145.

13. Anthony Spotti, "World Trade Center Bombing, 1993," in *Encyclopedia of Terrorism: Revised Edition,* ed. Cindy Combs and Martin Slann (New York: Facts on File, 2006), 236–240.

14. Steven Emerson, *American Jihad* (New York: Simon & Schuster, 2002), 168.

15. Retrieved on June 15, 2009, from http://news.yahoo.com/s/ap/20090613/ap_on_go_ot/ us_lone_wolf_terrorists.

16. Retrieved on June 15, 2009, from http:/eyeonhate/com/mcveigh/mcveigh6.html.

International Legal Perspectives on Terrorism

International and transnational terrorism are nothing more nor less than the wanton and willful taking of human lives, the purposeful commission of bodily harm, and the intentional infliction of severe mental distress by force or threat of force.

— Robert Friedlander

TERRORISM IS A CRIME

The world is now officially engaged in a "war on terrorism." If Friedlander's assessment of the nature of terrorism is correct, then one would assume that such acts would already be designated as common crimes in the legal codes of most countries today. One could also be forgiven for assuming that international law, if it truly reflects the laws and mores of the international community, would reflect a similar tendency to declare such acts illegal.

That this is not the case is perhaps due less to a lack of consensus about the desirability of such a law or even the criminality of "a willful and wanton taking of human life" than to two critical factors: the nature of the international system itself and the political problems in defining an act as "terrorism." The latter factor has already been discussed in Chapter 1, and the problems involved with defining terrorism are clear. Examining the international community's legal response to terrorism, however, offers insights into how the internal difficulties in defining terrorism translate into a global inability to create clear legal parameters for terrorist acts.

In the international community, although there has been general agreement on the undesirability of such things as war, racial discrimination, genocide, and other violations of basic human rights, there is still a reluctance to translate that agreement into workable treaties with enforcement powers. Why, if nations generally agree with the idea of reducing the incidence of such "evils," cannot workable methods of getting rid of these evils be constructed?

The answer to this question must be the same as that given by municipal leaders when confronted with a question as to why a society's evils (e.g., poverty, unemployment, and discrimination) are not being effectively eliminated. Unfortunately, consensus about the undesirability of these evils at any level is often difficult to translate into acceptable, enforceable rules and regulations that might remedy the situation. General policy directions are always easier to formulate than specific legislation.

Moreover, the constraints that make progress in creating such legislation difficult at the local and national levels are magnified many times at the international level. An examination of at least a few of these constraints may help us to understand the dearth of international law on terrorism.

The first problem involves a lack of legislative authority. However inept one may consider state and national legislators to be, at least lawmaking bodies can be said to exist at such levels. But on the international level, there is no body invested with such authority. The United Nations was certainly never designed to "rule" the nations of the world or to create rules for its governance.[1] The United Nations offers a forum for discussion, for cooperation, and for consensus building on issues. It does not make laws in the sense that governing bodies make laws for subordinate individuals and groups in the national arena.

There is too a distinct lack of central authority in the international community. To describe this community even as a confederation is to invest it with properties that it does not really possess. A confederal system has mechanisms for governing at the top level, whereas no such governing system exists in any real sense at the international level. Not only is there no legislative body empowered to make laws within the international community, there is also neither an autocratic nor a democratic chief executive who is able to speak with authority for and issue commands to the community of nations.

Moreover, there is no judicial system to which all have recourse and whose decisions are binding at the international level. The International Court of Justice's decision-making authority depends for the most part on the willingness of states to amicably resolve a difficulty and on their willingness to submit their disputes to the court for adjudication.[2]

So the most serious infractions of international law often go untouched by the court, because many states are *not* willing to submit their disputes for adjudication. A voluntary judicial system that can neither hail an offender to the bar of justice nor enforce compliance with its judgments, and that has no provisions by which entities other than states (e.g., individuals, groups, or corporations) can seek recourse for injustice, seems to be sadly lacking in judicial accouterments.

The international system governing states, then, has no central authority figure or figures, provides only a forum for debate rather than lawmaking, and possesses only a voluntary (and frequently ineffective) judiciary. It is, thus, even less able than municipal governments to deal with the difficulties inherent in enacting and enforcing laws designed to eliminate societal problems. The political and enforcement problems that hamper the making of effective laws within nations are even more capable of preventing the successful completion of treaties designed to deal with sensitive issues in the international community.

This incapacity is complicated by the absence of law enforcement officers. With the possible exception of **INTERPOL**, *the world's largest international police organization with members in 187 countries, created in 1923 to facilitate cross-border police cooperation* (and strictly charged to stay out of political problems), there does not appear to be anyone at the international level with the authority to act in this capacity. Just as there are few procedures for bringing a miscreant to justice, there is no one universally authorized to physically do so.

The absence of such international legal enforcement mechanisms is not unanimously regarded as a handicap for the community of nations. While it is true that the law, at the state level of analysis, does require enforcement apparatus, it is also true that most obedience to the law is dependent upon habits of compliance rather than the presence of a police officer at every intersection. At the international level, this is even more true. Certainly, the laws are agreements that states make among themselves to establish guidelines for acceptable behavior, but the states that make up the international community have expressed little consistent interest in creating enforcement units to patrol the international community. Such a force, in the views of some legal experts, might threaten state sovereignty and exercise power in ways that might be detrimental to international peace and security.

As international bodies lack these instruments of governance most commonly found at the national level, the construction of rules at the international level has become an extremely delicate and difficult task. Political considerations of the nations in the international community are usually accommodated as fully as possible, because compliance with any rules is largely voluntary.

The more highly politicized the issue and the greater the perception of national interests involved, the more difficult it becomes to construct an effective treaty—that is, one both strong and acceptable. This may derive, as one scholar suggests, from the nature and scope of national interests' inevitable tension with political reality. When diverse national interests appear to oppose perceived common goals, as they often do in discussions on terrorism, then this "tension" becomes heightened to unworkable levels, according to this scholar.[3]

History provides many examples of the hazards that abound when international law extends itself further than the limits of assured compliance within the community of nations. The most striking instance of such overextension may be attempts to outlaw war, notably through the Kellogg-Briand Pact.[4]

Despite the majority consensus that may exist on the undesirability of war, it is not within the power of international law to enforce a prohibition of it.

More successful, perhaps, have been efforts within the international community to restrict certain highly undesirable practices during times of war. This was partially accomplished by putting together "rules of conduct" for times of war. Conventions about the treatment of prisoners of war and innocent civilian personnel, and others involving prohibitions of certain methods of warfare and weapons of war, have been more effective in terms of compliance than the ill-judged and altruistic Kellogg-Briand Pact.

This success in creating laws to deal with specific aspects of generally undesirable behavior has important implications in terms of understanding the attempts by the international community to deal with the politically sensitive issue of terrorism. Attempts by the international community to construct general treaties dealing with terrorism were largely unsuccessful until the events of September 11, 2001. But on treaties or conventions that deal instead with specific aspects of terrorism, greater progress has been made. A quick review of the provisions and "success" record in preventing or punishing terrorism could make it easier to decide on the most effective ways for handling the problem of current and future terrorism.

First, let us examine portions of international law that do not deal specifically with terrorism but from which laws and regulations on terrorism have evolved. Three areas of international law come immediately to mind in this regard: laws of war, laws on piracy, and laws concerning the protection of diplomatic personnel and heads of state.

LAWS OF WAR

International law has been divided by some scholars into laws of war and laws of peace. This can be a somewhat confusing dichotomy, because some peacetime laws continue to apply even during times of war. However, it is true that the rules of behavior change in many respects during wartime. This change is usually in the direction of allowing greater latitude for suppressing or eliminating ordinary protections and courtesies. It is fair to say that during times of war, more types of violence may be employed against a wider range of targets with far fewer safeguards for human rights than are permissible during times of peace.

This is not a tautological statement. It is, instead, an important point when one considers that it is the laws of war that are most often invoked by terrorists to justify their acts. If, even under the rules that permit a broader range of acceptable actions, there are certain significant prohibited actions, then those actions could be said to be always prohibited, regardless of the provocation.

Although the mass of rules and laws that govern warfare today has grown to immense proportions, a number of fundamental rules meet the criteria described previously in that they involve the establishment of minimum standards of behavior, even for parties engaged in hostilities. Of these rules of war, perhaps the most significant for this study are those that affect the treatment of civilian noncombatants.

This category of persons is an extremely important one for students of terrorism. It is crucial to establish a clear understanding of the legal term *civilian*. Terrorists have asserted that "there is no such thing as an innocent person,"[5] suggesting that there is no one who is a "civilian" in their conflict, yet the Geneva Convention extends special protections to civilian noncombatants, defining them as *"persons taking no active part in the hostilities."*[6]

Innocence, as used by the laws of war, has much the same meaning as that found in any expanded international dictionary definition of the term. In both cases, **innocence** signifies *freedom from guilt for a particular act,* even when the total character may be evil. It is in one sense a negative term, implying as it does something less than righteous, upright, or virtuous. Legally, it is used to specify a *lack of guilt for a particular act or crime, denoting a nonculpability.*[7] Civilians who have no active part in hostilities are by legal definition innocent parties during the time of war. In contrast, a **combatant,** by legal definition, is *someone who takes a direct part in the hostilities of an armed conflict.*

Innocence is imputed to a thief found innocent of the crime of murder. By this logic, even a government official guilty only of indifference can still be said to be "innocent" of any crime committed by his or her government. That official, in other words, has been guilty of nothing that would justify his or her summary execution or injury by terrorists having a grievance with his or her government.

This concept of a lack of guilt for a specific act is particularly appropriate in examining the random selection of "any Englishman or any Israeli" by terrorists as acceptable targets.[8] If "civilian noncombatant" status can be removed by guilt only for a specific act or crime committed by the person (not by others of the same age group, nationality, race, religion, or other similar categories in the context of the hostilities), then there can be no legal justification for such a random selection of targets.

International law, like that of most civilized nations, neither recognizes nor punishes guilt by association. The Nuremberg trials records give credence to this point in terms of the efforts made to establish personal guilt for specific criminal acts (such as murder or torture), instead of prosecuting simply on the basis of membership in the Nazi Party or Hitler's SS troops.[9] In refusing to punish all Germans or even all Nazi Party members for crimes against humanity and crimes of war, the precedent was established for differentiating between a person guilty of committing a crime during a time of war and those innocent of actual wrongdoing.

The importance of this legal concept of innocence as an absence of guilt for a particular act cannot be overstated. The reason for its significance lies in the justification set forth by modern terrorists for their selection of victims. Many organizations that commit terrorist acts today do so on the premise that they are legitimately engaged in seeking to overthrow an existing government or to radically change existing conditions and are thus engaged in warfare.

Accepting for the moment this claim to revolutionary action, it is logical to assume the actions of these groups should still conform to the rules of warfare. If these groups seek to have their status of belligerency recognized and their cause understood by the wider audience, then they must also be held to the laws of war governing such conflicts.

The Geneva Convention on the Treatment of Civilians During Times of War demands special protections for "persons taking no active part in the hostilities." Civilian **noncombatant** status does not imply that the person is good, virtuous, or even disinterested in the outcome of the conflict. *A person need only be innocent of participation in the hostilities* to be protected by the convention.

This means that membership in the civilian population of a nation against which a group is waging war is insufficient reason for according a "guilty" status to a person, thereby removing those special protections. Thus, the waging of war against "any Israeli" or "any Englishman" is not acceptable behavior under the laws of war.

What, then, are the **special provisions in the Geneva Convention** relating to the treatment of civilian noncombatants?

Article 3 of this document lists actions that are prohibited "at any time and in any place whatsoever with respect to such persons." These prohibited acts include violence to life and person, in particular murder of all kinds; mutilations, cruel treatment, and torture; taking of hostages; and outrages upon the personal dignity, in particular humiliating and degrading treatment.[10]

Article 27 emphasizes the degree of legal protection afforded to these noncombatants, stating that they are entitled in all circumstances to respect for their persons, their honor, their family rights, their religious convictions and practices, and their manners and customs; at all times to be treated humanely; and to be protected especially against all acts of violence or threats thereof.[11]

Article 33 of the Geneva Convention for the Protection of Civilian Persons (1949) provides that no protected person may be punished for an offense he or she has not personally committed. Collective penalties and likewise all measures of intimidation or terrorism are prohibited. Pillage is prohibited. Reprisals against protected persons and their property are prohibited.

"**Protected persons**" in this convention are *civilians who have the misfortune to be living in a combat zone or occupied territory*. Not only does this convention specifically prohibit the use of terrorism against this civilian population, but it also in Article 34 prohibits the taking of hostages of any sort. Such rules make it clear that the kidnapping or murder of any civilian, even during times of war, to exact punishment for an injustice real or imagined, is not legal unless the victim was directly responsible for the injustice.

This prohibition against collective punishment applies to states as well as to revolutionary organizations. Control Council Law No. 10, used in the trials of war criminals before the Nuremberg Tribunals, makes this clear.[12] Neither side in an armed conflict, whether involved in the "liberation" of a country or in the efforts of the state to maintain itself while under attack, may engage in warfare against the civilian population.

Both terrorist acts against civilian noncombatants by the state and acts of terrorism by nonstate groups are as illegal in time of war as they are in time of peace. If terrorism by its very nature involves victimizing a civilian third party to achieve a political goal and to evoke a particular emotional response in an audience, then it seems reasonable to say that terrorism is illegal under the laws of war.

Although this convention was drafted with the protection of civilians in occupied territories in mind, Protocols I and II to the convention, drafted in 1976, extend these protections to civilians in nonoccupied territories. Article 46 of Protocol I codifies the customary international law doctrine that the civilian population as such, as well as individual citizens, may not be made the object

---

> **CASE STUDY 10.1**
>
> # Enemy Combatants
>
> In 2001, in response to the September 11 attacks, the United States launched the global "war on terrorism," which included specific military operations against the Taliban in Afghanistan and members of al-Qaeda operating there. Hundreds of the individuals captured during the following months were transported to Guantánamo Bay, Cuba, to a location designated as "Camp X-Ray," where they were held as "enemy" or "unlawful" combatants, a status vaguely defined as being a captured fighter in a war who is not entitled to prisoner of war status because he or she does not meet the definition of a lawful combatant (according to the Geneva Convention on Prisoners of War).
>
> During the last months of 2001, the United States also took into custody suspected al-Qaeda members, including Afghans, Pakistanis, Saudis, Yemenis, and others from other parts of the world. In January 2002, 482 of these detainees were flown to Camp X-Ray, and the struggle to determine the legal rights and statuses of these detainees began.
>
> The Bush administration also designated these detainees as "enemy combatants" and declared that they therefore could be held indefinitely incommunicado, with no access to the U.S. legal system. Bush used the term **enemy combatant** as it was generated by the United States in the 1942 ruling "Ex Parte Quirin" and articulated by former president Franklin D. Roosevelt in his proclamation number 2561. In this address, Roosevelt stated that this definition applied to
>
>> all persons who are subjects, citizens, or residents of any Nation at war with the United States or who give obedience to or act under the direction of any such Nation or any territory or possession thereof, through coastal boundary defenses, and are charged with committing or attempting or preparing to commit sabotage, espionage, hostile or warlike acts, or violations of the law of war.[13]
>
> The legal struggle continued until the change in presidential administrations, when the newly elected Barack Obama ordered the closing of Camp X-Ray. The final legal fate of these prisoners has not yet been determined as the legal status of "enemy combatant" remains essentially unresolved, even within this country. ■
>
> *Source:* William Haynes, "Enemy Combatants," Council on Foreign Relations, December 12, 2002, retrieved from http://www.cfr.org/international-law/enemy-combatants/p5312

of direct military attack. One significant provision in this article states, "Acts or threats of violence, which have the primary object of spreading terror among the civilian population, are prohibited."

This article goes on to prohibit indiscriminate attacks that are "of a nature to strike military objectives and civilians or civilian objectives without distinction." It further states that "a bombardment that treats as a single military objective a number of clearly separated and distinct military objectives located within a city, town or village, or other area which has a concentration of civilians is considered to be indiscriminate and is therefore prohibited."

What does this mean in terms of legal restraints on terrorism? For one thing, it means that a state may not commit an attack on a city or town as a whole just on the basis of information that insurgents or combatants may be making a base in that area. To do so would be to commit an act of terrorism under international law. These conventions, in other words, make it clear that states as well as groups are prohibited from punishing the innocent in efforts to stop the insurgents in guerrilla warfare.

Article 50 of Protocol I clarifies the precautions that a state and a revolutionary army must take in conducting attacks. This article also codifies customary international law concerning what is called the "**rule of proportionality.**" Generally speaking, this refers to *the need for the loss of civilian life to be minimal compared to the military advantage gained.* In simple terms, this provision, along with other provisions in the article, means that those launching or planning to launch an attack are legally responsible for making sure that the military objectives they expect to gain justify the minimal loss of civilian life that may occur. This provision is extremely practical. It recognizes a basic fact of life during war: There are inevitably civilians on and around military targets who will no doubt be injured or killed during an attack on those targets.

There are two important points here. One is that the objective is assumed to be a military, never a civilian, target. The law makes it clear that whereas legitimate attacks may be expected against military targets, there is no legal expectation or right to launch attacks against civilian targets. On the contrary, the civilians within the target zone are to be protected against the effects of that attack as far as it is militarily possible.

The other point is that although military reality makes note of the fact that some civilian injuries may occur during an attack, the injury or deaths of civilians should be incidental to the operations and on a scale proportionate to the military objective sought. If civilian casualties are expected to be high, then the attack cannot be justified under international law.

Two thoughts come to mind with respect to these provisions. One is that guerrilla or revolutionary groups who select predominantly civilian targets are in violation of international law, even if there is a military target that may also be hit. Thus, the fact that a cafe is frequented by members of an enemy military does not make it a legitimate target, because there would be a great likelihood of many civilian casualties in such an attack. If the target area is populated predominantly with civilians, then it cannot be a justifiable military target.

The other thought that this provision evokes is that states may not strike civilian settlements, even if there are guerrilla soldiers taking refuge or making their headquarters in such settlements. To attack such places would mean inflicting unacceptably high levels of civilian casualties in proportion to the military objective sought. Thus, those who seek to destroy Palestinian revolutionaries may not under international law drop bombs on Palestinian refugee camps or in residential sections of the West Bank or Gaza, because such areas have large civilian populations that include women and children, the sick, and the infirm.

CASE STUDY 10.2

Iraq: Differentiating Between Combatants and Noncombatants

Warfare today is more often unconventional than conventional, and the current U.S.-led "war on terror" is an excellent example of the legal problems presented by this type of conflict. The laws of war currently in effect were written primarily based on conventional warfare, with four criteria to help distinguish combatants from noncombatants. Combatants:

- carry their weapons openly
- wear uniforms clearly displaying a recognizable emblem or insignia
- conduct their operations in accordance with the laws of war
- have a command structure within their ranks

Two problems complicate the application of the laws of war to modern warfare, and both relate to the difficulty in determining who is truly a combatant. The first lies in the fact that there are thousands of deployed "peacekeeping" troops in conflict zones throughout the world today—troops, who are in uniform with insignias, are armed, and follow a clearly defined command structure. The problem is that the role of these soldiers ranges from the use of massive lethal force to that of a city police officer. This makes their status as combatant a continuous source of controversy, particularly in war zones such as Iraq, where the measure of peace in different parts of the country—and hence the role of the peacekeeping forces—varies widely. Peacekeeping forces charged with keeping a peace that does not fully exist is by definition a difficult role to define.

The second problem is equally difficult: Most insurgent groups today fail to meet at least one or more of these criteria for combatant status, making it a constant challenge to differentiate between a civilian and a combatant with any accuracy. In Iraq, as in most countries experiencing insurgencies or rebellions, few of those involved in insurgent or resistance groups wear uniforms with clear insignias or carry their weapons openly. With the increasing number of suicide bombings committed by people (men and women) who wear civilian clothing, distinguishing between combatants and noncombatants grows more difficult each day.

One final point is important here: If there is disagreement, legally, about who is truly a noncombatant, particularly among the armed forces, is the use of IEDs (improvised explosive device) at military checkpoints on civilian highways a terrorist act or legitimate insurgent violence? If the military at these points are acting as police rather than as warriors, can they be designated as innocent victims, noncombatants whose deaths make the IED explosion a terrorist act? Take a quick look at U.S. data on terrorism in Iraq since 2010, and note the difficulties that arise over this question. ∎

Source: Thomas W. Smith, "Protecting Civilians . . . or Soldiers? Humanitarian Law and the Economy of Risk in Iraq," International Studies Perspective (2008) 9, 144–164.

PIRACY OF AIR AND SEA

If, during times of war, terrorist acts against civilian noncombatants are illegal, then it seems logical to assume that such acts are also illegal during times of peace. Indeed, the term *crimes against humanity,* which was used to describe war crimes at Nuremberg, did not originate with laws of war but with laws of peace. The term was used in international legal writings to describe acts of piracy. The famous English jurist, Sir Edward Coke, in the time of James I, described pirates as *hostis humanis generis,* meaning *"common enemies of mankind."*[14]

National case law confirms this view of piracy as an international crime. The U.S. Supreme Court, in the case of *U.S. v. Smith* (1820), went on record through Justice Joseph Story as declaring piracy to be "an offense against the law of nations" and a pirate to be "an enemy of the human race."[15] Judge John Bassett Moore of the World Court reaffirmed this assessment in his opinion in the famous *Lotus* case (1927).[16]

In fact, from the Paris Declaration of 1856 to the Geneva Convention of 1958, the proliferation of treaties dealing with aspects of terror-violence on the high seas has helped to codify international law with regard to piracy.[17] Piracy—of the sea, at least—is one of the first and most universally recognized international crimes.

Nations have not been so willing, through international law, to deal with modern **skyjacking**, which some legal experts termed *air piracy.* One legal expert suggested that "the legal status of aerial hijackers could become the same as sea pirates through the process of novation wherein the former would be presumed to stand in the shoes of the latter."[18] Theoretically, this would provide a way to bring perpetrators of the modern crime of skyjacking under the existing legal restrictions and penalties imposed on crimes of a similar nature, that is, of sea piracy, which was more common at an earlier date.

Novation is not a complicated process. Legally, it refers to *the substitution of a new indebtedness or obligation, creditor, or debtor, for an existing one.* In other words, aerial hijackers would assume the legal "indebtedness" of sea pirates under international law. Thus, it would not be necessary to create new international law to deal with what is in many respects a very old form of criminal activity.

But modern nations have not seen such a process as an adequate or acceptable solution. Instead, three major agreements on aircraft hijacking have evolved, as well as a number of smaller agreements between nations concerned with this crime. But the three treaties have met with limited success since three issues that need to be addressed in any successful hijacking convention have not been adequately resolved. These are the problems of determining who has jurisdiction, of establishing a prosecutable offense, and of providing for prompt processing of extradition requests.

The Convention on Offences and Certain Other Acts Committed on Board Aircraft, signed in Tokyo on September 14, 1963, provided a general basis for the establishment of **jurisdiction**, that is, *legal authority to exercise control*. The hijacking of an aircraft is an act that often takes place in flight and thus between countries. Such planes are often registered to yet another country and carry citizens of many countries. So a decision as to who has the right to bring a hijacker to justice is often a difficult one.

Article 3 of the Tokyo convention provides that the state of registration is the one that has the first and primary right to exercise jurisdiction.[19] But this convention does not place the responsibility on any signatory nation to ensure that all alleged offenders be prosecuted. Thus, a nation may accept jurisdiction and then refuse or neglect to bring the offenders to justice.

The subsequent Convention for the Suppression of Unlawful Seizure of Aircraft, signed at The Hague on December 18, 1970, deals more specifically with the issues of extradition and prosecution. This convention obliges contracting states to make the offense of unlawful seizure of aircraft punishable by severe penalties.

This convention offers a definition for the actions that constitute the offense of skyjacking in Article 1, which states that any person commits an offense while on board an aircraft in flight if he or she "unlawfully, by force or threat thereof, or by any other means of intimidation, seizes, or exercises control of, that aircraft, or attempts to perform any such act; or, is an accomplice of a person who performs or attempts to perform any such act."

Although not as explicit as a later convention drawn up at Montreal, this convention does provide an important legal framework for prosecution of an offense that is reasonably and clearly defined in legal terms directly applicable in the legal systems of many states (meaning the states are thus not given the sticky political task of creating laws to make such acts a legal offense).

Under this convention, too, **provisions for jurisdiction** were extended. Three states were legally given the responsibility for jurisdiction, in the following order of precedence: (1) the state of registration, (2) the state of first landing, and (3) the state in which the lessee has his or her principal place of business or permanent residence. Moreover, this convention requires each contracting state to take measures to establish jurisdiction if the offender is within its territory and is not to be extradited.

This convention also addresses the issue of prosecution, obligating each contracting state to either **extradite**—that is, *to send the person to another state seeking to prosecute*—an alleged offender, or to submit the case "without exception whatsoever to its competent authorities for the purpose of prosecution." Although it does not create an absolute obligation to extradite, the convention states that the offense referred to is deemed to be included as an extraditable offense in any existing extradition treaties between contracting states and is to be included in every future extradition treaty concluded between such states.

The Convention for the Suppression of Unlawful Acts Against the Safety of Civil Aviation signed in Montreal on September 23, 1971, adds more detail to the description of the offenses affecting aircraft and air navigation. It includes

1. acts of violence against a person on board an aircraft in flight if that act is likely to endanger the safety of that aircraft; or
2. destruction of an aircraft in service or damage to such an aircraft which renders it incapable of flight or which is likely to endanger its safety in flight; or
3. placing or causing to be placed on an aircraft in service, by any means whatsoever, a device or substance, which is likely to destroy that aircraft, or to cause damage to it which is likely to endanger its safety in flight; or
4. destruction or damage of air navigation facilities or interference with their operation, if any such act is likely to endanger the safety of the aircraft in flight; or
5. communication of information, which is known to be false, thereby endangering the safety of the aircraft in flight.[20]

The Montreal convention also articulated what has come to be called the concept of **universal jurisdiction** for crimes of aerial hijacking. Building on the agreement included in the convention of the previous year, the signatories in Montreal made it clear that *aerial hijacking is an international crime for which every nation party to the convention has jurisdiction.* This means that regardless of where the crime is initiated or concluded or on whose territory it is committed, every state party to this convention agrees to treat the act as a crime under its jurisdiction. Thus, each state either extradites or prosecutes the person accused of this crime, under the laws of the state.

Table 10.1 offers a simple comparison of these three important treaty efforts to create international agreement on this type of terrorist activity. Although other agreements have emerged to deal with alternative acts of terrorism impacting aerial safety, such as bombing, these three conventions provide a relatively firm agreement on the part of states about this one type of terrorist crime.

In the succeeding decades, other protocols and conventions focusing on "the suppression of unlawful acts" that endangered civil aviation continued to be debated, rewritten, and occasionally accepted as law. The 1988 Protocol for the Suppression of Unlawful Acts of Violence at Airports Serving International Civil Aviation, supplementary to the Convention for the Suppression of Unlawful Acts Against the Safety of Civil Aviation (Montreal), attempts to clarify the nature of the offense. In the Montreal convention, the crimes being described only included an act of violence against a person on board an aircraft in flight; destruction or incapacitation of an aircraft in flight; placing

TABLE 10.1

Key Legal Issues in Hijacking Conventions

Treaty	Significant Legal Points
Convention on Offenses and Certain Other Acts Committed on Board Aircraft (Tokyo, September 14, 1963)	Jurisdiction given to state of registration
Convention for the Suppression of Unlawful Seizure of Aircraft (The Hague, December 18, 1970)	Jurisdiction given to state of registration—first claim state of landing—second claim state in which lessee has principal place of business or primary residence—third claim
Convention for the Suppression of Unlawful Acts Against the Safety of Civil Aviation (Montreal, September 23, 1971)	Definition of aerial hijacking jurisdiction Universal jurisdiction— obligation to extradite or prosecute

(or causing to be placed) of a bomb aboard an aircraft in service; destroying or damaging navigation facilities; and communication of false information to endanger flight.

The Protocol expands the crimes treated by this convention to include acts of violence against a person at an airport serving international civil aviation and damages to facilities at such an airport. This legal change reflected a change in the patterns of terrorist attacks, which by the mid-1980s had begun to include attacks in the airport in addition to aircraft bombings or hijackings.

In 1988 the laws of the sea, which had been the basis from which the laws of air piracy were drawn, were amended to include some of the new piracy laws just described in the context of similar acts at sea. The Convention for the Suppression of Unlawful Acts Against the Safety of Maritime Navigation, written in 1988, and the Protocol for the Suppression of Unlawful Acts Against the Safety of Fixed Platforms Located on the Continental Shelf were both in many respects a reflection of the earlier conventions relating to the safety of civil aviation described earlier. Terrorism became a recognized crime against both fixed and moving targets in the air and at sea, at least in terms of specific types of acts.

PROTECTION OF DIPLOMATIC PERSONNEL AND HEADS OF STATE

Similar difficulties have hindered efforts to create effective protections against attacks on diplomatic personnel and heads of state. In light of the seizure of American diplomatic personnel in Iran, which was never formally "punished" as a crime under international law, it could be argued that there still exists no effective international law concerning such acts. However, laws do exist (despite the fact that they are broken without punishment) on this politically sensitive subject. Since these laws concern terrorism of a specific sort, they deserve consideration here.

Perhaps the unwillingness to punish or even to condemn those guilty of attacks on these "protected persons" has its roots in the Western tradition of granting political asylum to offenders who have committed "political" crimes. Although concern for the preservation of societal order influenced some Western European governments to modify their positions on granting asylum for "political" crimes, political asylum remains the primary focus in extradition questions in many modern states.

In 1833, Belgium enacted a law providing for nonextradition of political offenders, a principle incorporated into a Franco-Belgium treaty in 1834.[21] Following both successful and unsuccessful attempts on the lives of heads of state in subsequent years, however, an **attentat clause** began to be incorporated into successive treaties. *This clause made the murder or attempted murder of any head of state or his immediate family a common (not political) crime.* These clauses stated essentially that such attempts "shall not be considered a political offense or an act connected with such an offense."[22]

In 1957, the European Convention on Extradition invoked the principle of the attentat clause by making assaults on heads of state and their immediate families nonpolitical offenses.[23] The Vienna Convention on Diplomatic Relations gave evidence of a broadening concern for diplomats as well as heads of state. Under this convention, it is made "the responsibility of the States" to prevent attacks on a diplomatic agent's person, freedom, or dignity."[24] The Convention on the Prevention and Punishment of Crimes Against Internationally Protected Persons Including Diplomatic Agents, which came into force in February 1977, declared it the responsibility of all states party to this convention to take all practicable measures to prevent and to either extradite or punish those committing "crimes against diplomatic agents and other internationally protected persons." This convention declared that acts that jeopardized the safety of such persons "are of grave concern to the international community."[25]

This broadly stated concern and general delegation of authority, however, has failed to secure significant enforceable protections for diplomats. As one expert expressed it, "what was needed, beyond the incidental tightening of police measures, is a constant vigilance on the part of states, acting individually and collectively in an organized way, to prevent the occurrence of incidents."[26]

But while subsequent treaties on this subject have attempted to make clear the specific acts prohibited and the fact that states have a right to claim jurisdiction over the crime, there remain serious flaws in the protection afforded to diplomatic agents today. No "collective, organized" approach to the problem has evolved.

Furthermore, the delegation of responsibility for protecting and punishing in the event of attacks on diplomats creates serious problems when the government of a state is itself a party or a tacit accessory to the taking of also diplomatic hostages. It is clearly useless to expect a government that actively or tacitly approves of such a crime to prosecute the perpetrators of the crime. Such a requirement could mean that the government must at some point prosecute itself for committing what it obviously did not regard as an illegal act—a most unlikely scenario!

One further development in the law regarding the protection of diplomatic personnel should be noted. The Venice Statement on Taking of Diplomatic Hostages, issued by the Heads of State and Government of the Seven Summit Countries during their meeting in Venice in 1980, not only expressed grave concern about the Iranian hostage situation but also called on nations to ratify the recently completed Convention Against the Taking of Hostages, adopted by the UN General Assembly on December 17, 1979. Thirty-nine states were signatories, and 167 states were parties to this convention as of October 2010.[27]

Completed shortly after the seizure of the American Embassy in Tehran, this convention effectively makes it a crime to take *any* person as a hostage. Through this convention, the protection of international law is extended to every individual, regardless of his or her position (or lack of one), with the exception of those in armed forces engaged in armed conflict.

This broadening of the law in this respect suggests that nations consider certain actions unacceptable to the community of nations. Just as in laws of war, we noted that certain actions were prohibited at all times, whether at war or at peace, so we note that there are some actions that the international community has come to believe are unacceptable regardless of the cause.

REGIONAL LEGAL EFFORTS TO PREVENT OR PUNISH TERRORISM

Although it is true that most regions have drafted and ratified a treaty to "prevent and punish" acts of terrorism, most of these conventions are no more specific than the international instruments in place today. The Organization of American States was the first region to draft such a treaty, creating the instrument in 1971. However, like the efforts by the international community at that time, it was vague and lacked a definition of terrorism or even a specification of types of terrorist acts. Instead, all member states simply agree to prevent and punish acts of terrorism, "especially kidnapping, murder, and other assaults against the life or physical integrity of those persons to whom the state has the duty according to international law to give special protection."[28]

Each regional convention, while fundamentally similar, has at least a few unusual qualities. The European Convention on the Suppression of Terrorism (1977), for instance, invokes the use of existing regional instruments such as the European Court of Human Rights to resolve disputes between states over the interpretation or application of the convention. No other regional instrument suggests such a yielding of sovereignty to a nonstate body in reference to the politically sensitive crime of "terrorism."

However, the Arab Convention on the Suppression of Terrorism, completed two decades later, offers in Articles 9–38 provisions for the arrest, extradition, or prosecution of individuals accused of terrorist acts, including the use of **judicial delegations**, *specially appointed delegations instructed to hear the testimony of witnesses and take depositions as evidence, examine and inspect evidence, and obtain relevant documents and records relating to the actionable offense.* Although each contracting state has a right to refuse to allow such a delegation, it must put into writing the reasons for its refusal. Thus, although the obligation to "extradite or prosecute" is similar to that in earlier conventions, this regional instrument creates the process for establishing a special tribunal with the authority to investigate charges of terrorism. This is a step that the international community has not yet taken.

More recent regional conventions, such as the Treaty on Cooperation among the States Members of the Commonwealth of Independent States in Combating Terrorism (1999) and the Convention on the Organization of the Islamic Conference on Combating International Terrorism (1999), make extensive reference to all the existing international documents on terrorism. Each of these, however, also includes types of terrorism not included in international conventions. In the Commonwealth of Independent States convention, Article 1 incorporates **technological terrorism**—*the threat or use of nuclear, radiological, chemical, or bacteriological weapons or their components, including the seizure, disruption, or destruction of nuclear, chemical, or other facilities posing an increased technological and environmental danger*—a type of terrorism not yet incorporated in any international instrument on terrorism. The Islamic Conference's convention adds to the category of terrorist crimes those that endanger the environment or other national resources—again a type of action not legally described as terrorism in any international convention to date.

There are currently seven regional conventions on terrorism on record at the United Nations. These are listed, with location and date of deposition, in Table 10.2.

Regions, then, although not necessarily moving a great deal faster than the international community in defining or creating a legal framework for terrorist crimes, have begun to offer new directions for international legal cooperation. Some of these new directions are ones that the international community, in the context of debate at the United Nations and related international organizations, is exploring with increasing vigor, particularly that of "technological terror," the financing of terror (mentioned in Article 3 of the Islamic Conference convention in terms of measures to prevent terrorism), and the need to halt the flow of arms to groups engaged in terror (discussed at length in the Islamic Conference convention). Each of these new directions is now or will soon be the subject of a new international convention.

TABLE 10.2

Regional Conventions on Terrorism

Conventions	Regional Organization	Date/Location of Adoption
Arab Convention on the Suppression of Terrorism	League of Arab States	April 22, 1998, in Cairo
Convention on the Organization of the Islamic Conference on Combating International Terrorism	Organization of Islamic States	July 1, 1999, in Ouagadougou
European Convention on the Suppression of Terrorism	European Union	January 27, 1977, in Strasbourg
OAS Convention to Prevent and Punish Acts of Terrorism Taking the Form of Crimes Against Persons and Related Extortion That Are of International Significance	Organization of American States	February 2, 1971, in Washington, DC
OAU Convention on the Prevention and Combating of Terrorism	Organization of African Unity	July 14, 1999, in Algiers
SAARC Regional Convention on Suppression of Terrorism	South Asian Association for Regional Cooperation	November, 4, 1987, in Kathmandu
Treaty on Cooperation Among the States Members of the Commonwealth of Independent States in Combating Terrorism	Commonwealth of Independent States	June 4, 1999, in Minsk

INTERNATIONAL EFFORTS TO RESTRICT INTERNAL STATE TERRORISM

In the wake of discovering just how ruthless some rulers could be in dealing with their subjects, leaders of victorious nations after World War II tried to create international laws that would restrict the ability of governments to use terrorism against their citizens. Attempts to create such laws by consensus were unevenly successful.

On December 10, 1948, the General Assembly of the United Nations adopted the **Universal Declaration of Human Rights** without dissent, calling on all member countries to publicize the text of the declaration and to "cause it to be disseminated, displayed, read, and expounded principally in schools and other educational institutions, without distinction based on the political status of countries or territories."[29]

This document states that *"everyone has the right to life, liberty, and security of person," and that these rights may not be taken away by any institution, state, or individual.* According to this declaration, it is not acceptable for states to administer collective punishment or to punish any person for a crime that he or she did not personally commit. The declaration emphasizes the necessity of fair trials and equal justice before the law. Since terrorism by a state often involves the summary punishment of individuals not for any specific crime but because their deaths or incarceration will result in a climate of fear among other citizens, this declaration would appear significant in the effort to curb state terrorism. However, it has no binding effect in international law. It is in some respects only a statement of concern among some states about the presence of state terrorism.

If this declaration is only a statement of principles lacking mechanisms for enforcement, the subsequent Covenant on Civil and Political Rights has tried to remedy that flaw.[30] Although this covenant has more explicit provisions for enforcing compliance, it has a much worse record for ratification. Less than one-third of the nations in existence today are a party to this treaty, which is designed in part to protect individuals from state terrorism. The United States, for instance, refused to ratify this covenant just as it also refused for over forty years to become a party to the convention outlawing genocide.

The problem, both in terms of ratification and enforcement, is largely a political one. States do not openly interfere in the domestic affairs of other states, because such interference would leave them open to similar intrusions. Conventions such as those protecting human rights are often viewed as dangerous, even by states with relatively clean records in terms of state terrorism, in that these conventions open avenues for hostile governments to interfere with the internal affairs of the nation.

George Kren and Leon Rappoport argue that within certain limits set by political and military power considerations, the modern state may do anything it wishes to those under its control. There is no moral ethical limit which the state cannot transcend if it wished to do so, because there is no moral-ethical power higher than the state. Moreover, it seems apparent that no modern state will ever seriously interfere with the internal activities of another solely for moral-ethical reasons.[31]

Most interference in the internal affairs of a sovereign state is based on national security rather than on ethical or moral grounds. Although the Nuremberg trials offered some evidence that the principle of nonintervention was being challenged by nations motivated by moral-ethical concerns, since that time few nations have indicated that crimes against humanity undertaken within a nation's own borders are a basis for international intervention. Even evidence of "ethnic cleansing" in Bosnia during the early 1990s, although generating the formation of an international criminal tribunal, did not produce on the part of nations a willingness to send indicted criminals to succumb to the justice process at The Hague. Justice remains largely within the purview defined by the rulers of the individual nation-states.

At least one action taken by a state in 2001, however, encourages hope that states will begin to effectively bring pressure on each other to comply with punishments for crimes against humanity. The carefully orchestrated arrest and extradition of Slobodan Milosevic, the former leader of Yugoslavia, by his successor as president of that state, to the War Crimes Tribunal meeting in The Hague suggests that pressure by the international community led the emerging leadership to submit former leaders to trial by the international community. This abrogation of the concept of immunity from prosecution in international courts of state leaders for actions, however outrageous and illegal, committed while in office suggests that the international norms for human rights are beginning to take a stronger legal hold in the international community than mere treaty ratification might imply.

The ability of the international community to use law to bring a state leader accused of genocide to a court of justice is very limited, however. The case of Milosevic is unusual in that the emerging leadership of the country that he had led and in which he was residing was willing to allow him to be taken by authorities for trial in The Hague. This was not the case in the efforts to bring Augusto Pinochet to trial for his actions as the leader of Chile, as he had secured amnesty in that country for his actions in return for his relinquishing of power. Thus, Spain's efforts to have the United Kingdom render him to Spain (where he had no immunity agreement and whose citizens were allegedly abused by his government) for trial when he traveled to the United Kingdom for medical treatment were ineffective, and Pinochet was able to return to Chile without being detained or rendered for trial.

International cooperation on efforts to contain state terrorism remains sketchy. Efforts to create an international criminal court, the focus of a conference in Italy in the summer of 1998, highlight the problem. Although agreement has slowly evolved on the need for such a court, its structure and mandate remain sources of contention. Moreover, the conference stated early in its meetings that the issue of terrorism by individuals or states would not be codified for such a court, because this issue presented too many points of controversy for successful resolution.

The linkage between revolution and violence has already been discussed. A similar relationship exists with respect to the right of a state to protect itself from revolutionary violence. Most modern states experienced a period of revolutionary violence. During and after such periods, the right of a state to protect itself remains restricted by more rules than those that apply to its revolutionary enemies. In addition to abiding by the laws of warfare, states are entrusted with the responsibility for preserving and protecting human rights and freedoms.

Thus, a state has an abiding obligation to restrain its use of violence against its citizens. Both at war and at peace, a state is supposed to recognize a legal commitment toward the preservation of the rights of the individual. If it is true that insurgent terrorists frequently try to provoke government repression in the hope of generating greater sympathy and support for the terrorists' cause, then it is obviously extremely important that governments *not* respond in kind.

This does not mean that governments are or should be held to be impotent in the face of flagrant attacks on law and order. Certainly a state is responsible for protecting its citizens from violence. But the means used to ensure law and order must be carefully balanced against the responsibility of the government to ensure the maximum protection of civil rights and liberties. Too great a willingness to sacrifice the latter in order to preserve stability within a state would not only be giving the terrorists the impetus for their cause but would also be placing the state in the invidious position of breaking international law in order to stop someone else from breaking it.

A state that violates international law by committing acts of genocide, by violently suppressing fundamental freedoms, or by breaking the laws of war or the Geneva Convention on the treatment of prisoners of war and civilians can be considered guilty of state terrorism.[32] If terrorism is defined to include acts of political violence perpetrated without regard to the safety of innocent persons in an effort to evoke a mood of fear and confusion in a target audience, then states have been as least as guilty of such acts as have individuals and groups.

CASE STUDY 10.3

Arresting Sudan's President

On March 4, 2007, the International Criminal Court (ICC) issued a warrant for the arrest of Sudan's president, Omar al-Bashir, for war crimes and crimes against humanity in Darfur. This was the first warrant issued against a sitting head of state by the ICC, which is based in The Hague, the Netherlands, and did not include a count of genocide. The conflict in Darfur had at this point, according to UN's records, resulted in as many as 300,000 people killed since its beginning in 2003. ICC Prosecutor Luis Moreno-Ocampo, an Argentine lawyer, accused Bashir of personally instructing his forces to annihilate three ethnic groups—the Fur, the Masalit, and the Zaghawa. The indictment did include seven counts of war crimes and crimes against humanity, which include murder, rape, and torture.

While international human rights groups hailed the decision and called on Bashir to turn himself in to international authorities, leaders of the African Union prepared to ask the UN Security Council to defer the ICC proceedings for a year. Aid workers in the Darfur region were advised to leave, and other aid agencies were ordered out by the Sudanese government, which accused them of helping to generate the warrant against Bashir.

UN and ICC actions have not ended the problem, and the ICC's lack of power has been made painfully clear. In May 2007, the ICC issued arrest warrants for crimes

(continued)

in Darfur against Sudanese government minister Ahmed Haroun and Janjaweed militia leader Ali Kushayb—warrants that the Sudanese government refused to honor. The ICC has no powers to enforce its own arrest warrants. According to the court's rules, only states can apprehend Bashir, as he can be arrested on the territory of any state that has signed the court's Rome Statutes. Bashir's government has rejected ICC jurisdiction, and he personally denies the charges. ■

Source: Human Rights Watch: ICC Warrant for Al-Bashir on Genocide July 13, 2010, retrieved from http://www.hrw.org/news/2010/07/13/sudan-icc-warrant-al-bashir-genocide

IS TERRORISM A POLITICAL CRIME?

The definition of what constitutes a "political" crime has become a crucial part of the modern legal debate concerning terrorism. The crux of the problem appears to be in deciding how one determines what is and what is not a political crime. It is a problem that is far from solved and one whose political ramifications may well make it, for the present, insoluble.

For centuries, the nature of a **political crime** *rested largely upon the intended victim of the crime.* That is, the assassination of a head of state or of a diplomat was regarded as political in nature and therefore to be handled differently—more leniently or more severely, depending upon the state's system of laws—than an ordinary, nonpolitical offense such as the murder of an ordinary citizen.

If such criteria were applied to many terrorist acts today, such as the hijacking of an airplane or the bombing of a cafe, then such acts would not, on the surface, qualify as being political. The argument could be (and indeed has been) made that the real intended "victims" of such crimes are the governments forced to helplessly watch and perhaps ultimately capitulate as the events unfold.

But to assume that there is a victim involved beyond the obvious captives or casualties, one is forced to rely upon knowledge or inference about the motives of the perpetrators. In other words, the action would be described as a political crime, not specifically by its intended victim but by the motives that prompted the commission of the crime.

There are at least two problems with this reasoning. The first is that to make such a determination concerning a motive for an action, the person rendering the judgment would need knowledge of why the terrorists committed the crime. How is such knowledge to be obtained? Does it come from propaganda put out by the terrorists, which is designed to persuade but is not necessarily truthful? Does it come from interviews with the perpetrators or their allies, assuming such interviews could be arranged?

Is there any way, indeed, to discover the facts concerning the motive for a crime? To search for a factual basis is not useless by any means, but the attribution of a motive for any crime, political or common, is essentially a judgment call. In the courts of most civilized nations, assessment of motivation may affect the degree of severity with regard to the prosecution or sentencing but has little effect on the decision as to whether or not a crime has been committed.

Yet if one allows motivation to be the determinant for delineating political from common crimes, there is reason to suspect that, for crimes judged political in motivation, there would in fact be neither prosecution nor sentencing. This is the second problem in allowing motivation to be the guiding factor in determining what constitutes a political crime. For under the laws of many nations, **political offenders** are accorded special status. *Those believed guilty of political offenses are eligible for the granting of political asylum by friendly states.* States granting such asylum are under no legal obligation to prosecute the perpetrator for the crime.

Even those who are prosecuted are afforded special treatment. Seldom are political criminals jailed with those who have committed common crimes. To be a political prisoner confers, in many nations, a unique status on the offender. There is nothing wrong with this: Political crimes are not the same as common crimes. Their perpetrators are often regarded as motivated by high ideals for political change for which they are willing to pay a high personal price.

That is another important point, however. Just like the perpetrator of any other crime, the political offender does so with the knowledge, even the acceptance, of the penalty that must be paid for the crime. Perpetrators of political crimes in earlier centuries committed their offenses in the full expectation of being required to pay the legal penalty for their crimes. Those who would classify terrorism as a political crime do so to enable its perpetrators to evade the payment of those penalties.

This **loophole in the law,** *which allows political offenders to escape extradition or even punishment,* has worried international legal experts for years. Attempts have been made to advocate the creation of an international criminal code and an ICC. Under these innovations, terrorism could be specified as an international crime, punishable in international court. But although the efforts to create an international criminal court have progressed dramatically in recent years, with the convention establishing such a court now open for signatures, the leaders working in Italy to construct the code for this court were unable to resolve both practical legal and political problems relating to international terrorism. Indeed, it is interesting and discouraging to note that the issue of terrorism was removed early in the conference as a crime for which this international criminal court would be expected to adjudicate. So the loophole of political offender still allows terrorists to commit heinous crimes for political purposes and escape the hand of justice.

THE UNITED NATIONS AND THE WAR ON TERRORISM

The issue of terrorism was brought before the UN General Assembly in 1972, after the massacre of Israeli athletes at the Munich Olympics by a Palestinian group. Since that time, the United Nations has sporadically worked on measures to combat the global problem. In the 1970s, the Ad Hoc Committee tasked with generating consensus for action on the issue became deadlocked in a struggle to define the term *terrorism*.

After a decade of effort, the committee reported that the issue was "too politically difficult" to define, making consensus on appropriate actions in response not possible. The problem in the General Assembly (GA) lay in differentiating between the legitimate struggles of peoples under colonial rule or alien domination and foreign occupation and terrorism. Self-determination and national liberation were processes that many member states had experienced, and most were reluctant to create law that could impinge on these fundamental rights.

The GA, in December 1985, passed a resolution containing these ambivalent feelings about causes as well as the effects of terrorism, but with sufficient strength to generate a new convention. Although GA Resolution 40/61 urged all states "to contribute to the progressive elimination of causes underlying international terrorism," it also unequivocally condemned "as criminal, all acts, methods, and practices of terrorism wherever and by whomever committed." In response to some of the explicit challenges of this resolution, and quoting it as the reason for the drafting of the treaty, the Convention for the Suppression of Unlawful Acts Against the Safety of Maritime Navigation was drafted in Rome on March 10, 1988.[33]

On November 26, 1997, the GA Third Committee condemned terrorism, drafting a resolution condemning violations of the rights to life, liberty, and security, reiterating its condemnation of terrorism. Provisions of this resolution, approved by a recorded vote of 97 in favor to none against, with 57 abstentions, called on states to take all necessary and effective measures to prevent, combat, and eliminate terrorism. It also urged the international community to enhance regional and international cooperation in fighting terrorism and to condemn incitement of ethnic hatred, violence, and terrorism.

Less than a month later, the GA adopted the International Convention for the Suppression of Terrorist Bombings. This convention referred to earlier UN action, notably the Declaration on Measures to Eliminate International Terrorism, annexed to GA resolution 49/60 of December 9, 1994, as part of the reason for the drafting of the convention. This convention was drafted, according to its preamble, because of the increasingly widespread use of explosives in terrorist attacks and because of a perceived gap in existing multilateral treaties in the context of such attacks.

Using the General Assembly Plenary Declaration in 1994, which stated that acts of terrorism could also threaten international peace and security, the Security Council (SC) became more involved in the struggle to deal with this issue. In unanimously adopting resolution 1269 (1999), the SC stressed the vital role of the United Nations in strengthening international cooperation in combating terrorism and emphasized the importance of enhanced coordination among states and international and regional organizations. It called upon all states to take steps to cooperate with each other through bilateral and multilateral agreements and arrangements, prevent and suppress terrorist acts, protect their nationals and other persons against terrorist attacks, and bring to justice the perpetrators of such acts. The SC continues to advocate exchanging information in accordance with international and domestic law, cooperating on administrative and judicial matters to prevent the commission of terrorist acts, and using all lawful means to prevent and suppress the preparation and financing of any such acts in member states' territories.

In other resolutions passed in the 1990s, the SC called on all states to deny safe havens to those who planned, financed, or committed terrorist acts by ensuring their apprehension and prosecution or extradition. These resolutions stressed that before granting refugee status, states should take appropriate measures in conformity with national and international law, including international standards of human rights, to ensure that the asylum seeker had not participated in terrorist acts.

The SC has been careful not to take actions on this issue that would replace the efforts of the GA but sought to interact with it on the basis of its competence within the charter. Noting that the degree of sophistication of terrorist acts and the increasingly globalized nature of those acts were new trends and that the extensive international networks of organized criminals were creating an infrastructure of catastrophic terrorism, the SC resolved that terrorism posed a serious threat to international peace and security, making it an issue that needed SC action as well as that of GA and Economic and Social Council (ECOSOC).

In the wake of the attacks on September 11, 2001, the SC passed Resolution 1368 condemning the attacks and obliging states to "combat by all means threats to international peace and security caused by terrorist attacks." Two weeks later, on September 28, the SC passed Resolution 1373, which called on states to control "the financing and preparation of any acts of terrorism" and to ratify and implement all relevant UN protocols and conventions.[34]

To date, 13 major conventions and protocols designed to combat terrorism have been adopted by the states within the United Nations and deposited with the Legal Office of that institution for further signatures. These conventions require states to cooperate on issues such as the suppression of unlawful seizure of aircraft (in the two conventions and protocol mentioned earlier in this chapter), the physical protection of nuclear materials, and the marking of plastic explosives for detection. Five of these conventions were adopted by the member states of the UN General Assembly and have been ratified by a sufficient number of states to become international law. Table 10.3 lists the five treaties generated by the GA to date.

The International Convention for the Suppression of the Financing of Terrorism that obliges states to freeze assets flowing to terrorist networks was adopted by the GA on December 9, 1999, and remains open for signatories. The preamble to this convention highlighted a growing conviction that "the financing of terrorism is a matter of grave concern to the international community as a whole" and focused on "the urgent need to enhance international cooperation among states in devising and adopting effective measures for the prevention of the financing of terrorism." It is interesting to note that this convention does not seek to create a new definition of terrorism; instead,

TABLE 10.3	
Conventions on Terrorism Adopted by the UN General Assembly	
Convention	Date Adopted
Convention on the Prevention and Punishment of Crimes Against Internationally Protected Persons, Including Diplomatic Agents	December 14, 1973
International Convention Against the Taking of Hostages	December 17, 1979
International Convention for the Suppression of Terrorist Bombings	December 15, 1997
International Convention for the Suppression of the Financing of Terrorism	December 9, 1999
International Convention for the Suppression of Acts of Nuclear Terrorism	April 13, 2005 (deposited)

it includes a list of treaties on terrorist acts in its annex and states in Article 2 that a terrorist act "constitutes an offense within the scope of and as defined in one of the treaties listed in the annex." The annex includes all of the treaties discussed thus far in this chapter, including those dealing with maritime acts and the International Convention for the Suppression of Terrorist Bombings.

This approach, including a list of all treaties dealing with the issue of terrorist acts rather than redefining the problem, is an apparently successful effort *not* to have to struggle once again with the political problems of definition but instead to concentrate efforts on preventive action and punishment. This convention on financing terrorism had, as of October 5, 2001, fifty-seven signatories and four parties (**signatories** are *states that have signed the convention,* and **parties** are *states that have both signed and ratified the convention, making it law within these states*).

The United Nations has created a **Terrorism Prevention Branch** (TPB), which *researches terrorism trends, assists countries in upgrading their capacity to investigate and prevent terrorist acts, and fosters international cooperation based on best practices and lessons learned from previous events*. This department works with the UN Office on Drugs and Crime (UNDOC), which promotes the adoption and implementation of major drug control treaties and assists governments with research, analysis, and information sharing on the illicit drug trade, which is believed a major source of funds for terrorist activities. This office also works to combat money laundering, also a key aspect of terrorist financing, and to coordinate the efforts of states and organizations within the international community in preventing, inhibiting, and punishing terrorist acts.

The UN Global Counter-Terrorism Strategy, adopted by the GA in resolution 60/288 of September 8, 2006, makes substantial reference to the work of the UNDOC, particularly in its TPB. The strategy encourages the UNDOC to enhance its technical assistance to member states, noting that the UNDOC has significant comparative advantages for delivering assistance in counterterrorism efforts. Through its TPB, it combines a range of expertise in the related areas of crime prevention and criminal justice, rule of law, drug control, transnational organized crime, money laundering, corruption, and related international cooperation in criminal matters with operational field-level capacity. The UNDOC can also help states become party to relevant international legal instruments.

The UN Security Council adopted Resolution 1373 on September 28, 2001, which declared that "acts, methods and practices of terrorism are contrary to the purposes and principles of the United Nations," and called upon member states to "become parties as soon as possible to the relevant international conventions and protocols" and to "increase cooperation and fully implement the relevant international conventions and protocols."[35]

This resolution also established the **Counter-Terrorism Committee** (CTC) *in the Security Council to monitor the implementation of the resolution by all states and increase the capability of states to fight terrorism, including bringing member states to an acceptable level of compliance with the terrorism-related conventions and protocols.* The CTC has since become the UN's leading body to promote collective action against international terrorism. In carrying out its functions, the CTC is supported by the Counter-Terrorism Committee Executive Directorate.[36]

The United Nations and its related agencies have been active in creating a framework of international law to define acts of terrorism. The resolutions, conventions, and protocols generated by this body also serve to articulate international concern and to generate cooperation in efforts to prevent terrorist acts and to bring perpetrators to justice. Although much clearly remains to be done in this arena, the generation of consensus by this body on this politically hot issue has increased markedly in the past decade, particularly in the wake of the September 11 attacks. The UN's Counter Terrorism Strategy is a continuously evolving effort to resolve the challenge of terrorism today.

CONCLUSIONS

International law is useful as a measure of international concern and opinion on an issue such as terrorism. Lacking methods and mechanisms for enforcement, it cannot be said to be an effective deterrent to terrorism, either on the national or the international level. Because its formulation is so ad hoc, relying on loose associations of states rather than on any legislative body to draft conventions, it is somewhat less than coherent and often indecisive. Political considerations often weaken the resolve of nations to deal with politically sensitive subjects.

In the absence of a judiciary empowered to adjudicate without the consent of all parties, and lacking an executive or police force to enforce the laws, international law on terrorism has evolved as a patchwork of treaties. Among the most successful of the international treaties are those relating to specific types of terrorism and the most recent conventions on terrorist bombings and the financing of terrorism. Even these treaties, however, have been seriously hampered by political concerns relating to issues of jurisdiction, prosecution, extradition, and political asylum. Nor will the new international criminal court, as it comes into fruition, be of significant help in filling this absence of international legal authority.

As a means for combating terrorism, then, international law appears a somewhat dubious tool. When agreements are entered into that have enforcement capabilities, then such laws can be used to curb terrorism. But to date, only a few such agreements are in force within the international community.

DISCUSSION

The international community has declared a "war on terrorism" and has created numerous documents in its effort to define this crime. Yet there is much confusion remaining about what constitutes terrorism, how it should be punished, and by whom. There are, however, two other types of international legal agreements on terrorism that have been attempted, and one serious international legal question generated by individuals captured or arrested during the war on terrorism declared by the international community in the wake of the events of September 11. Consider each of the following descriptions of international legal efforts to deal with terrorism. Decide which, if any, have a reasonable chance of success given what you now know about the problems of enforcement and adjudication.

1. The creation of an ICC could offer a solution to the politicization of the crime of terrorism. Several national leaders, including the president of the Sudan, have been indicted by the ICC in recent years of "crimes against humanity," but the ability of the court to bring these individuals to justice remains unclear, since it lacks the ability to serve warrants on and arrest most of these persons. Does this use of international law to indict, without being able to bring to justice, world leaders accused of types of terrorism help or hurt the war on terrorism? Does it make international law appear strong and useful, focusing on crimes in the international community, or does it diminish the stature of the law, making it appear weak when the individuals cannot be brought to court for trial. Would, in fact, placing such a person in the hands of the ICC create as many problems as it would solve, even with respect to the crime of terrorism?

2. As noted earlier, several hundred people were captured by U.S.-led force in Afghanistan after the attacks of September 11, 2001, in a declared "war on terrorism." Until 2009, hundreds remained detained at the U.S. Naval Station at Guantánamo Bay, Cuba. The United States has called these individuals "enemy combatants" rather than prisoners of war and argues that they have no right to legal counsel and may be held indefinitely without being charged with an offense. Is this a legitimate use of legal authority to combat terrorism or a violation of the rights of "protected persons" during times of war? What should be the legal fate of these detainees? What are the problems with just setting them free or returning them to their home countries?

3. The United States has been accused of using torture against the prisoners at Camp X-Ray at Guantánamo Bay in efforts to gain information considered vital in the war on terror. Reports about these alleged abuses raise serious questions, including whether torture was used, if the abuse was in any sense justified by the information gained, and if the use of illegal means of interrogation can be justified by the "need to know," which is prevalent in wartime. Can torture ever be justified for a cause, or is it, like as acts of terrorism, never a legitimate activity?

ANALYSIS CHALLENGE

If terrorism is a crime because it violates the laws of the community of nations, regardless of the cause for which the act is committed, then the apprehension, trial, and potential punishment of such acts must be carried out in full compliance with the rule of this law. Consider the legal questions raised by the U.S.' actions with regard to the capture and killing of Osama bin Laden while he was living in Pakistan in May 2011. Read at least two different accounts of this action, and consider two important questions:

1. Was this a legal use of force to bring to justice an individual accused in the international community of carrying, or causing to be carried out, acts of terrorism?
2. Was there any realistic legal alternative to using a U.S. special forces team to kill bin Laden, once his probable hiding place had been determined? Would putting Pakistan in the position of having to openly arrest him, or allow the United States to do so and to take him out of the country for trial, have destabilized the current Pakistani government (a potentially high price for the legal apprehension of bin Laden)? If he had been arrested, where would/could he have been taken to trial, with any degree of personal or operational security?

   http://articles.cnn.com/2011-05-02/world/bin.laden.catharsis_1_bin-world-trade-center-imam-feisal-abdul-rauf?_s=PM:WORLD
   http://www.msnbc.msn.com/id/42852700/ns/world_news-death_of_bin_laden/t/us-forces-kill-osama-bin-laden-pakistan/

What, in your opinion, should be done when there is a clear violation of international law by an individual, but there is no clear legal recourse for justice to be served?

KEY TERMS

SUGGESTED READINGS AND RESOURCES

Arab Convention on the Suppression of Terrorism (signed at a meeting held at the General Secretariat of the League of Arab States in Cairo on April 22, 1998, deposited with the Secretary General of the League of Arab States).

Convention for the Suppression of Unlawful Acts Against the Safety of Civil Aviation (signed at Montreal on September 23, 1971, deposited with the governments of the Russian Federation, the United Kingdom, and the United States of America).

Convention for the Suppression of Unlawful Acts Against the Safety of Maritime Navigation (signed in Rome on March 10, 1988, deposited with the Secretary General of the International Maritime Organization).

Convention for the Suppression of Unlawful Seizure of Aircraft (signed at The Hague on December 16, 1970, deposited with the governments of the Russian Federation, the United Kingdom, and the United States of America).

Convention on Offences and Certain Other Acts Committed on Board Aircraft (signed at Tokyo on September 14, 1963, deposited with the Secretary General of the International Civil Aviation Organization).

Convention on the Marking of Plastic Explosives for the Purpose of Detection (signed at Montreal on March 1, 1991, deposited with the Secretary General of the International Civil Aviation Organization).

Convention on the Organization of the Islamic Conference on Combating International Terrorism (adopted at Ouagadougou on July 1, 1999, deposited with the Secretary General of the Organization of the Islamic Conference).

Convention on the Prevention and Punishment of Crimes Against Internationally Protected Persons, Including Diplomatic Agents (adopted by the General Assembly of the United Nations on December 14, 1973).

European Convention on the Suppression of Terrorism (concluded at Strasbourg on January 27, 1977, deposited with the Secretary General of the Council of Europe).

Friedlander, Robert A. *Terrorism: Documents of International and Local Control.* Dobbs Ferry, NJ: Oceana, 1979.

International Convention Against the Taking of Hostages (adopted by the General Assembly of the United Nations on December 17, 1979).

International Convention for the Suppression of Terrorist Bombings (adopted by the General Assembly of the United Nations on December 15, 1997).

International Convention for the Suppression of the Financing of Terrorism (adopted by the General Assembly of the United Nations on December 9, 1999).

International Instruments Related to the Prevention and Suppression of International Terrorism. New York: United Nations Press, 2001.

OAS Convention to Prevent and Punish Acts of Terrorism Taking the Form of Crimes Against Persons and Related Extortion That Are of International Significance (concluded at Washington, DC, on February 2, 1971, deposited with the Secretary General of the Organization of American States).

OAU Convention on the Prevention and Combating of Terrorism (adopted at Algiers on July 14, 1999, deposited with the Secretary General of the Organization of African Unity).

Protocol for the Suppression of Unlawful Acts Against the Safety of Fixed Platforms Located on the Continental Shelf (done at Rome on March 10, 1988, deposited with the Secretary General of the International Maritime Organization).

Protocol on the Suppression of Unlawful Acts of Violence at Airports Serving International Civil Aviation, Supplementary to the Convention for the Suppression of

Unlawful Acts Against the Safety of Civil Aviation (signed at Montreal on February 24, 1988, deposited with the Secretary General of the International Civil Aviation Organization).

SAARC Regional Convention on Suppression of Terrorism (signed at Kathmandu on November 4, 1987, deposited with the Secretary General of the South Asian Association for Regional Cooperation).

Treaty on Cooperation among State Members of the Commonwealth of Independent States in Combating Terrorism (done at Minsk on June 4, 1999, deposited with the Secretariat of the Commonwealth of Independent States).

Tucker, David. "Responding to Terrorism," *21 Debated Issues in World Politics*. Upper Saddle River, NJ: Prentice Hall, 2000.

United Nations Global Counter Terrorism Strategy, updated regularly on its website http://www.un.org/terrorism/instruments.shtml.

NOTES

1. As Werner Levi points out in his text, *Contemporary International Law: A Concise Introduction* (Boulder, CO: Westview Press, 1979), a degree of political cooperation is only implied, not stated, in the UN Charter (pp. 265–268). Considerable differences of opinion as to a legal obligation for political cooperation by member states continue to exist today.
2. See the statute of the International Court of Justice, 6 U.S.T. 3517, T.I.A.S. No. 3043, 74 U.N.T.S. 244 (1944).
3. Stanley Hoffman, in his article, "International Law and the Control of Force" (*International and Comparative Law Quarterly* 32 [June 1995]: 22) suggests, for example, that "peace" as a common goal is a weak tool. He asserts that many states embrace doctrines that have stated goals of protracted confrontation and ultimate conquest—goals incompatible with this "common" goal of peace.
4. See the treaty for the renunciation of war (Paris: August 27, 1928), 46 Stat. 2343, 94 L.N.T.S., 57.
5. Statement credited to Emile Henry, a nineteenth-century French anarchist who bombed a crowded Paris cafe, killing one customer and wounding twenty others. At his trial Henry is reported to have said that his only regret was that more people had not been killed. Henry's reply to the judge's exclamations that "those were innocent victims that you struck" has formed the dogma of "collective guilt" that is often invoked to justify indiscriminate acts of terror.
6. Convention Relative to the Protection of Civilian Persons in Time of War, U.S.T. 3516, T.I.A.S. No. 3365, 75, U.N.T.S. 287 (1949).
7. See Funk and Wagnall's *Standard Comprehensive International Dictionary* (Chicago: Ferguson, 1987), vol. 1, 653.
8. Irving Howe, "The Ultimate Price of Random Terror," *Skeptic: Forum for Contemporary History*, 11, no. 58 (January–February 1976).
9. See the judgment of the International Military Tribunal, Nuremberg, September 30, 1946, vol. 22, *Trial of the Major War Criminals Before the International Military Tribunal Proceedings*, 411, 427, 459, 461, and 463 (1948).
10. Marjorie M. Whiteman, *Digest of International Law* (Washington, DC: Department of State, 1968), vol. 11, chap. 35, Article 2, 3518–3520.
11. Ibid., Article 32, 3528.
12. This law defines as criminal "atrocities and offenses, including but not limited to murder, extermination, enslavement, deportation, imprisonment, torture, rape or

other inhuman acts committed against any civilian population . . . whether or not in violation of the domestic laws of the country where perpetrated."

13. Accessed on June 18, 2009, from http://www.sourcewatch.org/index. php?title=Enemy_combatant.

14. Quoted by Robert Friedlander, *Terrorism: Documents of International and Local Control* (Dobbs Ferry, NJ: Oceana, 1979), 18.

15. *U.S. v. Smith,* 18 U.S. (5 Wheat.) P. 71, 73–75 (1820).

16. The case of the SS *Lotus,* P.C.I.J., Series A, No. 10 (1927), 2 Hudson, World Court Rep., 20.

17. See "Harvard Research in International Law: Piracy," *American Journal of International Law,* 26 (1932), 739, 754, 759–760. See also text of the Geneva Convention on the High Seas, 13 U.S.T., 2312, T.I.A.S. No. 5200, 450 U.N.T.S. 82, and Article 100 of the Third United Nations Conference on the Law of the Sea, A/ Conf. 62/WP. 10/Rev. 1 (April 28, 1979).

18. Friedlander, *Terrorism Documents,* 13. For further insights on this subject, see Nancy Joyner, *Aerial Hijacking as an International Crime* (Dobbs Ferry, NJ: Oceana, 1974).

19. Tokyo Convention on Offences and Certain Other Acts Committed on Board Aircraft, signed September 14, 1963.

20. Convention for the Suppression of Unlawful Acts Against the Safety of Civil Aviation, signed in Montreal on September 23, 1971.

21. Extradition treaty, November 22, 1834, France–Belgium, Articles 5 and 6, *Recueil des Traites* (France) 278, 84 Perry's T.S. 456.

22. See, for example, the extradition treaty between the United States and Venezuela, January 19, 1922, Article 3, 43 Stat. 1698, T.S. 675, 49 L.N.T.S. 435.

23. *European Convention on Extradition,* December 13, 1957, 24 Europe T.S., 173–175.

24. Signed April 18, 1961, 500 U.N.T.S. 95.

25. Convention on the Prevention and Punishment of Crimes Against Internationally Protected Persons, Including Diplomatic Agents. *United Nations Treaty Series,* vol. 1035, no. 15410 (1977).

26. See comments by Christos L. Rozakis in, "Terrorism and the Internationally Protected Person in Light of the ILC's Draft Articles," *International and Comparative Law Quarterly* 23 (January 1974): 72.

27. International Convention Against the Taking of Hostages. Adopted by the General Assembly of the United Nations on November 17, 1979. Entered into force on June 3, 1983. *United Nations Treaty Series,* vol. 1316, no. 21931.

28. Article 1, OAS Convention to Prevent and Punish the Acts of Terrorism Taking the Form of Crimes Against Persons and Related Extortion That Are of International Significance. Concluded in Washington, DC, on February 2, 1971. Entered into force on October 16, 1973. *United Nations Treaty Series,* vol. 1438, no. 24381.

29. This declaration was adopted with 48 states voting in favor, none against, and eight abstentions (including Saudi Arabia, the Union of South Africa, the Union of Soviet Socialist Republics, and Yugoslavia). For a full copy of the text of this declaration, see Louis Henkin, Richard Pugh, Oscar Schachter, and Hans Smit, *International Law: Cases and Materials* (St. Paul, MN: West, 1980), 320.

30. International Covenant on Civil and Political Rights, 21 U.N. GAOR, Supp. (no. 16), 52, U.N. Doc. A/6316 (1966). Entered into force March 23, 1976.

31. George Kren and Leon Rappoport, *The Holocaust and the Crisis of Human Behavior* (New York: Holmes and Meier, 1980), 130.

32. See Nicholas Kittrie, "Response: Looking at the World Realistically," *Case Western Journal of International Law* 13, no. 2 (Spring 1981): 311–313.

33. *International Instruments Related to the Protection and Suppression of International Terrorism* (New York: United Nations Press, 2001), 25.

34. Ibid., 105.

35. http://www.un.org/sc (accessed October 1, 2007).

36. http://www.un.org/sc/ctc (accessed October 1, 2007).

The Use of Force to Combat Terrorism

As soon as men decide that all means are permitted to fight an
evil, then their good becomes indistinguishable from the evil
that they set out to destroy.

—*Christopher Dawson*

Although international laws of war and peace make it clear that terrorist acts are illegal, there is no cohesive framework capable of implementing and enforcing these laws on those individuals, groups, or states found guilty of terrorist acts. In the absence of such a framework, the burden of regulating such action has fallen upon individual nation-states.

Recent history abounds with examples of individual state efforts to combat the problem of transnational terrorism, highlighting both the dangers and the success they have achieved. The success and failure of the efforts and an assessment of the price paid for both provide insights into the strengths and limitations of nations engaged in waging single-handed war on terrorism.

Moreover, if international law truly evolves from international norms, then it may be that the strategy for dealing with terrorism internationally will strongly resemble those strategies found successful among nations individually. Thus, a review of the responses of nations to terrorism today may provide some clues as to the shape of international responses in the future.

NATIONS WITHOUT DEFENSES

It has been said that the **Munich massacre** *of Israeli athletes by Black September terrorists at the Olympic games in 1972* marked the turning point in the Western world's indifference toward terrorism.[1] Until that event, few of the nations that were most frequently the victims of terrorist attacks had made any coherent policy for combating terrorism. Although Central Intelligence Agency (CIA) analysts conclude that "terrorists continue to prefer operations in the industrialized democracies of Western Europe and North America,"[2] the very characteristics that cause nations to be included in this category also make it difficult for them to organize defenses against terrorist attacks.

In liberal democracies, dissent is part of the very fabric of the social and political milieu. This adherence to an almost absolute right to disagree sometimes creates conditions that allow radical dissent to become violent opposition before governments are able to prepare for this transformation. In West Germany, for example, before the publicized exploits of the Baader-Meinhof gang, any hint of the formation of an elite army or police unit to combat terrorism would have provoked a storm of protest inside (and outside) the country.

Similarly, the United States, where both the army and the public bore scars from the traumas of Vietnam and Watergate, was in no condition to prepare for terrorist threats. This was partly due to the demoralizing effect of the Vietnam conflict on the army's special units and partly to the perceived need to curtail (rather than expand) domestic surveillance operations.

Nor were these nations alone in their lack of preparedness. In the wake of its protracted Algerian war, France shared Germany's abhorrence of secret or special armies while the British, with their problems in Northern Ireland, were perhaps too confident in their assumption that their anti-IRA network would deal effectively with any international terrorist. Italy at this time was oblivious to the growing potential for terrorism within its borders, misled by a belief that most contemporary terrorism was confined to participants in the Arab–Israeli conflict. In fact, virtually every Western nation except Israel lacked the equipment and staff to combat the growing terrorist threat; they also lacked a realization of the impending danger.

At Munich, this complacency and inattention was shattered. When a group of Black September terrorists, with logistical support from German and French sympathizers, captured the Israeli athletes' dormitory in the Olympic village in Munich in 1972, West Germany's response was firm, but it failed to prevent disaster. As the world watched, the Germans set up an ambush at Fürstenfeldbruck Airport. Five sharpshooters succeeded in killing five of the terrorists, but not before the terrorists had killed all nine hostages.[3]

STRIKE FORCES: A FIRST MECHANISM FOR RESPONSE?

This spectacular attack and the equally spectacular failure of the government troops to secure the hostages' safety prompted several Western governments to reevaluate the quality of their counterterrorism strike forces. Since 1972, the creation of effective **strike forces**, *military or police units specially trained, equipped, and organized to combat terrorism*, has become a fairly common practice—with varying degrees of success and legality. A review of the strike forces created by a few nations, their methods of operation, and their patterns of success and failure may help us understand the problems of the use of such forces.

Israel's Sayaret Mat'kal

Israel has been engaged in antiterrorism warfare for perhaps longer than any other nation. It has a more extensive history in the use of strike teams; as such, it serves as an interesting case to study to determine the strengths and weaknesses of this tactic for combating terrorism.

In Israel, the Talmudic injunction, "If someone comes to kill you, rise and kill him first," has become the slogan of the **Sayaret Mat'kal**. This *specialized Israeli antiterrorist strike force* is so secretive that the Israelis rarely even mention it by name. This unit was responsible for raids into Beirut to murder Palestinian leaders and for the Entebbe rescue operation in 1976.

Founded nearly a decade after Israel's establishment in 1948, the Sayaret Mat'kal was one of the country's early elite antiterrorist military formations. The application process is severe and only a tiny percentage of applicants are admitted to the training program. The Sayaret Mat'kal specializes in hostage-rescue operations in Israel. However, the unit also engages in foreign activities and is understood to have been involved in the 1976 Entebbe operation. Sayaret Mat'kal frequently cooperates with other Israeli counterterrorist organizations such as Sayeret Tzanhanim, the elite paratroop unit.

This unit has both successfully thwarted terrorist attacks and, in its zeal to "strike before being struck," has also been guilty of the murder of innocent persons. When Prime Minister Golda Meir unleashed "hit teams" the day after the Munich massacre, with orders to roam the world seeking out and summarily executing those responsible for the attack, the results were neither entirely legal nor wholly desirable.

One of these "hit teams" assassinated the wrong man. At Lillehammer, Norway, in 1973, an innocent Moroccan waiter was gunned down by a hit team in front of his pregnant Norwegian wife. The team had mistaken the waiter for the architect of the Munich massacre, Ali Hassan Salameh. International indignation forced Israel to temporarily restrain the hit squads.

This incident was only a brief setback in Israel's use of strike forces in its war on terrorism. In January 1979, one of Israel's hit teams succeeded in killing Salameh with a radio-controlled car bomb in Beirut. This bomb also killed his four bodyguards and five innocent people who happened to be passing by.

One of the ironies of Israel's response to this incident is that, as an excusatory footnote to their (unofficial) admission of regret at the loss of innocent lives, the Israelis suggested that these people were "in the wrong place at the wrong time."[4] This has unfortunate echoes of the "justification" offered by terrorists of harm to innocent people caused by their bombs.

The innocent people killed in counterterrorism attacks, such as Susan Wareham, a British secretary for a construction company in Beirut, committed only the mistake of being too near Salameh's car when it exploded. Callous uncaring or deliberate disregard for the safety of innocent persons—the difference may be in the degree of disregard for the sanctity of human life. The net result for the innocent bystander is unhappily the same.

Not all of Israel's counterattacks on terrorism have been counterproductive. Indeed, the Sayaret Mat'kal is one of the best-trained and equipped special forces units in operation today, with an impressive record of successful missions as well.

The Sayaret Mat'kal is not part of the regular army and reports only to the chief of intelligence. Its members do not wear uniforms. This unit does not rely on trained volunteers but instead draws on raw recruits from the Kelet (the recruit depot). Usually an officer of the Sayaret Mat'kal will go to the Kelet to select about 15 to 20 recruits to form a team.

The Sayaret Mat'kal does much of its training in enemy territory, where the bullets are as real as the enemy. Recruits who survive this basic training become permanent members of a squad. Such squads are trained in the use of a pistol as well as the Uzi, the Israeli-invented machine pistol, and the Kalashnikov, the Russian assault rifle.

The willingness of such teams to commit acts of terrorism in order to counter terrorism may lie in the roots of Israel's history. The joint British–Jewish **Special Night Squads,** of which Moshe Dayan was a member, operated during the 1930s. These squads *were trained by their leader, Orde Wingate, to kill rather than wait to be killed.*

The **Irgun,** *a successor to these squads in the increasing spiral of violence in the region of Palestine,* boasted Menachem Begin as a member. This organization was responsible for the *bombing at the* **King David Hotel** *on July 22, 1946, which took 91 lives—British, Jewish, and Arab.* The terrorists of the Irgun who perpetrated this violence still meet to observe the anniversary of this bombing—at the King David Hotel.

Given this concept that it is better to kill than to wait to be killed, which has pervaded Israel's brief and bloody history, it is easier to understand both the brilliant successes that reflect the intense training and the disasters that have occasionally resulted because of the ruthless determination of these special strike force teams.

The Sayaret Mat'kal conducted a raid inside Lebanon in December 1968 that was described as an attempt to force the Lebanese to prevent Palestinian terrorists from mounting their attacks from Lebanon. The group launched a commando raid against Beirut International Airport. Thirteen Arab aircraft, including nine jetliners, were destroyed. There were no casualties because all of the airplanes were cleared of passengers and crew first.

Although the raid was a tactical success, its long-term effects were less rewarding. French president Charles de Gaulle condemned the raid as a violation of the sovereignty of a nation-state and used it as a reason for cutting off all arms shipments to Israel. This cutoff came at a time when the Israeli Defense Forces were relying heavily on French equipment. Moreover, the other major supplier of Israeli arms, the United States, expressed its displeasure over the raid but stopped short of cutting off arms shipments.

Furthermore, the Palestinians acquired both publicity and a certain amount of public sympathy for their cause, two of the primary goals of terrorists with respect to the media. Finally, the airline company that owned and operated the planes, Middle East Airlines, was able to purchase a whole new fleet of jetliners—with the insurance money from the destroyed planes!

Other assault operations were equally "successful" but had less of a negative impact. It was the Sayaret Mat'kal that in 1972 successfully ended the hijacking of a Sabena Boeing 707 jetliner, Flight 517 from Brussels to Tel Aviv. When four members of the Black September Palestinian group hijacked the plane and forced it to land at Lod airport in Israel, they announced that they intended to blow up the plane, with its 90 passengers and 10 crew members aboard, unless the Israeli government met their demands for the release of over 300 Arab prisoners.

The Sayaret Mat'kal assault force succeeded in storming the plane and freeing the passengers and crew members. Although one passenger and two of the hijackers were killed, this minimal loss of life became the standard for similar feats, such as that carried out by Germany's GSG-9 at Mogadishu.

When the Palestinians struck again, it was at the Olympic Games in Munich, only months after the Lod airport rescue. Israeli athletes were the target, and the Sayaret Mat'kal was excluded from the attempts to free those hostages.

The Sayaret Mat'kal also was responsible for the successful **Entebbe raid** in *June 1976 when Air France Flight 139, en route from Tel Aviv to Paris, was hijacked after a stop at the Athens airport and Israel responded by organizing a brilliant and successful military rescue operation.* The plane landed at Entebbe airport in Uganda, carrying 248 passengers and crew members. All but 106 of the hostages were released by the terrorists before the Israeli raid. Only the Israeli citizens and Jews of other nationalities were kept hostage to increase pressure on Israel to agree to the release of 53 "freedom fighters" imprisoned in Israeli prisons.

The military incursion mounted by Israel succeeded in freeing all of the hostages held at the airport, with the exception of three who either misunderstood or did not hear orders by the commandos to lie down as they opened fire on the terrorists. All seven of the terrorists—two of whom were German and five of whom were Palestinian members of the Popular Front for the Liberation of Palestine—were killed, along with a number of Ugandan soldiers who tried to prevent the Israeli commandos from escaping with the hostages.[5]

International opinion for the most part supported Israel in spite of the fact that Israel militarily had invaded Uganda. Part of this approbation derives from a common love for a "winner." But part is due to the perceived legal right of a nation to intervene for "humanitarian" purposes in another country. Although this right of humanitarian intervention is limited, it seemed to most nations to be acceptable in this case.

Thus, Israel had the first and arguably the most highly trained of the strike forces. Their greatest liability may lie in the fervor with which they pursue their enemies. This zeal has caused them to not only cross national boundaries in their quest for vengeance but also to defy international law.

The British Special Air Services

On May 5, 1980, Britain's 22nd SAS, the Special Air Service Regiment, supported by special police units, carried out **Operation Nimrod,** *an assault on the Iranian Embassy in the heart of downtown London.* As thousands of people on the streets of London watched, black-clad SAS members swung down from ropes and burst into the building through windows. Wearing gas masks, the assault force moved from room to room throwing stun grenades mixed with CS (tear) gas. As they moved through the building, they identified the terrorists, shot them with Heckler & Koch MP5s or Browning automatic pistols, and bundled the hostages out of the building.

Operation Nimrod was not the only successful counterterrorist attack carried out by Britain's SAS, but it was unique in at least one sense. Most citizens do not have the opportunity to see their special strike forces in operation on their home soil. Most operations of such forces take place on foreign soil, far from home and the attention of citizens.

Even in Operation Nimrod, however, Britain worked hard to preserve the speed and secrecy that have become the hallmark of SAS operations. The assault team wore hoods, which served both to hide their identities and to frighten the terrorists. When the incident was over, the unit handed authority back to the police and quietly made its way to the St. John's Wood barracks before returning to its permanent station at Bradbury Lines in Hereford.

Secrecy and surprise have been *the watchwords of this regiment* ever since it was formed over sixty years ago. Lieutenant David Stirling of the Scots Guard is credited with creating this special unit. Under his plan, the SAS was designed to operate in units of five (later reduced to four) men, which continues to be the standard SAS team unit.

The units have tended to be made up of a high percentage of Scottish Roman Catholics. All of its members are volunteers, mostly from the Parachute Regiment. It is not a "young" regiment; the average age is about 27.

Each recruit is required to give up his rank and pay (most have already reached the rank of corporal or sergeant) and go back to the rank of trooper. Training in the Welsh countryside is rigorous.

The SAS is perhaps the best-known special operations group in existence today, and the Special Projects (SP) team of the SAS is an equally well-known counterterrorist organization. The SP team, normally comprising 80 personnel, is divided into four troops of 16 men each, plus officers. However, the SP squadron is not a permanent entity since all SAS squadrons are rotated through duty in the Counterrevolutionary Warfare (CRW) section. The CRW duty training cycles usually last about six months. Thus, all SAS operatives are considered counterterrorist-qualified, and refresher training is constant. In this, the SAS is unique among special operations groups.

The SP unit is normally broken down into 65-man Red and Blue Teams, each of which has snipers and explosive ordinance disposal-trained experts. Team members' proficiency in firearms, already very good, is refined for close-quarters battle in the "Killing House." The basic course lasts for six weeks, during which troopers may fire more than 2,000 rounds of ammunition. Their firearms proficiency is further developed during a squadron's SP duty.

These training exercises are intense and have added elements of realism, using live personnel as hostages during room-clearing operations. SAS counterterrorist and hostage-rescue training is helped by cooperation of the highest members of the U.K. governments, many of whom (including the prime minister) take part in actual training exercises. Contributing to the skill of the SAS is the Operations Research Unit, which develops equipment for use by the SP team, such as the stun "flash-bang" grenade, specialized ladders for train and airplane assaults, night vision goggles, and audio-video equipment.

Recruits are trained in combat survival, survival in Arctic conditions, and swimming fully clothed. They receive special parachute training, including night jumps from extraordinary heights. Emphasis is placed on weapons training, using the Heckler & Koch MP5 submachine gun, the Browning .45 automatic pistol, the pump action shotgun, and the Sterling submachine gun fitted with a silencer. In addition, they are given training in foreign weapons so that they can both use captured weapons and be familiar with weapons that their enemies may use on them.

Out of every 100 men who apply, only about 19 will meet the physical and mental requirements. The initial tests include a series of treks across the Welsh hills carrying weighted packs. *The final trek covers 37 miles while carrying a 55-pound pack over some of the toughest country in the Brecon Beacons. It must be covered in twenty hours, and it is literally a* **killer course**. Men have died trying to complete it.

Once they pass these initial courses, the men continue to receive specialized training in explosives, battlefield medicine, and the operation of communication equipment. They train in the use of various personal weapons, knives, and crossbows for "silent" killing. They learn about desert and jungle warfare and wilderness survival.

Recruits continue to specialize in such fields as medicine, languages, skiing, mountaineering, or underwater warfare. Individual skill development is encouraged at all times.

The SAS finds itself operating more often than most other national strike forces, with the possible exception of the Sayaret Mat'kal. This is due to the decades of violence in Northern Ireland. Although the SAS rarely figures in press reports on antiterrorist activities in that region, many operations were carried out by this unit. The SAS has also seen overseas service in Aden, Yemen; Oman; and Borneo. Indeed, much of its training for the guerrilla warfare that it faced in Northern Ireland finds its origins in the SAS experience in Aden in the mid-1960s.

In Northern Ireland, the SAS served as a backup for the regular army units and the Royal Ulster Constabulary. It was a largely thankless and often a very dangerous job. As members have somewhat cynically noted, if the "Sassmen" (as the Irish have called them) were killed or injured in an ambush, little public mention was made of the incident. But if the SAS was responsible, even indirectly, for the injury or death of any civilians, then public indignation was quite vocal.

Britain, unlike Israel, has been willing to criticize its own strike forces when their actions have resulted in needless injury or loss of life. One judge, in whose court two Sassmen were on trial for responsibility in the death of a civilian in a stakeout of an arms cache, stated that although terrorists might consider themselves outside the rule of law, the army could not.

The Special Boat Service (SBS) is also a special operations group deployed by the United Kingdom that has trained to some extent with the SAS, particularly training relating to the possibility that there could be an event that might require both of their personnel and skills, such as the simultaneous hijacking of two or more oil rigs in the North Sea. While each SAS squadron maintains its own Boat Troop, there exists a high degree of respect and cooperation between the SAS and the SBS. A bomb scare on the ocean liner *Queen Elizabeth II* offered one opportunity for the two groups to deploy together successfully.

Forty years of experience as a special force regiment has made the SAS one of the best counterterrorist strike forces in the world, the most sought-after exchange partner in the world of counterterrorism. Its men have trained troopers from many different organizations and states, including, but not limited to, the United States' Delta Force, the Federal Bureau of Investigation's (FBI) Hostage Rescue Team, France's Groupe d'Intervention de la Gendarmerie Nationale (GIGN), Germany's GSG-9, Spain's Grupo Especial de Operaciones (GEO), the Royal Dutch Marines, and the SAS groups from Australia and New Zealand. These organizations have let British SAS members train with their own units in a reciprocal swap of information. The result of these exchanges is that worldwide there has been a significant increase in counterterrorist skills.

The SAS has continued to improve its skills, looking always for "a better way of doing things." In fact, at least one or two SAS personnel have been present at every major counterterrorist operation involving a friendly country in the recent past. Six SAS team members—two officers and four senior noncommissioned officers—were sent to Lima, Peru, in December 1996 to provide assistance and advice to the Peruvian government prior to the April 1997 assault that resulted in the rescue of 71 of the 72 remaining hostages. Information culled from such experiences is brought back to Hereford, where it is both shared to other team members and applied in training exercises.

Until the 1990s, there was one exception to this cooperative exchange of personnel and information, rooted in a fundamental distrust that the British had of the Israelis, another of the world's best at counterterrorist operations.

Both units remember a time when the British, under the Palestine Mandate, formed Q Squads to hunt down Jewish terrorists, particularly those of the infamous Stern Gang. In one particularly nasty incident, Roy Farran, responsible for the formation of the Q Squads, was acquitted in a court martial of the murder of a suspected member of the Stern Gang. Israeli terrorists, not satisfied with the verdict, sent a book bomb to Farran's home in England. Roy's brother, Rex, opened the package and was killed. The memory of such tragedies and the vindictiveness that caused them has made the relations between these two special forces units strained, although relations improved in the late 1990s and the two units now enjoy a low-key but positive relationship.

Sassmen are still called upon by their government to protect the leaders of various Arab states. Because many of these states and their leaders were regarded by some in Israel as natural enemies, the SAS and the Sayaret Mat'kal often find themselves on opposite sides of these security situations, making their working relationship tenuous.

Germany's GSG-9

Grenzschutzgruppe 9 (called **GSG-9**) makes no claim to being a "killer troop" or "hit squad." This group, *formed when the Bavarian State police were unable to deal adequately with the Munich situation in September 1972,* has made a point of being less dependent upon weapons than upon the talents, discipline, and training of its men. The inadequate response of the German police to actions of the Black September group generated a determination on the part of the German government to create a response team capable of handling terrorist activity. Until this incident, German authorities had been reluctant to create an elite military unit of any sort, due in part to a desire to reassure its neighbors that it was no longer a threat to their security. Thus, Germany had until 1972 a very low-profile security system.

Given this low-profile security system, it was possible for members of Black September to penetrate the Olympic compound, kill two Israeli athletes, and take nine others hostage. The situation became a debacle when the on-site commander of the German police ordered his men to open fire on the terrorists as they were getting ready to board two helicopters in their escape at Fürstenfeldbruck military airfield. This led to an open gun battle, which, when the smoke had cleared, found all nine remaining hostages dead as well as all of the terrorists.

After this disaster, German authorities determined never to be caught unprepared again by terrorist actions, created a counterterrorist unit, GSG-9, designed to be manned and controlled by the Federal Border Police Force (Bundesgrenzschutz), instead of the military. Operational only six months after the Munich massacre, GSG-9 was unique among counterterrorist forces in many respects.

The Federal Border Guard became the parent unit for this special unit, which works out well since it is the only force in Germany directly under the control of the central government. GSG-9 became the ninth unit of the Border Guard, making its headquarters at St. Augustin, just outside of Bonn. It was formed along the same lines as the SAS, operating with five-man sticks, or units.

Within GSG-9 are a headquarters unit, a communications and documentation unit, and three fighting units. Its three technical units deal with weapons, research, equipment, backup supply, and maintenance services. Each of its three strike forces has thirty men, comprising a Command Section and five Special Tactical Sections (composed of four men and an officer)—the five-man stick.[6]

This group differs from the Sayaret Mat'kal and the SAS in that it is a civilian police force. Although much of the training given to its members is similar to that of the SAS, it is unique in the training its members receive in the law, particularly the law applying to counterterrorism operations. Members of this special force are more conscious of the law and of their need to stay as far as possible within its bounds than are other similar strike forces.

Selection for those interested in becoming GSG-9 members is demanding. All recruits must be volunteers and all must come from the Bundesgrenzschutz. Members of the German army who seek to become a part of GSG-9 are required to first leave the military service and join the border police to become eligible. This is similar to the requirement that those seeking to join the SAS must give up their military rank and start over as a private.

The first thirteen weeks of the twenty-two-week training course are devoted to learning the fundamentals of counterterrorism and police operations, including a serious amount of academic study.

The last part of the course is devoted to specialization of operator skills and advanced antiterrorist studies. In fact, Germany's elite force has one of the most sophisticated arsenals in the world. Because the deplorable shooting at Fürstenfeldbruck Airport demonstrated the need for marksmanship training, every man of GSG-9 is taught to be an expert marksman, using weapons such as a sniper's rifle equipped with infrared sights and light intensifiers for night shooting.

An attrition rate of 80 percent is not uncommon for the volunteers seeking to join GSG-9. However, some graduates do excel, and some are sent to attend NATO's International Long Range Reconnaissance Patrol School located in Weingarten, Germany.

Because they are required to reach any part of Germany ready for action within two hours, units are supplied with Mercedes-Benz autos of special design and BO 105–type helicopters. The personnel are trained to descend from hovering helicopters via special ropes. The troopers enjoy the full support of the government when it comes to their equipment and are issued two complete sets of combat gear: one tailored to daytime operations and one for use at night. GSG-9 had, at one time, its own aviation unit, known as Bundesgrenzschutz Grenzschutz-Fliegergruppe.[7]

But these units are trained in more than just combat. They spend a great deal of time studying the origins and tactics of known terrorists to determine how best to defeat them. GSG-9 practices assaults on hijacked airliners, training on mock-ups of aircraft and sometimes on aircraft on loan from Germany's Lufthansa airline. Such training placed them in good stead in **Mogadishu** in 1977. In October of that year, *in support of the Baader-Meinhof gang, Zohair Akache's terrorist team hijacked a Lufthansa Boeing 737 with 82 passengers.* After touring the Middle East in search of an airport willing to let them land, they finally landed at Mogadishu in Somalia.

Unlike the situation in Uganda faced by the Israelis, the Germans found Somalia more than willing to cooperate with them in their efforts to end the hostage situation. Twenty-eight handpicked men stormed the airliner, rescuing all hostages without harm. It was, if not a perfect raid of its kind (the original assault ladders were too short), a very good example of careful planning and execution. No laws were broken, no unnecessary injuries to innocent persons occurred, and both hostages and plane were recovered.

GSG-9 no longer carries out activities involving terrorist situations outside of German borders. Reclaiming, in some respects, the original role from which its name derived—Border Protection Group 9—GSG-9 operates wholly internally today, carrying out roles similar to those of the U.S. FBI's Hostage Rescue Team and responding to terrorism only when it occurs within Germany's borders. Their Target Search Teams and their spectacular rescues such as that which occurred at Mogadishu offer excellent examples of counterterrorism successfully carried out within the borders of the law.

TOO MANY U.S. OPTIONS?

American counterterrorist forces are based in the United States, far from the Middle East where the current war on terrorism is focused. The Joint Special Operations Agency, headed by a two-star general, is charged with preparing guidelines and plans for counterterrorist forces during their formation, training, and operations. But this agency has no command authority over the forces.

The **U.S. Special Operations Command** *was established by the Department of Defense, under congressional orders, on June 1, 1987, as a single command for all of the special operations units.* This command is located at MacDill Air Force Base, Florida, and commands the following units: the Special Operations Command (SOCOM) unit based at Fort Bragg, North Carolina; the Naval Warfare Special Operations Command; and the Joint Special Operations Command. The Air Force Special Operations Command is located at Hurlbert Field, Florida. At present, the U.S. Army maintains the highest number of special operations units, with three distinct parts. The U.S. Air Force and the U.S. Navy each have one unit, and the U.S. Marines also have one unit, arguably the world's largest special operations unit dedicated to amphibious beachfront assaults.

A brief look at some of these units will help make understanding the whole collection a little easier. It may also make clear the problems faced in successful use of such forces.

Special Forces, U.S. Army

The Joint Special Operations Command (JSOC) and the U.S. Army Special Operations Command (USASOC) are headquartered at Fort Bragg, North Carolina, under SOCOM. JSOC is a multiservice and interdepartmental command, with antiterrorism its primary job. It includes a command staff that oversees the training and operations of the Army's Delta Force, the Navy SEALs' Team Six, and in times of national emergency, the FBI's Hostage Rescue Team.

USASOC has more that 25,000 personnel and includes the **U.S. Army Special Forces Command** (SFC), the 75th Ranger Regiment, the 180th Special Operations Aviation Regiment (SOAR), the JFK Special Warfare Center and

School, the U.S. Army Civil Affairs and Psychological Operations Command, the U.S. Army Special Operations Support Command, and various chemical reconnaissance units. Each of these "communities" has special roles and missions. For example, SOAR, often referred to as the "Nightstalkers," is the most secret and technologically advanced unit in USASOC, while the SFC is home of the more widely known Green Berets and is regarded as the "brains" portion of the USASOC; the Rangers are referred to as the "muscle" of the SOCOM.

The SFC comprises *"trained professionals," who with high levels of technical, cultural, and combat skills, train to work together to solve problems.* It has the highest operations tempo of any community within SOCOM, because an SFC soldier on average spends more than half of every year in the field. In this sense, they are more like a Peace Corps team with guns than a counterterror unit. Yet they continue to be used in areas where terrorism is a serious threat, as in Iraq and Afghanistan during the early part of the war on terrorism.

Although a special forces unit has three types of teams (A, B, and C), the latter two teams are generally not deployable since they consist of staff and support personnel. Usually, an A-Team consists of 12 men, including a captain, a warrant officer, and 10 men who all are at least sergeants. All candidates for such a team must pass a rigorous training course, much like that of the SAS. This training includes a "selection" session, with intense physical and mental training, and a Qualification Class (or Q-School). The twenty-five-week process creates candidates who are experts in a variety of tasks, including but not limited to land navigation, basic weapons and demolition, water navigation, intelligence, and reconnaissance. Upon completing Q-School successfully, the candidate must then continue training in his chosen area of specialty, which can take from six to fifty-six weeks to complete.

First Special Forces Operational Detachment—Delta (Delta Force), U.S. Army

Delta Force *was commissioned under the command of Colonel Charles Beckwith on November 19, 1977, to be primarily a hostage-rescue and counterterrorism force.* Most of its people are drawn from the Ranger units or the special forces units by a desire to serve in this very secret unit. Delta Force is built on the premise of a critical need for secrecy, and its training is in many ways similar to that of the SAS.

Very little public information is available about this unit. It is designed to rapidly resolve hostage or hijacking incidents involving U.S. citizens abroad or on planes traveling beyond U.S. territory. Consequently, its members have a wide range of skills, from rappelling to parachuting (into hostile territory) to rapid repair of a wide range of vehicles. Most of the training is updated regularly to be certain the men are able to respond to current world situations.

Ranger, U.S. Army

Drawn usually from the Airborne Infantry units, candidates for **Ranger** units comprise *a highly mobile infantry unit able to deploy quickly anywhere in the*

*world and to lead through any terrain ground forces that will be deployed
to follow.* All accepted into Ranger training must be extremely physically fit
initially, since training involves intense physical challenges. The first stage involves successful completion of the Ranger Indoctrination Program (RIP), a
three-week course of physical and mental training, including building strengths
in swimming, land navigation, and endurance as well as classroom instruction.

The next nine weeks, if one successfully completes the RIP, has four
phases, each of which presents a different type of challenge. The first phase
is another week of RIP, designed to weed out those not completely motivated
or physically able to continue. The second-phase training takes place in the
swamps and forests near Eglin Air Force base in Florida, where the candidates
stay "continuously wet, continuously moving, continuously hungry."[8]

During the third phase of Ranger training, candidates operate in a
mountainous terrain near Dahlonega, Georgia, again with little sleep or food,
learning to rappel down cliffs and to navigate through difficult valleys. Finally,
the training groups are sent to the desert near Dugway, Utah, to learn how to
navigate without many discernable landmarks and to conduct patrols and ambushes without cover or concealment. The objective for such a multifaceted
form of training is to create a mobile rapid-deployment force, able to handle
virtually any terrain in the world when necessary.

Air Force Special Operations Command

The Air Force Special Operations Command is based at Eglin Air Force Base
in Florida. Although the **Air Force Special Operations Command** (AFSOC)
units cover four different types of mission areas, only one, the Special Operations Forces Mobility, is usually associated with counterterrorism. *This unit
consists of numerous fixed- and rotary-winged aircraft, with the pilots and
support crews used to insert and recover soldiers of other special operations
units of every service branch.* The AFSOC currently has units located strategically throughout the world, ready to deploy with little advance warning to
facilitate counterterrorism efforts by the other branches.

Naval Special Warfare Command

Although it has units stationed around the world, the Naval Special Warfare
Command has its home base in Coronado, California. A part of the Naval
Special Warfare Group, (DevGru) the **SEALs** (Sea, Air and Land), *is made
up of highly trained and intensely motivated seamen who have successfully
completed twenty-five weeks of difficult training.* If the volunteer candidates
make it through the first five weeks of Basic Underwater Demolition training
(the "toughening up" phase), they must then spend a week pushed to the
limits of their physical endurance (called "hell week" by the men). Those who
successfully complete this will then spend the next nineteen weeks learning
to navigate great distances underwater, and become proficient at underwater
demolition, reconnaissance and navigation, and a variety of other skills

essential for combat diving, including how to enter and exit a wide range of vehicles to carry out operations at sea.

These seamen receive jungle, desert, and Arctic training, as well as training at Fort Benning and the U.S. Army Parachute School. The final five weeks of their training is in simulations in which they are required to use their new skills to resolve real-world situations they might encounter.

Clearly, the United States has a wide range of military units that could be utilized in counterterrorism efforts. The problems with U.S. counterterrorism forces are equally obvious, particularly those brought on by the lack of cohesive command illustrated by *the abortive attempt to send a strike team into Iran to free Americans held hostage in the U.S. Embassy in Tehran.* **Operation Eagle's Claw,** as this mission was called, was characterized by a confusion of command, insufficient training, and critical equipment failure.

Cloaked in so much secrecy that even some of the military officers involved were not told the aim of the mission for which they were preparing, this operation became a model for what can go wrong in a strike force maneuver. In addition to too much secrecy, there were too many "chiefs" and not enough cooperation between military units. An army officer, Major General James Vaught, was in command overall; Colonel James Kyle of the Air Force had responsibility for fixed-wing aircraft, while Colonel Charles Pitman of the Marines also had command responsibility and Colonel Beckwith controlled the Delta Force unit.

The Delta Force squad lacked sufficient training and experience for such an operation. It had been created by Colonel Beckwith only two years earlier in 1977, and its training program was incomplete. Delta Force was underfunded and ill-equipped to handle the hostage raid, having trained primarily in guerrilla warfare and low-intensity conflict.

Today, the United States has taken steps to create a command unit in which to vest coordination for this specialized training and command. In the wake of Operation Eagle's Claw disaster, a call was made for a new special counterterrorism unit, with personnel drawn from all of the armed services, but there has been little success in creating such a unit. Interservice rivalries make its creation very unlikely in the near future.

According to government reports, the Delta Force unit has been deployed several times, other than the highly publicized Operation Eagle's Claw fiasco and the *Achille Lauro* incident. It was sent to Venezuela to advise the armed forces there on ways to retake a hijacked aircraft. It was sent on a similar mission to Oman to prepare to retake a hijacked plane in nearby Kuwait. But in each of these cases its activities stopped short of assault; it simply made or advised in preparations for the assault.

To always be preparing for but never performing counterterrorist activities is infinitely frustrating, as the men in GSG-9 and SAS could attest. But the United States was reluctant to field a strike force against terrorists until a war on terrorism was declared in 2001. The role that Delta Force plays in this war will remain secret for the foreseeable future, and hence its effectiveness today is impossible to gauge.

Delta Force remains one of the best that the United States has to offer in terms of a strike force. Since the Iranian fiasco, it has proved itself capable of successful missions. The "skyjacking" of the *Achille Lauro* hijackers was an outstandingly successful operation, the legality of which has been overshadowed by its brilliant execution, giving a much-needed boost to Delta Force's morale.

Because the United States did not have many indigenous groups engaging in domestic terrorism until the 1990s, unlike Germany and Britain, which were challenged by events in the 1970s to create units to deal with terrorism domestically, it was able to focus its attention on training its special forces to operate overseas. Emphasis was placed less on secrecy of identity than on rapid-response capabilities and combat training. If coordination of command problems can be surmounted, these forces may develop into units as efficient and respected as the SAS and GSG-9.

New Units—and New Technologies

In the wake of the Operation Eagle's Claw debacle, the Pentagon began to establish the closest thing this nation has ever had to a secret army. Small, specially trained units were developed that were designed to operate much more covertly than some of the older military units. In addition to being given rather exotic code names, such as Yellow Fruit and Seaspray, these units were armed with newer, more sophisticated equipment. These included such items as the small, high-tech helicopters with which Task Force 160, operating out of Fort Campbell, train.

More important than technological "toys," however, was the creation of the Intelligence Support Activity (ISA), a far-ranging intelligence organization that gave the Army, for the first time, the ability to engage in full-fledged espionage, fielding its own agents. Through this organization the strike forces were able to gather the information they needed to plan their counterterrorist activities. They were no longer dependent upon the CIA or other intelligence services for vital data that were too often not available or kept classified at a critical juncture in the planning process. Indeed, their intelligence and reconnaissance efforts in the early stages of the war on terrorism in 2001 facilitated U.S. military response options at this critical juncture.

Even with these innovations, however, these units have had difficulty in rising above the bureaucratic infighting and bungling that has plagued U.S. strike forces. Although the units still exist, their morale and even their preparedness are often in disarray. Seaspray, Yellow Fruit, and the ISA became involved in clandestine operations in Central America, which seriously impaired their credibility with Congress. The use (or misuse) of counterterrorism forces in this area jeopardized America's efforts to develop a credible and respected strike force respected by and capable of working with units such as the SAS and GSG-9. The struggle in Afghanistan has offered U.S. special forces units and the SAS opportunities for joint operations that, when they are more clearly evaluated after the war, may improve the international perspective of these forces.

A quick look at two different efforts by governments to use special forces to resolve situations involving terrorism may help to illustrate both the strengths and the weaknesses discussed thus far in using such special forces.

CASE STUDY 11.1

Operation Chavin de Huantar

On December 17, 1996, rebels from the Tupac Amaru seized the Japanese Embassy residence in Lima, Peru, during a festive cocktail reception. Demanding the release of 400 of their comrades who were in Peru's prison at the time, the 14 Tupac Amaru guerrillas gradually released hundreds of the hostages, retaining only 72 for the entire siege. Alberto Fujimori, Peru's president, saw little chance for resolving the situation peacefully, because he was determined not to release the prisoners. But he gave the negotiators an opportunity to try. He appointed Archbishop Luis Cipriani to be the special negotiator.

The 72 hostages held for the entire 126-day siege included senior Peruvian officials, Fujimori's brother Pedro, foreign diplomats, and the Japanese ambassador. Britain, Germany, Israel, and the United States all offered to help in the rescue attempt but were all officially turned down. Fujimori, however, was under intense pressure to resolve the situation as quickly and peacefully as possible.

But Fujimori resisted all calls for a quick solution, choosing instead to allow time for his military and intelligence units to create and implement **Operation Chavin de Huantar** (named in honor of a pre-Incan archaeological site that was honeycombed with underground passages), the rescue mission, using 140 Peruvian special forces troops and professional miners. During the weeks of the standoff, while negotiations continued, the professional miners were brought into the area near the residence to build large, ventilated, and lighted tunnels through which the troops could reach the inside of the compound.

During the months of the incident, listening devices were smuggled into the residence. With this intelligence access, those planning the operation were able to monitor the movements of the guerrillas and hostages each day, noting patterns of behavior. This information made a carefully timed assault possible.

Because the building plans were readily available to government forces, the special forces team had time to train on mock-ups of the building. Construction of the tunnels, if detected by the hostage-takers, could have triggered a violent battle and possibly a massacre of the hostages. To prevent this, Peru's leaders played blaring martial music day and night outside the embassy compound to mask the noise. This diversion also served to deny rest to the hostage-takers, demoralizing or at least weakening their resistance and stamina. The tunnels were built to offer as many as six different accesses to the compound, which would increase the rebels' confusion when the assault began.

(continued)

On the day of the assault, the hostages, who were being held upstairs as usual, were alerted by a hidden receiver held by a military officer who was among them. They moved a desk to block the second-floor entrance and took cover. Three minutes later, 9 pounds of explosives were detonated in the tunnel directly under the reception room, where a soccer game was in progress. This explosion killed four of the eight guards and opened a hole through which troops began to pour.

The patience exercised by the Peruvian government in talking with the terrorists through extensive negotiations, using the time to gather intelligence, to build tunnels, and to practice the assault, was amply rewarded when the hostages were successfully rescued with the loss of only one hostage's life. The rescue efforts broke no laws, it wasted only one innocent life (a civilian who was shot by a guard as the attack began), and the rescue team was given plenty of time to plan a successful final act. Patience and careful planning, based on timely intelligence information, were keys to the success of Operation Chavin de Huantar.[9] ■

Source: Cindy Combs and Martin Slann, eds. "Operation Chavin de Huantar," in The Encyclopedia of Terrorism (New York: Facts on File, 2002), 135–137.

CASE STUDY 11.2

Navy SEAL Team Six

After obtaining, in August 2010, the probable location of Osama bin Laden, based on the identification of a courier suspected of meeting regularly with him to take and deliver messages, the U.S. president approved an assault in April 2011 by a unit of the DevGru, SEAL Team Six a highly secret special operations unit, on the compound near Abbottabad, Pakistan. While the search for bin Laden had been openly in progress among many countries for almost a decade, with millions of dollars and man-hours invested in finding the individual held responsible for the planning and execution of the attacks on September 11, 2001, the actions of this special forces team on May 2, 2011, would bring the hunt to a close.

Based on intelligence gathered about the 3,000-square-foot compound between August 2010 and May 2011, the actual attack was carried out by two well-trained Navy SEAL teams, with two equally well-trained teams along as backup in case of problems. One team would come from the roof, the other from the ground. Approaching the compound near midnight in four Chinook and Blackhawk helicopters, one of the Stealth Blackhawks had mechanical problems and had to land hard in the compound's courtyard, spoiling the element of surprise. Instead, the assault team, consisting of twenty-three trained SEALS, one interpreter, and a search dog named Cairo, began moving through the building, room by room, from the ground floor up. They had practiced this type of assault intensely using two training models of the compound, so this "Plan B" did not impede the mission's success. The teams had been briefed about the layout of the compound and the path each should take to clear the building, and both teams now began to move up through the building toward what was believed to be bin Laden's bedroom on the top floor.

Moving from room to room, the team engaged in firefights. One compound inhabitant grabbed his assault rifle upon seeing the team, and pulled his female companion in front of him. Both were killed in subsequent shooting. Another compound member, one of bin Laden's couriers, took the same evasive action, pulling the woman with whom he was talking in front of him as a shield. The team carefully removed the 9 women and 18 children they found out of the live-fire area, being concerned that they might have suicide vests but also that they might be accidently killed in the crossfire. After less than half an hour, with most of the rooms cleared, it was determined that a third man killed was bin Laden's son.

As the team moved carefully up through the compound, clearing each room, one team neared the room designated by their intelligence information as the one most likely to be bin Laden's. As they reached the hall, they saw him racing into his bedroom. Commandos burst through the door and opened fire, spotting a man crouched behind a steel table, firing his weapon at the team approaching. Careful aim by one of the assault team sent a bullet through the man's head as he leaned around the table to shoot again. The shot sent the man sprawling on his back, and after careful examination it was determined that this dead man was indeed bin Laden. The communications officer made the call, only forty minutes after the assault on the compound began, that bin Laden was dead.

The SEALs lifted bin Laden's body and carried it to one of the remaining three helicopters, along with the women and children removed from the compound. Before these three choppers lifted off, the pilot of the disabled chopper ran back to set the detonation charges, giving the helicopters two minutes to fly away before the disabled chopper exploded. The helicopters, with the SEALs, returned to the USS aircraft carrier *Carl Vinson* with bin Laden's body, which was subsequently wrapped, placed in a weighted bag, and buried at sea.

The members of the SEAL team involved in this operation were killed in the crash of a helicopter in Afghanistan in August 2011. According to news reports, the team members were among the 38 people who were killed when the plane was shot down by Taliban fighters. ■

Source: Retrieved from http://www.telegraph.co.uk/news/worldnews/asia/pakistan/8488542/Osama-bin-Laden-dead-the-US-Navys-SEAL-Team-Six-behind-the-killing.html

CONCLUSIONS

The use of special forces to combat terrorism has both assets and liabilities. Too little commitment can result in an insufficiently trained and equipped force, as happened to the U.S. forces in the Operation Eagle's Claw disaster. Too zealous a desire to use such forces can result in the loss of innocent lives, as Israel has discovered.

Determination unsupported by sufficient training or equipment is also a recipe for disaster, as became evident in November 1985. An Egyptian airliner en route to Cairo from Athens was hijacked and diverted to Malta. Egyptian troops stormed the plane the next day, after the hijackers began to kill some of the hostages on board. As the troops rushed onto the plane, the hijackers tossed grenades at passengers. The death toll reached 60 people, 57 of whom died in the rescue attempt.

It is not enough just to have such a force. Nations must train and equip them with adequate information and weaponry to meet an increasingly sophisticated terrorist threat. Nations need also to instill in its strike forces, as Germany has sought to do, a respect for the law and its restraints on strike force activities. Thus equipped and trained, such forces can operate to significantly reduce not necessarily the number but the success of terrorist attacks worldwide. The use of U.S. Special Forces teams in Djibouti and Ethiopia to help communities build wells and schools has received less global attention but is perhaps one of the most effective uses of such forces today in the war on terror, as such actions win hearts and minds. Much of the world is not yet engaged either in terrorism or in the struggle against it; the use of special forces teams to win the allegiance of those who are potential allies may be as effective, in the long run, as building a team of expert marksmen. It takes a special kind of courage to engage in this type of "warfare," and will require training and commitment as serious as that of any "killer course."

DISCUSSION

There are many conflicting views on whether strike forces are legitimate and useful tools in combating terrorism. Some view such strike teams as potential threats to democracy, creating elite troops that could be used to quell demonstrations as well as to stop terrorist attacks. Others view them as essential to a nation's security, operating in ways not open to a large military unit to safeguard a nation's citizens, both at home and abroad.

The following are two quotations that reflect in part this divergence of view. Each viewpoint expressed is a bit extreme, tending toward opposite ends of the spectrum of opinion. Read each and decide which more accurately reflects the appropriate assessment of the need and use for such forces in today's world.

1. "The Israelis argue the case for pre-emptive strikes: it is better to kill their enemies in their own bases and so prevent them from mounting their operations, rather than conduct elegant sieges inside Israel. While appreciating the excellence of other forces' pieces of electronic wizardry and the skill of the talk-out experts, their aim is to prevent the need for such expertise arising. Such a policy has its attractions, especially for a beleaguered, small nation like Israel under continual attack from enemies based round its borders. When national survival is at stake all manner of actions become permissible that would not be countenanced in more secure societies."[10]

2. "The danger inherent in the war against terrorism is, of course, the prospect of desperate societies willing to substitute state terror for (non-state) terrorism, to trade individual rights and freedoms for relief from chaos and violence,

reconstituting what were once relatively benign governments into coldly efficient, centralized tyrannies, whose populations are held in close check by armies of secret police and informers, widespread electronic eavesdropping, and a constant deluge of propaganda."[11]

ANALYSIS CHALLENGE

As the war on terrorism continues to struggle with challenges to the stability of nations such as Afghanistan, Iraq, and Pakistan, the military in such countries have become willing to allow—or encourage—paramilitary groups to carry out "special" military actions against insurgents who may be involved in terrorist acts. Former U.S. Ambassador to Sri Lanka, Robert Blake, sent a memo in May 2007 to the U.S. State Department identifying paramilitary groups working with the Sri Lankan military as being involved in "extra-judicial killings," reporting that the Sri Lankan president's brother had ordered military commanders to "not interfere with the paramilitaries on the grounds that they are doing 'work' that the military cannot do because of international scrutiny."[12]

Some of these paramilitary are similar to "special forces units," like the SAS or the Navy SEALs, trained and equipped to deal within the law in counterterror efforts. Others are government-sanctioned groups, which engage in counterterror that too often approximates the terror they are seeking to counter. Explore some of the assessments of this "player" in counterterror efforts, and decide whether their role is uniformly good, bad, or a potential mix of both. Websites such as http://www. southasiaanalysis.org/%5Cpapers9%5Cpaper859.html and http://www.guardian. co.uk/world/2009/may/21/sri-lanka-tamil-tigers-ltte-tamil-refugees-in-camp make good starting points for this analysis of contrasting views.

KEY TERMS

Munich massacre   250
strike forces   251
Sayaret Mat'kal   252
Special Night
   Squads   253
Irgun   253
King David Hotel   253
Entebbe raid   254
Operation Nimrod   255

Secrecy and Surprise   255
killer course   256
GSG-9   258
Mogadishu   259
U.S. Special Operations
   Command   260
U.S. Army Special Forces
   Command   260
Delta Force   261

Ranger   261
Air Force Special
   Operations
   Command   262
SEALs   262
Operation Eagle's
   Claw   263
Operation Chavin de
   Huantar   265

SUGGESTED READINGS AND RESOURCES

Clancy, Tom. *Special Forces: A Guided Tour of U.S. Army Special Forces.* New York: Berkeley Books, 2001.

Clarke, Thurston. *By Blood and Fire: The Attack on the King David Hotel.* New York: G. P. Putnam & Sons, 1981.

"Country Reports on Terrorism." U.S. Department of State Publications, http://www. state.gov/s/ct/rls/crt/

Dobson, Christopher, and Ronald Payne. *Counterattack: The West's Battle Against the Terrorists.* New York: Facts on File, 1982.

Rivers, Gayle. *The Specialists: Revelations of a Counterterrorist.* New York: Stein and Day, 1985.

Robinson, Linda. *Masters of Chaos: The Secret History of the Special Forces.* New York: Perseus Publishing, 2005.

Strategic Assessment 1999: Priorities for a Turbulent World. Washington, DC: National Defense University's Institute for National Strategic Studies, 1999, http:// specialforces/com

NOTES

1. Christopher Dobson and Ronald Payne, *Counterattack: The West's Battle Against the Terrorists* (New York: Facts on File, 1982), xvi.
2. *Patterns of International Terrorism in 1980: A Research Paper* (Washington, DC: National Foreign Assessment Center, 1980), 1–6.
3. "International Terrorism: Issue Brief No. 1874042" (Washington, DC: Congressional Research Service, 1978), 41–42.
4. Dobson and Payne, *Counterattack,* 84.
5. Seventy-four-year-old Dora Bloch was not being held with the hostages at the airport. She had been transferred to a Ugandan hospital. After the raid, she disappeared amid reports that she was dragged screaming from her hospital bed and murdered on Ugandan president Idi Amin's orders. She has never been seen or heard from since that time.
6. Dobson and Payne, *Counterattack,* 96.
7. Cindy Combs and Martin Slann, eds. "GSG-9," in *The Encyclopedia of Terrorism: Revised Edition* (New York: Facts on File, 2006), 112.
8. Gary Mitchell, "Special Operations Units of the United States Government," in *The Encyclopedia of Terrorism,* ed. Cindy Combs and Martin Slann (New York: Facts on File, 2002), 297–301.
9. Cindy Combs and Martin Slann, eds. "Operation Chavin de Huantar," in *The Encyclopedia of Terrorism* (New York: Facts on File, 2002), 135–137.
10. N. C. Livingstone, "Taming Terrorism: In Search of a New U.S. Policy," *International Security Review: Terrorism Report* 7, no. 1 (Spring 1982): 20.
11. Dobson and Payne, *Counterattack,* 83.
12. "Terror Campaign Against Tamils Reemerges." http://www.wsws.org/ articles/2011/jan2011/sril-j25.shtml

The Use of Legislation and Intelligence Resources to Combat Terrorism

The greatest threat posed by terrorists now lies in the atmosphere of alarm they create, which corrodes democracy and breeds repression. . . . If the government appears incompetent, public alarm will increase and so will the clamor for draconian measures.

— Brian Jenkins

LEGAL INITIATIVES TO COUNTER TERRORISM

Politicians and scholars have expressed grave doubts about whether any government can remain strong but not oppressive in the face of severe emergencies. If a government is to make a measured but effective response to the emergencies generated by terrorist acts today, then coping strategies other than sole reliance on the use of strike forces must be considered.

It is not feasible to evaluate all of the options available to nations in their efforts to deal with terrorism, as both an internal and an external threat. Nations have experimented with a wide range of policy options in their attempts to deal with this recalcitrant problem. Some tried to fashion a broad spectrum of legislative initiatives designed to make it clear that terrorists and groups resorting to terrorism operate outside the law of the land and can expect neither sanctuary nor quarter to be given them at the hands of the law.

These efforts have met with mixed success, depending in large measure on the determination of the government to enforce the laws that it creates and on the degree of entrenchment that the terrorists enjoy within the society. Canada's efforts to curtail the activities of the **Front de Libération du Québec (FLQ)**, for example, met with considerable success. Italy's offer of pardon to "penitent" terrorists combined with its efforts to close all havens in which those engaged in terrorism might hide also enjoyed some measure of success. It is difficult to gauge the success, yet, of the legislative initiatives undertaken in the United States after the events of September 11, 2001, including the passage and implementation of the PATRIOT Act. Examining its initial steps in comparison to the approaches of other countries sharing a similar commitment to democracy and the rule of law may offer useful insights.

In the cases of Canada and Italy, legal initiatives were combined with efforts at social reform designed to reduce the grievances that terrorists voiced with the existing system. Italy's success in its efforts is less clear than Canada's due in part to Italy's geographic location. Canada, with the help of a friendly nation on its only border, was able to keep terrorists from escaping across its border or receiving help from other similar groups. Italy had to contend with both indigenous and imported terrorism. Middle Eastern terrorists, as well as terrorists from several other European nations, have been able to offer support in the form of training, arms, personnel, and safe haven to Italy's indigenous terrorists. Thus, *Italy's strongest indigenous terrorist group,* the **Red Brigade**, was able to survive several intensive police crackdowns. The Red Brigade's ability to revive after each of these efforts is due less to Italy's lack of diligence in its efforts to eradicate the group than its inability to effectively close its borders to other terrorist support groups.

A quick look at the cases of Canada, the United Kingdom, Italy, and the United States offers insights into the effectiveness—and the lack thereof—of legal initiatives in coping with terrorism. These cases were chosen to illustrate two crucial points: (1) Legal initiatives are useful, but alone are insufficient to eliminate a terrorist problem; and (2) the use of extraordinary legal measures is not without risk, particularly to democracies.

Canada's Legal War with the FLQ

Canada offers an instructive example of emergency legislation, enacted and applied on a limited scale, in both scope and time. As the first North American nation to face *a vigorous and violent native terrorist campaign,* Canada from the late 1960s throughout the early 1970s was forced to create its own answer to terrorism. Faced with a series of violent attacks by the **FLQ** in the early 1970s, culminating in the kidnapping of James Cross (the British trade commissioner for Quebec) and Pierre Laporte (the minister of labor for the Quebec provincial government), Prime Minister Pierre Elliott Trudeau decided to take firm but extraordinary measures.[1]

In 1970, Trudeau invoked the **War Measures Act,** *which empowered him to call in the army to enforce his refusal to be coerced by terrorists.* Although Trudeau agreed to deal with the kidnappers, allowing them to be flown to Cuba in return for Cross's release, he was determined to rid Canada of the FLQ terrorists. Trudeau was willing to use any means at his disposal to accomplish this aim. He was willing to subordinate civil rights for the preservation of public order. As he noted:

> When terrorists and urban guerrillas were trying to provoke the secession of Quebec, I made it clear that I wouldn't hesitate to send in the army and I did, despite the anguished cries of civil libertarians.[2]

Trudeau succeeded to a large extent in ridding Canada of its indigenous terrorist organization. To do so, he saturated the Montreal area with troops to pin down terrorist cells and the Royal Canadian Mounted Police to locate the cells that had organized the terrorist attacks. Using broad local powers of search and arrest, more than 300 suspects were apprehended.[3]

Excesses were no doubt committed during the course of this crisis. Nevertheless, the crisis had an end, with civil liberties restored, the army withdrawn, and local police once again constrained by strict laws on search and seizure operations. It may be true, as David Barrett, head of the opposition of New Democratic Party once stated, that

> the scar on Canada's record of civil liberties which occurred [at that time] is a classic illustration of how the state, in an attempt to combat terrorism, overstepped its boundaries and actually threatened its own citizens.[4]

But it is also true that after Trudeau's crackdown, Canada enjoyed a decade relatively free of terrorism, with civil rights and liberties fully restored. Trudeau was astute enough to accompany the repression of this period with political measures designed to end some of the grievances that may have contributed to the terrorism. These political initiatives included creating compulsory French courses for English-speaking people in Quebec and heavy government investment in the French-speaking minority areas. Such measures helped to deprive those advocating terrorist actions of the support of the moderates among the French community.

Ironically, the problems that Canada faced in the 1990s over the efforts of Quebec to secede stem at least in part from the success of the government in "co-opting" the frustrated French-speaking population that had offered some support to the FLQ. By making the option of "working with the system" to achieve their objectives more attractive, Canada diminished its terrorism problems but may well have increased the probability of secession.

The "Temporary" British Problem in Northern Ireland

At what point should the general welfare of a nation take precedence over the rights of its citizens in a democratic society? For how long and to what extent can rights be reduced or taken away to secure that "general welfare" without doing irreparable damage to the fabric of democracy within that society?

Totalitarian and authoritarian states often justify the suspension or severe curtailment of civil and political liberties based on a "need to secure the general welfare." But it is not only undemocratic states that have been guilty of repressing civil rights for this reason. This issue confronted the United Kingdom during the last three decades of the twentieth century in its struggle with terrorism in Northern Ireland.

The periodic outbreaks of violence in Northern Ireland prompted the British parliament to enact the **Northern Ireland (Emergency Provisions) Act** in 1973. Parliament renewed this act each year for the next two decades, retaining in its title the term *emergency*, even though it had been in effect for more than a decade. This draconian measure allows *suspects to be detained by the executive authority, gives police powers of arrest without warrant for up to seventy-two hours, gives security forces broad authority for search and seizure, and makes it possible for those charged with terrorism to be tried by a judge, without benefit of a jury.*

This extraordinary legislation was followed in 1974 by an act called the **Prevention of Terrorism (Temporary Provisions) Act.** Under this act, *the home secretary was given special powers to exclude from the United Kingdom, without court proceedings, persons "concerned with the commission, preparation, or instigation of acts of terrorism"; and, detain a suspect for up to seven days without bringing him or her to court* (after arrest by police officers without a warrant, as allowed under the Emergency Provisions Act).

The Temporary Provisions Act also allowed the prohibition in the United Kingdom of organizations considered to be connected with terrorism.[5]

Both acts were renewed annually by Parliament, although often after heated debates. Thus although they carried the titles of "Temporary" and "Emergency," such terms are not really appropriate. *Emergency,* by definition, refers to a "sudden condition or state of affairs calling for immediate action."[6] Used in reference to a state of affairs that has persisted for more than a decade, it is meaningless.

These two legislative acts demonstrate the extent to which a democratic state is willing to compromise on civil rights to combat terrorism within its borders. The prolonged curtailment of fundamental civil rights and the granting of extraordinary powers to police surely diminish the democratic ideals of a state, even one that has been as committed to democracy as has the United Kingdom.

To create some measure of social order, Great Britain gave away some rights and freedoms of its Northern Ireland citizens. Unlike Canada, whose restriction of liberties was of relatively brief duration, the United Kingdom faced a restrictive situation that, because it showed only sporadic signs of improvement, seemed likely to assume an indefinite, if not permanent, position in the governing of this nation. Only the agreement reached in 1998 offered substantive commitment to a change in this governing position.

In Canada's case, the terrorists were not well organized or well armed, and they lacked substantive support from either other terrorist groups or supporters in other nations, particularly from the nation with which the country shares a border. So a determined effort by the Canadian government succeeded fairly well in wiping out the terrorist threat. Given these conditions, the curtailment of rights and liberties was of short duration.

The situation that the United Kingdom faces is very different. The **Irish Republican Army (IRA)** was *a well-organized, heavily armed, and well-funded resistance group in this region*. It received both training and weapons from supporters in many places. Other terrorist organizations contributed to the arms and training of IRA operatives, and supporters and sympathizers from several nations, particularly the United States and the Republic of Ireland, have given this group, and many of its splinter organizations, resources that include money, arms, and logistical support.

There are many difficulties in fighting an entrenched and heavily supported organization committing terrorist acts on one's home soil. As Spain found in dealing with the **Euskadi Ta Askatasuna**, *militant Basque separatists*, the presence of a friendly or neutral border over which terrorists can escape and find safe havens makes counterterror operations almost impossible for a nation to carry out on its own.[7] Cooperation between nations to thwart terrorists (as between Canada and the United States) can help make counterterror legislation unnecessary or at least short term; the absence of such cooperation, particularly when linked with transnational support for the group engaged in terrorist acts, makes it very difficult for national "emergency" legislation to be effective in eliminating the terrorism.

Italy and the "Penititi"

Italy experimented with a unique legal strategy with considerable success. In June 1983, Italians voted for the first time in more than a decade without an array of urban guerrilla groups holding the nation's political system at gunpoint. As Italy was regarded as the Western European country most vulnerable to terrorist attack during the general upsurge of terrorism in the 1970s, many of the nation's politicians and media experts hoped their country was finally beginning to emerge from its terrorist nightmare.

The man credited with a large share in Italy's success in its war on internal terrorism was Interior Minister Virginio Rognoni, who assumed his office in the wake of the kidnap-murder of former prime minister Aldo Moro. At the time he took office, the Red Brigade terrorists appeared to be acting with impunity.

Statistics issued by the Interior Ministry indicated that in 1978 there were 2,498 terrorist attacks within Italy. Between 1968 and 1982, 403 people were killed in terrorist incidents in Italy and another 1,347 were injured. These people came from all walks of life. But the bulk of the dead and injured were ordinary citizens unlucky enough to be on a train or in a piazza when it was blown up.

After 1980, Italy's internal terrorist activity dropped significantly, apparently because of a combination of legal initiatives and coordinated police efforts. Nearly 2,000 convicted urban guerrillas, including most of the leading members of the Red Brigade, were imprisoned. The Italians gave the task of hunting down these people to a portly general of the *carabinieri* named Carlo Alberto Dalla Chiesa. Armed with about 150 carefully chosen men—his antiterrorist cadre—he was responsible only to the minister of the interior, Rognoni, and to the prime minister.

With Dalla Chiesa's support, the government enacted a number of decrees: strengthening sentences for convicted terrorists, widening police powers (allowing police to hold suspects longer for questioning and to search without a warrant), and making abetting terrorism a crime. Increased powers were also given to the police in matters of detention, interrogation, and wiretapping.

Rognoni, during this increased police activity, began to exploit what he saw as a growing disillusionment with the efficacy of terrorism as a problem-solving instrument. He helped to have enacted in 1982 a law that promised the **penititi**, or *"repentant" terrorists,* lighter sentences if they confessed. Beset by gathering doubts, large numbers of the *brigadisti* began to confess.

Terrorism was not in any sense eliminated in Italy. In 1981, right-wing terrorists were responsible for an explosion in the Bologna train station that killed 85 people. But for a time, terrorism was significantly reduced. Consider the following facts:

> During 1980, deaths from terrorism occurred every three days on average.
> In the first six months of 1983, in the wake of the government's police and
>   legislative initiatives, only one terrorist-related death was reported.

The cost to Italy's democracy was arguably substantial—due process was certainly impaired by the expanded police powers, for instance. But it is also possible that Italy's democracy could not have lasted much longer under the barrage of terrorist attacks. Citizens' right to vote, to security of person, as well as to life and liberty was under constant threat of attack by terrorists. To have stabilized the situation without a civil war and without transforming Italy into an authoritarian regime is quite an accomplishment.

Much can be learned from Italy's experience. The judicious blending of strong police investigative and arrest action, coupled with the offer of a government pardon for "penitent" transgressors, proved an effective mixture. By closing most of the places to hide while holding open a friendly government door to pardon, Italy made serious efforts to resocialize a large number of its disaffected youth.

That Italy remains under attack by terrorists is due in large measure to its ties in the Arab world; its position in the Mediterranean makes it a natural staging ground or pathway for terrorism from the region. Most of Italy's terrorist activities in recent decades were conducted by foreign terrorists, primarily those from the Middle East, who were easily able to enter and exit this democratic nation.

Thus, general legislative initiatives, as well as emergency legislation, can be effective in reducing the threat of terrorism within a nation, without undue damage to democratic institutions. As one government publication noted:

> There is an almost irresistible tendency to react to terrorism by enacting laws
> and practices that diminish the rights of the accused or increase the authority of
> the state. The adverse consequences of that reaction are magnified by the equally
> predictable tendency to apply these specialized laws and mechanisms to an ever-
> increasing class of investigations. While the facts may justify certain changes, we
> must guard against overboard, non-productive, or counter-productive changes.[8]

Clearly, Italy and the United Kingdom have sought to deal with terrorism by an integrated use of law enforcement and legislative action, with mixed results. Since the events in the United States during the fall of 2001, this country has created similar legal and legislative efforts to reduce the threat of terrorism domestically. A brief analysis of these efforts may be useful in this comparative context.

CASE STUDY 12.1

The PATRIOT Act

In the immediate wake of the terrorist attacks on September 11, 2001, the federal government of the United States of America rushed to create new measures to protect the nation from future terrorist events. Only six weeks after the attacks, President George W. Bush signed into law a legislation called the **U.S.A. PATRIOT** (*Provide Appropriate Tools Required to Intercept and Obstruct Terrorism*) **Act.** Supporters of this new law claim it was designed to help law enforcement detect and disrupt terrorist plots; critics contend that its provisions can be used to infringe the rights of U.S. citizens and immigrants. There is some truth in both assessments, which is unsurprising since the law was created very quickly in the emotional wake of devastating events.

According to the Congressional Research Service, the PATRIOT Act gives federal officials greater authority to track and intercept communications, both for law enforcement and for foreign intelligence-gathering purposes. It vests the secretary of the treasury with regulatory powers to combat corruption of U.S. financial institutions for foreign money-laundering purposes. The act also seeks to further close U.S. borders to foreign terrorists and to detain and remove those terrorists within the borders while creating new crimes, new penalties, and new procedures for use against domestic and international terrorism.

This assessment is very positive and does not reflect the concerns raised by constitutional scholars about the potential dangers inherent in the powers created by this act. Some portions of the act are perceived by constitutional scholars as being truly radical, while other parts are viewed as essentially benign clarifications or improvements of existing regulations. The act is not wholly "good" nor is it "bad"; instead, it has strengths and weaknesses that are becoming evident as it is applied.

Essentially, the PATRIOT Act enhances electronic surveillance authority for law enforcement, enabling greater access to communication by e-mail, telephone, and other electronic devices; permits the government to arbitrarily detain or deport individuals suspected of connection with terrorism; allows law enforcement to clandestinely survey records of political and religious organizations; monitors financial transactions; expands the monitoring of foreign students; and makes possession of any biological agent or toxin (except for bona fide research or a peaceful project) a criminal act. A brief look at a few of the more controversial sections of this act offers some insights into its strengths—and weaknesses.

(*continued*)

Section 215 modifies the existing rules on record searches, making it possible for the FBI to conduct searches of the financial, library, travel, video rental, phone, medical, or religious organizational records of someone—not necessarily a terror suspect but at least suspected of being connected to potential terrorism—with approval by a Foreign Intelligence Security Administration (FISA) judge. While such a search is not quite "warrant-less," the judge does not have the authority to reject the application for such a search. This is an extension of the FISA authority to include efforts at counterterrorism, not simply to combat foreign espionage. While it is deplored by civil liberties advocates, it is certainly similar to laws enacted by other democracies, including the United Kingdom and Italy, to enhance terrorism investigations.

Sections 213 and 214 authorize (1) surreptitious search warrants and seizures upon a showing of "reasonable necessity," eliminating Rule 41 of the Federal Rules of Criminal Procedure requiring immediate notification to owner of seized items; and (2) pen registers to ascertain the phone numbers dialed from a suspect's phone. The so-called **sneak and peak authority**, for *surreptitious searches authorized by warrants from FISA courts*, is not a new legal tool; the primary difference between this and earlier law is the "reasonable" length of time allowed before notification, which under the PATRIOT Act can be as long as ninety days (with potential extensions). Nor are the **"trap and trace" pen registers** permitted by the act a radical change in law; the act here *extends the FISA-based ability of the FBI to initiate a wiretap by making it necessary to certify to a judge only that the tap would be "relevant" to an ongoing terrorism investigation.* Trap and trace operations monitor the source of all incoming calls as well as the numbers dialed from a suspect's phone, creating a pen register of contacts.

Section 216 is actually a clarification of the rules for Internet surveillance, which occurred before the PATRIOT Act was passed but without clear regulations. It changes terms, such as "dialing, routing, and signaling," broadening them to cover Internet communications and serving to regulate the use of taps on e-mail by extending the existing rights to tap telephones and mail. This broadening and clarifying of the rules for surveillance designed to gather information "relevant to an on-going criminal investigation" is in some respects a protection of the democratic process (as rules are clarified), rather than an attack on them.

None of these legal changes are radical in terms of antiterrorism legislation in a democracy. However, coupled with the provisions of two other sections of the act, the legal changes are potentially radical, argued by civil libertarians to be an assault on U.S. democratic institutions.

Sections 206 and 505 offer serious challenges to democratic procedures.

Section 206 authorizes the use of **roving wiretaps**, *taps specific to no single phone or computer but designed to be applied to every phone or computer that the target of the investigation may use.* Since this expands FISA rules to permit the surveillance of any communication made to or by an intelligence target without specifying the particular phone line or computer to be monitored, it has been challenged in U.S. courts as a breach of the "particularity" requirement of the Fourth Amendment to the U.S. Constitution, which protects against unwarranted searches and seizures.

Section 505 has provoked numerous legal challenges, as it authorizes the attorney general, or his delegate, to issue **National Security Letters (NSLs)**, which are essentially *administrative subpoenas requiring no probable cause or judicial oversight provisions, compelling holders of the personal records of individuals to submit such records to the government.* These records include telephone logs, e-mail logs, court records, bank records, and credit reports, and they can be issued against an individual not even suspected of espionage or criminal activity on the assumption that his or her records are "relevant to an on-going terrorism investigation." Since they can be issued by FBI field offices, rather than only by senior officials, it is perhaps not surprising that as of September 2005, about 30,000 NSLs had been issued annually to a broad range of holders of individual information, from gambling casinos to universities.

Sections 411 and 412 are often referred to by critics of the act as the **Alien and Sedition provisions**, since these sections of the *act make even an unknowing association with terrorists a deportable offense, and gives the attorney general the power to order the detention of an alien without any proof before a judge or a court that the person is dangerous.* Referring, as this nickname does, to the legal provisions made when the United States was concerned about domestic espionage carried out by aliens within the country during either violent or cold-war conflicts, these provisions are regularly challenged by legal experts, seeking to at least provide court hearings for such detentions.[9]

The PATRIOT Act thus has provisions that are arguably antithetical to a democracy, just as the provisions devised by the British in their Emergency and Temporary legislation and by the Italians in their 1980s efforts. The expanded authority to tap phones or computer links given to local as well as national law enforcement authorities is a two-edged sword. Although the absence of this type of intelligence-gathering mechanism has been cited as one of the critical weaknesses that might have contributed to the nation's vulnerability to the September 11 attacks, these tools in the hands of law enforcement also offer serious potential for abuse of civil liberties, as does the ability of law enforcement to hold for extended periods of time persons not charged with any crime. ■

Source: http://www.epic.org/privacy/terrorism.hr3162.html. Retrieved October 20, 2007. This site contains the full text of the PATRIOT Act.

The areas of expanded law enforcement capabilities described in the PATRIOT Act are cited by their advocates as vital in the effort to secure sufficient intelligence in a timely fashion to prevent future attacks like those of September 11, 2001. Ironically, these tools judged by some to be vital to ensure U.S. security may also be dangerous to the liberties of the system they are being employed to secure. As Benjamin Franklin noted in his *Historical Review of Pennsylvania* (1759), "Those who would give up essential liberty to obtain a little temporary safety deserve neither liberty nor safety."[10]

Several of the provisions of the PATRIOT Act threaten a loss of protection for civil rights as well as civil liberties. A short-term loss of rights and liberties, such as that experienced in one region of Canada, may be tolerable in a free society for a short period of time to permit the system to resolve a problem. But the continuation of the loss of rights and liberties is less easily justified, as noted in the case of the British in Northern Ireland.

Moreover, although the PATRIOT Act has a so-called sunset provision, limiting its lifetime to five years until it is renewed, additional legislation expanding law enforcement capabilities has moved through Congress. The U.S. House of Representatives approved legislation that allows the government to conduct secret surveillance on *suspected terrorists or spies not affiliated with a foreign government or terrorist organization,* the so-called **lone-wolf terrorists.** The legislation also strengthens the NSLs—tools used by the FBI in counterterrorism cases to obtain business and financial records and electronic communications from third parties—without judicial oversight in the issuance of such letters.

The so-called Alien and Sedition sections of the PATRIOT Act are perhaps the most controversial initiatives undertaken by the Bush administration in the wake of the September 11 attacks. In a broad sweep of arrests (similar to that carried out by Italy under Dalla Chiesa), former U.S. attorney general John Ashcroft announced in the fall of 2001 that 5,000 men between the ages of 18 and 33 were being "picked up and detained" indefinitely for questioning by the FBI. These young men were ones who had been in the United States for two years and were from "suspect" countries. According to Ashcroft, the objective of this arbitrary detention was to obtain information that these men might have regarding terrorist elements at home or abroad.

This form of arbitrary arrest based on a type of "profiling," rather than on any known connection to a crime, is a serious violation of the civil rights and liberties on which this country was founded, and was denounced by many groups monitoring the protection of these rights, including the Center for Constitutional Rights, Amnesty International, and the American Civil Liberties Union. Few of the individuals picked up in this sweep have been charged with crimes and brought to trial. Many remain in detention, unable to obtain either freedom or the right to a trial.

Congress is frequently criticized for the speed with which it passed the PATRIOT Act, although the legislators were doubtless responding in a rush to satisfy a frantic public that had discovered, with the events of September 11, it was vulnerable to terrorism. Many members of Congress did not read the PATRIOT Act before the vote to approve the legislation. Subsequent executive orders from the White House and rules from the attorney general's office—including the rule permitting eavesdropping by the Justice Department on the confidential conversations of inmates and uncharged detainees with their lawyers, and the executive order directing Defense Secretary Rumsfeld to establish military tribunals to try noncitizens charged with terrorism—were drafted with equal swiftness and have evoked similar outcries of dismay.

Like the emergency and the temporary legislations created by the United Kingdom to deal with terrorism in Northern Ireland, these legislative and executive office efforts are not intended to be permanent, but their incorporation into the legal system of the United States diminishes its credibility as a democracy in which civil rights and liberties are cherished. Given the historical record of such an approach in a similar cradle of democracy, it appears unlikely that these measures will effectively resolve the problem of terrorism in the United States in the long term. But these increased surveillance and detention techniques may well have contributed significantly to efforts to curb terrorist attacks in the United States since the September 11 attacks. As proponents of the measures note, while attacks have occurred in other democracies since 2001—notably the attacks in Madrid, Spain, and London, England—no such attacks have been successfully perpetrated in the United States yet, although several plots have been discovered and their perpetrators arrested.

Furthermore, the value of a strategy's effectiveness in eradicating terrorism must be balanced against the concomitant loss of other democratic values and civil liberties when a nation decides to wage war on terrorism. Terrorists can be said to have "won" in some respects when emergency measures are enacted: Seeds of doubt and dissension about the government's commitment to democracy are sown, and the government might have been forced to take distasteful measures that could serve to reduce both its legitimacy and its stability.

New Zealand, which experienced a significant terrorist act in 1985 with the bombing of the "Rainbow Warrior," created an anti-terrorism law in April 2001, designing the legislation to operationalize two international conventions on terrorism to which New Zealand was a party: The 1997 International Convention for the Suppression of Terrorist Bombings and the 1999 Convention for the Suppression of the Financing of Terrorism. This legislation criminalized terrorist acts and was not controversial. In the wake of the terrorist attacks in the United States in September of that year, parliamentary committees and law enforcement entities worked to create legislation that would fulfill the mandates of the UN resolution passed in the wake of the attacks.

The law which emerged, many months later, reflects a careful balance between the need for security and that of civil liberties. The definition of "terrorism" created a high threshold by which an act—and an organization or individual accused of such an act—could be prosecuted. It was worded carefully to avoid impacting the ability of New Zealanders to donate to international humanitarian aid projects. Unlike the PATRIOT Act, it did not give sweeping police or investigative powers to detect and capture suspected terrorists; instead, it was crafted as much to protect civil and political rights to dissent as it was to provide security against potential terrorist attacks. The legislation was approved more than a year after 9/11, in its second reading. Unlike the PATRIOT Act, it did not generate a wave of detentions, arrests, or deportations; in spite of—or perhaps because of—its lack of strong counterterror provisions, New Zealand continues to experience little that resembles terrorism today.[11]

In Table 12.1, a quick comparison can be made between the legal initiatives and law enforcement measures taken by five democracies in their struggle with terrorism. It seems obvious that legal initiatives are not enough and

▶ **TABLE 12.1**

Comparative Efforts and Effects

Country	Legislative Initiative	Law Enforcement	Concession	Outcome
Canada	War Powers Act	Royal Canadian Mounted Police in Quebec—for a short time	French as primary language in province	Peace—and possible future session of Quebec
United Kingdom	"Temporary" and "Emergency" legislation for twenty years	SAS in Northern Ireland	Peace efforts in 1990	Continued conflict, but efforts toward a coalition government
Italy	Specific targeted decrees	Carabinieri involved in intense search for Red Brigade	Offer of opportunity to "repent"	Many arrests, and decrease in RB activity
United States	U.S.A. PATRIOT Act	Joint Terrorist Task Forces		Many arrests made and plots detected
New Zealand	Terrorism Suppression Act		Lengthy review and revision of act to protect human rights	Identification of individuals of interest, but no terrorism

that coupling those initiatives with aggressive law enforcement measures is also not sufficient. What appears to be needed in addition to those efforts are measures designed to diminish the focus of the anger that is generating the terrorist activity by offering some form of "carrot" of understanding with the "stick" being used to force compliance.

Significantly, the two-decade effort of the United Kingdom to use strong legal measures with strong enforcement tools began to move toward success only when it was replaced by efforts to generate alliances in common goals. Ironically, Canada's efforts to appease its citizens contemplating terrorism by giving them an ability to preserve a greater degree of their French culture may ultimately cost Canada the province of Quebec by peaceful secession, rather than by terrorist violence.

The governments of 11 countries (10 members of the Association of South East Asian Nations [ASEAN] and New Zealand) meeting in Vientiane, LAO

PDR (Laos) in July 2005, issued a **Joint Ministerial Declaration to Combat International Terrorism**, stating that these nations reaffirmed

> the importance of having a framework for co-operation to prevent, disrupt, and combat international terrorism through the exchange of information, intelligence and capacity bulding.[12]

Collectively, these nations pledged to strengthen the sharing of intelligence and information on terrorism and to promote mutual legal assistance and extradition. Within this region, the **International Centre for Political Violence and Terrorism Research,** *a counterterrorism institute based at Nanyang Technological University in Singapore* works to facilitate this cooperative sharing of information, intelligence, and capacity building. Under the extraordinary leadership of Dr. Rohan Gunaratna, this Centre maintains

- a terrorism database—the Global Pathfinder—which serves as a repository for current and emerging terrorist threats
- graduate courses and specialist training for law enforcement personnel, focused on capacity building
- strategic counterterrorism projects, including ideological, legislative, educational, financial, media, informatics, and developmental initiatives.

Conducting research, training, and outreach programs aimed at reducing the threat of politically motivated violence, the Centre offers hope that the Ministerial Declaration by the governments in this region can indeed combat terrorism effectively within the law.

INVESTIGATION: THE INTELLIGENCE INITIATIVE

The Ministerial Declaration, and the Centre, address the need to combine intelligence gathering and sharing with counterterrorism legal efforts. Because most nations and many terrorist groups are currently engaged in the use of the strategy of intelligence gathering, an examination of the promises and pitfalls offered by such a strategy provides some insights into the way in which nations can and cannot cope with the rising threat of terrorism.

Investigation is a technique used by governments in their efforts to combat terrorism. Its potential as an antiterrorism tool is enormous. It has been effectively used to both prevent and punish terrorism. At the same time, its potential for abuse has been all too evident in recent years because it has proven to be a powerful two-edged sword capable, when improperly applied, of resulting in serious loss of civil rights, although seldom of human life.

The successful use of investigative techniques to counter terrorism is of relatively recent vintage. Although for decades Israel had an intelligence operation that accumulated vast amounts of information about Arab terrorists, even Israel has been unable to keep pace with the internationalization of terrorism, particularly of the Palestinian movement and the vast amount of information generated by its expansion.

However, until West Germany turned its attention in the 1970s toward intelligence gathering, Israel had the most active antiterrorist information system. In fact, they flooded Western European governments and police forces with information about terrorists, their movements, and planned actions; the French complained at one point that the mass of information gathered by Israeli agents (who had infiltrated Arab groups in France) was just too much for them to manage.

INTERPOL, *the international police organization,* with its data banks on criminal activity worldwide, would appear to have many of the resources necessary for such investigations. Under its charter, however, this organization was restricted for many years to investigations of ordinary crimes.

Because not all of its charter members are as yet clear on what constitutes the crime of terrorism, INTERPOL was hampered in offering substantive assistance in intelligence research. In October 1984, changes in the rules governing this organization were made, broadening its ability to assist nations in investigation of terrorism. It is today an active participant in the gathering of intelligence information about terrorist activity.

Germany's Intelligence Gathering: Target Search Teams

Germany developed and shared what is doubtless one of the most sophisticated antiterrorist intelligence operations in existence today. In Wiesbaden, *a computer nicknamed* **"the Kommissar"** played a vital role in that country's battle against terrorism. Controlled by the Federal Criminal Investigation Department (the BKA), this computer database during the 1980s and early 1990s experienced an enormous growth in the amount of federal resources put at its disposal.[13]

The heart of this computer system was an index of information called **PIOS** (*Personen, Institutionen, Objekte, Sachen*), in which was stored every clue about known and suspected terrorists. Every address found in a suspect's possession, every telephone number, and the name of every person who wrote to him or her in prison was stored in this system. Information about every object found at the scene of a terrorist attack or in a place where terrorists had been became a part of this computer's data sheets.

This information was effectively used by another German intelligence investigative tool—a special unit of investigators operating in small teams on *Ziefahndung* (**target searches**). Target searches were instituted for the apprehension of terrorists wanted under an arrest warrant with priority given to a "hard core" of about 15 violent offenders. Every police officer in Germany carried at all times a set of cards bearing the photographs of and identification data on these "targeted" persons. This was perhaps comparable to the U.S. FBI's Ten Most Wanted list.

When in operation, a target search team focused on one terrorist and immersed itself in his or her life using the Wiesbaden computer. All of the information about a suspect, however trivial it might seem, could be useful to the search team. If the information suggested, for instance, that a suspect always telephoned his or her mother on her birthday, then the mother's phone could be tapped. Support indicated by the subject for a certain soccer team would lead investigators to attend that team's matches.

These intensive search methods had documented success. Using such methods, 15 terrorists were tracked down in one six-week period in 1978. After that point, however, the success rate became somewhat less impressive. Having tracked the terrorists to other countries, the difficulty became one of securing their arrest and return for trial.

Four of the previously mentioned 15 terrorists sought in 1978 were traced to Bulgaria. According to the lawyer for Till Meyer, Gabrielle Rollnick, Gudrun Sturmer, and Angelika Loder (the four suspected terrorists), four hired cars containing heavily armed German police drew up outside a cafe in Sonnenstrand (a Bulgarian resort). Meyer and the three women were overpowered, taken to a nearby bungalow, and tied up. At 2:00 A.M., they were taken to Bourgas Airport in a minibus with German customs license plates and put on a plane with 25 armed German police. The cooperation of the Bulgarian authorities in this "kidnapping" of terrorists makes this a remarkable instance of cooperation between a communist and a noncommunist state in the apprehension of terrorists.[14]

This does not mean that cooperation on all such intelligence ventures is guaranteed. Indeed, the French refused to extradite Abu Daoud, one of Black September's commanders, to either Germany or Israel. Daoud (under an assumed name) had arrived in Paris for the funeral of the PLO's representative. The French, who had photographed the funeral party, circulated the pictures to friendly governments, asking for information in their efforts to solve the murder of the representative.

When British intelligence identified Daoud from a photograph, French police promptly arrested him, much to the French government's embarrassment. Israel and West Germany immediately requested his extradition, but the French government quietly set him free—outside of their borders.

Daoud had been formally introduced, in fact, to senior government officials and had been entertained at the Quai d'Orsay, the headquarters of the French Ministry for Foreign Affairs. France's decision not to extradite or prosecute was partly due to the embarrassment of having officially entertained Daoud, but more a result of the French government's ties to Arab states, whose sympathies lay with the PLO.[15]

Similarly, France arrested the German terrorist Wilfred Bose (whose connection with Carlos the Jackal was known to them), but released him. In this case, an extradition request was made based on intelligence information on the crimes committed by this man. Although the intelligence information was made available to France, the French government decided to neither extradite nor punish the offender. Lacking a treaty or convention that could create a legal obligation to do one or the other, France was free to act, as it did, in what it perceived to be its best national interest.

Nor is France the only nation to refuse to either extradite or prosecute when given intelligence information about suspected terrorists. The former Yugoslavia, for example, refused to arrest Carlos when informed (in detail in an intelligence report issued by a West German target search team) of his presence and his crimes. Yugoslav officials did arrest four of West Germany's most wanted terrorists (Rolf-Clemens Wagner, Brigitte Mohnhaupt, Sieglinde Hofmann, and Peter Boock) on information given by a German target search team. Subsequently, however, these suspects were released without either a trial or extradition proceedings.[16]

The point is that intelligence gathering as a weapon against terrorism is often of erratic value. Today, if a government thinks that its national interests will be best served by letting a known terrorist go free, it can (and will) usually do so. Where no overriding national interests are involved, cross-national intelligence-gathering and arrest operations are feasible; where such interests are perceived to be at stake, they are far less likely to succeed.

U.S. Intelligence-Gathering: Multiple Tools

Prior to the events of September 11, 2001, the United States had many agencies and operations engaged in gathering intelligence about terrorism in what was known as the Intelligence Community. These agencies were, in theory but not in practice, coordinated by the Director of the Central Intelligence Agency (DCI), who was responsible for establishing priorities for intelligence collection and analysis of critical issues. The problem, as *The 9/11 Commission Report* made clear, was that most of the information gathered on terrorism was not shared among the agencies, nor was it cross-referenced. This created a substantial lack of focus in the counterterrorism investigations being carried out and caused the agencies to fail to anticipate the events of September 11.

In practice, the DCI had little authority over the members of the Intelligence Community, particularly in terms of the Defense Department (DOD) resources. Each arena of intelligence information—defense (within the DOD), international (CIA and NSA), and domestic (FBI, coordinating a host of others)—had separate intelligence data collections, and the information was not, by practice and often by law, shared across the "lines" of these arenas. The vast resources of the United States in intelligence gathering were collecting data from all corners of the globe, but pooling the data in carefully guarded reservoirs unavailable to each other, although all were engaged in counterterrorism operations. The *Commission Report* made clear how flawed such a system for counterterror intelligence gathering was, indicating numerous instances when one agency had information on a suspect which, since it was not shared with another agency, allowed the perpetrators of September 11 to carry out their attacks unhampered.

Unsurprisingly, in the wake of this intelligence disaster, the United States began to reorganize its intelligence efforts in counterterrorism. **The Intelligence Reform and Terrorism Prevention Act of 2004** *created a Director of National Intelligence (DNI) to serve as the head of the intelligence community, giving this official broad oversight responsibilities to manage national intelligence operations, with particular reference to setting the budget and intelligence priorities of the 16 agencies within this community.*[17] *This act also established*

National Counterterrorism Center, to operate under the supervision of the DNI, and to incorporate the existing Terrorist Threat Information Center (TTIC), created in 2003 by President Bush.

The potential for information gathering in the United States exists in smaller units as well, many of which are gathered within the FBI. This agency established a network of Joint Terrorism Task Forces (JTTFs) designed to link federal, state, and local law enforcement in the investigation of terrorist threats. These were in existence in some areas before the events of September 11 but, since that time, have expanded to include bases in more than a hundred cities. They are, as the FBI website puts it, "our nation's front line on terrorism: small cells of highly trained, locally based, passionately committed investigators, analysts, linguists, SWAT experts, and other specialists from dozens of U.S. law enforcement and intelligence agencies."[18]

The JTTFs follow leads, gather evidence, make arrests, provide security for special events, conduct training, collect and share intelligence, and respond to threats or incidents quickly, very much like the target search teams did in Germany. Each of the FBI's 56 field offices has one such task force, with the first one established in 1980 in New York City, and 65 created in a wide range of cities after the September 11 attacks. These task forces include special agents of the FBI, state and local law enforcement officers, and professionals from other government agencies, including the Department of Homeland Security (DHS), the CIA, and the Transportation Security Administration (TSA). There is a National Joint Terrorism Task Force (NJTTF) in the Washington, DC, headquarters incorporating representatives from 30 agencies, which collects the terrorism information and funnels it to regional JTTFs, other terrorism units in the FBI, and other intelligence and law enforcement bodies.

Within the FBI headquarters in Washington, DC, is the **Strategic Information Operations Center,** *the centralized location for all of the information obtained by the task forces as well as any other state, local, or federal information relating to terrorist activity.* Federal agents from numerous bureaus work together with task forces from other agencies to review, analyze, and further investigate the accumulated information.

While there are clearly many agencies and entities still involved in the gathering of intelligence about terrorist activities in the United States, the integration of these efforts is a priority. The creation and empowering (by budgetary authority) of a Director of National Intelligence to integrate the intelligence gathered can be vitally important, but it has not yet resolved the problems in integrating military intelligence with domestic law enforcement bodies. The fact that all are "brought together" under the roof of the new DHS does not resolve the issue. Much of the information remains in separate data banks, inaccessible to members of other agencies due to the security provisions regarded as vital to the agencies gathering the information.

The U.S. Department of Homeland Security also created state and local **Fusion Centers,** organizing efforts of states and larger cities to share intelligence information within their jurisdictions and with federal agencies. It is not yet clear how effective this new tool will be in facilitating the sharing of intelligence information across "turfs," but these centers provide a valuable link between federal, state, and local law enforcement and intelligence services.

The JTTFs appear to be highly successful in integrating both personnel and information. Since the attacks in September 2001, several high-profile cases have been resolved without incident, in part by the efforts of these task forces. These incidents include, but are not limited to, the breaking up of potential terrorist cells like the "Portland Seven," the "Lackawanna Six," and the "Northern Virginia Jihad." The task forces have also traced sources of terrorist funding, responded to anthrax threats, worked to halt the use of fake IDs, and quickly arrested suspicious characters with various deadly weapons and explosives.[19]

CASE STUDY 12.2

Department of Homeland Security

In June 2002, President George W. Bush proposed the creation of a new Department of Homeland Security (DHS), the establishment of which would mark the most significant transformation of the U.S. government in over a half-century, transforming and realigning the current confusing patchwork of government activities into a single department whose primary mission is to protect the U.S. "homeland." This new DHS was designed to help the men and women who daily protect the borders and secure the nation to do their jobs better with increased communication, coordination, and resources. Specifically, the DHS has three primary missions:

1. Prevent terrorist attacks within the United States.
2. Reduce America's vulnerability to terrorism.
3. Minimize the damage from potential attacks and natural disasters.

In order to accomplish these goals, during its first years the DHS focused on creating the new capabilities discussed in the July 2002 National Strategy for Homeland Security. This strategy is premised on the fact that in 2002, no single government agency had homeland security as its primary mission. Instead, responsibilities for homeland security were dispersed among at least 22 different federal organizations. The DHS sought to reform and realign the current overlapping patchwork of government activities into a single department. The department was designed to give federal, state, and local officials one primary contact regarding homeland security.

The DHS was intended to manage federal grant programs for enhancing the preparedness of firefighters, police, and emergency medical personnel. The DHS was also empowered to set standards for state and local preparedness activities and equipment.

The DHS initially had important strategic goals:

Awareness: Identify and understand threats, assess vulnerabilities, determine potential impacts, and disseminate timely information to homeland security partners and the American public.

Prevention: Detect, deter, and mitigate threats to the homeland.

Protection: Safeguard the people and their freedoms, critical infrastructure, property, and the economy of the nation from acts of terrorism, natural disasters, or other emergencies.

Response: Lead, manage, and coordinate the national response to acts of terrorism, natural disasters, or other emergencies.

Recovery: Lead national, state, local, and private sector efforts to restore services and rebuild communities after acts of terrorism, natural disasters, or other emergencies.

Service: Serve the public effectively by facilitating lawful trade, travel, and immigration.

Organizational Excellence: Value the most important resource, the people. Create a culture that promotes a common identity, innovation, mutual respect, accountability, and teamwork to achieve efficiencies, effectiveness, and operational synergies.

The Homeland Security Act of 2002 (HSA) provides certain flexibility for the Secretary of Homeland Security to establish, consolidate, alter, or discontinue organizational units within the department. The mechanism for implementing these changes is a notification to Congress, required under Section 872 of the HSA, allowing for the changes to take effect after sixty days. The organization currently includes functional departments in Border and Transportation Security; Emergency Preparedness and Response; Information Analysis and Infrastructure Protection; Science and Technology; Management, Coast Guard, Secret Service, Citizenship and Immigration Services; and Inspector General.

Tom Ridge was appointed by President Bush as the first Secretary of Homeland Security. He served in this post until early in 2005. On February 15, 2005, Michael Chertoff was sworn in as the second Secretary of the DHS, and Janet Napolitano became the third on January 21, 2009. ■

Source: http://www.dhs.gov/index.shtm. This is the website for this agency.

Computers as Tools of Investigation

The Internet and the abilities of intelligence officials to eavesdrop on e-mail and phone calls became primary tools in the efforts to track down the perpetrators of the September 11 attacks. Several Internet tools offer interesting options for investigators.

Surveillance. The use of an inexpensive computer that can be plugged into an Internet service provider's network to monitor the communications of suspects has become one of the most important tools for the FBI. The system, called Carnivore,[20] is a version of a common technology that system administrators use to maintain networks. Carnivore was designed to help law enforcement officers determine who receives a suspect's e-mail and who sends e-mail to the suspect. It can be programmed to capture whole messages; it does not interpret encrypted messages.

Cooperation. A system for listening in on conversations, developed by the United States, Britain, Canada, Australia, and New Zealand, consists of a network of satellite dishes known as *Echelon*. This cooperative effort to create a shared information system has at times been criticized by privacy activists. Nor does it solve the problem of the reluctance of law enforcement officials to jeopardize a source or an investigation by sharing the information with others.

Search. Information that can be digitally scanned can be electronically searched by law enforcement. Digitalized fingerprints, pictures of suspects, even passport stamps that have been scanned can be searched by computers utilizing software designed to rapidly sift through large amounts of information. The possibility of using retinal scans as a part of airport security is also being considered in the United States.

None of these computer tools make the investigation or prevention of terrorist acts simple, and all have been challenged by those concerned that civil rights may be violated by the intrusion of electronic surveillance. But such tools may well be crucial for future investigations of terrorist acts and for the prevention of terrorism through enhanced security measures.

CASE STUDY 12.3

Dark Web Project Tracking Terrorism

Funded by the U.S. National Science Foundation and other federal agencies, a team of computational scientists are using cutting-edge technology and innovative approaches in a **Dark Web Project** to track terrorism online, providing an invaluable intelligence-gathering tool in the global war on terror. Based at the University of Arizona, under the leadership of Hsinchun Chen and his Artificial Intelligence Lab, this project is engaged in systematically collecting and analyzing all terrorist-generated content on the Web. This is an enormous undertaking as there are more than 5,000 websites created and maintained by known international groups engaged in terrorism. Many of these sites are in multiple languages, and all use the speed and potential anonymity of the Internet in e-mail and forums as well as websites—providing communication channels for these groups.

Because of the important role noted earlier which the Web now plays in recruiting, training, and coordinating terrorist activity, this project offers a vital counterterror tool. This tool uses advanced techniques such as **web spidering**, *a process involving searches of discussion threads and other content to find the "dark corners" of the Internet where terrorist activities are being planned. One of the other tools developed in this project is known as Writeprint, a procedure that automatically extracts thousands of multilingual, structural, and semantic features to determine who is creating "anonymous" content online relating to terrorist activity.* Using Writeprint, postings on an online bulletin board can be studied and compared with writings found at other locations on the Internet. Analysis of this comparative data can determine with about 95 percent accuracy whether the same author has produced Web content in the past. The system can then alert analysts when this author produces new content, as well as where on the Internet someone is copying, linking, or discussing the content.

This Dark Web Project has already produced tangible results in the form of a study of online stories and videos about the creation of improvised explosive devices (IEDs) designed to train others in the creation of these explosives. Knowledge of the type of information about IED construction being conveyed and where that information was being downloaded has improved the countermeasures being developed to counter these devices. This linking of math, computer science, and terrorism experts is one of the more innovative efforts in using the Internet to counter the threat of terrorism today. ■

Source: Artificial Intelligence Laboratory, Dark Web Terrorism Research, retrieved from http://ai.arizona. edu/research/terror/ in October 2011.

GOVERNMENT USE OF INVESTIGATION AND INTELLIGENCE

Two interesting cases of the use of intelligence and investigation as tools in counterterrorism offer contrasts in the use of these techniques in the late 1990s. Both involve the use of violent force rather than legal initiatives to resolve the situation, but both also are critically dependent for success on intelligence gathering and investigation efforts by law enforcement agencies.

The first case, detailed in Chapter 11, involved the Tupac Amaru seizure of the Japanese Embassy in Lima, Peru, in December 1996. As indicated by the details of that incident, dubbed **Operation Chavin de Huantar**, a successful resolution of a tense hostage situation was achieved in part by the patient collection of information about the patterns of activity, resources, personnel, and other useful data about both the hostage-takers and the hostages.

Although the hostages were held for 126 days, and there was intense pressure to use force in a rescue attempt, Peru's president remained determined to resolve the situation with a minimum amount of violence.

The success of the rescue mission (only 1 of the 72 hostages was killed) can be attributed in large measure to superb intelligence. During the months of the incident, listening devices were smuggled into the residence, concealed in items that the Red Cross workers were allowed to deliver, including buttons placed on clothing brought to the hostages as changes of clothing were needed. Using every opportunity to gather intelligence, during the final four days intelligence agents posed as doctors and were allowed to enter to check on the health of the hostages, implanting matchstick-sized two-way microphones that allowed intelligence officers on the outside to communicate with the military and police commanders being held inside.

With this intelligence access, those planning the operation were able to monitor the movements of the guerrillas and the hostages each day, making a carefully timed assault possible. For example, intelligence officers were able to learn that the 14 Tupac Amaru guerillas had a regularly scheduled makeshift game of soccer each day at about 3:00 P.M. in the ground-floor living room and that prior to beginning the game, they stacked their rifles in a corner of the room.

Thus, when the listening devices indicated at 3:10 P.M. on the day planned for the assault that the regular afternoon soccer game had begun, with at least eight of the rebels participating, the hostages, who were being held upstairs, were alerted to move a desk blocking the second-floor entrance and take cover. The assault, initiated minutes later, began with the detonation of 9 pounds of explosives in the tunnel directly under the room where the rebels were playing soccer, killing four of them and opening a hole through which troops began to pour, without injuring the hostages.

Peru, in this case, offered the international community an excellent example of the value of careful intelligence and planning in such terrorist attacks. The rescue efforts broke no laws and wasted no innocent lives. Patience and careful planning based on up-to-the-minute intelligence were rewarded.

This success, when compared with the U.S. 1993 assault on the Branch Davidian compound in Waco, Texas, offers dramatic evidence of the importance of accurate and current intelligence. At Waco, as one analyst noted, "the assault went disastrously wrong in part because agents relied on months-old intelligence that those in the compound were always separated from their weapons at 10:00 A.M."[21] The inaccuracy of this information contributed to the loss of four agents. Clearly, intelligence is a critical factor in counterterrorism exercises.

The second case used here to assess the importance of intelligence gathering on counterterrorism actions by a government involves the U.S. actions taken in response to attacks in 1998. Bombings devastated U.S. embassies in Kenya and Tanzania on August 7, 1998. More than 250 people, including 12 Americans, were killed. Intense investigation by federal officials from the United States, working with officials from Kenya and Tanzania, identified several suspects, including Khalid Salim (a Yemeni citizen) and Mohammed Saddiq Odeh. Salim was sent to the United States to stand trial less than three weeks after the bombing, and Odeh was arrested by Pakistani authorities on a flight from Nairobi the day of the bombing. He reportedly confessed under interrogation in Pakistan to a role in the attacks.

Although continuing to seek evidence and to bring suspects in the bombing incident to trial in this country, the United States did not wait to complete the investigation. Instead, on August 20, 1998, it carried out a missile strike against two targets: camps in Afghanistan used by **Osama bin Laden,** *leader of the al-Qaeda organization* and the man believed to be responsible for orchestrating and funding the embassy attacks; and a pharmaceutical plant in Khartoum, Sudan, linked by intelligence information to bin Laden's operations.

Investigators at the time stated that gathering information admissible as evidence of bin Laden's connection to the embassy bombings would take at least weeks, perhaps months. The circumstantial evidence seemed clear but was insufficient to warrant an indictment in early August. However, political pressure at home to take action was intense, and the public and lawmakers were unlikely to accept the need to exercise patience while intelligence was accumulated. Hence, the bombings were ordered, although intelligence on the targets of the missile attacks was not clear.

The links of bin Laden to the embassy bombings were numerous and dated back at least five years to the first bombing attempt on the World Trade Center in New York City in 1993. By 1996, the United States was pressuring Sudan to cut its ties to the multimillionaire, indicating that the United States considered him to be masterminding and funding terrorism in the region. The ties of Salim and Odeh to bin Laden were not surprising to those tracking the actions of this dissident leader. But the gathering of sufficient admissible evidence to substantiate guilt is a very time-consuming operation.

The cruise missiles inflicted serious damage on the physical facilities at both targets, with minimal loss of life. This effort to prevent civilian casualties in Sudan was important, because the United States gave Sudan no warning of the attack or of its concern with the facility itself. This unprovoked attack, as Sudan and many of its neighbors viewed the bombings, was both illegal and unjustified. Had the attack resulted in a high civilian casualty count, the anger of the international community might have been formidable. Instead, the small amounts of evidence that the United States was willing to offer to public scrutiny concerning the alleged use of the facility frustrated many allies, who deplored the lack of firm intelligence prior to the attack and the lack of diplomatic interaction between Sudan and the United States that might have prevented its necessity.

The attack on Afghanistan in 1998, although it provoked less concern in the international community in terms of the legality of the action, was less clearly effective because there was little evidence gathered before the attack to indicate that bin Laden or any of his people were at the site when attacked. Destroying empty, relatively inexpensive shacks used for mercenary training may have satisfied domestic desire for "action" but did not eliminate the threat of bin Laden. Indeed, it may well have offered him further reason to hate the United States.

The lack of intelligence concerning the presence of bin Laden at his head-quarters and the lack of admissible evidence against the Sudanese factory diminished the value of the American actions in August 1998. While the productivity of both actions in terms of counterterrorism cannot yet be determined, both were impugned by the lack of up-to-date intelligence.

CONCLUSIONS

> For a democratic society, the issue is not merely survival, but
> the way in which society chooses to survive.
>
> *Robert Friedlander*

Just as terrorism is essentially a war against both the state and all of civilized society, so the struggle to eliminate, or at least to restrict, terrorism is also war of a sort. The cost of this war on terrorism, if carried by each state alone, can be high, both politically and economically. Moreover, as noted earlier, when a state tries to pursue a strategy unilaterally, its effectiveness can be limited.

It is clear that terrorism is transnational, and thus no nation can or should try to deal with it alone. Generating domestic legislation and building methods of gathering and sharing intelligence about terrorism is important, but states can learn from the successes and failures of other states to build laws that counter terrorism without weakening the fundamental rights and freedoms intrinsic to democracies. Formal and informal networks of international police cooperation structures do exist that facilitate sharing intelligence concerning terrorism. In Europe there is a permanent, though comparatively secret, structure code named **TREVI** for *terrorism, radicalism, and violence international.* This is a formalization of the "old boy" police network, which regularly brings together police chiefs from European Union countries. It also engages in day-to-day consultations through national bureaus. Furthermore, NATO has an antiterrorist network that allies Canadians and Americans with Europe. This system facilitates the exchange of information on terrorists, their organizations, techniques, and weapons.

Not all regions have this cooperative approach to intelligence-sharing, nor have all states built successful counterterrorism legislation or intelligence-gathering strategies. But the cost of the absence of such legislation and intelligence mechanisms can be high. Consider carefully the brief look in Case Study 12.4, focusing on the steps taken by the prime minister to improve those capacities after a serious terrorist attack.

CASE STUDY 12.4

Terrorism in Mumbai

In November 2008, more than 10 coordinated shooting and bombing attacks occurred in Mumbai, India's financial capital and largest city. Beginning on November 26 and continuing until November 29, the attacks killed at least 173 people and wounded more than 300. By the early morning of November 28, all of the attack sites had been secured by the Mumbai police and security forces, but the attack on the Taj Mahal Palace Hotel was not resolved until India's National Security Guards (NSG) arrived from their headquarters in Delhi, several hours after the attacks began.

Mumbai police, who were using standard police procedures and did not have counterterror training, had initially treated the situation at the hotel as a hostage-rescue problem, believing that the individuals carrying out the attacks were taking hotel guests as hostages and would issue demands but not kill their hostages unless threatened. For police in most democracies, the priority is to keep the hostages alive, not necessarily to kill the individuals taking the hostages. However, the attackers were going from room to room in the hotel, shooting guests rather than collecting hostages, so standard hostage-rescue procedures did not save lives.

Counterterror training is usually given in democratic systems to special military or intelligence units such as the U.S. FBI or the British SAS. These teams are taught a different priority in terrorist attack situations: Capture or kill those carrying out the attack while saving as many hostages as possible. These teams are also given greater intelligence materials and training, enabling them to more accurately assess the strengths and weaknesses of the attackers. With the arrival of the NSG from Delhi, the use of lethal force against the attackers increased, and the situation was resolved by November 29, with one member of the attack group captured alive.

This quick look at the events should not suggest that the Mumbai police were incompetent or were in any way responsible for the loss of lives in the hotel. But the lack of counterterror training, the lack of information in their hands about the group identified as responsible for the attacks, and the distance that the national response team had to travel before being able to work with local authorities to resolve the situation certainly contributed to the impact of the attacks. More important, however, are the steps which India's prime minister, Manmohan Singh, described in early 2009 in response to the attack and to the analysis of events that had emerged. He announced several critical steps to enhance the country's ability to deal with this type of attack:

- The strengthening of the legal framework of counterterrorism laws (the Prevention of Terrorism Act of 2002)[22]
- The establishment of a federal investigative agency tasked with gathering and facilitating the sharing of information on terrorism
- The creation of an anti-terror force called "Force One"
- The creation of four NSG hubs in various parts of the country
- The upgrade of weapons for the Mumbai police force

Noting that the single captured attacker, Ajmal Amir Kasab, disclosed that the attackers were members of Lashkar-e-Taiba, a Pakistani-based military organization. Evidence indicated that the attackers traveled by sea from Karachi, Pakistan. India accused Pakistan of aiding the attackers, an accusation which Pakistan denied. The relationship of India with Pakistan, already strained, has deteriorated in the wake of this event, and a sharing of intelligence across borders is unlikely at this point. ■

DISCUSSION

The international community, after the September 11, 2001, attacks in the United States, initiated efforts to strengthen international cooperation to combat terrorism. The United Nations became the forum in which nations came together to denounce terrorism and to pledge support in an international effort to combat this problem. On

September 28, 2001, the Security Council of the United Nations unanimously adopted Resolution 1373, proposed by the United States, which established a body of legally binding obligations on all UN member states. Its provisions required, among other things, that all member states prevent the financing of terrorism; deny safe havens to terrorists; and review and strengthen their border security operations, banking practices, customs and immigration procedures, law enforcement and intelligence cooperation, and arms transfer controls.

This resolution also mandated that each state report on the steps it had taken, and it established a committee of the Security Council to monitor implementation.

Intelligence gathering and legal initiatives as tools against terrorism can be formidable—or ineffective. The need for cooperation is real; securing it on an organized basis is very difficult. Similarly, strong intelligence efforts can help to prevent or resolve criminal activity but can also be the source of significant government abuse of civil rights. The choices that governments must make are critical in the use of the vital set of tools that intelligence can provide.

Consider carefully the following statements as you consider the lessons learned from analysis of the July 7, 2005 London bombings, as these were formulated by the United Kingdom:

1. Despite their great efforts to improve the quality of their intelligence on al-Qaeda's network, the UK's intelligence services seriously underestimated the al-Qaeda's network in the United Kingdom. Only weeks before the bombings, the UK's Joint Terrorism Analysis Centre stated that there were no extremist groups with the current intent or capability of launching an attack in the United Kingdom. Lesson learned: Counter terrorism officials and policy makers should not neglect analysis of worst-case scenarios and their implications.

2. Because it is inherently very difficult to prevent terrorists from carrying out no-warning suicide attacks in vital places, it is vital to develop and exercise emergency plans for police and other first responders. More resources, training for emergency service personnel, and appropriate modern equipment should be made available, and good contingency planning and training can save lives in the event of such an attack.

3. To prevent future attacks from *jihadi* recruited and indoctrinated within a country, more efforts need to focus on winning the hearts and minds of young, angry, and alienated Muslims to prevent such recruitment. This should entail the enlisting of moderate religious and community leaders, as well as the enlistment of the education system, the universities, and the mass media to help in this task.

ANALYSIS CHALLENGE

Theories for decision making offer useful structures by which to assess the choices for counterterrorism discussed thus far. Consider these two decision-making models, and decide in terms of their utility in assessing a state's decision on its selection of counterterrorism strategy:

1. The Rational Actor Model, rooted in economic theory, assumes two important things: Governments are the primary actor, and a government will examine a set of goals, evaluating them in terms of their utility, and then choosing the one that will give the greatest benefits. Using this model, the application of legal remedies, carefully constructed, would offer the least penalty, but not necessarily the greatest gain.

2. The Organizational Process (OP) Model posits that, when faced with a crisis, government leaders do not look at the crisis as a whole, but instead break it down and assign it according to preestablished organizational lines, following set procedures and preexisting plans. Using this scenario, the use of the military would be the OP model decision-making choice, as the military has, in most nations' histories, been the primary agency responsible for national security.

Look at the U.S. decisions concerning the initial seizure of individuals after 9/11, eventually offering some the option of military tribunal, under the Bush administration. Compare this to the Obama administration to try the individuals seized at sea near Somalia in civilian court in New York. Use one of the models to assess the decision-making process involved.

http://www.nytimes.com/2011/04/25/world/guantanamo-files-lives-in-an-american-limbo.html?_r=2

http://www.huffingtonpost.com/2010/01/13/abdiwali-abdiqadir-muse-s_n_420577.html

KEY TERMS

Red Brigade 272
Front de Libération du Québec (FLQ) 272
War Measures Act 273
Northern Ireland (Emergency Provisions) Act 274
Prevention of Terrorism (Temporary Provisions) Act 274
Irish Republican Army (IRA) 275
ETA 275
Penititi 276
U.S.A. PATRIOT Act 277
sneak and peak authority 278

"trap and trace" pen registers 278
Roving Wiretaps 278
National Security Letters (NSL) 279
Alien and Sedition provisions 279
lone-wolf terrorists 280
Joint Ministerial Declaration to Combat International Terrorism 283
International Centre for Political Violence and Terrorism Research 283
"the Kommissar" 284
PIOS 284

Target Searches 284
The Intelligence Reform and Terrorism Prevention Act of 2004 286
Strategic Information Operations Center (SIOC) 287
Fusion Centers 287
Dark Web Project 290
Web Spidering 290
Writeprint 290
Operation Chavin de Huantar 291
Osama bin Laden 292
TREVI 294

SUGGESTED READINGS AND RESOURCES

Bssaden, Thomas, ed. *Annual Editions: Homeland Security 04/05*. Guilford, CT: McGraw-Hill, 2008.

Howard, Russell D., and Reid L. Sawyer, eds. *Terrorism and Counterterrorism: Understanding the New Security Environment*. Guilford, CT: Dushkin, 2005.

Jenkins, Roy. *England: Prevention of Terrorism (Temporary Provisions)—A Bill*. London: Her Majesty's Stationery Office, 1974.

Mahan, Sue, and Pakmalal Griset. *Terrorism in Perspective*. Thousand Oaks, CA: Sage Publications, 2008.

"Ottawa Ministerial Declaration on Countering Terrorism." Released at the Ottawa Ministerial on December 12, 1995.

Sauter, Mark A., and James Jay Carafano. *Homeland Security: A Complete Guide to Understanding, Preventing, and Surviving Terrorism.* New York: McGraw-Hill, 2005.

U.S.A. PATRIOT Act, http://www.epic.org/privacy/terrorism/hr3162.html.

"U.S. Report to the Counterterrorism Committee." Patterns of Global Terrorism, U.S. Department of State. December 27, 2001.

NOTES

1. See Brian Moore's *The Revolution Script* (New York: Holt, Rinehart, and Winston, 1971), for an account of these kidnappings; see also Leonard Beaton, "Crisis in Quebec," *Round Table* 241 (1971): 147–152.
2. Quoted by Robert Friedlander, *Terrorism: Documents of International and Local Control* (New York: Oceana, 1979), vol. 1, 113.
3. Christopher Dobson and Ronald Payne, *Counterattack: The West's Battle Against the Terrorists* (New York: Facts on File, 1982), 113. For six months, Trudeau flooded the Montreal area with troops. It took nine weeks to track down those responsible for Laporte's murder.
4. Dobson and Payne, *Counterattack*, 113. It was Barrett's contention that "democratic governments cannot legitimately establish consent by the use of force."
5. For information on these two acts, see Great Britain, "Report to the Commission to Consider Legal Procedures to Deal with Terrorist Activities in Northern Ireland" (London: Her Majesty's Stationery Office, 1972). For analysis of the Temporary Provisions Act, see Roy Jenkins, *England: Prevention of Terrorism (Temporary Provisions)—A Bill* (London: Her Majesty's Stationery Office, 1974).
6. See Funk and Wagnall's *Standard Dictionary of the English Language*, international edition (Chicago: J. G. Ferguson, 1977), vol. 1, 413.
7. French Basques are living north of the Pyrenees, and there is little doubt that they give help to people they consider to be compatriots in Spain. ETA men on the run frequently cross the border to find refuge in safe houses in France. In 1979, the French government finally removed the political refugee status of ETA members.
8. "Report on Domestic and International Terrorism," Subcommittee on Civil Rights of the Committee on the Judiciary (First Session, April 1981) (Washington, DC: U.S. Government Printing Office, 1981), 4.
9. Retrieved on October 20, 2007, from http://www.epic.org/privacy/terrorism. hr3162.html. This is the site for the full text of this act.
10. Retrieved on May 15, 2005, from www.worldofquotes.com/author/ Benjamin-Franklin/.
11. John E. Smith, "New Zealand's Anti-Terrorism Campaign: Balancing Civil Liberties, National Security, and International Responsibilities. Retrieved from http://www.fulbright.org.nz/voices/axford/docs/smithj.pdf in October 2011.
12. "ASEAN-New Zealand Joint Declaration for Cooperation to Combat International Terrorism," released on the July 29, 2005.
13. "Report on Domestic and International Terrorism," Subcommittee on Civil Rights of the Committee on the Judiciary (First Session, April 1981) (Washington, DC: U.S. Government Printing Office, 1981), 18. This report includes an evaluation of German officials on the effectiveness of this intelligence system. The officials included Siegfried Froelich, state secretary; Gerhard Siegle, administrative head of

the terrorism office; Dieter Osterle, deputy head of the Director's Office of the Police Superior Commission; and Captain Ulrich Grieve, representative of GSG-9.

14. Dobson and Payne, *Counterattack*, 101.
15. See the *New York Times,* January 12, 1977, sec. 1, p. 1, for a concise recounting of this incident. This was not, of course, the only time that France refused to extradite known terrorists. However, recent French efforts to capture and prosecute Carlos indicate a significant change in French attitude toward the problem.
16. In this case, the reasons were both legal and political. The Yugoslavs demanded that the Germans give them in return a number of anti-Tito Croatian nationalists, some of whom were in German jails serving sentences for acts of terrorism against Yugoslav property and officials inside Germany. Germany could not, it decided, overcome the legal and moral complexities of meeting this demand.
17. Retrieved on October 20, 2000, from http://www.nctc.gov/docs/p1108_458.pdf.
18. Retrieved on October 20, 2007, from the FBI website http://www.fbi.gov/page2/dec04/jttf120114.htm.
19. Retrieved on October 20, 2007, from the FBI website http://www.fbi.gov/page2/dec04/jttf120114.htm.
20. For more information on Carnivore, explore http://corz.org/public/docs/privacy/carnivore-faq.html.
21. "Peru Takes No Prisoners," *U.S. News & World Report,* May 5, 1997, 38.
22. Retrieved on June 20, 2009, from http://www.satp.org/satporgtp/countries/india/document/actandordinances/POTA.htm.

Security Measures: A Frail Defense

> The costs of terrorism that are more difficult to define and understand are the ongoing costs in the form of security measures, intelligence gathering programs or husky men wearing rubber gloves in airports.
>
> —*B.J. Bodnar*

Confronted with a growing tide of terrorist destruction, governments have been forced to spend increasing amounts of time and money on problems related to security. Modern society is both fragile and complex with much interdependence within systems. As such, the possibilities for interference by terrorism are almost infinite.

Some aspects of security have received more attention than others due to their selection as targets of terrorism. It is possible that this focus will shift as new technologies make current security measures obsolete and as successful security systems harden certain targets against attack.

Technological developments during the past few decades have increased dramatically the potential targets and weapons available to persons committing terrorist acts. While the technology accessible to governments has also grown, governments are to some extent hampered by the technology boom. Governments with democratic principles are simultaneously confronted with a rapidly growing number of targets that must be secured and constrained from utilizing many technological devices to secure those targets. Creating an effective security system that protects against a wide range of terrorist attacks while it continues to afford a maximum exercise of democratic freedoms and privileges is a formidable task.

THREE FACETS OF SECURITY

Security is not a one-dimensional issue. Instead, those confronting security problems are faced with at least three aspects of the situation that must be considered: physical security, operational security, and personnel security. Each of these facets of security is closely related to the others and cannot be easily differentiated. Let us briefly examine each of these aspects of security.

Physical security has, as its objective *the hardening of the target against which an attack may be made.* Although no blueprint for successful physical security measures against terrorist attack has been adopted, there are certain considerations and countermeasures that have begun to achieve acceptance in both the government and the business community.

Both these communities are slowly recognizing that security measures against terrorism must go beyond the level of normal crime prevention. Terrorists are not "normal" criminals: their goals, their willingness to sacrifice innocent lives, and their willingness to die in their attacks make them extraordinary criminals against whom extraordinary measures must be taken if security is to be achieved and maintained.

In order to determine what, if any, extraordinary security measures are needed to protect against a terrorist attack, government and business have employed a number of relatively ordinary tactics. A physical security survey by professionals who are aware of the dangers in a particular area or to a particular business or region is standard procedure. This has in recent years begun to include the use of **penetration teams**, *whose job is to discover holes in security systems through which other teams, such as terrorist attack teams, could presumably penetrate and sabotage or destroy the target.*

The penetration team, or the organization conducting the physical security survey, may suggest in its report that the business utilize certain devices that have proven useful in guarding against attack or sabotage. For example, a variety of intrusion detection devices are available on the market today.

Or such an evaluation may emphasize the importance of such factors as lighting, access control, or physical security and access control codes. Organizations may be advised to inhibit surreptitious approaches by increasing lighting of entryways, fences, hallways, and other points of access. Greater access control is often recommended, usually in the form of limitations on the numbers of individuals cleared to work in the facility as a whole or in specific, sensitive parts of the operation. One of the more common recommendations for improved physical security is that security and access codes be changed fairly frequently to make penetration of the operation more difficult.

Some operations in which security has been a relatively minor problem are urged to consider the use of personnel, such as guards, whose specific duty is to ensure physical security. Others who have already taken this step have discovered from security surveys that they need additional guards or specially trained counterterrorist guards.

Physical security is clearly dependent upon other types of security—operational security and personnel security. Fortress walls, barbed fences, and barred gates are not, in modern times, either reasonable or sufficient protection against determined terrorist fanatics. The operation of the facility itself must be secure and its personnel well trained in security procedures, to circumvent modern terrorist attacks.

Operational security *has as its objective the denial of opportunity for terrorists to collect such information on either the facility or its activities as might enable it to predict those activities.* To be able to predict those activities would help the terrorist to successfully penetrate the facility or activity and disrupt or destroy it. By denying that information to terrorists, the risk to terrorists carrying out an attack against the activity or facility significantly increases.

Prediction of operational activities usually relies on discerning patterns of behavior, so operational security analysis focuses on identifying those patterns and how they are communicated to personnel. Emphasis is placed on making such patterns less predictable, randomizing activities as far as possible without creating chaos within the organization. Too often, repeated activities create in the minds of the individuals responsible for security a lack of alertness to small differences that may be crucial. The arrival of a particular car at the same time every morning, the use of a van of a specific color and model delivering goods at the same place and time—these routines can deaden the alertness of personnel to such factors as the identity of the driver or the presence of an authorized person in the vehicle. Such a failure to notice, to carry out a thorough security check, can prove fatal to the organization or to some of its personnel.

The training of personnel in operational security measures is also important. Organizations are advised to train personnel in the recognition of intelligence-gathering activities, so that they can more readily spot individuals engaged in such activities. Screening of both employees and casual but regular contacts—such as vendors—is also a major focus of operational security efforts, as all such individuals can constitute a threat to the operation.

Moreover, the organization as a whole is encouraged to improve its operational security by a variety of obvious but essential measures. These include but are not limited to:

1. maintaining a low profile so that the organization does not become an attractive, publicity-provoking target;
2. improving communications security so that it is less possible to penetrate the flow of commands or patterns of communications; and
3. developing counterintelligence capabilities within both management and security-related personnel.

Neither operational nor physical security can function effectively without the third crucial type of security: personnel security. **Personnel security** focuses on *the training of personnel to take responsibility on their own for security* by teaching them to know how to recognize and respond to a potential terrorist threat. For many years, this type of security was directed toward those whom the organization regarded as being at a greater risk of attack than most of the rank-and-file personnel.

Many organizations have developed individual crisis management files, which help management decide which individuals need special security training and protection. Using those files, these at-risk individuals are advised on how to randomize travel routes and maintain a low profile. Training is also given to certain individuals in special antiterrorism devices, such as bulletproof clothing.

But today, personnel security has taken on added dimensions. Organizations routinely schedule periodic training for all personnel in counterterrorism procedures. Such training is usually designed to heighten awareness among employees of the potential for terrorist attacks, and the preincident phases—particularly intelligence gathering—which may alert personnel to a terrorist attack in progress. The proper use of security measures at all times is stressed so that employees are less likely to be lulled by a sense of routine into a possibly fatal breach of security procedures.

Most of all, the need to tell someone about suspicious or threatening behavior and to alert the proper authorities to potential threats has become a major focus in the training of personnel in many organizations. The alertness of personnel to security breaches may well mean the difference between a successful terrorist attack and the failure of such an attempt.

CASE STUDY 13.1

NSA's Operation Eligible Receiver

Using a "penetration team" composed of a group from within the National Security Agency (NSA) in 1998 and software easily obtained from hacker sites on the Internet, **Operation Eligible Receiver** *demonstrated how easy it would be for computer-efficient cyberterrorists to cripple U.S. military and civilian computer networks.* The simulated attack was run during a two-week period, and the results were "frightening," according to a defense official involved in the simulation. This official noted that this attack, "run by a set of people using standard Internet techniques, would have basically shut down the command-and-control capability in the Pacific theater for some considerable period of time."[1]

The "game" played by the penetration team was simple: They conducted *information warfare attacks,* or **infowar,** on the Pacific Command (and ultimately on the United States) to soften its policies toward the communist regime in North Korea, with the hackers posing as paid agents for North Korea. The "Red Team" of NSA surrogate hackers, using computers, modems, and software technology that is easily accessible on what is often called the "dark side of the Internet" (network-scanning software, intrusion tools, and password-breaking "log-in scripts"), were able to inflict crippling damage. According to news reports, they were able to break into computer networks and gain access to the systems that control the electrical power grid for the United States, giving them the ability, if they had so desired, to disable the power grid and leave the country in darkness.

(continued)

This power knock-out option was only a sideshow: The primary target of the attack was the U.S. Pacific Command, which is in charge of the troops (about 100,000) who would be called on to respond to wars in North Korea or China. According to one defense official involved in the exercise,

The most telling thing for the Department of Defense, when all was said and done, is that basically for a two-week period the command-and-control capability in the Pacific theater would have been denied by the "infowar" attacks, and that was the period of the exercise.[2]

The attacks were not of course run against the infrastructure components since there was no desire to actually shut down a power grid or disable Pacific Command. But the referees monitoring the simulation were shown the attacks and the structures under attack, and they concluded that the attacks would be successful. Moreover, the pseudo-attackers foiled essentially all efforts to trace them, even though the FBI joined the Pentagon in trying to locate them. Only one of the numerous units of NSA groups (one based in the United States) was uncovered. The others operated without being located or identified.

These attacks, run by "friendly" agents working as teams of hackers to penetrate "secure" computer networks, offered useful insights to government officials in the departments of Defense and Justice responsible for the security of such systems. This operation also makes clear the response of the U.S. government in 2003 to a massive power failure in the northeast section of the country, including New York City. Federal agencies were able to announce fairly quickly that this power failure was *not* a terrorist attack, because the parameters for such an attack had already been studied in this operation and did not fit the pattern of the 2003 grid failure. Being able to eliminate the possibility of a security breach as the root of the failure no doubt enabled a more rapid assessment of the real cause and the initiation of appropriate measures to resolve the problem. Thus, security tests cannot only indicate weaknesses in a system; they may also make evaluation of disaster situations at least one step easier. ∎

Source: Center for Defense Information, retrieved from http://www.cdi.org/terrorism/cyberdefense-pr.cfm in October 2011.

CRITICAL INFRASTRUCTURE PROTECTION

With the increased networking of a wide range of public and private systems involved in transportation, banking, energy, and many other entities vital to the stability of industrialized countries, most states had in place an agency or bureau responsible for the protection of such infrastructure before the events of September 11, 2001. According to Presidential Decision Directive 63 in the United States, **critical infrastructures** are *those physical and cyber-based systems essential to the minimum of operations of the economy and government, including "telecommunications, energy, banking and finance, transportation, water systems, and emergency services, both governmental and private."*[3] The

U.S. National Infrastructure Protection Commission, instituted by President Bill Clinton, is charged with providing a national focal point for information gathering on threats to the infrastructure and with coordinating federal responses to incidents of attack, including mitigation efforts and investigation of attacks as well as response and recovery.

Critical infrastructure is a vast and complex network with a multitude of targets that can vary by a wide range of factors, including but not limited to the nature and skills of the group or individual initiating the attack, the country in which the attack occurs, and the vulnerability of the prospective targets at a given time or place. While airports, after the events of September 11, were the focus of U.S. infrastructure protection efforts, other nations have experienced attacks on other transportation systems, cyber networks, energy and water systems, and many critical infrastructures. All of these attacks and potential areas of vulnerability cannot be examined in this text, but a quick look at a few of them will offer insights into the problems of security today.

AIRPORT SECURITY

Nations such as the United States have tried to institute some security measures at one of the favorite targets of terrorism: airports. Even before the September 11 attacks, travelers of commercial airlines in this country were routinely subjected to electronic or manual luggage inspection and to electronic or physical body searches—a practice virtually unknown only a few years before 2001.

Weaknesses in the Security System

The airport security systems in the United States had obvious weaknesses before September 11, 2001. For decades, most security measures against hijacking with conventional weapons were incomplete and poorly enforced. Consider the results of investigations of airport security in several major U.S. airports. Federal auditors testing X-ray procedures for carry-on luggage reported that major airports missed, on the average, about 20 percent of the auditors' dummy weapons. One airport missed 66 percent of these weapons! This was clearly a breakdown in both physical and operational security.

Other surveys taken before the attacks in 2001 suggested that the problem did not lie exclusively with laxity in X-ray procedures. One audit, for instance, found that Los Angeles International Airport could not account for 6,000 employee identification badges. Two thousand were missing at Dulles International Airport near Washington, DC. Obviously, personnel security was also somewhat lax in this industry, contributing to breaches in operational security.

Indeed, experts suggest that airplanes were used as the "weapon" in the September 11 attacks precisely because of convenient flaws that existed within airport and airline security systems of this industry. A quick look at a few of these weaknesses will illuminate the logic of this claim.

Ease of Access to the Cockpit

Because none of the September 11 planes' pilots or copilots informed air traffic controllers that they were being hijacked, and because the planes were turned into "missiles" flown deliberately into buildings on the ground, it seems reasonable to assume the terrorists were able to take over the cockpits. This was probably done with one of three methods: by stealth, by the use of sudden overwhelming force, or by creating a disturbance that drew one of the crew out of the cockpit, thereby creating access to the flight deck for the hijackers.

Taking the cockpit by stealth would require access to a key to the cockpit of the plane. Unfortunately, prior to September 11, every flight attendant was required by the standards of the Federal Aviation Authority (FAA) to carry such a key at all times. On American Flight 11 (the first plane to fly into the World Trade Center [WTC]), one of the flight attendants reported that two other flight attendants had been stabbed. The second plane to fly into the WTC, United Flight 175, also reported that one flight attendant had been stabbed and two had been killed. Since each of these attendants had a key to the cockpit, it is reasonable to assume that the terrorists were able to take the cockpit by stealth.[4]

As one expert notes, prior to the events of September 11, "a normal-sized man with a karate kick or a shoulder shove could have broken down a cockpit door without too much exertion."[5] Numerous examples of this weakness were reported by news agencies, including attacks by a passenger on a Boeing 747-400 British Airways flight from London to Nairobi in December 2000 and by a young couple on a flight in February 2001 from Miami to New York. In these as in so many other cases, the passengers were able to breach the cockpit by force—and neither incident involved a large or well-trained attacker.

Finally, it was possible to take the cockpit by creating a distracting disturbance in the passenger area. This security weakness was possible because pilots were instructed, in the event of a disruptive incident in the passenger cabin, to intervene personally by leaving the cockpit and confronting the disruptive passenger. This instruction may have led to access for the terrorists on September 11. After the United flight crashed into the World Trade Center, the operations center in Chicago sent an electronic text message to the airliners (including United Flight 93) that read: "Beware, cockpit intrusion." This message could have been interpreted by the flight crew as an air rage incident, requiring that the pilot exit the cabin to confront the problem. The pilots responded to confirm receipt of the message, and a few minutes later the plane was taken over by four terrorists. The policy of having the pilot exit the cockpit to confront a disturbance may have facilitated the seizure of the aircraft.

Inadequate Screening Processes

As noted in the earlier account of penetration teams at airports, the screening processes for passengers and luggage prior to the events of September 11 were seriously flawed. Perhaps the most obvious evidence of the flaws in this process lies in the handling of at least half of the nineteen hijackers. Consider these points:

Nine of the hijackers were selected for special security screenings on the morning of September 11. Of these, six were chosen for extra security by a computerized screening system. Two others were singled out because of irregularities in their documents. One was listed on ticket documents as the travel companion to one who had questionable identification.

Yet they were all, in the end, allowed to board their flights, because on September 11, FAA security regulations required that passengers selected for further screening were only required to have their *checked* baggage further evaluated for possible weapons. Since only one or two of the terrorists actually checked any luggage, the security process in place at that time could not detect the weapons in the *carry-on* luggage of the terrorists.[6] Clearly, the process needed refining.

IMPACT OF SEPTEMBER 11 ATTACKS ON U.S. AIRPORT SECURITY

Although airport security clearly had flaws prior to the September 11 attacks, this demonstration of the dreadful consequences of airline hijacking dramatized the issue and forced the government and the industry to rapidly reassess and reorganize to reassure the public. The attacks caused airports across the country to be shut down in an effort to prevent further hijackings. It took several days before the airports could be fully reopened, leaving thousands of passengers stranded at airports at which their flights had been diverted when the closings were ordered.

Moreover, we learned that the September 11 hijackers cased airports in the weeks prior to the attacks and took test runs on flights to identify weaknesses within the system.

Confronted with the task of both reassuring the public that it was safe to fly and immediately taking effective measures to ensure (as far as possible) that such hijackings did not occur again, government and industry took several steps. These included banning curbside check-in of luggage, severely limiting the use of e-tickets, restricting access to areas beyond the security scanning checkpoints to ticketed passengers only, and assigning members of the National Guard to offer visible security at check points.

Not all of these initial steps remained permanent or were even applied at all airports, but they represented a significant effort to improve airport security and the public's perception of that security. At some airports, scrutiny of handbags and carry-on luggage was intense and resulted in the confiscation of fingernail files, pocketknives, letter openers, and a variety of other potential "weapons." Because those who carried out the hijackings in September 2001 apparently did not use guns or other conventional weapons for which baggage handlers had been trained to scan, this represented a serious change in the perception of dangerous personal items on the part of airport personnel.

Moreover, new potential threats continued to emerge, challenging previous patterns of security operations at airports. The potential of explosives in shoes became evident with the attempt of an individual to ignite what appeared to be a fuse attached to his shoes on a flight from Paris. Subsequently, airports at several major points around the country began to require passengers to submit to a scanning of their shoes for explosives.

That the terrorists who seized control of the September 11 airplanes did not initiate a conventional hijacking situation also demonstrated a need to change security patterns. Pilots had been trained to cooperate, if possible, with hijackers in efforts to get them to allow the plane to land in order to offer opportunities for negotiation or hostage-rescue operations. Plane cockpits were seldom equipped with locking systems that would prevent such a takeover of a plane by skilled pilots. Thus, the pilots' training had to be revised, and mechanisms have now been added to most passenger planes that enable the cockpit to be secured from the inside against passengers, if necessary.

The United States struggled with the question as to who should have the task of maintaining internal airport security: private industry or the federal government. Because the attacks on September 11, 2001, were made when airports contracted for their own security personnel with private agencies, the assumption was made that this process was flawed. But both the cost and the practical problems of making airport security a government enterprise are staggering, although it is the route currently being mandated. The hiring and training—including the setting of qualification standards for employment, training regimens, and quality enforcement—have become the responsibility of the federal government, which must also try not to create unemployment problems with its new rules.

In addition, physical security is still not completely effective. Weapons experts have testified before Congress about the possibility of smuggling guns through metal detectors by carrying them on certain spots on the body. Nor are the metal detectors, on which much airline physical security relies, effective at all calibrations. Although some airports now have technology to detect explosive materials, it is expensive and therefore will not be used in all airports. Training in the search for explosive materials, too, is not yet complete. A man whose shoes showed evidence of explosive materials was stopped in January 2002 at the San Francisco airport and then allowed to walk away before security personnel could check him out, resulting in a shutdown of flights for several hours as airport security tried to locate him, without success.

Until after the events on September 11, the United States had no system in place to X-ray checked baggage on domestic flights. The argument was made that the volume of such baggage was too high and that many weapons forbidden in carry-on baggage (for which the current detectors are designed) were still permitted in checked baggage. After September 11, a program to match luggage with passenger flight manifests was instituted, but only for the first check-in point. Unless all checked baggage is tested for weapons and explosives, a person could still get a bomb into a plane in checked luggage if his or her flight had at least one stop where the passenger could disembark, leaving the luggage (and the bomb) on the next leg of the flight. The argument against the more comprehensive scanning and baggage matching scheme continues to be that it is too expensive in terms of time and money, but the Transportation Security Administration (TSA) is working with industries engaged in developing biometric identification technology which could be utilized to facilitate luggage matching. Baggage scanning and matching is not yet mandatory, however.

In an effort to increase physical scrutiny of passengers, the TSA has begun instituting **whole-body image scanning,** *using X-rays or millimeter rays to generate an image of the passenger's body,* for ticketed passengers. This policy continues to spark controversy, as some people object to what they perceive as an invasion of privacy, a slowing-down of the process of check-in, and a problem for those who have medical equipment (e.g., wheelchairs) or conditions (like the need for portable oxygen) which make them ineligible for this process, forcing them instead to have a more intense physical pat-down by airport employees. Each step taken by agencies like the TSA to expand airport security measures continues to generate public resentment without demonstrably making the industry more secure. The multiple events of "stowaways" on commercial flights in the United States in recent times illustrate that security problems remain, in many forms.

CASE STUDY 13.2

Bombs *before* Security Check-Points

On January 24, 2011, at 4:32 P.M., a bomb blast shattered the international arrival section of Domodedovo Airport southwest of Moscow, killing 35 and wounding at least 100 people. The blast, in the arrival hall of the largest air hub in Eastern Europe, which serviced 22.3 million passengers and 75 airlines in 2010, occurred in the area where passengers and friends gather prior to ticketing and security check-in gates.

Like most international airports, Domodedovo Airport has fairly intense passenger and luggage security systems. However, this airport had increased security, because its security was breached in 2004 when terrorists bribed their way through security checks to board two different passenger planes, carrying explosives. Both planes were destroyed, killing all 90 people on board.

The suicide bombing filled Domodedovo's international arrivals hall with dense smoke, sporadic fires, killing passengers and taxi drivers, scattering thick drops of blood across the snow-covered tarmac outside and bits of human flesh on survivors. Casualties included at least nine from other nations, including two British citizens killed and French, German, and Italians injured.

As many as 70 ambulances were deployed to the airport, and casualties were transported on litters and baggage carts to be taken to medical facilities. Some flights landing and departing were delayed or diverted to nearby Sheremetyevo Airport.

Doka Umarov, a militant leader of separatists from the southern Russian region of Chechnya, claimed responsibility for these blasts. This region has been in

(continued)

continuous conflict with Russian leadership since Prime Minister Vladimir Putin launched a war in late 1999 by invading the rebellious republic. Umarov, in a video apparently made the day of the attack, stated that the bombing was carried out on his orders, and that his goal is to form an independent Muslim state governed by Shariah law in the Caucasus region.[7]

Unfortunately, like almost every airport today, there is little if any security system in place to prevent an attack in the open gathering areas prior to passenger ticketing and baggage inspection. This attack was carried out at in an unguarded area, one common to most airports. In the wake of this attack, airport officials in Europe and the United States agreed that it is unlikely that there will be efforts to close nonticketed passengers off from other sections of airports, although some may add increased surveillance and security to areas outside of the security checkpoints. Instead, most agreed that greater information, intelligence, and awareness will be more useful in preventing such attacks than greater security measures. This appears to be a type of attack for which there is no reasonable security measure that can be taken, without massive costs of reconstruction to move security checkpoints at the very entrances to the airport—which would not necessarily prevent a determined suicide attacker in a car at the passenger drop-off point. ■

Source: Retrieved in January 2011 from http://www.reuters.com/article/2011/01/24/us-russia-blast-airport-idUSTRE70N2TQ20110124

While aspects of increased airport security are potentially controversial measures involving some invasion of privacy and some searches without a warrant of persons not accused of any crime, few citizens today have serious objections to these measures. Even the presence of air marshals on randomly selected flights and the use of National Guard troops for airport security were accepted with complacency by most citizens, perhaps in recognition of the fact that the threat to their lives and property created by a terrorist is greater than that incurred in airline security measures.

Security, of course, offers only a measure of protection in one country against one type of terrorism. If similar measures are not universally applied in airports throughout the world, then the potential for skyjacking or bombing remains substantial.[8] Moreover, even measures in the United States until late in 2001 focused primarily on preventing the hijacking of airlines with the use of conventional weapons; most of these measures were clearly inappropriate in terms of security preparations for the events of September 11.

PROTECTING OTHER FORMS OF PUBLIC TRANSPORTATION

Public transportation networks in large cities are enticing targets for terrorists because they typically carry large numbers of people; they move in concentrated, predictable geographic areas under routine time frames; and they are highly accessible, since they are "public service" operations, and cannot be hardened easily against their primary users—the general public.

Thus, in terms of physical, personnel, and operational security, public transportation is an attractive target for those seeking to reach a large audience and disrupt a system with little effort. The U.S. State Department, in its record of international terrorist attacks in 1996, noted that 92 of these—almost a third—were against transportation and transportation infrastructures. While European, Middle Eastern, and Asian countries rely much more heavily on their public transit systems than the United States and have consequently developed more expertise in protecting these systems, officials were unable to prevent the sarin gas attack on the Tokyo subway in 1995, the bombings of trains in Madrid in 2004, the bombs on buses and subways in London in 2005, or the explosives on the trains in Mumbai in 2006.

CASE STUDY 13.3

London Transport Attacks 2005

At 0:58 A.M. on July 7, 2005, three bombs exploded within fifty seconds on the London Underground, the first on the eastbound Circle Line, the second on the westbound Circle Line, and the third on a southbound Piccadilly Line. Because the blasts occurred on the trains when they were between stations, causing the wounded to emerge from both stations, there was initial confusion as to the number of bombs detonated. A Code Amber Alert was declared at 9:19 A.M., and the London Underground began to shut down the network, bringing all trains into stations to halt all services.

At 9:47 A.M., an explosion occurred in Tavistock Square on a No. 30 double-decker bus traveling from Marble Arch to Hackney Wick. The bus had stopped at the Easton bus station, where crowds of people had been evacuated from the London Underground and were boarding buses, and was near the British Medical Association building. Fifty-six people were killed, including the four suicide bombers, and about 700 were injured in the four bombing attacks, the deadliest bombings in Britain since World War II.

Homemade organic peroxide-based devices were used, according to a May 2006 report from the British government's Intelligence and Security Committee. The explosive used was found to be chapatti flour powder mixed with liquid hydrogen peroxide, detonated by a booster charge.[9]

The four men responsible for the attacks were identified as suicide bombers, making the July 7 attack the first incident of suicide bombings in Western Europe. The bombings in Madrid the previous year had not been suicide attacks; those bombs had been set off by cell phones and the loss of life had been much greater (191 people killed by 10 bombs that destroyed four commuter trains during rush hour). The bombers in the London attacks were identified by British authorities as Muslim men ranging in age from 18 to 30, each of whom detonated one of the bombs while on the transport.

(continued)

The bombers were British citizens who had grown up or been born in Britain and were primarily from middle-class families and relatively stable environments. The oldest one, Mohammed Sadique Khan, was married and had a baby daughter. Although none had demonstrated any indication of discernable radicalism before the attacks, surveillance tapes (ubiquitous in London) indicated that the four bombers met with an apparent coordinator before initiating the attacks.[10]

In the wake of the Madrid and London transportation system attacks, other nations considered measures designed to increase non-airport-related transportation security. In the United States, Congress considered calls for sharp increases in spending on rail security, protection for chemical and nuclear power plants, and support for first responders. However, since this type of attack had not yet occurred on U.S. soil, Congress also reflected a loss of support for the more intrusive features of the U.S.A. PATRIOT Act, including the lowering of the standards for search warrants and the FBI to seize library and health records in a terrorism investigation; measures that were slated to "sunset" (disappear) in December of that year, unless renewed. Under §224 of the Act, several of the surveillance portions originally expired on December 31, 2005. These were later renewed, but expired again on March 10, 2006, and were renewed once more in 2010. ■

Source: National Institute of Justice website, retrieved from http://www.nij.gov/journals/261/coordination.htm in October 2011.

Attempts to share learning experiences and technologies have evolved among some of the nations with a shared interest in this security threat. The G-8 (Canada, France, Germany, Great Britain, Italy, Japan, the United States, and Russia) have met many times to discuss the need for cooperation. On July 30, 1996, these nations met at the Lyons Summit in France, adopting a 25-point plan for international cooperation to combat terrorist acts. Based on the progress made at this summit, two further meetings focused on land transportation security were held in Washington, DC, in 1996 and 1997. In April 1998, domestic and international presenters (primarily from the G-8) met in Atlanta, Georgia, to discuss current and emerging terrorist threats, results from case studies, lessons learned and techniques developed due to terrorist actions, and new technologies useful in protecting land transportation systems. Some of the developing technologies discussed at this meeting, potentially of particular service in this target area, included weapons detection systems that could identify a weapon containing little or no metal at a distance of 30 feet; less-than-lethal incapacitation technologies that are both legal and socially acceptable (e.g., laser dazzlers, pyrotechnic devices, enhanced pepper-spray delivery systems, and net devices); and sniper fire identification systems, capable of detecting and locating a sniper within a 10-by-10-foot area of an urban environment.[11] In the wake of September 11, regional as well as national counter-terrorism centers began to host meetings to facilitate a more global response to the threat of terrorism.

Cooperation between states is indispensable in the effort to provide security for land transportation systems. The techniques and equipment developed by other nations, if shared, may make future attacks on these vulnerable targets more difficult. But, as the officials at these meetings noted more than once, security for such accessible targets is not possible without a loss of freedom unacceptable to democracies. Furthermore, the events of September 11, 2001, demonstrated that cooperation came *after* the terrorist event, not before, and thus did not prevent the attack but made capture of others involved possible.

PORT SECURITY

In the DHS, the Customs and Border Protection unit is responsible for cargo security in U.S. ports. It bases its cargo security strategy on two programs: the **Container Security Initiative** (CSI) and the **Customs-Trade Partnership Against Terrorism**, *programs built on the premise that their purpose would be best served by keeping terrorists and their weapons as far away as possible, effectively "pushing the borders out" by stationing U.S. customs inspectors at foreign seaports to target and oversee potentially dangerous cargo before it begins its journey to the United States.* CSI began operations in January 2002 and by October 2005 had operations in 40 foreign ports—ports which account for about 79 percent of the maritime cargo sent to the United States each year.

Under CSI, containers are "targeted," which does not mean that they are inspected but that they are assessed to determine the level of risk that each poses to the security of the homeland. This targeting process, called the "Automated Targeting System," or ATS, is unfortunately not that effective, according to the Government Accounting Office, because the information on which the ATS is based is insufficient to determine with any degree of assurance a given container's level of risk.[12] ATS is based on manifests of cargo containers that are often too general to be of much use in making a determination of suspicious contents. Moreover, such manifests can be changed for up to sixty days *after* the shipments arrive in the United States, raising serious questions about their reliability when generated for ATS.

Consider for a moment those high-risk shipments that are inspected by foreign inspectors using either "intrusive" (to stop and open) or "nonintrusive" methods (scanning with X-ray or gamma-ray equipment). Radiation detection devices can also be used, but there are problems. Different kinds of potentially deadly radioactive material vary in the degree of ease with which they can be detected: The kind of radiation used in a "dirty bomb" is easily detected as it is highly radioactive; highly enriched uranium, however, is hard to detect because it gives off little radiation and it is often packed in shielding, making it harder still to detect.

In spite of the "Megaports Initiative" enacted by the U.S. Department of Energy to provide major international seaports with radiation detection equipment, it is unclear whether any of the CSI ports have any of the three potential devices. Only two CSI ports—one in Greece and one in the Netherlands—have Radiation Portal Monitors, which can detect and pinpoint radiation. This lack of detection equipment enabled ABC News to carry out not one but *two* successful experiments in smuggling a steel pipe containing a 15-pound cylinder of depleted uranium shielded with lead from a CSI port to one in the United States. In both experiments, which were carried out a year apart on the anniversaries of the attacks of September 2001, customs inspectors duly inspected the cargo as it had been targeted as a potential risk, but failed to find the uranium. Clearly, the CSI has many flaws and remains a questionable tool for security of U.S. ports against the import of terrorist weapons.

PREVENTIVE SECURITY

Security has not been exclusively concerned with the hardening of targets that terrorists may—or may not—select today. Some efforts are also being directed at what has been termed *preventive security*, meaning the making of terrorist attacks themselves less likely.

One such security technique in use today involves efforts to tag and trace various weapon components. There exist **taggants**—*chemically identifiable trace agents*—for many types of explosives today. It is also possible, although not as easy, to use **trace detectors** for chemical agents, which would enable security agents *to detect the presence of dangerous or hazardous chemicals in innocuous-looking containers*.

The use of tagging devices and trace elements for portable rocket security, in addition to more complete inventory control measures, is also under advisement. The advantage in the use of taggants, in addition to an ability to detect certain substances, is their ability to determine the country and sometimes even the company of origin. Although this would not necessarily be of immediate use in preventing terrorist attacks, it would be of considerable use in determining responsibility, perhaps making such future attacks less likely.

However, companies and countries manufacturing such materials, from explosives to handguns, from nuclear to chemical and biological weapons, have resisted many attempts to institute a comprehensive tagging effort. Most have argued that laws requiring such security measures violate the rights of businesses engaged in lawful enterprises.

Political reality has made it clear that nations cherish their right to sell arms to whomever they please, under whatever conditions they deem advisable. Even nations that have made no secret of the fact that they sponsor terrorist groups with arms and war materiel have little difficulty securing those arms on the world arms market.

Arms are increasingly available to anyone with the money (or a moneyed sponsor) to pay for them. This makes the efforts to limit terrorist access to weapons as a form of preventive terrorism largely futile. What terrorists cannot purchase legally on the open arms market they can procure illegally on the black market. Fake end-user certificates are readily available from several countries, such as Nigeria.

Moreover, it is difficult in the shadow world of illegal arms sales to use most preventive measures effectively. Shell companies, Swiss bank accounts, and the routing of weapons from country to country three or four times to hide the country of origin make the labyrinth of arms deals difficult to penetrate with regulation or preventive action.

The use of taggants might make tracing the country of origin feasible (even through the maze of sale and resale), but it is also highly probable that nations winking at such sales by their industries are going to be unwilling to force those industries to institute measures that might make it easier for a finger to be pointed accurately at violators of arms agreements. For monetary reasons they may have tacitly agreed to the sales; for political reasons they do not want such arms sales easily traced home. Preventing terrorism becomes in such cases less crucial than being held accountable for violation of arms control laws and agreements.

The issue of arms sales becomes particularly critical when the arms being sold are nonconventional weapons. The growing threat of chemical, biological, and nuclear weapons in the hands of terrorists willing and able to use them will be discussed in Chapter 14.

THE COSTS OF SECURITY

The costs of such antiterrorism measures are high, materially as well as politically. Unfortunately, a great deal more money is required to erect defenses against terrorist attacks than to commit such acts.

If the cost of defending just one industry against attack is high, then the cost of erecting coordinated international defenses against a multitude of types of terrorist attacks may well be prohibitive. The protection of specific targets, including air transport facilities, against terrorists would be a mammoth task. It is also a task which would not in itself be sufficient to secure entire nations and populations against terrorist attacks of all kinds.

The difficulty, as Robert Kupperman noted, is that potential targets for terrorist attacks are not limited to airports. As he pointed out, there are numerous vulnerable targets in our sophisticated society. Electrical power systems, for example, are very tempting as accessible targets. A well-placed bomb or shots from a high-powered rifle could conceivably cause a blackout in an entire city. The same is true about the potential for destructive attacks on telecommunication systems, gas pipelines, dams, water systems, and nuclear power plants.

Kupperman also noted that, with the extensive reliance on computer information systems—for banking, credit cards, real estate, and so forth—that now characterizes industrial societies, the potential for economic disruption by terrorist attacks on those systems may also be substantial. As any computer hacker knows, no matter how carefully a computer system's security may be designed, a blend of time, patience, knowledge, and a little bit of luck will usually suffice to break into it. The potential of cyberterror, using computers to destroy banking systems, public records, even water purification systems, presents a serious threat to many industries in the twenty-first century.

Concern has surfaced too over the protection of oil rigs in international waters. There are hundreds of oil rigs in the Gulf of Mexico and a growing number in the North Sea, all of which are vulnerable to terrorist attacks. Recent movies and novels depicting attacks on such rigs serve to highlight the plausibility of this potential disaster.

The oil industry, so vital to modern economies, is particularly open to attack, according to some experts, not only at drilling operations but at a variety of other points. Although established petroleum and natural gas operations, their pipeline interstices, and associated tanks and storage facilities have been the most attractive targets to date, there are many other points at which this industry is vulnerable, as events in the war in Iraq and terrorist attacks in Saudi Arabia demonstrated.

An attack on a North Sea oil rig, for example, would not only affect the cost of oil in Britain (and any nations that Britain supplies), but it could damage the fishing industries of the countries bordering the North Sea as well. A successful attack on the computerized international banking system could have serious consequences for many national economies. The poisoning of a water supply in one nation could affect other nations that share the use of that poisoned river or lake.

Just as no nation can entirely protect itself from terrorism by securing all potential terrorist targets, it is probably impossible for any nation, acting alone, to prevent or control the flow of weapons to terrorists. If targets cannot be fully protected, the next logical security step may be an effort to curb the number and types of instruments of destruction available to terrorists. But again, the vast array of security measures required are staggering.

Some of the security measures in place or under consideration involve what is called **hardening the target,** which *involves efforts to make targets less accessible.* These include the installation of metal detectors and X-ray machines at points of entry, the use of sensor or closed-circuit TV to monitor access ways, and other similar technical devices. Such measures can also include the erection of fences, vision barriers, and heavy barriers around the perimeters of an installation. Related security measures can involve increased use of such items as armored cars, security guard forces, and bulletproof vests. An increasing number of executives are enrolling employees in expensive **training programs** designed *to teach skills in such things as high-speed car chases, surviving a kidnapping, and how not to look like a businessman traveling abroad.*

Indeed, companies offering to help make a business or a businessman more secure from terrorism have proliferated. One enterprising woman launched a business in 1987 that offered fake passports from nonexistent countries. Most of her clients were military men and businessmen traveling in the Middle East, South America, and Europe. Donna Walker, president of International Documents Service, pointed out, "When you're up against a bunch of gun-waving crazies, you should have an option"—such as a passport that does not label you as an American.[13]

Whether such exercises in protecting the target are useful or not, they continue to generate both interest and money for the companies providing them. What is not clear is the extent to which they offer real protection against a terrorist attack that is commensurate with the money expended on them.

Nor is it clear whether such measures are either legal or acceptable in a democratic society. Fake passports could be used by criminals to baffle legitimate customs officials. The erection of heavy barriers and guards around public buildings, although perhaps necessary to protect them from attack, is still unpopular with a democratic public accustomed to easy access to, for example, its nation's capitol buildings. It is, as the United States found in the wake of the Oklahoma City bombing, neither popular nor practical to harden all buildings that have federal offices against the public that they serve. Similarly, even though the general public supports as a whole the *idea* of strengthening airport security in the wake of September 11, 2001, people still do not want to wait longer or pay more for tickets in order to achieve that enhanced security.

THREAT AND RISK ASSESSMENT

How do nations or businesses decide what threats are of the most concern, how vulnerable they are to these threats, and which of their operations or activities are likely at risk to terrorist attacks? Each of these aspects—threat and risk—needs to be considered carefully, as the cost of preparing for and responding to terrorist attack today grows.

Threat Assessment

Nations and individuals use three types of indicators to assess the potential threat of terrorism. These can be described as general threat indicators, local threat indicators, and specific threat indicators. Let us look briefly at each of these types of indicators.

General threat indicators are used to *determine whether, within the nation or state, there exist conditions that might stimulate or provoke terrorism.* Such indicators are of little use in predicting the likelihood of a specific terrorist attack. Instead, they are used to assess the climate—political, ideological, religious, and so on—that might influence the willingness of a portion of the population to resort to terrorism. Politically, for example, the presence of an unpopular, repressive, or corrupt government is considered a positive indicator of the probability of terrorism. Similarly, an economic climate that includes extreme poverty and/or high unemployment is regarded as conducive to terrorism. Wars of occupation or invasions can also generate attacks within the country participating in the occupation of another, or in what is perceived as the invasion of another, as indicated by the suicide bombing attacks in London and the Madrid bombing attacks.

This does not mean that any nation or region experiencing these political or economic conditions will necessarily have a large degree of terrorism. It simply means that the presence of such conditions makes the likelihood of terrorism greater in such places than it might be in areas that do not have similar political or economic climates. These are only indicators, not predictors of terrorism. For instance, one geopolitical indicator has been the concentration of large foreign populations within a nation. In occupied territories or in nations involved in border disputes, such populations have been useful indicators of the probability of terrorism as proven each year by Israel, its occupied territories, and Palestine.

Local threat indicators are used *to assess more specific and localized possibilities for terrorism.* Usually, such indicators focus on the forms that dissent tends to take on the local level and the degree of violence involved in the expression of such dissent. The formation of radical groups; reports of stolen firearms, ammunition, and explosives; violence against local property, including looting and arson; violence against individuals, including murders, beatings, threats, and abductions; and the discovery of weapon, ammunition, and explosives caches are considered local threat indicators. Again, this does not mean that any radical group that forms must necessarily be a terrorist threat, nor that any demonstration against a government or a company must be the prelude to a terrorist attack. High-profile events with a high concentration of spectators, often attractive and accessible targets for terrorists, should also be on the local threat indicator list. These are just some indicators of the possibility of terrorism in a particular location.

Specific threat indicators are used *to evaluate the vulnerability of a particular target to terrorism,* not the likelihood of terrorism in a nation or neighborhood. These indicators include such things as the history of attacks on similar targets, the publicity value of the target, the target's access to infiltration, its counterterror capability and its communications capability, the tactical attractiveness of the target, and the availability of the police or other security personnel. Some of these indicators are essentially judgment calls, such as the determination as to whether the industry involves a "sensitive" installation, which is generally used to refer to a nuclear, chemical, or other similar facility. Others are very easily quantified, such as the population density in the immediate area.

Risk of Terrorist Attacks

Risk, in terms of terrorist attacks, is *the expected lives lost, persons injured, property damaged, and economic activity disrupted due to a terrorist attack.* **Risk management,** then, *is the estimation of the magnitude of a particular risk and an evaluation of how important the risk is.* There are two components to this: **risk assessment,** *the quantification of the risk from data to generate a risk probability;* and **risk evaluation,** *the judgment that a society places on the risks that face them in determining what to do about the risks.* Each of these elements of risk will be examined briefly.

The first part of risk management—risk assessment—involves assessing the probability of a terrorist event happening in a location or region and follows three steps: determining the probability of such an attack; identifying the elements at risk; and assessing the potential damage to individuals, businesses, and society as a whole if such an attack occurred. Data on terrorism attacks over time in each region of the world as well as the number and types of groups or cells in those regions do not exist in a single databank, but in many different locations and, therefore, is not always therefore compatible. Since the definition of terrorism differs widely, the data centers gathering information about groups, individuals, cells, and attacks will (and do) include differing data. In the United States alone, many different terrorism databases have evolved, including the Global Terrorism Database created at the National Consortium for the Study of Terrorism and Responses to Terrorism Center established by the DHS at the University of Maryland, the FBI's Domestic Terrorism reports, and the National Counterterrorism Center's dataset. Each uses a different definition of events tracked and limitations regions covered. Lacking consistency, domestically and internationally, the ability to quantify accurately the risk of terrorist attack remains challenging.

The second part of risk assessment—identifying and making an inventory of the persons, property, commerce, or systems at risk which would be affected if a terrorist incident occurred, and estimating the cost involved to each potential target—is also a challenging but vital task. As discussed in earlier chapters, the list of potential targets for terrorist attacks is quite long, and still growing. Certain types of buildings that are essential to a nation's infrastructure—banks, transportation centers, government buildings, energy hubs, water treatment plants, and many others—have been identified either by having been victims of such attacks or threatened by attacks at some time.

The final part of risk assessment entails using the identification of potential targets as a basis from which to estimate the cost of both the loss (for a period of time) and the replacement of these facilities or systems in the event of an attack. Again, mathematical formulas, which can facilitate the estimation of such costs, are often generated, but there exists as yet no universal formula to make this task easier on local, state, or national authorities.

Risk evaluation, the last part of risk management, is not numerically based, but requires a value judgment that a society places on the risks that face it. This evaluation of the risk of terrorism is impacted by the type and level of other risks that a society faces daily. Since most societies face multiple risks each day—of natural disasters, of accidents and criminal behaviors, and any other dangers—terrorism is not always evaluated as the greatest threat, unless or until an incident of some magnitude occurs to disrupt the daily patterns of life.

Moreover, in democratic societies the risk of losing liberties and rights in efforts to counter terrorist attacks is often evaluated as a greater risk than that of the potential for such an attack. Thus, the cost of eliminating one type of risk—terrorist attack—is judged to be too high if it entails serious infringements on those rights and liberties in an attempt by the government to mitigate the likelihood (and thereby reduce the risk) of such an attack.

None of the indicators can be said to predict the probability of a terrorist attack, nor can risk analysis necessarily generate the political will to take mitigating actions. Nevertheless, government and industry are beginning to rely increasingly on such indicators and risk analysis measures to help them decide what, if any, terrorist threat exists, what direction such attacks may take, and what actions should or could be taken to reduce the risks. With the spiraling cost of installing, staffing, and maintaining security systems, no one is eager to spend more than is warranted on protection against a threat that

CASE STUDY 13.4

Allocating Resources Based on Threat and Risk Assessment

Threat and risk assessment is a vital part of counterterrorism. The threat of terrorism is seldom fully understood or appreciated until a catastrophic event occurs, and then the demand for "government action" to remedy the vulnerabilities may generate legislation or the use of force, which may be counterproductive. It certainly would be wiser to mitigate as far as possible, without damage to civil rights and liberties, the vulnerability of targets to attack.

Using this logic, the DHS offers grants to state, local, and tribal governments to prevent, protect against, respond to, and recover from terrorist attacks (as well as natural disasters). The allocations are risk-based in three of the grant programs: Urban Areas Security Initiative, State Homeland Security Program, and Law Enforcement Terrorism Prevention Program (LETPP). The risk model for these grants considers the potential risk of terrorism to people, critical infrastructure, and the economy to estimate the relative risk of terrorism in a given area, using the three elements discussed earlier: the likelihood of an attack (probability), the relative exposure to an attack (vulnerability), and the expected impact (cost) of an attack.

The DHS risk analysis is based on a methodology using factors such as the Intelligence Community's best assessment of areas of the country and potential targets most likely to be attacked; the potentially affected populations; the economic impact of an attack; the presence of infrastructure that is considered critical to the nation; and other key national security concerns. More than $12 billion have been allocated by the DHS since it began this process in 2002.[14] To some extent, the successful thwarting of at least 19 terrorist attacks against the United States domestically since September 2001 can be attributed to these efforts by the DHS in threat and risk assessment. ■

Source: US Dept of Justice, "Assessing and Managing the Threat of Terrorism." Accessed from https://www.ncjrs.gov/pdffiles1/bja/210680.pdf.

may never materialize. But at the same time, few are willing to risk remaining unsecured where strong indications exist that terrorist attacks may cripple or destroy costly facilities and irreplaceable lives.

CONCLUSIONS

The question is how much a company, a government, or people are willing to sacrifice in order to achieve greater security from terrorist attacks. For some, as long as the attack happens to "somebody else," the sacrifice of rights to prevent terrorism will always seem too high a price. To others, the prevention of terrorism will justify the loss of precious rights and freedoms. Governments trying to strike a delicate balance between the need for their citizens to be secure and the need to protect their citizens' rights have an increasingly difficult task.

Terrorism is fundamentally an attack on the state. Just as offshore maritime terrorism is a crime waiting to happen, terrorism with nuclear, biological, or chemical weapons is an international disaster waiting to occur. Neither national nor international security measures have proved adequate in terms of either protecting targets or preventing the dissemination of such agents of mass destruction.

As governments and industries come to grips with the rocketing costs of securing themselves against terrorism, serious questions continue to be raised concerning the priority that security should have in the allocation of resources. However real the terrorist threat may be, few are willing as yet to meet the exorbitant costs, both political and economic, of providing adequate security against that threat. The costs that the United States is incurring in the wake of September 11, 2001, are enormous; to date it is not clear how long the general public will support the continued use of finite government resources, in a time of recession, to meet the threat of terrorism. Consider the threat today to what is termed *cyber security,* noting the "costs" associated with such security.

CASE STUDY 13.5

Cyber Security and Cyberterror

In April 2007, the government of Estonia (a nation occupied by the former Soviet Union for much of the cold war) moved a controversial Soviet-era World War II memorial from a central location in the capital city of Tallinn to a more secluded location, angering Russia and the large Russian population in Estonia. Weeks of cyber attacks followed, targeting government and private Internet sites. Some of the attacks took the form of **distributed denial of service (DDoS) attacks,** *in which hundreds or thousands of "zombie" computers were used by hackers to pelt Estonian websites with thousands of requests per second, boosting Internet traffic well beyond normal capacity levels.*

These attacks shut down some Estonian sites for a time, "denying services" to those who truly needed them. The government did not lose any infrastructure, but combating the events was time-consuming, expensive, and highlighted the weakness of a modern "wired" country to such cyber threats.

The actual attacks in Estonia occurred a year after several countries began to assess the risk of such attacks in order to plan strategically to meet this challenge. *In early February 2006, the United States and 115 partners, including major corporations, government agencies, and security organizations from the United States and five other countries, conducted a group of cyber war games labeled as* **Cyber Storm.** This exercise was designed to test the effects of cyber attacks against government, business, and private Internet sites. The fake attacks in this simulation caused blackouts in 10 states, infected commercial software with viruses, and caused important online banking networks to fail.

(continued)

As cyber attack scenarios and real cyber attacks increase awareness of this security threat, the United States has created a "first-responder" network to cope, including members of intelligence agencies, the Department of Defense, and the military (particularly the military's special unit at Barksdale Air Force Base in Louisiana, where 25,000 of its members work on electronic warfare, network security, and defending the country's Internet infrastructure). This **US-CERT**, *the United States Computer Emergency Preparedness team established in 2003,* is responsible for protecting and defending the nation's Internet infrastructure from attack.[15]

In May 2009, President Barack Obama announced the creation of a cyber security chief's office as part of his national cyber security strategy, without immediately appointing anyone to that office. In June of that year, Gordon Brown, prime minister of the United Kingdom, appointed his first national cyber security chief, announcing that work was continuing on a national cyber security plan and that a major exercise would take place later in the year to test the country's ability to withstand a serious attack on its communications network.

The attacks on Estonia demonstrated that cyber attacks can happen, and they can be costly. This would certainly be true if hackers could shut off power supplies or infiltrate a major banking system or disrupt the stock market. So far, most of the hackers who have initiated attack have at worst gained entry or carried out DDoS damage without carrying out actual damage while "inside" the system. But the learning curve for carrying out such attacks may be much smaller than that of protecting against such acts; hackers—or terrorists—need win this technology only once to cause potentially catastrophic damage to a system. ■

Source: Cyberterrorism Defense Analysis Center's website http://www.cyberterrorismcenter.org.

Protecting technology from cyber attacks has become a priority in many nations' homeland security initiatives. For many countries, almost every aspect of existence is dependent on reliable and secure technology. Accurate data are vital for everything from medical care to air traffic control, and without the increasingly important Internet for communication and marketing and the power sources that make the technology work, many national systems would be, as one expert notes, "dead in the water."[16] While nations continue to spend vast sums on physical security threats, protecting the core digital infrastructure has only recently come to the top of security agendas.

Unlike the issues raised with intelligence gathering and investigative counterterrorism measures, most security measures costs in the United States are reckoned less in terms of political ideals such as civil liberties than in terms of convenience, and more important, money. Until terrorism seriously pinches the pocketbook of nations and businesses, that pocketbook will be slow to open to defeat or prevent that "pinch." Once that pinch is felt, however, the willingness to pay may allow significant steps in security at airports, water systems, nuclear power plants, and many other vulnerable points to evolve.

DISCUSSION

Making a decision to take on the cost—in economic, political, and public relations terms—of installing and enforcing security systems is seldom easy. Rarely is there a clear indicator that makes such a decision effortless or obvious. Governments and industries continue to wrestle with the problems, and while their solutions seldom satisfy everyone, it is often difficult to state unequivocally what they should do in a given situation.

Consider the following cases, and try to formulate an appropriate response. Remember to take into account both the monetary and political costs of any decision. Could you justify your decision to a corporate board or an irate citizen in terms of cost-effectiveness? That is, does the security measure that you may recommend pay for itself in terms of the security gained in a way that would recommend itself to a stockholder or taxpayer?

1. In spite of the deaths caused by the bombings in the airport in Russia in early 2011, most airport officials and security experts agree that creating additional checkpoints before the passenger ticketing areas is not a feasible solution, due to both cost and public resistance to the inconvenience. Instead, many suggest that better intelligence gathering and more general scrutiny for intelligence purposes would be a better tool in preventing such attacks. The choice, then, is between enhancing intelligence-gathering capabilities or enhancing physical security as the primary counterterrorism weapon in this situation. Which do you believe would be more effective? Using either the Rational Actor or the Operational Model of decision making (discussed in Chapter 12), which is the best policy decision for Western democracies to make on this issue?

2. The 2004 bombings of the trains in Madrid, Spain, were clearly timed to impact the upcoming national elections, which they did. As other nations approach similarly critical transition points in their national government, should additional security be taken to prevent such incidents, or should the events be postponed or cancelled? What types of targets should be protected? Will any type of security really be effective if individuals or groups engaged in a crusade are determined to carry out such attacks? Should public events, such as the Olympics or other types of international sports competitions, be restricted, postponed, or cancelled due to security concerns?

3. Technology that can detect plastic explosives now exists and is used in some airports. The equipment is based on the detection of plastic and is similar to a metal detector but is much more expensive (about $1 million per unit). Because it was a plastic explosive that caused the destruction of the flight over Lockerbie, Scotland, in 1989, this seems an important technological breakthrough. But in order to detect the amount of plastic material used in the Lockerbie bombing, the machine's calibrations would have to be set so low (since it was a small amount) that the machine would detect every credit card that passengers had in their wallets. Setting it high enough not to set off an alarm for every credit card and driver's license (with the ensuing passenger frustration and endless delays) would mean that the Lockerbie bomb would not have been detected by the machine. Even though they are very expensive, should airports be required to have such devices to prevent the bombing of an airplane? How low should the calibrations on the machines be set—low enough to detect the Lockerbie-type bomb, even though to set it that low would mean long lines and much passenger frustration

at having to surrender, even for a moment, credit cards? What if the airport cannot afford the machines? Should the government provide them, as well as training for the security personnel to use them? How real does the threat of a bomb on a plane have to be before the security devices and the ensuing hassles are worth the trouble and the cost?

4. **Shoot-ats** are incidents in which in-flight aircraft (commercial and general or charter planes) are fired at from the ground (generally by SAMs, antiaircraft artillery, or small arms fire), or from the air. In November 2002, an Israeli charter jet was shot at by two SA-7s (SAMs) as it was traversing over Mombasa, Kenya. In May 2002, a U.S. military aircraft experienced a shoot-at by an al-Qaeda member also using an SA-7. Can commercial passenger aircraft be secured against this type of attack? What would it cost? Should such protection be mandatory for all civilian aircraft? Who would pay for it?

5. There were reports in 2004 that American troops in Iraq had discovered two CDs containing photographs, an evacuation plan, and other crisis management-related information regarding eight school districts in six U.S. states. Although authorities asserted that there was at that time no link to terrorism found, it raised serious concerns. The deadly siege of a school in Beslan, Russia, by Chechen rebels, claiming the lives of 340 people (most of whom were children), was featured in the news at the time, highlighting fears in the United States of attacks on schools. Claims by al-Qaeda to "the right to kill four million Americans, including one million children" raised levels of concern. Are American schools potential targets for terrorist attacks? Should security at schools, both public and private, be a priority, infringing if it must on individual liberties of students? What type of security—personnel, physical, or operational—would be most effective and least disruptive for most schools to institute?

ANALYSIS CHALLENGE

Cost of security measures today have become a "hot topic" of intense political debate. As concerns about security increase, the need to consider both the costs and the benefits of security measures becomes of critical public interest. The costs of such measures can be operationalized in terms of both direct and indirect costs, of the mitigation/security measures implemented and of the attack itself. The "benefits" of such security is less easily quantified, but equally important. Visit one of the following websites, and use a framework suggested to assess the costs and benefits of a specific security measure (at an airport, at a country border, for a shopping mall, for a business) that you believe will be "beneficial" to the community.

http://www.homelandsecurity.org/DHSUnivSummit2011/Rose_Chaterjee_%20
    White%20Paper_09May11.pdf
http://terrorism.about.com/od/issuestrends/a/EconomicImpact.htm

KEY TERMS

physical security   301
penetration teams   301
operational security   302
personnel security   302

Operation Eligible
    Receiver   303
infowar   303
critical infrastructures   304

whole-body image
    scanning   309
Container Security
    Initiative   313

SUGGESTED READINGS AND RESOURCES

Baer, Martha, Katrina Heron, Oliver Morton, and Evan Ratliff. *Safe: The Race to Protect Ourselves in a Newly Dangerous World.* New York: HarperCollins, 2005.

Ervin, Clark Kent. *Open Target: Where America Is Vulnerable to Attack.* New York: Palgrave Macmillan, 2006.

Howard, Russell D., and Reid L. Sawyer. *Defeating Terrorism: Shaping the New Security Environment.* Guilford, CT: McGraw-Hill, 2004.

"Jane's Terrorism and Security Monitor." http://jtsm.janes.com/public/jtsm/index.shtml

Laqueur, Walter. "Postmodern Terrorism." *Foreign Affairs,* 75, no. 5 (September/October 1996): 24–36.

Liddy, G. Gordon. *Fight Back: Tackling Terrorism, Liddy Style.* New York: St. Martin's Press, 2006.

National Strategy for the Physical Protection of Critical Infrastructures and Key Assets. Department of Homeland Security. Retrieved from http://www.dhs.gov/xlibrary/assets/Physical_Strategy.pdf

Thomas, Andrew R. *Aviation Insecurity: The New Challenges of Air Travel.* Amherst, NY: Prometheus Books, 2003.

Wallis, Rodney. *Combating Air Terrorism.* Dulles, VA: Potomac Books, 1998.

NOTES

1. Bill Gertz, "NSA's Operation Eligible Receiver," *Washington Times*, April 17, 1998. Retrieved from http://www.landfield.com/isn/mail-archive/1998/Apr/0089.html.

2. Ibid., 2.

3. Testimony of Ronald L. Dick, Director, National Infrastructure Protection Center, FBI Before the House Committee on Governmental Reform, Government Efficiency, Financial Management and Intergovernmental Relations Subcommittee. "Cyber Terrorism and Critical Infrastructure Protection." July 24, 2002. Retrieved from http://www.fbi.gov/congress/congress02/nipc072402.htm (accessed June 22, 2009).

4. Andrew R. Thomas, *Aviation Insecurity: The New Challenges of Air Travel* (Amherst, New York: Prometheus Books, 2003), 33.

5. Ibid., 37.

6. Ibid., 38–39.

7. "Explosion at Moscow Airport." http://www.newsweek.com/2011/01/24/explosion-at-moscow-airport.html (accessed July 11, 2011).

8. One CIA official (who requested anonymity) noted that in many less developed nations, the lack of any real security at airports constitutes "a terrorist attack waiting to happen."

9. "Report into the London Terrorist Attacks on 7 July 2005," Intelligence and Security Committee (May 2006). Retrieved from http://news.bbc.co.uk/1/shared/bsp/hi/pdfs/11_05_06_isc_london_attacks_report.pdf

10. "London terror attacks, July 7, 2005," Cindy Combs and Martin Slann, eds. *Encyclopedia of Terrorism*, Revised Edition (New York: Facts on File, 2006), 177–79.

11. "Protecting Public Transportation from Terrorists," *National Institute of Justice Journal* (March 1998): 17–24.

12. Clark Kent Ervin, *Open Target: Where America Is Vulnerable to Attack* (New York: Palgrave Macmillan, 2006), 121.

13. Walter Laqueur, "Postmodern Terrorism," *Foreign Affairs,* 75, no. 5 (September/October 1996): 24.

14. Homeland Security, *FY 2007 Homeland Security Grant Program.* Retrieved from http://www.dhs.gov/xlibrary/assets/grants_st-local_fy07.pdf (accessed June 22, 2009).

15. Jacob Silverman, "Could Hackers Devastate the US Economy?" Retrieved from http://computer.howstuffworks.com (accessed June 24, 2009).

16. Kevin McDonald, "Are We Prepared for a Potential Digital D-Day?" Retrieved from http://www.nationalcybersecurity.com/articles (accessed June 24, 2009).

The New Terrorist Threat: Weapons of Mass Destruction

Science and technology have made enormous
progress, but human nature, alas, has not changed. There
is as much fanaticism and madness as there ever
was, and there are now very powerful weapons of mass
destruction available to the terrorist.

— *Walter Laqueur*

CONTEXT OF THE THREAT

As noted earlier, terrorism is not a new phenomenon; it is instead a pattern of behavior with deep roots in the history of most modern nation-states and peoples. Nor are all weapons of mass destruction (WMDs) new; biological and even chemical agents have been used in conflicts for centuries. But most analysts of contemporary terrorism assumed, until recently, that the costs—financial and political—were too high for modern terrorists to seriously attempt the use of such weapons today.

This reasoning contained several errors. The first is the assumption that the financial costs of all forms of WMDs are too high to be paid by individuals or groups willing to commit acts of terrorism. Although the cost of building a nuclear bomb is still quite high, access to nuclear material and the technological skills to develop such weapons have become much less restricted since the fall of the Soviet Union. So-called backpack nukes and other small-scale tactical nuclear weapons have made it to the black market in arms sales fueled by the Soviet collapse. Nuclear waste material continues to be generated at an alarming rate, although secure storage of a permanent nature for such material remains a serious problem, making the possibility of a nuclear dirty bomb as a terrorist weapon quite feasible.

The second flaw in the logic is the assumption that terrorists would not use nonconventional weapons today, because to do so would bring down attacks using similar weapons on a sponsor state. To deliberately jeopardize the patron state, thus perhaps causing the cutting off of all lines of support, would be an irrational move. Nor, it was reasoned, would patron states be willing to put such weapons in the hands of groups carrying out terrorist acts, because such retribution would surely fall on the state if the group used the weapon.

This reasoning is based on the assumptions that terrorists are rational actors and that all terrorist groups are supported by states and would thus be unwilling to damage that relationship by the use of such weapons. As the attacks of September 11, 2001, demonstrated, terrorist groups today are not necessarily funded by or networked with any particular state and so cannot be assumed to be unwilling to use such weapons for this reason. As noted in Chapter 3, discussing the motivations of terrorists, it is also probably erroneous to assume that terrorists are rational actors in the commonly accepted sense. Because they define their world in ways that often make little sense to those who do not see the struggle or the enemy as they do, assuming that their rationale for the use or nonuse of WMDs would meet the world's criteria for logic is itself irrational.

Furthermore, as Walter Laqueur discusses in his book *The New Terrorists: Fanaticism and the Arms of Mass Destruction*, there are now many terrorists who are **fanatics**, *individuals who are overenthusiastic, zealous beyond the bounds of reason*. Because reason is clearly not, by definition, going to be a factor in the decision-making process of a fanatic terrorist, then to assume that he or she would not use WMDs is a foolish hope, an irrational act on our part. To know that such weapons exist, to be aware they are much more accessible now to potentially fanatical users, and *not* to attempt to assess the potential for such destructive attacks and their probable consequences, would be irrational— as irrational as the fanatic who may well seek to use such weapons today.

The greater the understanding of the reality of the threat, the potential for destruction of these weapons, and the capability of groups to utilize such weapons, the better will be our ability to deal with the current world situation without either paranoia or desperate security measures. This chapter will deal with these three aspects of terrorism and WMDs: a historical analysis of the use of WMDs, a survey of the types of such weapons that currently exist and their lethality, and an analysis of the ability of current groups engaged in terrorism to use such weapons.

HISTORICAL USE OF WEAPONS OF MASS DESTRUCTION

Modern WMDs have one new component—nuclear weapons—but the other two major types of WMDs, biological and chemical, have been part of the arsenal of warriors for much longer. The oldest of these, **biological weapons**, *warfare agents that include living microorganisms and toxins produced* *by microorganisms, plants, or animals,* have the longest history to explore. **Chemical weapons,** *often composed of binary compounds of chemicals that separately would not be lethal,* are not necessarily a completely different category of weapon, since agents like strychnine and ricin (which will be discussed later) are called biotoxins. We will begin with the oldest of these weapons—the biological ones—and progress through chemical to nuclear, taking a quick look at each type.

A Brief History of Biological Weapons

During the 1990s, there was a widespread belief that biological and chemical weapons were the greatest danger facing humanity. Biological weapons treaties, including the one signed by the United States and the Soviet Union twenty years earlier, declared that nations would no longer produce such weapons and would destroy their current stocks of these weapons. But the use of such weapons had already been part of the history of conflict throughout the world.

The **plague** of the fourteenth century, *reported to have killed about a third of the population of Europe, was supposedly spread by the Tartars in their siege of the fortress of Caffa in the Crimea.* According to legendary accounts, the Tartars used catapults to hurl plague-infected corpses into the city, becoming one of the first armies in history to engage in germ warfare. Other plagues were alleged to be either the result of or to be enhanced by the deliberate use of infected skins, corpses, or both by military groups. This includes the account in Chapter 9 discussing terrorism in the United States of the use of blankets infected with smallpox as "peace offerings" to Native Americans in Pennsylvania in the 1760s.

During World War I, Germany was accused of trying to spread cholera bacilli in Italy, the plague in St. Petersburg, and anthrax in Mesopotamia and Romania. In 1915, German agents in the United States were believed to have injected horses, mules, and cattle with anthrax on their way to Europe during World War I. The germs were produced in Silver Spring, Maryland, a Washington, DC, suburb, at a small German laboratory headed by Dr. Anton Dilger, who produced a liter of anthrax and glanders. The original seed cultures had reportedly been supplied by Berlin.[1]

In the mid-1930s, *Japan created a special biological warfare force* called **unit 731,** led by General Ishi in Manchuria, and many biological agents were produced in the laboratories of this unit. During the Japanese invasion of China in 1937, fleas were infected with many of these agents, including plague, smallpox, typhus, and gas gangrene. Evidence has emerged that these fleas were put in wheat and dropped from Japanese planes over Chinese towns toward the end of the war, resulting in hundreds of deaths.

The United Kingdom and the United States also developed germ warfare capabilities during World War II. The United Kingdom's experiments with anthrax at Gruinard Island off the coast of Scotland resulted in contamination of the island, which remained contaminated until the late 1990s. The U.S.

biological warfare program, initiated in 1942, continued after the end of the war, headquartered in Fort Detrick, Maryland, during the 1950s and 1960s.

Germ warfare installations also suffered from problems due to accidents. One of the most famous of these occurred in Sverdlovsk, in the Ural Mountains of the Soviet Union in April 1979. Intelligence assessments, later confirmed by Russian files found after the collapse of the USSR, indicated that a large airborne release of anthrax spores used for bacteriological warfare resulted in fatalities. Similar, if smaller, accidents have reportedly occurred at facilities around the world, making the production of such weapons more visibly hazardous.

A Brief History of Chemical Weapons

There are today a wide range of potential chemical weapons. Unfortunately, many chemicals used regularly for nonlethal purposes can be easily obtained and used—in combination with other chemicals—as chemical weapons. Chemical agents can be divided into many categories, but at least a cursory look at some of the major types of chemical agents will make a discussion of this type of weapon more easily understood.

Biotoxins, mentioned earlier, are one type of chemical agent. This category includes agents such as ricin, abrin, and strychnine. Another type of agent used by the military in many contexts in the twentieth century are the blister agents, including sulfur mustard, also known as mustard gas.

Chemical weapons are a much more recent addition to the arsenal of nations and warriors. For the most part, this type of weapon was not used in conflict until the twentieth century, existing only in the form of plans never carried out in the decades at the end of the nineteenth century. The idea of using poison gas against an enemy has been reported in connection with several groups, including the Fenians, who allegedly planned to spray it in the House of Commons in London in the 1870s. Similar plans for the use of poison gas were made but never implemented during the Boer War and the Japanese War with the Russians in 1905.

It saw not until World War I that a chemical weapon—chlorine gas—was used on a large scale with shocking success by the Germans at the battle of Ypres in 1915. The gas killed 5,000 Allied troops and injured many more. Five months later, in Loos, Belgium, the Allies used poison gas against German troops, again with dreadful success. The military on both sides continued to use gases as weapons with varying levels of success. Although chlorine gas continued to be used in gas artillery shelling in a number of battles, including but not limited to the battles of Fey-en-Haye, Verdun, and the Somme, an equally effective mixture of chlorine and phosgene (mustard gas) was also used.

About 25 poison gases were used in World War I. The exact casualty count from this type of weapon is unclear; estimates vary between 500,000 and 1.2 million troops and civilians from both sides. History indicates that the Russians may have suffered the worst losses from this weapon when it was used against them in conflict east of Warsaw in 1915. They reportedly lost about 25,000 soldiers in the first such attack, with countless casualties among civilians in towns near the front line.

Gas attacks, though clearly technologically possible, do not appear to have occurred in World War II. Even the Germans, who had clear technical superiority in the range of available chemical weaponry, decided for a variety of reasons not to use these weapons. Believing, apparently, that Allied forces had also developed tabun and sarin, toxic gases that were produced in Germany by 1944, Hitler decided not to use these newest lethal weapons.

Another reported use of chemical weapons occurred when Iraq used them during its war with Iran, both against Iranians and later against members of Iraq's own citizenry. Here are a few of the accounts of the use of these agents in this eight-year conflict:

1983. Mustard gas was used at Haj Umrah.

1984. Nerve gases again used, at Al-Basra, when Iraqi troops were in retreat.

1985 and 1986. Thousands of Iranian soldiers reportedly killed by gas attacks at Um Rashrash, Hawizeh Marsh, and other locations.

1986 and 1987. Poison gases used against the Kurds at Panjwin and Halabah. Reports indicate that Saddam Hussein used tabun in these attacks. News reports depicted men, women, and children lying in agonized death sprawls on the streets after planes passed over the villages spraying the toxins.

A Brief History of Nuclear Weapons

The history of the actual use of nuclear weapons is quite brief. This recently developed WMD has been used only on the occasion of the bombing attacks by the United States on the Japanese cities of Hiroshima and Nagasaki in 1945, bringing about an end to the war in the Pacific during World War II. Although atomic, and later nuclear, weapons were in the hands of only a few nations for several decades, this situation has rapidly changed in recent years.

To date, there are at least eight states with openly declared national nuclear weapons capabilities: the United States, the United Kingdom, France, Russia, the People's Republic of China, India, Pakistan, and North Korea. However, many more states, including Israel, Iran, South Africa, Iraq, and a few others, have secretly developed, and have arguably tested, nuclear weapons. Moreover, several states that emerged from the former Soviet Union, in addition to Russia, have nuclear weapons still within their arsenals, although most have agreed to turn these over to Russia for the purpose of bilateral United States–Russian disarmament, as initiated in the Strategic Arms Reduction Talks, documents, and discussions of the 1980s and 1990s.

Proliferation of nuclear weapons has occurred and is no doubt still occurring. This trend makes it unlikely that the history of the use of nuclear weapons will terminate with the two attacks in 1945.

TYPES OF WEAPONS OF MASS DESTRUCTION AVAILABLE

Clearly, WMDs have been used by groups of warriors and nation-states for many years. The possibility that terrorists today would use such weapons cannot be assessed, because there is no history of previous use by others involved in intense struggles. Moreover, such weapons have not been used exclusively, or even primarily, by nondemocratic states or individuals. Instead, a variety of states, many of them democratic, have been the major forces employing these weapons. Remember that the *only* use of atomic weapons, nuclear weapons, or both was by the United States against predominantly civilian targets (of military significance but civilian populations).

The next step is to examine the types of WMDs available to terrorists today and the relative capacity of each to create mass destruction. Although many of these weapons have been untested on human populations, estimates can be made as to their lethality based on laboratory tests. Such tests cannot be definitive, but information provided about these weapons in such tests offers some indication of the toxicity of the substances.

Biological Agents

There are four categories of living microorganisms: bacteria, viruses, rickettsiae, and fungi. **Bacteria** are *small free-living organisms*; they can be grown on solid or liquid media and produce diseases that often respond to specific treatment with antibiotics. A familiar example of bacteria used recently in a terrorist attack is anthrax, an acute infectious disease caused by the spore-forming bacterium *Bacillus anthracis*. Although anthrax most often occurs in hoofed mammals, it can also infect humans, as the anthrax attack in the mail system of the United States in the fall of 2001 proved.

Viruses are *organisms that require living cells in which to replicate*. This type of organism does not respond to antibiotics but is sometimes responsive to viral compounds, few of which are available. Again, the most familiar example of viruses as a weapon of terror is smallpox, an infection caused by the Variola virus.

The latter two groups are less familiar to the general public. **Rickettsiae** are *microorganisms that have characteristics of both bacteria and viruses*. Like bacteria, rickettsiae have metabolic enzymes and cell membranes, utilize oxygen, and are susceptible to a broad spectrum of antibiotics. Like viruses, they grow only within living cells. Q-Fever, a zoonotic disease caused by the rickettsia *Coxiella burnetii*, is a form of rickettsiae. **Fungi**, *primitive plants that do not utilize photosynthesis, are capable of anaerobic growth and draw nutrition from decaying vegetable matter*, are a little more familiar, but not in terms of a biological weapon. A diverse group of more than 40 compounds produced by the fungus *Trichothecene mycotoxins* has been generated in recent years because these compounds can inhibit protein synthesis, impair DNA synthesis, alter cell and membrane structure and function, and inhibit mitochondrial respiration. T-2, as these are called, used as a biological warfare agent aimed at causing acute exposure via inhalation, could result in the onset of illness within hours of exposure and death within twelve hours.

Biotoxins, *poisonous substances produced naturally by microorganisms, plants, or animals that may be produced or altered by chemical means*, will be discussed later in the context of chemical weapons. This category would include agents such as ricin, abrin, and strychnine.

As one news analyst noted,

> While the list of the most likely weapons in a bioterror attack is short, it includes agents that, if acquired and effectively disseminated, could cause a significant public health risk. The challenge would be to recognize the danger early to limit the number of casualties.[2]

A quick look at five biological agents currently available illustrates the breadth of the threat of attack from such weapons. A more in-depth case study of one of these—anthrax—will offer further clues as to the danger that such agents pose.

Botulinum toxin *(Clostridium botulinum) is the single most poisonous substance known*. While it is usually food borne, it could be developed as an aerosol weapon. Within twenty-four to thirty-six hours of infection with this biological agent, symptoms generally include blurred vision as well as difficulty swallowing and speaking. This agent, a nerve toxin, paralyzes muscles, thus leading to respiratory failure and death. The Aum Shinrikyo cult in Japan was accused of trying to spray botulinum toxin from airplanes over Tokyo, fortunately without success, at least three times in the 1990s.

Plague *(Yersinia pestis) is an incredibly virulent, but not always lethal, biological agent*. If 110 pounds of this agent were released over a city of 5 million people, about 150,000 of them would contract the disease but most would survive if treated early in the infection period. Within one to six days after exposure to the plague bacteria, victims would begin to show symptoms of severe respiratory and gastrointestinal distress. Treatment with antibiotics would be effective as long as they were administered within the early stages of infection.

Tularemia *is a potentially lethal infectious organism developed by the United States as a possible weapon in the 1950s and 1960s*. As a weapon, it could be sprayed in an aerosol cloud. Within three to five days of infection, victims would suffer fever, chills, headaches, and weakness. Subsequent inflammation and hemorrhaging of the airways can be fatal, and no vaccine is currently available.

Smallpox *is an infectious agent that several nations have tried for decades to effectively weaponize* but which was eradicated in 1980. However, some strains of this disease are officially maintained in two nations: the United States and Russia. The former Soviet Union reportedly stockpiled large amounts of this virus for use as weapons, and several other nations, such as Iraq and North Korea, may have covert stashes of smallpox today. The smallpox virus is highly contagious and would quickly spread, because vaccinations for this disease stopped more than twenty-five years ago. An aerosol release of smallpox infecting only 50 people could easily unleash an epidemic that would kill about 30 percent of those infected with the painful, disfiguring disease.

Anthrax *is an acute infectious disease caused by the spore-forming bacterium Bacillus anthracis.* It most commonly occurs in mammals such as cattle, sheep, goats, camels, and antelopes but can also occur in humans exposed to infected animals or tissue from infected animals. Anthrax is unusual in that its spores are hardy: They are resistant to sunlight, heat, and disinfectant and can remain active in soil and water for years. Anthrax spores tend to clump together in humid conditions, making it somewhat difficult to spray as an aerosol. Anthrax, unlike smallpox, is not contagious—that is, it is highly unlikely that it could be transmitted from direct person-to-person contact.

Since this particular bacterium was used in 2001 as a biological agent, a closer look at anthrax as a biological weapon would be useful at this point.

CASE STUDY 14.1

Anthrax

Anthrax has been linked to several devastating plagues that killed both humans and livestock. In 1500 B.C., the fifth Egyptian plague, which affected livestock, and the sixth, known as the plague of boils, were linked to anthrax. The Black Bane of the A.D. 1600s was also thought to be anthrax and killed 60,000 cattle in Europe.

Robert Koch confirmed the bacterial origin of anthrax in 1876. Not long after this discovery, anthrax began to emerge as a biological weapon. Biological weapons programs involving anthrax continued after World War II and throughout the 1950s and 1960s at various military bases. In the United States, Fort Detrick in Maryland became the focal point for this program until 1969, when President Richard Nixon formally ended the United States' biological weapons program. In 1972, Nixon signed an international convention outlawing the development or stockpiling of biological weapons.

The ratification of this convention did not end the production, testing, and use of biological agents, including anthrax. Evidence of continued development of anthrax as a biological weapon emerged in 1979 when aerosolized (weaponized) anthrax spores were accidentally released at Compound 19, a military part of Sverdlovsk in the Soviet Union. An explosion at this secret military base near an industrial complex in the Ural Mountains sent a cloud of deadly microbes over a nearby village. Reputed death tolls from this accident vary, with as few as 68 to as many as 1,000 eventually dying from contact with this weaponized form of anthrax.

The group Aum Shinrikyo released anthrax in Tokyo several times between 1990 and 1993, but without any reported deaths or infections. Anthrax, even in weaponized form, is difficult to disseminate over a city because warm air generated by the traffic and compression of people generally forces the air up, not down. In theory, a cloud of anthrax spores inhaled by a city's population would create widespread severe, flu-like symptoms, killing 80 percent of those infected within one or two days after their symptoms appeared. As yet, no successful dissemination of this sort has been attempted. Nevertheless, in 1995, Iraq admitted to UN inspectors that it had produced 8,500 liters of concentrated anthrax as part of its biological weapons program.

In 2001, a letter containing anthrax spores was mailed to NBC's offices in New York City one week after the September 11 attacks on the United States. This was the first of a number of incidents in the eastern part of the country, including letters mailed to a tabloid newspaper in Florida and in Washington, DC. Five deaths were attributed to these anthrax attacks.

Anthrax infection can occur in three forms: cutaneous, inhalation, and gastrointestinal.

Cutaneous. About 95 percent of cutaneous anthrax infections occur from a cut or abrasion on the skin, such as when someone is handling the wool, hides, or hair products of infected animals. It begins as a raised itchy bump that resembles an insect bite but soon turns into a painless ulcer about one to three centimeters in diameter, with a black center in the middle. About 20 percent of untreated cases of cutaneous anthrax result in death. An employee of news anchor Tom Brokaw who contracted anthrax in the U.S. incident had the cutaneous form of anthrax.

Inhalation. Inhalation anthrax occurs when anthrax spores enter the lungs, requiring from two to forty-three days for incubation. Initial symptoms for this form of anthrax may resemble a common cold but lead to severe breathing problems and, after several days, to shock. Inhalation anthrax was thought to be fatal in about 90 percent of the cases because its symptoms initially appear in a form that does not require a visit to a doctor. However, this assumption was based on incomplete data from the Russian accident mentioned earlier. The data did not include information on those people who were treated for infection and who survived or those who were not infected. It only identified the deaths from the infection. The employee of the Florida tabloid and four U.S. Postal Service employees handling mail going through New Jersey died of inhalation anthrax in the 2001 attack.

Gastrointestinal. Gastrointestinal anthrax generally follows consumption of contaminated meat. It is characterized by an acute inflammation of the intestinal tract and includes symptoms of nausea, loss of appetite, vomiting, and fever, followed by abdominal pain, vomiting blood, and severe diarrhea. Usually, between 25 and 60 percent of cases of this form of anthrax are fatal. This is the type of anthrax that the Soviet Union initially blamed for the deaths in Sverdlovsk.

Anthrax is not contagious and can be treated with antibiotics. To be effective, the treatments must be initiated early, because if not treated in a timely fashion, the disease can be fatal. A cell-free filtrate vaccine for anthrax exists that contains no dead or live bacteria in the preparation.

Anthrax is a particularly attractive candidate for a bioweapon because its spores are hardy. However, manufacturing sufficient quantities of any bacteria in stable form is a technical and scientific challenge, and dissemination of anthrax also remains a challenge. The use of crop duster planes, for instance, as a tool for dissemination is difficult because the planes are designed to spray pesticides in a heavy, concentrated stream. In contrast, anthrax as a bioweapon would perform better if scattered in a fine mist over as large an area as possible. The nozzles of

(continued)

crop dusters are best suited to discharge relatively large particles—100 microns in diameter—not tiny 1-micron specks of bacteria.

In its natural state, anthrax has a low rate of infection among people. The organism *Bacillus anthracis* can be grown in a lab to produce a weapons-grade form of the bacteria. Removed from a nutrient-rich environment, the bacteria turn into spores, which naturally clump together. These spores are then purified, separated, and concentrated. Finally, they are combined with fine dust particles to maintain separation and increase the time that they can be suspended in the air.

Used as a weapon in the 2001 attacks, this powdery mixture was apparently put into an envelope. When released into the air, such as during processing of mail at post offices, a high concentration of spores can be drawn deep into the lungs. The spores return to their bacterial state in the lungs and rapidly develop an anthrax infection by releasing deadly toxins into a person's system.

In addition to the apparent use of anthrax as a weapon sent through the mail system in the United States after the September 11 attacks, several other countries reported mail that initially tested positive for anthrax contamination. In Pakistan, at least one of four suspected letters received at three locations in Islamabad contained anthrax; in Lithuania, one mailbag at the U.S. Embassy at the capital tested positive, revealing trace elements of anthrax. The potency of anthrax as a weapon for disruption and expensive response was clearly demonstrated by the limited attacks occurring in the autumn of 2001. ■

Source: Federal Bureau of Investigation website: http://www.fbi.gov/about-us/history/famous-cases/anthrax-amerithrax

---

CASE STUDY 14.2

Viral Hemorrhagic Fevers

Although biological agents such as anthrax and smallpox have been used as biological weapons in the past, neither is as potentially lethal as some of the viral hemorrhagic fevers studied at the Centers for Disease Control and Prevention (CDC) in the United States.

Viral hemorrhagic fever (VHF) is a term used to describe *a syndrome that severely affects multiple organs in the body, caused by several distinct families of viruses.* Although some of the VHF viruses can cause relatively mild illnesses, many of them cause severe, potentially fatal disease. With a few noteworthy exceptions, there is no cure or established drug treatment for VHF.

The survival of VHFs is dependent on the animal or insect host, called the natural reservoir, and humans are not the natural reservoir for *any* of the VHFs. But humans may become infected when they come into contact with infected hosts and, in the case of some of the more lethal VHFs such as Ebola and Marburg, may transmit the disease from one human host to another. This type of secondary transmission, from infected human to infected human, can occur directly (through close contact with infected people or their body fluids) or indirectly (through contact with objects contaminated with their body fluids).

VHFs such as Ebola and Marburg have terrifying symptoms. Initial signs include marked fever, fatigue, dizziness, muscle aches, loss of strength, and exhaustion. As the diseases progressed, however, the person would exhibit signs of bleeding under the skin, in internal organs, and from the mouth, eyes, ears, or all three. Although the loss of this blood externally would appear shocking, the patient would not in most cases die from it. Instead, the patient's body would be assaulted with the collapse of many organs within the system, nervous system malfunction, coma, delirium, seizures—and finally death, which would in many respects be a release.

There is no known cure for Ebola or Marburg VHF. Outbreaks of Marburg and Ebola have occurred through human-to-human transmission. The potential for a crusader willing to be a "suicide patient" rather than a suicide bomber, deliberately infecting himself or herself with one of these lethal VHFs to infect people within an "enemy" nation, is still remote given the fortunate scarcity of the virus. But the possibility exists, and if the virus was obtained and replicated in a lab with deliberate intent to use it as a weapon, the results for humankind might be unthinkable. ■

Source: Center for Disease Control and Prevention website: http://www.cdc.gov/ncidod/dvrd/spb/mnpages/dispages/vhf.htm

Bioterrorism Defense

A few disturbing trends in the new biosecurity landscape are worth noting here, as they impact both the potential for future bioterror attacks and our ability to cope with or prevent such attacks. Christopher Chyba and Alex Greninger suggest that these trends came together in the 1990s and confront us today with new challenges.[3]

The first trend suggested by these researchers is that of emerging infectious diseases. This is not to imply that there have not been many catastrophic pandemics. But during the 1970s and 1980s, research indicated that a new disease was emerging at the rate of about one every year. Moreover, the dramatic outbreaks of diseases such as Ebola and the emergence of many versions of known diseases that are increasingly drug resistant, such as tuberculosis, lend new importance to this threat.

The increased occurrence of mass-casualty terrorism is the second trend in modern biosecurity. While there are historical records of such attacks, the destruction by bomb of the passenger plane over Lockerbie, Scotland, in the late 1980s, the first attempt to destroy a World Trade Tower in 1993, the sarin gas attack on the Tokyo subways by the Aum Shinrikyo cult in 1993, and the 1995 Oklahoma City bombing lend credence to the claim of this as a trend. The events of September 11, 2001, certainly strengthen this conclusion.

The third disturbing trend suggested by Chyba and Greninger is the increasing evidence of gross violations of the 1972 Biological and Toxic

Weapons Convention (BWC). The end of the cold war brought to light the extent to which the former Soviet Union had built a biological weapons program in spite of being a signatory of the convention. As the researchers noted, in July 2001, the administration of George W. Bush declared the BWC to be "inherently unverifiable," but withdrew from negotiations to create a compliance protocol for the convention.[4] Iraq's purported development of such weapons was a stated element in the U.S. decision, under Bush's leadership, to invade the country to verify the existence of, and then to end, bioweapon development programs.

The anthrax mail attacks in 2001 reminded us of our vulnerability to bioterror attack. Four lessons learned from that attack may help to shape our response to such attacks in the future. The first is that the volume of the agent may not be the critical point, as the amount may be small but may produce a large effect. While only a few deaths occurred from this attack, it cost the federal government, states, and businesses billions of dollars as anxiety caused use of the mail service to decline and thousands to bring mail—or sick family members—to be tested at a limited number of biolabs.

The use of the mail as an agent for disseminating a biological agent, suggested in fiction for years, was surprisingly effective, offering another lesson in modern vulnerability to terrorism. Diagnosis of the anthrax infection was complicated by the skepticism of many about the likelihood of such an agent being used in such a manner. Perhaps the challenge is to be willing to accept the potential for unexpected but possible attacks like this, as Leonard Cole suggests.[5]

The need for cross-training and exploration of "unlikely" potentials is also, according to Cole, another lesson that could be derived from the anthrax attacks, as those charged with the task of local counterterror response—such as law enforcement or emergency response personnel—may not have the training necessary to deal with WMD terrorism. Such training is being encouraged and sponsored by the DHS, by grants, and by the establishment of Centers of Excellence tasked with generating programs for such training.

This need to extend training and awareness is related to the fourth lesson learned from the anthrax attacks, as those attacks affected people not only in cities but also in remote communities. If anyone, in any location, can be the target of such attacks, then training and resourcing for such attacks must be much more widespread than previously planned. While the DHS is certainly moving resources and directing efforts in the direction of improving local preparedness, there is clearly much that still must be done.

As Cable News Network (CNN) revealed in a study conducted after the anthrax attacks in 2001, neither local emergency management nor public health centers were prepared to cope effectively with this crisis. A quick look at the situation in Las Vegas, Nevada, as the anthrax crisis evolved in 2001 offers useful insights. The medical system of that city collapsed due to a number of factors. The population in the greater Las Vegas region had exploded, so that when the crisis occurred, there was an insufficient number of hospital beds for the population: Las Vegas needed about 200 beds per 100,000 people (according to CDC statistics), but was about 600 beds short. Having only 11 hospitals, Nevada ranked 50th of the 50 states in the United States in nurse-to-patient ratio. When the crisis occurred, as hundreds of people rushed to emergency rooms for treatment and admission, the overcrowded and under-staffed emergency rooms had to close to new patients about 40 percent of the time. Had there truly been a large-scale anthrax attack, hundreds, even thousands, might have died for lack of access to adequate care. CNN's study of hospitals in 25 cities evaluated in this context found that most were severely lacking in this critical hospital bed/patient care area.

The CDC in Atlanta noted problems in the health care systems's ability to respond to a biological crisis involving a contagious disease. In the event of a need for mass vaccinations for smallpox, for example, local emergency managers would need to open hundreds of vaccination centers and train large numbers of vaccinators (it usually takes about two hours of training to qualify a vaccinator because they are insured by the federal government due to liability issues). For every 1 million people receiving the vaccination, about two will probably die. All of those vaccinated must remain in the vaccination site unexposed to others for up to twenty-one days. The responsibility of planning for and paying for such a comprehensive medical response program, including vaccinator recruitment and training, the establishment of vaccination centers capable of housing those vaccinated for up to twenty-one days, and the payment for the workers needed at these centers to care for those vaccinated, would be huge, and it is unclear on whom this burden would fall.

David Franz, director of the National Agricultural Biosecurity Center at Kansas State University, states the problem of security from bioterrorism clearly when he says that "[a]lthough we have some understanding of threat, vulnerability and impact of a biological attack, risk is impossible to quantify."[6] This makes knowing how to allocate vital resources in preparation for an unknown bioterror attack very difficult. We can take an "all-hazards" approach, like the Federal Emergency Management Agency (FEMA) does in its preparation for natural disasters, but in this case use the same medical preparedness training for a bioterror attack as we would for any emerging infectious disease, adding the fact that the disease is being intentionally spread with an intent to harm. We may not spread the preparation efforts far enough to cover all possible targets—and we may prepare for the wrong type of disease, as a contagious agent must be treated differently from an agent that must be ingested. But we must prepare ourselves, as trends indicate that such attacks will occur with increasing frequency and perhaps increasing lethality as well.

Chemical Weapons

Although there are potentially thousands of biological agents that terrorists could use, there are, in all probability, even more poisonous chemical agents available. Chemical agents come in a variety of forms, most often as a liquid rather than a gas, usually dispersed as droplets. Biotoxins are one type of chemical agent, which include agents such as ricin, abrin, and strychnine. *Chlorine* and *phosgene* are **choking agents** that were used during World War I and *cause pulmonary edema. Mustard gas, lewisite, and others that cause chemical burns and destroy lung tissue* are called **blistering agents. Blood agents** include other types of chemicals, such as *hydrogen cyanide* and *cyanogen chloride, which attack the respiratory system and usually rapidly result in coma followed by death*. The *neuromuscular system is attacked* by the **nerve gases** examples of which include *sarin* (used in the Tokyo subway incident), *tabun* (found in Iraq after the Gulf War), *soman, and VX*. These agents *block the enzyme cholinesterase, which causes paralysis of the neuromuscular system, resulting in death*.

Most of the substances used to create chemical weapons have a legitimate use. Some, like eserin (a nerve gas), have been used for medicinal purposes. Others are used as cleaning agents, insecticides, herbicides, and rodenticides. This makes many of them commercially available in some form. As the United States learned in the bombing at Oklahoma City, truckloads of fertilizer can be easily obtained and can be a very lethal weapon in the hands of a terrorist.

Chemical weapons are prolific in number, relatively easy to acquire and stockpile, and not too expensive. However, they are difficult to manufacture in sufficient quantities for a large-scale attack. More likely, they would be used successfully in isolated attacks of a relatively small nature. Chemical weapons are also difficult to disperse effectively. The attack by the Aum Shinrikyo on the Tokyo subway system in Japan illustrates both the strengths, in terms of the psychologically disruptive effects, and the weaknesses, in light of the relative nonlethality of the attack and the problems in dissemination, inherent in the use of chemical weapons by terrorists today.

At least three possible types of chemical terrorism are identified by Jonathan Tucker, a senior fellow at the Center for Nonproliferation Studies in Washington, DC:

1. the release of a military-grade chemical warfare agent against a civilian target (intending to inflict mass civilian casualties);
2. the sabotage of a chemical manufacturing plant or storage facility (including a rail tank car) containing toxic materials, intending to release toxic gases or vapors; and
3. the contamination of public water or food supplies with toxic agents.[7]

A database compiled by the Monterey Institute's Center for Nonproliferation Studies indicated that only a relatively small number of chemical terrorism attacks have been recorded in the past four decades. While this is reassuring and may, as Tucker suggests, be because few terrorist organizations are motivated to inflict indiscriminate casualties, it would be unwise to be complacent about this threat. Osama bin Laden had declared that it was his "religious duty" to acquire chemical and other nonconventional weapons to use against the United States. Clearly, lack of motivation may not be true for all contemporary terrorist groups.[8]

Chemical weapons can be made from ordinary products. Thiodigycol, an immediate precursor to mustard gas, is used to make the ink in ball point pens. All that is needed to produce mustard gas is a simple acid, which is easy to obtain. While the production of such an agent requires some skills in chemistry, "how-to" manuals such as the *Anarchist Cookbook* and even jihad manuals with instructions in this process are available on the Internet, making the production challenge less of an obstacle.

Fortunately, acquisition of military-grade CW agents, such as sarin and VX, is not simple, nor is the process of "weaponizing" a toxic chemical. To be "weaponized," a toxic chemical must be stabilized to extend its shelf-life, and a delivery system must be developed that will spread the toxin through a target population. The delivery system would need to be mechanical, pneumatic, or explosive, with the most effective being an aerosol generator producing tiny droplets of the substance to float in the air and be inhaled by the victims. This is a complex and difficult delivery system to perfect, as the Aum in Japan discovered. They were able to obtain and produce a substantial quantity of sarin, but the delivery of the agent failed to effectively reach most of the target audience.

The potential for a chemical terror attack taking the form of sabotage of chemical industry plants is much greater. Detonation of a conventional explosive in a plant containing a hazardous chemical could be extremely disruptive and destructive. The 1984 accident (allegedly carried out by a disgruntled employee) at a Union Carbide plant in Bhopal, India, that caused more than 2,500 deaths is a dramatic example.

Examining one toxic chemical, ricin, may help to make clearer the dangers that exist today from the potential of chemical terrorism.

CASE STUDY 14.3

Ricin

Ricin is a *biotoxin found in the bean of the castor plant, Ricinis communis,* and it is one of the most toxic and easily produced plant toxins. Originally cultivated in ancient Egypt as a lubricant and a laxative, castor beans are today used to produce castor oil, which is a brake and hydraulic fuel component found throughout the world. Ricin can be made from the waste left over from processing castor beans.

Because it is both highly toxic and easily produced, ricin was studied and developed by the United States during both world wars in the twentieth century. Unfortunately, these same characteristics have made ricin an attractive weapon of interest to radical individuals, groups, and governments in recent years as well.

Like anthrax, ricin may cause toxic reactions in people from three possible routes of exposure: inhalation, injection, and oral ingestion (the least toxic method). Inhaling ricin, according to one group of experts, would produce symptoms within eight hours and depending on the dose, death within thirty-six to seventy-two hours. There is, unfortunately, no known vaccine for ricin and no antidote to the poison.[9]

Although ricin poisoning is not contagious (it cannot be spread from person to person from casual contact), it has already been used as a weapon in recent history. In 1978, Georgi Markov, a Bulgarian writer and journalist who was living in London, died after he was attacked by a man with an umbrella—an umbrella that had been fixed to inject a poisonous ricin pellet under Markov's skin. Reports

(continued)

indicate, too, that ricin was used in the Iran–Iraq conflict in the 1980s. Quantities of ricin were reportedly found in caves in Afghanistan used by al-Qaeda prior to the 2001 attacks on the United States, and information about ricin appears in the so-called *Jihad Encyclopedia* discovered after the September 11, 2001, attacks. Ricin is intensely more lethal than sarin, which was used in the Tokyo subway attack.

In November 2011, four men in the United States, from the state of Georgia, were charged with plotting to use ricin to attack government officials. Traces of ricin were found in the possession of the four. ■

Source: Centers for Disease Control and Prevention website: http://www.bt.cdc.gov/agent/ricin/facts.asp

Radiological Weapons

While radioactivity was discovered more than a century ago, the effects of lower levels of radiation on human cells have only begun to be understood in recent years. Although only uranium and a few other elements can be turned into explosive weapons, there are many elements that emit radiation, some of which are used today in legitimate biological and medical work.

Since radioactive materials are plentiful—waste from nuclear power plants includes highly radioactive cesium, tritium, and strontium, for instance—the possibility of "dirty bombs" using such materials increases rapidly.[10] **Dirty bombs** do not require the theft of large amounts of carefully guarded plutonium, nor does their construction require great technical skills or a well-equipped laboratory. These weapons can be made with *nonfissionable radioactive materials, such as cesium 137, cobalt 60, and strontium, and are exploded by conventional means*. Even though such a bomb would not cause the vast number of fatalities generated by a nuclear blast, it spreads nuclear contaminant over water supplies, crops, and other essential parts of a system. These bombs could be used in shopping malls or train stations to disrupt as well as to destroy.

A dirty bomb could cause extraordinary costs, not all of them financial. Fear of radiation poisoning from the particles dispersed in the atmosphere, scattered like dust on the surfaces of furniture and buildings, would drive many to leave their homes and business until they could be reassured that decontamination was complete. The decontamination would be extremely expensive and could take months or years to complete, depending on the size of the blast and the weather conditions. Public confidence in the safety of decontaminated areas would be difficult to achieve.

As one expert described it, "If a casket of spent fuel from a nuclear power plant was exploded in downtown Manhattan, more than 2,000 people might die quickly and thousands more would suffer from radiation poisoning."[11]

The immediate health effects from exposure to the low radiation levels expected from a dirty bomb are expected to be minimal and would be determined by several factors, including the amount of radiation absorbed by the body, the type or radiation (gamma, alpha, or beta), the distance from the ration to the individual, whether the exposure resulted in radiation being absorbed through the skin or inhaled or ingested, and the length of time of exposure. However, panic would be rampant; hospitals might be overwhelmed; and local first responders would be challenged to subdue the panic, diagnose the ill, and stem the flood of demands for treatment before supplies are exhausted. A small device in heavily populated areas could cause catastrophic damage, generating public panic.

Attacks on nuclear power facilities are also a form of nuclear terrorism possible. This has happened many times, in many countries, but without evidence that such attacks have yet generated a major accident with catastrophic loss of lives. Nevertheless, in the wake of the attacks on September 11, 2001, nuclear facilities were recognized as vulnerable to the same type of attack—one using a large, well-fueled plane as a "bomb" flown into the facility.

Nuclear Weapons

Several types of nuclear weapons may be feasible for use by terrorists in the twenty-first century, although none have yet been used in an attack. A **small plutonium device**, *requiring at least 2.5 kilograms of plutonium, is constructed with a core made of a sphere of compacted plutonium oxide crystals in the center of a large cube of Semtex (or one of the other new, powerful explosives)*. The bomb, when complete, would weigh about a ton and would require at least a van or a truck to get it to the target.

A home-produced or stolen nuclear device of moderate size, about 10–15 kilotons, detonated in a major city would destroy several square miles of territory and could cause up to 100,000 casualties. The bomb would have to be transported and strategically placed for maximum effect. The technical skills required, the facility necessary, and access to a large quantity of plutonium are impediments to the use of such a weapon by a group engaged in terrorism.

As one expert noted, however, if terrorists obtained 60 kilograms of highly enriched uranium (HEU), "they could make a nuclear explosive similar to the 'Little Boy' atomic bomb that leveled Hiroshima, Japan at the end of World War II."[12] Large quantities of HEU are stored in nuclear research facilities worldwide, many of which are in Russia, where the security for such facilities is often minimal.

An important point needs to be recognized here with respect to the motivation of terrorists to make—and use—a nuclear bomb. While a state seeking to create—and deploy—such a weapon would not want to have only one, which might or might not seriously incapacitate an enemy, a terrorist (or terrorist group) will seldom be seeking to destroy an enemy with one blow, one bomb. Thus, the bomb need not be the best made, or foolproof—it need only work to some extent, to make the political point of the terrorists. Moreover, a state, on its own, would surely be expected to hesitate to use such a weapon unless it could survive the reprisal for the act. If a terrorist group were openly responsible for a bomb, it would have a much greater capacity to evade reprisal and thus a greater likelihood to use such a weapon, given the chance.

Bin Laden made clear his desire for nuclear weapons for use against the United States and its allies, calling the acquisition of WMDs a religious duty, and referring to the need to inflict a "Hiroshima" on the United States.[13] Material found in al-Qaeda camps in Afghanistan proved that the group had downloaded information on nuclear weapons, including crude bomb designs, and tried to recruit nuclear weapon scientists to work with them. Clearly, this group at least is strongly motivated to acquire and to use nuclear weapons in terrorist attacks today.

The black market for weapons has had, since the demise of the Soviet Union, incidents in which small, backpack nuclear devices, and even devices as small as landmines, were for sale. Although obviously no records exist of such sales, the leaders of the international community have expressed their concern about the possibility of a group engaged in terrorism or a "rogue state" acquiring such fully manufactured devices. This possibility has been the subject of discussion at numerous UN meetings and resulted in resolutions condemning such sales and pledging not to facilitate them, but little documented success in the control of such weapons exists.

Terrorists and groups appear more willing to experiment with the use of biological or chemical weapons than nuclear weapons today. If terrorists want chemical weapons, they can make potent agents from such substances as isopropyl alcohol (easily available at drug stores and supermarkets), from pesticides and herbicides (available at most home and farm supply stores), and from a host of other equally accessible products.

Most experts also agree that it does not take great skills in chemistry to manufacture many different chemical agents. Some are more difficult than others, of course; but a wide range is possible for someone with perhaps a few graduate courses in chemistry.

ACCESS TO AND USE OF WEAPONS OF MASS DESTRUCTION

Chemical Agents

As weapons of terrorists, chemical agents are relatively easily accessible and potentially very lethal, but they are limited in usefulness to date by the difficulty in dissemination, unless the desired effect is primarily psychological rather than physical in nature. Most chemical weapons have been available since World War I, and the processes for manufacturing most usual war gases have been published in open literature. Several nations possess chemical weapons, making it possible for them to supply a group with this type of weapon. Yet only the Aum Shinrikyo cult in Japan has attempted to procure and use a chemical weapon in a large-scale terrorist attack.

The reason for this lack of use may be simply practical rather than political, moral, or monetary. Most toxic gases are very difficult to handle, control, and deploy effectively. Even toxic industrial gases such as chlorine and hydrogen cyanide, which are easy to procure, are very volatile. These types of agents could only be used in an attack on a target population in an enclosed area with limited exits (so that those targeted could not escape, and/or to keep the gases from escaping into the atmosphere outside). As one researcher noted, if a terrorist wanted to use a nerve agent by introducing it into the air-handling system in a building (whose inhabitants are the target population), the device must be of a size and shape that is easily carried by one person; be leakproof; and have an activation process that will result in the agent being dispersed in a way that will not endanger the terrorist operating the device (unless the terrorist is a crusader, willing to die in the attack), yet be strong enough to reach the population in a sufficiently high concentration to cause a high casualty rate.[14]

Nevertheless, trainees at terrorist camps in Afghanistan learned how to use chemical weapons, according to testimony in U.S. courts in July 2001. Ahmed Ressam told the court that his training for chemical attacks included testing the effect of cyanide and sulfuric acid on a dog. "We wanted to know what is the effect of the gas," Ressam told the court.[15]

CASE STUDY 14.4

Aum Attack on the Tokyo Subway

On March 20, 1995, Aum Shinrikyo (Supreme Truth), a Japanese cult, placed containers of sarin gas on five trains of the Tokyo underground subway network, which came together at Kasumigaseki station, near many government offices. This attack killed 12 people, injured 5,500, and caused serious chaos in the subway system for days afterward.

The timing of the attack, as well as its focus on trains full of government workers, was significant. Japanese police were actually planning to raid cult leader Shoko Asahara's Tokyo compound on March 22, expecting to find the chemical agents the group possessed. Aum had been able to infiltrate the police department with two supporters who warned Asahara of the coming raid. Aum chose to launch the subway attack on March 20 during the police shift change to divert attention from the planned raid.

The subway attack had many flaws and consequently left fewer victims than might have been expected. The sarin used was not pure, and the means of distribution—polyethylene bags that had been punctured—was primitive and ineffective. The attack was carefully planned, but rushed into place earlier than anticipated, thus relying on improvisation rather than tested techniques.

The Tokyo attack in 1995 was not the cult's first attempt to use a chemical weapon. Aum spent more than $30 million developing poisonous gases, even constructing a special facility called Satyan 7 to produce sarin gas. In 1994, 7 people were killed and another 264 injured at Matsumoto, a resort west of Tokyo. The event was thought to be an accident, although members of this cult

(continued)

later admitted to spraying sarin from a van. There had been other minor incidents involving toxic vapors linked to Aum, and the police had received anonymous threats referring to future attacks. Some of these letters even named the Tokyo subway as the probable target, but the authorities took only limited action.

Because the cult owned a billion-dollar computer empire in Japan, it invested much of its profits in the building of fully equipped laboratories, where it attempted to create or modify deadly chemical and biological toxins. Aum sent scientists in research teams worldwide in search of deadly biological agents, even exploring the possibility of securing a culture of the Ebola virus during that virus's outbreak in Zaire.

Evidence gathered after authorities searched the warehouses and labs indicated that Aum had tried to develop weaponized forms of botulinum and anthrax as well as other toxic agents. In 1993, the cult tried twice to spray what it believed to be a weaponized form of anthrax, in aerosol form, from the top of its compound in Tokyo. After the 1995 attack, it also admitted to spraying botulinum on the walls outside the American Embassy in Tokyo. No injuries or deaths were reported from either of these attempts to use biological agents. The willingness of the group to spend millions to acquire these lethal agents and its eagerness to use them was balanced, apparently, by its inability to produce effective strains or to disseminate them efficiently. ■

Source: Centers for Disease Control and Prevention website: http://wwwnc.cdc.gov/eid/article/5/4/99-0409_article.htm

Biological Agents

In the early 1990s, perception of the possibility of biological attacks was radically altered by two dramatic events. The first was the discovery of enormous quantities of such weapons in Iraq after the Gulf War, particularly as there was reason to believe that only a portion of them had been found. Moreover, there was also a growing realization that Iraq and other countries were continuing preparations for BC (biological/chemical) warfare. While suspicions existed before the Gulf War, since Iraq had used chemical weapons against both the Iranians and the Kurds in attacks that had resulted in thousands of deaths, the realization of the buildup of BC had been underestimated.

At the Al Muthanna laboratories in Iraq, 2,850 tons of mustard gas were found to have been produced, along with 790 tons of sarin and 290 tons of tabun. Iraq was found to have 50 warheads with chemical agents in place at the beginning of the Gulf War. In terms of biological weapons, Iraq had also produced anthrax, botulinum toxin, and other biological agents since 1988, with the result that when inspectors began investigating in 1991, they found that 6,500 liters of anthrax and 10,000 liters of botulinum had been weaponized.

Libya also engaged in intense production of biological agents. With help from biological firms in Germany, Switzerland, and several other countries, Libya constructed large underground laboratories at Tarhuna and Rabta. Specialists suggest that such facilities could be transformed in less than one day from weapons factories to peaceful pharmaceutical labs. This makes tracking the production of biological agents difficult, and given Libya's long-term relationships with many groups engaging in terrorist acts, made the access of terrorists to such weapons feasible. Recent events in Libya, including the death of Qaddafi and the emergence of a fledgling government seeking to unite the many militias who had helped to end his leadership, left it unclear the status of the stock of these weapons.

The second source of world shock on the issue of biological agents came with the breakup of the Soviet Union. Although Russia promised to destroy its BC weapons, it soon became obvious that the country was failing to adhere to its promise and was instead preventing access by foreign inspectors after 1993. Records of the amounts of such weapons in existence, and even of the location of facilities manufacturing or storing them, were lost, destroyed, or hidden, with the result that few are certain of precisely how many BC weapons were produced and who currently possess them.

This type of weapon has been linked to several earlier terrorist groups and activities. It was reported in the late 1970s that the Red Army Faction (RAF) in Germany was training Palestinians in the use of bacteriological warfare. A raid by police in Paris uncovered a laboratory with a culture of botulism. The RAF threatened to poison the water supplies of about 20 German cities unless their demand for special legal defense for three of their imprisoned comrades was met. Microbiologists were believed to have been enlisted by groups in Italy and Lebanon in efforts to generate biological weapons for terrorist use. In the United States, 751 people in the small town of The Dalles, Oregon, were poisoned by salmonella planted in two restaurants by followers of self-proclaimed prophet and spiritual leader Bhagwan Shree Rajneesh.

A special issue of the *Journal of the American Medical Association* published the first systematic survey of biological agents in 1997. This survey included brucellosis, the plague, tularemia, Q-fever, smallpox, viral encephalitis, VHFs, anthracis, and botulinum. The latter three were described as the greatest potential danger given their toxicity and contagion rate, and because both were found in large quantities in Iraq, where they had already been weaponized.

Although vaccines could be used to neutralize many of the existing agents, and antibiotics could be used to both treat and prevent most, the weaponizing of these agents presents a problem. Through this process, the agent is changed in ways that could make the majority of the safeguards and remedies ineffective.

It is believed that 30 to 40 countries have the capacity to manufacture biological weapons, because many have a pharmaceutical industry to aid in this production. The greatest concentration of existing weapons is believed to be in the Middle East, including not only Iraq and Iran, but also Syria, Libya, and the Sudan. The U.S. bombing of the pharmaceutical factory in the Sudan in 1998 when this laboratory was linked by intelligence information with Osama bin Laden illustrates the rising concern over the possible use of this type of agent by terrorists.

Biological agents have been called "the poor man's nuclear bomb." They are difficult to trace, cheap to manufacture, and potentially incredibly lethal. Botulinum, the most deadly toxin available—100,000 times more poisonous than the sarin gas used in the Tokyo subway attack—is theoretically capable, in a quantity as small as one gram, of killing all the inhabitants of a city the size of Stockholm, Sweden. An aerosol distribution is the ideal method of delivery for such an agent. It has been estimated that botulinum, in optimal weather conditions, could kill all living beings in a 100-square kilometer area. Fortunately, ideal weather conditions seldom last, but many would certainly die from such an attack.

CASE STUDY 14.5

Agroterrorism

As concern mounts about the potential for terrorist attacks utilizing WMDs, one of the possibilities receiving special attention is that of agricultural biowarfare, or **agroterrorism**, which involves *the deliberate introduction of a disease agent either against livestock or in the food chain for purposes of undermining stability or generating fear.* At least 13 nation-states have developed, or are suspected to have developed, biological agents with antilivestock or anticrop properties. Specific, verifiable information on such programs is difficult to access since most biowarfare programs are clandestine. The list of diseases developed in these programs by just two countries, the United States and the former USSR, is staggering and includes (but definitely is not limited to) anthrax, brucellosis, equine encephalitis, foot-and-mouth disease, fowl plague, glanders, African swine fever, avian influenza, contagious bovine pleuropneumonia, Newcastle disease virus, wheat blast fungus, rye blast, and tobacco mosaic.

Concern about the potential for agroterrorism led the United States in February 2003 to conduct a terrorism scenario focused on a domestic agroterror attack, **Operation Silent Prairie**, a *simulation of an attack generating an epidemic of foot-and-mouth disease (FMD).* The national livestock population has had no natural immunity to this disease since 1929, when FMD was eradicated in the United States. Given this lack of immunity, by the conclusion of the exercise, FMD hypothetically had ravaged livestock herds from North Carolina to the San Joaquin Valley in California, with what would have been devastating economic consequences.

Organized by the National Strategic Gaming Center and held at the National Defense University, the simulation was designed to give senior government officials (18 members of Congress, the surgeon general, the deputy secretary of agriculture, the deputy secretary of defense, and representatives from the FBI, FEMA, the North Carolina Department of Agriculture, the National Guard Bureau, the Joint Chiefs of Staff, and others) insights into the complexities of the emerging global biosecurity challenges. It certainly served to highlight the devastating potential of the bioterror threat. ■

Source: US Department of Justice website: https://www.ncjrs.gov/pdffiles1/nij/214752.pdf

Nuclear Devices

Hundreds of pages of photocopied, handwritten, and printed documents, written in a mixture of Arabic, Urdu, Persian, Mandarin, Russian, and English, were recovered from a number of al-Qaeda houses in the Afghan capital of Kabul a day after its fall to the Northern Alliance forces in November 2001. These pages confirmed, among other things, that al-Qaeda cells were examining materials to make a low-grade, dirty nuclear device. The pages also indicated that al-Qaeda's understanding of bomb-related electronic circuitry at least matched that of the Provisional IRA's experts.

According to John Large, a British nuclear consultant, while the organization would not have been able to make a large-scale missile or nuclear device from the documents found, "it was obviously prepared to consider the use of such weapons, so that if it could not manufacture such for itself then, given the opportunity, it would acquire such for use."[16] Included in the documents acquired by *the Times* relating to nuclear physics was a chart depicting a portion of the periodic table of elements dealing solely with radioactive materials. This portion, according to Large, contained all of the elements needed if one were constructing a dirty bomb. Access to nuclear materials is problematic depending on which type of material is sought. The most carefully guarded elements, weapons-grade uranium and plutonium, are perhaps the least accessible. However, numerous attempts have been made to smuggle nuclear materials out of the former Soviet Union, and there are unconfirmed rumors that some nations, and perhaps even a group like al-Qaeda, may have obtained a nuclear warhead. Thus far, police and customs officials in Europe have seized only low-quality nuclear waste that could, in sufficient quantity, be used to build a dirty bomb that would spread nuclear contamination.

The easiest means by which a terrorist group might make a nuclear bomb would be to find a government willing to allow access to its laboratories or its arsenals, but few, if any, governments are willing to take such a risk today. After the Gulf War, UN inspectors found that Iraq had come within months of building an atomic bomb, but the effort apparently took about a decade and cost nearly $10 billion. There is no evidence that any government today has helped terrorist groups to acquire nuclear weapons at such prohibitive costs. The potential cost of being linked to the bomb if the terrorists deploy it successfully has also apparently deterred access to this type of weapons through state conduits.

But the number of potential suppliers of nuclear weapons technology continues to expand. Countries such as North Korea, once dependent on external help from other nations in crafting a nuclear weapons program, enjoy a vigorous missile- and technology-export business with a number of Middle Eastern countries, including Iran, Pakistan, and Syria. Moreover, all technologies become less expensive with the passage of time and proliferate as more people begin to use them. Although there is no immediate threat of nuclear bombs in the hands of terrorists, the next plane flown into a symbolic target such as the World Trade Center may have something more lethal aboard than aviation fuel.

Study of the potential for access to nuclear weapons capabilities would not be complete without examining the impact of Pakistan's nuclear expert: Abdul Qadeer Khan. Khan, widely viewed as the father of Pakistan's nuclear weapons, has, with the help of associates, bought and sold key nuclear weapons capabilities for more than two decades, in spite of the efforts of the world's best intelligence agencies and nonproliferation organizations. Khan's network sold the equipment and expertise necessary to produce nuclear weapons to states such as Iran, Libya, and North Korea, countries that have in turn marketed materials and expertise to groups engaged in terrorism.

Created in the 1970s to supply Pakistan's gas-centrifuge program, Khan's network slowly expanded its network of sales in gas centrifuges, which were used to produce weapons-grade uranium for Pakistan's nuclear weapons. Khan exported gas centrifuges and production capabilities to other, mostly Muslim, countries, driven by a desire for profit, but also by his pan-Islamism and by his hostility to Western efforts to control the supply of nuclear technology. While Egypt reportedly refused Khan's offers of assistance in the development of nuclear technology, the response of Syria is less clear, as is whether the offer was also made to Saudi Arabia, birthplace of Osama bin Laden and of many of the perpetrators of the September 11 attacks. There is considerable suspicion that, due to his travels in Afghanistan between 1997 and 2003, Khan may also have offered nuclear assistance to al-Qaeda.

The Khan network certainly exploited loopholes in the nuclear nonproliferation network, expanding the number of nations with nuclear technology and significantly expanding the potential for groups engaged in terrorism for access to both the technology for nuclear weapons production and the waste products of that production. Iran, Libya, and North Korea, at least, were provided with nuclear technology that seriously enhanced their nuclear weapons potential. Since each of these states has been linked to various terrorist support networks, the potential for nuclear terrorism has been seriously impacted by the Khan nuclear smuggling network.[17]

Radiological Devices

To date, there have been no attacks involving the detonation of radioactive devices, or dirty bombs, although two such devices were reportedly discovered, undetonated, in Russia and attributed by authorities to a Chechen resistance group. Radiological accidents, including the one that occurred the late 1980s in Brazil, causing more than 150 injuries and 5 deaths, offer insights into the pattern of contamination and the potential for illness and deaths from such radioactive agents.[18]

RISK ASSESSMENT: COMPARATIVE EFFECTIVENESS OF WMD

Risk assessment for biological, chemical, radiological, and nuclear weapons could be based on the distinctive qualities of each of these weapons, as these qualities impact their effectiveness and likelihood of use. Table 14.1

TABLE 14.1

Characteristics of Weapons of Mass Destruction[20]

	Biological	Chemical	Radiological	Nuclear
Complexity of production	2	3	1	5
Cost of production	2	3	3	5
Difficulty of acquisition	2	2	2	5
Difficulty of delivery or dispersal	1	2	1	4
Worst-case consequences	5	4	4	5

is part of an assessment developed by Leonard Cole, based on studies produced by the U.S. Congress' Office of Technology Assessment, and supported by other literature comparing WMDs.[19] Table 14.1 offers insights into the relative effectiveness of these four types of weapons, comparing how difficult they are to produce and to acquire; their cost of production; the difficulty of their delivery or dispersal; and the "worst-case" scenario of consequences in their use. The weapons are compared on a scale of 1 to 5 in each category, with 1 denoting "lowest or least" and 5 representing "highest or most."

This type of assessment is based on generalizations since all biological agents differ, some significantly, in terms of their accessibility, the symptoms they produce, and their probable method of delivery. The numbers presented for biological weapons are somewhat subjective, as they must represent a range of agents. The conclusions of much of this assessment are not surprising. Nuclear agents are more complex to produce than chemical agents; nuclear bombs are most likely, in general, to be the most effective and the most destructive, but probably also the most difficult to acquire and the most expensive.

The comparisons make a strong case, however, for the need to expend considerable efforts to prepare for, and, if possible, prevent, terrorist attacks utilizing WMDs. Although there have been, to date, few attacks with any such weapons on a scale to produce mass casualties, the potential for catastrophic injury is clear. With biological and radiological weapons, the costs and complexity factors are not great, but the potential for worst-case scenarios (with catastrophic damage and mass casualties) is very high. WMDs in the hands of terrorists must be assumed to be possible and to carry the potential for unthinkable consequences.

CONCLUSIONS

There is growing concern that the use of WMDs may become more common in the near future. The legal, political, and financial restraints that have discouraged states from the use of these types of weapons appear less likely to be sufficient to limit the willingness of a group to use such weapons if it could acquire them. Because access to such weapons is clearly growing and groups are already training in the use of the more easily accessed materials, the likelihood of a threat by terrorists deploying a WMD seems credible.

Documents obtained from some of the al-Qaeda houses in Afghanistan not only described the organization's efforts to obtain nuclear capabilities but also outlined this group's plans for chemical weapons. These plans were drawn with large-scale production in mind, with each recipe containing a step-by-step guide explaining how to produce batches that would kill thousands of people. Some of the pages contained photocopies explaining how a device or chemical agent could best be put to devastating effect.

The use of WMDs by terrorists, not just al-Qaeda, is clearly not a remote possibility but an actively sought goal today. Smallpox, which is estimated to have killed 120 million people in the twentieth century alone, offers an incredibly lethal weapon in weaponized form or in the hands of a **suicide carrier,** *a terrorist willing to be infected with the disease in order to carry it into the target audience to spread it among this group.* If smallpox had not been eradicated, according to the World Health Organization, "the past 20 years would have witnessed some 350 million new victims—roughly the combined populations of the United States and Mexico—and an estimated 40 million deaths—a figure equal to the entire population of Spain or South Africa."[21]

The biological threat is small in at least two respects: Most biological agents are hard to produce and hard to make into weapons. The preparedness of governments to deal with even this small threat, however, was demonstrated in the fall of 2001 by the anthrax attacks in the United States and elsewhere.

In spite of the fact that ordinary airplanes were used as WMDs in the September 11, 2001, attacks, the difficulty in generating and appropriately dispersing biological, chemical, and nuclear weapons remains high. But that attack has changed, to some extent, the world's perception of modern terrorists. The suicidal zealotry, the malevolence, and the determination of the individuals who flew the airliners into buildings; their willingness to prepare for the attacks for years; and their clear desire to cause mass casualties have confirmed the possibility that such terrorists would willingly use chemical, biological, or nuclear weapons.

DISCUSSION

The prospect of terrorists armed with, and willing to employ, WMDs generates a mood of fear, even without an actual attack. As Russell Howard, editor and author of numerous books and articles on terrorism, points out, "The best we may be able to achieve is to understand that we live in danger, without living in fear."[22] Building an awareness of the types of weapons that could be utilized, of the risk that such weapons pose, and of the documented attempts by terrorist groups to acquire and to use these weapons may help us cope with the "war on terrorism" more effectively, without fear but with clarity of understanding that makes us better able to respond to and, ultimately, to prevent such attacks.

Knowing that there have already been numerous documented efforts to achieve and use such weapons can help to build our security and response provisions. Study carefully the following list of cases in which the acquisition of WMDs, their use, or both has been linked to a current terrorist organization. We can learn from these examples in terms of: ability of groups to acquire materials to create WMDs, potential for construction of WMDs, motivation and willingness of groups to use WMDs to generate mass casualties, capacity for utilization of WMDs to maximum effect thus far, by groups today.

a. Jemaah al-Islamiya (JI), a group based in Indonesia that was responsible for the bombings in Bali in 2003 that killed more than 200, produced a manual that explains how to carry out chemical attacks with chemical hydrogen cyanide. According to the manual, "30ml of the agent can kill 60 million people, God willing." Dr. Rohan Gunaratna, an expert who has long studied this al-Qaeda–linked group, stated that JI had plans to use the chemical agents against Western targets in May 2006. Australian newspapers carried headlines stating that JI planned a "Holocaust gas attack in building" using this chemical agent, as Gunaratna suggested. While the attack did not occur as planned, the intent revealed here is disturbing.

b. Al-Qaeda's views on the acquisition and use of WMDs are well known. As operational leader and ideologue of al-Qaeda, Abu Musab al-Suri stated in an open letter to the U.S. Department of State, if he were consulted about the use of WMDs against the United States,

> I would advise the use of planes in flights from outside the U.S. that would carry WMD[s]. Hitting the United States with WMD[s] was and is still very complicated. Yet, it is possible, with Allah's help, and more important than being possible—it is vital.[23]

c. The first *fatwa* on the use of WMDs was pronounced on May 21, 2003, by Saudi religious leader Shaykh Naser bin Hamad al-Fahd, who said that if "the Muslims could defeat the infidels only by using these kinds of weapons, it is allowed to use them even if they kill them all, and destroy their crops and cattle." Al-Fayd went on to say that since the United States had killed about 10 million Muslims, the Muslim world was allowed to retaliate and kill as many Americans. Another al-Qaeda leader also used this analogy, suggesting that al-Qaeda was allowed to kill at least 4 million Americans, including 2 million children.[24]

d. Based on interviews with scientists and senior officials, Judith Miller, Stephen Engelberg, and William Broad posited, in their book, *Germs,* that "In the coming years, those willing to die for their cause may well choose . . . to become smallpox carriers or Marburg martyrs." Sharing this point of view, Bruce Hoffman, one of the world's preeminent terrorist experts, expresses the dilemma posed to us today by the prospect of WMDs in the hands of terrorists:

The issue here may not be as much ruthless terrorist use of some WMD, as calculated terrorist use of some unconventional weapon to achieve far-reaching psychological effects in a particular target audience. We may therefore be missing the point and sidestepping the real threat posed by terrorists in this regard. It will likely not be the destruction of an entire city—as portrayed by writers of fictional thrillers and government officials alike—but the far more deliberate and delicately planned use of a chemical, biological, or radiological agent for more discrete purposes.[25]

ANALYSIS CHALLENGE

The Commission on the Prevention of Weapons of Mass Destruction Proliferation and Terrorism issued a "Report Card" on the U.S. government's effort to take necessary steps in this critical area in January 2010. If we agree that the potential use of WMDs by terrorist is growing, then the actions to prevent access to such weapons are essential, particularly for a nation which is both the target of choice for many individuals and groups engaged in terrorism today, but also the producer of a wide range of WMD resources.

Visit the website of this commission, which has now become an independent research group, at http://www.preventwmd.org/1_26_101/. Which of the failing or nearly-failing grades causes you the most concern? What can be done to improve U.S., and Allied, efforts to improve the grades? Will unilateral action be sufficient to truly make terrorist attacks with WMDs less likely? Read the report attached to this website, and analyze the suggestions for multilateral actions.

KEY TERMS

fanatics   328
biological weapons   328
chemical weapons   329
plague   333
unit 731   329
bacteria   332
viruses   332
rickettsiae   332
fungi   332

biotoxins   333
botulinum toxin   333
tularemia   333
smallpox   333
anthrax   334
viral hemorrhagic   fever   336
choking agents   339
blistering agents   339

blood agents   339
nerve gases   340
ricin   341
dirty bombs   342
small plutonium   device   343
agroterrorism   348
operation silent   prairie   348
suicide carrier   352

SUGGESTED READINGS AND RESOURCES

Butler, Richard. *The Greatest Threat: Iraq, Weapons of Mass Destruction, and the Crisis of Global Security.* New York: Public Affairs, 2000.

Cole, Leonard A. *The Eleventh Plague: The Politics of Biological and Chemical Warfare.* New York: Freeman, 1997.

Howard, Russell D., and James J. F. Forest, eds. *Weapons of Mass Destruction and Terrorism.* New York: McGraw-Hill, 2008.

Laqueur, Walter. *The New Terrorism: Fanaticism and the Arms of Mass Destruction.* Oxford: Oxford University Press, 1999.

Miller, Judith, Stephen Engelberg, and William Broad. *Germs: Biological Weapons and America's Secret War.* New York: Simon & Schuster, 2001.

Stern, Jessica. *The Ultimate Terrorists.* Cambridge, MA: Harvard University Press, 1999.

NOTES

1. Walter Laqueur, *The New Terrorism: Fanaticism and the Arms of Mass Destruction* (Oxford: Oxford University Press, 1999), 61.
2. "Guide to Toxic Terror," *The Charlotte Observer*, September 30, 2001, 11A.
3. Christopher F. Chyba and Alex L. Greninger, "Biotechnology and Bioterrorism: An Unprecedented World," in *Weapons of Mass Destruction and Terrorism*, ed. Russell D. Howard and James J. F. Forest (New York: McGraw-Hill, 2008), 198.
4. Ibid., 199.
5. Leonard A. Cole, "WMD and Lessons from the Anthrax Attacks," in *Weapons of Mass Destruction and Terrorism*, ed. Russell D. Howard and James J. F. Forest (New York: McGraw-Hill, 2008), 96.
6. David Franz, "Bioterrorism Defense: Controlling the Unknown," in *Weapons of Mass Destruction and Terrorism*, ed. Russell D. Howard and James J. F. Forest (New York: McGraw-Hill, 2008), 190.
7. Jonathan B. Tucker, "Chemical Terrorism: Assessing Threats and Responses," in *Weapons of Mass Destruction and Terrorism*, ed. Russell D. Howard and James J. F. Forest (New York: McGraw-Hill, 2008), 213.
8. Ibid., 216.
9. "A Focus on Ricin Toxin," *Counter-Terrorism Training and Resources for Law Enforcement*, http://www.counterterrorismtraining.gov/focus/focus.html.
10. Cole, "WMD and Lessons from the Anthrax Attacks," 90.
11. Ibid., 91.
12. Alexander Glaser and Frank N. von Hippel, "Thwarting Nuclear Terrorism," in *Annual Editions: Homeland Security*, ed. Tom Baden (Dubuque, IA: McGraw-Hill Publishers, 2008), 110.
13. Matthew Bunn and Anthony Wier, "The Seven Myths of Nuclear Terrorism," in *Annual Editions: Homeland Security*, ed. Tom Baden (Dubuque, IA: McGraw-Hill Publishers, 2008), 126.
14. Raymond A. Zilinskas, "Aum Shinrikyo's Chemical/Biological Terrorism as a Paradigm?" *Politics and the Life Sciences*, September 1996, 238.
15. Sharon Theimer, "Special Report: Attack on America," *Washington Post*, September 21, 2001, A27.
16. "Scientists Confirm bin Laden Weapons Tests," *Sunday Times*, December 30, 2001, 2A.
17. David Albright and Corey Hinderstein, "Unraveling the A. Q. Khan and Future Proliferations Networks, in *Weapons of Mass Destruction and Terrorism*, ed. Russell D. Howard and James J. F. Forest (New York: McGraw-Hill, 2008), 317–330.
18. Two metal scavengers broke into an abandoned radiotherapy clinic and stole a capsule containing powdered caesium-137. They opened the capsule at the home of one of the thieves, contaminating the home, the family, and a number of others before the radiation sickness was detected at a hospital and steps to limit contamination were taken. Retrieved on June 15, 2009, from the International Atomic Energy Association's website, "Radiological Accident in Goiania" (1988) at http://www-pub.iaea.org/MTCD/publications/PDF/Pub815_web.pdf.
19. U.S. Congress, Office of Technology Assessment, *Proliferation of Weapons of Mass Destruction: Assessing the Risks* (Washington, DC: Government Printing Office, August 1993); and U.S. Congress, Office of Technology Assessment, *Technologies Underlying Weapons of Mass Destruction* (Washington, DC: Government Printing Office, December 1993).

20. David Ensor, "Biological Attack Threat Real, but Small," *CNN Washington Bureau,* September 24, 2001.
21. Russell D. Howard, "The New Terrorism and Weapons of Mass Destruction," in *Weapons of Mass Destruction and Terrorism*, ed. Russell D. Howard and James J. F. Forest (New York: McGraw-Hill, 2008), 19.
22. Howard, "New Terrorism," 17.
23. Robert Wesley, "Al-Qaeda's WMD Strategy after the U.S. Intervention in Afghanistan," Jamestown Foundation, *Terrorism Monitor,* 3, no. 20, October 21, 2005. Retrieved from http://www.jamestown.org/programs/gta/single/?tx_ttnews%5Btt_news%5D= 590&tx_ttnews%5BbackPid%5D=180&no_cache=1 (accessed November 11, 2009).
24. Bruce Hoffman, "CBRN Terrorism Post-9/11," in *Weapons of Mass Destruction and Terrorism*, ed. Russell D. Howard and James J. F. Forest (New York: McGraw-Hill, 2008), 275.
25. Cole, "WMD and Lessons from the Anthrax Attacks," 93.

Future Trends

> The greatest threat posed by terrorists now lies in
> the atmosphere of alarm they create, which corrodes
> democracy and breeds repression. . . . If the government
> appears incompetent, public alarm will increase
> and so will the clamor for draconian measures.
>
> — *Brian Jenkins*

IDENTIFYING TRENDS IN TERRORISM

In a world engaged in a "war on terrorism," understanding the changes in the nature of terrorism and the responses to terrorist acts is vital. Terrorism continues to increase in diversity in terms of geography, demography, and method: Terrorist acts now occur in almost every nation, involve a widening range of ethnic communities, and employ an expanded arsenal of weapons. The redefinition of terrorism at the local, national, and international levels has made data collection and tracking of trends in this phenomenon difficult, contributing to disagreements over "who" the war is engaged against and what rules apply in this increasingly violent conflict. Unlike earlier U.S.-led "wars" on drugs or poverty, the war on terror is a violent conflict, making the establishment of a definition of the act of terrorism critically important. Let us first examine a few of the significant changes in terrorism highlighted in this text.

Suicide bombing has become a much more common tactic of terrorists from many groups. From 2005 to 2007 in Iraq, suicide vehicle-borne improvised explosive device attacks outnumbered person-borne improvised explosive device attacks by approximately three to one.

Terrorism is increasingly carried out by individuals, by women as well as men, and "lone wolf" terrorism is more common but still difficult to predict. In Iraq, the number of female suicide bombers increased from five in 2007 to thirty-three in 2008. From the Liberation Tigers of Tamil Eelam, in Sri Lanka, the first group in the past century to advocate and practice suicide bombing, grew the Women's Liberation Front in 1985, which continues to train its members in suicide terror today.

Terrorism today is almost completely *transnational*. In the past, terrorism was planned and carried out within one state; today, acts are much more likely to have international planning, performance elements, and victims. Globalization and increased capabilities in mass transit and communication make this linkage formidable.

Terrorist networks today are *increasingly better financed and more loosely structured*. The Baader-Meinhof gang in Germany, the Red Brigades of Italy, and the Quebec Liberation Front (FLQ) of Canada were generally underfunded, certainly compared to the funding enjoyed by groups such as al-Qaeda today. The cell structure of terrorists today is much more difficult to infiltrate than those of earlier decades. The all-channel network structures of terrorist cells make bribes, sting operations, and the capture of one member to gain entry to a group much less effective than similar counterterror actions against the earlier chain networks.

Twenty-first-century terrorists are, as a whole, much *better trained and equipped* than those of earlier decades. As Chapter 7 indicated, terrorists today have not only organized camps but also training manuals and a growing arsenal of weapons, including weapons of mass destruction (WMD). The bombs and other explosives are still popular today, as the growing use of improvised explosive devices (IEDs) makes clear. However, according to evidence collected for a French court, training camps in chemical and biological weapons operated in the Pankisi Gorge in the Caucasus state of Georgia, where individuals with ties to al-Qaeda completed their training before returning to their home countries (mainly in Europe). The use of such weapons by groups such as Aum Shinrikyo and the efforts to create WMDs by many other groups make the threat of WMDs today much greater.

Terrorists today are much *more adept at using the Internet and other forms of modern mass communication*, reaching worldwide audiences and targeting many different types of audiences effectively with their messages. The Internet "showcases" terrorists' work very effectively, as hostage videos from Iraq have demonstrated. Terrorists are no longer dependent on getting local newspapers to carry their messages. These new skills also highlight the increasing vulnerability of computer networks to cyber attacks, making the critical infrastructure of many developed nations at risk for cyberterror.

Terrorists today can sponsor states, rather than being dependent upon a state for sponsorship. Whereas terrorist groups of the late twentieth century had state sponsors such as Libya and Cuba, modern terrorists have resources that make such sponsorship unnecessary. This means that the limits on state actions and the vulnerability of state actors to reprisal or punishment for open sponsorship no longer can be assumed to limit the actions of terrorist groups. Failed or failing states can give terrorist groups a safe haven without ties or responsibility for adherence to international law, as the increasing piracy around the coast of Somalia makes clear.

These attributes of the terrorism emerging in this new millennium do not offer a complete, or even a final, picture of terrorism today. Law enforcement and security agencies, in order to cope effectively with modern terrorism, not only had to be aware of these changes but also had to develop methods of counterterror to cope effectively with the new threats. But counterterror policymakers had to not only "catch up" on the **learning curve**—*a graph of progress in the mastery of a skill against the time required for such mastery*— they had to learn faster than the terrorists. The first step in this organized counterterror effort was the war on terror declared in 2001.

A WAR ON TERROR

The late Hannah Arendt, in her controversial book on the trial of Gestapo Lieutenant Colonel Adolf Eichmann, coined the phrase *the banality of evil*. She used this phrase to describe the way in which a "terrifyingly normal" person was able to help turn the murder of a people into an ordinary bureaucratic routine. Eichmann became the quintessential government bureaucrat—highly efficient and mindlessly, remorselessly obedient to orders.

The individuals who carried out the September 11, 2001, attacks were banal, but in a different manner. Many of the men who hijacked and flew the planes into the targets had come to the United States much earlier to complete the planning and training. They were so banal, so *ordinary,* that none of their neighbors or coworkers noticed them. Yet they were planning to carry out one of the most dramatic and lethal terrorist attacks in modern history.

The suggestion by Brian Jenkins, consultant and author on terrorism, that until the events of 2001 terrorism had achieved a similar level of **bureaucratic banality** in that *its perpetrators carry out heinous crimes with increasing efficiency, while a worldwide audience becomes increasingly "unshockable" when viewing those acts,* seemed an accurate assessment of contemporary terrorism. Statistics appeared to have replaced headlines in referring to the escalation of terrorism. Terrorism had become so much the norm that it was commonplace, not unthinkable.

The events of September 11, 2001, *were* unthinkable, however. The magnitude of the attack; the cost in lives, property, and economic stability; and the multinational network that worked to carry this out, after years of planning, staggered the United States and much of the world. For the first time, rapid international action was taken to focus attention on the problem of terrorism, in the form of U.N. resolutions, treaties moving toward ratification as well as signatures, and the declaration of a **war on terror**, *a statement of action by a coalition of nations led by the state that was a victim of the September 11 attacks.* Yet, the problem remains unresolved.

The spending and personnel involved in terrorism itself and in the fight against it have increased exponentially in the twenty-first century. After the events of September 2001, the United States annually designates a dramatically increasing portion of its budget to the external and internal efforts to combat terrorism. In establishing a new Department of Homeland Security (DHS), the United States parallels the United Nations, which has created an office to monitor the agreements and efforts nations are now making to control the funding and arming of terrorists. Terrorism has become a bureaucratic reality in a completely new and extremely expensive fashion.

Although we had come to accept the existence of terrorism in our daily lives, the events of September 2001 made such a tolerant attitude less prevalent. Instead, a "war on terrorism" was declared and is being fought, first in Afghanistan, home of the Taliban and refuge of Osama bin Laden and his al-Qaeda network, and later, as a factor in the U.S.-led war in Iraq, in part to remove a regime that had sponsored terror for decades. States such as Libya and Syria that had been refuges for, and even supporters of, groups carrying out terrorist acts were quick to condemn the September 11 attacks and offered to work to end the threat of future attacks.

Efforts are under way to eliminate terrorism now, not only in terms of a successful war on terrorism, but, perhaps more importantly, in terms of working to ensure that such virulent anger does not fester in other places. The developed world today is more conscious that desperate poverty and hunger can provide a breeding ground for terrorism, and that, to win a war on terrorism, it must first win a nonlethal war for the hearts and minds of the audience of terrorists, as discussed in Chapter 8.

THE COUNTERTERRORISM LEARNING CURVE

We have suggested that terrorism today is more prevalent but less structured, more prone to suicide bombing and lone-wolf attacks than to group efforts, better funded but less structured, and is mastering modern technology at an alarming rate. Counterterror efforts have also developed significant learning trends, which are important in assessing the tools of counterterror and the pattern which the global war on terror may take.

Globalization, and Understanding the "Why" of Terror Attacks

As terrorist groups have become more loose networks than structured organizations as they expand globally, states countering terrorism have of necessity become *more* linked to one another. In attempts to come to grips with ensuring that such terrorist attacks would not recur, nations are not only trying to improve their security measures and to track down and destroy the networks of individuals responsible for attacks, but also to understand *why* people might feel such hatred toward another country. Understanding the causes of the anger became as important, in many respects, as the ability to punish the perpetrators.

Two important factors that may trigger terrorist violence have emerged: the impact of the widening gap between the rich and the poor nations of the world, highlighted by the trend toward globalization; and the lack of understanding between the West and the Middle East, particularly religious understanding.

Just as terrorism has become globalized, networking groups and nations in struggles across national boundaries, economic **globalization**—*the networking of national economies on a global scale,* puts businesses large and small in competition for markets across the world. Globalization is recognized as part of the reasons for the anger directed at countries such as the United States, a vocal advocate for global free trade. It has left at least 20 percent of the world's population destitute, as small businesses and family farms, lacking the technology and resources to compete effectively with international corporations, are crowded out of a global market as nations lower their protective tariffs to participate more fully in global trade. More than 925 million people in the world today are chronically undernourished, a condition with devastating consequences to health and community welfare. The poverty and hunger in many developing countries provide fertile soil for those who want to blame the West for these conditions.

Understanding that the economic divide is huge and getting wider did not, of course, lead to a sudden decision on the part of nations to create some kind of egalitarian communal society. But awareness of the problems created by this divide is growing; with this awareness, solutions of a more realistic and permanent nature are being sought, primarily through the United Nations but also through other secular and religious organizations. The commitment to stay and help to rebuild Afghanistan after the war, offering the people hope instead of poverty and despair, suggests that this awareness may produce positive results.

The West discovered, in the search for the answers to the *why* questions of the attacks, that most of its people did not understand Islam, nor did most in the Islamic world understand Western culture or religion. The open and concerted effort *not* to make a "war on Islam" in its war on terrorism led the West to host many forums, create many websites, and seek out many scholars to better understand Islam, its tenets, and its misuse as a tool by Islamic radicals. This effort to build cultural bridges of understanding offers hope for a lowering of tensions that can make progress toward peace possible.

Using the Internet

The virtues of the Internet—including but not limited to the ease of access, lack of regulation, large potential audiences, and the rapid flow of information—have begun to be used with increasing skill by groups committed to using terrorism to achieve their goals. Almost all active groups that have engaged in terrorism today have established a presence on the Internet, with hundreds of websites now serving terrorists and their support networks. The dynamic quality of the Internet enables groups engaging in terrorism to establish their own website, modify their profiles, disappear and reappear with startling speed, and evade efforts by law enforcement to infiltrate or suppress.

This networking of cells of groups challenged states with access to new technologies to seek ways to mathematically search the Internet for clues of groups forming and plans being made. For example, research suggests that individuals who are willing to carry out violent acts as part of a group may exhibit distinct patterns in their use of e-mail or online forums such as chat rooms. As an operations researcher noted, while most people amass a wide variety of contacts on the Internet over time, those planning criminal activity tend to keep in touch with only a very small group of people—a pattern discernible on a search of the Web with the proper mathematical model, as it is a very predictable type of behavior.[1]

These developments suggest that the Internet is a rapidly expanding tool for networking by individuals and groups engaged in terrorism, but that it is also being examined by technological groups seeking to track the growth. The vulnerability of critical infrastructure to terrorism is very real, and nations with advanced technology resources are encouraging research and development in this field as being essential to the security of the companies and communities that depend on this technology for their lifestyle—and their existence. The Pentagon is creating a new military command for cyberspace as it prepares to wage both an offensive and a defensive war, if necessary, against terrorist attacks in cyberspace.[2]

CASE STUDY 15.1

Globalization: Sharing Intelligence and Laws

In the wake of 9/11, the costly efforts to carry out a "war on terror" using military forces, and a growing realization that terrorism cannot be countered by an single nation or tool (military, security, investigation, or law), there is an increasing global effort to counter the globalization of terrorism with a concomitant globalization of shared intelligence and legal cooperation. Recognizing the truth in the assessment of experts who noted that transborder terrorism cannot be controlled without bilateral or regional cooperation, a regional approach to counterterror strategy has emerged, with a wide range of centers being facilitated by the United Nations as well as individual states.

Not all of these centers have experienced success in establishing the level of cooperation desired to counter terrorism. In South Asia, for example, the South Asian Association for Regional Cooperation (SAARC) adopted, more than twenty years ago, a Regional Convention for the Suppression of Terrorism, but most of the cooperation exists primarily on paper. In the wake of the 2008 attacks in Mumbai, when gunmen travelled from the port of Karachi in Pakistan into India, the need for transborder cooperation is clear. While efforts to bring individuals to justice, or to extradite for prosecution, continue to be a problem, India and Pakistan shared an unprecedented amount of intelligence information on Lashkar-i-Taiba in the aftermath of the 2008 attacks, facilitated by the SAARC structures and agreements.

The United Nations today, through its Office on Drugs and Crime, which houses its Terrorism Prevention Branch, has undertaken to work closely with a wide range of regional partners to provide specialized legal expertise, technical assistance, and experts on each region as needed. The experts provide specialized national and subregional input and perspectives, facilitating effective follow-up to intelligence-sharing and legal cooperative ventures. By assigning experts to South-East Asia, the Pacific, Central Asia, North Africa and the Middle East, East and West Africa, and Latin America, the United Nations is able to help nations within each region build expertise on counterterrorism issues.

This cooperative effort is channeled by the United Nations through existing regional and transnational bodies, such as the African Union, INTERPOL, the International Monetary Fund, the International Maritime Organization, the International Law Enforcement Academy (ILEA-Bangladesh), the Organization of American States (Inter-American Committee Against Terrorism), and the Council of Europe. There are also training institutions in which partnerships offering technical assistance and capacity building activities are available, with the United Nations facilitating the cooperative efforts.

Legal institutions, such as the International Court of Justice and, more recently, the International Criminal Court, have also become "players" in the global counterterrorism efforts. Nongovernmental organizations such as Human Rights Watch have brought to the attention of the ICC recommendations for the indictment of the Syrian president for the actions taken during the uprisings in that country in the wake of the "Arab Spring," as Syrians engaged in peaceful protests demanding system changes. The ICC has issued indictments for the president of Sudan for endorsing acts of terrorism by the Janjaweed, and indictments were pending for the Libyan leader, Qadafi, prior to his death, accusing him of crimes against his people during the democracy uprisings in 2011.

Globally, and regionally, the international community is responding to terrorism with efforts to share intelligence, expertise, and technical assistance. Applying the rules of law appears to be a more attractive, less expensive, and potentially successful tool for counterterrorism in a globalizing world. ■

Source: The United Nations webpage: http://www.un.org/terrorism/strategy-counter-terrorism.shtml

Deterrence as a Tool against Suicide Bombing   In the wake of the cold war, when deterrence—a strategy of defense in which the threat of massive retaliation (as a form of punishment) is used to prevent an attack—was employed, apparently successfully, in deterring attacks with WMDs, the use of such a strategy against terrorism was attractive but difficult to construct. Since terrorism was seldom carried out by a state actor against another state (although state terrorism clearly occurred when carried out against the people of the state), it was difficult to use deterrence, with the threat of massive retaliation directed against the nonstate actors carrying out the terrorist attacks, since most such actors were not all in one place at one time. The U.S. attacks on the al-Qaeda bases in Afghanistan after the attacks in 2001 were, perhaps, a massive retaliation, intended to punish and to deter such future attacks.

Deterrence against individuals, or even small groups, is very difficult to direct, or to enforce. Deterrence in law enforcement works on individuals in systems in which the rule of law is regularly enforced, and the habit of obedience to such laws is customary. Drivers in the United States will obey, in general, speed limit laws not because there is always an officer of the law lurking near to issue a ticket, but because there is potentially such an officer near, and the habit of generally obeying the laws is a cultural norm. Deterrence by threat of punishment for breaking the rules can work if there is a belief that the rules are important and that punishment for breaking the rules is likely.

The problem, in terms of suicide bombing, is that individuals prepared to engage in acts of terrorism are already committed to breaking the rules, since terrorism itself, as noted in earlier chapters, breaks the most fundamental rules of law. A person intending to be a suicide bomber, moreover, will not be deterred by threat of punishment—what punishment can he or she be threatened with, if the person is planning to die in a violent explosion? What massive retaliation would deter such an act, unless it were threatened against innocent people, such as the bomber's family—an option not acceptable to the laws of the civilized world today?

The instinct for self-preservation has, in Western cultures, been assumed to be a fundamental drive inherent in every individual. But a person who has decided to carry out a suicide bombing attack clearly is not driven by such an instinct. So threatening to massively retaliate, with the probable loss of life, will not deter a suicide bomber from his or her plan of action. Traditional deterrence is clearly not a viable tool in countering this type of terrorist action.

DEALING WITH WEAPONS OF MASS DESTRUCTION

Terrorism could grow much worse, with terrorists' access to biological and chemical agents as well as nuclear materials and the technical skills to effectively construct and utilize such weapons becoming more widespread. The ability of governments to deal with the threat of WMDs is unclear, and events to date suggest that it is also unpromising.

U.S. federal officials found out in June 2001 how complicated and destructive a bioterrorist attack could be. In *a war game played at Andrews Air Force base outside Washington, DC, an exercise code-named* **Dark Winter** *began with a report of a single case of smallpox in Oklahoma City.* When the exercise was terminated, after thirteen days of simulated time, the epidemic had spread to 25 states and 15 other countries, killing over 24 million people. As the exercise unfolded, the government quickly ran out of vaccines, forcing officials to make life-and-death decisions about who should be protected—health workers, soldiers, only citizens of Oklahoma, or citizens of all neighboring states—and whether the military would be needed to quarantine the patients. After the exercise, officials were convinced that the United States was unprepared to deal with bioterrorism.[3]

In the wake of this learning experience and spurred by the events of September 11 and the subsequent anthrax attack, the U.S. DHS planned a third **TOPOFF** (Top Officials) exercise, *an exercise designed to improve the nation's ability to prevent, respond to, and recover from terrorist attacks.* TOPOFF 3 involved a series of exercises of increasing complexity that simulated a terrorist WMD campaign. In the third exercise, the simulated attacks occurred in the states of Connecticut and New Jersey and were intended to enable government officials to respond more efficiently, based on the lessons learned from the earlier scenarios.

The DHS has contracts for the development of a variety of technologies for defense against biological and chemical threats. These research teams will seek to develop many new systems, including Bioagent Autonomous Networked Detectors (to detect and treat biological agents in outdoor urban areas) and a Rapid Automated Biological Identification System (a "detect-and-protect" system for round-the-clock, distributed indoor monitoring of buildings and selected outdoor locations for bacteria, viruses, and toxins). In fact, in spite of years of intensive research and development and implementation programs to meet this threat, at a cost to DHS of more than $50 billion, almost all of the significant targets are as vulnerable today as they were a decade ago.[4]

The events of September 11, 2001, taught us that WMDs need not be biological, chemical, or nuclear. The airplanes flown into the World Trade Center towers were certainly WMDs but did not fall under the parameters of such weapons in most planning scenarios. Today, special efforts to secure airports and air transport against use as WMDs are being made as the world adjusts to this new type of "weapon."

As N. C. Livingstone noted more than a decade ago,

> As the nations of the globe learn to live with routine low-level violence, it can be expected that there will be a movement by terrorists toward more dramatic and increasingly destructive acts of terrorism designed to ensure that the public does not forget about them and their cause.[5]

The explosive growth of technology that has brought with it new vulnerabilities to highly industrialized societies will continue to provide incentives for increased destruction.

Japan was fortunate, in 1995, that the group carrying out the sarin attack had ample supply of the toxin but little experience in its effective use; consequently, the death count from this attack was low. Similar "luck" befell the United States in the 1993 bombing of the World Trade Center. Court accounts of the incident revealed that those organizing the attack had planned to place sodium cyanide in the vehicle as well as the explosive materials that they did use. The intent was to create sufficient heat to vaporize the sodium cyanide, creating a lethal cyanide gas that would have been sucked into the north tower, killing thousands. Although the physical destruction and the injuries caused by the bomb were dramatic, the death toll was very low compared to what was intended, had the materials been correctly utilized.

The United States was similarly fortunate in the anthrax attack it experienced in the fall of 2001. The anthrax sent through the mail was to be lethal, but only a few people died. The attack cost billions of dollars nationwide and created a feeling of paranoia among many U.S. citizens similar to the "fear of flying" experienced after September 11, but the casualty count was small, given the potential for serious casualties in the system's lack of preparedness.

Within the United States, evidence of efforts by individuals and groups to secure and even to use chemical or biological agents continues to grow. A list of only a few such attempts will make clear the reality of the threat:

> In 1991, sheriff's deputies in Alexandria, Minnesota, learned of a shadowy group of tax protestors called the Patriots Council. One informant reported discussions of blowing up a federal building. Another turned over a baby food jar containing ricin, one of the most deadly poisons known. In 1995, three of the plotters, whose plans included the assassination of IRS agents, were convicted under the Biological Weapons Anti-Terrorism Act.
>
> In December 1995, Thomas Levy, an Arkansas man with survivalist connections, was arrested by the FBI for possession of a biological agent for unlawful purposes. He had 130 grams of ricin that, used with skill, was enough to kill thousands of people.
>
> In May 1995, an Ohio member of the Aryan Nations allegedly ordered bubonic plague bacteria from a Rockville, Maryland, research supplier. He received the bacteria, but the supplier became suspicious over the man's persistent phone calls about delivery of the material and alerted officials. Larry Harris was subsequently arrested.[6]

There is growing evidence of nuclear smuggling from the former Soviet Union, at first across Europe but later in southerly directions where border controls are less stringent. Although no individual or group has yet used or openly threatened to use such weapons, nuclear technology can no longer be dismissed as an "unthinkable" weapon in this new century.

So our world is, and will for the foreseeable future continue to be, afflicted with the "condition" of terrorism, which, in the view of most experts, will probably become worse rather than better. As the global public becomes inured to low-level violence, that violence has escalated in very undesirable ways that utilize the incredible innovations in modern technology.

TRENDS IN TERRORIST INCIDENTS

Some of the changes in terrorism discussed at the beginning of this chapter can be documented graphically in terms of incidents of terrorism; others cannot. A quick review of those that can be statistically verified is useful but will not make clear all that must be said about contemporary trends in terrorism.

Volume and Lethality of Incidents

The **volume of terrorist incidents,** *the number occurring annually,* has dramatically increased since the turn of the millennium, but the pattern of growth since the world began to track terrorist incidents globally has been erratic.

After the 1972 attack on Olympic athletes in Munich and continuing through the mid-1980s, the number of terrorist incidents rose at an annual rate of between 12 and 15 percent. This rate of increase was not constant throughout that time frame. In the 1980s, there was a marked acceleration, which brought the average rate up. From 1983 to 1991, for instance, there was an increase, although certain types of incidents became less common (e.g., aerial skyjacking).

Unfortunately, terrorism has also increased in the **lethality of attacks**— that is, in *the number of people killed*. There is an increasing tendency toward large-scale indiscriminate terrorist attacks in mundane, everyday locations such as airplanes or railway stations. In 1993, 109 people were killed and 1,393 were wounded in terrorist incidents around the world, the highest casualty total in five years. But the attacks on the Madrid trains in 2004, the London subways and buses in 2005, and the Mumbai trains in 2006 provided dramatic evidence of the increased lethality of terrorist attacks in the twenty-first century. Of course, the attacks on the World Trade Center and the Pentagon in 2001, with thousands of casualties, meant that the new millennium began with a new record in terms of the lethality of terrorist attacks as well.

Since a contemporary trend in terrorism is the "internationalization" of most groups, and since significantly different definitions of terrorism are being used by various agencies and organizations to track incidents of terrorism globally, it should not be surprising to discover that there is no consensus on the "pattern" of terrorist attacks based on incident data. One data source is a U.S.-based organization, Memorial Institute for the Prevention of Terrorism, established after the Oklahoma City bombing in 1995. In spite of the 1993 World Trade Center bombing attempt in New York City, this center still classified most terrorist acts as international rather than domestic; using this criterion, the Oklahoma City bombing by Timothy McVeigh would not be statistically relevant as it was domestic rather than international.

In 1998, the United States altered the State Department database to include both domestic and international terrorist incidents, significantly increasing the number of incidents reported each year from this point forward. A similarly radical change occurred in 2006 when the United States sought to separate the events occurring in Iraq and Afghanistan from other data records of terrorist events, in part because of the problem discussed earlier in differentiating between insurgency and terrorist attacks in those areas. The new database, funded by the DHS and based at the START Center established at the University of Maryland, is called the Global Terrorism Database and tracks a wide range of incident types, including those with "doubt" as to such items as the perpetrators, targets, and political motives.

Generating charts of terrorist incidents from these diverse databases will, of course, yield confusing and potentially conflicting results. All statistical measures have potential flaws, and terrorism, with its multiple definitions and increasingly complex nature, too often generates confusing and contradictory data patterns.

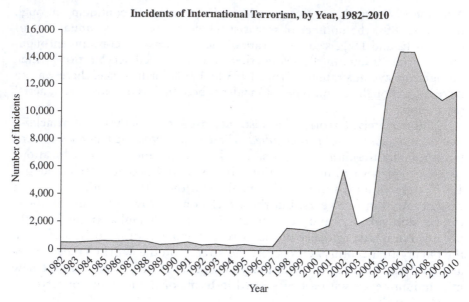

FIGURE 15-1

Number of Terrorism Incidents over Time [12]

Source: http://www.nctc.gov.

Keeping in mind the potential for error in such analysis, we will review only one trend statistically, rather than depend on just case studies and examples to establish the points. Figure 15.1, using data collected for the U.S.

Department of State for use in its annual terrorism reports, suggests that the number of terrorist incidents has grown dramatically in recent years.

The dramatic increase in the number of incidents is startling until one considers that the definition of terrorist acts was broadened to include those termed *domestic* prior to the revisions made in 1998. Until that point, incidents carried out within one country were defined as domestic, even if the group planning and carrying out the operation had international ties. Thus, most of the incidents occurring inside of Israel and the Occupied Territories carried out by HAMAS or Hezbollah were not included in the data pool, as they were domestic by this definition. The change in definition clearly provided a large number of new incidents for inclusion, but the definition was not retroactive in the data pool.

This trend also draws attention to the challenge that the ongoing conflict in Iraq has made to the efforts to define "terrorist incidents" when they are mingled with a "war" and an "insurgency," often in difficult-to-distinguish forms. Even separating the data from Iraq and Afghanistan, as the U.S. Department of State attempted to do in 2005 and 2006, does not alleviate the confusion or mitigate the graphic illustration of a dramatic upsurge of terrorism activity. When terrorist incidents rise from a relatively modest 184 in 1997 to a startling 1,286 in 1998, the impact of the redefinition is clear. But when, as in Iraq, the conflict becomes both more intense and more difficult to separate (terrorist acts and acts of insurgency are not always clearly distinguished, either on the ground or in the data), the change is equally dramatic.

Radicalization of Religion and Terrorism Today

But the rapid increase in the number of terrorist incidents each year is not the only trend of concern. Another significant change has been in the surge in **radical religious terrorism,** *carried out by militant, conservative, and fundamentalist individuals and groups in the name of a faith.* If the 1960s can be described in terms of left-wing terrorism, with the 1970s carrying that trend to its logical conclusion by witnessing the involvement of liberation struggles in terrorism, the 1990s and the first few years of the twenty-first century witnessed a resurgence of right-wing terrorism. This was particularly true in Europe and the United States initially, but it is now becoming the norm in Southeast Asia, North Africa, and to a lesser extent Latin America. The activities of such organizations as the neo-Nazi youth groups against refugees from Eastern Europe in Germany provided grim reminders of the existence of right-wing groups increasingly willing to resort to violence. The attacks of September 11, 2001, by religious fanatics and subsequent attacks by al-Qaeda cells and related groups throughout the world, including the dramatic bombing of the trains in Madrid in 2004 and London in 2005, indicate the range and diversity of the threat of radical religious terror today.

Radicalization in religion is not a new phenomenon. But building an understanding of the process of radicalization and of the impact of radical fundamentalism with the emerging "crusader-type" terrorists may help us learn to deal with this phenomenon.

Psychologists assert that the "radicalization" toward religious-based terrorism is a dynamic process with identifiable phases, which include the process of becoming involved in a group engaged in acts of terror, being involved in the group activities, and, for some, disengaging from the group. "Involvement" means different things to different people, with a wide variety of roles from passive support to violent action included in the spectrum of involvement. All who belong to a particular religion or religious group are not involved to the same extent, nor do they see their involvement as requiring violent action. As history indicates, any religion can be "radicalized" by members who interpret its tenets differently, forming groups who seek to impose their will on the community by violence if necessary.

There is no single catalyst for "being involved" in a group. Often, the desire to belong to a group and to socialize may prompt an individual to become involved. The **risk factors for initial involvement** in this stage are generally identified as *personal involvement with a victim who needs to be avenged, an expectation that involvement will improve a social or political situation, socialization with others already involved, and access to relevant groups.*

In the second phase, described here as "increased involvement," individuals become more than peripherally involved; they begin taking part in activities and making decisions rather than just providing nominal support by simply attending meetings. The **factors encouraging increased involvement** include *the process of the group (incorporation), confirmation by the group of inclusion, learning capabilities, ideological commitment, and sometimes prior commitment patterns of the individual.* Only a portion of any group truly becomes involved with the activities of that group, moving from simple membership to active participant. In the radicalization process, as a person becomes more intensely and personally involved in the activities of a radical religious group advocating violent actions, the potential for violent action by that person becomes greater.

The role or function of the individual who is increasingly involved in the group will be determined by a variety of factors as well. The will of the group leaders for a specific action, the desires of the individual to be actively involved, the "value" placed on the more active role by the group, the external climate in which both the individual and the group exist, and the incidence occurrence that may make future activity more or less desirable or feasible—these factors will limit or expand the options for an individual's role to change within the group.

Understanding this dynamic of radicalization toward violent behavior helps us understand the actions of some of the young people in the Palestinian territories today who seem to become willing to be suicide bombers "overnight." Knowing this, the action is not so much defensible as perhaps preventable if the motivating causes are addressed before the active role is picked up by the next "crusader" willing to die and to take the lives of others for the cause.

Fortunately for mankind, most people who are even peripherally a part of a religious group focused on a need to carry out violent attacks will disengage rather than assume the active role of attacker. But religious fundamentalism advocating, encouraging, or simply tolerating terrorist violence presents serious challenges to the world, as "crusader terrorists" can be generated by any faith. The term **fundamentalism**, like the adjective *terrorism*, is often selectively and inappropriately applied, leading to serious misunderstandings and a lack of coherence in policy.

For the purpose of the study of terrorism here, fundamentalism will be used to refer to *an approach to a religious faith that seeks to maintain or return to basic tenets and that rejects the modern world as a threat to the faith.* Thus, the basic differences between mainstream religious groups and fundamentalists would be that fundamentalists believe that their faith is threatened by the modern world; believe that they must draw a clear line therefore between "self" and "the world" to protect their faith; and believe that they are confronted on all sides, with "their backs against the wall" as they seek to protect the tenets of their faith.

Unsurprisingly, such an approach would lead to a view of the secular world as a foe rather than a friend and would view globalization as a force that is inherently damaging and that destroys cultures and religions as it expands across borders rather than linking people. Agents of socialization provided by fundamentalist groups, such as schools and churches, will therefore not teach support for the secular state, but may instead foster a sense of a struggle for "good" by the group against the "evil" of the state—unless the state is linked with or a part of the group's network. Thus, the concern on the part of Western countries regarding the role of the madrassas (schools run by the Muslim community of faith) in Saudi Arabia is valid. The madrassas indeed have, in some cases, fostered a radical fundamentalist view of the world, making a transition to participation in a terrorist group easier for young people. Similar concerns may emerge about Christian private elementary and secondary education schools, particularly with the growth of religious fundamentalism on the far-right in the United States, as exemplified by Timothy McVeigh and Eric Rudolph.

One last note on the impact of the increased role of religion in terrorist violence today: Religious "crusaders," firm in their belief that they are doing the will of a supreme being and that the world will be better for their efforts, will be more willing than any state has ever been to use WMDs. Even during the cold war, as the two superpowers that were the United States and the Soviet Union built massive stockpiles of nuclear, chemical, and biological weapons, states refrained from the use of those weapons for a variety of reasons, at least two of which are important to note here. One reason for nonuse was the fear of retaliation and the consequent destruction of massive portions of mankind. Another reason, less clearly identified but certainly present in the memoirs of leaders of that time, was concern over the "rightness" of their actions—not the morality, but the sense of how history would view what they contemplated doing.

Neither of these constraints would hamper radical religious cults from using such weapons. As terrorist groups are less tied to state sponsors today and consist more and more of networked cells that transcend state boundaries, the potential for massive retaliation that restrained the superpowers during the cold war will not limit terrorist groups today. Nor will concern over the legitimacy of their actions, as their religious beliefs in many cases will enable them to believe that their actions are divinely inspired.

SUICIDE BOMBING

While suicide bombing is not a new tactic, it has certainly become the tactic of choice for a wide range of individuals and groups today. Statistically, the trend is staggering, as the number of suicide bombings has grown from fewer than 5 per year in the 1980s to more than 200 annually from 2006 to the present. While radical religious extremism, particularly Muslim extremists, have been the most frequent users of this tactic, the organization which initiated its recent use was the Liberation Tigers of Tamil Eelam (LTTE) of Sri Lanka, who were nationalists rather than religious extremists.

Suicide bombing in recent years has occurred in a variety of tactical formats. A few examples indicate the diversity of ways in which modern suicide bombing is accomplished:

Explosive belt or vest. Assassination of Indian Prime Minister Rajiv Gandhi
   Explosives hidden inside the body. The 2009 nine attack on Saudi Prince Muhammad bin Nayef
   Attack on a bicycle with explosives. Assassination of Sri Lankan president Ranasinghe Premadasa
   Attack by boat with explosives. USS *Cole* in Aden, Yemen
   Suicide car bombs. Multiple incidents in Iraq since 2003
   Attack with commercial jets laden with fuel. September 11 attacks on United States

This is by no means a comprehensive list of incidents or tactics but does serve to suggest the wide variety of forms that this type of terrorist attack takes today. The London subway and bus bombings in 2005 and similar bombing attacks on transit in Madrid and Mumbai illustrate the challenge of this type of tactic to modern states today—and the high casualty rate such attacks can generate, even in states with strong counterterrorism programs.

There is significant difference of opinion among researchers about the reasons why suicide bombing is a tactic of choice, and about the demography of those who choose to utilize this tactic. The war in Iraq alone has seriously skewed the data, as in 2004 there were reported to have been more than 400 suicide attacks generating 2,000 casualties in that country. Whether the motivation for all of these attacks was religious (Islam) or political (perception of the United States as "occupiers") is difficult to determine with any objectivity.

Moreover, motivation for these acts, even when the announced reason is religion, is less clear than it would appear. The motives and justification used for carrying out suicide bombings in the name of Islam are often by fellow Muslims, who point out that suicide is clearly forbidden in the Quran. The killing of innocent bystanders, even the harming of plants and animals in such attacks, is, according to these critics of suicide bombers, a violation of Islamic law. Perhaps it would be more accurate to say that those carrying out such attacks have a mixture of religious and political motives, making it difficult to determine the desired result of such actions and difficult to anticipate and prevent them.

One final important point about suicide bombing in modern times is important here. While most of those engaged in this tactic, throughout history, have been males, at least a few groups/movements are beginning to involve women at least as often, if not more often, today. The LTTE have for years recruited and trained women in this tactic, but more recently the rebel groups in Chechnya and the Kurdistan Workers Party have begun to draw women into the role of suicide bombers. This change in demographics presents a challenge to Western nations engaged in counterterror efforts, as many of the women in these groups wear loose-fitting robes, making the concealing of explosives easier, and the desire norm of seeking to preserve "privacy" for women from intrusive personal searches makes it difficult to prevent such attacks.

Impact of Generational Differences within Terrorist Groups

Generational differences exist *between young militants and older leaders* in terrorists groups operating today. Today's terrorists seem less likely to be involved in pickets and demonstrations before resorting to violence. Instead, they seem more willing to throw a bomb first and then talk later (if at all) about their grievances.

This "do something now" mentality has caused some difficulties and even embarrassment for some of the older leaders of established movements. During the 1990s, the PLO witnessed a number of splits, frequently between older, more "institutionalized" members of the organization and younger members who wanted to take immediate violent action against the existing situation.

HAMAS, *a radical element seeking the establishment of an Islamic state,* which is supported by Iran and active in the West Bank and Gaza, strongly rejected any such renunciation of terrorist tactics. The difficulties experienced by Yasser Arafat in governing Gaza during the last decade of the 1990s and the first years of the twenty-first century illustrate the deepening splits between the older leadership, who are willing to compromise in order to achieve a portion of that for which they fought, and the younger factions that are willing to continue the struggle with violence and are unwilling to settle for less than full success. The takeover by HAMAS of political leadership in Gaza in 2007, in which the group split violently with the more traditional leadership of the Palestinian National Authority, makes clear the potential for long-standing groups to splinter into new factions less willing to compromise to reach a political solution.

IED: Weapon of Choice

Although the international community is concerned over the potential for the use of WMDs by terrorists in the future, terrorists today are making extensive use of a weapon, which, although small, is difficult to detect and can inflict serious casualties. Improvised explosive devices, or IEDs, are hidden killers that are easily made from readily available materials in regions of conflict such as Iraq. Hidden along roads in Iraq and detonated as a convoy or group of vehicles passes, these devices have been set off to explode sometimes simultaneously, creating a lethal "kill zone" for vehicles and pedestrians. Within communities in Iraq, IEDs have been sunk into manhole covers or buried beneath the road and covered with a pressure plate, packed in a vehicle and driven by a suicide bomber, or hidden in buildings and detonated after troops or targeted civilians are inside. Since the detonation of the first IED in Iraq in 2003, more than 81,000 IED attacks have occurred in that country. The death toll from these attacks is extraordinarily high, but many of these incidents do not meet the criteria for terrorist attacks as the majority of victims are military personnel. More than two-thirds of combat deaths in Iraq by 2007 were caused by IEDs.

U.S.-led forces in Iraq initially had no contingency plans for the security of thousands of ammunition caches, estimated to have held at least 650,000 tons of explosives. Since IEDs depend upon access to explosives, Iraq continues to be a ripe ground for use of this type of weapon. In spite of intense counter-IED measures by the U.S. Navy and Marine Corps in recent years, the problem is growing and is spreading to other countries. Insurgents coming into Iraq to fight the U.S.-led coalition are returning home after a time trained in the construction and use of these devices, secure in the knowledge that a vast supply of ammunition is "available" in Iraq. Use of IEDs by returning fighters in several neighboring countries has made this growth potential another serious concern.

In 2006, the U.S. Department of Defense established a Joint Improvised Explosive Device Defeat Organization, tasked with devising methods to detect and defeat these devices. The number of U.S. and Iraqi casualties from the devices began to decline in 2008, but attacks and casualties in Afghanistan began to increase during that time.

THE THREAT AND REALITY OF CYBERTERROR

Terrorism today is engaged in a new form of netwar called cyberterror, an area of concern in terms of domestic security from terrorist attacks that has emerged in recent years. **Cyberterror** is a difficult term to define. Using the operational definition adopted in this text, cyberterrorism would include *the calculated use of unlawful violence against digital property to intimidate or coerce governments or societies in the pursuit of goals that are political, religious, or ideological.*

This definition draws several distinct lines to differentiate cyberterrorism from other types of cyber crime. Like all forms of terrorism, cyberterror must have a political, religious, or ideological motive, not simply a desire to disrupt, destroy, or simply annoy. Thus, not all computer hackers who send worms into an e-mail system to destroy or disrupt other users are committing cyberterror, although their acts may well be cyber crimes under both state and national law.

Actions intended to destroy innocent persons, when motivated by political objectives and designed to create a mood of fear in an audience, can readily be called terrorism, even if the attack is made in cyberspace. For example, an attack on a computer system that routes airlines or passenger trains would clearly fit the parameters for this text of "terrorism." So cyberterror must involve destructive acts against innocent persons or against the systems vital to their survival and must be motivated by political goals.

But most of what is called cyberterror today is plagued by very fuzzy definitional boundaries. Would, for instance, a cyber attack on the stock market of a country be a form of cyberterror, even though it involves no immediate, tangible violence and though there might not be universal agreement on the essential nature of the stock market to the survival of those living in the system? What about an attempt to corrupt information within a system, such as that pertaining to blood types in a hospital? If the only result is additional costs in terms of time delay and effort, not lives lost or medical emergencies, is this still terrorism?

Technology in the last two decades has radically altered the patterns of organization and interaction of individuals, groups, and governments. As one scholar noted,

> The headlong rush of the U.S. and other advanced nations into the information age involves new risks. The information systems central to national security, the conduct of government and commerce have significant weaknesses that can be attacked.[7]

Thus far, attacks on such systems have achieved only limited impact, but the potential for such attacks and the clarity with which the definitional line can be drawn to separate ordinary cyber crime from cyberterror must be subject to careful study. Efforts to generate categories for different types of cyber attacks would be useful.

A white paper produced at the Center for the Study of Terrorism and Irregular Warfare in Monterey, California, in 1999 offers useful tools for this study of cyberterror. The authors of this study suggest that there are three levels of cyberterror capability:

Simple-Unstructured: This level of capability has the ability to conduct basic hacks against individual systems with tools created by others. An individual or organization operating at this level possesses few target analysis, command and control, or learning capabilities. Hacker groups are psychologically and organizationally ill-suited to mount such offensives. They tend to feature loose affiliations without the centralized direction necessary for sophisticated attacks on infrastructure targets. Perhaps more importantly, it is against their own self-interest to cause mass disruption to the information infrastructure, as they have more reason to want the Internet to function.

Advanced-Structured: This level includes the capability to conduct relatively sophisticated attacks against multiple systems or digital networks. It may also have the capacity to modify or even create basic hacking tools. Thus, the individual or organization would possess fundamental target analysis, command and control, and learning capabilities. The technical skills associated with the advanced-structured level include mastery of at least one operating system and one network protocol, as well as programming for both stand-alone and networked computers.

Complex-Coordinated: Groups and individuals operating at this level have the capacity for coordinated attacks capable of causing mass disruption of integrated, heterogeneous defenses (including cryptography). They would also possess the ability to design and create sophisticated hacking tools and would be capable of target analysis, command and control, and organizational learning. At the complex level we add knowledge of industrial and control network protocols to the obvious expansion of the topics in the previous level. Closely tied to technical skill is analytic ability. The cyberterror organization must be able to perform a detailed target analysis. Finally, the group must be able to plan and orchestrate the event to within very narrow tolerances.[8]

Groups operating at the simple-unstructured level will use the openly available tools to interfere with computers used by the government, hacking into systems to cause problems but not widespread disruption. Those at the complex-coordinated end of the spectrum could attempt to disrupt a basic service over a wide area or multiple services within perhaps a smaller geographic region.

A good indicator of a terrorist group's potential for cyberattack may well be the degree to which it is itself linked to the use of the Internet for communications, management, and intelligence gathering of its own. Cyberterror will not, in all probability, be a tool utilized by a large number of groups against the vulnerable cyber-services of the modern world. There are many reasons for this no doubt brief period of relative safety from devastating cyber attacks, some of which are related to the nature and goals of terrorist groups today. Let us consider how these two aspects will, for a time, limit the probability of high-end cyberterror attacks.

Nature of Groups as Limiting Factor

The nature of the group will probably limit the likelihood of its use of cyberterror. Groups that are "old" are less likely to be capable of the necessary cyber-proficiency than those that are "young," as cyber technology is a fairly recent phenomenon. Groups that are largely leaderless movements and those that use the Internet to connect cells scattered across large geographic areas will also be less likely to use devastating cyberterrorism, since such groups rely on the Internet for recruitment, planning, and even training operations. The more **informatized** the group is (*the more it uses the Internet in recruitment and training of members, propaganda distribution, even the transfer of resources*), the less likely the group will be to attack the computerized system on which it depends. The nature of groups will be a limiting, but not a prohibitive, factor, at least for a time.

Goals of Groups as Limiting Factors

Groups that seek to disrupt or destroy on a large scale are the exception rather than the rule in most studies of terrorism today. Religiously motivated groups engaging in "crusades" across wide geographic boundaries are perhaps the most likely to be willing to engender mass destruction, as is evident in the recent activities of some of these groups. Single-issue groups, such as those engaged in the protection of animal rights, the environment, or both against the incursions of modern technologies, may be the most willing, in spite of the use of the Internet for recruitment and propaganda, to engage in complex, widely disruptive terrorism. Such groups would also be more likely to have as a goal disruption without destruction and would thus be willing to generate disruptive Internet attacks. Moreover, such groups and their targets are prevalent in societies rich in information technology, making such attacks easier to launch and offering a wide range of targets. As noted in a white paper, "These groups have, by far, the best match between desire, ideology and environment to support a near term advanced-structure attack threat."[9]

Cyberterror is not just a "weapon of the future." In May 2007, Estonia, a country enormously dependent on the Internet for everything from parliamentary elections to banking, suffered a cyber attack. The attack was launched through software known as "bots," generating a giant network of bots banded together to simultaneously flood the country's computer networks. This "denial of service" attack generated serious concern among NATO allies, who were aware of the vulnerability of many modern systems to this "nonviolent" but extremely disruptive form of assault. The waves of attacks continued for several days and seriously impacted the economy and government services of this state.

Nearly a decade before this attack, in 1997, a Presidential Commission on Critical Infrastructure Protection was created by U.S. president Bill Clinton to assess the threat to vital infrastructures of communication, electrical power systems, transportation and air traffic control, emergency services, and banks posed by cyber hacking and cyberterrorism. This commission continues to offer reports on the escalating scale of potential cyber attacks and on the efforts taken, as well as those needed, to improve security to such infrastructure.

Awareness of the potential for dramatic cyberterror attacks against U.S. targets appeared in the attacks detected in 1998 by the U.S. Department of Defense. An official interagency investigation was launched in response to several computer attacks. These attacks appeared to be originating from, among other places, the Middle East, and at least 11 of the attacks were launched on a number of navy, Marine Corps, and air force computers worldwide. The attacks appeared to be primarily focused on denial of service and exploited a well-known vulnerability in the Solaris operating system. Since the U.S. military was at that time preparing for possible combat operations in Iraq, the investigation engaged the FBI, the CIA, and the Department of Justice, as well as the military intelligence forces, in what was dubbed the "Solar Sunrise" attacks.

After a flurry of court orders, the culprits were found: two California teenagers and their eighteen-year-old Israeli mentor.[10] In light of the seriousness of the breach of security, the results were somewhat anticlimactic but served to illustrate the extent of cyber vulnerability of even the most secure of government infrastructures. Had the teenage hackers been terrorists, the results could have been incredibly destructive.

Cyberterror is a threat but not yet necessarily an eminent threat. Three factors limit the credibility of the threat, and each is rapidly disappearing:

1. Public and private interest in erecting firewalls against cyber breaches of security is growing rapidly. There are barriers to entry into most cyber systems that are vital parts of U.S. infrastructure that are beyond the

capability of most, with individual hackers presenting an annoyance, but not a threat of terrorism, to date.

2. Terrorists generally lack the funds essential to mount a large-scale, computer-driven cyber operation on most critical infrastructure. While the vulnerability of such infrastructure to physical and operational attacks is real, cyber attacks are less likely due to the resources essential for such an attack, at this point.

3. Most terrorist groups lack the human capital needed to mount cyberterror operations on a meaningful level. Most computer hackers are not part of groups with strong political agendas, and most members of such groups lack the formidable computer skills necessary to carry out such attacks, so far.

Thus, given the difficult technical paths that must be followed, and the fiscal and human capital essential for serious cyberterror events, cyberterror remains a threat, but not of imminent destruction—yet.

CONCLUSIONS

The world community is now required to deal with unprecedented problems arising from acts of international terrorism . . . which raise many issues of a humanitarian, moral, legal, and political character for which, at the present time, no commonly agreed rules or solutions exist.[11]

The world community must meet the challenge of terrorism. If it is indeed a condition for which there is no known cure, then we must at least seek to understand the phenomenon in order to better cope with its presence in our lives.

To recognize the existence of terrorism is not to recognize its right to exist or its inevitability. A doctor faced with an epidemic must first recognize the problem and then take steps to deal with it, at least in terms of containment and perhaps prevention. Similarly, students of world social, legal, political, and security issues today must study the phenomenon of terrorism in order to better cope with its presence in the world.

Just as that hypothetical doctor facing that epidemic has restraints on what he or she may do to handle the problem, so nations searching for ways to cope with modern terrorism must exercise restraint in their responses. Nations must weigh the cost, in terms of the loss of liberties and freedoms, against the gains in subduing terrorism, recognizing that to sacrifice too many liberties may well be to give terrorists the victory they seek: the destruction of democratic systems. The cost of winning some battles against terrorism may be too great. Terrorism is a crime, in any context, for any cause. In order to combat it successfully, we must keep our responses within the law which we have created, and which defines the act of terrorism as a crime.

But to concede that there are some ways in which a nation or a people may not combat terrorism is not to concede that terrorism cannot be fought. Regardless of the cause, terrorism is not an acceptable mode of behavior and cannot be permitted to prevail unchecked. The end does not, and can never, justify the means.

We cannot "stop" all opportunities for terrorism to occur. We *can* understand what causes terrorism, how it works, and the individuals or groups that are willing to commit terrorism. Understanding and predicting can make us better able to cope without over-responding and without being blind to the reality of the threats that confront us.

DISCUSSION

Terrorism has contributed to changes in the mode of conflict both between and within nations. Conflicts today appear less coherent than in the past, at times exhibiting not two clear sides but several confusing and shifting alliances. Such conflicts are also less decisive, with no clear "winner" or "loser." As states use terrorism to engage in irregular warfare against other states, the stakes in the conflict become confused, the rules less clear, and the heroes hard to find.

Terrorism is not new, but it is changing. The ability to understand and to predict terrorist attacks is growing with the explosive waves of globalization fueled by the Internet and other forms of mass media, mass transportation, and new technologies—but so is the potential for destruction from both sides of the struggle. Those engaged in terrorism are increasingly able to cause more casualties and to destroy more buildings and infrastructure, while those seeking to protect such targets are tempted constantly to sacrifice liberties to provide security from attack. The balance in the struggle is constantly in flux, and each decision—by a group to use a weapon or by a government to impair essential freedoms—could bring about destruction on an unimaginable scale.

Policy is made by prioritizing the disposition of resources, and in the effort to "deal with" terrorism, this is vitally important. Take a careful look at the following list of potential measures suggested to alleviate this problem, in terms of awareness, prevention, mitigation, or response. These are the "all-hazard" phases particularly relevant to terrorism today, and they offer critical choices of action:

1. *Train and equip first responders to terrorist events.* First responders in the Tokyo subway sarin attack were not trained for this type of weapon and were themselves victims of the attack.
2. *Build bridges of cultural awareness.* Before the events of September 11, 2001, most U.S. citizens were unaware of where Afghanistan was on a map and had no real knowledge of or interest in the economic problems or the religious turmoil of that area. Since that time, Christian–Muslim panel discussions and community information-sharing groups have helped to defuse the concept of a "clash of civilizations."
3. *Win the war of hearts and minds.* Much of the war on terrorism will be won not on a battlefield, but on the Internet or in the mass media, in the presentation of ideas and concerns in ways that foster cultural understanding.
4. *Make terrorism a crime that can be taken to the International Criminal Court.* Without this option, there is no place to take those accused of terrorist acts except courts within a state, where justice may be problematic. If the United States had captured bin Laden instead of killing him, where could he have been taken to court?

5. *Expand special forces to have sufficient manpower to handle terrorism, when necessary, in other countries.* The use of Navy Seal teams in the attack on bin Laden's compound was not only successful, it also saved the lives of many women and children in the compound who would doubtless have been killed in a bombing raid. There is a need for more such highly trained special forces teams, able to carry out targeted attacks without endangering civilians in the area.

ANALYSIS CHALLENGE

In January, 2009, in Tizi Ozou, Algeria, at least 40 members of an al-Qaeda cell were killed in a cave when a weaponized form of the Pneumonic plague escaped its containment and infected most of the members based there. Clearly, Al Qaeda in the Land of Islamic Mahgreb, as this cell is called, has been planning to use this biological agent in an attack.

This and many other disturbing incidents are reported in the Global Terrorism Database (GTD) website (http://www.start.umd.edu/gtd/). Go to this website and initiate a search to determine a trend in terrorism that interests or concerns you. You can track data by region, perpetrator, weapon, and a variety other factors. The GTD will generate a graph for you to help you visualize this trend in terrorism today.

There are no "magic formulas" for resolving the problem of terrorism in the world today, but there is a growing sense of urgency in our efforts, as this incident illustrates. Consider this final set of questions:

Has humankind formulated a weapon for its own destruction by fomenting the conditions from which terrorism arises? By putting WMDs in the hands of individuals willing to commit terrorist acts, are we creating the arrow that will destroy our world?

> So in the Libyan fable it is told
> That once an eagle, stricken with a dart,
> Said when he saw the fashion of the shaft,
> "With our own feathers, not by others' hands
> Are we now smitten."
>
> AESCHYLUS, WISDOM OF THE AGES

KEY TERMS

learning curve 359
bureaucratic banality 359
war on terrorism 359
globalization 361
Dark Winter 364
TOPOFF 365
volume of terrorist
  incidents 366

lethality of attacks 367
radical religious
  terrorism 369
risk factors for initial
  involvement 369
factors encouraging
  increased
  involvement 370

fundamentalism 370
generational
  differences 373
HAMAS 373
cyberterror 374
informatized 376

SUGGESTED READINGS AND RESOURCES

Huffman, Bruce. *Inside Terrorism*. New York: Columbia University Press, 2006.

Kegley, Charles W., Jr., ed. *The New Global Terrorism: Characteristics, Causes, Controls*. Upper Saddle River, NJ: Pearson Education, 2003.

Lacqueur, Walter, ed. *Voices of Terror: Manifestos, Writings and Manuals of al-Qaeda, Hamas, and Other Terrorists from Around the World and Throughout the Ages*. New York: Reed Press, 2004.

Nyatepe-Coo, Akorlie A., and Dorothy Zeisler-Vralsted, eds. *Understanding Terrorism: Threats in an Uncertain World*. Upper Saddle River, NJ: Pearson Education, 2004.

"Patterns of Global Terrorism: 2003." U.S. Department of State. Washington, DC: U.S. Government Printing Office, April 2003.

Reich, Walter, ed. *Origins of Terrorism: Psychologies, Ideologies, Theologies, States of Mind*. Washington, DC: Woodrow Wilson Center Press, 1998.

Weimann, Gabriel. *www.terror.net: How Modern Terrorism Uses the Internet* (United States Institute for Peace: Special Report 116, March 2004).

NOTES

1. "Mathematical Methods in Counterterrorism," Retrieved on November 12, 2007, from http://www.rit.edu/-cmmc/conferences/2007/index.php3.
2. "Pentagon Plans New Arm to Wage Cyberspace Wars," *New York Times*, May 29, 2009. http://www.nytimes.com/2009/05/29/us/politics/ (accessed June 25, 2009).
3. http://www.homelandsecurity.org/darkwinter/index.cfm.
4. http://www.homelandsecurityresearch.com/2010/10/u-s-bio-detection-homeland-security-defense-technology-market-2011-2016/.
5. N. C. Livingstone, "Taming Terrorism: In Search of a New U.S. Policy," *International Security Review* 7, no. 1 (Spring 1992): 17.
6. Jonathan B. Tucker, "Chemical/Biological Terrorism: Coping with a New Threat," *Politics and Life Sciences* 15, no. 2 (September 1996): 169.
7. Gregory J. Rattray, "The Cyberterrorism Threat," in *Terrorism and Counterterrorism*, ed. Russell D. Howard and Reid L. Sawyer (Guilford, CT: Dushkin/McGraw-Hill, 2002), 227.
8. Bill Nelson, Rodney Choi, Michael Iacobucci, Mark Mitchell, and Greg Gannon, "Cyberterror: Prospects and Implications." Prepared for the Defense Intelligence Agency, Office of Counterterrorism Analysis (October 1999). Retrieved on September 24, 2007, from http://www.nps.navy.mil/ctiw/files/Cyberterror%20Prospects%20and%20Implications.pdf
9. Ibid., 4.
10. Retrieved on October 13, 2009, from http://www.globalsecurity.org/military/ops/solar-sunrise.htm
11. Bruce Hoffman, "Defining Terrorism," in *Terrorism and Counterterrorism: Understanding the New Security Environment*, ed. Russell D. Howard and Reid L. Sawyer (Guilford, CT: McGraw-Hill, 2003), 3.
12. U.S. State Department, "Report on Terrorism," compiled annually from 1982–2010.

INDEX

Note: Page numbers followed by 'f' indicate a figure; and those followed by 't' indicate a table